The first fifty years

*The Secretary-General in
World Politics 1920-1970*

ARTHUR W. ROVINE

The first fifty years

The Secretary-General in World Politics 1920-1970

A.W. Sijthoff | Leyden | 1970

ISBN 90 218 9190 5

Library of Congress Catalog Card Number: 75-124501

© A. W. Sijthoff's Uitgeversmaatschappij N.V., 1970

Printed in the Netherlands by A. W. Sijthoff, Printing Division, Leyden.

For Phyllis

Acknowledgements

This study was first suggested by Raymond B. Fosdick, who served as Under Secretary-General in the earliest days of the League of Nations when Sir Eric Drummond was Secretary-General. After I completed a portion of the basic research for him, Mr. Fosdick and I considered for a time that a co-authored book on the Secretaryship-General would be advisable. We finally agreed that separate works from differing points of view would be preferable. I owe Raymond Fosdick an enormous debt of thanks for his insight and encouragement, and for his untiring efforts in helping me gain access to private papers and to key officials, both in the League and United Nations.

Research on the League of Nations Archives in the Palais des Nations in Geneva, Switzerland was made very much easier by the assistance of the former Acting Chief Librarian, Mr. Norman Field, and his chief aide, Mr. Badr Kasme, the Law Librarian. Interviews granted by Frank Walters, Thanassis Aghnides, Edward Phelan, Pablo de Azcaraté, Jonkheer van Asch van Wijck, and Adrianus Pelt were essential for the development of the material on the League Secretary-General. Thanks are due also here to Jean Siotis and Stephen Schwebel for their general assistance, and to Katherine Pfitzer and William Kemp for their generous help in combing through the League Archives. Dr. Arthur G. Kogan of the U.S. State Department's Historical Office kindly granted permission to study the Department's records for the period 1919 to 1940, covering the administrations of Sir Eric Drummond and Joseph Avenol. I am indebted further to Mario Toscano for his assistance in providing material from the Italian Foreign Office Archives dealing with the Avenol era.

Perhaps my deepest felt appreciation for help in preparing the chapters on the League Secretary-General is for the late Arthur Sweetser, formerly of the League Secretariat. Mr. Sweetser was extraordinarily generous with his time, both in granting interviews and in making available his collection of papers dealing with the League. He was most helpful in going through the papers with me, and in permitting an examination of letters and other documents that are crucial for an understanding of the critical period in 1940 that witnessed Joseph Avenol's resignation and the assumption of responsibility by Sean Lester as Acting Secretary-General. Given the resources presently available to scholars of the League period, it is probably not too much to assert that the chapter devoted to the Lester administration could not have been written without the aid of Arthur Sweetser.

Preparation of the chapters on the United Nations Secretary-General was very substantially assisted through interviews granted by Andrew Cordier, Oscar Schachter, Ernest A. Gross, Ralph Bunche, C.V. Narasimhan, José

7

8

Rolz-Bennett, Brian Urquhart, David Owen, Martin Hill, Piero Vinci, Richard Pedersen, Seymour Finger, Bo Beskow, Wallace Harrison, and Kenneth Thompson.

I am indebted for general administrative assistance and typing to Nora Allen in New York, and Judith Levin, Peggy O'Neil, Lois Rolley, and Shirley Zimmerman at Cornell University.

Ithaca, New York   Arthur W. Rovine
February, 1970

Introduction

The establishment in 1920 of a world organization whose primary purpose was the maintenance of peace among nations marked one of the great watersheds in the history of international relations. National policies were to be subject to the norms and processes of global institutions, and world order sought through cooperative relationships created and maintained in part by the new League of Nations. One of the crucial segments of the League system was the international secretariat, a permanent body of officials devoted to no single national policy, and working for the interests of the League itself, as defined by decision of its Council and Assembly. At the head of the Secretariat stood its Secretary-General, the world community's first "chief executive", administrative head of the international staff, and world diplomat.

The first fifty years of the Office have revealed a rich history of political activity by the Secretary-General, both in the League and United Nations years, and while the evolution has been gradual, with more than an occasional backsliding, the general direction has been toward an expansion of the chief executive's powers and responsibilities in the maintenance of peace. As a result, after five decades, we are confronted with an issue of outstanding importance for contemporary international relations, that is, whether the nations of the world community wish the Office to become still more vital and perhaps independent or whether the experiment begun in 1920 should be restricted and confined to the current limit of political action and capabilities. Nations are far more conscious of the potential of the Office and its capacity for action in international conflict than they were in 1920, particularly when the Organization itself intervenes on a large scale. They also appreciate the risks of creating an additional international actor whom they cannot entirely control nor expect to be anything but neutral and impartial in most cases of inter-state dispute. Thus the crucial question of how far the Office will be permitted to develop, and to what effect upon the slow evolution of world order.

My own strong preference is for an expansion of the capabilities and prerogatives of the Office as an essential element among the institutions required for the development of a rational world order system. Effective neutral third parties may be vital and are certainly useful in the process of conflict resolution, as the historical narrative and the subsequent functional analysis in this study attempt to demonstrate. Thus the concentration herein will be upon the political activities of the Secretary-General from 1920 to 1970, with the primary emphasis on his role in particular political disputes, but including material with a direct bearing upon the development of the Office. The chief executives of the League and UN have had an enormous range of responsibilities in areas other than political conflict, such as economic development, human rights, and international law creation, but in terms of the Office, the critical variable has always been their work in peaceful settlement, and thus the bulk of the data will deal with that aspect.

There are, to be sure, several different frameworks within which this material might properly be presented. The choice here is to present a straightforward historical account of the first fifty years of the Secretary-General's political activity, followed by a more abstract analysis of his resources and functions in world politics. Information in the historical chapters has been selected primarily on the basis of importance to the Office as an effective international institution. The body of data on the Secretary-General's previous career is significant only insofar as it might be relevant to the training required of future chief officials. Some of it permits a flexibility in the writing of a continuous narrative. Material on a Secretary-General's subsequent career is kept at a minimum, although given Sir Eric Drummond's experience, this might well have a bearing on the work of the Office. Information on a Secretary-General's selection, his political and constitutional views, or any data touching directly on the international staff or integrity of the Office have been included as having a very direct relevance to the capabilities of the institution. Yet the basic attempt here is to present a study that permits the reader some understanding of the great sweep of history since 1920 from the perspective of the Secretary-General and his role in conflict resolution.

The most obvious alternative mode of presentation is a functional model allowing analysis of the Secretary-General's role within the framework of a discussion of each of his tasks in world diplomacy. This has been done by some writers with varying degrees of success, although to date the functional theory has served more as heading for what turned out to be traditional historical narrative. The decision here to set forth the record in traditional fashion, and to devote a separate section to more abstract theory, is based on several considerations. First, a substantial portion of the historical material herein is new. Despite a comparatively large body of literature on the Office, there have been no studies made of the Drummond or Lester periods, and to date only one history of Avenol's administration. Stephen Schwebel's outstanding study of the UN's first chief executive, Trygve Lie, and a few books and articles on Dag Hammarskjold comprise the serious historical literature on the UN Secretary-General. No single work attempts to encompass the entire period 1920 to 1970. Thus even the large body of work on the Office currently available leaves us without political histories of three of the six Secretaries-General, and without easy access to an historical review covering the past five decades. This study tries to fill these gaps.

Given the newness of much of the material, it is far more satisfactory to present it in traditional form, rather than dissect it through an abstract model. Sir Eric Drummond's work in the Sino-Japanese conflict in the early 1930's, for example, is best learned as just that, rather than by bits and pieces through an analysis of his mediation work that includes part of his role in that conflict, his communications functions, containing another part, and so on. A basic knowledge of the essential material on the Secretary-General's activities from 1920 to 1970 is vital to the formulation of models explaining his behavior in more abstract terms.

This consideration is reinforced by the paucity of any serious theoretical work on the Office of the Secretary-General. There are many ways of slicing into the mass of material forming the record of the first fifty years. The functional analysis based on resources and tasks presented in the last chapter is one method of making a start toward theory, but there are other, perhaps more fruitful techniques, and further effort should not be hindered by the selectivity and special emphases that accompany any conceptual framework for political analysis. The decision here is thus to present a relatively complete historical account and make a separate beginning toward theory. The idea is to make available a record of political activity for historians of international organization, and sufficient data for theoreticians to construct conceptual frameworks with some assurance of familiarity with most of the critically important information.

It is, of course, impossible to record in a single volume a very detailed political history of the six Secretaries-General. Each is obviously entitled to a book-length study, although to date only Avenol, Lie and Hammarskjold have received such close attention. The attempt in this work is to present as concisely as possible the most significant political activity and events affecting the Office so as to engender understanding of the Secretary-General's role in international conflict rather than offer an exhaustive analysis of his work for fifty years, while setting forth sufficient material to permit a start toward theory. The hope is that both the descriptive and more abstract sections of this study will generate further work in the history and theory of the Office.

One of the great difficulties in a work of this kind is the unavailability of essential documentary sources. The UN archives are of course closed and most of the information on the period from 1946 was gathered from secondary sources, published UN documents, and interviews. It is almost impossible to gain access to material bearing on behind-the-scenes activity of the UN Secretary-General, and this is a severe limitation on the value of the material presented. The voluminous secondary sources and even interviews cannot compensate for a study of the Secretary-General's private negotiations as depicted in his own records of conversations, memoranda, etc. The problem with the League is markedly different. There are very few secondary sources on the League Secretary-General and original documentary materials are unevenly available. The League archives may be examined, but the destruction by the Secretariat of a great portion of Sir Eric Drummond's papers during the war (because of fear of a German invasion of Switzerland) has deprived researchers of some extraordinarily valuable data. Some of the files have remained intact, and they offer a glimpse of his outstanding service. Joseph Avenol left few papers, and Sean Lester headed a moribund League during the war and had little to do. National archives, particularly the American and British, are essential, and as the French and other national records become available, far more will be known of the Office during the League era. Private collections of papers and interviews with former League officials are of great assistance in any study of the Organization, its staff, and the Secretary-General's Office. In sum, data on the League Secretary-General is frequently based on original documentary sources and is therefore of great importance and interest, although at times woefully incomplete. Information on the UN Secretary-General is based on a great volume of secondary sources and interviews, but must remain more superficial and less interesting until UN and national archives for the period from 1946 are open.

The decision to begin with the record of the League Secretary-General in 1920 is based upon the rather clear difference in political role between that official and the "international" staffs of earlier organizations. The League Secretary-General was an international civil servant at the head of a global and multi-purpose organization whose primary goal was the maintenace of world peace. There are several examples of earlier public unions and organizations with international staffs, but they are largely single-task oriented, and most frequently involved with non-political technical areas. Even then, violations of international staffing rules were not uncommon. Needless to say, the international bureaux of the several public unions had no direct political work of any significance. This was true as well of the Secretariat of the Supreme Council established by the Allies in 1917, and the staffs of the several subordinate Councils.

Table of Contents

ACKNOWLEDGEMENTS   7

INTRODUCTION   9

Chapter I
SIR ERIC DRUMMOND
Secretary-General of the League of Nations 1920-1933   17

Sir Eric Drummond and his Appointment as the First Secretary-
    General   19
The Functions of the League Secretary-General   27
Drummond and the International Civil Service   33
Drummond's Views on the League and the Secretariat   43
The Secretary-General's Political Role   51
The Sino-Japanese Conflict: 1931-1933   77
Drummond's Resignation and Later Career   96
Sir Eric Drummond's Contribution to World Order   100

Chapter II
JOSEPH AVENOL
Secretary-General of the League of Nations 1933-1940   105

The Selection of Joseph Avenol as Secretary-General   108
The Sino-Japanese Conflict and Japanese Withdrawal from the League 116
The Italo-Ethiopian War   124
The Decline of the League and the Rush Toward War   137
The Crisis in the League Secretariat: 1938-1939   141
The Bruce Report   146
The League's Last Political Action—The Expulsion of the Soviet
    Union   149
The Princeton Transfer   152
The Resignation of Secretary-General Avenol and his Attempt to
    Shut Down the League   158
The Afterward   166

Chapter III
SEAN LESTER
Secretary-General of the League of Nations 1940-1947   173

14

Chapter IV
TRYGVE LIE
Secretary-General of the United Nations 1946-1953   201

The Election of Trygve Lie as Secretary-General   207
The Iranian Issue   213
Palestine: 1947-1949   217
The United Nations Guard (Field Service)   224
The Berlin Blockade   226
The Peace Mission and Chinese Representation   230
The Korean War   236
The Issue of American Communists in the UN Secretariat   251
Lie's Views on His Office and United Nations Political Functions   256
The Extension of Lie's Term and His Final Resignation   264

Chapter V
DAG HAMMARSKJOLD
Secretary-General of the United Nations 1953-1961   271

Hammarskjold at Peking   279
Crisis in the Middle East: 1956-1957   283
The Hungarian Revolution   295
Lebanon   298
The Laotian Crisis   305
The Congo   309
Hammarksjold's View of the UN and the Office of Secretary-
    General   327

Chapter VI
U THANT
Secretary-General of the United Nations 1961-   341

The Election of U Thant   344
The Congo Crisis   350
West New Guinea   362
The Cuban Missile Crisis   368
The Yemen Observation Mission   375
The Federation of Malaysia   377
Peacekeeping in Cyprus   381
The Kashmir Question   386
Secretary-General Thant's Re-election   390
The Arab-Israeli War and the Withdrawal of UNEF: 1967   393
The War in Vietnam   400

Chapter VII
THE SECRETARY-GENERAL IN WORLD POLITICS:
Resources and functions 415

Resources
neutrality 416
political information 420
diplomatic skill 422
prestige 424
structural position 426
constitutional theory 427
record 428
political constituency 431
authorizations or grants of power 433
skilled personnel 436
tangible resources 438
Political Functions 440
diplomatic functions 441
communication 441
articulation and aggregation of interests 442
legitimization 445
rule-making 447
conflict-management functions 448
participation 449
mediation 451
arbitration 452
accomodation 453
mobilization of resources 455
policy planning 456
field operation 457
interposition 458
integration functions 459

SELECT BIBLIOGRAPHY 465

INDEX 469

CHAPTER I

Sir Eric Drummond
Secretary-General of the League of Nations
1920-1933

It is, of course, quite natural that the League will have ups and downs. After all, we are only a mirror—a very faithful mirror—of what happens in the world; and, if the world suffers, the League reflects that suffering. But I have no doubt whatever as to its permanence. One of its great elements of strength is the fact that the Secretariat, which is one of its essential organs, has a definite continuity, and the strength of the Secretariat lies greatly, to my mind, in the fact that that continuity rests on the spirit of the Secretariat, which is to serve the League. It does not matter if persons come or go, if Governments fall or change; as long as that spirit continues all will be well with one of the main organs of the League.
Sir Eric Drummond, June 30, 1933

The creation of the League of Nations fifty years ago signified a critical turning-point in the history of nations, for the international community, statesmen and publics alike, decided the time had come to commence the construction of a rational and ethical world order in which relationships among states would be influenced and shaped, if not governed, by cooperative international institutions. Derived immediately from the agonies of the World War, the League of Nations was also the culmination in 1920 of a slow growth of internationalist thought and practices founded on an appreciation of the economies and potential for peace of world-wide collaborative activity. Of crucial importance was the radical shift away from the sweeping positivism of the nineteenth century toward a more general acceptance of the proposition that there are limits, legal as well as moral, upon the right of a nation to go to war, that nations should judge others and try to prevent, through peaceful means, and by coercive measures if necessary, resort to force perceived as unjustified by the world community, and all within the framework of international institutions and rules.

To be sure, the League of Nations constituted only the most fragile of governmental structures, but the notion that sovereign states would willingly join together in a world-wide body was a striking departure from the immediate past, particularly given an appreciation of the League's emphasis on peacekeeping procedures limiting independent discretion, the commitment to economic and social development, disarmament, public judgments of state acts, and the establishment of a permanent secretariat service whose staff were responsible to no nation and no interest save the League of Nations itself.

The League, however, was never a universal organization in any fundamental sense, notwithstanding that almost all of the world's independent states were members at one time or another, for several key international actors were not significantly involved in its workings. The greatest disappointment, of course, was the failure of the United States to associate itself, thereby creating an organized community deprived of substantial resources of wealth, influence and power. And the Soviet Union did not become a League member until the Organization's second decade, with Europe already sliding toward a second world war. Germany participated in the League only from the mid-1920's to the rise of Hitler, and Japan took no part in the global body's political work after 1933. Latin America was far from League centers and never the beneficiary of sustained interest from Geneva, and of course, the whole of the colonial world, encompassing most of Africa, the Middle East, and South and Southeast Asia were not associated and never a central concern of the League's proceedings. The Mandates System was narrow in scope, and the great majority of non-self-governing territories in no way affected by the processes of the new world organization. The League was largely an institution of liberal democratic Europe, and when that Europe later turned inward to settle its conflicts violently, and with a level of destruction unknown to man, the League too was destroyed, even while its essential framework and ideology were resurrected in the United Nations.

If lack of universality limited the initial domain of League activity, the Organization's impoverishment of power was the critical determinant of its marginal relevance in world politics. Despite the apparent Covenant automaticity of League sanctions in case of unjustified resort to force, the institution's members interpreted their obligations evasively, and freedom of choice rendered the League's collective security system impotent in all but the case of the Italian-Ethiopian conflict in 1934-1936. The organized community of nations had no armed forces at its disposal, and the concept of a small international peacekeeping force used essentially for buffer purposes had to await the United Nations era.

Finally, the League was confronted with an international system far more harsh and unsuited to the successful maintenance of international organization devoted to peace than the successor United Nations Organization. The League possessed no nuclear umbrella, and the risk of total war was far greater as a result; there was no large group of neutral nations standing between the principal antagonists and serving in part as a channel for the expansionist energies of dynamic and often grasping states; and there was an economic depression of world-wide dimension that was of crucial importance in the development of the totalitarian governments that viewed war as the most propitious technique for solving economic problems.

Yet for all its vulnerability and institutional frailties, the League of Nations marked the initiation of governmental acceptance of a world order perspective, and it thus stands in the history of international relations as a turning point of supreme consequence for the peace and well-being of mankind. The League's political, economic and social bodies were charged with tasks necessitating more constant communication and planning than was known to state practice in the years prior to 1920, even though on a scale that appears evanescent in 1970. And one of the great contributions of the League of Nations was the concept and reality of an international secretariat, a group of civil servants devoted to international service, rather than the bureaucracy and government of any one nation. This too was a radical departure from past practice, and it stamped 1920 as the year of inauguration for the slow and gradual development of meaningful organs of world order.

There is little question that the greatest legacy left by Sir Eric Drummond, the first Secretary-General of the League of Nations, was the international civil service, for while the Versailles Conference had not settled the issue, Drummond insisted that the officers who served the League's political, economic and social bodies should be international servants devoted primarily to League interests, as defined by those bodies. He created a core of public officials continuously at work for the League, and since the international secretariat was the only League organ to work continuously, it came to be the embodiment, in many respects, of the League of Nations itself. At the apex of the Secretariat structure stood Secretary-General Drummond, the quiet and efficient administrator whose intimate knowledge of League history, procedures, personalties and political issues, combined with a scrupulous impartiality and devotion to peaceful settlement, prepared the foundation and illuminated the techniques for the development of a political role for the Secretary-General unforeseen and unintended by the League founders, and carried to peak importance in the United Nations era.

Sir Eric Drummond and his Appointment as the First Secretary-General

James Eric Drummond, of Scottish descent from a family that can claim relationship with most of Europe's royal families, was born in Yorkshire, England on August 17, 1876. He was educated at the Bedford Grammar School and Eton, from which he won the Prince Consort's Prize for French in his last year. Young Drummond had no university training, but spent a year on the Continent traveling and studying language, primarily in Germany.

There was relatively little wealth in Drummond's immediate family, or even in the larger clan, for the great Drummond Castle and massive estates had been confiscated by the British crown when the sixth Earl of Perth, a former Lord High Chancellor of Scotland, had his titles and land attainted by Parliament at the end of the seventeenth century for his loyalty to the Stuart cause. More than a century later the estates were restored to James Drummond, who died without male children, but when, some forty years later still, Queen Victoria had Parliament repeal the act of Attainder of the Earldom of Perth in favor of the fourteenth Earl, the estates were beyond recovery. The fourteenth Earl died in 1902, predeceased by his son and grandson, and James Eric Drummond, a distant cousin, became the heir presumptive as his older half-brother assumed the title. Drummond, who was knighted in 1916 while still working in the British Foreign Office, became the sixteenth Earl of Perth in 1937 upon the death of his half-brother without children.

In 1900, at the age of twenty-four, Drummond entered the British Foreign Office as a clerk, but his work was considered outstanding and his rise was very rapid, for by 1906 he was appointed private secretary to Lord Fitzmaurice, Parliamentary Under-Secretary of State for Foreign Affairs. He worked at this level, and also as a precis writer to the Foreign Secretary, Sir Edward Grey, until 1912. From 1912 to 1915, Drummond served as one of the private secretaries to Prime Minister Herbert H. Asquith, and he worked in a similar capacity for Foreign Secretary Grey from 1915 to 1916. Finally, in 1916 he became private secretary to Sir Arthur Balfour, who had succeeded Lord Grey as head of the Foreign Office, and he remained with Balfour for three years until his appointment as first Secretary-General of the League of Nations.

Drummond's path to the League's highest office lay initially through his friendship with Colonel Edward M. House, President Wilson's closest adviser on matters relating to America's relations with the Allies, the post-war settlement, and the League of Nations. Drummond and House first met in 1915 when Drummond was secretary to Sir Edward Grey and House was in Britain representing President Wilson. Later, on April 2, 1917, Sir Eric cabled House just after Wilson's speech asking Congress to declare the existence of war between Germany and the United States:

May I offer you my warmest congratulations on magnificent speech of the President. We are all deeply moved at its terms and tone. When Congress has responded to the great ideals which he has expressed, we trust consideration will be given to a commission, technically expert, being sent from here to place at the disposal of the United States Government the experience gained in this country during the war.

It has been suggested that Mr. Arthur Balfour should be the head of such a commission for a short time to coordinate its activity and to discuss wider issues involved.[1]

This was a proposal for Balfour's famous Special War Mission, accepted almost immediately by Wilson, and shortly after the Congressional declaration of war, the Mission was on its way, landing at Halifax on April 21, and proceeding by train to Washington, where for the first time Drummond

---

[1] Charles Seymour, *The Intimate Papers of Colonel House* (Boston: Houghton Mifflin Company, 1928), Vol. III, p. 33.

met President Wilson. Shortly thereafter similar missions arrived from France, Belgium and Italy, all for the purpose of securing the joint effort essential for the defeat of Germany.

Drummond was quite active in the talks between Wilson, Balfour, and House, and on many occasions presented the policy viewpoint of his Government or Balfour to House in separate conversations. Much of the policy planning was actually done through Drummond and his formulations were important in the final decisions taken. Thus House wrote to Wilson on May 20, 1917 that he and Drummond had "gone over the situation of the Central Powers and he has given me the views of his Foreign Office on many points... I convinced Drummond that the most effective thing we could do at present was to aid the German liberals in their fight against the present German Government".[2] House wanted to stress the notion of a war for the liberation of all peoples, including the Germans, with no Allied wish to destroy the German state, but an insistence upon no dealings with the military autocracy. Drummond drafted a memorandum spelling out these considerations, and it came to be known as the House-Drummond memorandum, subsequent to approval by Balfour and Wilson. The salient points were that the United States and the Allies were totally committed to the destruction of German militarism, and that a clear distinction should be made between the German Government and the people it governed, the essential idea being there was no thought of dismembering Germany. The primary motivation was to weaken German morale and will to fight, and according to one outstanding scholar of the time: "The points outlined in the House-Drummond memorandum deserve careful appraisal, since they formed the basis for the public statements of President Wilson during the remainder of the War".[3]

The Balfour Mission was of great significance for Drummond's later career, for it was during the course of the visit that Wilson broached the idea of the League of Nations to Balfour, and it is reported that the Foreign Secretary, apparently not particularly interested in or attracted by the plan, turned the matter over to Drummond, whom he was later to call "the perfect private secretary".[4] Wilson found Sir Eric extremely interested and

---

[2] *Id.*, pp. 57-58.

[3] *Id.*, p. 59.

[4] See an article by Robert Neville in *The New York Times*, September 27, 1931, Section 9, p. 5. The author cites Balfour's Memoirs as the source of the statement. However, the unfinished autobiography left by Balfour in 1930 includes no such phrase. There is a mention of Eric Drummond as his private secretary, however, within the context of a brief discussion of his visit to Washington in 1917 on the Special War Mission. There is little question that Balfour thought highly of Drummond, of whom he said: "I was fortunate in securing his services when I took Grey's place, and from then onwards either in that capacity or in the infinitely more important one of Secretary-General to the League of Nations, he has done incalculable service to the cause of European peace. I attempt no catalogue of the others of our Mission with whom I had such happy

enthused, and of course, under those circumstances, the President was not likely to forget him. And indeed, when Wilson and Drummond met again at the Versailles Peace Conference, Balfour's "perfect private secretary" was one of the few present to whom he could turn for both advice and sympathy on the League project, for Sir Eric had studied the issue closely, was still enthused, and able to discuss the matter in all its complexities with the President and assist him with the intricate diplomacy required to steer the project through the Conference. According to one account, Drummond "became his principal confidant in the matter" and the President "came to look upon Sir Eric as the man of all others who appreciated his ideals, who understood and sympathized with his views about the League of Nations".[5]

But notwithstanding his devotion to and deep appreciation of the League idea, Drummond, with his quiet behind-the-scenes training and experience in the British Foreign Office, was not necessarily what the great powers were seeking in the executive head of the new Organization. A primary issue for the League founders was whether the Secretariat's first officer should have political responsibilities and functions, or merely administrative tasks, and the problem was reflected in the choice of titles—that is, whether a Chancellor or a Secretary-General should be appointed.

Sir Robert Cecil of the British delegation to Versailles, in a draft he gave to Colonel House on January 1, 1919, initially proposed the title "General Secretary", but two weeks later revised it to read "The General Secretary or Chancellor" and finally, on January 19, he decided on "Chancellor". The draft plans suggested by the British were the only ones, prior to the publication of joint American-British proposals, that even mentioned an office of Secretary-General. The first official British draft plan, dated January 20, 1919, referred to a Chancellor to be appointed by the Council, and to hold office "during the pleasure of the Council". Concerning the issue of the nationality of the Secretariat's highest officer, Cecil's January 14 draft would have had the General Secretary or Chancellor appointed by the Great Powers, but if possible, not one of their nationals. His January 20 draft left the problem unresolved.[6]

The essential question, discussed quietly, was the availability of acceptable candidates, for a Chancellor obviously had to be an international statesman of some note if he were to have serious political tasks, whereas a Secretary-General with more routine administrative functions might well be a lesser figure. The question was formally decided in the League of Nations Commission, established on January 25, 1919, to work out in

---

associations". (Arthur James Balfour, *Retrospect* (Boston: Houghton Mifflin Company, 1930), pp. 240-241.

[5] *The New York Times*, February 7, 1926, Section 2, p. 4.

[6] The several drafts are to be found in David Hunter Miller, *The Drafting of the Covenant* (New York: G. P. Putnam's Sons, 1928), Vol. II, *passim*.

detail the provisions of the Covenant and the League's general functions. The various drafts all listed tasks for the executive head which fell primarily in the administrative category, but the Hurst-Miller draft, a combined British-American effort, still referred to a Chancellor and this draft served as the basis for the League Commission's discussions. The Chancellor, according to Hurst and Miller, was to appoint and have general direction and control over the staff, act as Secretary at meetings of the Council and Body of Delegates, make arrangements for the investigation and consideration of disputes referred to the Council, and register treaties. These are administrative tasks, the first three of which became the responsibility of the Secretary-General; the fourth was entrusted to the Secretariat itself.

During the next few weeks, the decision was taken to appoint a Secretary-General, for on February 13, 1919, the Drafting Committee of the League Commission substituted "Secretary-General" for "Chancellor"[7] and this was accepted throughout the remainder of the negotiations. Apparently it was not possible to secure an outstanding political leader for the post, and it therefore became necessary to downgrade it somewhat, at least in title, for certainly the published drafts give no evidence of any political functions even for the proposed "Chancellor". Further, it was also apparently decided to select a Secretary-General from among the key western states, preferably England, for House cabled to President Wilson on February 27 "Having an English-speaking Secretary-General will lessen our difficulties and not put us at disadvantage as would a French or Italian Secretary-General. It would also enable us to take the Chairmanship of the Executive Council if we so desire. Please give me your views".[8] The message here seems to be that the Secretariat head should be a British national, for only then would the U.S. have been able to take the Chairmanship of the Council.

Finally, at the twelfth meeting of the League Commission, on March 24, the French representative recommended the adoption of an addition to the proposed Article 11 that would have enabled the Secretary-General "at the request of any one of the Associated Governments" to convoke a meeting of the Council in case of "any occurrence calculated to imperil the maintenance of peace".[9] This was adopted, and was of great importance, for if there was any one political task to be entrusted to the Secretary-General or Chancellor, it was in this—that a strong political figure might call the Council on his own initiative; an administrative head would have to secure a request from a member state. The League founders opted for the latter alternative, probably in the light of their failure to secure an important statesman of the time to head the new Organization. Indeed, the search for a Chancellor might already have been abandoned by the time the League Commission began its discussions, for there is some evidence that the

[7] *Id.,* p. 305.
[8] Seymour, *op. cit.,* Vol. IV, p. 352.
[9] Miller, *op. cit.,* p. 347.

British gave up the notion of an international statesman in the face of political objections from the French and Italian Governments, and then merged their administrative conception into the Hurst-Miller draft.[10]

There were several possibilities for Chancellor discussed at Versailles. Wilson himself at one time toyed with the idea, and among others mentioned were Cecil and Maurice Hankey of Great Britain, Thomas Masaryk of Czechoslovakia, General Jan Smuts of South Africa, and most prominently, Eleutherios Venizelos of Greece. Venizelos was the most long-lived of the candidates, but when he finally refused the post, the Chancellor idea collapsed. As Drummond himself put the matter:

"The first idea was to have an important and well-known political statesman... He would have wide political powers, even wider than the Secretary-General of the United Nations... The League Secretary-General was supposed to be an international civil servant, the Chancellor an international statesman. It hinged on trying to get Venizelos. Whey they found they couldn't get the highest caliber man for the job, they had second thoughts about it... They decided they didn't want an international 'dictator'." [11]

This was confirmed by Lord Cecil in 1941,[12] and has been generally accepted, notwithstanding the incompleteness of the official documentation.

Sir Eric Drummond was now in a perfect position for the Secretary-General post, given his administrative talents, British nationality (evidently attractive to House), and his friendship with Wilson. On April 28, 1919, the Covenant was accepted by the Peace Conference in a Plenary Session and Drummond was named in an Annex to the Covenant as the first Secretary-General of the League. He is the only individual whose name appears either in the League Covenant or the Charter of the United Nations.

The choice was certainly fortunate from the standpoint of the League of Nations and the Office of the Secretary-General, for indeed, Sir Eric, just forty-two at the time of his appointment, was the "perfect private secretary". Analyses of the League era are in virtual agreement on the personal qualities of the man, and in every case the picture is that of the quiet, even shy, but extraordinarily gifted administrator, with a passion for anonymity, great tact and discretion, and an intimate knowledge of the issues confronting the new Organization. Drummond was extremely modest, and given his lack of oratorical capacity and his general policy of rarely speaking out in public, the Secretary-General impressed most observers as something less than a dynamic figure. "Sir Eric's modesty fits him perfectly", wrote one sympathetic observer. "In appearance he might be compared with a small-town banker who was a bit preoccupied. But a cartoonist once de-

---

[10] See Jean Siotis, *Essai Sur Le Secretariat International* (Geneva: Publications de l'Institut Universitaire de Hautes Etudes Internationales, No. 41, 1963), p. 64.
[11] Stephen M. Schwebel, *The Secretary-General of the United Nations* (Cambridge: Harvard University Press, 1952), p. 4.
[12] Lord Robert Cecil, *A Great Experiment* (New York: Oxford University Press, 1941), pp. 89-90.

picted him as a choir boy, and it is hard to lose the impression of him in this character".[13] Yet the shyness and evident lack of humor in the Drummond known to the public were apparently not at all evident in his behind-the-scenes work as administrator and advisor to League representatives and staff members, for here was Sir Eric at his best, shrewd, extremely well-informed, but impartial, and with a real ability to inspire trust and confidence in the statesmen and international civil servants with whom he dealt.

Drummond recognized himself the essential differences between his public and private images. He is quoted in Stephen M. Schwebel's outstanding study of the Secretary-General as saying that "I don't think people are influenced by public speeches or documents. They are by private talk. The behind-the-scenes work of the Secretary-General is more important". He added that "Behind-the-scenes activities suited my temperament and previous experience. I was neither a Parliamentarian nor a politician and totally unaccustomed to making speeches in public, though I was compelled to make numerous speeches when I went on official tours".[14] If Sir Eric was not a forceful public figure, certainly the League representatives and key political figures of the day were content, for he gave full credit and responsibility to the Council and Assembly for decisions taken, thus keeping any independent initiatives of the League Secretariat deliberately in the background, and minimizing any tendency to create another actor in the complex system of international relations prevailing in the post-war period. Further, given his tact, state representatives could rely upon his refusal to betray a confidence, and his impartiality meant trust on the most delicate of issues. There is no question that Drummond was well-informed, and at the same time imaginative in the formulation of proposals or ideas that politicians might find acceptable and rivals agree upon for compromise solutions to vexing problems.

Apparently Sir Eric got on well in personal terms with the diplomats at the League, for if he had no real political power or public political skills, certainly he was the social equal, as a knight and heir presumptive to a peerage, of the men with whom he worked, and he had the substantial assistance of Lady Drummond, the second daughter of the eleventh Baron Herries, in his manifold social duties as Secretary-General. And while Drummond generally worked long hours, his relaxation was normally devoted to social activities, such as tennis, golf, and bridge.

In terms of the development of the Organization and the Office of the Secretary-General, the Drummond style was probably essential, for the evidence indicates that the statesmen of Europe in the 1920's would not have permitted a strong politicized executive head, and had Drummond made attempts along these lines, the alienation almost certain to follow

[13] *The New York Times,* September 27, 1931, Section 9, p. 5.
[14] Schwebel, *op. cit.,* p. 7.

would have hindered the growth of international institutions. Certainly the idea of an international secretariat was new and untested, and Drummond's behavior and general practice were well-suited to encourage the development of reliance upon his good faith and equity, and to permit probing and examination of the possibilities and limitations inherent in the structure of the Office. The statesmen at San Francisco in 1945 were certainly more knowledgable and confident about the nature of the Secretaryship-General because of Drummond's careful and methodical development of the Office than might have been the case had he opted for a strong political leadership role.

The usual contrast here is that of Drummond and Albert Thomas, the dynamic French Director of the International Labour Office, whose style of executive management was precisely that of the energetic initiator of political action. With no greater constitutional authorization than the League Secretary-General, Thomas took the lead in publicly proposing specific measures to the ILO Conference, even when governments disagreed with the substance of his recommendations, and did not hesitate to present publicly, through statements to the Conference, his annual reports, speeches on tour, the press, and contacts with representatives from governments, employers and trade unions, his perspective on the critical issues confronting the ILO and the international community generally.[15]

The ILO, to be sure, a specialized agency devoted to a particular sphere of activity, and having as its constituency representatives of unions and employers, as well as governments, was not the League of Nations. A dynamic role is usually more feasible in the narrower context, and even though it may reasonably be argued that Drummond might well have utilized at least some of the Thomas techniques (stating political views in the annual report, for example) without degrading in any way the strength of the Secretaryship-General, political influence for Sir Eric had to be exercised through his knowledge and imagination. At least from the start of the League of Nations, time was required to arrive at an appreciation whether the Secretary-General was going to be, in any fashion, even a minor rival to government decision-makers. Drummond could combine assurances on this issue with a meaningful political influence only by a self-effacing public image coincident with a large input of diplomatic capacity behind the scenes. The League's political bodies were clearly suspicious of Secretariat initiatives, as was made manifest from the outset by the Second Assembly:

We recommend with special urgency that in the interests of the League, as well as in its own interests, the Secretariat should not extend the sphere of its activities; that in the preparation of the work and the decisions of the various organizations of the League, it should regard it as its first duty to collate the relevant documents, and to prepare the ground for these decisions without suggesting what these decisions should

---

15 *Id.*, p. 12.

be; finally, that once these decisions have been taken by the bodies solely responsible for them, it should confine itself to executing them in the letter and in the spirit.[16]

Given this kind of attitude, it is hardly likely that Drummond would have succeeded with the Thomas strategy, and it is in no small measure due to Sir Eric's work that the UN Secretaries-General, while certainly opposed at particular junctures, have never been confronted with an entire Assembly united behind a severely inhibiting directive.

Thus the name of Sir Eric Drummond, while very well known to the Foreign Offices of League members, went largely unrecognized by the general public. The Secretary-General addressed Assembly committees or the Council only in a discreet administrative capacity, never as a political leader, and in fourteen years he made not a single statement to the plenary sessions of the Assembly. In sharp contrast to Thomas, his annual reports merely reviewed in straightforward manner the League activity for the previous year, and Sir Eric made no public statements diverging from any governmental viewpoint, never appealed in any way to public opinion, and rarely went so far even as to push the League or its importance in world politics. His talks justifying the Organization tended to be formal analyses of its structure, with but mild intimations that the international system might be more peaceful and orderly would states make more substantial use of it.

But for all that, Drummond was eminently successful in establishing an efficient international civil service, while demonstrating that the Secretary-General could influence the processes and direction of world organization and politics, and that quiet diplomacy might result in a very significant political role for an Office with no power or influence in the traditional sense at its disposal.[17] We have come to accept the international civil service and the political activity of the Secretary-General in 1970, and for both, the community of nations is indebted to Sir Eric Drummond.

The Functions of the League Secretary-General

The Covenant of the League of Nations was consistent with the intentions of the Organization's founders at Versailles that the highest staff officer be a Secretary-General rather than a Chancellor, for its provisions contained little authorizing a role of any significance for Drummond, although vagueness in formulation also permitted the Secretary-General an opportunity to develop his own powers as political conditions warranted and experience dictated. Article 6, the only Covenant clause devoted to the Secretariat, states simply that the first Secretary-General shall be the person named in the Annex and thereafter he is to be appointed by the Council

[16] Quoted in C. Howard-Ellis, *The Origin, Structure and Working of the League of Nations* (London: George Allen & Unwin, 1928), pp. 197-198.
[17] See pp. 51-96, *infra*.

with the approval of an Assembly majority.[18] The Secretary-General is to appoint the secretaries and staff with Council approval, and is to act "in that capacity" at all meetings of the Assembly and Council. Since the precise capacity in which Drummond was to function was nowhere specified or agreed upon, this clause appears to allow some room for interpretation, but the context precluded anything more than administrative tasks, and was certainly no mandate for active intervention by the Secretary-General in political debates, although Drummond might well have accomplished more in this regard had he so chosen.

Articles 11 and 15 authorize a limited political role for the Secretary-General, for in case of war or threat of war and on request of any League member, he is to "forthwith summon a meeting of the Council" and in case of a dispute submitted to the Council and likely to lead to a rupture, to "make all necessary arrangements for a full investigation and consideration". Summoning a Council session on request of any League member is considerably less power than the UN Charter's Article 99 authorization for the UN Secretary-General to convene the Security Council on his own initiative if he perceives a threat to the peace, but in practice the difference need not have been substantial, for a strong League Secretary-General, as Felix Morley points out, would have had little difficulty in securing the agreement of one of some fifty-five members to request a Council meeting in a particular case.[19] Schwebel quotes Drummond as having stated "I wish Article 99 had been at my disposal",[20] but the Covenant Article 11 formulation, while narrower, still permitted room for maneuver for an energetic and politically active Secretary-General.[21] The provision for an investigation

[18] There was no set term for the first Secretary-General, and in the case of Drummond, no disposition to seek his replacement until Sir Eric announced his resignation. The salary of the Secretary-General was set at £ 4000, with entertainment and house allowances totalling another £ 3500. The sum of £ 7500 was about half the salary and allowances of an important British Ambassador. See Howard-Ellis, *op. cit.*, p. 179.
[19] Felix Morley, *The Society of Nations* (Washington: The Brookings Institution, 1932), p. 309.
[20] Schwebel, *op. cit.*, p. 17.
[21] Within the context of the League's discussion on economic sanctions under Article 16 of the Covenant, the Assembly, on December 10, 1920, passed a resolution that included the following clause: "It shall be the duty of the Secretary-General to call the attention of the Council to any facts which in his opinion show that a member of the League has become a Covenant-breaking State within the Meaning of Article XVI;
"Upon receiving such an intimation, the Council shall, on the request of any of its members, hold a meeting with the least possible delay to consider it..." (*Records of First Assembly*, Plenary, 1920, p. 409).
As originally drawn up, the Secretary-General alone would have called the Council into session automatically by calling attention to facts indicating a League member had violated the Covenant within the meaning of Article 16, but after objection, the clauses were modified to require a request for a meeting by a Member. Lord Robert Cecil formally proposed that the procedure be made "the same as Article 11 of the Covenant... It will not be left entirely to the Secretary-General to summon a meeting:

by the Secretary-General under Article 15 also permits a certain latitude, for again a dynamic figure might advise a government in a given case to invoke Article 15, thus paving the way for an inquiry by the Secretariat head, and it might even have been possible for an investigation to be carried out between Council sessions.[22]

But the formal constitutional stipulations had very little relationship with the key functions, administrative, parliamentary, and political, performed from the outset of his tenure by Secretary-General Drummond, and continued by his successors to the present time. The salient political function of the Drummond administration was mediation and negotiation with government representatives at the League, by correspondence, and in the many capitals he visited. In this context, the League's Secretary-General, working quietly and with no publicity whatever, was able to influence the procedural and substantive direction of many issues confronting the Organization, and with no constitutional authorization or League resources beyond his central position in world affairs, his knowledge of the issues and personalities of the time, and his own creative capacity and imagination in formulating proposals likely to be acceptable to parties with widely divergent interests and outlooks. Covenant Articles 11 and 15 never played an important part in the political history of the League Secretaryship-General, for as will be seen,[23] diplomatic negotiation and recommendation were clearly the most significant of the executive head's diverse roles. Drummond's office was the scene of many "secret" Council sessions, and the forum for countless discussions with individual representatives on League political bodies.

Closely related to Sir Eric's mediation function was communication of

---

he will have to get the approval and initiative of one Member of the Council". (*Id.,* p. 405) His amendment carried without debate. Cecil had made it clear, however, that he was not in agreement with the objections raised, and was compromising to reach the widest possible agreement.

In 1921, the Assembly passed a second resolution on the issue, and one of its clauses clearly gave the Secretary-General more power. On the second try, Cecil had no trouble whatever gaining acceptance for a provision that read as follows:

"All cases of breach of Covenant under Article 16 shall be referred to the Council as a matter of urgency at the request of any Member of the League. Further, if a breach of Covenant be committed, the Secretary-General shall at once give notice thereof to all the Members of the Council. Upon receipt of such a request by a Member of the League, or of such a notice by the Secretary-General, the Council will meet as soon as possible". (1921 *Assembly Resolutions,* October 4, 1921, p. 25)

Schwebel (*op. cit.,* p. 231) cites Drummond's explanation for allowing this authority to go unused as resting with its Article 16 context. That is to say, Sir Eric felt that in the absence of war, the resolution was not applicable. Yet, the provision refers to "a danger" of a Covenant breach. There is very little, if any, difference between this Assembly authorization and Article 99 of the UN Charter.

[22] Morley, *op. cit.,* p. 310.
[23] See pp. 51-96, *infra.*

information, a key mission for a figure centrally placed in the international arena. The talks held by political figures and staff members with Drummond were crucial in assisting the general negotiatory and bargaining process, for the Secretary-General was well situated to inform decision makers of important data and to pass on to them likely responses to particular positions. At times the Secretary-General was the most convenient channel for communication between parties who might otherwise have had very little contact, and in the case of states outside the Organization, the executive head was important as a central link to the world community. In the latter role, Drummond was particularly active as spokesman for the League, trying to secure support for the Organization, explaining its policies, and acting to smooth the way for nations wanting to join or strengthen their relationship with the organized international community. Sir Eric travelled widely, including trips to Germany, Italy, and Latin America.

All of Drummond's important political work, however, was done quietly and with no hint of a strategy to develop the international importance of the Office, for this was expected of a man appointed precisely because of his administrative, rather than political training and experience. Many students of the League era consider Drummond mistaken in failing to utilize at least two methods for making public statements of his position on key political issues. The annual report, of course, was a convenient vehicle for considered analyses of questions before the League, but as noted, Drummond chose to use it only for cataloging the Organization's activity for the previous year, and the current practice was inaugurated only under the administration of Trygve Lie in the late 1940's. Second, since it was open to Drummond to appear before the Assembly, its Committees, and the Council, he might have used the many opportunities to publicize his views, and thus perhaps augment the prestige and importance of his Office. Indeed, the League Assembly provided, in its rules of procedure, that the Secretary-General "may be invited by the President to make verbal communications concerning any question under consideration".[24] Egon Ranshofen-Wertheimer, a former League official and outstanding student of the Secretariat, has argued:

The tradition of the Secretary-General addressing the Assembly or the Council could and should have been established in the early days of the League when everything was still in flux. The novelty of the spectacle might have caused a slight initial fluster on the part of some delegates and diplomats wrapped in outdated traditions. But their susceptibilities were then being also tested by other features of the new instrument for international cooperation and they were becoming accustomed to seeing many of their cherished traditions upset at Geneva.

Had the Secretary-General personally presented his annual report and had he

---

[24] Quoted in Egon Ranshofen-Wertheimer, *The International Secretariat: A Great Experiment in International Administration* (Washington: Carnegie Endowment for International Peace, 1945), p. 38.

availed himself of this opportunity to expound and interpret international trends and possibilities of action, the general discussion of the Assembly might have been lifted into a real exchange of views instead of becoming a mere sequence of set speeches and official declarations.[25]

Ranshofen-Wertheimer thought that the League founders quite deliberately restricted the Secretary-General's political power "on the assumption that his functions and role would automatically increase with the League's growing influence".[26] The problem was that Drummond and Avenol after him did not avail themselves of at least two avenues of influence, however marginal, open to them, thereby artificially confining the Office to a lesser place in world politics. If Drummond was in no position to emulate fully the Albert Thomas model, his refusal to utilize League forums and reports was probably as unnecessary as it was unfortunate. In sharp contrast to the political history of the United Nations Secretaries-General, the international role of the League executive head changed very little in the two decades of its active existence, circumscribed as it was by the chosen framework of private and quiet discussion.[27]

Drummond's parliamentary and staff functions were extensive, and the practices established and maintained by Sir Eric are still the core of the internal powers exercised by the Office today. His primary tasks in the Council and Assembly were procedural, for the most part guiding the Presidents of those bodies through the often bewildering mass of rules governing their functioning, and in this capacity Drummond attended almost all Council sessions and plenary Assembly meetings. As noted, his interventions were almost always in an administrative role, frequently to impart information on a staff or budgetary question. Sir Eric spent a great deal of time defending and explaining the budget before the Assembly's Fourth Committee, and working with the Supervisory Commission for the same purpose, as he was responsible for drafting the budget estimates, and for all final League expenditures. Drummond's concern with parliamentary tasks followed naturally from his assignment to suggest Assembly and Council committee structures and representation, and to select rapporteurs for particular questions before the Council. The Secretary-General was accountable for all Secretariat reports and position papers communicated to the Assembly or Council, and he prepared many himself. And of course, the Secretariat was responsible for the execution of decisions taken by the League's political organs, insofar as an international civil service possessed the ability to supervise the implementation of agreed upon resolutions.

The Secretary-General had full power, in theory, over staff appointments, although as we shall see, political pressures severely limited his discretion to select his aides in the Secretariat upper level offices. Drummond

[25] *Id.,* pp. 39-40.
[26] *Id.,* p. 38.
[27] See pp. 100-103, *infra.*

was also instrumental in the shaping of the staff regulations governing all Secretariat members, including their working conditions, terms of employment, promotions, and the like. His basic administrative techniques, derived from his experience in the British Foreign Office, resulted in greater reliance upon English rather than French bureaucratic practices in the Secretariat until the Avenol administration began in 1933. Essentially, this meant a great deal of discretion granted to lower level personnel, as the preparation of documents and Secretariat planning commenced in the Sections and if necessary, particular problems were brought to higher levels and finally to the Secretary-General only in cases of political sensitivity or administrative difficulty beyond the discretionary authorization of the "Haute Direction", as the top-level structure came to be known. The French system entails more initial responsibility for the Secretary-General followed by delegations of authority to lower-level personnel. Drummond had very little contact with lower-level staff, although he worked closely with his Directors and Under-Secretaries, both in private conference and in the weekly meetings.

A good deal of Sir Eric's internal staff work was done through written messages, most commonly in the form of comments made on memoranda sent up by any of the Directors. The League Archives are replete with notations from the Secretary-General, frequently a simple "I agree" or "approved", and at times rather detailed explications of alternative suggestions or analyses of why he disagreed with a particular approach. The original work and development of plans commenced in the Sections, although the Secretary-General always gave final approval, and in Drummond's case, frequently influenced the direction of a particular item as well. Most communications from the Sections were read first by Frank Walters, the head of Sir Eiric's "cabinet", who reviewed the entire matter for Drummond, noted his own opinion, and made any recommendations he felt appropriate, thus contributing to the normal rapidity with which Drummond worked. According to several former League officials, very little of consequence was decided at Directors' Meetings, which were held for information puposes and informal discussion of pertinent issues. The great majority of internal Secretariat decisions were taken by the Secretary-General and the Director of the Section involved, either through personal conference or written notes and memoranda.

Drummond also had a unique task of construction, for a new multipurpose global institution was confronted with the enormous mission of establishing the several organizational systems designed to implement the rather nebulous Covenant framework. The Mandates and Minorities systems, for example, had to be built from scratch, and the constitutional and procedural principles to guide their proper functioning had to be written, tested, and developed quickly, and in this the Secretary-General had a large role, for he supervised the staff work involved and helped his Directors establish such principles. This was not just a matter of fashioning a particular Secretariat model, although that in itself was one of Drummond's greatest contributions to world organization, but a question of how particular sections of the Secretariat were going to serve the League's political bodies in implementing the obligations outlined in the Covenant and in Council and Assembly resolutions. Sir Eric wrote many of the basic rules and helped shape the initial groundwork for several of the League's systems, including the economic, financial, mandates, minorities, and to a lesser extent other Secretariat sections.

The League Secretary-General thus combined a complex series of administrative and political-diplomatic assignments, although in the first years of the Organization, the distinction between the two was never very evident, for the construction and administration of a new international bureaucracy at least ostensibly neutral in the nation-state conflicts of the time was a departure of considerable political import in the 1920's, and tended to assume a diplomatic significance. Administrative and diplomatic functions were both of political interest to League members, and Drummond's administrative expertise and efficiency essential resources for the political success of global institutions.

Drummond and the International Civil Service

The same Plenary Session of the Versailles Peace Conference that accepted the Covenant on April 28, 1919, and appointed Drummond the first Secretary-General, also established a Committee on Organization of the League of Nations to make plans for the establishment of the official machinery of the League pending ratification of the Covenant. The Organization Committee, consisting of representatives from the states with seats on the first Council—the Principal Allied and Associated Powers plus Belgium, Brazil, Greece, and Spain—held two formal meetings, one each on May 5 and June 9, 1919.[28] At the first of these sessions Sir Eric (in the capacity of Acting Secretary-General until the Covenant came into effect in January, 1920) was instructed to prepare proposals for the League structure, and with a credit of £ 100,000 open for his use, he was authorized to engage a temporary staff and offices.

Between the May 5 and June 9 meetings of the Committee, Drummond secured the services of several officials to assist him in the Secretariat, including a few of outstanding merit in the work of the League. By June 9, he could report the acceptances of Jean Monnet of France, and Raymond B. Fosdick of the United States as Under Secretaries-General, Paul Mantoux, a French historian, to serve as director of the Political Section, Arthur

[28] Press summaries of the Organization Committee's meetings, setting forth the resolutions passed and a very brief summary of discussion are available in the League Archives at the United Nations European Headquaters in Geneva.

Salter, an outstanding British civil servant, selected to head the Economic and Financial Section, Erik Colban of Norway, originally slated for the directorship of the Section on administrative commissions, and Joost Van Hamel, a Dutch jurist to head the Legal Section.

The June 9 session of the Committee resolved that the League had to be fully informed of political, economic, financial and social considerations relevant to its work, and that every member should supply the Secretariat "with all appropriate information". Further, League members were requested to "count as meritorious the service of their nationals on the International Secretariat of the League".[29] This was not altogether consistent with the concept of an international civil service, but the Secretary-General, in later writings of his own,[30] asserted that the Committee generally accepted his conception of the Secretariat.

Perhaps the first published declaration of the Drummond theory of the Secretariat came on May 31, 1919, in an interview Sir Eric granted to the *Manchester Guardian:*

We are working out plans for a truly international secretariat. Its members will have an international character of mind. They must divest themselves of national preconceptions. Its members are not to be appointed by or to be regarded as the representatives of their respective nations. When important national interests are involved it will be found essential that Prime Ministers and Foreign Secretaries should attend meetings of the Council and Assembly.

The secretariat must show an entirely impartial aspect. There must be one guiding principle—that of securing really first-rate men and women interested heart and soul in the success of the League.[31]

The Secretary-General subsequently stated, in an article published in 1931, "When I was appointed Secretary-General in April, 1919, I found that there were two utterly opposed ideas as to how the Secretariat should be constituted".[32] The first, of course, was the conception based upon the models of the several inter-allied cooperative organizations during the war, in which the secretariat would consist of government representatives. "The second idea", wrote Sir Eric, "which was the one I personally had cherished, was the constitution of a truly international civil service—officals who would be solely the servants of the League and in no way representatives of or responsible to the Governments of the countries of which they were nationals".[33] Drummond states that he placed both views before the Organization Committee, naturally endorsing the second, and "[h]appily

[29] Press Communique, 9 June 1919, p. 1.
[30] See footnote 32.
[31] The *Manchester Guardian,* 31 May 1919, p. 10; quoted in Helen M. Moats, *The Secretariat of the League of Nations: International Civil Service or Diplomatic Conference?* (University of Chicago: unpublished doctoral dissertation, 1936), p. 89.
[32] Sir Eric Drummond, "The Secretariat of the League of Nations", *Public Administration* (Vol. 9, 1931), p. 228.
[33] *Id.,* p. 229.

from my point of view, the members of the Committee were unanimously in favour of it. It was therefore on this foundation that the further building was undertaken". From Sir Eric's perspective, an international secretariat "would not only result in fresh progress in international affairs but was essential if the League were to become what its founders hoped it would be".[34]

Drummond lost little time in setting up the Secretariat along the preferred lines, and given the fact that the Council did not meet until January, 1920, he had several months with relatively few distractions. Immediately after the Organizing Committee's second meeting, and in order to distinguish the League from Versailles, Sir Eric departed for London, where the Secretariat's very first headquarters had been established temporarily in a back drawing room at Manchester Square. The Acting Secretary-General had one assistant, Lord Colum Cricton-Stuart, one stenographer, and one office keeper. Larger quarters were then secured at Sunderland House in Mayfair, and this served as the real first home of the League of Nations for over a year, as it was not until September, 1920, that the Secretariat moved to more permanent quarters in the old Hotel National in Geneva, Switzerland. The final and permanent Headquarters, the Palais des Nations in Geneva, was ready for occupation in 1936, and is utilized today by several bodies of the United Nations system as the UN European Headquarters.

Political pressures concerning the top-level posts in the Secretariat were exercised from the start, even during the negotiations among members of the Organizing Committee. Sir Eric felt that from the administrative viewpoint, a Secretary-General and one Deputy would have been sufficient, but this of course raised the nationality issue, and the Committee decided upon two deputies. Monnet and Fosdick were selected, representing France and the United States, but Japan and Italy, the two remaining great powers slated for permanent Council representation, were then without nationals in the Secretariat's "Haute Direction". The final compromise agreed to by Drummond with the members of the Committee was one Deputy from each of the four powers, although with the resignation of Fosdick in January, 1920, the number was cut back. Drummond's top-level "cabinet" then consisted of Monnet as Deputy, and Dionisio Anzilotti of Italy and Inazo Nitobe from Japan as Under Secretaries-General. Sir Eric later insisted that the pressure was not simply a matter of political prestige, but an understanding by Committee members that it would be to the Secretariat's advantage to secure the services of outstanding and prominent people, and to achieve this, the rank and conditions had to be attractive.[35] Nevertheless, the great powers in 1919, and in the years since, insisted upon a represen-

---

[34] *Ibid.*
[35] *Ibid.*

tation of political interests at the Secretariat's key decision-making level, indicative perhaps of the prevailing conception that even a weak administrative body may exert political infuence, and that national interests had therefore to be protected.

Drummond organized the Secretariat into several substantive sections in accordance with League functions as depicted in the Covenant, thus rejecting an alternative suggestion of geographic division, but the top-level staff, ranging from Under-Secretary through Director and Member of Section, were overwhelmingly Western European, with the great powers dominant throughout.

Sir Eric finally reported to the League Council in May, 1920 on his initial construction of the Secretariat, and apparently the great powers were satisfied with their representation in the Haute Direction, for there was little discussion and a general acceptance of Drummond's efforts and the conception of an international service. The Council established a committee to examine Sir Eric's work, and the report of this committee,[36] known as the Balfour Report (although Drummond had contributed heavily to its writing), was significant as the first formal League legitimization of the international civil service:

By the terms of the Treaty, the duty of selecting the staff falls upon the Secretary-General, just as the duty of approving it falls upon the Council. In making his appointments, he had primarily to secure the best available men and women for the particular duties which had to be performed; but in doing so, it was necessary to have regard to the great importance of selecting the officials from various nations.[37] Evidently, no one nation or group of nations ought to have a monopoly in providing the material for this international institution. I emphasize the word "International", because the members of the Secretariat once appointed are no longer the servants of the country of which they are citizens, but become for the time being the servants only of the League of Nations. Their duties are not national but international.[38]

Sir Eric reported to the First Assembly of the League in December, 1920, just after the Secretariat move from Sunderland House in London to the new quarters in Geneva. For the first time, he was publicly challenged by a number of representatives on his organizational achievement, but

---

[36] League of Nations, *Official Journal,* I, No. 4 (June, 1920), p. 137.

[37] Cf. the wording of the UN Charter's Article 101, paragraph 3: "The paramount consideration in the employment of the staff and in the determination of the conditions of service shall be the necessity of securing the highest standards of efficiency, competence, and integrity. Due regard shall be paid to the importance of recruiting the staff on as wide a geographical basis as possible". The League commonly referred to "distribution of nationalities" while for the United Nations the counterpart phrase is "geographical distribution".

[38] Sir Eric's wording, the direct forerunner of Article 101 (3) in the UN Charter was as follows: "The object, in making these appointments, is to secure the best available men and women for a particular post, but due regard has been and will be paid, so far as possible, to the selection of persons of different nationalities". (Proces-Verbal, 5th Sess. of the Council, Annex 5, p. 219)

while most of the issues raised were important—such as the Secretary-General's right to dismiss staff, nationality distribution, desirability of short terms, methods of recruitment, pensions, etc.—there was no disposition to challenge the fundamental structure or theoretical foundation of the administration. Basic functions were hardly discussed, and since the Council had not seriously considered the matter, Drummond had successfully shaped the Secretariat tasks within the framework of his own appreciation of what the political system might permit.

The Expert Committee appointed by the Assembly, known as the Noblemaire Committee for its Chairman, approved of Drummond's general work in its report of May 7, 1921,[39] and went into great detail on the structure of the Secretariat organization, covering problems of post classifications, salaries, terms of appointment, recruitment techniques, distribution and merit as determinants of staff hiring, and general conditions of work. Secretary-General Drummond defended the organization he had established, particularly the distribution of nationalities, both at lower levels and in the Haute Direction. As for functions, the Noblemaire Report tended to stress the purely administrative tasks, citing the preparation of material for meetings of the political organs and the publications of decisions.

The next several years witnessed the steady growth and consolidation of the Secretariat under Drummond's direction, but with continued great-power dominance, representation of national interests at the top-level, and the repeated appointment of diplomats to posts in the Haute Direction—all tending to weaken the fabric of internationalism in the Secretariat, but certainly in response to political representations that were persuasive to the Secretary-General and for the most part accepted by the greater portion of the League's membership. The practice of assuring the great powers "representation" in the top-level structure was an issue of controversy in the 1920's, although it has become common enough practice in the United Nations era.[40] At times, however, the political influences at work were in the context of demands well beyond representation. Thus, for example, Drummond paid a visit to Premier Mussolini in Rome shortly after the Corfu crisis in 1923, later quoting the Italian leader as asserting that Italy's place in the Organization should be more "adequately established".[41] British and French dominance had obviously rankled Mussolini, and in 1924, Drummond doubled the number of Italians in the Secretariat.

[39] Report of the Committee of Experts (Noblemaire Report), 7 May 1921, *Records of Second Assembly,* Minutes of Fourth Committee, Annex 2.
[40] The emergence in the Secretariat of "national islands" was still another practice in the weakening of the League staff's internationalism. Each of the top-level officers had a kind of "cabinet" of his own, composed primarily of co-nationals. For example, as of December, 1926, Drummond's office had four assistants of English nationality, and one New Zealander; Avenol's cabinet was composed of six Frenchmen, and usage in the offices of the Under-Secretaries was not significantly different.
[41] *The New York Times,* 7 November 1923.

The first blatant attack against the integrity of the Secretariat came in June, 1927, in the form of a law promulgated by the Fascist Parliament in Rome requiring Italian nationals to obtain the permission of the Government prior to entering the service of international organizations, including the League, or foreign governments. The consent was at all times subject to revocation, and those holding foreign or international posts were obliged to maintain contact with local Italian Government representatives.[42] The Italian, and from 1926, the German Secretariat officials were apparently in no position to take seriously their obligations as international civil servants, for national allegiances were made manifest, including the practice of reporting particular Secretariat items deemed to be of interest back to the home government. There was little the Secretary-General could do given the necessity of maintaining Italian and German membership in the League, although British and French dominance did little to assuage the suspicions of those who were essentially revisionist in European politics.[43]

With the entrance of Germany into the League in 1926, the stage was set for the great debate of the next several years on the Secretariat, particularly the Secretaryship-General and the entire top-level structure, for Italy was quickly joined by Germany in an attempt to limit British and French hegemony, and to limit the independence of the Secretary-General by means of group decision-making, a procedure that would have significantly curtailed the development of the Office. By this time, it was obvious enough that the upper strata of the Secretariat were filled with political appointees responsible in fact not to Secretary-General Drummond, but to their respective foreign offices, with their primary functions being advisory, representative, and liaison with home governments.[44] Sir Eric himself remained generally above suspicion, although this judgment was certainly not shared by the German and Italian governments, but the principles of the Balfour Report were eroding through concessions made to political pressures and the constant and conspicuous failure of the German and Italian staff members to observe the most fundamental of staff regulations.

Drummond, as was to be expected, defended himself and his administration from small-power charges that he had insufficiently protected the integrity of the Secretariat from attacks by the dominant states in the Organization. Responding to assertions made in 1928 by Carl Hambro of Norway in the Assembly's Fourth Committee that Sir Eric had failed to

[42] *Gazetto Ofiziale* (Rome), No. 1487, 16 June 1927. Cited in Moats, *op. cit.,* p. 143.
[43] And so too rationalizations were easily constructed—"It is always something of a shock", wrote Felix Morley in 1932, "to note the Fascist badge displayed in the button-holes of Italians on the Secretariat. But it may be argued that these disciples of Mussolini are only exhibiting openly a national allegiance which others feel as deeply". (Morley, *op. cit.,* p. 301)
[44] See Rowland Egger, "Road to Gethsemane", *Public Administration Review,* (Vol. 6, Winter, 1946), p. 76.

resist governmental pressures and had appointed too many diplomats to staff positions, the Secretary-General replied: "It might be that a Government had suggested certain names for a given post, but he had never taken from amongst those names any one whom he did not think was really fit for the position".[45] Drummond also attached little significance to the previous career commitments of staff appointees, maintaining that "if a man was really the right man for the post, whether he was a university professor or a diplomatist or a politician, he ought to be appointed without taking into consideration the career which the followed". He also insisted that the Organization Committee had not given him a free hand, that the Fourth Committee had acquiesced, and if any monopoly of great-power posts existed, he was not responsible.[46]

The Fourth Committee ended by endorsing the Balfour principles and stressing the Assembly's reliance on Drummond to uphold them, but it also followed an Italian suggestion to carry the debate further by calling on Secretariat officials to consider what amendments to the staff regulations might ensure "the best possible administrative results" and to submit the findings of the inquiry to the League's Supervisory Commission which in turn would report to the next Assembly. The Supervisory Commission was an expert group advising on technical questions of staff and budget. In 1929, the Fourth Committee decided to engage in a complete analysis of the Secretariat, including the Haute Direction, and it established a Committee of Enquiry, known also as the Committee of Thirteen, to present a final report to the Eleventh Assembly in 1930. The Committee's report dealt with virtually every aspect of the League Secretariat, as well as that of the International Labour Office and the Registry of the Permanent Court, but for our purposes, only the problem of the Secretary-General and the upper staff level will be considered.

The essence of the German-Italian complaint was that the British, through Drummond, and the French, through Deputy Secretary-General Jean Monnet for the first few years and Joseph Avenol thereafter, dominated the politically important Secretariat, while the German and Italian Under-Secretaries held posts only nominally significant. Their primary strategy was to reduce the individual standing of the Secretary-General, and increase their own, both to protect national interests should the Secretariat deal with sensitive issues, or at least increase their participation at the top to augment national prestige. The Committee's minority report, the work of the German and Italian representatives and clearly reflecting the views of their Governments, began by emphasizing the increased political "influence" of the Secretariat's work through its interpretative and judgmental tasks. "The political influence of the Secretariat, and especially of its principal

[45] *Records of Ninth Assembly,* Minutes of Fourth Committee, p. 37.
[46] *Ibid.*

officers", they wrote, "is, in fact, enormous and it would be a mistake to close our eyes to this fact".[47] As the "have-not" nations perceived a dominance ill-suited to serve their own interests, the minority report dismissed the possibility of a "truly international civil service" as conceptualized by Drummond and Balfour: "So long as there is no Super-State, and therefore no 'international man', an international spirit can only be assured through the co-operation of men of different nationalities who represent the public opinion of their respective countries".[48]

The crux of the complaint, however, that both Italy and Germany had long harbored was that only Drummond and Avenol were responsible for the general direction of the Secretariat, and were the only persons "required and entitled to be informed of everything that happens in the Secretariat, and of everything which is of political importance or involves a principle".[49] They asserted that apart from title and salary, there was no difference between an Under-Secretary and a Director of Section, and that the weekly meetings of the top-level staff, including Directors, did not allow the discussion of delicate questions because of the large number of persons present.

The minority report set forth two recommendations, the first of which was evidently regarded as more satisfactory by the authors, and the second as perhaps politically more realistic. Under the first proposal, the Under-Secretaries would form a Governing Board, with the Secretary-General as chairman, and each "on a footing of equality" with the others. The Governing Board would discuss all general policy questions (calling in Directors when necessary), would decide what actions were necessary in pursuance of Assembly or Council directives, ensure liaison with member states, examine draft agendas and documents of the League's political bodies, authorize missions in the field, and examine their reports.[50]

The second recommendation provided that "The Secretary-General, who would be solely responsible, would be assisted in his duties by a Committee consisting of the Under-Secretries-General, which would be required to keep itself informed of all political questions and all questions involving a principle, and to give the Secretary-General its opinion on all such matters". It was suggested that this Advisory Committee be kept fairly small, enabling it to keep in constant contact with the Secretary-General and to deal with urgent and sensitive issues in the Secretariat. The minority report also proposed that the Advisory Committee "in a general way ... should have the

---

[47] *Records of Eleventh Assembly,* Minutes of Fourth Committee, Annex 8: Report of the Committee of Enquiry on the Organisation of the Secretariat, The International Labour Office, and the Registry of the Permanent Court of International Justice, p. 314. Concerning this point of the minority report, Schwebel quotes Drummond as having said in 1951: "I am afraid that the judgment of the minority was entirely right". (Schwebel, *op. cit.,* p. 10)
[48] *Ibid.*
[49] *Ibid.*
[50] *Id.,* p. 315.

right to give its opinion, if it so desired, before any measures involving important political issues or principles were taken by the Secretary-General". This was not to preclude the Secretary-General from taking action in an emergency without consultation.[51]

The majority report, reflecting the views of Britain and France, emphasized the essential administrative virtues of impartiality and neutrality which barred any arrangement involving staff members in the pursuit of national aspirations or policy, equality among states, enabling nationals from any member to reach the highest posts, and the desirability of allowing all staff members the opportunity for promotion to the principal ranks in the Secretariat. In terms of efficiency, the majority asserted that an Advisory Committee would impair rapidity of decision, erode the Secretary-General's capacity to communicate with the Directors since they "could not freely give him advice differing from that of their respective official superiors" and would perhaps "lead to overinsistence on divergent national points of view". Speed of decision-making was of crucial importance for the League, argued the majority, since "Certain duties in times of emergency are assigned to the Secretary-General, and a delay of a few hours caused by a difference of opinion in an advisory body might well be fatal to the success of his action".[52] Concerning the control exercised by Drummond and Avenol, the response was that any point might be discussed at the weekly meetings of Under-Secretaries and Directors, and quite apart from that, all significant telegrams and papers were sent immediately to the Under-Secretaries, as were any files they might wish to consult. They had every opportunity to make representations to Drummond on any subject, including opinon in their countries.[53]

The German and Italian proposals naturally satisfied no one, for the notion that there was no "international man" ran counter to the views of not just the British and French, but to small powers who saw in the Drummond model a practical technique for augmenting their standing and relative power position in international affairs. Further, the Advisory Committee plan simply added to the dominant position of the great powers by legitimizing the practice of permitting only nationals from powerful states to exercise the most important decision tasks. Thus, for example, Sweden complained that the minority plan had the "irremediable defect of placing every high official belonging to a country which is not represented permanently on the Council under the orders of an official who is a national of one of these countries".[54]

Just prior to the vote in the Fourth Committee on the minority recommendation for an Advisory Committee, Secretary-General Drummond

[51] *Ibid.*
[52] *Id.*, p. 299.
[53] *Ibid.*
[54] *Records of Eleventh Assembly,* Minutes of Fourth Committee, p. 59.

made a strong and persuasive plea for rejection. "I quite frankly believe", he declared, "that the constitution of the Advisory Committee would be contrary to the efficiency of the Secretariat, and that is the only thing I have at heart". He argued that such an arrangement would put an intolerable burden on the Secretary-General and other staff members, calculating that he would have to spend from one to two hours each day in consulting the Committee. Further, all Under-Secretaries were fully informed, since they received advance copies of all important telegrams simultaneously with the Secretary-General, and also all synopses of the papers that came into the Secretariat. Drummond naturally emphasized his availability to staff members:

I am not an isolated person. I am always at the disposal of any Under-Secretary-General if he wishes to come to me and express his views. I like talking over questions, and am perfectly ready to talk them over. I think, therefore, there is no necessity for this Advisory Committee, and I am convinced that it would place an intolerable burden on the Secretary-General if he had to consult that body on every point. I hope [the German and Italian representatives] will forgive me, but it is a question which intimately concerns me. If I had not devoted ten years of my life to this administration, I would not have ventured to take sides on this question.[55]

The Fourth Committee could not agree on most of the issues concerning the Haute Direction, including the proper number of Under-Secretaries and their nationality, and decisions on those questions were deferred pending the report of still another Committee of Thirteen and the retirement of Sir Eric. But there was near consensus in rejecting the German and Italian proposal, thus preserving for the time being the administrative integrity of the Secretaryship-General and the fundamental principle that however imperfect in application, the Drummond-Balfour creation of a "truly international civil service" remained the working model for the League of Nations and the best hope for the construction of meaningful world order institutions.

The debate on the German-Italian proposal was crucial for the success of the Secretariat, for there is little doubt that its efficiency would have been impaired and its capacity for decision reduced to items of pure administration or political insignificance. The Advisory Committee plan was in effect an attempt to secure a veto over the workings of the Secretariat, and the recommended technique would have transformed the international service into another political conference with a four-power directorate in control. The Secretary-General's influence, muted as it was, would have been further diminished by a system paying the traditional deference to the notion that there is no "international man", for if Drummond as a British national had failed to distinguish his work from the dictates of London's foreign policy, then surely the experiment was worthy of another attempt

55 *Id.*, p. 153.

through the appointment of a Secretary-General from a small and neutral nation, much as the United Nations has done since 1946.

The fact was, of course, that the great majority of League members perceived Drummond's work as almost totally satisfactory from the standpoint of devotion to League interests and impartiality. As noted, Sir Eric had built through the years a reputation for independence and fair dealing that enabled him to work closely with great numbers of League representatives as friend and confidant. His advice was sought after, and the general feeling among most delegates and staff members was that notwithstanding British nationality and close ties to the Foreign Office in London, Drummond was close to impeccable in his role as an "international man". In terms of the development of the Office, this was fortunate indeed, for had the German-Italian proposal prevailed, the climate of the 1930's and the difficult administration of Joseph Avenol would certainly have contributed little to the resurrection of the Drummond model in 1945. As it was, the international community after the war could refer to Drummond's tenure and the success of the international experiment as evidence that even with a great-power national in the Secretariat's highest post, independence and impartiality were attributes to be expected from a Secretary-General, and even within the context of bitter great-power revalries.

In this sense, Drummond's service for fourteen years built a legacy of internationalism in the Secretariat that remains today as his greatest contribution to world institutions and politics. He established a new system and did it well, managed it through its early years, and successfully withstood a grave challenge that might well (given the political system of the 1930's and the war) have destroyed altogether the organs of global service based on neutral principles. The Secretariat, to be sure, was to face a very similar challenge in the 1960's [56] from another dissatisfied great power, and while it is impossible to trace a direct line of influence from the Drummond defense in 1930 to Dag Hammarskjold's in 1960, the Secretaryship-General was certainly in a stronger position than would have been the case without the work of "the perfect private secretary".

Drummond's Views on the League and the Secretariat

Secretary-General Drummond, as has been noted, very rarely made public addresses or granted interviews, and the few published statements or declarations available in the League and national archives tend toward formal and rather bland descriptions or accounts of the Organization's work and structure, and are usually devoid of meaningful political analyses or content. There were no attempts at theoretical pronouncements, so characteristic of

[56] See pp. 316-319, *infra.*

Dag Hammarskjold's work a few decades later, nor were there any serious investigations of the real role of global institutions in world politics. While Sir Eric, particularly at the beginning of his administration, was compelled rather frequently to justify the Organization in positive terms, in fact a good deal of his public discourse was devoted to defense against criticism of particular aspects of League structure or method.

Drummond was quite naturally disposed to depict the League of Nations as central to the concerns of world politics and statesmen, despite its all too frequent marginal influence in important conflicts. Thus, in a letter to Raymond Fosdick in 1925, the Secretary-General asserted that "A year or a year and a half ago we found the League somewhat outside the main currents of political international life, and negotiations. It has now become the pivotal point".[57] Similarly, in 1933, he stated that "the League has become the centre around which international life has been built up. If it were to disappear today...[a] state of chaos would arise in international relations. In short, as has been rightly said, the first task which would confront statesmen on the League's disappearance would be to reinvent the League".[58] For Drummond, speaking in 1933, the "development and increasing authority of the League is one of the most comforting features of the last decade".[59]

Drummond was also apparently convinced of the superiority of League procedures over any of the available alternatives—he much preferred the League Council, for example, to the Supreme Council of the Allied and Associated Powers. "We have had experience of what the Supreme Council is", he wrote, "and of its difficulties".

In the first place, the Prime Ministers are too much occupied with internal affairs to be able to meet immediately, should foreign policies necessitate it. In the second place, if one Prime Minister does not wish for a meeting, he can easily find excuses to put off a Supreme Council, and there is no binding pledge which forces him either to attend himself at a given time, or to send a representative. At one moment...Lloyd George was very anxious to have a Supreme Council immediately, but Briand, by making excuses, was able to delay it for a considerable period. Now the great force of the Covenant is that it provides for meetings at very short notice, and its representatives of the Members of the Council must attend or otherwise their case goes by default.

Further, the smaller States dislike the Supreme Council, and are very unwilling to conform to its decisions. In fact, in the near future, I think it quite possible that they will refuse to obey. Their position in the League is, however, quite different, since, being Members of it, they regard compliance to its requests as much more dignified than obedience to the commands of the Supreme Council.[60]

---

[57] Letter from Drummond to Raymond B. Fosdick, 30 March 1925.
[58] Sir Eric Drummond Broadcast, printed by The British Broadcasting Corporation, Broadcasting House, London, 1933 (no. 681), pp. 5-6.
[59] Id., p. 6.
[60] Letter from Drummond to Arthur Sweetser, 2 December 1921.

Indeed, the Secretary-General reported to a weekly meeting
in 1921 that "as a result of his visit to England, he had com
clusion that the opinion of a number of influential people whc
Supreme Council was a better instrument for international peace than
Council of the League, had been very sensibly changed".[61]

Yet at the same time, Drummond was extremely cautious with regard to
the capacity of the League to take the initiative in any given case, and he
realistically assumed that states would have to bring a problem to the
Organization before it could properly take a position. And this was particularly so in the context of the immediate post-war European issues of boundaries, reparations, and the like, even though the practice of settling such
problems outside the League framework for the first few years left the
institution with very little important political work. Thus, the Secretary-
General, in a discussion in 1922 with the Directors of the Secretariat sections, argued that the League must expect the Allies to settle most post-war
issues themselves, referring only "small matters" to the Organization, with
the question thereby raised whether "you could keep the League active
during this period through the work of its technical Organizations and the
smaller political questions. This pointed towards a considerable development of the technical work".[62] Drummond apparently refused to be dis-
heartened by the incapacity of the League in its formative years to settle
issues of consequence:

We must not forget that the League was founded for a settled world. What we must
expect is that if we can keep the League alive for the difficult period mentioned it
will assume the dominant position in the world as soon as we arrive at this settled
condition. Our position is certainly stronger today than in the past, even though we
have not had to settle the big political questions. We should not, therefore, be discouraged if we do not get them referred to us. We are building for the future, and
should take a long view of the situation.[63]

In the early years, Drummond tended to measure the League's success not
so much by the decisions taken or implemented, as by the easier test of
how many and what questions were discussed in its forums. In an interview
at the end of 1924, Sir Eric declared that the League was here to stay, and
responded to a question on the institution's prospects for 1925 by declaring
it was impossible to answer without rearranging the inquiry so as to read
"what is the League program for 1925?" He listed the many questions
before the Organization and concluded:

At the first meeting of the Council in Paris in 1920, there was but one small question
on the agenda. At the thirty-second meeting in Rome in December, 1923, there were
forty items, covering nearly every field of international interest. Or, to put it in still

---

[61] Minutes of the Directors' Meeting, 3 August 1921, p. 1.
[62] Minutes of the Directors' Meeting, 8 June 1922.
[63] *Ibid.*

another way, there were in the first eights months of 1924 no less than seventy-four meetings of international conferences and committees. Comment seems to be useless.[64]

By the end of the decade, and despite the world-wide economic depression, the League had yet to suffer a serious political reverse, and the Secretary-General's words were stronger still. "The League of Nations progresses", he asserted, "and I have noticed with surprise the change that has taken place, even in its own attitude. Some years ago the League of Nations made its recommendations or issued its decisions with a halting voice and appeared as though it was not sure that it would be heard. Today, the League of Nations speaks with unquestionable authority and knows that its word will be heard".[65]

Drummond, much in the manner of a spokesman for the Organization and setting a pattern for each of his successors, argued persistently throughout his administration for universality of membership, a conception of particular consequence for a League of Nations missing the United States, the Soviet Union until 1934, Germany until 1926, and with only the most tenuous of links to Latin America. In the cautious Drummond style he asserted that "any initiative or proposition that has a tendency to make stronger and more evident the universality of the League will always be received in an especially favorable manner. Universality is, in effect, with equality, justice and the respect of rights, one of the principal fundamentals of the League of Nations".[66] For Sir Eric, the absence of the United States and Soviet Union "greatly weakened the League's action outside Europe", and he contended prophetically in 1933 that Washington's non-participation in League consideration of non-European disputes "may prove to be a tragedy not only for the League, but also for America".[67] The statement was made against the background of the League's failure to settle peacefully the Sino-Japanese conflict that marked so clearly the turning point toward failure for the Organization, and the fateful sign of impending world war.

It is possible, however, that Drummond's conception of universality was narrower than that of the United Nations Secretaries-General, for there is evidence that while he worked and argued for universal state membership, he never truly believed that fundamentally conflicting social and political systems could coexist within world-wide organizations. There are no public statements to that effect, but the League archives reveal something of his understanding of the League as essentially a western liberal democratic institution incompatible with totalitarian ideology and method. Later to

[64] The *Border Cities Star,* Windsor, Canada, 31 December 1924.
[65] National Archives of the United States, Foreign Affairs Division, Washington, D.C. 032. Drummond, Sir Eric/42, 30 December 1930, p. 4 (hereafter referred to as *National Archives*).
[66] *Ibid.*
[67] Drummond Broadcast, *op. cit.,* p. 10.

become an important figure in Great Britain's Liberal Party, Drummond was strongly anti-communist, and on occasion this was revealed in his conversations with state representatives and officials. For example, during his trip to Latin America in late 1930 and early 1931, he was told by the President of Cuba that the one real danger to his nation was communism, that nations ought to cooperate to "combat the communist peril", and that was one reason why he believed so strongly in the League. "I said to him", wrote Sir Eric in his notes on the visit, "that I agreed on this point, and that I thought there were two great antagonistic forces in the world today: (1) communism, and (2) the League. Obviously these forces were opposed, and though they could for the time being live side by side, ultimately a choice might have to be made between the two".[68]

Even on issues which permitted a peaceful settlement and compromise, however, Drummond had no very clear conception of just what precise functions the League could undertake, and his pronouncements were repetitious declarations of the Organization's utility as a forum for discussion and serious negotiations, both in the public debates of the Assembly and Council, and the private talks in the corridors and offices of the League Headquarters.[69] The Secretary-General did view the League machinery as a valuable face-saving device, however, thus pin-pointing one function of great consequence for global institutions and their members. Sir Eric agreed that "an institution had been created to which a Government, perhaps in the past constrained unwillingly by public passion or by sense of honour to go to war on a particular issue, could, without losing face, appeal for a peaceful settlement. Prestige has up to now played so important a part in national policies that the value of the League as a 'face-saving machinery' should not be under-estimated".[70] In fact, this has always been one of the key tasks for world organization, including the League and United Nations, and will remain so as long as global bodies are without real military power as neutral third-party intermediaries. This is discussed in greater detail in Chapter VII.

There seems little question that Drummond viewed the Secretariat as in essence the League itself, since it was the only body continuously at work, and therefore at the center of international diplomacy, certainly well-informed, and possessed of a large body of officials truly devoted to a peaceful and rational world order, rather than the parochial interests of a single state or group of states. This was reflected in his distaste of the

[68] League Archives, 1928-1932, General and Miscellaneous 50/25677/722, 31 January 1931.
[69] Yet at times he tended even to minimize those efforts, as in the declaration made in 1928 that "It is infinitely preferable that countries should settle their difficulties by direct negotiation rather than by the help of third parties. The League is not jealous, it rejoices in every settlement made, in every step towards peace, whether taken under its own auspices or not". (*The London Spectator,* 3 November 1928)
[70] *Ibid.*

permanent missions accredited to the League by many of the smaller powers, for he believed that the task of liaison between national capitals and the Organization should have been performed by Secretariat staff, especially, of course, members of the Haute Direction. It was Drummond's set policy to minimize the significance of the permanent delegates stationed in Geneva and to grant them the slightest possible recognition, for otherwise such institutions might have become well-established alternatives to Secretariat liaison work particularly if the great powers established permanent missions. This would reduce the Secretariat and Secretary-General, so Sir Eric believed, to secondary instruments in terms of diplomatic functions. In early 1933, the American consul in Geneva declared that Drummond's policy in this context was

based on the theory that should the League powers, particularly the great powers, set up diplomatic establishments in Geneva, the result would be that all important matters of policy and procedure would be worked out in private conversations between these establishments, and the Secretariat would be relegated to the secondary place of an instrument for carrying out such measures. Moreover, it is felt that the presence permanently in Geneva of diplomatic officials of high rank, would greatly reduce the position and prestige of the Secretary-General and the other officials of the Secretariat in their role of liaison with their respective capitals; and for this reason in particular Sir Eric is described as having been most apprehensive and resentful of the suggestion (once brought forward) that London accredit an Ambassador to Geneva.[71]

It would appear that Sir Eric's fears were largely unfounded, for permanent missions have become a fixture in the life of the United Nations, and without injury to the work or prestige of its Secretariat.

Drummond's view tends to enunciate a political role for the Secretariat never intended by the League founders, despite an early British draft of the Covenant under which the proposed Chancellor would "maintain current relations at the capital of the League with any official representatives whom the member States may accredit to the League".[72] This was probably intended as a statement of obligation with regard to state representatives on League bodies, such as the Council or Assembly, rather than the permanent missions later established. And indeed, Drummond was never enamored of the popular conception that the Secretariat avoided policy-making and merely implemented or prepared the material for decision-making by the diplomatic organs of the League. He never publically expressed a contrary view, but in his private discussions, a different conception seemed to prevail, even from the early years of his administration.

In 1923, for example, speaking at a meeting of the Directors, the Secretary-General "while agreeing that technically the Secretariat must not be held to have any policy of its own, recognized that the individual Directors did, in fact, exercice a considerable influence on opinion in League matters within their respective countries". Thus, he argued, "it was essen-

[71] National Archives, JA 500. C 001/802, 2 May 1933, p. 2.
[72] Miller, op. cit., Vol. II, p. 115.

tial that they should all speak with the same voice, and, therefore, desirable that they should agree in advance on the line to be taken".[73] The Secretary-General also perceived his Office as essential in what was in effect the process of deciding Secretariat policy:

The Secretary-General might be regarded as a dictator, or, on the other hand, every decision might be the result of discussion at a meeting of Directors forming in fact a Cabinet. Neither of these theories seemed to him applicable. The present system—something between the two—did not seem to him to work badly. He recalled the important questions, with regard to which the common view of the Secretariat had been settled by discussion at a special Directors' Meeting—views which had proved to be right...He felt bound to protest against the suggestions that he was not easily accessible, and that he had ever discouraged the giving of information at Directors' Meetings. He, however, agreed with Sir Herbert Ames as to the desirability of thinking out beforehand a list of suitable subjects.[74]

And of course, if the Secretariat was the true embodiment of the League of Nations, then the success of the Organization as a whole depended upon the maintenance of the international spirit of the staff and the continued excellence of its work. Drummond placed somewhat greater reliance upon the former, contending that if Secretariat belief in the League should diminish, the League experiment would fail, and indeed, he argued, "it is not perhaps too much to say that in such an event the whole basis of the present structure of the League of Nations will have to be re-examined".[75]

As noted, the Secretary-General devoted a good deal of effort in his public statements to rebutting criticisms comonly directed against the League, and he did so in a relatively non-technical and facile manner calculated to educate mass opinion. For example, Sir Eric addressed himself to the frequently-voiced objection of voting equality in the League with the obvious response of distinguishing the vote of a great power from the influence it wields over many lesser members. "[D]o not let us mix up voting power and influence", he argued, for clearly "a great Power, with all its responsibilities, must and does exercise more influence in League deliberations than a small Power". Yet he defended the voting procedures with the assertion that "a small Power has an interest equal to that of a great Power in the preservation of peace. In fact, such interest may often be greater, because a small Power is more exposed to pressure and violence from its neighbours in time of war".[76]

Drummond vindicated the League's much criticized and now abandoned unanimity rule through reference to the traditional view holding that the system necessitated "considerable give and take on all sides" commonly resulting in a middle-course decision and only rarely in an actual vote. Further, while the rule in theory permitted any state to block League

[73] Minutes of the Directors' Meeting, 28 February 1923.
[74] *Ibid.*
[75] Drummond, "The Secretariat of the League of Nations", *op. cit.*, p. 235.
[76] Drummond Broadcast, *op. cit.*, p. 7.

50

activity, if any nation did so, "its objective would be recognised to be so cynically destructive that methods would assuredly be found by its co-members to compel its withdrawal from the League".[77]

In confronting the manifest weakness of an Organization without military power and a paucity of resources for securing compliance with its decisions, Sir Eric enunciated a two-fold rejoinder:

[I]s it a small thing that the League can concentrate on a particular country, in case of need, all the moral force, all the public opinion of the world? Can such a condemnation be lightly faced by any state, however powerful? And even if this moral pressure fails, the League's resources are not at an end. And here I feel bound to turn on the critics, and remind them that the League is composed of the Governments which form its members. It is those Governments which give strength or weakness to the League. The League is as powerful as the Governments which compose it desire to make it. The theory that the League is something apart from, and foreign to, the Governments is utterly untenable.[78]

These are themes repeated by each of Drummond's successors in the Secretaryship-General, although the success of the United Nations in developing a limited peace-keeping capacity has somewhat lessened dependence upon the retort of "moral force" to every charge of institutional impotence.

The oft-repeated stricture of intolerable delay in League handling of important disputes, including the adjournment of issues from one Council session to another, was met with the response that "Time must be given for the moral pressure of world public opinion to exert its force. The Council meets every three months, but the settlement of disputes between individuals, between national organizations, often requires years: why should the League be expected more rapidly to solve international problems which deeply affect national feelings and perhaps national interests"?[79] For Drummond it was sufficient that "the League works by persuasion, not by force: and it cannot immediately impose its will on a recalcitrant party".[80]

To cries of extravagance, Sir Eric replied simply that the entire Organization, including the World Court and the ILO, had a budget for 1933 (to take one representative year) of less than two million pounds, with the British share of just under two hundred thousand pounds "a sum considerably less than that required for the combined annual stationery and printing bill of the Navy and of the Air Force".[81]

In sum, Drummond developed no consistent theory of the League in world politics, while bravely picturing the Organization as centrally placed in the international arena and as the pivotal point of global decision-making. He was a western liberal who pleaded for universality of membership without any faith that the Organization had the capacity to accomodate

[77] *Id.*, p. 8.
[78] *Id.*, p. 9.
[79] The *London Spectator*, 3 November 1928.
[80] *Ibid.*

widely differing systems. He defended the League against its critics, doing so largely for the benefit of the "man in the street [who was] not yet fully awakened to the vast importance of international questions as affecting his country, his family and himself". Sir Eric decried the fact that "in many, indeed in most, countries [the common man] knows little of the League beyond the mere fact of its existence".[82] And for Drummond, the Secretariat, which had a political role to play with himself at head and with a prevailing international spirit, was the key without which there could be no true League of Nations.

As important as the words were the hesitancy and general reluctance of Drummond to speak out frequently on behalf of the Organization and to establish himself as a visible and known spokesman for world order. Sir Eric's near silence was an unfortunate antipode to the strident claims of state representatives, for one of the few voices of rationality in international politics was muted, uncommunicative, and formalist when heard. This was an impediment to the development of the Office of Secretary-General, and a tragedy for the League of Nations.

The Secretary-General's Political Role

It has generally been considered by writers on international institutions that Secretary-General Drummond was fundamentally an efficient administrator who, because of personal choice, temperament and political realities, never developed a political role of any consequence during the fourteen years of his service to the League.

As noted, "political role" in the context of the Secretaryship-General refers essentially to activities in the realm of international bargaining, particularly in cases of inter-state conflict, and the capacity in such cases to influence governments and the Organization's political decision-making bodies, the Assembly and Council.[83] Given this framework for analysis, there can be no question that Drummond did indeed carve out for himself and the Office of Secretary-General a vital political role in the series of issues confronting the League between 1920 and his resignation in 1933.

There are perhaps two important reasons why a contrary view has prevailed for many years. In the first place, Sir Eric's deliberate policy of working unobtrusively and without fanfare or publicity of any kind was

[81] Drummond Broadcast, *op. cit.,* p. 15.
[82] The *London Spectator,* 3 November 1928.
[83] See pp. 100-103, *supra.* Any issue, of course, may take on political significance, depending upon its importance to the parties concerned and the manner in which it is processed or handled. In the League context, material on the Organization's relations with the United States and Latin America (which in essence means another aspect of League-United States relationships) is included because of the obvious political importance to the international community of such issues.

somewhat misleading. His public silence was apparently taken as evidence of inactivity in the important cases of conflict before the League, or at best, as an indication of concentration on administrative tasks, such as the preparation of position papers and draft resolutions, unworthy of public attention. The assumption often was that a figure in international life who never spoke out and whose name was not to be found in the press, even during the most critical times, was most unlikely to be engaged in serious political activity. And obviously, while number-two men and private secretaries often enjoy a large measure of political influence behind the scenes, Drummond was no one's assistant. As Secretary-General he headed an important international bureaucracy. The unjustified conclusion was that Sir Eric's self-effacing manner and general quietude derived from the relatively unimportant tasks assigned to the Secretariat. Politics was for the League Council and Assembly, and for the statesmen gathered at Geneva, but not for an international staff of experts who prepared the ground for the politicians.

Second, and most unfortunately, the destruction in 1941 of a large portion of Drummond's papers because of fears of a German invasion of Switzerland and the seizure of the League buildings has deprived students and scholars of the League era of extraordinarily valuable sources of information on Sir Eric, and the best evidence of his contribution to the political development of the Office. Drummond made it a practice of recording his conversations with state representatives and even staff members if the subject was deemed important enough, and of preparing memoranda of his views for the staff and delegates. His comments on the papers prepared in the Sections often indicated his strategies and perspectives on particular issues, and in some cases there are sufficient papers left to trace his political role and influence. But much has been lost, and it may be that history has been permanently dispossessed of a satisfactory record of Drummond's most important work. As national archives for the League years are opened, and the remaining League archives thoroughly searched, evidence is becoming available that indicates just how extensive was Sir Eric's diplomatic role. While the data cannot be complete in any given case, enough is accessible at the moment to sketch, even though incompletely, a summary and illustrative accounting of a part of Drummond's political activity.

A third, and less significant factor, was the relative unimportance of the conflict situations that came before the League in the 1920's, the larger portion of Drummond's administration. While European politics during the decade involved issues of the most fundamental importance for world peace, such as the stress of the relationships between status quo oriented Britain and France and revisionist Germany and Italy, the new League of Nations was influential only in comparatively minor inter-state disputes, and not until the Sino-Japanese conflict, beginning in 1931, was the Organization confronted with a major threat to international stability.

Finally, there were the very obvious and severe contraints upon the Secretary-General's political capacity, regardless of the nature or consequence of any given case. Drummond naturally had no political base or source of support, no military power or League contingents at his disposal, and only a tiny Secretariat staff to provide essential expertise. The set of circumstances made any meaningful political activity appear almost contrary to reason, and when added to the original expectations of the League founders in 1919, there seemed to be no doubt that Drummond's contribution had nothing whatever to do with the politics of conflict.

Nevertheless the appearances are deceptive. In fact, Sir Eric fashioned a political role that has come to serve as a model for each of his successors in terms of his quiet and behind-the-scenes activity. Innumerable resolutions were prepared under Drummond's supervision for the Council and Assembly, and strategies for settlement worked out in bargaining sessions between the state representatives concerned and the Secretary-General. Reports, recommendations, and an extraordinary portion of the Council and Assembly's output were written in the Secretariat, and at times by Drummond himself. There was no important political issue before the League that escaped his attention, and rarely did a problem emerge untouched by his influence. At the very least, his Office served as a convenient channel for communication between states, as Sir Eric acted as liaison with governments involved in particular cases and used his central position to pass on data and evaluations of likely responses.

Indeed, the two key differences between his political role and that of the United Nations Secretary-General are that since 1946, the UN's executive head has spoken out publicly and made his viewpoint known on any issue, regardless of sensitivity and national interest, and in the 1950's with the rise of the Afro-Asian group in the UN and the establishment of UN peace-keeping forces, the Secretary-General developed a substantial discretionary power unknown in the League era. But the importance of Drummond's political work should no longer be under-estimated. He evolved most of the techniques accepted and expanded upon by the UN Secretaries-General, and through the excellence of his work, induced the founders of the UN Organization in 1945 to accept and even extend the notion of a political role for the Secretary-General.

Perhaps one unusual feature of Drummond's diplomatic performance and functioning was that the real power of his Office changed very little between 1920 and 1933. One might have expected at least gradual growth, particularly since his position as the first Secretary-General left substantial room for experimentation and development of techniques acceptable to actors in the world arena. Development of power was certainly characteristic of Trygve Lie's and Dag Hammarskjold's administrations from 1946 to 1961. Yet Sir Eric acted very much in 1920 in the Aland Islands question as he did in 1931-1933 in the Sino-Japanese conflict. His performance was more extensive in the later case, but that was due primarily to the nature and importance of the conflict rather than to an expansion of political influence. This is probably explained by the deliberately chosen framework of quiet and private political work without benefit of publicity and public statement. A Secretary-General who utilizes the press and other mass media to appeal to public opinion and create a certain reknown for his Office may well find his influence growing if he can effectively establish any significant support capable of influencing governments or particular international decision makers. There are obvious risks, of course, for the alienation of a power may spell the decline of influence or even result in unacceptability as Secretary-General.

Drummond took none of the risks, but neither did he reap the benefits of a more public performance. His framework for political activity and influence was restricted to the resources of his own imagination and knowledge. At times his influence was substantial indeed, but inherent in the framework was a certain rigidity, for his impact was unlikely to change over the years unless there were marked alterations in his sources of data or personal characteristics. Since either was unlikely, Drummond went through fourteen years of service to the League without any significant enlargement of his political power. Fortunately, he took the utmost advantage of his comparatively sheltered position to become well-informed, and thus able to exert whatever influence was open to a third-party neutral intermediary devoted fundamentally to world peace and the maintenance of institutions of world order.

The first conflict of any consequence to come before the League Council was the question between Sweden and Finland in 1920 concerning sovereignty over the Aland Islands in the Baltic, an issue derived from Finland's newly-won independence from Russia.[84] Finland successfully maintained control of the Islands, but the population there was Swedish and strongly committed to union with Sweden, with Stockholm quite willing to comply with the Islanders' wishes, even to the point of using force to settle the matter.

Drummond and his top aides in the Secretariat began to prepare possible solutions and plans even prior to the formal establishment of the League, and while the entire matter was being dealt with by the Peace Conference and the Supreme Council. Sir Eric's first thought was a League High Commission to govern the Islands, associated with local representation along the lines of the Danzig model. Erik Colban of Norway, at that time appointed by Drummond as Director of the Secretariat's Section of Administrative Commissions (which later became the Minorities Questions Section) prepared a long memorandum on the subject surveying the many problems

[84] For a thorough account of the dispute, see James Barros, *The Aland Islands Question: Its Settlement by the League of Nations.* (New Haven: Yale University Press, 1968).

involved, including implementation of the Treaty of Paris of 1856 against the fortification of the Islands, and their neutralization under a League guarantee. The Secretary-General was cautious, but predicted that the issue would be brought before the League, and wished to be informed of developments. His handwritten note attached to Colban's August 26, 1919 memorandum states "I quite agree that the question ought not to be brought before the Council or the Assembly except at the request of the Peace Conference or of some Power member of the League. I think, however, that either sooner or later it will come before the League. Meanwhile I will write a discreet letter to Paris reminding them of the report of July 4 [of the Baltic Commission] and asking whether any further developments have occured as it would naturally be useful to us to know of them in view of our foreshadowed task".[85] Sir Eric wrote to the British delegation in Paris and was kept informed.

Drummond was correct, for the Supreme Council eventually decided that any change in the Islands' status would have to be made by the League of Nations and associated with the new Organization rather than the great powers. By December, 1919, Drummond was receiving representatives of the Islanders in his office, hearing their case on the merits and advising them, in response to questions, that "the Council of the League in considering any question would begin *de novo,* and that their proper course would seem to be for the Islanders to send their statement to the Secretary-General for transmission to the Council, and at the same time to ask that the Delegates might be heard personally by the Council, a request which he was convinced the Council would grant".[86]

Unsuccessful negotiations continued throughout the first several months in 1920, with tensions rising between Sweden and Finland and a growing disposition in London to place the matter before the League Council. Again Drummond's assistance was sought, this time by Ossian Donner, the Finnish Minister in London, who, on June 4, 1920 inquired first as to Finland's application for League membership, and then presented the heart of Finland's argument to Sir Eric. Donner declared that Finland had granted the Islanders a "large measure of autonomy in the hope that thereby the agitation among the Islanders to join Sweden would cease". But this had not satisfied them, and they had sent a delegation to Stockholm to request action by the Government there. He had heard that Sweden was "likely to make a Proclamation that Swedish protection was extended to the inhabitants" and this would raise the dispute in acute form, for "Finland

---

85 League Archives 1919, Political 11/468/468, 31 August 1919.
86 League Archives 1919, Political 11/2440/468, 12 December 1919. The Islanders were concerned at the delay likely with Council proceedings, but Eir Eric advised them that if the issue "were remitted to the Council of the League he thought under normal conditions it would come under discussion within a month of its being laid before the Council". (*ibid.*)

could never admit that the Islands should be taken away from her by such methods". The essence of Finland's position was that the population was so small that the inhabitants' wishes could not be controlling, and the territorial and naval considerations involved "make it impossible for Finland to give way... [and] the Finns would be prepared to fight to the last on the point".[87]

Drummond's record of his conversation with Donner then contains an extraordinary paragraph in which the Secretary-General evidently gave the Finnish representive advice on the best case he might make before the League Council:

He then asked me if there were any stipulations in the Covenant which were applicable. I told him that I could not give him a considered opinion, but I reminded him of Article 11 and of Article 15, *calling his special attention to paragraph 8 of the latter article.*[88]

Sir Eric was apparently suggesting to Donner the utility to Finland of the Covenant's domestic jurisdiction clause, and indeed, this certainly became the core of the Finnish legal case before the Council. Drummond's record concludes: "I added that as far as I could see, since both the Swedes and the Finns considered they had an excellent case, the question was one which might well be referred to the arbitration of the Council, but Mr. Donner gave me the impression that the Finns considered the matter as domestic, and would with difficulty brook interference by any outside body, no matter how impartial the latter might be".[89]

Later in June, Lord Curzon of Great Britain finally referred the dispute to the League Council, and on June 23, Minister Donner paid another visit in London's Sunderland House to the Secretary-General, fearing Finland's disadvantage since she was not a League member as was Sweden, and viewing Britain's action as unfriendly. Drummond asserted that Britain's action was consistent with the Covenant and justified. Further, according to Sir Eric's record of conversation, "I gave him a formal assurance that I felt convinced that the Council would desire entire equality of treatment for the two parties concerned, and that I would use any influence which I had in this direction".[90] Donner also asked Drummond for advice concerning what action Finland should take, and here Sir Eric retracted somewhat his emphasis on the domestic jurisdiction argument:

I told him that while this question put me in a very awkward position, I was prepared to tell him personally that I thought that it would be a mistakse for Finland absolutely to refuse discussion of the question in the Council, on the ground that it was a purely domestic matter, falling, therefore, solely within the competence of Finland. This claim could, of course, be put forward by Finland, but it should be done in such a way

---

87 League Archives 1920, Political 11/4639/468, 4 June 1920.
88 *Ibid.,* italics added.
89 *Ibid.*
90 League Archives 1920, Political 11/5024/468, 23 June 1920.

as to imply that if the Council did not accept it, Finland would be ready for the question to be discussed and dealt with by the Council.[91]

The minutes of the Directors' Meeting held later the same day by the Secretary-General indicate Drummond's thinking on the most appropriate League procedure for dealing with the dispute. First, he wanted the Special Meeting of the Council to be held in London in early July if Bourgeois would attend, and he was opposed to a meeting in Brussels "as it would make the Meeting of the Council appear a side-show to the Meetings of the Supreme Council of the Allies".[92] Drummond felt that "the Council should first propose to the parties that they should accept a Commission to enquire and report, the Members to be selected by the League from among persons chosen from three impartial States, e.g., Switzerland, Spain and Czechoslovakia, and that the parties should undertake in advance to accept the findings of this Commission. If they refused to give such an undertaking, the Council should then as an alternative propose that the Commission of Enquiry should report with recommendations to the Council at a later date. In either case, the Commission would endeavour to settle the matter by mediation, and to secure agreement between the parties".[93]

The Directors were far happier with Sir Eric's second plan, as the first amounted to binding arbitration, and they perceived too many political, military and social issues involved to settle the dispute by reference to law or juridical principles. Drummond had already suggested arbitration to the British Foreign Office in a letter written on June 22, and while he maintained this position in the Directors' Meeting of June 23, he wrote again to the Foreign Office after the Meeting, suggesting the second procedure, and the idea was accepted. Lord Hardinge of Penshurst, Permanent Under-Secretary of the Foreign Office, wrote to Drummond on July 7 that "The procedure you propose...of despatching an impartial Commission of Enquiry to the Islands—is I feel surely preferable to your first idea of submitting the question to arbitration. Both parties to the dispute will certainly expect a decision by the League itself".[94] The Secretary-General, in the meantime, busied himself in the preparation of legal memoranda for the Council covering the many Covenant issues, including the problem of domestic jurisdiction, likely to be raised in the debates which took place from July 9 to 12, 1920.

The Council's first decision was that the Finnish argument invoking Article 15, paragraph 8 of the Covenant necessitated the expert advice of international jurists, and since the Permanent Court had not yet been established, the issue would be submitted to an ad hoc Commission of

[91] *Ibid.*
[92] League Archives 1920, General 40/5039/854, Minutes of the Directors' Meeting, 23 June 1920, p. 1.
[93] *Ibid.*, p. 2.
[94] League Archives 1920, Political 11/5526/468, 7 July 1920.

Jurists. This meant delay in implementing Drummond's plan for a commission of enquiry, but the Secretary-General was not disturbed by the
decision. In early July he reported to a Directors' Meeting that he had been
informed by Finnish representatives that the Russians declined to regard
the Islands as covered by the recognition of Finnish independence and now
claimed them as part of Russia. Bourgeois was of course troubled by the
same problem, and not anxious to have the Council commit itself on the
point.

At a meeting with the Directors on July 14, Drummond asserted that "the
decision reached on the Aland Islands question was better than could have
been hoped'.[95] He now felt that the Polish-Russian situation pointed to a
general conference on Baltic questions, including Russian and German
boundaries, at which the Aland Islands status would be raised. It followed
for Sir Eric that "if the Council had definitely committed itself, there would
have been difficulties in re-opening the matter with Russia as a party to
the discussion. Reference to a Jurists Commission had... turned out to be
a wise plan".[96] Very much concerned with possible Russian claims, Drummond suggested in August a League Committee to help Sweden and Finland reach an amicable settlement.

In the event, however, the Commission of Jurists soon returned the
matter to the Council, for they decided the matter was not purely internal,
given the Swedish claim and Russian interests in the Islands, and that the
Swedish-Russian-British treaty of 1856 stipulating non-militarization of the
Islands was still valid and in force. Thus by September, 1920, the dispute
was once again before the Council, which accepted the Jurists report, and
agreed, in accordance with Drummond's alternative plan, to establish a
Commission of Inquiry to examine the problem, and report back. At this
point the Secretary-General's efforts were directed toward the proper
representation on the commission. He now wanted British and French
members to serve to insure the greatest possible weight for its report,
although this was strongly resisted in London and Paris. In September, Sir
Eric recommended Britain's former Prime Minister Herbert Asquith,
France's former Colonial Minister Etienne Clémentel, and Felix Calonder,
former President of the Swiss Republic, as a group that "would make the
best Commission".[97] As for a United States voice on the Commission,
Drummond wrote that "An American could I fear not be appointed without much delay in view of the approaching election. I will, however, discuss
the question with M. Balfour..."[98] Britain and France turned down Sir

---

[95] League Archives 1920, General 40/5547/854, Minutes of the Directors' Meeting,
14 July 1920.
[96] *Ibid.*
[97] League Archives 1920, Political 11/7065/468, 27 September 1920.
[98] *Ibid.*

Eric's recommendations, although the United States agreed to serve, along with representatives from Belgium and Switzerland.

By April, 1921, the Commission's report was ready, and in essential matters, it accepted Finland's substantive claims to sovereignty over the Islands, while recommending League insurance of the inhabitants' rights and the negotiation of another convention providing anew for non-militarization. The report rejected the plebiscite plan advocated by Sweden and the Islanders, but suggested improvements in the autonomy laws governing the Islands, particularly in education and Swedish language. Drummond's last task was simply to communicate the contents of the report to Sweden and Finland even prior to its publication. This was prompted by a visit to the Secretary-General by Count Albert Ehrensvard, the Swedish Minister in Paris, who urgently requested information. The Secretary-General did not feel justified in giving the contents of the report to one party and not the other, but Ehrensvard pressed his demand and assured Drummond the information would be kept confidential. "Under these conditions", wrote Sir Eric in his record of the interview, "I agreed to his seeing Mr. Nielsen [the secretary of the Commission] and putting various questions to him. The interview took place in my presence. Mr. Nielsen answered the different questions. Comte Ehrensvard, although clearly somewhat unhappy as to the replies he received, expressed his thanks for the courtesy shown him".[99] The next day, Drummond communicated the same information to Carl Enckell, the Finnish Foreign Minister. Late in June, 1921, the Council adopted the Commission's Report, and after acceptance by the parties, the Aland Islands question disapppeared from public debates at the League of Nations until the coming of war in Europe in 1939. It had been the first significant issue before the League in 1920, and was to be the last in 1939.

The conflict was of great importance for Sir Eric Drummond, who was still in the process of establishing his new Secretariat and the principles upon which it was to be based when the dispute was placed before the League. His discussions and communications with the key decision-makers involved indicated clearly that the Secretary-General's role could be politically important. The pattern for the Drummond model was determined from the start—he would work quietly and his diplomatic activity would take the form of recommendation and suggestion, even on consequential procedural or political matters. He made great efforts to remain well-informed, and his prestige was sufficient even in 1920 to enable him to deal effectively with the statesmen of his time. Not all his suggestions were adopted, but the fact that an administrative appointee of the new Secretariat could properly recommend (to the great powers and the concerned states) arbitration, or a League Commission, and the composition of such a body, as well as give procedural and substantive advice to state representatives, was a

[99] League Archives, 1921, Political 11/12295/468, 22 April 1921.

ıg indication of the potential inherent in the Office of the Secretary-ral. Most of the functions to be executed by the League's highest ɛr were seen in his work in the Aland Island issue—mediation, communication, evalation of proposals, liaison work with national capitals, legal analysis—and since it was done privately, there were no objections to his work from any source. Sir Eric had created the precedent of an active political role for the Office of the Secretary-General even before he had won firm acceptance of his plans for an international civil service.

Drummond's diplomatic tasks were not confined, obviously, to cases of conflict between States. He was active in the politically important work of establishing or maintaining links between the League and particular nations whose membership he regarded as vital for the Organization's success, and in this context his efforts with regard to the United States, Latin America, Germany, and Italy were politically significant.

The crucial issue of American membership was naturally quite beyond the capacity of Drummond to exert any meaningful influence, but he worked at the margin of events to bring the United States into the League. Developments in Washington were watched closely, and Drummond responded to them if he felt League proceedings might be affected. He rather optimistically appointed several Americans to the Secretariat staff, and while this was somewhat disturbing to League opponents in the Senate, it did help to create an awareness of the new Organization among several outstanding officials who were able to communicate some of what the League was to an American public that appreciated very few of the issues involved in the relationship between the United States and the world community.

Drummond's first major appointment of an American to the Secretariat was Raymond B. Fosdick as Under-Secretary-General, one of Sir Eric's top aides during the several months in London's Sunderland House. Others were Arthur Sweetser in the Public Information Section from 1919 to 1941, George Beer, originally selected as Director of the Mandates Section, Manley Hudson in the Legal Section, and Captain Huntington Gilchrist, an assistant to Fosdick and a staff member for nine years. Fosdick's services were to be important, for the Secretary-General hoped to benefit from his links to the American Government, and with Sweetser, to create some favorable publicity for the Organization in the United States. In early October, 1919, Drummond selected Fosdick as his representative to the International Labour Conference in Washington, D.C., where the American Under-Secretary maintained liaison between the League Secretariat and the International Labour Office, and simultaneously informed Sir Eric of the Senate debates that were rapidly destroying hope of U.S. participation in the League. Fosdick also, with difficulty, spent some time consulting with the State Department about matters of interest to the League, such as disarmament, mandates, and of course, American membership. His contact with the State Department was insubstantial, however, and given Wilson's illness and House's loss of influence, he had lost touch at the White House.

By the autumn of 1919, there appeared little reason to hope the Senate would act favorably, and the communications between Drummond, Fosdick and Gilchrist were dispirited, revealing the hopelessness of the Secretariat's position. On November 11, Sir Eric cabled to Fosdick that "It has been suggested that U.S. situation might be affected favourably by judicious publicity particularly with a view to explaining difficulties which smaller States are suffering as a result of delay. Am personally doubtful whether it is not all too late, but should be glad to have your opinion".[100] Fosdick replied that publicity had already been given but without result. "[The] Senate is virtually isolated from public opinion", he wired, "and constant misrepresentation of League from various interested sources causes situation throughout country to be much confused".[101] Even the matter of Americans serving on the Secretariat was questioned, as Senator William Borah put forward a resolution requesting the State Department for names of Americans on the staff, the ultimate aim being to prohibit such service. Drummond cabled to Fosdick in Washington that the "State Department could say, first, that they know officially of no American on League, and, second, that they had made no appointments or suggestions".[102] This was done, and the Americans stayed on without undue difficulty, particularly at the lower levels.

Drummond also brought to the attention of Fosdick and Sweetser the statements of intent to join the League made by a large number of South American states, the point being to use the information in publicity releases in an attempt to influence Senate debate. At a Directors' Meeting on December 3, 1919, the Secretary-General conceded that the move had had little if any effect, although he agreed it might be useful for the Secretariat's Information Section "to bring it to the notice of some of the American press men in London".[103] The Minutes of a Directors' Meeting of December 17, 1919, however, reveal that the Secretary-General was opposed to the idea of League representatives travelling to the United States (on the invitation of the Senate) to present the League case from the European standpoint. The record does not reveal his reasoning, although by that time it appeared quite late to influence the course of Senate debate.[104]

In a letter to Fosdick[105] written on December 15, 1919, Drummond tried to rest the essentiality of American membership largely on economic grounds. Sir Eric stated three general themes in a kind of overview of the

---

[100] League Archives, 1919, General 40/2709/1866, 11 November 1919.
[101] *Id.,* 14 November 1919.
[102] League Archives, 1919, Establishment. General 30/2073/2073, 19 November 1919.
[103] League Archives 1919, General 40/2287/854, 3 December 1919.
[104] League Archives 1919, General 40/2495/854, 17 December 1919.
[105] Raymond B. Fosdick, *Letters on the League of Nations* (Princeton: Princeton University Press, 1966), pp. 82-84.

League's relationship with the United States. First, until the Senate came to a definite decision, the Americans on the Secretariat should remain in their posts "unless this would unfavourably affect the chances of the League in the Senate". Second, it would be wise to accept all the Republican reservations to the Peace Treaty; indeed, "it is worth paying almost any price to obtain ratification". Third, and the central theme, "The economic position of the world has become such that disaster in Europe of a most appalling kind is imminent unless American cooperation can be secured without delay".

The Secretary-General predicted economic breakdown unless international cooperation included American participation, and spoke in terms unusually strident for the quiet civil servant he was: "Unless international action is taken, all the most prominent economists predict such economic conditions in practically every European country as must lead to what will be equivalent to revolution and the break-up of civilization in its present form". Of course, it was possible for the United States to cooperate without joining the League, but in that case the Secretary-General doubted whether "the League would ever be an international instrument of really first class importance. It would become a centre for those subjects of international life where no conflict is likely to arise". Fosdick passed on Drummond's views to several people in the U.S. Government, including William H. Taft, but to no avail.

Drummond was also inclined towards Brussels as the seat of the League, if the United States refused to join, and he went so far as to render his acceptance of Geneva dependent upon American membership. At the least, he wished to delay the decision on location until the Senate's final decision was taken, a point on which he had the agreement of his staff and most League members. He told his Directors in a meeting in December, 1919 that

If the U.S. were going to join whole-heartedly in the League and make the Council its channel for dealing with international affairs, it would be safe to go straight to Geneva, because the cooperation of the United States was so necessary to European countries that their leaders would go to whatever place they would find a plenipotentiary of the United States. If, however, she did not join, or joined only in name, the League would have to rely mainly on the Western Powers. A meeting such as that which had just taken place between Mr. Lloyd George and Monsieur Clemenceau in London could hardly be hoped for at Geneva. If the League were there, it would probably be ignored, and the Prime Ministers would meet in Paris or London. They would however, he thought, be willing to go to Brussels. The matter, therefore, could not be settled until the decision of the United States was known.[106]

As the League was formally established in early 1920 and still without a final decision from the U.S. Senate, Under Secretary-General Fosdick resigned his post, cutting a most tenuous link between the League and the United States. Fosdick cited his "inability to establish contact either at the State Department or in the White House" as leading to his final decision

[106] League Archives 1919, General 40/2495/854, 17 December 1919.

and felt that after the League had become a going concern his position was intolerable. "I did not feel that without the positive support of some government authority I could myself assume the responsibility of continuing in my relationship to the Secretariat".[107] Fosdick advised the other Americans in the Secretariat to remain, for his own decision resulted from his rank, and was not properly viewed as a precedent for the remaining U.S. citizens on the staff.

The American decision not to join the League naturally had a crippling effect on the Office of Secretary-General, as well as the entire Organization. Drummond had no efficient method for maintaining contact with the State Department, thereby weakening enormously his own potential influence and the efficacy of his diplomatic endeavors. Washington's policy planning and any cooperative efforts associated therewith had to be discerned and regulated solely through traditional diplomatic channels. And the State Department lost no time in emphasizing its studied avoidance of the League structure. Given President Wilson's illness, it was decided, for example, by Secretary of State Robert Lansing that Wilson's invitation to the Powers to attend the first meeting of the Council in January, 1920, would be issued through the normal diplomatic route rather than through the Secretary-General's Office. The official explanation was lack of time, but as Fosdick informed Drummond, the real reason was quite different. "Lansing . . . doesn't really believe in the League of Nations and is entirely out of sympathy with our whole plan. He is not going to play any more closely with us that he absolutely has to. In the matter of the invitations, the President was not and could not, of course, be consulted, and Lansing had the thing his own way".[108] Léon Bourgeois, who presided over the Council's first formal session in Paris on January 16, 1920, made a rather different gesture as he invited Secretary-General Drummond to take a seat at the Council table, thus placing him among the great statesmen of his time.

The State Department went further after the inauguration of the Harding Administration in 1921, for it was then decided not to communicate at all with the Secretariat, even to the point of refusing to answer League notes sent to states throughout the world, including the United States. On June 30, 1921, Drummond's record of an interview states that the American Consul in Geneva read to him a telegram signed by Secretary of State Charles Evans Hughes:

Please inform the Secretary-General orally and unofficially that his notes of the 18th November and the 22nd May have been received, but as this Government has no relations with the League of Nations, no reply will be sent to them.[109]

From this low point, relations between the United States and the League of Nations gradually developed throughout the 1920's, thanks in large

[107] Fosdick, *op. cit.*, p. 107.
[108] *Id.*, p. 101.
[109] League Archives 1921, General 40/13843/1866, 30 June 1921.

measure to the patient and quiet work of the Secretary-General, aided by the Americans on his staff, particularly Arthur Sweetser, Manley Hudson, and Huntington Gilchrist. Washington was encouraged to participate in whatever manner it desired, and slowly the contacts multiplied, mostly unofficial, but including a few Governmental decisions to participate in one or another League Committee or Conference, until by 1925 America took part in disarmament meetings and most conferences concerned with economic and social matters. Political issues and international conflicts, however, were the forbidden areas, and not until the Sino-Japanese conflict began in 1931 was Drummond able to secure even marginal American participation in League discussions of the key problems of world politics. The Secretary-General never criticized nor complained, but gave positive encouragement to the slightest expressions of willingness to cooperate, and the strategy had its success, notwithstanding continued refusal to join the Organization or even to adhere to the Permanent Court, for the association between the League and America was far more substantial by the end of the decade than at the start, and Sir Eric's position strengthened accordingly.

Drummond's work in connection with Latin American relations with the League turned primarily on the vexing political issue of the Monroe Doctrine, its place in the League system, and effect on Latin American members of the Organization. The difficulty stemmed from the inclusion in the Covenant of Article 21, which provided that nothing in the Covenant was to affect the validity of international engagements or regional understandings like the Monroe Doctrine. This was inserted to mollify the United States, although with no success, and it raised the question whether the League had any capacity to act in cases of conflict in the Latin American region. From the start, Secretary-General Drummond supported the view that the clause did not preclude League action in South and Central America, thereby generating conflict with Washington, but throughout the 1920's the Secretariat and most League members backed a minimalist construction of Article 21.

As early as 1919, Sir Eric, in response to a Pan American Union draft program declared that "a possible solution might be found in the League of Nations delegating to the Pan American League certain of its powers as regards American disputes, but the League of Nations cannot and must not relinquish its position as the final court of appeal and supreme authority in all matters relating to international disputes".[110] Drummond was thus willing to utilize special procedures in cases of conflict confined to the Monroe Doctrine area. In a memorandum circulated to the Under-Secretaries and Directors in July, 1920, the Secretary-General suggested that "in the case of a purely American quarrel, the Council of the League should designate its American Members, plus three Representatives of other

[110] League Archives 1919, General 40/1011/1011, 14 May 1919.

American States, to act as a Sub-Committee on its behalf, investing it for the purpose with similar powers to those which it itself holds".[111]

Yet there were obvious political difficulties even in getting "a purely American quarrel" before the Council. At the end of February, 1921, Drummond brought to the attention of the Council, then meeting in Paris, a border dispute between Panama and Costa Rica that had already led to fighting. He did so prior to the receipt of any official information from either of the contending parties or any League member, and the reaction in the United States was sharp. "I would assume", said Senator Borah, "from Sir Eric Drummond's action...that he is desirous of destroying the last vestige of the League. This action confirms every possible objection which has been made to the League by those who are opposed to it and is utterly violative of the Monroe Doctrine in its very essentials".[112] The parties quickly accepted Washington's mediation, and the League was no longer concerned with the matter as a settlement was reached, but the political significance of Sir Eric's action was not lost on League members, and the Secretariat was shortly to become involved again in the complexities of regionalism in Latin America and its relation to the League.

The Latin American states had made manifest their own interpretation of Article 21 as no bar to League action in the Western Hemisphere, but their attitude generally toward the Organization turned on whether the League could give the assurances they wanted. From an early date, Drummond refused to announce an official Secretariat interpretation of Article 21, while leaving full room for League assistance. When the issue of Mexican membership was discussed in 1924, for example, Sir Eric declared:

I entirely agree that the League certainly cannot and should never refuse any legitimate request for help from a Member, whether a Latin American country or not, but I am equally clear that it would be a mistake for the Secretariat to give any official advice as to the exact scope and meaning of that Article [Covenant Article 21]. If any country wishes to raise a question as to the interpretation of any article of the Covenant, it clearly has an opportunity to do so at the Assembly.[113]

Drummond's refusal to pronounce an official interpretation was frequently coupled with a statement of League competence over international conflicts involving any of the Organization's members, and on occasion he appeared quite willing to utilize the Secretariat to underscore the latter point. For example, at a meeting of the Secretariat committee on Latin American questions in February, 1928, Drummond stated in a discussion on Article 21 that he had "discussed with the Argentine Minister for Foreign Affairs in Paris the general question of the attitude to be adopted by the Secretariat

---

[111] League Archives 1920, Political 11/5549/5549, 20 July 1920.
[112] *The New York Times,* 1 March 1921, p. 3.
[113] League Archives 1923, Admissions to the League 28/31501/30762, 5 February 1924.

towards any discussion of League matters in the Argentine, and...in particular asked whether the Secretariat could undertake any useful propaganda".[114]

Sir Eric's general view of Article 21 and its relation to League activity in Latin America was actually adopted by the League Council in 1928. The Council had formally requested Spain, Brazil, and Costa Rica to reconsider their decisions to withdraw from the League, and unexpectedly, the Costa Rican government's reply was a request to the Council to explain the League interpretation of the Monroe Doctrine "and the scope given to that doctrine when it was included in Article 21 of the Covenant". The Secretary-General immediately requested the advice of his staff, including suggestions of the most appropriate wording for the Council to use in reply to Costa Rica, and on September 1, 1928, the Council cabled a response in accordance with the Secretariat's viewpoint. There would be no interpretation of the Monroe Doctrine as such, and Article 21 "In declaring that such engagements are not deemed incompatible with any of the provisions of the Covenant...refers only to the relations of the Covenant with such engagements; it neither weakens nor limits any of the safeguards provided in the Covenant".[116] The Articles of the Covenant "confer upon all the Members of the League equal obligations and equal rights".[117] The Council position did not result in Costa Rica's return to the League, but it was important, for as Frank Walters was later to write, "the Council's reply gave much satisfaction to the Latin American Members. From that time on until the period of the Spanish war, their interest in the League, their inclination to use it and support it, were steadily growing".[118] The Secretary-General and his staff had well prepared the way for the Council, demonstrating the political significance of a relatively simple and acceptable legal analysis by the international civil service.

Drummond worked hard to strengthen the relatively weak relationship between the Organization and Latin America, and was active in the attempts made over the years to induce Argentina, Brazil, and Mexico to become active members. Throughout his administration, he directed some kind of special arrangement in the Secretariat for liaison work, whether in the form of a special Latin American Bureau, the system of correspondents in Latin America, or special consultation with Latin American Section members concerning communications with South or Central American states. There were also regularly held meetings of the Latin American staff

[114] League Archives 1928-1932, General and Miscellaneous 50/882/882, Latin-American Meeting/P.V. 12., 10 February 1928, p. 6.
[115] League Archives 1928-1932, General and Miscellaneous 50/6472/2857, letter of 19 July 1928 from Costa Rica to the President of the Council.
[116] League Council Doc. C.451.M.137.1928, 1 September 1928.
[117] *Ibid.*
[118] Frank Walters, *A History of the League of Nations* (London: Oxford University Press, 1952), p. 392.

members to discuss committee appointments, membership problems, and issues of interest to the area. In a 1926 circular to staff members, Sir Eric emphasized the importance of liaison through Latin American Secretariat personnel:

Liaison work is executed by means of personal contacts and of unofficial, personal and confidential correspondence. The object of such work is to develop and fortify the relations existing between the League and its members. It is therefore likely to be more effective when in charge of nationals of each country. Subject to this proviso, the work of liaison with Latin America will be entrusted as a whole to nationals of Latin American states, who may at any time be in the Secretariat...[119]

In late 1930 and early 1931, Drummond made his first visit as Secretary-General to South America. The immediate occasion was an invitation to take part in Uruguay's centenary celebrations, but Sir Eric then accepted further invitations, including those of Brazil, Argentina, Chile, Peru, Colombia, Panama, and Cuba. His receptions were generally warm, and the Secretary-General spoke several times on behalf of the League and the interest of Latin-American states in the Organization. The main idea was to gain some publicity through press coverage for the League, and perhaps in that way to influence governments.[120]

Drummond naturally toured European countries with greater frequency and in the cases of Italy and Germany this was significant. He made a few trips to Berlin to make arrangements for Germany's admission to the League in 1926, and was a frequent guest of the Italian Government in Rome, to strengthen Italy's links with the Organization and to increase her Secretariat "representation". The Secretary-General's trips to various member states frequently had for their purpose discussion of particular administrative matters, such as Secretariat posts, membership on League committees, and the like. Such considerations were important in bringing Germany into the League and in maintaining Italy's allegiance. In sum, Drummond spent substantial time and effort on problems of membership —generally far more so than the United Nations Secretaries-General, and in the League era membership issues were of great consequence for the Organization and world politics. This was an area in which the quiet and subtle efforts of the Secretary-General helped expand the scope and meaning of a League of Nations committed to peaceful settlement among all

[119] League Archives 1926, General 40/56227/56227, 27 October 1926.
[120] The difficulty, according to the American Consul in Geneva, was that "It was felt that only a small group in each [Latin-American] country is interested in the League or knows anything about it. To be or not to be a member of the League seems everywhere to depend chiefly on presidential decision, so that the fate of the League in Latin-America appears in general to rest in the hands of the respective Presidents". (*National Archives*, H/P 032 Drummond, Sir Eric/60, 25 March 1931, p. 4) In fact, Drummond's press coverage was spotty, and quite bad in Brazil; while his governmental receptions were always cordial, it is not likely that the trip had any significant impact.

nations, and therefore, at least in the view of its executive head and the Secretariat, committed as well to universality of membership.

The pattern set by Drummond in the Aland Islands conflict was maintained throughout the League's first decade in the settlement of relatively minor disputes and border problems. While the destruction of a major portion of his papers in 1941 has left great gaps in the data available on his political role in the 1920's, the general functions and role appeared the same throughout. His records of interview and memoranda reveal Sir Eric's skill in mediation and his value to representatives as a source of well-informed advice. Drummond had a quick sense for the relevant issues, and his views frequently influenced decision-makers in their handling of a case. But his political work was on occasion important more in terms of its long-range consequences for shaping the institutions of world order than for its immediate role in assisting settlement of a conflict. This is seen particularly in the Corfu dispute in 1923 between Italy and Greece, a conflict finally brought to resolution by the Conference of Ambassadors with some aid by the League Council, and raising the issue of the proper relation between League institutions and outside agencies, and the Organization's task in cases of resort to force short of war.

The Corfu case was triggered by the murder on Greek soil of an Italian member of a commission of the Conference of Ambassadors and three of his assistants while engaged in the demarcation of the Greek-Albanian border in late August, 1923. The Fascist Government under Mussolini had recently come to power in Rome, and was attempting to strengthen its diplomatic position in Europe and to embark on a policy of territorial expansion. Italy's response to the murder was a twenty-four hour ultimatum to Greece demanding apologies, a rapid inquiry, execution of the guilty parties, and a payment of 50 million lire. Greece's partial rejection led Mussolini to occupy the undefended Greek island of Corfu after a bombardment that killed several persons. Rome at once denied the competence of the League Council to handle the conflict, viewing the Conference of Ambassadors as the more friendly forum, but the Council did forward its own suggestions to the Conference and for the most part had them adopted. The key decision-making body, however, was the Conference, with the Council subordinate in the role of mediator and advisor. Greece made her apologies to the Delimitation Commission of the Conference, and while the Conference at first agreed to the Council's recommendation that the Permanent Court be asked to decide the proper compensation, Italy's refusal to evacuate Corfu resulted in a reversal whereby the 50 million lire were paid to Rome without reference to the Court.

The fact of settlement without further violence was gratifying, but the method created fears for the League's future, particularly in light of the Italian arguments that denied the Council's competence as no war was declared, that the occupation was proper under international law, and that another international body was dealing with the matter. The Council did not reject or accept the arguments, but simply handed the matter to the Conference of Ambassadors, thereby setting a precedent that permitted an interpretation of constitutional incapacity. The small powers understood France's wish to remain on good terms with Mussolini, and Britain's wish to keep Italy in the League, as well as Rome's dissatisfaction with the Versailles settlement. But they insisted the Council must reassert its rights to deal with international conflict, and it was here that the Secretary-General's influence was felt.

On September 14, 1923, almost two weeks prior to Italy's evacuation of Corfu, Drummond wrote a long memorandum on the conflict, setting forth his perspective on its effect upon the League and the questions raised for the future.[121] For the Secretary-General, League action had to be evaluated in terms of its effect upon the dispute in question and upon the League, for the Council's role was not only to secure pacific settlement, but also to build a tradition and practice to prevent dangerous conflicts from developing in the future.

Referring to the Corfu incident, Sir Eric wrote that "It cannot be doubted that, for the moment at least, the events of the last two weeks have done much to weaken both the moral authority of the Council and the general confidence that the precise obligations of the Covenant will be universally accepted and carried out". He felt that unless something were done to restore general confidence in the Covenant, "a severe blow will be struck at the future usefulness of the League". The Secretary-General left little doubt of his view of the Corfu bombardment and occupation, stating that it was "very generally believed" that a powerful League member had violated the Covenant with impunity and perhaps even with an increase in prestige. He asserted that it was "generally held... that this challenge has brought in question the fundamental principles which lie at the root of the public law of the new world order established by the League". Still further:

Everyone who had taken the trouble to read the Covenant, believed it lay upon the members of the League an absolute obligation to submit their disputes to arbitration or to enquiry by the Council, and an absolute obligation not to resort in the conduct of its disputes to methods of coercion until measures of pacific settlement had been tried without success.

These fundamental principles have been called into question, and until they are re-established in the minds of Governments and peoples, there will be a sense of uncertainty which will rapidly disintegrate the power of the League.

The Secretary-General felt that the overwhelming majority of League members agreed with his view, but that public discussion within the context of the Corfu conflict might exacerbate the quarrel, while an analysis in

---

[121] League Archives, 1923, Political 11/30889/30508, 14 September 1923; the full text may also be found in James Barros, *The Corfu Incident of 1923* (Princeton: Princeton University Press, 1965), pp. 317-320.

abstract terms would be of assistance. He suggested an advisory opinion from the Permanent Court on several questions raised by the Italian action in Corfu and arguments before the Council. First, he asked whether there were any disputes between League members that did not fall within the League's competence under Article 12, 13 and 15 (aside from the domestic jurisdiction clause of Article 15, paragraph 8) because they concerned national honor and dignity, or fell within the competence of another international authority, or did not threaten the immediate outbreak of war, or because the Government of one of the parties had not been accorded full diplomatic recognition by all League members. Second, Drummond inquired whether resort to "methods of coercion, such as the forceable occupation of territory" was legitimate before the dispute had been submitted either to arbitration or to enquiry by the Council. His own view was that while international law may have accorded recognition to acts of force short of war prior to the League, Articles 10 and 12 made such measures illegal, although the point had to be clarified or the Covenant amended. Sir Eric asked finally for interpretation concerning the extent and character of the responsibility of a state upon whose territory members of a diplomatic or international mission are murdered.

Six days later, on September 20, Viscount Ishii of Japan, the Council's President, proposed to the Council that it study, with the aid of legal experts, "certain questions of interpretation of various articles of the Covenant dealing with the powers of the Council".[122] Italy resisted, but at the end of several meetings, the Council agreed upon a set of five questions to be submitted to a committee of jurists. The issues posed covered most of the ground previously outlined by the Secretary-General, the first three questions dealing with the Council's capacity under Article 15 if one of the parties claimed the Article to be inapplicable, the fourth inquiring whether acts of force short of war were consistent with Articles 12 to 15 when taken without recourse to the procedures set out therein, and the fifth question asking in what circumstances and to what extent the responsibility of a state is engaged by the commission of a political crime in its territory.[123]

The jurists' reply of March, 1924 satisfied the majority of League members on the first three and fifth questions, but its response on the all important fourth issue was ambiguous, and the result was to leave to the founders of the United Nations the task of prohibiting "the threat or use of force against the territorial integrity or political independence of any state, or in any other manner inconsistent with the Purposes of the United Nations".[124] Yet the Council's authority had been vindicated, and much as he had with the Monroe Doctrine problem, the Secretary-General had

---

[122] League of Nations, *Official Journal*, 4th year, 1923, p. 1317.
[123] *Id.*, pp. 1350-1351.
[124] United Nations Charter, Article 2, paragraph 4.

formulated a method for satisfying the contending parties in the particular case while maintaining the position that the League of Nations was competent in all cases of international conflict, regardless of regional interest or the involvement of outside organizations. As well, Sir Eric tried to fill an obvious gap in the Covenant, and while this was left by the Council to the San Francisco Conference in 1945, his quick grasp of the issue and the emphasis he placed upon it, and with persuasiveness for the Council, was important in terms of the Secretary-General's eventual influence on the construction of global institutions. Today there is no doubt that force short of war is illegal except in case of self-defense or UN-sanctioned measures, and the Charter's provisions in this context are traceable to the Corfu conflict of 1923 and Drummond's imaginative use of his power as Secretary-General.

The Greco-Bulgarian border incident of 1925 marked the apex of League Council prestige and efficiency in settling a brief but violent encounter that threatened war in the Balkans.[125] Greek forces had entered Bulgarian territory in force a few days after a border skirmish on October 19, 1925 resulted in the killing of a Greek officer advancing with a white flag to stop the shooting. The Secretary-General and his staff were active primarily in an effort to urge caution in Athens and compliance with the League Covenant, and with Drummond, Arthur Salter, Director of the Economic and Financial Section, and Deputy Secretary-General Joseph Avenol involved in this effort, the impression of British and French pressure on Greece was easily inferred.

On October 21, under instructions from Drummond, Salter telephoned the Greek chargé d'aiffaires in Bern, Switzerland informing him that London had sent information to Geneva to the effect that Greece had given Bulgaria an "ultimatum" necessitating a reply within forty-eight hours. He said that Drummond believed Greece wished to comply with the Covenant. The next day, the same officer wired Athens that Secretary-General Drummond felt disturbed over the Greek action, and that the Secretariat had informed him that Council members were seeking information in case Council action became necessary. After Bulgaria appealed to Drummond on October 22 to call a Council session on the matter, the Secretariat advised Greece to withdraw her troops from Bugaria and to inform the Secretary-General that orders had been given for that purpose. At the same time, Deputy Secretary-General Avenol, through his Secretariat associate Thanassis Aghnides of Greece, urged caution and compliance with the Covenant. Sir Eric, in accordance with Bulgaria's request, convoked a

---

[125] This account relies upon the detailed history of the dispute by James Barros, "The Greek-Bulgarian Incident of 1925: The League of Nations and the Great Powers", *Proceedings of the American Philosophical Society*, Vol. 108, No. 4 (August 27, 1964), pp. 354-385, particularly at pp. 362-364.

Council meeting for October 26, the earliest possible time, and President Briand, in agreement with Drummond's move, also telegraphed to the parties the equivalent of a ceasefire order, urging them to halt military movements and to withdraw troops behind their frontiers.

After great-power pressure induced the Greeks to withdraw, and the fighting had ceased, the Council dispatched a commission of inquiry to investigate the incident and make recommendations concerning reparations and future procedures in the area. With the very substantial assistance of the Secretariat, whose suggestions were of course approved by Drummond, the commission called for reparations from Greece, neutral patrols for frontier supervision, and methods for handling private property claims. There was general compliance with the Council's actions, and the settlement of the dispute followed shortly.

It is difficult to assess the impact of the Secretary-General's role in the Greco-Bulgarian conflict, although it is evident that British and French strategy were critical in determining the outcome while the Secretariat's influence was marginal at best. Yet Drummond, as always working quietly, attempted to exert some authority in matters of vital concern to the League and world politics, and in so doing, he maintained the reality of a political function for the Secretary-General as mediator and aide in shaping the terms of settlement, and as a leading channel for communication between the parties to the conflict and the international community.

Sir Eric was actively engaged in negotiations even in the two important cases of conflict in the Western Hemisphere, the one between Bolivia and Paraguay over the Gran Chaco in 1928 and 1933, and the other involving Colombia and Peru in a 1933 dispute over the Leticia Trapeze. The border issues in question were of little interest to European powers, but the problem of League competence in the face of determined United States insistence upon regional settlement confronted the Secretary-General with difficult applications of his long-held view according primary deference to the procedures of the global institution he headed.

Drummond worked hard to keep the League involved in these conflicts while attempting to strike a balance with the United States and even with Latin American states who preferred a weak or restrictive view of the Monroe Doctrine clause in the Covenant, but nevertheless often preferred regional settlement efforts. Sir Eric put the issue of the 1928 outbreak of fighting between Bolivia and Paraguay to the Council, but he tried to assure the Bolivian Minister at Bern, who came to discuss the matter with him:

I replied [to the Minister] that I felt sure that the Council would do everything it could to help forward a settlement of the matter, but I felt bound equally to observe that all that the Council desired was that the problem should be settled by peaceful means. The Council had no special desire to be the instrument to effect such a settlement, and, if other means were preferred, such as, for example, the arbitration of the

Argentine Republic, the Council would be equally happy. I thought it well to make this remark as the Minister rather seemed to imply that it was the desire of the League to settle the matter itself.[126]

Shortly after the 1928 outbreak, the crisis passed as both parties agreed to the good offices of the Pan American Arbitration Conference to settle at least the conflict caused by the eruption of fighting. The larger territorial issue was left unsettled and under the authority of the American established and based Neutral Commission, composed of representatives from the United States, Colombia, Cuba, Mexico, and Uruguay.

During the summer of 1932, fighting began anew, and throughout the remainder of his administration, Drummond remained active in bargaining sessions that oftentimes resembled a competition for jurisdiction between the League Council and the five-nation Neutral Commission. Washington and both contending parties preferred the Commission forum, but the smaller powers on the Council wanted a more substantial role for the League, and Sir Eric, in September, 1932, recommended a Council cable to both parties pointing out their Covenant obligations, their apparent acceptance of mediation, and urging strongly that they confide the case to the Neutral Commission and abide by its recommendations and decisions.[127] Drummond told Hugh Wilson, the American Minister in Switzerland, that he could "readily persuade the Council to undertake" [128] the suggested plan, and indeed, he succeeded. He asked only for frequent reports of the Commission's progress, in order to "keep the matter entirely within the bounds of cooperation" with its work.[129]

The Secretary-General cooperated rather closely with the Neutral Commission's efforts during the last few months of 1932, going so far as to attempt to prevent the Council committee dealing with the Chaco dispute from meeting as scheduled in early November in order not to interfere with the Commission's work.[130] Within two weeks, however, the Secretary-General felt he could no longer stave off Council activity, both because of the almost daily accounts in the press of fighting in the Chaco area, and since many Council members wished to take a position on this conflict in order to have some influence over the contemporaneous Leticia dispute

[126] League Archives 1928, Political 1A/8946/2042, 12 December 1928.
[127] *Foreign Relations of the United States* (Washington: Department of State), 1932, Vol. V, p. 229. Hereinafter cited as *FRUS*.
[128] *Ibid.*
[129] *Id.*, p. 235.
[130] The failure of the Commission to keep the Council adequately informed made Drummond's task of delaying Council activity somewhat awkward and difficult, prompting Wilson to suggest to Secretary of State Henry Stimson that "we must do what we can to help Drummond in this connection and ... full and continuous communication from the Chairman of the Neutrals to the Chairman of the Council is the only hope of stemming off action by the Council". (*Id.*, p. 244)

between Colombia and Peru.[131] U.S. Secretary of State Henry Stimson insisted on patience, arguing that League action would unravel the progress made over a period of four years, but Drummond went ahead with recommendations that the Council note the negotiations under the Commission's auspices, call upon the parties to cease the hostilities and accept the Commission's proposal for a military committee to examine the facts and make arrangements to ensure no further outbreaks, and conclude that a refusal by either party to stop the fighting would constitute a violation of the Covenant.[132] The Council acted in accordance with Sir Eric's suggestion, adopting all but the last of his four-part proposal, but it had little influence over the course of the conflict. Both sides accepted the notion of a commission of inquiry in principle, but wished to delay its functioning so long as the four neighboring states of Argentina, Brazil, Chile, and Peru, on appeal from the Neutral Commission, tried to settle the conflict.

Drummond also supported the idea of a small Council committee of three members that would visit the capitals of the two parties and the disputed area if necessary, the idea being to negotiate an agreement through League political representatives.[133] He urged this course on Bolivia, Paraguay, and the United States, but to no avail. An attempt by Britain and France to organize an embargo by League members also fell through as the U.S. Senate rejected it.

On May 10, 1933, after months of fruitless negotiations and Council inactivity, Paraguay declared the existence of a state of war with Bolivia, and at this point, the Neutral Commission finally gave way to the League Council, which now insisted on action and a commission to negotiate a cessation of hostilities and an arbitration agreement. The committee was also to inquire into all the circumstances of the dispute and the role of the Council. For the Secretary-General, nearing the end of fourteen years in office, it was a "wretched business",[134] and he again wearily urged the United States to cooperate. By the end of June, and coinciding with the effective date of Drummond's resignation, the Neutral Commission formally bowed out of the diplomatic role it had undertaken since 1928, and Sir Eric simply communicated his hopes to the parties for cooperation with the Council's efforts. He wrote to U.S. Minister Hugh Wilson informally, asking the United States Government to take diplomatic action at La Paz to ensure Bolivia's acceptance of the Council's recommendations, as Paraguay had accepted them earlier.[135]

The Chaco Commission did not begin its work until well after Sir Eric's resignation, and the final settlement, produced effectively only by the

---

131 *Id.*, p. 248.
132 *Ibid.*
133 *Id.*, pp. 262-263.
134 *Id.*, p. 330.
135 *Ibid.*

parties' military exhaustion, came in 1938, and without the participation of the League. Drummond's role had been the commonly accepted function for the Secretary-General of neutral mediator, and once again his real political impact was marginal (as was that of the great powers) even while he maintained the strength of his Office in international diplomacy. His negotiating skills and the Office's communication functions enabled Sir Eric to take part in the political discussions very much on a par with the statesmen of Europe and Latin America, and his suggestions were those finally adopted by the League Council. His capacity to influence the League's supreme peacekeeping organization seemed remarkable given his administrative position and inconsequential political base, and was attributable primarily to his imaginative application of the mediator's role in international politics.

In the Leticia conflict between Colombia and Peru in 1932-1933, the League achieved a peaceful settlement in the disputed area known as the Leticia Trapeze, ceded by Peru to Colombia by treaty in 1928, but seized by Peru in 1932 and contested again during the final months of Drummond's administration.

The first attempt at mediation came from Brazil, the suggestion being that Peru should surrender the territory to a Brazilian military contingent which would in turn, a few days later, turn the area back to Colombia. In a discussion on January 27, 1933 with the Colombian and Peruvian representatives at the League, Drummond received the impression that Peru wanted a solution that might permit it to "climb down" from an untenable position, and he urged support of the Brazilian plan. The problem was that the proposal called for the termination of the Brazilian occupation in ten days, deemed by Peru to be too short a time span, and Drummond therefore suggested the occupation might be prolonged to a period of a month or six weeks, emphasizing that this was a personal suggestion on his part and in no way binding on the League or any member.[136]

Between this discussion in late January and the middle of February, 1933, the recommended temporary occupation by Brazil was set at sixty days, but in the midst of difficult negotiations concerning the precise wording of the Brazilian plan, hostilities broke out as Peruvian planes bombed Colombian ships moving toward the Leticia territory, and public sentiment for war developed in both countries. By February 15, Brazil had ended her mediation effort, and from this point forward the United States raised no objection to consideration of the matter by the League.

The Secretary-General supported, and the League Council recommended, a plan under which Peru would hand over Leticia to a League Commission for a year, during which negotiations between Colombia and Peru would go forward, and after which, in the absence of a contrary agreement,

[136] *FRUS,* 1933, Vol. IV, pp. 433-434.

the territory would be restored to Colombia. A small Colombian contingent would be constituted an international force to keep order, but the League commission and its command over the Colombian troops would guarantee Peruvian inhabitants against mistreatment during the year-long negotiations. Drummond wanted a commission with representatives from the United States, Brazil, and one other country, and to have them as near as possible to the Leticia territory so as to arrive quickly if the proposal were accepted by both parties.[137]

By the first week in March, Peru was balking at the Council's terms, insisting on international troops, rather than a Colombian contingent, and urging arbitration of the issue. Most Council members felt that Colombia had every right to occupy what was clearly her territory under international law, and that her sovereignty over Leticia was not a proper matter for arbitration. The Council therefore prepared to issue its own report under Article 15, paragraph 4 of the Covenant, although Drummond wanted to go much further. According to Hugh Wilson's communique to Stimson on March 7,

Drummond pointed out that he hoped that the matter would not stop merely with the adoption of a report under paragraph 4 of article 15. This is a clear-cut issue on which all states agree as to the violator. He is doubtful himself of the advisability of breaking diplomatic relations since he recognizes the danger and even disaster that this might bring to foreign interests in Peru. He does believe, however, that an arms embargo could be applied against Peru followed perhaps by other forms of embargo.[138]

The Secretary-General's concern with "foreign interests" was a reference to American economic investment in Peru. An arms embargo, however, would avoid any substantial clash with foreign businessmen, and might well be sufficient to induce Peru to cooperate with the League Council. In a series of talks with Peruvian representatives, Sir Eric received the impression that they were "hesitant as to the course to pursue and... particularly apprehensive at the thought of sanctions". He was anxious to know the United States view of an arms embargo, for he considered "the mere possibility of such action would be sufficient to turn the tide with the Peruvian Government and make them accept the League's proposal".[139]

Stimson informed Drummond the United States could not take part in an arms embargo, and the Secretary-General's sanctions proposals were put aside pending the Council's report, which was adopted on March 18, 1933. Peru was to withdraw her forces from Leticia, and once this was accomplished, negotiations between the parties could begin. An Advisory Committee was established to help implement the Council's resolution, and to ensure that League Members did not hinder in any way the recommendations on withdrawal and diplomatic negotiation. Peru naturally re-

[137] *Id.*, pp. 490-491.
[138] *Id.*, p. 495.
[139] *Id.*, p. 496.

jected the report, and the Advisory Committee itself I
sanctions, particularly the proposed arms embargo.

In April, Lima agreed to the League Commission i
of Leticia by that body until negotiations between f
satisfactory conclusion, but Peru rejected a new s
mendations on May 10 calling for a Commission to ac
name of Colombia for a maximum period of one year. Wᴵᴸᴸᵉ ·
proceeded in the Advisory Committee as to the most efficient method or
implementing the Council's report of March 18, the danger of war increased
as Peru sent a cruiser and three submarines into the Atlantic and then
toward Iquitos, where the warships were to join Peruvian troops for an
expected battle with Colombian contingents. The Advisory Committee
tried to persuade Members at whose ports the ships would stop to refuse
assistance, but to no avail. Britain and the Netherlands, whose responsibility
was paramount, hesitated long enough to enable the ships to take on sufficient food, fuel and other supplies to proceed toward the Amazon. The
Secretary-General, speaking immediately after the British delegate in the
Advisory Committee on May 13, said that in his view "Peru was playing
for time until the squadron could arrive in the Upper Amazon" and that
"giving of facilities to the warships was playing Peru's game". He concluded
that withholding of facilities and delaying the arrival of the Peruvian fleet
was the best possible support for the Advisory Committee.[140] This was one
of Drummond's rare political statements in a League body, and all the
more significant for its direct criticism of British policy.

By the end of May, however, war was averted, for Peru finally acquiesced
in the proposal for a League Commission to administer Leticia for a
maximum period of one year, and a few weeks after Drummond's resignation, the Commission, including representatives of the United States, Brazil
and Spain, arrived at the disputed territory to begin its year-long administration prior to returning it to Colombia. It was the Secretary-General's final
success in the political arena, although it came simultaneously with his
failure in the Chaco dispute, and the far more consequential inability to
assure a favorable outcome for the League in the Sino-Japanese conflict.

The Sino-Japanese Conflict: 1931-1933

It was the misfortune of the League that the first great test of its power to
prevent aggression should have come in the fall of 1931 during the financial
panic that had swept the world. Another misfortune was that it came at the
same time the League was planning for the opening of the World Disarmament Conference, scheduled for February, 1932. The rape of Manchuria by

[140] *Id.*, p. 532.

apan was the most shattering blow the League had encountered, and because the Organization never succeeded in controlling the course of events, the effect on its prestige was obvious. The irony of the action in Manchuria lay in the fact that until 1931 Japan had been one of the League's most effective and loyal members, deeply respected by her associates. Japanese representatives like Nitobe, Adatci, Sato and Sugimura were outstanding in their services.

Although Manchuria was part of the Chinese Empire, it had had an unfortunate history, for it had been ruled by a series of war-lords and there were times when its government was little more than chaos. The Japanese had built a railroad system there and had established some industries, but that they should send in an army to seize the country came as a complete shock to Members of the League and to the entire world.

On September 18, 1931, the Japanese army, which had been lawfully guarding the zone of the South Manchurian Railway, suddenly attacked Mukden and other centers in Manchuria. Chinese troops offered feeble resistance, and Japan's occupation of Manchuria had begun. Word of the fighting reached Geneva on September 19, and it was immediately discussed by the Council.

China, represented by Alfred Sze, a man of great diplomatic ability, claimed that the situation was rapidly worsening, with cities not only being occupied, but bombed with great loss of life. He called upon the Council to act at once, and said that his country would accept any decision taken. Kenkichi Yoshizawa of Japan frankly conceded what he called the vital importance of Manchuria to Japan, but asserted that the army's action was only a local incident and would be settled without delay. In any case he must ask for an adjournment because he had no instructions from his government. The Council reluctantly agreed, while warning both sides to do their best to prevent the situation from deteriorating.

For Sir Eric Drummond, this was the beginning of a long and complex involvement in an international conflict of the gravest significance. Drummond's role demonstrated more clearly than ever that the Secretary-General of the League was far more than the quiet, unobtrusive administrative official that most accounts would have us believe, for he was in a key position among the participants in the protracted negotiations that attended the League's first great crisis. The League of Nations Council and Assembly were the primary arenas for the negotiations that stretched out from September, 1931, to the spring of 1933, and the centrally placed League Secretary-General was invaluable to governments as a constant source of data on the views of other representatives, and of policy alternatives that might be acceptable to the powers concerned. Drummond's knowledge of League procedures and Members' views gave his opinions great weight among the delegates at Geneva, and the foreign offices of the world. Again, he took part in negotiations almost as an equal to any of the Foreign

Ministers present at the League, making recommendations of substance and procedure, evaluating policy alternatives presented by the states concerned, and serving as the key to effective liaison with the United States. This was all accomplished, of course, behind the scenes, and in a manner that generally sustained the reputation Drummond had built as a remarkably impartial League official dedicated to the League and a peaceful world.

The alarm over the action of the Japanese invasion swept around the world, for the action not only ran counter to the Covenant, but also violated the Nine Power Treaty on China of 1922, as well as the 1928 Kellogg-Briand Pact. Washington was shaken, and Secretary of State Stimson, a man clearly sympathetic to the League, determined that something should be done about the Japanese threat, although he was far from clear as to just what the United States response should be. The first thought at Geneva was to have a Commission of Inquiry, composed of national officials in the area, report to the Council on conditions at the railway zone. Drummond pressed hard for United States cooperation. In the Secretary-General's view, there were two ways in which Washington might assist the League: either an American might be invited to sit on the League Council, or a small Council Committee could request the United States to appoint an American representative. Drummond naturally preferred the first step as "the boldest and perhaps the most effective possible because of its effect on public opinion in Japan",[141] and after some hesitation, Stimson adopted this course.

The Secretary-General also was anxious to have the United States take part in the special investigating committee. He suggested to Stimson that the invitation to serve on the committee might be based upon U.S. interest as signatories either of the Nine Power Treaty or the Kellogg Pact, or on a basis of general world concern.[142] Stimson opposed the investigation committee idea, however, primarily on the ground that it would make it more difficult for civilian rule to maintain itself in Japan against the army, and the idea was dropped for the time being, despite the support of Drummond and of Norman Davis, an American who was in Geneva at the time as a member of the League's Financial Committee.

A few days later Yoshizawa, having received his instructions from Tokyo, presented his nation's case as essentially one of self-defense against attacks from the Chinese in the area, asserting that Japan had no territorial designs and was already withdrawing most of its troops back to the railway zone. The Council apparently believed this to be the position of the Japanese Government, for its resolution of September 30, 1931 was an optimistic call upon both parties to prevent a widening of the conflict. The Council

141 *FRUS*, 1931, Vol. III, p. 39. The quoted passage are the words of Hugh Wilson. Drummond felt that only Japan would be unhappy with United States participation, but would not protest publicly.
142 *Id.*, p. 50.

was willing to accept the Japanese promise of evacuation given in return for Chinese assurances on the safety of the lives and property of Japanese nationals.

In fact, however, the situation in Manchuria deteriorated rapidly. The Japanese Army disavowed Yoshizawa's statement, and embarked on a full scale military occupation in China that did not stop until Shanghai had been attacked in early 1932. Chinchow was bombed on October 8th, 1931, and the promised evacuation did not take place, nor would it, stated Tokyo, until negotiations between China and Japan produced Chinese agreement on the fundamentals of Japanese influence in China.

At this point, however, Drummond was still hopeful of a peaceful solution, believing that if Japanese withdrawal to the railway zone were achieved, the League could properly call upon both parties to adjust all outstanding issues through direct negotiation. In view of the worldwide economic depression, the Secretary-General agreed with the United States, Britain, and France that pressure on the Japanese through economic sanctions "would be entirely out of the question",[143] although he felt that if Japan refused to accept the Council resolution, the great powers might withdraw their mission chiefs from Tokyo. Sir Eric argued that this kind of pressure might be difficult for the Japanese to resist.

The Council met again on October 13th, this time under the chairmanship of Aristide Briand, who had been premier of France on ten different occasions. Drummond had just received a letter from Secretary Stimson commiting Washington to reinforcing League action even while acting independently. Upon receipt of the letter, Briand suggested the United States be invited to participate in the Council discussion, and after Yoshizawa's strenuous objection was overruled, the invitation was extended. Stimson promptly accepted, and Prentiss Gilbert, the American Consul in Geneva, took his seat at the horseshoe table of the Council. Unfortunately, the step increased domestic pressure on Stimson, who then limited Gilbert's role quite severely, and the U.S. representative was never able to play an effective part in the proceedings, but the moral effect of his presence was deemed important and he also served faithfully as the key liaison between Stimson and Drummond.[144]

---

143 *Id.*, p. 130.
144 Stimson sent much valuable information to the Secretary-General, but Drummond was usually enjoined to keep the source confidential. Sir Eric was not altogether satisfied with the arrangement. The following passage from one of Prentiss Gilbert's reports is revealing:

"Drummond then discussed his role of Secretary-General of the League of Nations and its relation to a matter of this nature. He pointed out that in no way was his position analogous to a Foreign Minister's. In a relationship between the League and various governments, he is in effect only an agency of transmission. Accordingly, to exchange information with him alone is not in any way tantamount to an exchange with either the Council or its members. In regard to this valuable

At this point began a long series of bargaining sessions leading toward a Council resolution submitted by Briand, and finally rejected by the Japanese on October 24th. This was a critical juncture, for it indicated clearly that Tokyo was no longer interested at all, if indeed she had been at the beginning of the crisis, in peaceful settlement. Secretary-General Drummond played an important role along with Briand in the talks, but all to no avail.

Stimson had earlier raised the possibility of an invocation of the Kellogg-Briand Pact by the League Council. Drummond resisted this, thinking it more proper for the United States alone to address a note calling the attention of Japan and China to the Pact of Paris.[145] He also feared the danger of invoking the Pact in a manner that might indicate war had already taken place. Apparently convinced, Stimson delivered a note on October 20 to the Chinese and Japanese calling attention to the Pact, and expressing the hope that the two nations would refrain from measures that might lead to war. The United States had wanted the appeal to public opinion to help the Japanese toward a more conciliatory attitude in the Geneva discussions, but this was not to be.

According to reports sent to the U.S. State Department by Gilbert, the important developments now occurred in the direct conversations between the Secretary-General, Lord Reading (the British representative to the Council), Briand, Dino Grandi (the Italian delegate), Sze, and Yoshizawa.[146] The critical issue was whether the Japanese would withdraw at the same time as security for Japanese lives and property was assured by China (the thrust of the September 30th resolution), or whether Japanese troops would withdraw only after all outstanding questions between China and Japan had been settled. Japan insisted that the latter position represented no change from the September 30 resolution, but Drummond, Briand, and Reading thought otherwise.

The Secretary-General, together with the British and French representatives, finally drew up a draft resolution he must have known would be unacceptable to the Japanese. The text included a provision calling for Japanese troop withdrawal to be completed by the next meeting of the Council, scheduled in three weeks, and for direct negotiation on all out-

---

information you have supplied, he remains handicapped in his use of it in any practical fashion so long as he is restrained by the injunction not to reveal its source. Should he communicate it to anyone, the first question he would be asked would be as to the source of the information. From the kind of reply he would give, the information either would not be accorded its due weight or its source would be surmised". (*Ibid.*, p. 156)
Stimson insisted, however, that the source of the information he sent to Drummond be kept confidential.
[145] *Id.*, p. 168.
[146] *Id.*, p. 272.

standing issues as soon as the withdrawal had been accomplished. The resolution was due for presentation to the Council on October 24, and to the last, Drummond tried to reach agreement with the Japanese representative. Yoshizawa, in a conversation with the Secretary-General on October 22nd, insisted that prior to evacuation China agree to respect certain treaties between the two countries relating to railways in Manchuria. The treaties were a matter of dispute as their validity was not recognized in all respects by China, but Drummond could not agree that the Japanese had the right, under the Covenant, to use force to gain compliance with disputed treaty rights.[147]

The Secretary-General saw no way to meet Japan's position. The furthest he would go was a simultaneous evacuation and provision of security, with direct negotiations covering both to take place at the same time. A memorandum by U.S. Under Secretary of State William R. Castle, Jr., lists these points as having been made by Drummond on October 20th, 1931, and accepted by the Japanese Government on October 22nd. According to Castle's report, Yoshizawa hurried to Lord Reading with his Government's acceptance of Drummond's plan, but Reading refused to discuss the matter further.[148]

Drummond made another attempt at compromise on the evening of October 22nd. He suggested to Yoshizawa that the latter ask Sze in the public session of the Council whether China was prepared to carry out its obligations under the treaties. If the answer were yes, then Japan would have its undertaking. If the problem of the validity of the treaties arose, the issue could be submitted to the Permanent Court of International Justice at the Hague. Yoshizawa replied that his Government was not inclined to take the matter to the World Court, and had probably said its last word on the subject.[149]

Briand formally submitted the resolution on October 24th, and Japan, taking advantage of the fact that the Council was acting under Article 11 of the Covenant (allowing even a party to a dispute to vote, under the then current League theory), vetoed the draft. The Japanese Army continued to extend its occupation in Manchuria. Within a few days theres were signs that the Japanese position was stiffening further, and Drummond stated his belief that Tokyo's next move would be the establishment of a puppet government in Manchuria.[150] In the meantime, the Secretary-General and Briand continued to handle the negotiations for the Council.

The problem was where to go from the veto of the October 24th resolution. Drummond and Briand emphasized the importance of the defeated resolution's fifth point, namely, the appointment of representatives from

147 *Id.*, pp. 299-301.
148 *Id.*, pp. 333-336.
149 *Id.*, pp. 300-301.
150 *Id.*, p. 341.

both countries to negotiate the evacuation and taking over of the evacuated territory. The Secretary-General felt that once the discussions on this point had begun, the question of a fixed date for withdrawal would become relatively unimportant. He requested the United State Government to try to induce Japan to appoint representatives to get the talks started,[151] but despite Washington's support for Drummond, Japan was in no mood for compromise.

The Council met again for a third try in Paris on November 16th, 1931. The Secretary-General and those members of the Secretariat staff working on the Sino-Japanese conflict moved to Paris with the Council members and occupied quarters in the Quai d'Orsay. Drummond made it known that he would not give way to Japanese demands for settlement prior to evacuation, and the search for further League alternatives continued.

Writing to Deputy Secretary-General Joseph Avenol on November 6, 1931, Drummond stated:

The Japanese aims are now quite clear. They are:
(1) To obtain the recognition by China of certain Manchurian agreements which China up to now has contested.
(2) To subtract Manchuria from any direct dependence on Nanking.
Obviously, China can never agree to such demands nor are the methods used to obtain them in accordance with the principles of the League. Further, if the League fails in this matter, not only is the value of the peace-keeping clauses of the Covenant destroyed ... but also the success of the Disarmament Conference is seriously endangered ... This is why ... I regard this matter as absolutely vital from the League point of view and for the general principles for which the League stands.[152]

Sir Eric felt strongly that the fate of the Disarmament Conference, and of the peace in Europe depended largely upon a successful outcome of the Sino-Japanese conflict. He wrote to Avenol on November 10, 1931, that it was the extreme nationalist press in each country, in addition to the military and to those interested in armaments manufacture who were "clamouring against any further pressure being put on Japan in the present circumstances; and it is those elements which are equally opposed to any successful issue being found at the Disarmament Conference".[153]

While the Weimar Republic in Germany staggered toward its tragic end, the Secretary-General wrote in his precise and careful style of the obvious lesson to be learned from a League failure in China:

as you say, the general public in Europe does not distinguish between the present case and one which might occur in Europe. I cannot help feeling that, to a certain degree, there is justification in this theory. If it is admitted that, because treaty rights are being violated, a country has the power to occupy the territory of the violating power, and

---

151 *Id.,* pp. 352-353.
152 Letter from Sir Eric Drummond to Joseph Avenol, 6 November 1931. Special Drummond file, United Nations Library, Geneva.
153 *Id.,* 10 November 1931.

not to depart from that territory till they have obtained satisfaction, then obviously such an admission must alarm a considerable number of powers in Europe.[154]

Drummond now began to talk of an appeal from China under Article 15 of the Covenant. The advantage of Article 15 was that decisions could be taken without the vote of the parties to the conflict, and a commission of inquiry could be established for purposes of studying all the circumstances of the case and to serve as an impartial fact-finding body. For the Japanese, it had the advantage of further delay, and if for no other reason, was thus attractive to them. On the other hand, Article 15 involved a threat of sanctions, and was thus not looked upon favorably by most members of the Council, particularly Great Britain.

Sir Eric pointed out that "up to now ... we have done our best to persuade the Chinese Government not to utilise that Article. Briand was much opposed to its being invoked, and I think this was the general feeling among the other members. I am inclined to believe that there had not been sufficient examination of Article 15 and of its delaying effects".[155]

The Secretary-General was also still willing to attempt a legal approach insofar as the contested treaties were concerned. He held it important to obtain from Tokyo a statement as to the treaties she was relying upon, and if the Chinese objected to the validity of such agreements, the Council could ask the World Court for an advisory opinion. Drummond actually felt that the answers given by the Court would probably favor Japan, but that Tokyo was unwilling to take the risk, despite further opportunities for delay.

Drummond also viewed the Japanese Government as disposed to tolerate deliberately provocative acts by the military, and he decried the change in Tokyo's negotiating position from the first days of the crisis. He wrote that on September 30th, when the Japanese made evacuation dependent on effective assurance for the lives and property of their nationals, they "had not then in mind that this safety depended on the execution of the treaties they now refer to. This claim has been an after-thought, and ... they now talk, not only of the safety of the lives and property of Japanese nationals, but also of a return to normal conditions".[156] Sir Eric claimed, however, that the Japanese Delegation had been ready to make a definite statement that the evacuation to the railway zone was not dependent upon direct negotiations between Japan and China on other issues, but that this was abandoned "through a blunder on the part of the Chinese".[157] He did not state what the blunder was.

In the meantime, Drummond had Under-Secretary-General Yotaro

[154] *Ibid.*
[155] *Ibid.*
[156] *Ibid.*
[157] *Ibid.*

Sugimura of Japan working on the entire set of issues, and he sent Frank Walters to Tokyo to try to persuade the Government there to make some conciliatory gesture. Perhaps Walter's mission met with some success, for Yoshizawa agreed with Drummond at a secret meeting of the reconvened Council that the League should send a Commission of Inquiry to investigate the situation and report its findings. Given the deterioration of the situation in Manchuria, and the ascendancy of the military in the Government at Tokyo, it is fair to conclude that Japan's primary motivation in making the proposal was delay, but the Council had almost no alternative to offer, and the plan was accepted once it was known that the United States supported it.

On November 21st, 1931, Yoshizawa made the recommendation at a public Council meeting, and after a few weeks of wrangling over details, the Council, on December 10th, adopted a resolution establishing a League Commission of Inquiry to the Far East. It had no authority to recommend terms of settlement, but was empowered merely to investigate the situation and report on any facts that threatened peaceful relations between Japan and China.

The Commission, consisting of five members drawn from the great powers, was not actually established until early January, 1932. Lord Lytton of Great Britain was selected as chairman, and the Commission shortly became known to history as the Lytton Commission. The United States was represented by General Frank McCoy, an officer who had served with General Pershing in France. The Commission did not leave for China until February, and given the slow westward route chosen, did not arrive in Manchuria until April. In the meantime, negotiations continued in Geneva, London, and Paris, and Japanese control became more extensive and firm in Manchuria.

The talks preceding formal approval of the Lytton Commission were once again carried forward by the British and French delegates to the Council, along with Sir Eric Drummond. Briand continued to represent France, and Sir John Simon, the new British Foreign Secretary, remained in Geneva for a short while to represent Great Britain.

The Chinese were naturally not happy at the thought that the Commission of Inquiry would simply mean more delay, but Drummond, in long discussions with Sze, urged the Commission idea as being very much in China's interest. The Secretary-General asserted that he had tried every argument possible, finally inquiring as to what alternative the Chinese might propose.[158] Sze insisted that China could not agree to the Commission if it were not accompanied by a time limit for Japanese evacuation. Simon and Briand also had prolonged talks with Sze, and China finally agreed to the Commission without a time limit for troop withdrawals.

Drummond was also active, of course, in enlisting American support

[158] *FRUS, op. cit.,* p. 551.

for the Commission. He went so far as to suggest statements that the American Government might make concerning the importance it attached to the Commission, and that if the Council decided that a U.S. citizen should be one of the members, that it would look with favor upon an appointment.[159] Sir Eric also assisted the President of the Council in the selection of the Commission members.

Drummond was perhaps overly optimistic as to the positive results the Commission might achieve, although he realized full well the danger of delay. Yet there were no further concessions to be gotten from the Japanese, and the Secretary-General was thus willing to make any move that provided the slightest ray of hope. In a message to Dr. Ludwik Rajchman at the end of November, 1931, Drummond argued that if evacuation was not completed when the Commission arrived, the "pressure caused by their presence and enquiries will be very great".[160] At the same time, the Secretary-General refused to ask the Japanese to comply with the time-limit demand for withdrawal, as this might wreck chances for their final agreement on the Commission: "We have succeeded in wringing great concessions from [the] Japanese and I am terrified that if they are now pressed too hard they will withdraw them, as [the] extreme National Party there are indignant".[161]

As the year 1931 drew to a close, it was clear that the League of Nations had suffered a shattering blow. And the Secretary-General who had lead the League in its decade of success, only to witness the economic collapse and now the failure of the Organization to keep the peace, was forced to compromise with what almost every member of the world community viewed as an unjustified resort to force.

In terms of his Office, however, Sir Eric had done well. Building on the trust and confidence placed in him over the years from 1919, Drummond was able to play a key political role, for his work, while almost completely private, was obviously important, particularly in the delicate negotiations throughout the fall and early winter of 1931. He had succeeded in keeping the League actively involved, and had been able to work closely with the United States, which only ten years before had refused even to answer his communications.

If there were criticisms of Drummond's work at this time, they were certainly few and far between. Disapproval did come from Sir Eric's old friend Lord Robert Cecil, who, writing from London on December 18, 1931, stated to Drummond that secrecy in the negotiations had been harmful:

I cannot tell you how much harm the secrecy of the recent negotiations seems to have done in this country. For the first time there is a real movement against the League

---

159 *Id.,* p. 650.
160 *Documents on British Foreign Policy,* Second Series, Vol. VIII, 1931, p. 973.
161 *Id.,* p. 974.

which has extended to the Disarmament Conference... If I could believe with you that secrecy materially assists success, that, of course, would have to be considered. But I confess the evidence... seems to be slight. Unless you struggle against it, the tendency of all Foreign Offices will always be in favor of secrecy, and most Foreign Ministers will share their views because it seems safer, and besides, increases their personal importance.[162]

To this Drummond replied on December 29th. "Unhappily I agree with you that the Manchurian affair had dealt a severe blow to the League, but I cannot but disagree entirely when you suggest that this is due to the secrecy of the recent negotiations... It is my absolute belief, and I think I had more to do with the negotiations than anybody, that if we had tried to negotiate in public, we would never have gotten anywhere... Of this I am quite content to take the responsibility, but I am not prepared to take it as regards the limits within which the Great Powers, and chiefly Great Britain, forced us to work... We must do our best to pull through in circumstances which are going to be of exceptional difficulty".[163] There were also some critical press remarks somewhat later, charging Drummond with overly close cooperation with the Foreign Office and a tendency to compromise too far with unjustified Japanese demands.

The new year opened with some hope as Secretary of State Stimson's historic non-recognition doctrine attracted world-wide attention. In a note dated January 7, 1932, addressed to both China and Japan, the United States declared that

The American Government... cannot admit the legality of any situation *de facto*, nor does it intend to recognize any treaty or agreement entered into between these governments, or agents thereof, which may impair the treaty rights of the United States or its citizens in China, including those which relate to the sovereignty, the independence, or the territorial and administrative integrity of the Republic of China, or to the international policy relative to China, commonly known as the open-door policy; and that it does not intend to recognize any situation, treaty or agreement which may be brought about by means contrary to the covenants and obligations of the Pact of Paris of August 27, 1928, to which treaty both China and Japan, as well as the United States, are parties.[164]

The Stimson Doctrine fell like a bombshell on Japan, but the British Government refused to subscribe to it. This aroused Drummond. Writing to Lord Cecil, with the suggestion that his letter be shown to the British Secretary for Foreign Affairs, Sir Eric said he was greatly disturbed at the British attitude, and suggested with emphasis that "if we return a discouraging answer now, we shall certainly cause great resentment in America with all its possible consequences, and encourage the Japanese Government

---

[162] *Id.,* Vol. IX, p. 22.
[163] *Id.,* pp. 56-57.
[164] See Westel W. Willoughby, *The Sino-Japanese Controversy and The League of Nations* (Baltimore, The Johns Hopkins Press, 1935), p. 206.

in the view that they are not going to meet with any real opposition whatever they do".[165]

But Drummond's advice was disregarded. Instead the British Government told Washington it was concerned about the possibility that trade with Manchuria might be adversely affected and that Japan already understood this situation. Therefore, it argued, a note such as the United States had sent was inadvisable, and to compound the damage, London published its reply in the newspapers, to the great satisfaction of the Japanese. The Council, and later the Assembly accepted the non-recognition doctrine, but without the common front of the United States, Britain, and France (which followed the British lead on the matter), the League's voice meant little.

The Council met again at the end of January, 1932, at the same time that the Disarmament Conference was about to open. The Lytton Commission had still not left for Manchuria, and in the meantime, the Japanese had struck at Shanghai. China finally asked for consideration of the question under Article 15 of the Covenant, rather than Article 11, a course the Council and Secretary-General Drummond had successfully headed off until the attack on Shanghai. Under Article 15, the parties to the dispute could not veto League action, as had occurred with the Council's October 24 draft resolution.

Naotuke Sato, Japan's new delegate to the Council, and Baron Matsudaira, her Ambassador in London who came to Geneva to try to exert pressure, protested with every legal argument at their command, but the Council, following Drummond's lead, could not agree that Article 15 was improperly raised by China. Sato and Matsudaira tried hard to convince Drummond, but to no avail. The Secretary-General informed the Japanese representatives that the Council had no option here, and that Japan had no capacity to limit the question submitted by China. Sato felt that the Council could not deal with the issue both under Article 11, as it had done, and Article 15 at the same time. In the Secretary-General's view, the two articles ran concurrently, and could be used together. Drummond's memorandum on his talks shows the impasse to which Japan and the League had come:

M. Sato again emphasized the fact that public opinion in Japan was violently excited because they considered that the Council had accepted to treat the Manchurian questions under article 15 in spite of Japan's protests.

I said that was greatly to be regretted; but I could not see that there was any other alternative. I heard that the Japanese Government was contemplating the very grave step of withdrawing from the League owing to this popular feeling. Nobody could be more sad if such a thing happened than myself; but really I would prefer such withdrawal to the abandonment of the principles laid down in article 15. To agree with the Japanese contention would be simply to destroy the effective value of the Covenant. I hoped at any rate that before any such step were taken the Japanese Government

---

[165] *Documents on British Foreign Policy, op. cit.,* Vol. IX, p. 221.

would consider very carefully the third paragraph of article 1 that stated that a state could only withdraw after 2 years' notice provided it had fulfilled all its international obligations and obligations under the Covenant.

M. Sato answered that while it might be true that Japan was legally bound to remain a member of the League for 2 years it might well be that in practice she might retire and having nothing more to do with the League even if she had not fulfilled her international obligations.[166]

China was thus enabled to obtain at least a formal judgment from the League (without the vote of the parties to the dispute) concerning the validity of Japan's action in China, thereby also raising the threat of sanctions. Further, China requested the Assembly to consider the issue as well, thus trying to maximize world public opinion on her side.

Secretary-General Drummond had responsibilities under Article 15 for making arangements for an investigation and these were carried out almost at once. The initial idea was to use the Lytton Commission, which was just about to set out on its journey to Manchuria, but the Commission, set up under Article 11 for a full-scale investigation into conditions in Manchuria, could not provide quickly the detailed information needed immediately on the situation at Shanghai. Drummond at once established an Investigation Committee, made up of the consuls of several powers with interests in the area, to send in reports to the Secretary-General for consideration by the Council. The Secretary-General emphasized that the Lytton Commission, operating under Article 11 of the Covenant, was concerned with fundamental aspects of Chinese-Japanese relations; the Shanghai Committee, on the other hand, was acting under Article 15, and only for purposes of fact-finding. The consular committee sent in several reports that were valuable as a source of impartial information on conditions and events at Shanghai.

Prior to the Assembly meeting requested by China (and scheduled by the Council for early March, 1932), Secretary-General Drummond took another initiative. He proposed that the twelve neutral members of the Council issue an appeal to the Japanese Government alone, reminding her of the

---

[166] *FRUS*, 1932, Vol. III, p. 204. Drummond's memorandum of his talk with Sato makes it clear that the Japanese Government had no understanding of the legal requirements of the Covenant:

"M. Sato told me that he had received a telegram from his Government saying that they could not accept the application of article 15 to Manchuria. If that application were limited to Shanghai events the Japanese Government would not oppose it but they definitely refused to allow the Manchurian question to be considered under that article.

I replied that I feared that the Japanese Government were under some misapprehension. This was not a question which lay within their competence to refuse or to accept. China had asked that the dispute as a whole should be submitted to the Council under article 15. There was no option but for the Council to consider the dispute under this article. It was not within the power of the Japanese Government to limit the question submitted by China under article 15". (*Id.*, pp. 202-203)

Covenant obligations of peaceful settlement.[167] He believed that public opinion in Japan distinguished between the Manchuria and Shanghai actions, and that a movement was developing against the Shanghai attack. On February 16 the appeal was made, perhaps weakening Japan's political position, but the military occupation in China continued unaffected.

The Secretary-General understood that Great Britain's insistence upon trade relations with Japan rendered League sanctions out of the question. Appeals could be made, and judgments passed, but the great powers would not agree to punish Japan for aggression, and Sir Eric had no choice but to go along. U.S. Minister Hugh Wilson, reporting on Drummond's views as of the end of February, 1932, stated that the Secretary-General

felt that there had been much loose talk on the subject of severance of trade and financial relations mostly from countries with nothing to lose and that it was certainly most important to avoid giving Japan any pretext to declare war either on the League as a whole or on any member thereof. Nevertheless, everything should be done short or giving an excuse for such extreme action. It was his opinion that at the present moment the Japanese state of mind might be ready to go to war with even Great Britain "should economic sanctions be undertaken". For these reasons, he did not feel that any proposal of such a nature would obtain support and would surely be rejected. One danger was that the Assembly might try to pass judgment on Japan to the effect that she had violated the Covenant which would seem to entail the application of article 16. The Secretary-General agreed, however, that it would be an error to punish a prisoner before sentence was passed and thus it would be better to avoid passing any judgments till all the facts were at the disposal of the body, since the Covenant provides that the judgment itself would entail the immediate punishment.[168]

Just as the Secretary-General was expressing these views, a "declaration of independence" for Manchuria—now called Manchukuo—was issued by a Japanese-sponsored government desirous of having a *fait accompli* for the forthcoming Assembly and the Lytton Commission, now en route to the Far East. Despite the League's efforts, Japan took possession of the entire territory, and held it for fourteen years until driven out by the armies of the Soviet Union at the close of World War II.

Without the Lytton Commission's report, the Assembly could do little more than offer political encouragement to China, although when it met in early March, 1932, the fighting at Shanghai had stopped and the situation seemed more hopeful. The Assembly formally adopted Stimson's non-recognition doctrine, and established a Committee of Nineteen to try its hand at negotiating a settlement. The Shanghai armistice was finally agreed upon on May 5th, 1932, and all that remained was for the Assembly to await the Lytton Report, due in September of the same year.

There was never any doubt concerning the basic conclusions the Commission would reach. As early as July, 1932, Drummond was able to outline the League procedure after receipt of the Report. He felt it "improbable"

[167] *Id.*, pp. 351-352.
[168] *Id.*, p. 547.

that Japan would accept the report, but the Assembly, on recommendation from the Committee of Nineteen, would adopt it, as the Lytton Commission would make it "clear that the present Manchurian Government is not there by the will of the people but is purely a creature of the Japanese and dependent upon them for its existence".[169]

The Report of the Lytton Commission was presented in September, 1932, one year after the first Japanese attack at Mukden, and at last the world had an authoritative report on the Manchurian conflict, and one generally considered to be candid and unbiased. Drummond's prediction was quite correct. The report took great pains to describe the weaknesses of the Chinese administration in Manchuria, but it was *in toto* a clear justification of the Chinese position. In Chapter VI of the report it was declared that the independence movement in Manchuria had never been heard of until September 18th, 1931, and that it was "conceived, organized and carried through" by Japanese troops.

Japan sent one of its ablest diplomats, Yosuke Matsuoka, to present its case and to defend against the conclusion of the Lytton Report. China also sent a new delegate, Wellington Koo, who had served on the Commission, under Woodrow Wilson, that had created the League of Nations. It was a formidable debate, for both were skillful, and the argument dragged on for two months, due in part to Matsuoka's delaying tactics, and in part to the League's wish to give both sides an ample opportunity to present their material. Many more weeks' delay resulted from attempts by the Committee of Nineteen to reach a negotiated settlement on the basis of the Lytton Report. All was to no avail, and the Committee of Nineteen finally reported to the Assembly its own recommendations, based almost entirely on the Lytton Report.

On February 24th, 1933, the Assembly agreed with its Committee of Nineteen, and with the Lytton Commission, avowing that members of the League would not recognize the new state of Manchukuo. The Assembly affirmed, as had its Committee before it, and the Lytton Commission itself, that Japan had violated the Covenant, and with this passage of judgment, Matsuoka, on the orders of his government, dramatically and ostentatiously walked out of the Assembly, taking his delegates with him. A month later, on March 27, 1933, Japan announced her withdrawal from the League.

This was precisely the result Drummond had tried his best to avoid, for during the period from September, 1932 to February, 1933, he worked almost desperately for conciliation. At the end of October, 1932, he raised the possibility of convening (outside the League framework) a conference of the parties to the Nine-Power Treaty for consideration of the Sino-Japanese conflict. The Secretary-General felt that the Treaty had been formulated with the Far East in mind, and that the parties to the Treaty

[169] *FRUS,* 1932, Vol. IV, p. 182.

were actually better fitted to consider the matter than League bodies, including the Committee of Nineteen.[170]

Drummond admitted that an invocation of the Nine-Power Treaty would mean still more delay, but at this point, he did not think that would prove disadvantageous. The Secretary-General felt that Japan was facing financial difficulties in Manchuria, and that the army there was "not particularly enjoying itself", thus causing a certain loss of enthusiasm among the militarists in Tokyo. In any event, further consolidation of Japan's position in Manchuria would not result from delay because the Japanese had consolidated themselves already insofar as was possible in the area.

The Secretary-General was not in favor of a total transfer of the question from the League "as it would be quite impossible to work out anything satisfactory which would have the aspect of leaving the League to one side or present the failure of League efforts".[171] But Drummond was unable to say just how the League would fit into a program of action under the Nine-Power Treaty.

At the same time, Sir Eric began to speak of strengthening the position of the Chinese Nationalist Government, particularly through financial support. He felt that "to introduce the idea that a support of the present Chinese Government would also be a move against communism, would be highly impolitic, although it could, of course, be kept in mind that such an end would indirectly be served".[172]

As U.S. Consul Prentiss Gilbert reported to Stimson, Drummond was "doubtlessly somewhat preoccupied with relieving the League of certain embarrassments"[173] under which it was obviously suffering. He wished dispairingly to continue a process of conciliation and to avoid a total League failure. Given the substance of the Lytton Commission's report, the consensus of opinion in the Assembly, and Japan's insistence on maintaining an "independent" state of Manchukuo, the only method left was to remove the issue from League jurisdiction.

On November 14, 1932, just one week before Matsuoka began the first full-scale public Japanese reply to the Lytton Commission, Stimson turned down Drummond's idea of calling a conference under the Nine-Power

---

[170] *Id.*, pp. 323-325.

[171] *Id.*, p. 324. Prentiss Gilbert, the U.S. Consul with whom Drummond raised the Nine-Power Treaty idea, recalled that Germany was not a party to the treaty, and had objected on that ground when the treaty had been discussed at the end of October, 1931. Drummond replied to this that during his recent visit to Berlin he had sounded out the German Foreign Office on the matter and that officials there were favorable to the invocation of the Treaty, and a meeting of the powers for purposes of discussing the Far Eastern conflict. They informed Drummond that they were even considering adhering to the Pact, but had not for fear of appearing to prejudge the case in advance of the Lytton Report. (*Ibid.*)

[172] *Id.*, pp. 324-325.

[173] *Id.*, p. 325.

Treaty. Stimson's view was that Japan would probably not even attend such a conference (and there was no treaty obligation to do so) and that any attempt to shift the jurisdiction of the problem would "tend to divert attention from the real issue and would weaken the position of the League" in support of the post-war peace treaties and pursuit of the "common objective of peace".[174] Drummond received no support from other quarters, and the proposal was dropped. Technical assistance to China, however, did become the basis of League policy after Japan's notice of withdrawal was given in March, 1933, and only to this extent were Drummond's ideas for avoiding a total League failure carried out.

The Secretary-General also pressed hard for conciliation within the League framework even after receipt of the Lytton Report. He viewed the League, in December, 1932, as faced with the alternatives of conciliation through the Committee of Nineteen, or recourse to a report and recommendations under Article 15, paragraph 4 of the Covenant which would result in Japan's quitting the League. He successfully urged the former course, although conciliation did not result in a more moderate Japanese position. The negotiations between China and Japan during this period were carried out by Paul Hymans of Belgium, Chairman of the Committee of Nineteen, and by Secretary-General Drummond. At the same time, however, as the year 1933 opened, Drummond made it perfectly clear that while he preferred conciliation "in order to forestall if possible the menace of a real war in the Far East", if there was no agreement, then Article 15, paragraph 4 had to be utilized to "maintain intact the Covenant of the League".[175]

After a long series of fruitless discussions with Matsuoka, Drummond finally drew up a letter which the Committee of Nineteen approved, putting the question for the last time to Japan: would Japan accept in Manchuria the sovereignty and administrative integrity of China? The answer was essentially no, and the attempted conciliation was finished.[176]

---

[174] *Id.*, pp. 342-343.

[175] *FRUS*, 1933, Vol. III, p. 93. The Secretary-General pointed out that England and France maintained the same view. There was to be an attempt at conciliation, and if this failed, while there would be no sanctions, the principles of the Covenant would be maintained and a judgment of Japanese aggression made by the League Assembly. To ignore Article 16 of the Covenant on sanctions, however, was to let drop the basic foundation of the League system. Given the depression and western trade patterns with China and Japan, Secretary-General Drummond could not realistically hope to maintain the Covenant intact.

[176] Secretary-General Drummond was the subject of criticism in the British press in January, 1933, for his role in the attempted conciliation with Japan. Certain Japanese counterproposals to the Committee of Nineteen's recommendations had been put forward, and there were reports that these were the result of an agreement between Drummond and Under Secretary-General Sugimura. The proposals, of course, avoided any condemnation of Japanese actions in China. Drummond insisted at a private meeting of the Committee of Nineteen that he had merely been consulted by the

At this point, the Committee of Nineteen completed its statement (based almost entirely on the Lytton Report) to the Assembly, and called on the parties to open negotiations to reach the recommended settlement. At Drummond's suggestion, a new Committee to help in these discussions was established, one purpose being to try to associate the United States more closely with the League's work. Drummond attempted to make the idea more palatable to Washington by emphasizing that the new Committee's mandate fell under Article 3 of the Covenant (allowing the Assembly to deal with any matter "affecting the peace of the world") rather than Article 16, and sanctions would thus be no obstacle.

The new Committee was able to establish the principles for League Members to follow in their responses to Manchukuo, but the Japanese walkout and withdrawal from the League in March meant the end of an active role for the world organization in the Sino-Japanese conflict. Secretary-General Drummond worked with the new Committee until the effective date of his retirement from office, June 30, 1933, at which point, responsibility for the League role in the Far East fell to the new Secretary-General, Joseph Avenol.

For Drummond, the Sino-Japanese conflict marked the first great failure of the League to keep the peace, and in that sense was his first serious setback. He had been intimately involved in the negotiations from the beginning, and while his influence with most League members was substantial, he was unable to persuade the Japanese to pursue a more moderate course in China. Given that the United States, Britain, and France also failed in this objective, there seems little reason to fault the Secretary-General, but it was his first important defeat, as well as the League's.

On the other hand, the conflict presented Drummond with the opportunity to develop the potentialities inherent in the Office of Secretary-General, and he did just that, for never had his political activity been so intense as during the critical days from September, 1931, to March, 1933. Drummond's part in the negotiations was more extensive than that of any other single individual, and his recommendations and influence clearly not insubstantial.

Perhaps the primary reason for this was his knowledge and comprehension of the problems, maintained by the expertise of the Secretariat in Geneva, and the innumerable personal discussions he held with representatives of the powers concerned. Above all, Drummond was knowledgable.

Japanese, and had given advice as he would to any League member. The Secretary-General would not issue a public statement on the matter, but stressed that the Secretariat had been instructed to prepare a report under Article 15(4) should resort to that paragraph become necessary. (See R. Bassett, *Democracy and Foreign Policy* (London, Longmans, Green and Co., 1952), pp. 341-343; also *FRUS,* 1933, Vol. III, pp. 95-96.)

This had always been the greatest merit of his administration, and consequently his opinions, evaluations, suggestions, and predictions of probable responses were almost always accorded the most careful consideration. Most of the resolutions and proposals for settlement were actually drafted in the Secretariat at Drummond's direction, and often his personal touch was obviously present.

Everything was done quietly. The League Secretary-General could not publicly take a position that might involve conflict with the policy of any League Member, but working unobtrusively and taking advantage of the trust in his impartiality, Drummond was able to push his views even on unwilling ears, and in many cases was quite successful in influencing the direction of the negotiations, in terms of both procedure and substance. The fateful period from the fall of 1931 to the spring of 1933 thus marked the lowest point yet reached by the League as an organization devoted to peace-keeping, but the peak of the development of the Office of Secretary-General.

The League had failed, of course, primarily because the great powers were unwilling to take any action against Japan. The Disarmament Conference was used as an excuse, but it was clear that the necessity of trade relations during the grip of the greatest depression of modern times was the essential factor. Further, neither the United States nor any of the major Member powers, intended during depression times to be responsible for a war over Manchuria. Japan had flouted the League, but only the small powers appeared willing to bring her to account.

Looking back on the Manchurian affair, Drummond commented in 1933: "Japan's final argument was to the following effect: if you say we were wrong, you will create a dangerous position, and even imperil the peace of the world, which the League was formed to preserve. What you should do is to tell China to accept the situation created by our action, and to negotiate with us on that basis. Thus peace will be assured".

"This line of thought really will not do. A state cannot occupy the territory of a neighboring state, set up a so-called independent Government, and then plead that anyone who does not accept the position thus created is likely to endanger the peace. The argument is too easy, and could be made to cover almost any international wrong-doing... During the early stages of the dispute, I remember saying to a Japanese friend, 'The Members of the League will do everything to meet you, but they cannot abandon the principles of the Covenant. Rather than that this should happen, the League had better disappear because otherwise it would become a sham'. I added that we should all hate to see Japan leave the League, but if the sole choice was between that and the League being untrue to itself, there could be only one answer. That answer has now been given, and though the League had been weakened by the announcement of Japan's withdrawal, it has been strengthened morally by its own decision to face honestly and without fear of the consequences the hardest situation with which it has ever been confronted".[177]

Drummond's Resignation and Later Career

On January 23, 1932, twelve years after he assumed the post, Drummond submitted to the League Council a letter of resignation as Secretary-General. "It has for some considerable time past", he wrote, "been my intention to resign this post; but I did not think it right to do so while certain questions relating to the organization of the Secretariat were under consideration by the Assembly, and in view of the meeting of the Conference for the Reduction and Limitation of Armaments". Sir Eric added that he wished the resignation to take effect "as from a convenient date during the first six months of 1933".[178]

There had been speculation that the resignation, coming as it did at the height of the economic depression, in the early and critical stages of the Sino-Japanese conflict, and in the midst of the Disarmament Conference, had political significance as an indicator of a failing League of Nations, but there is little to support it and more substantial evidence pointing to purely personal reasons. It is clear, obviously, that the resignation was closely tied to the whole question of the Secretariat's Haute Direction, its composition, form, and distribution of nationalities, but the agreed upon settlement, including the election of Joseph Avenol as Secretary-General, seems to have followed Sir Eric's announcement, rather than the reverse. Drummond's retirement letter was apparently the spur required by the Assembly to reach agreement in the autumn of 1932.

As for the Disarmament Conference, Drummond indicated in several letters to friends and associates in 1932 that the end of the Conference (which he evidently expected to be in 1933) would be a convenient time to leave the League. In February, 1932, for example, he wrote that "the fact that the Conference on Disarmament will have finished by next year will mark, I think, the accomplishment of the first stage in the League's work so that the moment I have chosen seems to me to be appropriate".[179] The Sino-Japanese conflict does not appear as a relevant factor at all, for Drummond repeatedly stressed his long-standing intention to resign, and several months prior to the Japanese attack on Mukden, the Second Committee of Thirteen appointed to reach agreement on the Secretriat's top-level structure decided to shelve the problem for three years unless Drum-

---

[177] Drummond Broadcast, *op. cit.*, pp. 20-21.
[178] League Archives 1928-1932, General and Miscellaneous 50/39242/39242, 23 January 1932. In his original draft letter, Sir Eric asked that the effective date be January 1, 1933 or no later than April 1 of that year.
[179] *Id.*, 5 February 1932.

mond's retirement forced an earlier reopening of the discussion. The Committee's report, dated February 5, 1931, is persuasive evidence that Sir Eric was seriously considering resignation in early 1931.

The American Consul in Geneva at the time (Prentiss Gilbert) cabled the State Department in Washington on January 30, 1932 that "Speculation is of course rife as to the 'political' reasons, particularly those connected with the Manchurian affair or disarmament, governing Drummond's resignation coming at this juncture. While it is probably inevitable that his action will have political consequences, I am personally convinced through having had knowledge of his intentions for some time and from conversations with him that his decision to resign is based almost entirely on personal considerations".[180]

Drummond gave little indication of his own motivation. He wrote in February, 1932 that "It has... been my intention for some years past to resign, as I find the strain very great, and, in addition, there are personal reasons of a serious character".[181] In a letter to Ake Hammarskjold, Registrar of the Permanent Court and older brother of UN Secretary-General Dag Hammarskjold, Sir Eric stated that "the strain of the last twelve years has been very great" [182] and to an associate in London he wrote that "The strain of the post is too great to continue in it for more than 12 years, and I shall have had 13 next year".[183]

The League Council requested Sir Eric to withdraw the resignation, but he would not comply and the letter was thus circulated to members, with the Council reserving "any decision this situation might demand desiring not to give up all hopes of being able to retain Drummond's 'valuable services'." [184] On September 27, 1932, the Acting President of the Council, Eamon de Valera, announced the Council's acceptance of Sir Eric's resignation, it being understood that it would not take effect earlier than June 30, 1933. The Council also placed on record a beautiful tribute to Drummond:

It would be impossible to summarise in any adequate form the achievements of the retiring Secretary-General. But the record of these achievements is written in the history of the twelve years which have passed since he undertook the great public duty which he is now relinquishing. His unremitting industry, his loyalty and devotion to the work of the League, his wide knowledge of the subjects which fall to be considered by that organisation, and his executive ability as the officer charged with the execution of its decisions will remain as an example to those who carry on the work in the years to come.

Sir Eric Drummond, however, brought to the task entrusted to him by the nations

---

180 *National Archives*, 500. C 113/66, 30 January 1932.
181 League Archives 1928-1932, General and Miscellaneous 50/39242/39242, 5 February 1932.
182 *Id.*, 11 February 1932.
183 *Ibid.*
184 *National Archives*, 500. C 113/66, 30 January 1932.

rarer gifts than these—gifts which especially fitted him for his unique place in the Assembly of the world. His judgment, tact, impartiality and unfailing courtesy are known to all who come to Geneva on the business of their governments. Not one of them but must recall occasions of which the solution of problems of great difficulty and delicacy was made easier by the efforts of the Secretary-General to find the highest common measure of agreement.[185]

The Council concluded that in congratulating Sir Eric they were "congratulating themselves on the fact that during the first phase of the greatest experiment in international co-operation ever undertaken, they had the services in the capacity of Secretary-General of a statesman and diplomat who reflected in his own person the ideals in which that experiment was conceived and will be carried forward".[186]

The Council characterization of Sir Eric as "statesman and diplomat" and the emphasis on his role in solving problems "of great difficulty and delicacy" indicate the League's perception of Drummond's primary worth to the Organization. The Secretary-General was being lauded for his political work, despite his appointment over twelve years earlier as the "perfect private secretary" whose administrative talents were tapped in lieu of the political skills of a Venizelos or Hankey. Drummond's reply was a brief statement in praise of his Secretariat colleagues and an expression of regret at leaving, coupled with an assertion that "a change in the leadership of the Secretariat after a period of fourteen years may result in very real advantage to the League itself".[187]

All that remained was the completion of the negotiations in the Fourth Committee concerning the Haute Direction, and with agreement finally reached, the Council, on October 17, 1932, formally nominated Joseph Avenol of France as the second Secretary-General. This decision was confirmed by the Assembly on December 9, and on June 30, 1933, Sir Eric relinquished his post after fourteen years, counting the several months of 1919 in which he served as Acting Secretary-General prior to the official establishment of the League. He held the position for several years longer than any of his successors.

In his last statement as Secretary-General, a farewell address to the Secretariat staff on June 30, Drummond voiced his hopefulness even during the League's darkest hours: "I notice that there is, even among us, perhaps, a certain feeling of pessimism as to the future of the League. Before I go, I want to say that I am convinced that that pessimism is neither justified nor well founded. It is true that the political outlook may be a little black to-day, but I feel—and M. de Madariaga once told me that if an Englishman feels he is probably right; it is only when he begins to reason that he goes wrong—that the League is really in an unassailable international position,

[185] League Council Doc. C.L. 154, 1932, 27 September 1932.
[186] *Ibid.*
[187] *Id.*, 1 October 1932.

that it has come to stay and that we need have no fears on that score".[188]
The next day, July 1, 1933, Joseph Avenol, the French Under-Secretary-
General since 1923, became the League's second Secretary-General, and
the Organization began the long period of collapse, ending in its virtual
abandonment in 1940 as war engulfed Europe and the Far East.

The years after the Secretaryship-General were active for Drummond, as
he returned to Great Britain's Foreign Office for several years, and held
other government and Liberal Party posts. From 1933 to 1939, he served
as London's Ambassador to Rome, a key assignment in the period when
one of the pillars of the British appeasement policy was the goal of preventing Mussolini from joining in alliance with Berlin against the European
liberal democracies.

It is generally considered by students of international organization that
Sir Eric erred badly in taking the post in Rome, for the precedent set was
obviously damaging. As Secretary-General he had come into possession of
very substantial amounts of confidential information concerning Italy and
its relationships with other nations which he could now use to advantage.
Further, if a Secretary-General is justified in assuming a high-level post
subsequent to his service as executive head of the Secretariat, there is a
strong risk that any Secretary-General will pattern his behavior while in
that Office in accordance with his best advantage in the later employ of his
own Government. The United Nations was later to establish rules prohibiting this, although to date, of course, they have been applicable only in the
case of Trygve Lie. Several of Drummond's associates at the League pleaded with him not to take the post, citing the sensitive nature of the Secretary-
General's position, but whether for financial or other personal reasons, Sir
Eric would not be dissuaded.

In 1937, upon the death of his half-brother, Sir Eric became the sixteenth Earl of Perth, and in May, 1939, he retired from foreign service and
returned to Great Britain as chief adviser on foreign publicity in the
Ministry of Information, a post he held for one year. He was a representative
peer of Scotland from 1941 to his death in 1951, and took an active part in
House of Lords debates. In 1946 he was appointed Deputy Leader of the
Liberal Party in the House of Lords, and served also in that capacity until
1951.

He was not called upon to assist the United Nations in any way, in line
with the UN's general policy, begun at San Francisco in 1945, of avoiding
any significant connection with the discredited League, and Lord Perth was
generally silent throughout the UN's formative years on issues of substances
or procedure confronting the new world institution. In 1944, as Chairman

[188] League Archives 1933-1940, General and Miscellaneous 50/346/346, 30 June 1933.

of the Liberal Party's Permanent Policy Committee, he published in a report on "Germany After the War" some perspectives on international organization very much in accord with British foreign policy, calling for a new international organization with a primary task of maintaining peace and concurrent obligations to promote social and economic progress. The report also stressed the importance of sufficient military force at the disposal of the new organization, although recognizing some of the difficulties involved, the Committee stated that "it might be sufficient and effective to confine its composition to air power alone". If this were found impractical, the powers concerned should "earmark a certain proportion of their air forces for the use of the international organization in case of emergency".[189] It is impossible to say how much of the report was influenced by the views of Lord Perth, although during and after the war he generally favored a strengthening of global institutions, including the Office of the Secretary-General.

Lord Perth died on December 15, 1951, and a few days later the United Nations, through a moment of silence in the General Assembly, paid tribute to him and at long last to the League of Nations. The President of the Assembly, Mr. Luis Padilla Nervo, stated that much of the initial success and prestige of the League was due to Sir Eric Drummond's "untiring efforts, wisdom and common sense" and that he had "organized an international secretariat and raised it to a position of authority and prestige". He concluded that Drummond "must therefore be regarded as one of the founders of the United Nations, and his memory will always be remembered and honoured by this Organization".[190] Sir Gladwyn Jebb, representative of the United Kingdom, spoke of Drummond as "a perfect example, if I may say so, of a diplomat who shed his national character and became a genuinely international civil servant". The Secretariat he founded "was certainly an example for the future and its tradition has been worthily carried on by the present Secretary-General of the United Nations".[191] Drummond's death was one of the very rare occasions when the theme of continuity between League and United Nations was underscored by UN representatives, and this in itself was a well-deserved tribute to the first Secretary-General of world organization.

Sir Eric Drummond's Contribution to World Order

It is difficult to overestimate the significance of the contribution made by the League's first Secretary-General to the development of institutions devoted to the construction of a peaceful world order system, for several

---

[189] "Germany After the War", Liberal Publication Department (London, 1944), p. 20.
[190] GAOR: Sixth Sess., Plenary, 356th mtg., 20 December 1951.
[191] *Ibid.*

of the techniques and requirements for such development were first understood and worked out in careful and skillful fashion by Drummond. The
direction taken today by structures aiming at a more meaningful integration
in the international community were first set by Sir Eric, and the current
capacity of international organization to muster any kind of independent
corporate and discretionary power is in large measure a function of the
patterns set by the Drummond model of executive leadership.

Of primary importance was his success in legitimizing the conception of
an international civil service, both at the beginning of his administration as
an experiment in institution building, and through several years of
auspicious service to the world community. This was fundamental to the
future of global organization, for clearly if international governmental
structures of any significance were to exist, then an executive staff relatively
independent of national policy and with some discretionary powers would
have to become an established fixture. By his skill in administration and
the good fortune to have as his closest assistants men of outstanding talent,
Drummond in effect operationalized what had been but a daring conception
a few years earlier. The world community was convinced in a relatively
brief time that an international secretariat was highly functional in the
complex arena of continuous transnational negotiation and bargaining, and
most of the credit must go to Sir Eric, whose construction of the executive
branch and extraordinary sound judgment and well-informed decision-
making on administrative and political matters endowed the new institution
with a legitimacy and acceptability that might not have been forthcoming
under a lesser figure.

He was also successful in defending the experiment against the traditional
and parochial attack of Germany and Italy in the late 1920's and early
1930's, and as has been noted, the defense was essential, given the collapse
of the League and its Secretaryship-General during the Avenol administration. The Drummond contribution had been convincing enough so that in
1945, and notwithstanding the Avenol lapse and a period of twelve years
without an effective Secretary-General, the statesmen gathered at San
Francisco to establish a new world organization had little difficulty in
agreeing upon the desirability of a Secretariat based on the Drummond-
Balfour principles, and a Secretary-General with enhanced political power.
The UN Charter articles on the subject are in reality a fixed tribute to
Sir Eric Drummond.

Drummond's political work was, of course, an unintended benefaction
that redounded to the benefit of the Office and the diplomatic utility of
international organizations acting as neutral intermediaries in cases of
inter-state conflict. The prestige he built up over the years, derived basically from his tact, discretion, insistence upon being well-informed, and
imagination in formulating proposals acceptable to contending parties,
permitted him a latitude as mediator and adviser that has strongly in-

fluenced the development of the Office in current world politics. He demonstrated that even within the context of a genuine international bureaucracy serving essentially administrative tasks, a political role was possible, and indeed, that diplomatic functions at several levels might be performed by the Secretariat's highest officer. Sir Eric's Office served mediation functions, as a communications channel for state representatives, as a liaison with national decision-makers, and as an evaluator of programs and ideas. The Secretary-General made hundreds of recommendations of procedure and substance, proposed draft resolutions, and provided legal analyses when necessary. Much of this work had political significance, but Drummond was able to expand his prestige and acceptability so that after fourteen years it had never been higher. And similarly to the administrative contribution, the pattern was repeated in 1945 and even enlarged, as the insertion of Article 99 into the UN Charter, enabling the Secretary-General to convene the Council on his own initiative in case of a threat to the peace, signified the intention of the UN founders to perpetuate the Drummond diplomatic work and augment it if possible. This too was agreed upon without difficulty, and despite the weak political performance during the seven years of administration of Secretary-General Avenol. Again, Sir Eric's work had been convincing enough to persuade world political leaders in 1945 that a political role for the executive head was highly desirable.

As noted, Drummond was perhaps too cautious in his diplomatic work, for while the constitutional and political limitations were confining, he failed to take advantage of opportunities that might have endowed him, even marginally, with more substantial international reknown. This was a matter essentially of temperamental and personal limitation rather than political realities, although it is not at all clear that the diplomatic significance of the Office would be any the greater today had Drummond spoken out more frequently and on more sensitive issues. Trygve Lie, during his administration from 1946 to 1953, certainly compensated for Sir Eric's public reticence and shyness, and it is doubtful he could have accomplished more had the first League Secretary-General attempted to establish rights of intervention in Assembly or Council debates or utilized the annual report as a vehicle for asserting his political viewpoint.

But if Drummond succeeded in legitimizing and maintaining the notion of an international civil service and an important political role for its first officer, he also contributed to the United Nations a virtual catalogue of the essential attributes of an outstanding Secretary-General. To date the closest to the Drummond model has been Dag Hammarskjold, who himself recognized the similarity in approach and style. Perhaps the salient factor in Sir Eric's work was his uncommon capacity for mastering the complexities of the issues confronting the League, which, combined with creative skills in fashioning acceptable solutions or formulations, made him a formidable diplomat indeed. He had opinions on almost every administrative and diplomatic problem handled in the Secretariat, and since much of the decision-making was done through written communication channeled through his Office, or conferences with staff members and state representatives, his influence was ever-present and in organizational issues, often decisive. The tact, discretion, and willingness to work quietly without publicity of any kind were consistently displayed by Drummond throughout his fourteen years as Secretary-General, and have now become closely associated with his name. In all, the general behavior pattern has served as a model for future Secretaries-General, and can itself properly be adduced as one of Drummond's outstanding contributions to world order.

Sir Eric was fortunate in serving the League during its prosperous years, and was subject to little undue strain because of his British nationality. There were few conflicts of consequence between League and British policy during the Drummond era, although the Sino-Japanese conflict not infrequently placed Sir Eric in a position of some difficulty. In the final analysis his political efforts failed, as the depression and military conquest in the early 1930's finally ushered in the decline of the League, but his work even under the worst of circumstances was of the same high order, leaving no doubt that the Organization's failures could not be attributed in any measure whatever to the Office of the Secretary-General. If the Office was not significantly more powerful in 1933 than it had been in 1920, at the least it had been well-established and maintained with efficiency. Drummond's legacy to world order had been the international civil service, a political role for the Secretary-General, and the precedent of the remarkable virtues that gave to both an impelling vitality.

CHAPTER II

Joseph Avenol
Secretary-General of the League of Nations
1933-1940

"...except for Germans and Italians who have a program, a doctrine and a method, no one seems to me to have one. The expression 'new order' is a slogan, but who can say what it means.

1941 will remain the starting point of a historic era; it is the end of the world of the 19th century. We are at the beginning of a great revolution.

...[The German and Italian programs] must not be rejected wholesale; they contain things which one can no longer reject."
Joseph Avenol, September 1, 1940.

Joseph Avenol, the second Secretary-General of the League of Nations, assumed office at a tragic period in world and League history. The global economic depression, the Japanese attack in China, and the advent of Hitler all pointed to war and the collapse of meaningful institutions of world order. And Secretary-General Avenol was not devoted in great measure to the ideals of the League Covenant, or of western liberal democracy.

The seven years' administration of a Secretary-General who indentified closely with the most conservative financial circles in inter-war France was characterized by a consistent backing for British and French appeasement policy and sympathy for the dictators of the right. It was not the lukewarm support of a League official compelled to implement great-power strategies he found distasteful. Rather, it was the backing of a man whose weak commitment to democracy and growing appreciation of a "new order" in Europe left little room for support of the League of Nations and its Covenant.

How could a former French Treasury official without political training or experience or commitment to world order become Secretary-General? The answer lies in the tangled thicket of League and European politics in the early 1930's, and a situation that dictated compromise in a world organization devoted to peace. The result was that Avenol's unhappy administration, which lasted from 1933 to 1940, made little or no attempt to strengthen the League's peace-keeping capacity or to develop, in any appreciable manner, the influence of the Secretary-General's Office.

Avenol's primary efforts were aimed at minimizing League activity that might run counter to the ideas of the totalitarian states, and to extending the non-controversial technical work of the Organization. When war came, however, and the League stood helpless, Avenol resigned his position, tried to liquidate what remained of the Organization, and joined the Pétain regime at Vichy, France.

Joseph Avenol was born in Melle (Deux-Sèvres) France on June 7, 1879. As a young boy, he wanted to be a seaman, but his nearsightedness blocked that early plan. He attended secondary school at the Collège de la Rochelle, and at the age of seventeen, went on to the University of Poitiers. He completed his higher education in Paris, studying law there and also attending the School of Political Science at the University of Paris. Until he began his university training, Avenol's background had been extremely conservative, religious, and politically far to the right, an orientation he retained throughout his life. His powerful anti-communist posture, coupled with authoritarian sympathies, shaped his entire career, even to the point of antipathy for the League of Nations he would serve for over seventeen years.

In 1905, Avenol, then twenty-six years old, won first place in an examination given by the French Treasury for neophytes in finance, and he remained with the Treasury until 1923, rising to the position of Inspecteur Général. His assignments during this period were increasingly important; he travelled throughout France and North Africa, and upon the outbreak of war in 1914, was entrusted with the financial reorganization in the departments of France in which Army zones were located. Toward the end of 1916 he was named Finance Delegate to the French Embassy in London, a post he held for seven years. Thereafter he had a number of important assignments, including service on the Interallied Commission for Reconstruction and the Permanent Committee of the interallied Supreme Economic Council.

In 1922, Premier Raymond Poincaré persuaded Avenol to present himself for the post of Deputy Secretary-General of the League of Nations. Jean Monnet, the original French choice for the post, had devoted his efforts to the Finance and Economic Section of the Secretariat, and to general policy questions concerning the Brussels Financial Conference. Monnet, however, left the Secretariat after a few years, and the need for a French financial expert in the top-level structure of the League prompted Poincaré to suggest Avenol.

Sir Eric Drummond accepted the recommendation, and Avenol, who had initially indicated a preference for a post in the Bank of France, yielded to Poincaré and in 1923 became Deputy Secretary-General of the League. It was an important but a narrow and highly specialized job. His first significant work was financial reconstruction in several European countries, of which Austria was the most important. The League Council, of course, under Arthur Balfour, laid down the foundations of the plan. This was followed by financial assistance, for which Avenol also served as the Secretariat's leading expert, to Hungary, Bulgaria, Greece, and Estonia. In 1929, he went on mission to Nanking, China, to advise the government there on financial reconstruction.

There are few indications of Avenol's views on the League Secretariat or on the functions of the Secretary-General prior to his accession to office. On the key Secretariat issue of the time, however, he strongly opposed the German-Italian plan for a top-level advisory board for the Secretary-General. Avenol insisted, as did Drummond, upon an individed responsibility in the Office of Secretary-General that could not be shared or diluted.[1]

As for the role of the Secretary-General, Avenol expressed himself only in the most formal of terms, and then in a cautious manner quite similar to Drummond's. He seemed to have no notion whatever that the Office might be developed and its powers extended beyond the point at which Drummond had left it. Avenol had no theory of the Secretary-General's powers, and no concept of acting in any but the most quiet and unobtrusive fashion, behind the scenes, and without fanfare. Despite the political and economic crises shaping the background of his accession to the Secretaryship-General, he was clearly content, at least at the beginning of his administration, to permit the great powers, particularly Great Britain and France, to shape League policy as far as possible. He would not oppose in any meaningful fashion the political programs, such as they were, of the western democracies, nor would he articulate a viewpoint that might be characterized as "League policy".

Avenol's reticence was to change as Europe rushed headlong into war, but not in a manner that one might expect of the highest official of a world organization whose primary concern was the maintenance of peace. His administration commenced at a most difficult time in European and world politics; it ended in tragedy. The question here is the contribution made by Joseph Avenol, second Secretary-General of the League of Nations, to the cause of peace and world order.

---

[1] Letter from Avenol to Drummond, June 30, 1930. Special file of Avenol papers, United Nations Library (Library of the Palais des Nations), Geneva, Switzerland. Avenol wrote that while it was useful to retain the post of Under Secretary-General, this was only as a corollary to the generally accepted notion of maintaining "entirely and without division the responsibility and authority of the Secretary-General". He was pleased that the French had supported the British in opposing the advisory board plan, for in Avenol's view, it was "not so clear from the strictly national point of view, there would not have been interest in supporting the principle of the Italian proposal". (*Ibid.*)

The Selection of Joseph Avenol as Secretary-General

As noted, Sir Eric Drummond resigned in 1932, but was persuaded to remain until June 30, 1933 while the question of his successor was approached by the Council and Assembly in 1932. Throughout the prolonged negotiations, the only significant opposition to Avenol was expressed by Germany, although Berlin was unhappy with the notion of a French Secretary-General, rather than with Avenol himself. The League of Nations Union, an influential private organization of League supporters in London, alone spoke out strongly in public against his appointment. The Union accused the League Council of taking "the line of least resistance"[2] in supporting Avenol when "his qualities, in themselves quite notable, do not, in most people's opinion, happen to fit him" for the post of Secretary-General.[3] The plan to appoint him, argued the Union, rested primarily on the belief that his promotion to the top position would "arouse less opposition than the appointment of some man of outstanding ability from outside".[4] The developing political role of the Secretary-General, particularly as evidenced by Drummond's work in the Sino-Japanese conflict, was stressed by the Union:

Only the closest observers of the League appreciate at their full importance the personality and political background of a Secretary-General. He is much more than the administrative head of a big international framework. He must conduct delicate negotiations with many governments day in and day out. On frequent occasions he must stand behind the President of the Council or the Assembly and guide them—and the whole League—through difficult political waters. His alertness and ability to lead have absolutely unlimited opportunity. They are matched only by the necessity for tact and discretion.[5]

Essentially this was a call for another Sir Eric Drummond, but that was clearly impossible. Quite aside from what appeared to many as a German and Italian willingness to accept a Frenchman only "as a kind of sitting tenant",[6] and the resulting reluctance to appoint a prominent diplomat from outside the Secretriat, there was the issue of the original leadership of the Secretariat and the International Labor Office. In 1932, Albert Thomas, the brilliant, eloquent and driving head of the I.L.O. died, and was succeeded by his able assistant, Harold Butler, an Englishman. Under the circumstances, since the first League Secretary-General had been British, it seemed a natural course to balance the line-up by the selection of a French national from within the Secretariat as thè next League Secretary-General. This was also in accordance with an understanding reached at Paris in 1919 during the drafting of the Covenant. Balfour had agreed that Drummond's

2 *Headway* (publication of the League of Nations Union), October, 1932, p. 181.
3 *Id.*, p. 182.
4 *Ibid.*
5 *Id.*, p. 186.
6 *Ibid.*

successor should be a Frenchman, and Sir Eric's initial expectation, or at least hope, was that it would be his Deputy, Jean Monnet. In 1932, Drummond at first opposed Avenol's appointment, and leaned to a national of a small state for purposes of maintaining great-power harmony. He suggested Willem van Eysinga, a Dutchman on the Permanent Court, but van Eysinga declined.

According to Prentiss Gilbert, the United States Consul in Geneva, "That the Secretary-General must be a European now almost goes without saying".[7] At one time Japan had been considered, and it was thought by Drummond that Under Secretary-General Sugimura might succeed to the Office, but the Japanese attack on Manchuria and the Sino-Japanese question generally eliminated that possibilty. Latin America had played a minor role in League affairs, and a candidate from that region was never considered at all. Norman Davis and Newton Baker of the United States were suggested, but given the American determination to remain outside the Organization, and the fact that "the League would scarcely wish to face the implication that the League powers were bankrupt in the matter of available men",[8] the United States was also eliminated as a serious possibility.

Of the great powers, it was clear that neither a German nor an Italian national could hope to secure election, and yet the views of Berlin and Rome had to be accomodated. Gilbert revealed that:

Leading Italians have told me quite frequently that they would prefer the post to go to a "representative" of a great power whose policy would thus be clearly defined and who could in a way be held responsible therefor and could be bargained with on that basis. They assert that they would prefer such an arrangement rather than to have the position go to a national of a small power who would very possibly be under British or French influence. They feel that, this influence being disguised, such a Secretary-General would be a difficult person to deal with.[9]

---

[7] *National Archives.* 500. C. 113/71, p. 2.

[8] *Id.,* p. 3.

[9] *Id.,* p. 4. Given the inter-war system of alliances, the Italians were saying essentially that a candidate from Sweden, Norway, Denmark, or the Netherlands might be acceptable as neutrals. But even here, the candidate would have had to be "of an age sufficiently advanced to regard the position as the final point of his career" (*Id.,* p. 7) and would have to be elected for five or ten years so as to ensure that no further political aims would interfere with his political independence. This meant that men such as Benes of Czechoslovakia, Politis of Greece, and Titulescou of Rumania were ruled out at once. Van Eysinga from the Netherlands, Ekstrand of Sweden, and Colban of Norway became serious candidates.

The only realistic alternative to a national from one of the neutral Northern European states was a national of France, and Joseph Avenol thus became a leading choice. Louis Brouckère, a Belgian Socialist and Senator famous for his knowledge of the League, was discussed, but failed to meet the independence test required by the Italians of a national from a small power. René Massigli, a French delegate to the League known for his political and organizational abilities was also suggested.

Given these considerations, Avenol seemed to be in an excellent position. The biggest stumbling block was Germany, but after the Lausanne Economic Conference, in which Avenol was quite active, Berlin let it be known that it would not oppose the election of a French national as Secretary-General. Italy backed Avenol in return for more Italian representation in the Secretariat, a rather persistent demand from Rome over the years.

Avenol was also supported by many League members on the theory that he would not centralize power and influence in his Office as Drummond had done throughout his administration. "Avenol is much less industrious than Sir Eric", wrote Gilbert, "and it is felt that under his direction there would be more decentralization of authority which the representatives of a number of powers have long been anxious to bring about in League affairs".[10]

The choice of a new Secretary-General was intimately bound up with the complex issue of the entire top-level structure of the League Secretariat. Agreement on both problems had to come simultaneously. When two successive Committees of Thirteen failed to reach agreement, however, and with Drummond determined to leave his post by the spring of 1933, it was clear that immediate decisions had to be taken. The Fourth (Administrative and Budgetary) Committee of the League Assembly established a sub-committee in September, 1932, and it was this agency that made the formal decisions concerning the choice of a new Secretary-General, and the nature and structure of the Secretariat's top direction. Over a period of ten days the sub-committee met privately, and finally worked out a series of compromises subsequently approved by the Assembly.

First, it was agreed that Avenol should be Secretary-General, his functions to begin on the retirement of Sir Eric, scheduled for June 30, 1933. In return for acceptance of a Frenchman as Secretary-General, Germany was assured that one post of Under Secretary-General would be assigned to her, with the post to entail supervision of the League's economic and financial work previously under Avenol's direction.

The sub-committee agreed further to establish two posts of Deputy Secretary-General, one for Italy (after strong demands by Rome), and the other for a smaller European power. At the same time, in order to gain the agreement of Latin America, it was decided that the post of Legal Adviser, held by a citizen of Uruguay, would be raised to the rank of Under-Secretary. The German-Italian plan for an advisory board for the Secretary-General's Office was voted down.

There was also agreement on the "national islands" issue, as it was stipulated that the private staffs of the Secretary-General and the Deputies

---

Gieuseppi Motta of Switzerland was supported. The inside track, however, obviously belonged to M. Avenol.

10 *Id.*, p. 5.

Secretary-General should not include more than one member of section who was a national of the same country as the holder of those posts. It was further agreed, on the demand of Germany, that there should be no more than two nationals of the same country at the top level. This was important primarily because at the time, Avenol, Robert Haas, and Pierre Comert, all Frenchmen, held posts in the high command.[11]

Another important feature of the 1932 settlement was the terms of office for the top posts. The Secretary-General was appointed for ten years, renewable for three years. Avenol's term was thus set to expire as of June 30, 1943, with a possible renewal to 1946. The Deputy Secretaries-General were limited to eight years, renewable for five, and the Under-Secretaries were assigned a term of seven years, renewable for another seven-year period.[12]

There can be little question that the elaborate series of compromises finally agreed upon in the bargaining sessions of the Fourth Committee and its special sub-committee did little to sustain the conception of an international civil service as created by Drummond. Member states were patently jockeying for position to enhance their interests in the Secretariat, and it was assumed by all that appointments to the highest Secretariat posts were

[11] It was decided that since Comert's contract expired before that of Haas, he would not be reappointed. Comert resigned, and this left Arthur Sweetser of the United States as Acting Director of the Information Section. It was generally felt, however, that a post as high as Director should not be held by a national of a non-Member state, and Adrian Pelt of the Netherlands became the new Director.

[12] This left the question of the identity of the holders of the principal posts in the Secretariat. With Avenol selected as Secretary-General, it was agreed to give one Under-Secretary post to Dr. Ernst Trendelenberg of Germany, formerly Secretary of State in the German Ministry of Economy and Chairman of the League's Economic Committee. Trendelenberg took over Avenol's former responsibilities in the Secretariat. The two Deputy posts were assigned to Massimo Pilotti of Italy and Pablo de Azcaraté of Spain. Pilotti, a diplomat, was given the prize of a Deputy post (next in line after the Secretary-General and thus higher than the Under-Secretaries), but he was placed in charge of the Secretariat sections dealing with Intellectual Cooperation and the International Bureaux, not positions of any political significance. Azcaraté, the Director of the Minorities Section, was given charge of the Secretariat's internal administration. Again, the post was not important, but assigning Spain a Deputy post represented a victory for the smaller and medium powers not permanently seated on the League Council.

Frank P. Walters of Great Britain, for many years Sir Eric Drummond's chef de cabinet and right-hand man, became an Under Secretary-General and Director of the Political Section. Walters was thus not in the higher Deputy position, as Avenol had been under Drummond, but his appointment was politically far more important than either of the two Deputy posts.

Japan was no longer represented at the top level of the Secretariat as Under Secretary-General Sugimura resigned his position as of March 31, 1933. This coincided with Japan's notice of withdrawal from the League. It also relieved M. Sugimura of the embarrassing and difficult task of serving as Director of the Political Section at the time of the Sino-Japanese conflict.

made by a conference of League members in committee assembled, rather than by the Secretary-General.[13]

Avenol was nominated by the League Council on October 17, 1932, and on December 9, the nomination was approved by the Assembly. His functions as Secretary-General were to commence on July 1, 1933. Avenol was the first and only Secretary-General of the League to have been selected by the ordinary constitutional rules of the Covenant prescribed in Article 6, paragraph 2. Drummond, of course, had been named in an Annex to the Covenant itself, and Sean Lester took over in the emergency period of 1940 as Acting Secretary-General.

While it was clear from the outset that Avenol was not likely to demonstrate the political capacities of Sir Eric Drummond, there was a disposition to emphasize the new Secretary-General's economic expertise and ability as essential for finding solutions to the world-wide economic depression. The press indicated that given the depression and the new Secretary-General's experience, "it is fortunate that a man like Joseph Avenol has been placed at the head of the League of Nations".[14] Even the League of Nations Union in London agreed: "That a financial expert should be at the head of the World's Civil Service at the present juncture in its affairs is most opportune".[15]

It is also evident, however, that the new Secretary-General's personality did not match the early expectations. Avenol had been regarded by many, at the time of his election, as more "approachable" than Drummond, who had tended to be somewhat aloof from the lower echelons of the Secretariat. It was felt that under Avenol, a more satisfactory "esprit de corps" might develop throughout the Secretariat. But this was not to be. As recalled by some of his associates, Avenol was an extremely quiet and secretive man, who often struck his colleagues as being quite cold. There seems to be agreement that he was not particularly interested or well-informed on many political questions, and was rarely asked for his views or advice.

According to one former League official who worked closely with both Drummond and Avenol, "Avenol was less interested in being informed on anything. One could always see Drummond and get help from him, but it was useless to go to Avenol. He was not *au courant* the situation. The Sections were much less supported by Avenol than by Drummond". An-

---

[13] There was little that either Drummond or Avenol could do about it, however, and they were content with the small gains made. One was their insistence on selecting Pablo Azcaraté of Spain as the small state "representative" in the Secretariat. Naturally enough, the small powers had wished to select their own candidate, and led by Sean Lester, the Irish Free State delegate, they proposed Edward Phelan of the I.L.O. Drummond and Avenol stood firm, and finally prevailed. Other small gains were the stipulation that no state have more than two nationals in the high direction, and the "national islands" limitation as described heretofore.

[14] *Petit Journal* (Paris), 6 June 1933.

[15] *Headway,* June, 1933, p. 124.

other League officer, while conceding Avenol's intelligence in economics and finance, thought him "an indolent man who hated work. He was a sybarite and was happy if someone else did the job". Frank Walters believed Avenol was "open to flattery",[16] and that this affected his work in at least two important cases—the Italo-Ethiopan war, and the decision to expel the Soviet Union from the League after its attack on Finland in 1939.

Without exception, former League staff members recall the constant consultation of League delegates and Secretariat officials with Drummond and on all manner of political question. This was one of Sir Eric's chief contributions during his years as Secretary-General. But as one former League official asserted, the same delegates "did not go to see Avenol. One cannot compare the moral authority of Drummond with that of Avenol". The latter judgment is corroborated by the League Archives in Geneva. The files are filled with records of conversations between Drummond and other Secretariat officials or representatives of Member States. The same Archives have far fewer records of conversations, interviews or requests for opinions during the Avenol administration.

Moreover, there was never a close or even satisfactory working relationship between Drummond and Avenol. According to Pablo de Azcaraté, of the League Secretariat, personal relations between the two were always "extremely cold", and during Sir Eric's administration, neither had confidence in the other, with Avenol consulted by Drummond only on questions of direct interest to the French Government.[17]

Azcaraté's analysis of the problem places significant weight on the personality of Avenol's predecessor as the "French" Deputy Secretary-General, Jean Monnet. Monnet was quite close to Great Britain and the United States, spoke fluent English, and worked very well with Drummond during the formative years of the League Secretariat. Drummond assumed that Monnet would always serve as one of his most immediate collaborators, and perhaps even as his successor. It was evidently something of a shock to Sir Eric to have Monnet replaced by Avenol, who thus found himself in the difficult position of succeeding an official whose relationship with the Secretary-General had been exceptional.[18] Avenol's narrow financial training and lack of political experience did not assist him in achieving a closer rapport with Drummond.

Nor was Avenol able to achieve better relations with the Secretariat staff generally. Arthur Sweetser, an official in the Secretariat's Information Section, concluded simply that he was "a very distant person who did not

[16] Interview granted by Frank P. Walters to the author on July 2, 1966, Grenoble, France.

[17] Interview granted by Azcaraté to Professor George Codding, Jr., of the University of Colorado, on March 25, 1966, under the auspices of the European Office of the Carnegie Endowment for International Peace.

[18] *Ibid.*

succeed in obtaining the loyalty of his staff".[19] Avenol was "very astute in economics", said Huntington Gilchrist. "A very complex and enigmatic personality, an easy going administrator, but one could not be with him long without realizing the corrosive effects of his cynicism".[20] The combination of extreme right-wing views, lack of political understanding or skill, and, according to his associates, a set of personal attributes that included cynicism, vanity, laziness, and opportunism, culminated in a disastrous administration.

Avenol occupied the house, La Pelouse, that the League had built for the Secretary-General, with his mistress, Vera Lever, a highly educated woman, who served as his hostess at the lunches and dinners he gave. He was very much interested in art, and spent a great deal of time on the gardens of La Pelouse and on the details of the architecture and construction of the new Palais des Nations on the shore of Lake Geneva. During the Spanish Civil War, he managed to have a great number of Spain's most famous art treasures, particularly El Greco paintings, stored in Geneva until the war was over.

Avenol was credited, at least in the early stages, with a "natural bent for administration" and it was considered that certain changes he instituted in Secretariat procedures were made with a view to increased efficiency.[21] Azcaraté has stated that in fact one of Avenol's primary interests was administration, and in this respect he was significantly different from Drummond. Indeed, he often put political questions aside in order to deal with administrative issues, and even details, and then, in Azcaraté's words, "lorsqu'il se mêlait des questions politique, c'était une catastrophe".[22]

One of Avenol's more important contributions to the Secretariat was the initiation of the "French System" of administration. Drummond had utilized basically British techniques during his fourteen-year term. As noted, this entailed substantial discretion and authority for lower level officials, with problems passed to higher officials and to the Secretary-General, if at all, only if the proper responsibility did not exist at lower levels.

The French system entailed starting at the top and working down. The Secretary-General's highest aides would assume greater immediate responsibility, and distribute the work as they saw fit. Drummond's British experience had been reinforced by his training in the Foreign Office, an institution very different from the other parts of the British Civil Service. The Foreign Office gives advice and follows events, but does very little in the way of administration. Drummond had adopted the Foreign Office method. Avenol, and Albert Thomas of the International Labor Office,

[19] Letter from Arthur Sweetser to Raymond B. Fosdick, July 18, 1965.
[20] Letter from Huntington Gilchrist to Raymond B. Fosdick, undated.
[21] *National Archives,* 500.C/725, January 11, 1935, p. 34.
[22] Azcaraté interview, *op. cit.*

used the ordinary techniques of a French Minister, modified by the habits of British administration, and by the presence in the Secretariat of many English subjects who could not easily adapt to newer methods.[23] Avenol established a Central Section in the Secretariat for coordination purposes, and in due course the new section had succeeded in absorbing most of the initiation functions in the League civil service.

The French system has been criticized by some writers as leading to a rigid over-centralization in the Secretariat resulting in a loss of incentive and prestige; in fact, however, Avenol evinced so little interest in much of the work, that there was often as great a personal initiative under his administration as in the Drummond era. As we have seen, this likely result was one of the factors prompting support for Avenol in the first place, and according to several of Avenol's colleagues in Geneva, the centralization did not restrict initiative for any of the more important questions with which the League was dealing.

Although Avenol was not an effective speaker, he did make a number of public addresses on the League of Nations. His speeches were extremely formal, often dealt with League procedures, avoided direct responses to the question of League prospects in the face of the dictators, and gave the impression that the new Secretary-General had little hope for the Organization he headed. Like Drummond, Avenol spent substantial time defending the League against uninformed criticism, and several of his statements resembled talks made in the United States in 1920 by League supporters who were trying to arouse public opinion against the frustrating action of the Senate.

Avenol thus spoke of the Covenant as "the first and only measure of a practical nature which humanity may have for the purpose of establishing the reign of law in relations among nations".[24] He insisted that despite the Organization's rapidly declining prestige, "the world must choose not between the League and some other more satisfying system of international relations, but between the League and an almost total anarchy".[25] He stated that the abandonment of the Covenant would mark aggression for a period of incalculable length, and were this to happen, he predicted, "neither the present generation nor the following would ever regain the advanced position which we occupy today".[26]

His general stress was upon the oft-repeated theme that however imperfect the Covenant, it was best not to try to change it, and in any event,

[23] For more details, see Egon F. Ranshofen-Wertheimer, *The International Secretariat: A Great Experiment in International Administration* (Washington: Carnegie Endowment for International Peace, 1945), pp. 152-156.
[24] "Discours prononcé par le Secrétaire général de la Société des Nations à la Chambre des Communes le Lundi 11 décembre 1933" (Imprimerie Berger-Levrault, Nancy-Paris-Strasbourg: 1934), Library of the Palais des Nations, Geneva.
[25] *Ibid.*
[26] *Ibid.*

such efforts would clearly be futile. On the key issue of treaty revision, which meant the Versailles limitations on German sovereignty, Avenol admitted the impossibility of achieving a satisfactory solution within the Covenant framework. On the closely related problem of the connection between the Covenant and the Treaty of Versailles, he asserted that the question was not textual, but rather "moral" and "psychological", and the only solution lay in a "moral agreement, which ought to be indissolubly linked to an agreement on disarmament".[27] Given the conditions of European politics when Avenol became Secretary-General in 1933, he was essentially conceding the improbability of settlement, within the League framework, of the most crucial problems of the time.

There was no attempt by the Secretary-General to legitimize any of the suggestions for Covenant "reform" that had already begun to circulate in League corridors, nor was there yet any disposition to emphasize the Organization's economic and social work in lieu of political activity. Avenol's views were neither optimistic nor original, nor did they evince inspired leadership. His opinions followed closely those of the British Foreign Office and the French Quai d'Orsay, and as such had not developed into a meaningful theory of League possibilities in a Europe divided by irreconcilably hostile forces. Essentially, his only prescription for action was a bland statement that it would be "useless and imprudent, indeed dangerous, to abandon the careful conservation of the assets that still remain to us, and for which we are responsible, in exchange for what is unknown and uncertain".[28]

The Sino-Japanese Conflict and Japanese Withdrawal from the League

The Sino-Japanese conflict that began in 1931 and marked the first serious reversal for the League was also the initial opportunity for Joseph Avenol to take part in one of the crucial political issues confronting the Organization. The result was not a happy one for the Office of the Secretary-General, for the League, or for world peace.

Three factors characterized Avenol's role and views in the Manchurian crisis: first, in sharp contrast to general sentiment at the League, he demonstrated what appeared to be a certain sympathy for the Japanese position, and a hesitancy to utilize the Organization to resist aggression; second, not until after he became Secretary-General in 1933 was Avenol able to become well-informed on League activities concerning the dispute,

[27] Avenol, J., "The Future of the League of Nations", translation of Address given at Chatham House on December 12, 1933, and published in XIII International Affairs (Royal Institute of International Affairs, March-April 1934, No. 2), pp. 143-153, at p. 152.
[28] Id., p. 153.

and his work was deliberately kept at a minimum; third, as Secretary-General, he was perfectly content with a minimum League technical aid program in China that was intended to have no political significance whatever, and he refused to countenance a League program to which the Japanese could not agree.

All this was somewhat surprising in view of Avenol's previous interest in China, derived from his visit there in 1928-1929, and his obvious appreciation, at the time, of the political importance of League assistance to the Nationalist regime. It is true that as Deputy Secretary-General, Avenol came away from his visit with an essentially financial prescription for League action. He had felt that the Kuomintang Government might request the Organization to devise a plan for economic reconstruction in China, and more particularly, for the rehabilitation of her financial system. The evidence indicates that Avenol perceived Nanking's economic difficulties as turning upon the necessity of convincing American bankers that investments in China would be productive.[29]

There was no question, however, that Avenol looked to League assistance in China as one means of preventing war with Japan. Having visited Japan as well during his Far East voyage in 1929, he wrote that Tokyo had "only one foreign policy: China".[30] Japan had become accustomed to considering China as a huge amorphous territory without its own political life, and an area in which Japan might assume a place analogous to that of the English in Egypt. But the Japanese, felt Avenol, had been seriously disillusioned. China had become a nation once again, under a government, and with a strong reaction against foreigners generally, and the Japanese particularly.[31] It followed for the Deputy Secretary-General that "regular cooperation between China and the League of Nations may be a factor of the first importance for the good relations of the peoples bordering on the Pacific".[32]

Indeed, he felt that the Japanese Government (assuming the continuance of a purely military policy in China) would fall, and he cited the possibility of his being able to influence Tokyo's strategy more considerably than he could have hoped for prior to his visit.

Japanese military conceptions did not change, however, and the attack on Mukden in September, 1931 marked the first serious blow to the League's fortunes. From this point forward, Avenol, who continued as Deputy Secretary-General until the middle of 1933, and served as Secretary-General thereafter, appeared to lose all interest in a politically

[29] Joseph Avenol, "The League and China: New Links Between Nanking and Geneva", *Headway* (June, 1929), p. 105.
[30] Extract from letter by Avenol (no addressee), dated 29 March 1929. Avenol file, Library of the Palais des Nations, Geneva, Switzerland.
[31] *Ibid.*
[32] Avenol, "The League and China...", *op. cit.,* p. 105.

significant role for the Organization. At the same time, he was kept in the background by Sir Eric Drummond until the latter's retirement in June, 1933, and was not to assume a role of any importance until it was clear that the League had failed to keep the peace in the Far East.

The key Secretariat figure in the conflict was, of course, Drummond. Ordinarily the head of the Secretariat's Political Section might also be expected to play an important part, and Under Secretary-General Yotaro Sugimura did just that, but his position as a Japanese national was difficult, and his influence therefore somewhat muted.[33] Frank Walters, Drummond's chef-de-cabinet, thus took on added responsibility, and was sent on mission to Tokyo in November, 1931. This was deeply resented by Avenol.

While it might be assumed that the second ranking Secretariat official, Deputy Secretary-General Avenol, would enjoy a role somewhat comparable to that of Drummond, Sugimura, or Walters, this was not the case. In November, 1931, Avenol complained bitterly to Drummond at the failure to include him in secret Council meetings dealing with the conflict, and stated flatly to his chief that "you have assumed alone all of the work" concerning the dispute, and of maintaining relations between the Secretariat, the two parties, and the United States observers.[34]

Avenol wrote to the Secretary-General that Sir Eric's assumption of sole responsibility for the Secretariat work in the conflict would run the risk "of weakening confidence which had been based on the collective action of the Secretariat and on an organic division of the work".[35] He stated:

I came here [Paris] [36] with the hope of assisting at a difficult time. Since my arrival, I have remained in complete ignorance of your actions and plans.

---

[33] Frank Walters said of Sugimura that "he was the finest character of anyone I knew in the Secretariat. He was the one person who would have sacrificed himself for the League. And it was taken for granted that if he was an active participant in the behind-the-scenes negotiations, he was advocating the Japanese cause. This was true to a great extent, but far more moderately than almost all of the Japanese. He was convinced that the League had to bring about the peace—and agreement of some sort was necessary to save the face of both sides in the Far East". Interview granted the author in Grenoble, France, July 2, 1966.

[34] Letter from Avenol to Drummond, dated November 26, 1931. Special file at the Library of the Palais des Nations, Geneva.

Avenol sketched briefly what he felt were the inherent risks in Drummond's policy. Formerly on all important issues, wrote Avenol, there were discussions and consultations between the Secretary-General and several other members of the staff. This was useful and desirable because the process resulted in an objective treatment of the issues. "The Secretariat was thus easily able to perform its proper function, which was not to map out policy, but on the contrary, by reason of its detachment and impartiality, to inspire the confidence of the parties".

[35] *Ibid.*

[36] The secret meeting of the Council to which Avenol referred was actually held in the offices of the French Ministry for Foreign Affairs.

I might observe in passing that these conditions make it impossible for me to remain "au courant" for purposes of carrying out my eventual duties.[37]

By the time Avenol became Secretary-General, on July 1, 1933, Japan had given its notice of withdrawal, and the League had failed completely in its attempt to resist aggression in China. Yet the Secretariat's top office evidently had little effect upon Avenol's role in what remained of League efforts to try to deal with the problem. For a substantial period he remained uninformed, and again much of the political work was handled by other Secretariat officials.

Only three weeks after Avenol assumed the Secretaryship-General, for example, the Secretariat was confronted with the issue of practical measures to be taken by states to implement the non-recognition of "Manchukuo" strategy agreed upon by the League. The Assembly's Manchurian Advisory Committee (appointed to follow the situation in the Far East and to assist Members in concerting their action) had drawn up a circular covering measures to give effect to the Stimson Doctrine. Insofar as concerns the United States response, Minister Hugh Wilson reported to the State Department on July 22, 1933 that "Avenol returned to Geneva this morning and leaves again tonight. I have just seen him. He is not sufficiently familiar with the work of the Manchurian Committee to discuss this matter usefully".[38] Two days later Wilson telegraphed the needed information, obtained in a talk with Walters.

On the other hand, it became clear from the beginning of Avenol's administration that the new Secretary-General was very much interested in and well-informed on the issues of League technical assistance to China. This was perhaps a reflection of his prior training and experience, as well as his interest in the Far East derived in part from the trip in 1928-1929. The new Secretary-General argued that the Organization could be useful in China only if it assiduously avoided political issues and concentrated instead upon a technical assistance program. Avenol followed closely the work of the Special Committee on Technical Collaboration created by the League Council in 1933. The Special Committee's task was to coordinate the many technical aid programs for Nanking established since the Manchurian crisis. The Secretary-General sought widespread cooperation with the Committee, calling technical cooperation with China "a matter of international importance".[39]

Yet he appeared totally uninterested in the program's political impact. As reported by Prentiss Gilbert in April, 1934, Avenol's statement of the Organization's position in the Far East "bore no resemblance whatever to the League's attitude at the outbreak of the Manchurian affair in 1931,

---

[37] Letter from Avenol to Drummond, November 26, 1931, *op. cit.*
[38] *FRUS*, 1933, Vol. III, p. 378.
[39] *Id.*, p. 498.

either technically or in its more general political aspects".[40] In Gilbert's estimation, Avenol was quite deliberately minimizing any political import of the League work in China.

The Secretary-General insisted that he had no information concerning the policy of the League powers, and he willingly assumed full responsibility for the views he expressed. He described the situation in China in 1934 as different from what it had been during the original Manchurian crisis and asserted that he

did not perceive that the League was involved in it in any way and that in so far as his control or influence reached it was his intention that the League should not be involved.[41]

League strategy in the Far East was to be confined to a "modest" program of technical assistance and any interference with this "appropriate activity" would be resisted.

Gilbert stated that while Avenol spoke only in his capacity as Secretary-General and, despite his disclaimers, knowledge of the policy preferred by the principal League powers "was in the background of what he had to say".[42] This, of course, tends to render Avenol's views as mere reflections of British and French policy. Avenol naturally denied this was the case, and willingly presented his opinion as his own without any indication of disagreement with London or Paris.

When asked whether the Organization's posture in the Far Eastern situation could rightly be thought of as illustrative of general League policy, the Secretary-General replied that

the League for an indefinite future in so far as it could consistently do so would avoid the handling of new political questions and likewise in so far as possible would seek to avoid action in those which were now before it which would jeopardize continued League support by the League states particularly concerned.[43]

As early as the spring of 1934, then, the Secretary-General of the League was stating that the world organization would have no political role "for an indefinite future".

It was certainly obvious that within the context of the Manchurian affair, Avenol went quite far to avoid giving any political connotation to the League's work in China, and to prevent any action displeasing to Tokyo. One of the League officers sent to China was Dr. Ludwik Rajchman, a Polish national who also served as Director of the Secretariat's Health Section. According to official reports from Geneva, Dr. Rajchman and a number of other League officials saw in the technical assistance program an opportunity to maintain interest in China that might help in the expansion of its trade and finances. One result might be increased diplomatic

[40] FRUS, 1934, Vol. III, p. 145.
[41] Ibid.
[42] Id., p. 146.
[43] Id., pp. 146-147. The quotation is Gilbert's rendering of Avenol's statement to him.

support "with a consequent strengthening of the international and national position of China's central government".[44] The U.S. Consul declared that "there was no hint of any such League purpose in my conversations with Mr. Avenol".[45]

I cannot express too strongly my impression of a decided intent to denude this League endeavor, insofar as may be possible, of any political connotations which might be offensive to Japan or embarrassing to any important government, notably perhaps the British.[46]

Not surprisingly, in response to pressure from Tokyo, Avenol informed Dr. Rajchman that his services in China could not be renewed after his one-year term expired on August 1, 1934. While Rajchman formally resigned his China post, there is no question that his action was not voluntary.

Avenol thus evinced warm support for what later came to be known as "appeasement", and indeed, his statements to the effect that he had no official intimation of great power policy in the League underscored his intent to make that policy his own. Several factors combined here: Avenol had little knowledge of world politics and had demonstrated, according to his colleagues, a singular lack of political sagacity. The League had failed in the Far East, and assuming the desirability of even minimum contact with Japan, technical assistance stripped of political import seemed the only useful service it could perform, there and elsewhere. The result was a Secretary-General who seemed to ignore the Covenant, and as the Organization's political capacities diminished, Avenol would make no move, take no risk, nor utter a word to revive them.

Finally, toward the end of March, 1935, the Secretary-General made a statement to the press concerning Japanese withdrawal from the League. The two-year notice required by Article 1, paragraph 3 of the Covenant had run, and as of March 27, 1935, Japan ceased to be a member of the League. The occasion was not extraordinary in itself, although its implications were ominous enough. However the Secretary-General's statement was evidently made on his own initiative, and appeared to involve an unusual interpretation of the Covenant. Perhaps most important, his statement seemed to absolve Japan from past wrongs.

Article 1, paragraph 3 of the Covenant provided that any Member could withdraw after two years' notice *"provided that all its international obligations and all its obligations under this Covenant shall have been fulfilled"*. Avenol, without authorization from the Council or Assembly, asserted that "Now that the separation is an accomplished fact, the legal bond of connection between Japan and the League ceases to exist. Japan had no longer any right or obligation as regards the League, and it is therefore unhappily

[44] *Id.*, p. 411.
[45] *Ibid.*
[46] *Ibid.*

impossible for her to retain the position she has hitherto occupied in connection with the League".[47]

The Japanese Consul General at Geneva issued a statement to the press at the same time in which he repeated Avenol's "no right or obligation" formula, and went on to say that Japan would not ignore the Organization's efforts in humanitarian and technical endeavors, that her experts would continue to serve on League organs concerned with technical activities, and that Tokyo would continue to send reports to the League Mandates Commission.

The Chinese Minister at Geneva, Victor Hoo Chi Tsai, protested at once that the Secretary-General had no right to interpret the Covenant, much less construe it in a manner contrary to its terms. Avenol's interpretation, said Minister Hoo, would tend to weaken the Covenant. "Any member whatever of the League of Nations could violate the Covenant and then leave the League of Nations. It would be absolved from every obligation with respect to the League of Nations in spite of the formal terms of article 1".[48]

Avenol's defense, summarized in a letter to Hoo, was weak, although perhaps he made the best of a bad case. The Secretary-General argued that any League member had the right to contest that the conditions of Article 1(3) had been fulfilled, but that no member did so. This being the case, Japan ceased to be a member, although there "does not ensue from this . . . a certificate that it has fulfilled all its international obligations, including those of the Covenant".[49]

The episode is important because it raises basic questions concerning Avenol's role as Secretary-General, as well as the question whether the

---

[47] League of Nations Archives 1933-1940: Political 1/3198/3153. The statement was evidently drawn up on March 22, 1935. It was made to the press on March 27. See also *National Archives,* 500.C 001/1087, enclosure No. 1. The full statement was as follows:

It is most regrettable that the League of Nations should have to part with one of its original members that has cooperated with it for nearly fifteen years.

Now that the separation is an accomplished fact, the legal bond of connection between Japan and the League ceases to exist. Japan has no longer any right or obligation as regards the League, and it is therefore unhappily impossible for her to retain the position she has hitherto occupied in connection with the League.

We are, however, given to understand that the Japanese Government has the intention of pursuing a policy of international co-operation in the spirit of the "Imperial Rescript" promulgated two years ago. Such an intention is a cause for great satisfaction. We cannot say what form it will take, but for my part I am decided to do nothing that could prejudice the relations between Japan and the League. We cannot foretell the future and I do not think that we should abandon the hope of the League's universality.

[48] *National Archives, op. cit.,* enclosure No. 3.

[49] *Id.,* enclosure No. 4. Hoo accepted this, but Avenol's response very clearly does not meet the objections raised.

Western democracies intended at all to resist aggression and to insist upon compliance by members with their Covenant obligations.

On the latter point, United States Consul Gilbert reported to Washington that "From knowledge of Avenol's character it is difficult to view his action other than as being definitely motivated either by what might be termed League policy or in respect to the policy of some League powers... [I]t is difficult to believe that [the statement] was made without prior knowledge of Paris and probably of London".[50] Other close observers of League and great power policy in the Sino-Japanese conflict tended to agree. Frank Walters wrote that the small powers in the League believed that "there was in London, Paris, and Rome a certain current of sympathy for the State which had dared to use its military preponderance to impose its own justice".[51] "Great Britain was pleased", he said, "that the Chinese Government was not powerful, and that it received a good strong kick from the Japanese. It was a bad error..."[52]

By March, 1935, when Avenol made his statement to the press, the Italo-Ethiopian conflict was under way, and the Western democracies were faced with the second great test of their willingness to challenge aggression. Their failure in the first case, a failure which Secretary-General Avenol did little to resist and just enough to sanction, marked the beginning of the end of the League's prestige, and indeed, the start of its collapse.

The protest generated by Avenol's statement demonstrates clearly the restricted nature of the League Secretary-General's role. What has become commonplace for the United Nations Secretary-General, that is to say, a public interpertation of the Charter, was not readily considered proper for the League Secretariat's first officer. Minister Hoo naturally protested, although it is common enough for a state unhappy with a Secretary-General's interpretation to question his right to make it. Avenol, however, offered no reply to the Chinese assertion that a Secretary-General had no right to interpret the League Covenant without authorization from one of the League's political organs. Gilbert, as a relatively disinterested observer at Geneva, raised the same question:

It is a marked departure from precedent for the Secretary-General to issue such a pronouncement of political policy especially one interpretive of the Covenant and there is further the thought that no obvious circumstances render such a pronouncement other than gratuitous.[53]

Gilbert found Avenol's statement "significant not only as respecting Japan but in relation to the entire principle and practice of obligations of states under the Covenant".[54]

[50] *National Archives*, 500.C001/1080, p. 4.
[51] *A History of the League of Nations* (London: Oxford University Press, 1952), Vol. II, p. 499.
[52] Interview granted the author, July 2, 1966, Grenoble, France.
[53] *National Archives*, 500.C001/1080, p. 3.
[54] *Ibid.*

Minister Hoo conceded that the Secretary-General's interpretation of the Covenant did "not result from an initiative on the part of a member of the League",[55] and as such, was again revealing of the Secretary-General's own thinking. He had, as already noted, made private judgments tending to evidence a certain hesitancy to resist the dictators, even when their plans included military aggression. The statement to the press on the Japanese withdrawal was a public judgment, and if taken on his own initiative, is consistent with the picture of Avenol as a League of Nations official who rather frequently found himself poorly attuned to general sentiment at the League.

The March, 1935 incident was, however, neither the first time nor the last that Secretary-General Avenol was to take a step reflecting little sympathy for the ideals of the League Covenant.

The Italo-Ethiopian War

The last nail in the coffin of the League was driven by Mussolini in his brutal conquest of Ethiopia. If the Sino-Japanese conflict was the first indication of the League's helplessness in the face of aggression, and the real turning point for the Organization, the Italo-Ethiopian war was the final seal on the League's demise. The British and French tried this time, after initial hesitation, and coordinated their efforts for a short while through the League, but to no avail. When League economic sanctions finally failed, it was clear that the global body had no further political role to play in world affairs.

The League's inability to prevent the conquest of Ethiopia was due almost entirely to the mistaken notion of the British and particularly of the French that Mussolini's Italy might subsequently become a valuable ally against Germany, and that nothing should be done to drive Fascist Italy into the arms of Nazi Germany. If this entailed a free hand for Italy in backward Ethiopia, little was lost. Aggression might be a violation of the Covenant, but too strong a resistance might antagonize Rome, and what could be more dangerous for the safety of Britain and France? This was appeasement in full bloom, and nowhere could a stronger advocate of that strategy be found than in the Office of the League Secretary-General.

Throughout the crisis, which lasted from December, 1934 to the autumn of 1936, Avenol forcefully supported British and French hesitancy to enforce the Covenant against Italy, and even when London, led by Anthony Eden, and Paris, rather reluctantly, finally agreed on economic sanctions, Avenol actually disapproved, making manifest his preference for a "peaceful" solution that in effect would have given Italy all she wanted in Ethiopia.

[55] *National Archives,* 500.C001/1087, enclosure No. 5.

Within the context of British and French foreign policy, Avenol's public position was not surprising. But the Secretary-General gave no indication whatever, even privately, that perhaps another strategy would have been preferable, nor were his ideas on the crisis substantially different from Mussolini's. Above all, he apparently did not deem it desirable to support the League, its Covenant, and the accepted procedures of the world organization for the settlement of international disputes.

His thinking was perhaps best summed up by Anthony Eden. Writing in his *Memoirs* of the very natural Italian wish to negotiate with Ethiopia directly and outside the League framework, Eden stated:

When I returned to the League meetings, Madariaga told me that he was disturbed at the attitude which the Secretary-General had taken up. At luncheon on April 16th [1936] I found this well justified. Avenol surpassed the French Ministers in excuses for Mussolini's attitude. I asked whether it was the view of the Secretary-General of the League that the victim of aggression was not entitled to ask that negotiations to settle his fate should take place at Geneva in the presence of the League. To this I got no clear reply.[56]

Eden was referring here to Italy's final proposals to Ethiopia just prior to completion of the military conquest in the spring of 1936. From the inception of the conflict, however, Avenol seemed to do his best to avoid the Covenant obligations, both in the interests of French foreign policy as he perceived them, and from personal conviction that military conquest of an African nation was insufficient reason to insist upon enforcement of the League constitution.

As far back as April, 1933, shortly before Avenol became Secretary-General, Baron Pompeo Aloisi, the Italian Delegate to the League, wrote in his Journal that he believed Avenol to be "a supporter of a French-Italian rapproachment".[57] This was something of a major understatement. The League followed a dual procedure[58] in the crisis, involving League proceedings on the one hand, and private negotiations between Great Britain, France, and Italy, on the other. The Secretary-General was clearly more interested in the private negotiations, although these were consistently based upon the assumption that Covenant obligations were of minor significance.

Avenol's first efforts in the dispute occurred shortly after the Wal-Wal incident of December, 1934.[59] After some hesitation, Ethiopia, through its Delegate, Bajirond Teclé-Hawariate, expressed the wish to inscribe the matter on the Council's agenda. The Secretary-General, in meetings with

[56] Anthony Eden, *Facing the Dictators* (Boston: Houghton Miflin Company, 1962), p. 426.
[57] Baron Pompeo Aloisi, *Journal* (25 juillet 1932-14 juin 1936) (Paris, 1957).
[58] Walters, *op. cit.*, Vol. II, p. 628.
[59] The Wal-Wal incident involved a clash between Italian and Ethiopian troops at Wal-Wal, a water source more than fifty miles within Ethiopia's somewhat vague boundary. The Italian military units were from Italian Somaliland.

Aloisi, Eden, and Pierre Laval, the French Foreign Minister, supported a formula whereby Ethiopia agreed that the issue should not be discussed by the Council, in return for Italy's promise to arbitrate the question under Article 5 of the Italo-Ethiopian Treaty of Friendship of 1928.[60] The Italians considered that a public discussion of the matter by the Council would prejudice chances for a friendly settlement, and of course, Rome had no interest in anything other than private negotiations with Ethiopia.

Avenol had first tried a compromise. Ethiopia, he warned, might insist upon having the Council add the item to its agenda, as was its right. In that case, suggested the Secretary-General to Massimo Pilotti, the Italian Under Secretary-General, perhaps it would be possible to avoid a public discussion, but have instead a rapporteur follow the direct negotiations.[61] Italy rejected this as implying Council intervention, precisely what Mussolini wished to avoid.

Avenol's meetings during this period in January, 1935 were with Laval, Eden, and Aloisi on the one hand, and with Teclé-Hawariate and his legal adviser, Professor Gastion Jèze of the University of Paris, on the other. Avenol was also in touch with Aloisi through Under-Secretary Pilotti.

On January 18, with Eden insisting on a role for the League Council in case of further incidents in Ethiopia, the Secretary-General recommended another compromise, this time with more success. The representatives of both Ethiopia and Italy would address letters to the Secretary-General, one demanding and one accepting adjournment of Council consideration of the matter in view of direct negotiations under the 1928 Treaty, and each promising to take necessary measures to avoid further incidents. On January 19, postponement pending arbitration under the Treaty was accepted, and Italy thus won the first round. Had the 1928 Treaty been taken seriously in Rome, the agreement would have been reasonable enough, but with no disposition to settle the issue by arbitration, Italy had the advantage of preventing public consideration of the issue by the Council.

The arbitration on the Wal-Wal incident was slow in coming, and for several weeks after the January 19 agreement, there was no meaningful negotiation or attempt to arbitrate. In March, Ethiopia finally requested consideration of the dispute (after continued Italian military moves in Italian East Africa) under Article 15 of the Covenant, the provisions of which outline procedures for disputes not submitted to arbitration or judicial settlement. Secretary-General Avenol, utilizing Rome's reply to the Ethiopian complaint, suggested to Ethiopia that action under Article 15 was not

[60] See *Foreign Relations of the United States* 1935 (I), p. 597; Armand Cohen, *La Société Des Nations Devant Le Conflit Italo-Ethiopien* (Geneva: Librairie E. Droz, 1960), pp. 61-62; Baron Pompeo Aloisi, *Journal, op. cit.*, pp. 251-252; Diary notes kept by Secretary-General Joseph Avenol from 15 January-19 January, 1935; in special file at the Library of the Palais des Nations, Geneva.
[61] Avenol's Diary Notes, *op. cit.*, entry for 16 January 1935, p. 2.

"immediately appropriate" inasmuch as direct negotiations between Rome and Addis Ababa were in progress.[62] Council sessions in April and May, 1935 provided no assistance, however, as Italy each time promised to implement the arbitration procedures of the 1928 Treaty.

During the summer months of 1935, negotiations continued between Italy, Britain, and France, with representatives from Addis Ababa excluded from the talks. In June, Avenol recommended that Italy take the offensive by arguing Ethiopia's "barbaric" nature and unfitness to remain a League member. He openly advocated Italian dominance in Ethiopia, and whether in the form of a protectorate or League mandate made little difference. Late in July, he asserted that London "had finally become convinced of Italy's need to expand"[63] and was ready to comply with the terms of the French-Italian entente of January, 1935. (Foreign Minister Pierre Laval had visited Rome in early 1935 and while there signed agreements with Italy covering African affairs generally. Apparently there was also a secret accord under which Laval gave Italy assurances that France would not resist an Italian conquest of Ethiopia.)

In London, Paris, and Geneva, Avenol outlined his conception of a proper agreement. The entire question was to be removed from the League agenda, and he again proposed that Italy might do well to raise the question whether Ethiopia was entitled to its seat in the League of Nations.[64] The central idea, of course, was to permit Italy a free hand in Ethiopia after the formation of a preliminary alliance of Italy, Great Britain, and France. The Tripartite Pact of 1906, according the three powers particular zones of

[62] *National Archives,* 500.C113/110, p. 3.
[63] Luigi Villari, *Storia diplomatica del conflitto italo-etiopico* (Bologna: Zanichelli, 1943), p. 119; Gaetano Salvemini, *Prelude to World War II* (New York: Doubleday and Company, Inc., 1954), p. 247.
[64] See Cohen, *op. cit.,* p. 88; Salvemini, *op. cit.,* p. 247; Villari, *op. cit.,* pp. 119-120. Villari's account is as follows:
"According to Avenol, the two objectives to be pursued were to avoid a conflict between Italy and the League of Nations, and to assure the former of the possibility of acting independently, since this would give Italy much greater freedom of action in dealing with the situation, and hence would reduce the military force which might prove necessary. Italy would have to come to an understanding with Great Britain and France in order to withdraw the Ethiopian question from the attention of the League of Nations.
Avenol displayed a certain understanding of Italian aspirations, and seemed to believe that the British government was disposed to answer Italy's January proposal. He held that it would be wise to help the British government to extricate itself from the embarrassing situation into which it had been driven by its intimate relations with the League and by its electoral necessities. He believed that the Tripartite Pact could serve as a starting point for obtaining from Great Britain recognition of Italy's broadest rights, and he thought Italy would do well to raise the issue of Ethiopia's right to belong to the League of Nations". (pp. 119-120; translation from the Italian by Mr. Julian Pace, graduate student in the Department of History, Cornell University.)

influence in Ethiopia, was Avenol's favored framework for negotiation. He suggested to Renato Bova-Scoppa, the deputy Secretary-General of the Italian Delegation to the League, that tripartite conversations have as their object the recognition of Rome's preponderant position and control in Ethiopia. The only exceptions to this would be French rights over the Djibuti-Addis Ababa railroad, and British jurisdiction over Lake Tsana. French and British diplomatic pressures combined with Italy's diplomatic and military activity would be sufficient to persuade Emperor Haile Selassie of the wisdom of the plan. Finally, the League of Nations, under Avenol's scheme, would assume the task of reorganizing Ethiopia's administrtion, and this would be accomplished with due respect for Italy's preponderance there. In the words of one observer, "the Secretary of the League of Nations, no less than Laval and Hoare, had 'disannexed' Ethiopia from the League, while waiting for the moment when it would be the turn of Spain, Austria, and Czechoslovakia".[65]

In August, after the initiation of talks by the Tripartite Pact powers, Laval and Eden agreed on the essentials of the settlement recommended by Avenol, but in negotiations with Aloisi, it became apparent that Mussolini was not prepared to accept such proposals. He wanted outright annexation, and as the Council met once again on September 4, the issue was at a head. Italian military preparations were in full swing, and the recent closing of the Wal-Wal question with the report of the Arbitration Committee (neither side was held responsible for initiation of the fighting) meant little to Italy.

At the suggestion of Avenol, first broached in June by the Secretary-General, Aloisi presented to the Council on September 4 a 246-page printed memorandum, replete with documents, maps, photographs, affidavits, eye-witness accounts, facsimiles, and annexes of all kinds. The point was to confirm beyond doubt that Ethiopia was a barbaric, violent, and lawless country that consistently failed to meet its Covenant obligations and was thus unfit to remain a member of the League. Professor Mario Toscano of the Italian Foreign Office Archives, wrote in his introduction to Aloisi's Journal that the memorandum was an effort "to resolve the Ethiopian issue within the framework of the League and of European solidarity" by developing the theory of continued aggression by Ethiopia against the European powers. The Secretary-General hoped this would be sufficient for purposes of resolving the entire dispute in accordance with Italian wishes.[66] In line with dominant French policy, Avenol maintained throughout that Mussolini might join in an alliance against Germany, and to that end wanted a settlement that would not involve an Italian break with London or Paris.

Military preparations had gone far, however, and public opinion in Italy did not oppose war in Ethiopia. London was thus confronted with an im-

65 Salvemini, *op. cit.*, p. 248.
66 Aloisi, *op. cit.*, p. XIV.

possible choice. On the one hand, Britain might permit Italy a free hand in Ethiopia and hope to retain Mussolini's friendship; yet this would constitute an announcement that the League great powers were unable or unwilling to prevent aggression, and would be tantamount to allowing Germany a free hand in Europe. In the alternative, Britain might impose sanctions in an attempt to thwart aggression; but this risked driving Mussolini into an alliance with Berlin against the democracies.

Attention shifted to the League Assembly in September, 1935, as Great Britain formally announced her support of the Covenant obligations to resist aggression, and it appeared that an Italian attack would be met by the League after all, in the form of economic sanctions. Secretary-General Avenol, however, along with Salvador de Madariaga, the Spanish delegate who had been appointed Chairman of the Council's new Committee of Five to work out a settlement, continued to press for a compromise that would give Italy essentially all it wanted short of conquest. Aloisi wrote in his Journal on September 9, 1935 that Madariaga and Avenol

appear animated by a desire to give us satisfaction within the framework of the League of Nations... If I were free in my actions, I feel that I would be able to arrange everything, while gaining for Italy all the satisfaction that I wish, and to remain in the League.[67]

On September 18, the Committee of Five proposed an elaborate "scheme of collaboration and assistance" for Ethiopia and of "territorial readjustments" between Ethiopia and Italy. Basically, the plan was derived from the scheme first proposed by the Secretary-General in July and further developed in August during the Paris negotiations. On September 22, Mussolini formally rejected the proposal, and on October 3, Italian armies and planes attacked Ethiopia. The critical hour was now upon the League, but the dual policy continued, as the Organization decided to impose sanctions (in the form of an armaments ban and a prohibition on financial loans to Italy) while it continued to support private talks, the hope being that Mussolini might yet be persuaded to accept a compromise.

After an initial support for sanctions, taken even so far as an attempt to persuade Paris to align itself with London and the League on the issue, Avenol's views began to diverge from those of the Foreign Office. After a time he again accepted only that segment of the double policy aiming for a settlement acceptable to Rome, and refused to support League sanctions against a state found by the Council to be an aggressor. According to Frank Walters

Avenol did not like the sanctions against Italy. I don't think he ever worked with the League committee [committee of 18] dealing with sanctions. Avenol inclined to the Foreign Office at this time but still he was not keen on the work of the sanctions

---

[67] *Id.*, p. 302.

committee and he did not attend its meetings. He did not try to prevent sanctions, but he did not support them as he could have.[68]

In one respect, the Secretary-General might be said to have tried to weaken the sanctions effort. In late November, Avenol put to U.S. Consul Gilbert at Geneva the question of what effect the League's recent postponement of an oil embargo might have on the U.S. position on oil exports. Secretary of State Cordell Hull answered that any prediction of the nature and duration of the American "moral" embargo would be viewed as a commitment of cooperation with the League, and this would seriously embarrass the U.S. Government. Gaetano Salvemini, in his study of the Italo-Ethiopian crisis in *Prelude to World War II,* asserts that Avenol raised the issue "The better to utilize the American alibi" and that "Avenol only needed to be enabled to say that it was impossible to foresee what the United States would do, and that, therefore, it was advisable not to do anything".[69]

With even limited and far from universally-applied sanctions showing some effect, however, the League was stunned in December, 1935, to hear that British Foreign Secretary Sir Samuel Hoare and French Foreign Minister Pierre Laval had reversed course and agreed upon still another plan that Italy might find acceptable. The Hoare-Laval plans involved a cession of some 60,000 square miles of Ethiopian territory to Italy in exchange for some 3,000 square miles ceded from Italy to Ethiopia to provide Addis Abada with an outlet to the sea. A second plan suggested by Hoare and Laval was the demarcation of the southern half of Ethiopia, about 160,000 square miles in all, as a zone in which Italy would be preponderant; Ethiopia would have legal sovereignty, but Italy would possess full power of economic exploitation with public administration to be accomplished by Italian officials acting in the name of the League.

The proposals were rejected by almost every League member, including Italy and Ethiopia, and finally were dropped by France and Great Britain. Frank Walters, Under Secretary-General of the League and Director of the League's Political Section at this time, was later to characterize the Hoare-Laval plans as "the consecration and reward of aggression", as a "breach of faith towards Ethiopia, and towards all Members of the League",[70] with the sole purpose of delaying further discussion and possible extension of sanctions. Avenol was angered by the incredible reversal in British policy, but he viewed the proposals as "substantially just".[71]

---

[68] Interview of July 2, 1966 at Grenoble, France.
[69] Salvemini, *op. cit.,* p. 382; see *FRUS,* 1935, Vol. I, pp. 862-867.
[70] Walters, *op. cit.,* pp. 669-670.
[71] Report from Under Secretary-General Massimo Pilotti to the Italian delegation at Geneva, transmitted to Rome on December 19, 1935; our thanks to Professor Mario Toscano of the Italian Foreign Office Archives for providing a copy of this report, as

Indeed, the Hoare-Laval plans, which went beyond anything Avenol offered previously, were viewed by the Secretary-General only as coming too late. He tended to blame British diplomacy for a situation he viewed as "confused". According to Pilotti, Avenol emphasized the contradictions of British diplomacy, which had too late decided upon an appeal to Rome to avoid war, had executed the appeal tactlessly, and against all good sense, had abandoned the idea of a friendly settlement.[72] The Secretary-General also underscored the reaction he saw setting in against Great Britain on the part of some of the medium and smaller powers. They were naturally not happy with making sacrifices under the sanctions plan, only to see England seek an accord with Mussolini that would reward his aggression.

The Secretary-General now totally rejected League policy. Even the very conception of the Organization appeared to mean little to Avenol. Italy's gold reserves had fallen off badly under the sanctions, and at Christmas-time, 1935, several Italian Secretariat officials presented as a symbolic act a bar of gold to Mussolini with money from their salaries as international officials. There were no objections from the Secretary-General.[73]

In early 1936, the Italian armies and air force, with the help of lethal gas, scored repeated victories and enthusiasm for sanctions quickly waned. In April, Italy offered Ethiopia only direct negotiations, and on April 16, Avenol indicated to Anthony Eden, as cited above,[74] a reluctance even at that point to permit the victim of aggression to utilize the League for negotiations. Aloisi, however, recorded in his Journal on April 16 that Madariaga and Avenol "brought strong pressure to bear on me to grant some *formal* concession. I appeared to acquiesce while remaining intransigent".[75]

On May 6th, 1936, Addis Abada was captured, and Mussolini announced the war was over. There was no statement from Avenol, nor were there any objections the following day when Pilotti, and several Italian Secretariat members attended a celebration given by the Italian colony in Geneva. A French official of the International Labor Office paid tribute to Rome and its struggle against the League. The Secretary-General had no comment to offer.[76]

For Italy, the independent nation of Ethiopia had ceased to exist. On May 9th, Mussolini proclaimed the establishment of the Fascist Empire, and his representative at the League, Baron Aloisi, refused to sit at the

---

well as the information from several reports to Rome setting out Secretary-General Avenol's opposition to the League sanctions.

[72] Pilotti report, 19 Dec. 1935.
[73] Salvemini, *op. cit.*, p. 416, footnote 1.
[74] See p. 125, *supra*.
[75] Aloisi, *op. cit.*, pp. 374-375. Italics added.
[76] Salvemini, *op. cit.*, p. 448.

Council table with the Ethiopian representative. Aloisi recorded in his Journal on May 10 that he had conferred with Avenol and had told him that if the Ethiopian delegate were introduced at the Council session called for May 11, "I will pose the alternatives: either him or me".[77] For the Council it was the Ethiopian delegate, and Mussolini ordered his delegation to leave Geneva. Aloisi was ordered to depart without presenting any explanation other than the order itself. He gave Avenol the news, and records in his Journal for May 12 that the Secretary-General was "nonplussed" and requested explanations that were not forthcoming.

Italy had thus ceased all meaningful cooperation with the League, although attempts were still made to encourage her return. Mussolini did not pronounce official notice of withdrawal until December, 1937, and in the meantime, there existed some slim hope, believed Britain and France, that Rome might yet cooperate with the European democracies and the League of Nations. On July 4, 1936, the League Assembly formally removed the sanctions, a move strongly supported by Avenol, but the hopes were clearly in vain. Italy announced it would return to Geneva only if Ethiopia were excluded from the Organization, and Avenol, supported by the Quai d'Orsay, strongly backed Rome's demand for formal recognition of its sovereignty in Ethiopia, and the exclusion of Ethiopian representatives from Geneva. For the Secretary-General, there was still a role to play.

On September 7, 1936, Avenol, without authorization from any League body, and without public announcement, arrived in Rome for talks with Mussolini and Foreign Minister Galeazzo Ciano. In Frank Walters' terms, "Avenol was open to flattery, and was induced to come to Rome".[78] Ostensibly the visit was for purposes of discussing the Italian members of the Secretariat. There was a much greater significance.

The primary issue was whether or not Italy would attend the Assembly session scheduled for September 21st. Avenol fully appreciated that the Italian delegation would not be present if the Ethiopian delegate was recognized. His strategy was simply to have the Ethiopian representative's credentials refused, and to avoid the more fundamental issue of membership. Shortly after his talks with Ciano and Mussolini, Avenol informed Edward Ingram, the British Chargé d'Affaires in Rome, of their substance. This report was passed on to the U.S. Chargé, who sent it to the United States Department of State.[79]

Avenol, according to Ingram's report, asserted to Ciano that he had come to Rome solely in his capacity as Secretary-General of the League, without a mandate from anyone, and for the purpose of ascertaining Italy's conditions for resumption of collaboration with the League. He advised that the expulsion of Ethiopia could not be placed on the agenda of the Council

77 Aloisi, *op. cit.*, pp. 382-383.
78 Interview of July 2, 1966, at Grenoble, France.
79 See *National Archives*, 500.C111/935, Sept. 10, 1936.

or Assembly. However, upon inquiry of Foreign Minister Ciano as to what the League attitude would be should an Ethiopian delegate insist upon taking part in the Organization's meetings, the Secretary-General replied that

the views of the League Secretariat were to the effect that the credentials of an Abyssinian representative might be rejected either on the basis that since Abyssinia no longer existed as an entity there could be no representative of something that did not exist, or on the basis that since the Emperor of Abyssinia no longer exercised effective sovereignty over his territories his representative could not be admitted.[80]

While it is not known what the views of the League Secretariat as a whole happened to be on this issue, it is far more likely that Avenol was expressing his own opinion and a subtle strategy. There was no marked tendency at Geneva to accord such complete recognition to Italy's conquest.

In any event, the Secretary-General reported that "Both Mussolini and Ciano...were obviously pleased with this formula"[81] and wished therefore to return to Geneva. Ciano suggested that Italy wait until the Assembly's Credentials Committee rejected the Ethiopian delegate. Italy would appear only after receiving absolute assurances that no Ethiopian delegate would have his credentials validated. Avenol agreed to this procedure, but was convinced that in any event, the Assembly would indeed refuse to recognize the validity of the Ethiopian delegation's credentials. Evidently both Ciano and Mussolini had their hopes raised by the Secretary-General, and only upon the basis of his personal opinion. The final decision was for the League to take.

Gilbert reported from Geneva one week later that the atmosphere was "charged with rumors and denials as to what actually took place in the Avenol-Mussolini conversations",[82] and that the Secretary-General simply stated he had been able to achieve "an adjustment" in the issue of Italian-League cooperation. Avenol did disclose, however, that Italy would not attend the Council sessions during the week preceding the Assembly, or the opening session of the Assembly. There would be a "small delegation" ready to come to Geneva after the League gave "satisfaction" to Rome.

Avenol further revealed that Italy had made known her position on three other points: Rome opposed a disarmament discussion in the Assembly; opposed a discussion of Covenant "reform" until after a European settlement; and demanded changes in the Italian Secretariat personnel. The latter issue was essentially a problem of a replacement for Under-Secretary Pilotti.

The Secretary-General was evidently disturbed at the reaction to his visit, for on September 18, he issued a statement of explanation to the

[80] *Ibid.*
[81] *Ibid.*
[82] *National Archives,* 500.C111/940, Sept. 17, 1936.

Council and later presented the statement to the Assembly.[83] He said he had gone to Rome "in the normal performance of his duties" and discussed the conditions of Italy's resumption of collaboration with the League. He insisted that the legal status of Ethiopia could not be raised, and that Italy "intended to make its collaboration depend exclusively on the presence *de facto* of an Ethiopian delegation".[84] He then asserted that if that were the issue, the question was only whether the Ethiopian delegation would submit valid credentials, and this was a problem within the competence of the Credentials Committee. This explanation, of course, does not at all square with the report sent to Washington from Rome. The Secretary-General concluded with a claim that he

had made it clear to the Italian Government that his visit had been made in the discharge of his duties. He had stated quite definitely that he had not received any instructions to negotiate from any authority of the League, and that his visit had been made for purposes of information, namely, to enable him to inform the competent authorities of the League.[85]

Gilbert wrote from Geneva on October 15 that it was "almost certain that Avenol must have carried to Rome undertakings in some form from Paris and London".[86] A few weeks later he reported that

It was generally understood that Avenol on his mission to Rome had carried with him undertakings from Paris and London to the effect that France and Great Britain would endeavor to have the Italian desires met. I was, in fact, told that this was the case by a responsible member of the British Delegation.[87]

Gilbert's report emphasizes British and French support for the Secretary-General's attempt to gain Italian cooperation by sacrificing Ethiopia. He felt it "highly improbable" that Avenol would have gone to Rome without British and French backing, supporting this view by reference to the fact that both Eden and Yves Delbos (the new Foreign Minister in the French Popular Front Government) did all they could to prevent the seating of the Ethiopian Delegation. Gilbert continues:

After it had been found that this was impossible due to the opposition of a large number of League states, the British Delegation gave out that London had in no way been a party to M. Avenol's visit to Rome and that indeed Great Britain had no objection to the seating of the Ethiopians. This was resented by the French and also caused no little stir in Geneva as reflecting very directly upon M. Avenol. It was observed that from a practical point of view proceeding on a mission under the direction of the two most important League powers was something entirely different from proceeding upon his own initiative and responsibilty. There was even talk that the situation which was created might bring about M. Avenol's resignation.[88]

---

[83] League of Nations Document A.38. 1936, Sept. 23, 1936.
[84] *Ibid.*
[85] *Ibid.*
[86] *National Archives,* 500.C111/1003, Oct. 15, 1936.
[87] *National Archives,* 500.C113/122, November 9, 1936, p. 12.
[88] *Id.,* p. 13.

This report casts substantial doubt on the generally accepted view that the Secretary-General made his famous visit to Rome solely on his own initiative. The implication is that the trip was undertaken at the direction of Britain and France, and that having failed in its purpose, London disavowed Avenol.

In any event, the normally drab Credentials Committee became a political body of first-rank importance as Eden, Delbos and Maxim Litvinov of the Soviet Union joined the deliberations. The British and French tried for a short while to exclude Ethiopia, but majority pressure proved too much, the Committee permitted the Ethiopian Delegation to take its seat, and the full Assembly agreed. The Italian Delegation remained in Rome, and was never again to resume active collaboration with the League of Nations.

Until the Foreign Office archives for this period are open, it will not be possible to set down the definitive story of Avenol's role in the Italo-Ethiopian War. He very clearly, however, supported the appeasement strategy of the French and British Governments, even to the point of refusing support to the League-sponsored sanctions against Italy. He endeavored almost desperately to bring about Italian cooperation with Geneva, and was willing to sacrifice Ethiopia for that purpose. The visit to Rome in September, 1936, was the last meaningful step in that direction, though it failed completely.

Avenol had done little to enhance the role of the Secretary-General during both the Sino-Japanese and Italo-Ethiopian crises. Independent initiatives were of no value, primarily because there was so little support for the steps taken. In addition, from September, 1936 on, many of Avenol's colleagues in the Secretariat believed he had changed still further, and significantly so, in the direction of antipathy for the western democracies and support for the dictators. The Spanish Civil war had now begun, and according to one of Avenol's colleagues, "his sympathies were clearly with the [Franco] rebels".

The visit to Rome is frequently perceived as the true turning point for the Secretary-General. In the words of one of Avenol's closest associates in the Secretariat, "from that time on he was a different man". The same associate relates that upon his return from Rome, Avenol was greeted by a high official of the International Labor Office who inquired as to what news the Secretary-General brought from Mussolini and Count Ciano. According to the former League official, and his account to the author was confirmed in all substantial respects by the International Labor Office official concerned, Avenol stated that "left-wing organizations like the I.L.O. are finished". From then on, Europe "would be governed by Hitler, Mussolini, and..."—then he stopped. Both officials agreed that he meant to say "and Avenol". Rome had advised him he would be Secretary-General of the League within the framework of a "new order" in Europe, and

ain stood in his path. Both officals agreed further that
t forward, the Secretary-General emerged as strongly

during the Italo-Ethiopian conflict was consistent with his
ring the Sino-Japanese crisis, and in each case tended to
diminish the capacities of the Office of the Secretary-General and the
League. The one man who symbolized the League of Nations pressed hard
for an approach that could leave no doubt of the Organization's impotence
in the face of aggression. Perhaps European politics would have been much
the same had Avenol urgently demanded compliance with Covenant
obligations, but at least his Office and the Organization would have suffered
less damage. As it was, the Secretary-General joined his voice and influence
to those who finished by destroying the League's capacity to keep the peace,
and thus the League itself. While a public denunciation of aggression was
not to be expected of the League Secretary-General, even privately Avenol
refused to resist an unjustified resort to force, and while he preferred a
peaceful solution, it was only by way of a "compromise" that bordered on
Ethiopia's destruction. Avenol's role and views during this critical hour for
world organization reflected quite closely the conservative French opinion
of the day. Above all, war with Germany was feared, but the possibility of
such war necessitated almost any concessions to Italy in the desperate hope
of maintaining her friendship.

The Secretary-General's activity during the crisis demonstrated once
again, as Sir Eric Drummond had clearly shown during the Sino-Japanese
war, how active a political role the League Secretary-General might undertake. Even given the unwritten code that prohibited him from making public
his most important political ideas, and from appealing to any national
leadership or public opinion, the Secretary-General did take part in the
political maneuvering and negotiations throughout the conflict. Behind the
scenes, he influenced the course of the procedures agreed upon at the
League, including a few of political importance. Of greater substantive
impact, he proposed solutions that some of the great powers found acceptable, and in fact, his detailed recommendations served as a basis for the
negotiations prior to the Italian invasion of Ethiopia.

But whereas Drummond utilized whatever political influence he possessed to uphold Covenant norms, and was active behind the scenes
primarily for purposes of resisting Japanese force in China, Avenol worked
to implement French foreign policy as he understood it, rather than the
ideals and obligations of the League. This was true even after Britain and
France finally supported sanctions.

It was primarily for these reasons that Avenol accomplished so little in
terms of enhancing the Office of the Secretary-General. His insistence upon
supporting his own notion of French foreign policy to the exclusion of
League Covenant prescriptions, and of the clearly expressed wishes of the

great majority of League members, could not eventuate in an extension of his powers.

For Secretary-General Avenol, his primary responsibility in fact was not to support a strategy outlined by the great majority of members, nor even the policy of the great powers. Rather, he wished to represent what he viewed as correct French foreign policy. At no time did he evince support for the short-lived French willingness to cooperate in the sanctions against Italy; at no time did he emphasize legal obligations of League members under the Covenant; at no time did he endeavor to modify British and French willingness to permit Italy full latitude in a poor and weak African nation that also happened to be a member of the League.

Finally, of course, at no time did Secretary-General Avenol indicate appreciation of Sir Eric Drummond's vision and creation of an international civil service. Avenol acted in most important respects as if he were merely another member of the French delegation to the League, and not as an impartial League Secretariat official whose primary obligation was support of League interests as defined by the Covenant and the political bodies of the Organization. It was now manifest that while the Drummond administration had generated a strong political role for the Office of the Secretary-General, no further progress would be possible during Joseph Avenol's term.

The Italo-Ethiopian war and the League's failure in Africa marked the end of the Organization's political usefulness, and as Europe rushed toward war, the world body began to dissolve. It fell to Secretary-General Avenol to oversee the Organization's decline, and to salvage as much as possible. There was substantial doubt in Geneva that Avenol was best suited for the task, but the only work remaining was to render the League useful in technical areas while hoping for a European settlement, and for the great powers to avert the war that seemed inevitable.

The Decline of the League and the Rush Toward War

For the Secretary-General the four years between the collapse of League resistance to Italy and the fall of France in 1940 were years of frustration and doubt. The Organization was unable to deal in any meaningful way with the problems of maintaining the peace, and had thus lost its primary reason for being. After the Italian-Ethiopian war, there were no significant opportunities for leadership, even behind the scenes, for the Secretary-General. The League was in no position to resist German rearmament, the militarization of the Rhineland, and further Japanese aggression in China. The world body might condemn, but could do no more. As Hitler annexed Austria and provoked the crisis with Czechoslovakia, Avenol was silent, the Organization helpless, and finally both all but ignored the Covenant.

"Reform" of the League was a subject of some interest just subsequent

Mussolini's victory in Ethiopia, as was, of course, the issue of how the ɔbal institution might play a useful role in a Europe threatened by war. Avenol expressed himself on both topics, and in a manner attuned to a changing and fearful sentiment among League Members.

There had been several changes and proposed "reforms" of the League during the successful first decade. Most of these, such as the Treaty of Mutual Assistance, the Geneva Protocol, and the Kellogg Pact, were designed to strengthen the Organization. In 1933, Mussolini proposed reform as a means of weakening the League, and in 1936, after sanctions were officially abandoned, "reform" generally implied the question of how League Members might properly evade the sanctions obligations of Article 16 of the Covenant. Italy's earlier proposals, first put to Avenol and then published in the Italian press, were not seriously considered until the 1936 League collapse. Indeed, the Secretary-General is reported to have said, after hearing the earlier "reform" plans: "The trouble with Mussolini is he has never read the Covenant".[89]

By 1936, however, Avenol fully supported the movement for reform of the Covenant. Indeed, in an address delivered at Oxford and Cambridge Universities in November, 1936, the Secretary-General suggested that while the obligations concerning the settlement of international conflicts (Articles 12, 13 and 15 of the Covenant) were unconditionally binding on states, the obligations for collective action were "relative".[90] This meant that sanctions provisions were "absolutely binding only if all the political conditions which they postulate are in fact realised".[91]

The political conditions emphasized by Avenol were armaments, revision of treaties, and universality. The Secretary-General argued that certain nations whose forces were below "the lowest point consistent with national safety and the enforcement by common action of international obligations" (quoting the language of the Covenant's Article 8) would incline toward neutrality. The implication was that such states were not strictly obligated under Article 16. As for treaty revision, Avenol cited the case "of a country which systematically obstructs proposals for the application of Article 19 which have been put forward in good faith and in the due exercise of constitutional rights".[92] He asked whether that state would be entitled, if attacked, to require the Council to advise upon the means to preserve its territorial integrity. Lastly, he complained that certain states "and those not the weakest—are outside the League, and have their hands free".[93]

The Secretary-General was stating quite simply that sanctions under

[89] *National Archives,* 500.C Covenant/117, Dec. 21, 1933, p. 15.
[90] Address delivered at Meetings held at Cambridge on November 20th and at Oxford on November 21st (1936), p. 9; Library of the Palais des Nations, Geneva.
[91] *Id.,* p. 10.
[92] *Ibid.*
[93] *Ibid.*

Article 16 could not be enforced through the League because weak states could not assume the risk, Germany had been frustrated in its legitimate demands for revision of the Treaty of Versailles, and the United States as a non-member could not be required to join in collective security efforts, thus frustrating the effectiveness of those efforts. In short, political conditions were not ripe for implementation of the League's collective security system, and in this, the majority of the Organization's members were in firm agreement.

There is some evidence that at least until Munich, Avenol favored a kind of regional mutual assistance system under a League aegis. In early 1938 the Secretary-General discussed the possibility of having the League committee on reform of the Covenant propose that the Scandinavian countries, Belgium, Holland, Switzerland, and all the Latin American nations be relieved of their responsibilities under Article 16 in case of conflict that did not directly concern them.[94] At the same time, he suggested that the committee recommend that "temporary mutual assistance ultimately be made within the framework of the League between the powers particularly concerned to cover certain special areas (a) the Mediterranean; (b) Eastern Europe; and (c) central powers".[95] By the autumn of 1938, however, even this kind of thinking could not seriously be considered. The peacekeeping provisions of the Covenant were totally inoperable, and the League to be useful at all, had to serve other purposes.

The Secretary-General, however, at least in his public pronouncements, spoke in terms of a minimal political education role for the Organization. There is no question that Avenol feared a European war, and he knew well, once Italy had commited itself to the Axis and withdrawn from the League, that only the determination of the British and French might prevent a conflagration. He spoke repeatedly of the need to make the League "a place where the forces of public opinion may be rallied, for the purpose, not of making war, but of maintaining peace".[96] As late as August, 1937, Avenol stated in a speech delivered during a visit to Lithuania, that

What the League of Nations should be above all is a center of public opinion for the respect of obligations assumed, for the maintenance of peace, for the resistance to the fear of war and prevention of the spread of panic.[97]

He felt that the League would not meet "with a really serious crisis unless the members of the League of Nations shall resign themselves to the regime of force as before an inevitable fate".[98]

As war approached, however, even this most minimum of League

94 *National Archives*, 500.C Covenant/246, Jan. 8, 1938.
95 *Ibid.*
96 Address Delivered at Meetings held at Cambridge, etc., *op. cit.*, p. 11.
97 *National Archives*, 500.C113/126, August 19, 1937 (enclosure to Despatch No. 245 from the American Legation at Kaunas, Lithuania).
98 *Ibid.*

political functions was eliminated from the Secretary-General's public rhetoric, and in private he insisted that the League attempt nothing of a political nature. In early March, 1939, Avenol asserted that "it was no time to make political pronouncements or to undertake political maneuvers".[99] A few weeks laters he repeated that theme and added that

the great powers at the moment considered the League politically dead and an attempt at the present moment to bring it back to life might be taken by the totalitarian states as a despairing effort to belabor the dead body of the League into a further instrument of encirclement.[100]

He concluded that he "would not feel justified in suggesting or even encouraging any action through the League in the present situation".[101]

Was anything left for the Organization? With political activity ruled out, the Secretary-General turned naturally to the area he knew best. He began to accentuate the essentiality of extending the League's technical services, and indeed, it was here that Avenol made perhaps his greatest contribution as Secretary-General. It was Avenol who finally led the drive for a new economic and social organization to save the League, and its establishment served to inspire the creation of the United Nations Economic and Social Council in 1945. This will be set out in greater detail below.[102]

Further, if not committed to the League Covenant, Avenol understood that no permanent peace could exist without some rational international order. In a long interview in mid-January, 1939, with Carlos Pardo, of the Argentine Delegation and a member of the League's Supervisory Commission, the Secretary-General stated that almost the entire world was engaged in a "demi-guerre" in which the ordinary principles of international law and order were suspended. He believed that the political League must lie dormant until this "demi-guerre" came to an end. A general war, declared Avenol, was "by no means improbable" but in his personal view "would be avoided".[103] In any event, there would subsequently emerge a restoration of peace, and of the fundamental principles of international order, and for this reason "it would be an enormous advantage if at this time an organization such as the League with its trained staff were in existence".[104] It might then be necessary to abolish or perhaps strengthen Article 16 concerning sanctions, but such amendment should not take place now. It would be a "fatal mistake" and he added that "Article 16 was at present dormant but not dead". Yet the mere existence of the League, even though inactive, was of great importance.[105]

[99] *National Archives,* 740.00/654, March 10, 1939.
[100] *National Archives,* 500.C/971, April 5, 1939.
[101] *Ibid.*
[102] See pp. 146-149, *infra.*
[103] *National Archives,* 500.C/960, Jan. 16, 1939.
[104] *Ibid.*
[105] *Ibid.*

The Secretary-General thus expressed his basic belief in a world-wide organization devoted primarily to the maintenance of peace. It was a stand upon which almost all could agree, but the mission still remained of endeavoring to salvage and to expand, if possible, the technical services of the League, and at the least to keep the Organization alive should war come to Europe. There was no reason to think, in early 1939, that Secretary-General Avenol, if not skilled in his job, was not firmly committed to both tasks.

The Crisis in the League Secretariat: 1938-1939

As the League began its slow death after the abandonment of sanctions in 1936, the organizational structure itself began to wither. The number of state withdrawals mounted, and the League's political work evaporated. Delegates to conferences and meetings tended to stay away, and were frequently not replaced. Funds available to the League decreased, and the Secretariat began to shrink. Mobilization for armed services caused further decline in the staff ranks. The key issue was money, and it was soon apparent that economy measures would have to be taken, and the League staff deliberately cut. This was a difficult period for the Secretary-General, for he was ultimately responsible for final decisions on Secretariat structure. As war approached and finally began, still another issue emerged—the physical location of the Organization.

In September, 1938, the League Assembly decided that the Secretary-General, acting with the approval of the Supervisory Commission,[106] should have discretionary power "to take any exceptional administrative or financial measures or decisions which appear necessary".[107] Such measures and decisions were to have the same force as if taken by the Assembly.

In less than a month the crisis of the Secretariat had begun. The Secretary-General was obliged to dismiss a large number of staff members, in part for economy reasons, but also because the decline in the Organization's political work resulted in an over-sized Secretariat. One of the first to go was Marcel Hoden, Avenol's chef de cabinet and a man who had worked in the Secretariat for eighteen years. Hoden was a strong supporter of the Popular Front Government in France, had been critical of the recent Munich Agreement, and opposed the appeasement strategy. The suspicion was strong that Avenol, even as late as the end of 1938, was still attempting

[106] The Supervisory Commission of the League was a body of seven members appointed by the Assembly for three years. Its task was to give advice on financial and administrative questions, and to examine the closed accounts and budget estimates. At least one of the members of the Commission was required to be a financial expert. The Supervisory Commission has a counterpart today in the United Nations Advisory Committee on Administrative and Budgetary Questions.

[107] League of Nations, *Assembly Minutes,* 28 Sept. 1938, pp. 55-56.

to placate Italy and Germany, and rumors of a "purge" of left-wing Secretariat officials that swept Geneva were widely publicized in the press.

United States Consul Howard Bucknell reported to the State Department on October 28, 1938 that Secretariat officials had informed him that fifty to sixty officials would be dismissed within a few months:

Ostensibly economy will be given as the reason and in some cases this may be the true reason particularly as I understand that a reorganization of the Secretariat including the amalgamation of some of its services is also being contemplated. It is reported, however, on good authority that the British and French Governments are bringing pressure on the Secretary-General to "purge" the Secretariat of officials who have leftist tendencies or who for other reasons have been outspoken in their reply to the dictatorships and to recent British and French policies particularly as regards the Munich Agreement.[108]

It is not known how intense, if any, was the pressure brought to bear by Britain and France, but Hoden's "resignation" quickly became known as the "Hoden affair", and it was correctly assumed that Avenol had in fact dismissed him. Bucknell reported his conviction that Hoden's resignation was involuntary, and not for the sake of economy.[109] Avenol had simply eliminated the post of chef de cabinet after charging Hoden with partisan political activity and with failing to keep him informed of his work. Frank Walters was later to state simply that Avenol "fired Hoden".[110] The dismissal came shortly after the Secretary-General visited Paris where he was reported to have discussed League circumstances with Georges Bonnet, the new French Foreign Minister. Secretariat officials linked Hoden's dismissal with the visit, with Hoden's political views, particularly his opposition to Munich, and implied that Avenol was endeavoring to establish the impression of setting a good economy example by permitting his own chef de cabinet to depart.

After Hoden left, interest centered on which higher level Secretariat officials would follow. Bucknell reported on October 28 that according to his Secretariat sources, Avenol had also requested and received the resignations of Frank Walters, Ludwik Rajchman of Poland, and Thanassis Aghnides of Greece. Several Secretariat members asserted that the German and Italian Governments had drawn up a "blacklist" of officials who would have to be purged as prerequisite for their return to the League.[111] The list was said to include, among others, the names of Hoden, Walters, Rachjman, and Henri Vigier, a Frenchman who today is serving in the United Nations Secretariat. It is difficult to believe, however, that anyone took seriously

108 National Archives, 500.C113/160, Oct. 28, 1938. Press accounts may be found in the National Zeitung (Basle), 27 Oct. 1938; the Manchester Guardian, 31 Oct. 1938; the New York Post, 29 Oct. 1938; the New York Herald Tribune, 28 Oct. 1938; L'Europe Nouvelle, 5 Nov. 1938.
109 National Archives, 500.C113/161, Nov. 7, 1938.
110 Interview of July 2, 1966, at Grenoble, France.
111 National Archives, 500.C113/161, Nov. 7, 1938.

the notion of either Germany or Italy returning to the League. In Bucknell's tactful language:

One of the most persistently rumored reasons for the purge is the desire to pave the way for the return of Germany and Italy to the League. It is not seen here, however, how such an endeavor could be successful under present circumstances.[112]

Secretary-General Avenol, however, was evidently struck by the strong press reaction to the Hoden affair and to the rumors that fifty to sixty officials, including some of the higher personnel, would be dismissed for political reasons. On November 1, 1938, the Secretariat issued a communiqué characterizing the reports as "without foundation". Walters in fact stayed on until his contract ran out, and finally resigned in May, 1940. Aghnides also remained. The only other higher level official about whom there was a political question was Rajchman, whom Avenol wished to fire, but without a reaction similar to that following the dismissal of Hoden. The Secretary-General simply allowed his contract to run out in 1939, and did not reappoint him. Other Directors dimissed were those for the Minorities, Economic, and Mandates Sections.

On January 20, 1939, the Secretary-General publicly announced reorganization plans and defended himself against the charges of dismissals based on political opposition. He reviewed the history of the budget cuts proposed by a special Committee on Budgetary Economies, and the organizational changes proposed by that group.[113] The proposed reorganiza-

---

[112] *National Archives,* 500.C113/160, Oct. 28, 1938. Bucknell reported on November 7, 1938, that the "more conservative members of the Secretariat", particularly those handling personnel questions, denied that any "purge" was to occur, and stressed that any reductions were for reasons of economy. Other officials, "both in and outside of the Secretariat who are equally trustworthy" were convinced that the Secretary-General was about to try to dismiss several Secretariat officials who opposed the appeasement policies of Britain and France. The background of the situation in the Secretariat, and an excellent description of the feeling in that body, were provided by Bucknell as follows:

"For several years, and recently at an increasing tempo, a feeling of discouragement and disillusionment had been prevalent in the Secretariat due to the failure of the major League powers to carry out a policy representative of fundamental League principles and as a consequence the gradual disintegration of international order and the recession of the League into the background to the point of its almost complete elimination from any part in the settlement of political questions. This discouragement has been experienced not only by those who have been influenced by ideological concepts, but also by the most liberal and unbiased. The trend of concessions to Italy, Japan and Germany, and also in a minor way to other states, culminating in the Munich Agreement, was felt by many members of the Secretariat to be not only at the expense of League principles, but contrary in general to the maintenance of a world order and opposed in many cases even to the national interests of the countries represented on the Secretariat. The Munich Agreement brought this situation to the foreground and created a kind of moral crisis". (*National Archives,* 500.C113/161, Nov. 7, 1938)

[113] The Committee had been established by the Assembly in September, 1938, as an independent body to examine the standing charges of the Secretariat and the Inter-

tion, accepted by Avenol, entailed an arrangement of the nine Secretariat sections into three groups. The first group would include the Political, Minorities, Disarmament and Mandates Sections. The second would merge the Economic and Financial Section with the Transit Section, and the third group would join the Opium, Social Question and Health Sections. The financial savings were substantial. The Secretary-General contended that the entire matter had been "distorted by rumors and Press campaigns" [114] and that he

need hardly say that his decisions would not be based on any political, philosophical, religious, racial or other such considerations. It would certainly never have spontaneously occurred to him to make that observation. But since it was what had been said and written, he would simply state, out of respect for the Council, that it was absolutely false and absurd.

How would it be possible, in an administration including persons of forty nationalities belonging to different races and possessing different religions and customs, to maintain discipline otherwise than on a basis of justice and impartiality? How could it be imagined that the plan he had just outlined could be carried out by arbitrary decisions? He was prepared to face the test of the reorganisation precisely because he was convinced that the members of the Secretariat had confidence in the justice and impartiality of their chief.

After all, everyone would be able to judge by the results. They would afford the best evidence.[115]

The Secretary-General insisted he would be influenced "neither by representations nor by recommendations".[116] In any event, the League Secretariat began to shrink rapidly. In 1939 the number of principal officers went from 17 to 12, and first division officials from 148 to 86. By January 1, 1940, the entire Secretariat numbered only 488 officials.[117] There is no sufficient evidence indicating an overall attempt by the Secretary-General to dismiss only, or primarily, officials who opposed British and French policy, but at the highest Secretariat level, it is probably justified to conclude that Avenol again deferred to British and French pressure. He was also to make further attempts along these lines at a later time.

As war approached in 1939, the Secretary-General was further confronted with the basic question of the Secretariat's location, and on this issue he had no consistent policy. Initially he appeared to favor a quick move out of Switzerland, and the establishment of at least part of the

---

national Labour Organization. The Committee consisted of M. Jean Reveillaud, Chairman of the Supervisory Commission for 1938 (France); M. Carl J. Hambro, Chairman of the Supervisory Commission for 1939 (Norway): His Excellency Count Carton de Wiart (Belgium); Sir Russell Scott (United Kingdom); Mr. Carter Goodrich, representing the Governing Body of the I.L.O. (U.S.A.).

[114] League of Nations, *Official Journal*, 20 January 1939, p. 93.

[115] *Id.*, pp. 93-94.

[116] *Id.*, p. 94.

[117] *Report of the Supervisory Commission for 1940*, League of Nations Doc. C.152, M.139. 1940. X., 4 November 1940, p. 12.

Secretariat in America. Subsequently, and when a decision had to be taken, he reversed this line of thought. In April, 1939, he announced that if war should break out, he would evacuate the League from Swiss territory at once, whether or not Switzerland were involved. Avenol reported that while he had informed Swiss Foreign Minister Gieuseppi Motta of his decision, the Swiss authorities had made no request for a League evacuation. The Secretary-General maintained that in case of war, the Organization's location on Swiss soil might constitute an excuse for Germany to violate Swiss neutrality.[118] Avenol added that he had considered the possibility of establishing the Economic and Financial Section "somewhere on the American continent",[119] emphasizing that many considerations pointed to such a move, the most important being that this section could not operate effectively under war-time conditions.

A few weeks later, the Secretary-General called a confidential meeting of the Permanent Delegates in Geneva to inform them of detailed plans for the evacuation of the League to Vichy, France in the event of war. He announced his intention to consult member states as soon as possible after an evacuation "regarding a permanent seat for the League preferably in a neutral country".[120]

By August, 1939, however, there had been a complete change of plan. The Secretariat and the Swiss Government were both at that time of the opinion that if war came Switzerland would not be attacked, and Avenol decided that the Secretariat would remain in Geneva unless Switzerland were invaded, or Bern requested the Secretariat to leave, or if communications should be rendered so difficult as to make it impractical to remain.[121] When war finally came just a few days after this decision, there was no indication that Switzerland would be attacked, and the League remained in Geneva.

As the Second World War began, the League Secretariat found itself smaller and weaker, and in a more precarious position than ever. The Assembly renewed the 1938 authorization of emergency powers for the Secretary-General in consultition with the Supervisory Commission. Further mobilization orders and economy cuts had reduced the staff to little more than skeleton proportions, and the once mighty League Secretariat was little more than a symbol of international cooperation.

The top-level staff had nearly disappeared. Under-Secretaries Sugimura and Trendelenberg had resigned when Japan and Germany withdrew from the League. Deputy Secretary-General Pilotti left his post when Italy finally quit the League at the end of 1937. The entry of the Soviet Union in 1934 had resulted in the appointment of Marcel Rosenberg as Under-Secretary.

118 *National Archives,* 500.C/971, April 5, 1939.
119 *Ibid.*
120 *National Archives,* 500.C/972, April 22, 1939.
121 *National Archives,* 500.C/983, August 29, 1939.

He was later replaced by Vladimir Sokoline, who remained only until the expulsion of the Soviet Union in 1939. Pablo de Azcaraté resigned his Deputy post in 1937 to become the Spanish Ambassador to London, and was replaced by Sean Lester of Ireland, who was brought back from Danzig where he had been High Commissioner. By the end of 1939, only Britain and France of the seven major powers during the inter-war era had nationals in the League's top direction. After Avenol as Secretry-General, the only top officers remaining were Lester and Walters as Deputies, and Aghnides of Greece as Under-Secretary.

The Bruce Report

As noted, after the political role of the League collapsed in 1936, greater attention was devoted to its functions in economic and social questions, and Secretary-General Avenol strongly supported the shift in emphasis. Non-political questions were not likely to irritate anyone, and given the state of European politics, it was clear that the League could seriously concern itself only with technical matters.

However, there had been discontent over the years with the structure of the League's non-political systems. All of the Organization's specialized agencies were under Council jurisdiction, resulting in delay, disinterest, and uninformed judgments, to the extent that any were made at all. The Council had little interest in economic and social issues, and thus even when it did more than accord formal approval to particular programs or measures, little was gained. Further, the United States, finally becoming associated with the League's non-political work in the 1930's, had no share in the making of Council decisions.

One result was a movement to establish an international organization devoted solely to economic and social issues, and to maintain it completely apart from the League of Nations. The 1938 Assembly requested non-Members to present their views on these questions. The only reply was from United States Secretary of State Cordell Hull on February 2, 1939. Washington not only wished to maintain the link between economic and social work and the League, but generally praised the global body's accomplishments in these areas, pledged continued support, expressed the hope that the work would be extended, and undertook to consider how to make its collaboration more effective.[122]

[122] Secretary-General Avenol was evidently much encouraged by the United States' reaction. The New York World's Fair was scheduled to open on May 1st, 1939, and Avenol intended to come to the League Pavilion to deliver a speech that emphasized the League's role in economic and social matters. He also was scheduled to meet with the Secretary of State and with President Roosevelt in Washington. On April 11, Avenol cancelled his trip and had Adrian Pelt, Director of the League's Information Section, read the speech at the League Pavilion.

Avenol was not long in taking the initiative, and making the most of Hull's reply. At a private meeting of the Council on May 23, he referred to the Hull note and suggested that a study be made of the measures that might render America's proposed collaboration more effective. Avenol formally recommended the establishment of a small expert committee[123] and selected as its chairman Stanley M. Bruce of Australia, one of the League's outstanding economic experts. The group was instructed to examine the League's entire organization of economic and social work, as well as methods for ensuring active collaboration of all nations, meaning essentially the United States. Bruce, in consultation with Avenol, appointed the remaining members.[124]

The Secretary-General recommended even before the Bruce Committee submitted its report that the Organization's technical activities should be separated completely from its political work, and removed from the Council's supervision. He suggested that the technical work be organized on "a semi-autonomous basis under the direction of an executive committee"[125] whose members would be appointed by the League Assembly. Under Avenol's plan, the committee members would be government representatives, rather than independent experts, and as such would have substantial discretion in initiating and organizing the League's economic and social activities. Avenol declared that these were his personal views, and he would not urge them upon the Bruce Committee. However, the thinking on the Committee obviously ran along very similar lines. Sean Lester, the Deputy Secretary-General [recently recalled from Danzig after a three-year term as High Commissioner] asserted that Avenol's policy was to take "only a slight initiative in making suggestions or otherwise guiding the Committee's deliberations".[126] Frank Walters, however, was later to state that "Avenol was the moving spirit behind the entire movement".[127]

There is no question that on this issue the Secretary-General pushed as hard as circumstances would permit. The Bruce Report was made public on August 22, 1939, just ten days before the outbreak of World War II. In all essentials, it embodied Avenol's suggestions for a new economic and

[123] *National Archives,* 500.C/974, May 24, 1939.
[124] Besides Bruce, the "Special Committee with regard to the Development of International Cooperation in Economic and Social Affairs" consisted of Harold Butler of Great Britain, formerly the Director of I.L.O. and at the time the Warden of Nuffield College, Oxford; Carl J. Hambro, President of the Norwegian Parliament, and Chairman of the Supervisory Commission; Charles Rist of France, a professor of Political Economy at the Law Faculty of the University of Paris and one of the leading financial experts in France; Maurice Bourquin of Belgium, a professor at the University of Geneva; Dr. Francisco Tudela of Peru, a former Minister of Foreign Affairs; and Professor K. Varvaressos of Greece, a Deputy Governor of the Bank of Greece, and professor of political economy at the University of Athens.
[125] *National Archives,* 500.C/982, July 28, 1939.
[126] *National Archives,* 500.C/980, July 20, 1939.
[127] Interview of July 2, 1966, at Grenoble, France.

148

social structure. It was proposed that a Central Committee for Economic and Social Questions be established for purposes of exercising control over the specialized agencies, and open to League Members and non-Member States alike. The war, of course, prevented its functioning, but the underlying concept for the United Nations Economic and Social Council had been born.

The Secretary-General was quite anxious that the 1939 Assembly approve the Bruce Committee's Report, and establish the new Central Committee. Such approval might have been impossible as the war made a full meeting of the Assembly not only difficult for delegates, but sensitive politically for Switzerland as host country. Bern wished to fulfill its obligations to the League, but certainly not at the price of antagonizing Germany, and it was clear that nothing of political importance could take place in the Assembly. Avenol therefore devised a possible method of approval for the Bruce Report failing full Assembly ratification. He contemplated calling a conference of states, both Members and non-Members of the League, to draw up a protocol to implement the Report's principles, particularly the establishment of the Central Committee.[128] An alternative he had in mind was calling the Fourth Committee as the continuation of the 1938 Fourth Committee. This body would adopt the budget for 1940, and then formally accept (after a transformation into the Second Committee) the Bruce Report.

Avenol considered the Report's recommendations as absolutely essential to the further functioning of the League. He spoke to U.S. Consul Harold Tittmann on November 17, 1939 of the "necessity of creating the Central Committee as soon as possible",[129] arguing that of the three principal League organs, only the Secretariat could function, as the Council and Assembly were finished because of the war. The Secretariat was a civil service body only, while the several economic and social committees were advisory bodies without the Council direction that was constitutionally necessary. It followed for Avenol that if the Central Committee could not be established, "the League might as well close down".[130]

The limited Assembly that met did approve the 1940 budget and the Bruce Report, and the Central Committee was formally established, although it was clear that the war would prevent its functioning. Avenol appreciated that Germany, Italy, and Japan would refuse to take part, although he believed that eventually Japan might be the most willing of the three to cooperate in technical fields. The most substantial hope was that the United States would join.

The Secretary-General wrote a year later that he had had "the great hope of creating out of the League a new organization, much more adapted

128 *National Archives,* 500.C/993, Oct. 31, 1939.
129 *National Archives,* 500.C111/1116, Nov. 17, 1939.
130 *Ibid.*

to the world situation, since the League had become useless by the lack of employment of the political institutions of 1919".[131] While this was not to be, the United Nations Economic and Social Council is the result of Avenol's plans for a technically directed League, and without doubt, constitutes his greatest contribution as Secretary-General to the cause of international organization and cooperation. Avenol was first and foremost an economic and financial technician, and it was befitting that his most significant contribution should have been in the area he knew best, and in which he was best qualified to serve.

The League's Last Political Action—The Expulsion of the Soviet Union

If Secretary-General Avenol was the driving force behind the movement for a new world-wide economic and social structure, this was due primarily to the League's inability to deal with political questions and Avenol's desire to maintain a League of Nations. Yet at the end of 1939 the League took another important political action by expelling the Soviet Union for its unprovoked attack on Finland, with the main effort and inspiration underlying the action provided by the Secretary-General. The Soviet attack, after more than a year of negotiations for territorial exchanges considered essential by Moscow for its defenses in time of war, came on November 30, 1939. The League had never considered the expulsion of Japan or Italy for their acts of aggression, but the inconsistency counted for little.

Avenol, on one of his frequent trips to Paris, was invited by the U.S. Ambassador to France, William Bullitt, to visit the American Embassy to discuss the matter. Bullitt proposed to the Secretary-General, and Avenol readily agreed, that the attack on Finland provided an excellent opportunity to expel the Soviet Union from the League. The step would perhaps add to the Organization's prestige, and to Avenol's at the same time. The Secretary-General returned at once to Geneva and requested Thanassis Aghnides to take charge of the matter.

United States Consul Harold Tittmann saw Avenol on the afternoon of December 1, 1939, and reported that the Secretary-General "was full of the ideas he had gained from conversations [in Paris] with various personalities including Ambassador Bullitt".[132] Avenol asserted that his conversations in Paris and his own conviction brought him to the conclusion that "it was his duty to bring about a situation... that would result in the expulsion or the separation of Russia from the League of Nations".[133] If

---

[131] Letter from Avenol to Frank Boudreau of the United States, Sept. 8, 1940; quoted in Stephen M. Schwebel, *The Secretary-General of the United Nations* (Cambridge: Harvard University Press, 1952), p. 216.
[132] *National Archives,* 500.C001/1432, Dec. 1, 1939.
[133] *Ibid.*

there were to be no meeting of the Council or Assembly in the near future, "it was up to the Secretary-General to take the initiative". Tittmann's report indicates the strength of Avenol's feeling on the issue:

He stated that his indignation was so strong that he could not deliver the usual address at the meeting as long as the Russian delegates were present and intimated that his address instead would take the form of a denunciation of Russia.

The Secretary-General spoke with great vigor and determination with no semblance of his usual caution.[134]

The Secretary-General received an appeal from the Finnish Government under Articles 11 and 15 of the Covenant, and thus convoked the Council for December 11. The entire procedure was apparently worked out by Avenol himself. He informed Tittmann of his initiative in bringing about Finland's appeal, and declared that without his "encouragement", the appeal would not have been made.[135] Avenol also recommended the procedure that was subsequently utilized, i.e., an Assembly report followed by Council action. He said that while the Council was competent to take the action alone, he preferred an accompanying Assembly recommendation since its approval of the expulsion would carry greater weight. The Secretary-General argued that while there was a possibility that Council members "would not have courage enough to take the necessary action for the expulsion of Russia", he did not consider this probable because "unlike previous instances of aggression that had come before the League, opinion for such action seemed to be unanimous in the present case".[136]

In sum, the Secretary-General according to Tittmann's understanding, "was most anxious to have Russia's expulsion take place. He felt that such action would serve to increase immeasurably the prestige of the League".[137] The U.S. Consul reported further that he was "becoming increasingly convinced that the present resumption of political activity of the League of Nations is due entirely to the efforts of the Secretary-General".[138] He asserted that the extent to which Avenol "played a lone

134 *Ibid.*
135 *National Archives,* 500.C001/1438, Dec. 3, 1939. Avenol's action here consisted in urging the Finnish Minister in Paris to try to persuade his Government to send a formal appeal to the League. Avenol reported that before he left Paris (where he had talked with U.S. Ambassador William Bullitt) he had had no assurances that the appeal would be forthcoming. Upon his return to Geneva on December 1st, 1939, he found the Finnish delegate "too upset" to take action, and found that direct communication between Geneva and Helsinki was not possible. Avenol thought that no Assembly meeting would take place, but he devised an alternative plan under which a meeting of the Fourth Committee scheduled for December 4th would result in the separation of Russia from the League. On December 3, the appeal from Finland came, and the Secretary-General was thus legally obligated to call a meeting of the Council. (See *National Archives,* 500.C111/1119, December 6, 1939.)
136 *National Archives,* 500.C001/1438, Dec. 3, 1939.
137 *Ibid.*
138 *National Archives,* 500.C111/1119, Dec. 6, 1939. Tittmann went on to say that "With the League discredited and sinking into a state of torpor, Avenol, taking ad-

hand" in the move to expel the Soviet Union was not generally realized in Geneva, and that political risks were involved in the maneuver:

As [Avenol's] role becomes progressively clearer to the public the approbation he may receive as the champion of a popular cause will necessarily be tempered by the criticism of those who find an Assembly meeting at this time a source of embarrassment. Events will soon reveal, however, whether or not his decision to take the action he did was a wise one.[139]

The Secretary-General did have obstacles to overcome. The Swiss Government, under pressure from Berlin, was obviously worried over the Assembly session due to meet on December 9, and informed Avenol of its wish that the agenda include no political items except the Finnish-Russian issue, and that the public discussion of even that question be kept to a minimum. Bern intimated to the Secretary-General that if other questions were raised and resulted in public discussions embarrassing to the Government, in term of maintaining its neutrality, it might be forced to ask the League to leave Switzerland. Avenol then outlined a plan under which the Russian-Finnish question would be referred by the Assembly to a committee that would hold secret sessions.[140]

Another problem for the Secretary-General was the attitude of the Finnish Government. The Finns were in no mood to antagonize the Soviet Union still further, and indeed, Finnish Foreign Minister Välnö A. Tanner informed the Scandinavian powers of his opposition to the expulsion plan. The Secretary-General was evidently upset by this, for he requested Tittmann to see the Finnish Minister to Paris, Harri Holma, who was in Geneva at the time, in order to "bring Tanner into line".[141] This was rejected as inappropriate by Tittmann, whereupon Avenol requested that the conversation be reported to the State Department in the hope that the Finnish Minister in Washington might be persuaded to take some acion. It was clear that the Secretary-General wanted nothing to stand in the way of his drive to expel the Soviet Union.

The Assembly, on December 14, pronounced its verdict against the Russian aggression, declaring that the Soviet Union had placed itself out-

---

vantage of the unique opportunity offered by the widespread indignation caused by the Russian attack on Finland, aroused himself to action and is now making a determined effort to restore the institution as an active moral force and thus augment the chances of its maintenance and perhaps even its usefulness during the period of the war. In evolving his plan to expel Russia from the League one way or another, the genesis of which may be traced to his conversations in Paris last week, the indications are that Avenol limited his consultations to the minimum and purposely refrained from approaching the British or any other governments which might show reluctance although he undoubtedly received informal encouragement from several quarters in Paris". (*Ibid.*)

139 *Ibid.*

140 *National Archives,* 500.C111/1121, Dec. 7, 1939.

141 *National Archives,* 500.C001/1447, Dec. 9, 1939.

side the Covenant. The Council later the same day formally expelled the Soviet Union from the League, the only such case in League history. It was clearly not an action that would antagonize Japan, or Germany, or Italy.

The Secretary-General's role thenceforward was primarily administrative. The Assembly called upon League members to provide Finland with "such material and humanitarian assistance as may be in its power", and the Secretary-General was authorized to organize the assistance, and to consult with non-Member states "with a view to possible cooperation". After some hesitation,[142] Avenol dispatched telegrams to League members, and consulted with the chief non-Member, the United States. For some three months several Members and the United States provided assistance to Finland, but by the beginning of March, 1940, the Finns' resistance collapsed, and Russian demands were met. The League's and the Secretary-General's role abruptly came to a halt.

Avenol had demonstrated his capacity for very strong political action so long as it was not inconsistent with the appeasement strategy he had so long supported. The evidence available seems to indicate he was motivated by a desire to increase his own, as well as the League's prestige by driving the Soviet Union out of the Organization, and neither political nor legal difficulties were permitted to stand in his way. It was an error, of course, for the war that had already begun in Europe had reduced the League to a symbol of its former structure and function, and the only remaining question was how to maintain some form of non-political international organization in the midst of the raging Second World War. Neither the League nor Secretary-General Avenol gained from a program that might better have been applied several years earlier.

The Princeton Transfer

In the spring of 1940, only a month after Finland's resistance to the Soviet Union finally collapsed, the "phony" war became real in Europe. German armies invaded and occupied Denmark, Norway, Luxemburg, the Netherlands, and Belgium, and in June, 1940, France fell. At the same time, Italy

---

[142] According to one highly placed League Secretariat official, Avenol seemed to lose all interest in the project after the expulsion, and indeed, indicated that he had turned against it. Thannasis Aghnides had drafted the text of the communication to all League Members, and presented it at a Directors' Meeting. The Secretary-General, according to the former League official, appeared angry, refused to sign it, and said the message would never be sent. Aghnides later went to La Pelouse, the home of the League Secretary-General adjoining the Palais des Nations, and insisted that since the Assembly had made its decision, it would be impossible to have a "dereliction of duty". The Secretary-General signed the message. The former League official attributed Avenol's sudden opposition to the project to the fact that Ambassador Bullitt, who had gone "very far in flattering Avenol", now showed no more interest in him.

declared war on Britain and France. The League was now almost totally isolated in Geneva, and Switzerland could not be certain that it would not be occupied as well. Indeed, it seemed for a period that the German invasion of France would come through Switzerland.

With the League insecure in a Geneva under state of alert and under pressure from Bern, Deputy Secretary-General Sean Lester obtained a camion, loaded onto it a selection made by Aghnides of the more confidential League files, and sent it to Vichy in unoccupied France. Then the invasion by German armies came through the north of France, and pressure on Switzerland eased. Shortly thereafter, the German drive seemed to threaten even Vichy, and Lester returned the files to Geneva only a few days after they had been removed from the Palais des Nations.[143] Swiss pressure also abated as Bern was not anxious to give the impression of fearing an imminent German invasion.

It was clear, however, that the League Secretariat had entered a new period of crisis. Economy cuts were still being made, naturally, and the entire staff now numbered little more than one hundred persons. Avenol had Aghnides prepare circulars that in effect requested all Secretariat members to offer their resignations as part of the general retrenchment.[143a] According to former League officials, one idea here was to accept the resignations of those the Secretary-General disliked, and most particularly, the British nationals. League Secretariat officers considered that one of the strongest motives was to eliminate Sean Lester, although Lester was forewarned, and of course, stayed on. Many Secretariat staff members had been mobilized, or had joined their own governments for other reasons. Arthur Sweetser wrote at the time that the Administration "did all it could to encourage departures", but that

The dearth of leadership and inspiration was unbelievable; the office seemed without soul. One who had known the Secretariat in the old days of its glory would not have thought it could have sunk so low.[144]

At the end of May, 1940, Frank Walters resigned from the Secretariat and returned to England, announcing to his colleagues on the staff that his

---

[143] Letter from Lester to Arthur Sweetser, May 15, 1946.

[143a] The most important of the circulars were 41.1940, May 10. 1940; 43.1940, May 15, 1940; and 49.1940, June 25, 1940. The first of these circulars contains the following paragraph:

1. The headquarters of the Secretariat remain in Geneva, but it is not the intention of the Administration to oblige members of the staff to remain at Geneva against their wishes. Those who desire to do so are free, both morally and administratively, to ask for the suspension of their contracts; or, if they so wish, to resign. Such requests will be granted on the terms already laid down by the Assembly.

The last of the circulars noted above contains a statement to be subscribed to by the Secretariat members, in which they ask to resign, the resignation to be accepted or not according to the needs of the Secretariat.

[144] Arthur Sweetser, "Exit Geneva", May 1940.

departure was for personal reasons and unconnected with the war. Walters had obviously been unhappy with the paucity of meaningful work in Geneva, but he insisted that

The Secretariat has still its place in the world and its work to do; and after more than twenty-one years in its ranks I am convinced that if any real form of international collaboration can be maintained or rebuilt after the war the Secretariat will from the first, by public opinion and by the Governments also, be called upon to play a central part.[145]

On May 29, Walters, in a last note to Avenol, affirmed that despite his retirement, he remained at the disposal of the Secretary-General "for any assistance that I could possibly give to the work of the Secretariat, which will never cease, so long as I live, to be my spiritual home".[146] The top-level staff of the League Secretariat now consisted only of Avenol, Aghnides, and Lester.

Given the threat of German invasion, and Geneva's isolation, it was evident that if the Secretariat, as the only functioning League body, were to achieve anything during the war, it would necessitate a location other than Geneva. Indeed, as noted above,[147] in April, 1939, Avenol had already revealed his consideration of the possibility of establishing the Economic and Financial Section "somewhere on the American continent". That section's work was completely dependent upon free communication with many nations, and this had become impossible from Geneva. Avenol was insistent in May and June, 1940, however, that the seat of the League remain in Geneva, and this insistence was to form the basis of strong opposition to the notion that the League technical work move to the United States.

Arthur Sweetser, almost immediately after his return to America from Geneva at the end of May, 1940, initiated consultations on the possibility of transferring the Organization's technical sections to Princeton University. He had earlier begun preliminary talks on the matter in Geneva, but from the beginning, Avenol's resistance to any move was apparent. Sweetser reported on a meeting he held on June 7 with officials at Princeton, the Institute for Advanced Study, the Princeton branch of the Rockefeller Institute, and the Rockefeller Foundation. It had been agreed that the idea of a move from Geneva to Princeton would be put before the Boards of Trustees of these institutions. But on June 9, Sweetser received a telegram from René Charron, a French official on the League Secretariat, stating that Avenol had decided to maintain the entire Secretariat at Geneva unless actually compelled to leave, and that he could not consent to the plans outlined by

[145] Statement by Frank Walters to the Secretariat, May 27, 1940; Library of the Palais des Nations, Geneva.
[146] Letter from Walters to Avenol, May 29, 1940.
[147] See page 145, *supra.*

Sweetser. The projected move involved only a handful of officials and their families.

By June 12, however, after Washington approved, the official invitation was sent. The carefully worded cable to the Secretary-General made no mention of the legal seat of the League, but requested Avenol to "consider the possibility of removing the technical sections of the Secretariat, including both the personnel and the records, to Princeton, New Jersey, for such period as may prove to be advisable".[148]

On June 13, Avenol called in U.S. Consul Harold Tittmann, and told him that the invitation could not be accepted. The seat of the League was Geneva and it would not be abandoned. To do so would be to "desert our duty" and would mean grave "moral prejudice". The Secretary-General also raised with Tittmann the question of the international status of the officials concerned, and contended he had no right to take a decision depriving them of that status.[149] Avenol replied to Princeton on June 15 that he had no power even provisionally to change the seat of the Organization "unless the initiative were taken by one or more states" and the final decision would be subject to approval by League Members.

Pressure on the Secretary-General to accept the invitation was immediate. The U.S. Government had no objection to the Princeton invitation, although there were serious doubts in the State Department concerning the possibility of diplomatic status for League officials. The British Government urged acceptance, as did all the Dominion Governments, and Norway. Carl Hambro, Chairman of the Supervisory Commission, cabled Avenol that the Princeton move would not entail a transfer of the League's seat, but simply the establishment of a working center for technical activities rendered impossible by Geneva's isolation.

At a long meeting on June 28 with Sir David Kelly, the British Minister in Bern, the Secretary-General again defended his position. He denied that he had refused the invitation, and maintained that

The value of the work done by the technical services was chiefly due to the fact that their international status enabled them to obtain from Governments, through the Secretary-General, such data as no private institution had so far been able to procure.

---

148 The invitation, signed by Harold W. Dodds, President of Princeton, Carl Ten-Broeck, a Director of the Rockefeller Institute for Medical Research, and Frank Aydelotte, Director of the Institute for Advanced Study, cited the accomplishments of the League technical sections, and the fears for the work and the trained personnel caused by the hostilities surrounding Geneva. "We are extending this invitation because of the great importance which we attach to the scientific and scholarly work of the technical sections of the League. We understand the difficulty of building up such an effective personnel as these sections now contain, and are most eager that they should not be dispersed and that the work of these sections may not be interrupted by the war".

149 Memorandum of conversation between Avenol and Tittmann, June 13, 1940; Sweetsers papers.

Had the Secretary-General immediately accepted to send his technical staff to the U.S.A., that staff, as from the time they disembarked in America, would be treated as private persons by the U.S. authorities. He, as Secretary-General, had no authority therefore to bring about such a fundamental change in the status of those international officials, a change inevitably bound to detract from the value of their work so much that that work would be reduced to the level of any other unofficial academic publications, produced all over the world by other eminent statisticians and experts.[150]

Finally, Avenol insisted, it was for the American Government to decide "whether it could, if not actually invite all or part of the Secretariat, at least to authorise such transfer as is implied by the invitation of the Princeton University, such authorisation involving the safeguarding of the international status of our officials".[151]

The problems posed by the Secretary-General were of fundamental importance, but he did not appear at all disposed to solve them. Essentially, his attitude was one of disapproval. When asked by the British Minister if the League budget would contribute in case there should be a transfer to Princeton, Avenol responded that he had no right "to spend money for which one could not expect any returns". The reply to this was that perhaps the British Goverment might contribute beyond its normal quota, whereupon Avenol declared he could not "contemplate asking any Government for fresh funds for so uncertain a purpose".[152]

Avenol met with Tittmann the same day, and repeated the substance of his arguments. He maintained that the question was not so much the diplomatic privileges of the officials concerned, as it was the maintenance of their international status "which alone enabled them to communicate with States officially".[153] Following Tittmann's report of this conversation to the State Department, Secretary of State Cordell Hull wired back on June 29, 1940, that the U.S. Government could not extend a formal invitation. Citing the necessity of obtaining Congressional approval, which he thought impossible, Hull cast doubt on the entire project with the statement that

in spite of the great interest of this government in the technical and non-political work of the League, serious doubt is held in the Department that the transfer of the technical sections to this country would be entirely understood and approved by members of the Congress and by large sections of the people of the United States.[154]

Avenol immediately brought Hull's reply to the attention of the British.

Meanwhile, Carl Hambro, who was in New York, wired Avenol again, urging him to accept. He conceded that major questions of principle could

---

[150] Memorandum of conversation between Avenol and British Minister Kelly at Geneva, June 27, 1940; Sweetsers papers.
[151] *Ibid.*
[152] *Ibid.*
[153] Memorandum of conversation between Avenol and Tittmann, June 27, 1940; Sweetsers papers.
[154] *FRUS 1940,* Vol. II, pp. 320-321.

not be resolved, but that acceptance was justified as a provisional emergency measure to make unhampered continuance of the technical work possible.

On July 12, 1940, after further consultations with the State Department, a new invitation was issued from Princeton. The difficulties were characterized as formal rather than real, and the conditions at Princeton described as more favorable for the work of the Economic and Financial Section than those in Geneva, despite the legal limitations. In almost pleading terms, the second invitation affirmed that the legal seat would remain in Geneva and with the understanding that after the war, the personnel would return to Geneva. "Surely the League has power to authorize part of its personnel to proceed to the United States on mission..."

Avenol did not reply at once, and the following two weeks (just prior to Avenol's resignation announcement) witnessed rather intense conflict in the Secretariat between Avenol, on the one hand, and Alexander Loveday, head of the Economic, Financial and Transit Section, and Sean Lester on the other. Loveday and Lester of course favored the move; Avenol did not. He was convinced that Germany and Italy would triumph and reorganize Europe with a new League that would exclude Britain and the United States, and a transfer to Princeton would associate Washington far too closely with the Organization at a time of revolutionary change in Europe. The Secretary-General who had done so much to emphasize and improve the economic and technical work of the League now relied upon legal formalities in war-time to prevent that work from being carried forward, and only to maintain his position in the new order. Vichy's sudden insistence that he resign altogether, however, made further opposition rather pointless.

Hambro, still in the United States, reported to Avenol that the facilities at Princeton and the working conditions were "perfect", and that support would be forthcoming from the remaining League members, and from the Rockefeller Foundation. Reluctantly, the Secretary-General, on July 26, 1940, gave his consent to the move and at the same time, under instructions from Vichy, announced his resignation to take effect at the end of August, 1940. Avenol cabled to President Dodds of Princeton that he was authorizing Loveday and the collaborators he considered essential for the work to proceed to the United States "on mission".

On July 30, Avenol formally instructed Loveday that the mission did not involve a transfer of the headquarters of the Economic, Financial, and Transit Department, which remained at Geneva. Further,

[t]he work normally incumbent on this Department will be carried on at Geneva, your mission being to make studies of world economic problems. For this purpose, you are authorised to carry on such correspondence of a technical character as may be required.[155]

---

[155] League Archives 1933-1940, 18B/40469/37845, July 30, 1940.

The staff at Princeton was placed under the direct authority of Loveday, to whom the Secretary-General's powers were delegated for that purpose. With minor exceptions, the staff continued to be subject to the provisions of their contracts and of the League Staff Regulations. Locally hired staff were not to be Secretariat members.

By the second week in August, Loveday, seven other officials of his Department, and their families arrived at Princeton. They had travelled by bus from Geneva through the south of France, and after a delay caused by a minor accident at Grenoble, continued on through Spain to Lisbon and from there to the United States by plane. Thus did the League find a home in the nation that had been so instrumental in creating it some twenty years earlier, and which had then ignored it until its failure.

The Economic and Financial Sections were not the only international bodies to leave Geneva. The League Treasury, under Seymour Jacklin, moved to London, the center of the League's remaining financial support. The International Labor Office transferred its headquarters to Montreal, Canada, where international status was accorded the officials. The League Section dealing with drug traffic came to Washington, D.C. The Palais des Nations in Geneva was no longer the active center of the community of nations.

The role of the Secretary-General in the Princeton transfer was, of course, closely tied to his resignation, which is treated separately. It seemed to most observers at the time that the Secretary-General's reliance upon legal objections to the transfer masked his plan to close down the League altogether if it could not be fitted into the new order. Whether the Pétain regime in France had indicated to Avenol its wish that the League come to an end is not known. In any event, however, if the Organization's technical sections were to serve any useful function at all, the United States seemed much the better location, despite loss of international status. Avenol appreciated this, and his resistance to the transfer must therefore be traced to other motives. This leads to perhaps the most unfortunate event in the history of the League Secretary-General's Office—the resignation of Joseph Avenol.

The Resignation of Secretary-General Avenol and his Attempt to Shut Down the League

From 1938 until Avenol actually resigned in July, 1940, there had been many rumors of impending resignation, but each time they had been denied forcefully. As late as July 6, 1940, the Secretary-General told Tittmann he would prefer to resign, but considered it his duty to remain under the circumstances.[156] At that time he spoke of plans to reduce the League staff to

156 *National Archives*, 500.C/1020, July 6, 1940.

about 40 persons, to close the main building of the Palais des Nations, and to move the remaining offices into the Library. He asserted even then, while the Princeton transfer issue was at its height, that his task was "to maintain a nucleus in being as long as possible".[157] Eleven days later the Secretary-General's attitude appeared to have undergone a complete transformation. On July 17, Tittmann sent a telegram to the U.S. State Department in which he reported that the Secretary-General favored the complete liquidation of the Secretariat, although he cited the possibility that Avenol would defer to other officials (meaning Lester, Aghnides, and Loveday) who wanted to maintain at least a portion of the Organization.[158]

What had occurred in the interim? Avenol had written to the newly installed regime at Vichy, pledged his support to the Pétain authorities, and formally offered his resignation. By mid-July Avenol had received word from Vichy that he was expected to resign. He had no real choice in the matter, but preferred to maintain his position, even if semi-retired and with someone (preferably Aghnides) to act on his behalf. Lester, of course, as an Irishman, would not do. On July 18, 1940, Tittmann reported that Vichy had at first intended to withdraw altogether from the League, but had reconsidered and decided to remain a member. It was also, decided, however, that France would remain inactive, and in accordance with that decision, wrote Tittmann, "it has requested that Avenol resign his position as Secretary-General in view of his French nationality".[159] At the same time, however, René Charron of the Economic and Financial Section, was requested to stay on, and he agreed. Tittmann believed it was unlikely that a new Secretary-General would be appointed to succeed Avenol, but that a committee would administer the League. Pétain had probably concluded that a French Secretary-General would indicate a strong French attachment to the League, and this was not the image Vichy wished to project. On the other hand, to have Charron also resign would have been going too far in the other direction—thus the compromise.

Early in July, 1940, before Avenol's July 6 statement on his intention to remain as Secretary-General, rumors circulated in Geneva that Avenol was preparing to transfer the League properties to the Germans and Italians should they wish to use them, and was simultaneously attempting to force the resignation of the British nationals remaining in the Secretariat. Avenol, according to Tittmann's report of July 6, 1940, "emphatically denied" the rumors. Stephen M. Schwebel, in his "Notes on the Resignation of Joseph Avenol"[160] cites a statement by a former League official that Avenol went to Bern for the purpose of handing over the League to the Nazi and Fascist

157 *Ibid.*
158 *National Archives*, 500.C/1024, July 17, 1940.
159 *National Archives*, 500.C/1025, July 18, 1940.
160 Appendix to *The Secretary-General of the United Nations* (Cambridge: Harvard University Press, 1952), p. 219.

Ambassadors there. This was denied with "considerable indignation" by Avenol. Jean Siotis, in *Essai Sur Le Secrétariat International,* states that "numerous observers of the time" affirmed that Avenol made such an offer to the German and Italian ministers at Bern several weeks before his re-signation.[161] The rumors still persist, although there is no adequate proof.

There is absolutely no question, however, that the Secretary-General believed at this time that Germany and Italy would win the war, and there were significant indications that he welcomed the prospect. One former League official stated flatly to the author that Avenol "was sure the Germans would win the war, and he was very pleased". Another relates the following conversation he had with Avenol just subsequent to the German occupation of Paris: "Avenol stated 'It's all over' and I asked 'what's all over?' He answered 'what the English prevented my country for three hundred years from doing. We should work together with Hitler to expel the English from Europe'. I told him that the British might defeat the Germans in the war, and he replied that they would be 'prostrate in two weeks'. I said the United States might enter the war, and Avenol asked whether I had read of the isolationist sentiment in America. I said there was still the Soviet Union, and Avenol replied that they were allies of the Germans". Avenol's initial fear of war with Germany had given way to the conviction that Hitler could not be defeated, and with war now raging, he did not seem displeased.

On September 1, 1940, the first day after his resignation became effective, Avenol wrote a long letter to Arthur Sweetser in New York in which he argued that "except for Germans and Italians who have a program, a doctrine, and a method, no one seems to me to have one. The expression 'new order' is a slogan, but who can say what it means?" For Avenol, "1941 will remain the starting point of a historic era; it is the end of the world of the 19th Century. We are at the beginning of a great revolution". Furthermore, the German and Italian programs "must not be rejected wholesale; they contain things which one can no longer reject".

The former Secretary-General conceded that "if the war should last too long, Germany's chances, which today must be evaluated at 90%, would decrease greatly".[162] Avenol never specified precisely what portions of the German and Italian programs should not be rejected wholesale, nor why the "revolution" of which he spoke might be characterized as "great". But these were very clearly not the sentiments of a man committed in any manner to the League of Nations.

On July 25, 1940, one day before he finally consented to the Princeton transfer, Avenol announced his intention to resign.[163] He said that up to September 1936 (the date of his famous trip to Rome) he "believed that

---

[161] Jean Siotis, *Essai Sur Le Secrétariat International* (Geneva: Librarie Droz, 1963), pp. 108-109.
[162] Letter from Avenol to Sweetser, Sept. 1, 1940. Sweetser papers.
[163] League of Nations Document C.121.M.111, 1940, July 25, 1940.

certain inevitable reforms" would enable the League to "regroup" the forces that were "moving away from it". While the situation constantly deteriorated, the remaining hope was the establishment, on a wide basis of collaboration, of "great economic, social and humanitarian work". This was thwarted by the war, and since that time it had been his "painful duty" to reduce the expenses of the League because of the declining level of its resources. He stated further that since the Assembly, Council and Committees were unable to meet, the constitutional powers of the Secretary-General were in suspense and that the remaining duties, principally the administration of a small body of staff officials and the management of the League finances, "no longer justify maintenance of the political High Direction, which is no longer consistent with the realities of the situation". He expressed gratitude to League Members who accorded him their good will and confidence, and requested them to "relieve me of the task with which they have entrusted me". He concluded by saying that the date upon which his resignation would become effective would be subsequently announced, and that he was "anxiously considering appropriate measures to ensure that the administration and work of the Secretariat shall continue". He promised proposals on this subject in due course.

On July 26, Carl Hambro, Chairman of the Supervisory Commission, cabled Avenol from Washington and asked him to reconsider. He assured Avenol that his "experience, wisdom and tact" were indispensible for saving the future of the League, that the world organization was of vital importance to a future peaceful settlement, and that the resignation might mean the "final destruction" of the League as an international organ.[164] Sean Lester reacted with great dismay to this message,[165] but Hambro's plea made little difference.

Avenol soon indicated, however, that in fact he did not wish to renounce all his authority. On August 5, Tittmann reported that Avenol had informed him that the resignation would become effective on August 31 but that

he did not contemplate separating himself entirely from the administration of the League of Nations. What Avenol's future position would be or what form the executive authority would take after his resignation was not forthcoming but I gathered, however, that he was not pleased at the present time with the prospect of technical sections of the League of Nations operating elsewhere than Geneva.[166]

But apparently pressure on Avenol from Vichy to withdraw entirely was maintained and by mid-August, the Secretary-General, not very hopeful of retaining any kind of authoritative role at Geneva, found a method for winding up the League altogether. The chosen weapon was the Organization's budget.

---

[164] League Archives 1933-1940, *General and Miscellaneous:* 50/40543/40543.
[165] See p. 179, *infra.*
[166] *National Archives,* 500.C/1034, August 5, 1940.

On August 9, Avenol called a Supervisory Commission Meeting for August 20. On August 16, the Secretary-General addressed a letter to Council President Adolfo Costa du Rels of Boliva. He quoted his resignation letter of July 25th with regard to ensuring "that the administration and work of the Secretariat shall continue" but added "the difficulties that have to be overcome are very serious".[167] In the same August 16 letter Avenol announced his intention to resign as of August 31, stating his willingness to remain at the disposal of the Council President, of the Supervisory Commission, or of any other League body, "for the purpose of any information, explanations, or opinions, for which I might be asked".

Avenol's offer was turned down shortly thereafter. The crucial portion of this document, however, is found in an annex to the August 16th letter. The annex constitutes a report by the Secretary-General on the history of the Princeton transfer and the budget problems for the following year. The report was intended for consideration by the Supervisory Commission, whenever it could meet. The section dealing with the Princeton transfer is a straightforward account of Avenol's negotiations prior to his consent to the transfer, and is in no way controversial. The section of the report on the budget, however, is essentially an argument for the winding up of the League.

"Under what conditions", asked the Secretary-General in his report, "could the budget for 1941 be voted or authorized?" Since the beginning of the League, he argued, it had been acknowledged that the regular vote on the budget required the unanimous approval of all League members, and this had never been lacking. The issue now, of course, was how to obtain that approval when war made it impossible for League political bodies to meet. In 1939 there had been a plenary Assembly, and this allowed for the normal application of the rules. But in 1940, there was no Assembly, no Fourth (Budgetary) Committee, and thus no way to validate the budget. "It is in fact", wrote the Secretary-General, "a generally accepted principle that without a budget or without authorization taking place, *an administration loses all right to spend*".[168]

The same Secretary-General Avenol who refused to let legal problems stand in the way of the Bruce Report approval, or the expulson of the Soviet Union from the League, could find no resolution of the problem he posed. Other monetary accounts of the League provided no solution, he argued. The total in the floating capital account would be exhausted before the end of 1940 and "how and by virtue of what decision will it be re-established?" asked Avenol. Indeed, the Secretary-General wrote in his report, "None of the accounts of the League of Nations can be allocated, without the decision of the Assembly, to uses other than those assigned

[167] League of Nations Document C.131.M.120, 1940, August 24, 1940.
[168] *Id.*, Annex, p. 2. Italics added.

them by the Assembly. One can thus say that without such a decision, they must be considered immobilized".[169]

The Secretary-General's position, then, was that there could be no budget as there was no political body to vote a budget, and existing accounts could not be utilized for other than their originally intended purposes without a decision of a political body. Without a budget, naturally, the League would have to close down altogether, even if there were no formal dissolution.

Avenol's position on the budget and his evident wish to immobilize the League, is highlighted by the "null and void" affair of August 31st, the last day of Avenol's administration. On that day, Sean Lester transmitted to the Council and to the League Members generally a statement agreed upon by Council President Costa du Rels and Avenol. The statement simply declared that the two officials agreed that League document C.131.M.120. 1940 "should be regarded as null and void".[170] The document referred to included Avenol's letter to Costa du Rels of August 16th, the annexes, including Avenol's budget views, and Costa du Rels' reply, which gave no response to the budget argument.

It would seem clear that the document was declared "null and void" for the purpose of preventing Avenol's budget argument from being publicly circulated. There is nothing of substance in Avenol's August 16th letter itself, or in Costa du Rels' reply that cannot be found in other League documents of this period. Only the annexes were different, and of the annexes, only the section on the budget could in any way be regarded as controversial.

Further support for this view is found in the transcription of a telephone message from Sean Lester in Geneva to Carl Hambro in New York, on August 27, 1940.[171] Lester informed Hambro that Avenol's August 16th letter had been distributed as a League document to the Members. However, the message continues, the *annexes* to the letter had been referred to the Supervisory Commission "*but not otherwise circulated. Lester said he attached special importance to this*. The first [annex] refers to finances and in form presented seems to be an *argument for an implied liquidation*".[172]

Lester and Council President Costa du Rels obviously believed that the Secretary-General was endeavouring to dissolve the League. Not wishing to publicize the fact, however, Avenol's budget arguments were not distributed to League Members at all. Yet since his views were set forth in what had already been labelled an annex to a League document distributed to members, and referred to by that document, it seemed natural, if one

---

[169] *Id.*, p. 3.
[170] League of Nations Document C.136.M.125.1940, August 31, 1940.
[171] Transcription made by Arthur Sweetser on August 27, 1940. Sweetser papers.
[172] *Ibid.* Italics added.

wished to prevent circulation of the budget argument altogether, to declare the entire document "null and void".

Why Avenol himself agreed to the "null and void" procedure is not known. He stood alone on the issue as there was a united front against him at this point, and his influence in the Secretariat had been totally destroyed. In addition, he was making demands upon Lester for privileges (office space and allowances) that were not legally due him, and this might have been a factor.

The attempt made by Avenol to shut down the Organization, was, of course, a failure. The Supervisory Commission met at the end of September, 1940, and itself passed a budget for 1941 that was distributed to League members, and there was no dissent. The solution that eluded the Secretary-General was a relatively simple one. Acting Secretary-General Lester wrote to Hambro shortly thereafter that "We are very gratified indeed that a budget has been passed four weeks after it was the declared policy here [Geneva] that it neither should be nor could be".[173]

The Secretary-General who had stressed his wish to "ensure that the administration and work of the Secretariat shall continue" was, in July and August of 1940, opposed to the transfer of the technical sections to a location where they might work effectively, and was opposed to having a budget at all for the League in the war-time emergency. The correspondence that passed between League officials at this time indicates, as might be expected, that the conflict between Avenol on the one hand, and Lester, Aghnides, and Loveday, on the other, was rather intense.

Avenol's attempt to liquidate the League in fact, if not in law, was intertwined with the procedures of his resignation, and his simultaneous request to stay on for limited purposes. On August 20th, Avenol informed the League members that Sean Lester had been Acting Secretary-General since July 26th.[174] Evidently, however, Lester's authority was rather limited, for Loveday declared that Avenol's intention was to give Lester authority on all matters except the budget and the Princeton mission,[175] clearly the two most important current matters.

From this point forward, the only problem for the other Secretariat members was how to accept Avenol's resignation gracefully without making any commitments for the future. On August 21st, Avenol went to Vichy for a week's visit, and during that week, the protocol was worked out. On August 24th, Hambro, still in the United States, wired to Costa du Rels in Geneva a proposed response: August 31st would be accepted as the effective

---

[173] Letter from Lester to Hambro, October 4, 1940. Sweetser papers.
[174] League of Nations Document C.127.M.116.1940, August 20, 1940. This communication also repeated that portion of the Secretary-General's message to Council President Costa du Rels in which Avenol stated that his resignation would be effective as of August 31st, but that he would hold himself at the League's disposal for purposes of information, explanations, or opinions that might be asked of him.
[175] Memorandum by Arthur Sweetser, August 25, 1940. Sweetser papers.

date of the resignation; the offer to be at the disposal of the Supervisory Commission was "highly appreciated"; and note should be taken that Lester was automatically the Acting Secretary-General.

It was hoped by Hambro that Costa du Rels, Lester and Avenol would work together, but this proved impossible due to Avenol's trip to Vichy. Thus there were separate acceptances of the resignation by Costa du Rels, as Council President, and Hambro in his capacity as President of the Assembly and Chairman of the Supervisory Commission. None of the League Members replying to Avenol's original letter of resignation raised any question.

The only demands made by Avenol, according to Lester, were the right to stay on for a time at La Pelouse, the Secretary-General's official residence, the assignment of two secretaries, and the sum of sixty francs per day. Lester agreed on the condition that such rights were understood to be temporary and not permanent.[176] Avenol accepted this and also agreed, upon his return from Vichy, to the "null and void" declaration.

Lester considered it important that Hambro and Costa du Rels accept the resignation in more careful terms than Hambro had proposed. Lester's view was that Avenol, "in taking his action at the request of his government did so reluctantly and with the *arrière pensée* of keeping control".[177] Hambro agreed, and his official message of August 27th simply conveyed his acceptance of August 31st as the effective date, and of the devolution of the duties of Secretary-General to Sean Lester.[178] The "highly appreciated" wording was eliminated, and Avenol was thereby informed that his offer to remain at the League's disposal had been declined.

Joseph Avenol thus ended a seven-year administration as Secretary-General on August 31st, 1940, and Sean Lester became the "Acting Secretary-General", a title he was to keep until 1946. The Secretary-General had always been a symbol of the League, and the one official who might be said to stand for the entire organization. At a time when the League had little more than symbols, Joseph Avenol weakened it still further by destroying one of its primary offices.

Whether his attempt to wind up the League was also made at the request of the Pétain regime at Vichy is not known. As to the resignation, it would appear that this step was taken at Vichy's request. Why did Avenol comply? There were, to be sure, the several reasons articulated in his original resignation letter of July 25th. The Secretary-General's powers were in fact in a state of suspense, the League had failed on all fronts, with even the future for technical activities being dim, an idle Secretariat would only

---

[176] Memorandum of telephone conversation between Lester (at Geneva) and Sweetser (at New York), August 25, 1940. Sweetser papers.
[177] Telephone message from Lester to Hambro, Geneva-New York, August 27, 1940; transcription made by Arthur Sweetser. Sweetser papers.
[178] League of Nations Document C.134.M.123.1940, August 29, 1950.

"degenerate",[179] and Avenol did not wish to remain as the "privileged beneficiary"[180] of the economies he had carried out.

The isolation of the Office, particularly after the break in diplomatic relations between Great Britain and France, was also cited by the Secretary-General as one of his primary reasons.[181] Perhaps most important of all, however, was his loyalty to Vichy France. "In this heartbreaking hour, I found ease in the simplest duty: being faithful to my country".[182]

There were, obviously, different ways of remaining faithful to one's country, as many Frenchman were then demonstrating. But the question remains whether loyalty to his country or to the international organization he serves (assuming conflict between the two) is the more proper focus for a Secretary-General. The question is of critical importance at a time of crisis, and will be answered in accordance with the political views of the Secretary-General confronting the challenge.

Joseph Avenol felt no overriding attachment to the League of Nations, and when the Organization had reached the end of its usefulness, he not only abandoned it, but endeavored to destroy even its symbolic value to the international community. At a time of war and under pressure from occupied France, Avenol's reaction was understandable, but it is perhaps not asking too much of the world organization's highest official that his first devotion be to his international obligations.

The Afterward

There is little evidence of Avenol's plans after his resignation. One of his first acts was to write a long letter to Arthur Sweetser in New York, setting out his general views and stating that perhaps he would "travel outside of Europe".[183] This seemed to imply a desire to come to the United States, perhaps even to Princeton.

Avenol finally had some kind words for Princeton. "If Princeton", he wrote, "instead of being simply an asylum for refugee officials, should become the focal point for preparation for the future, then its role could be great".[184] Indeed, he went so far as to ask

Why shouldn't Princeton University become a center of studies, calling not only upon the officials of the Secretariat, who will necessarily have a great deal of trouble in thinking outside of their customary surroundings, but who would bring great experience to it, as well as new, carefully selected elements.[185]

---

[179] Letter from Avenol to Sweetser, Sept. 1, 1940. Sweetser papers.
[180] Schwebel, *op. cit.*, p. 220.
[181] *Id.*, pp. 220-221.
[182] *Id.*, p. 221.
[183] Letter from Avenol to Sweetser, Sept. 1, 1940. Sweetser papers.
[184] *Ibid.*
[185] *Ibid.*

Sweetser discouraged Avenol at once, however, and in fact the former Secretary-General never travelled outside of Europe.

After a short stay at Vichy, he lived in the Haute-Savoie until early January, 1944, when he returned to Switzerland after receiving warning that the Germans were about to deport him. He obtained political refuge from the Swiss Government, but was warned to abstain from all political activities. In Switzerland, at Duillier sur Nyon in the Canton of Vaud, near Geneva, Avenol lived quietly, and in almost total isolation, until his death in 1952.

The former Secretary-General's only activity was a moderate amount of writing. Aside from defenses of himself written to a few former League officials, and to Geneva newspapers, Avenol published in 1944 a small volume entitled *L'Europe Silencieuse.*[186] He now wrote on the assumption that Germany and Italy would not win the war, and there was nothing more heard of a "new order" or of a "great revolution" or of German and Italian "programs" that "contain things which one can no longer reject".

Avenol concentrated on the future organization of Europe, one that would eliminate tarriff barriers, while maintaining individual sovereignty, constitutions, and administrative organizations. He called for a European police force to act against aggression, and proposed a Council of Europe for purposes of defining principles of action and bases of authority and responsibility. Technical details were to be handled in committee, but the basic coordination of the several European economies would be arranged by the Council. Avenol was confident that Europe, now "like a lost continent" would "find itself", and that while the process might be complicated, the common interest would win over old memories. The book was published just after the liberation of Paris.

Every analysis so far made of Avenol's administration has been highly critical, and no defense has been forthcoming save one. Vera Lever, onetime private secretary and mistress to Avenol, wrote to Stephen Schwebel on February 9th, 1952, shortly before Avenol's death, setting forth in brief terms her comments on the accepted image of the League's second Secretary-General. Miss Lever wrote of a "campaign" against Avenol that had the benefit of a "war psychosis" enabling it "to spread with all the distortions attached to it by certain people for their own aims".[187] She wrote that Avenol lived in isolation by his own choice. Military men who shared his views in 1940 might continue their careers, but politicians without the support of a party, had to "intrigue", and this the former Secretary-General would not do. Concerning his relations with the Quai d'Orsay, Miss Lever wrote

---

[186] Editions de la Bacernière, Neuchatel, 1944.
[187] Letter from Vera Lever to Stephen M. Schwebel, February 9, 1952.

although he was always considered there with the greatest respect his total independence was not always appreciated, and this all the more gave him as S.G. of the League a far greater international vision than Sir E. Drummond had. M. Avenol cherished this independence of his above everything, and he kept himself too aloof from other people to be popular. This attitude gained him special esteem and respect from all delegations whilst he was S.G., but of course on the other hand left him isolated when he resigned. You are right in saying he was not a politician in the French sense of the word...but he was a diplomatist.[188]

For Miss Lever, the resignation was a "purely personal, patriotic act", taken under "no pressure whatever". She insisted that Avenol "perfectly understood and shared the real feelings of his country" and that "a great majority of French people in 1940" felt as he did. She quoted with approval Anthony Eden's statement on the day of the liberation of Paris: "We who have not been occupied by foreign armies have no right to judge those who have".

Secretary-General Avenol has been judged, nevertheless, and harshly, by whose with whom he worked, perhaps because in large measure he demonstrated so little sympathy with the ideals of the League and its Covenant long before France was occupied by foreign armies.

It is extremely difficult, however, to provide an accurate analysis of Avenol's political views. The available evidence provides no clear answer to the question of the extent of his commitment to League norms. Throughout the years of his administration, there is no question that he feared war with Germany, and was devoted, at least until 1936, to peaceful solutions to European problems. At the same time, however, he indicated a certain ambivalence toward the totalitarian states. Until the famous trip to Rome in 1936, he is represented as believing that the democracies of Europe had to stand together (and with Italy, if possible) to resist Germany. Subsequently, Avenol gives the impression of sympathizing more strongly with Berlin and Rome. One is never quite certain where the Secretary-General stood, and indeed, it is not clear that Avenol himself was certain.

Of course he was far more discreet in his public pronouncements than in private statements to Secretariat colleagues. The total impression gained, however, is a sum of conflicting perceptions and emotional biases that gradually shifted in the later 1930's, until by September, 1940, Avenol felt able to describe Europe as at the beginning of a "great revolution". "Conflicts" is a word that crops up repeatedly in correspondence among Secretariat colleagues to describe Avenol, and the phrase "moral collapse" was just as frequently used at the end of, and subsequent to, Avenol's administration.

The harsh judgments of the men who knew Avenol best were not based entirely on his political views, to be sure, but also on what was perceived to be his failure to carry out adequately the functions of his Office. With the

[188] *Ibid.*

exception of the Bruce Report and certain early administrative changes, none of his colleagues have been willing to credit him with positive achievements during his years as Secretary-General, whether in terms of political leadership, development of the Office, or strengthening international organization generally.

In 1946, further criticism was directed against the former Secretary-General at the last Assembly of the League of Nations, and there was no one to defend. When Avenol died, on September 2, 1952, little notice was taken by the press or by governments, and in sharp contrast to the death of Sir Eric Drummond, there was no tribute at the United Nations.

There can be little question that the Office of the Secretary-General suffered at the hands of Joseph Avenol. The Office had been very successfully established by Sir Eric Drummond, for given the constitutional and political limits within which he was forced to work, the League's first Secretary-General demonstrated that an administrative leader, if well-informed, conscientious, and devoted to the Organization, can inspire confidence and trust sufficient to enable him to perform an important political role.

This is not to say that Drummond did all that he might for the Office. His shy, retiring nature, and his preference for the behind-the-scenes methods of the British civil service were not calculated to thrust him into a commanding position of political leadership. But above all, Drummond was knowledgeable, thereby giving his opinions great weight among both Secretariat aides and League delegations, and his impartiality and discretion easily gained him the confidence of most political figures of his day.

Joseph Avenol exhibited almost none of the characteristics essential for the further development of the Office, shared Drummond's more inhibitive traits, worked within the same narrow constitutional limits and served at a time of intense conflict that destroyed the League and greatly aggravated for international civil servants the fundamental contradiction between loyalty to nation and to international organization. The result was a clear loss for the position of the Secretary-General.

Avenol's public role, of course, was as severely limited as Drummond's. He rarely spoke to the Council, and almost never on political matters. In the Assembly, his appearances were usually before the Fourth (Administrative and Budget) Committee, and his presentations were not likely to touch on political questions. There was no Article 99 for the League Secretary-General, enabling him to bring to the attention of the Council on his own initiative any matter which in his opinion threatened the maintenance of international peace and security. Nor was it the custom for him to hold press conferences in which he might articulate his own perceptions of world problems and recommend possible terms of settlement or negotiation for international disputes. Avenol delivered some public addresses, but as in the case of Sir Eric, these were couched in formal terms, confined themselves to League structure, or to non-controversial aspects of League issues and activity. Avenol, perhaps a bit more than Drummond, touched on graver questions of politics, but in extremely cautious terms, and never in a manner likely to offend a government. Neither Drummond nor Avenol ever publicly disagreed with a particular state position on any important international dispute.

In addition to this, Avenol was also a shy and retiring individual, and like Drummond, not temperamentally capable of assuming a leadership role akin to that of the International Labor Office's Albert Thomas. In two senses then, Avenol shared with Drummond a set of circumstances that severely restricted his capacity to develop the Secretary-General's Office—legal and constitutional restrictions, and personal inhibitions.

Beyond these points, however, the comparison changes swiftly, and again, both publicly and privately. Drummond was Secretary-General during the time of the League's success, and while his administration lasted long enough to witness the economic depression spread over the world, and the Japanese attack in China, Drummond resigned before it was entirely clear that the League had no political future. For Avenol, there was no doubt. His administration coincided with the breakdown of European security, the outbreak of world war, and the collapse of the League itself as Geneva became less and less relevant to the statesmen of Europe. Avenol was Secretary-General at a time of severe threat to his own nation and thus his conception of the League as primarily an instrument for the preservation of the status quo and later as an international reflection of a "new order" in Europe were not surprising. There was an insoluble conflict for Avenol between the obligations of the Covenant and the foreign policy of his country. Avenol stood with France, rather than the League, and for this he has been censured. It was a conflict that never existed in such acute form for Sir Eric Drummond.

At the same time, there is substantial justification for the critical judgments of Avenol by those who knew him best—his Secretariat colleagues. If Sir Eric Drummond was well informed on all League issues, whether administrative or political, Joseph Avenol was much less frequently *au courant* the primary questions confronting his administration. This was perhaps the first key to his failure. The League Secretary-General, inhibited by constitutional and customary limitations, could accomplish little if his opinions were not valued. Avenol made comparatively little effort to remain well-informed, and the result was, in the words of one of his colleagues, he "was not a real Secretary-General".

Whereas Drummond had been extremely hard-working and industrious, Avenol was much less so, despite his initial lack of political training and experience. Avenol had been prepared for a role in economic and financial undertakings, but not for a serious role in political disputes, and this, in addition to his unindustrious nature markedly diminished the moral authority of the Office. Delegates and Secretariat staff members did not seek his advice on important questions, and the influence of the Office obviously waned throughout the seven years of his administration.

While Avenol did take a few significant independent initiatives, he remained unable to augment the accepted powers of the Secretary-General. He moved boldly only for purposes of implementing the appeasement strategy he so strongly supported, and this was most unlikely to provide the kind of precedent essential for further expansion of the Secretary-General's role.

In short, then, the behind-the-scenes role of the Secretary-General so carefully nurtured and cultivated by Drummond was largely lost by Avenol. The functions performed were the same, but they were not served so often, nor so well. Avenol, as well as Drummond, was useful as a channel for communications; he took part in negotiations with League disputants, presenting his own views, and commenting on theirs; he made recommendations of substance and procedure on his own initiative and by request, and engaged in a process of evaluation of information, views, and programs; he presented legal analyses of Covenant articles and official recommendations, and helped draft League resolutions; perhaps most important, he served as a liaison between national governments and Council representatives, and more particularly, between France and the League. The consensus of his colleagues, however, is that none of these tasks were carried out with the skill or grace, or indeed, frequency, of Sir Eric Drummond.

Unfortunate also was Avenol's failure to make a vigorous effort to retain the League, or at least the Secretariat and the Office of Secretary-General, as symbols of international cooperation. He was never able to rally the staff, and with the onset of war, and his attempt to prevent the transfer to Princeton, and to dissolve the League, he lost all influence among the remaining top-level Secretariat officials. His resignation marked the end of an effective Office until the war ended and Trygve Lie could begin anew to construct a meaningful role for the United Nations' first official. This final failure, or "moral collapse" as it has been characterized by several of his colleagues, reflected his unwillingness to serve the League itself, and the norms legitimized by its Covenant, rather than the interests of his nation, as he perceived them.

What of the real impact of Secretary-General Avenol? Can one properly conclude that his Office was a factor of any importance in European politics? Was his influence significant or decisive in any instance? In the cases of the Bruce Report and the expulsion of the Soviet Union from the League, his role was probably decisive. But in the context of the crucial issues confronting the League in the 1930's, Avenol's work was important only insofar as he supported British and French foreign policy, and placed no obstacle in the path of those who would avoid war by ignoring the

Covenant. Beyond this, his role was clearly of very minor significance, both because of the inherent limitations constricting the Office, and the failure to preserve what Drummond had built.

The Office will obviously not become an important factor in politics until a far more highly integrated world community with an international organization of much greater corporate capacity exists. The League and Sir Eric Drummond were important historically because each undertook the first significant efforts to organize a meaningful international community. The League failed in these attempts in the 1930's, and Secretary-General Avenol made few moves to impede the process of disintegration. He was an economic technician devoted primarily to his country, and did not possess a deep understanding of the international civil service concept, or of the movement toward a system of world order represented by the League of Nations. It is tempting to speculate what might have happened to the League, and perhaps to European history, if that other Frenchman, Jean Monnet, with his sensitive appreciation of international relations, had been appointed in Avenol's place. Perhaps the result would have been the same, but at the very least, the League would have died in dignity. As it was, the League flame went out in 1939, with no one there to save it.

CHAPTER III

Sean Lester
Secretary-General of the League of Nations
1940-1947

The German troops are marching along the Jura and may be in Bellegarde to-day. There seems to be absolutely no military or political reason now for them to come into Switzerland and we may well be kept as an island... The world is crashing round our ears but [we] are keeping our heads up, if our hearts are broken...
Sean Lester, June 19, 1940

To Sean Lester, a diminutive and shy Irishman, fell the lonely task of keeping alive the idea of a League of Nations while the Second World War raged about him, and the obligation to oversee the formal death of a discredited world organization that had failed in its primary purpose of keeping the peace.

The conditions under which Lester was forced to work, in the attempt to achieve not altogether consistent ends, were discouraging, but the one man who fought for the League in the war years was determined that the Organization would go out in dignity, that the conception of a world peace organization would live on, and that the United Nations would be the better because a League of Nations had gone before it.

Sean Lester was born in County Antrim, Ireland, on September 27, 1888. He received his schooling in Belfast, and at the age of twenty began a career in journalism in Dublin, where he worked for thirteen years, from 1909 to 1922, with two of the city's leading newspapers. At the same time, he was associated with the Sinn Fein movement for Irish independence, and after the establishment of the Irish Free State, served in that nation's Department of Foreign Affairs from 1922 until 1929.

At this point Lester began an association with the League of Nations that was to last until the League's final transfer to the United Nations in 1947. In April, 1929, he was appointed the Free State's Permanent Delegate accredited to the League, a post he held until 1934, and from which he was able to represent his Government at every international conference held in Geneva throughout the period. During the Free State's membership on the League Council, Lester usually served as his Government's representative, and for a short while was Council President. He was also appointed President of several Council committees, including those that dealt with the Letitia dispute between Peru and Colombia, and the Chaco conflict between

Bolivia and Paraguay. He also served as Council Rapporteur on Minority, Health, and Opium questions.

Lester was generally held in high esteem by League delegates and officials during his service on the Council. His diplomatic capabilities, and the fact that he was a national of a small state, provided him with numerous opportunities for political initiatives. "Lester was one of the best members the Council ever had", wrote Philip Noel-Baker to Lord Robert Cecil, in July, 1933.[1]

As a representative of a small power in the League, Lester felt strongly the opportunity accorded small states by the League to assist in the settlement of international disputes. The future Secretary-General could not know how prophetic his words were, both for the League and for his own role, when he spoke in 1933 of the Sino-Japanese conflict:

If by the process of time, by the exhaustion of argument, the patient and indeed tragic learning of experience, the representatives of some small States were found in the role of advocate for the defence of the League it was not by any desire of their own; it was rather by the failure of leaders who would not lead. Voices which should have been authoritative and firm were, at best, silent; and sometimes when they had been heard it might have been better otherwise. A few small States with no axe to grind, independent, and with some courage, did, I believe, save the League from complete bankruptcy. Of that history must judge. Their task was not pleasant nor easy but they realized that behind them, not quite as articulate but equally convinced, stood dozens of others, many of them most anxious and seriously concerned for the fate of the League idea.[2]

From 1934 to 1937, Lester served as High Commissioner in Danzig, and under the rising tide of Nazism, worked to maintain some semblance of balance between Polish and German influence in the Free City. The position was, of course, impossible, as the Nazis during this period in Danzig destroyed the Constitution of the Free City, the procedures for League administration, the rights of the Danzigers, and made personal attacks on Lester. The League and its High Commissioner were compelled to retreat before the Nazi menace.

Secretary-General Avenol, at a secret meeting of the League Council on September 30, 1936, informed the members of the Council of his intention to appoint Lester to a three-year term as Deputy Secretary-General.[3]

[1] Letter dated July 22, 1933. Cecil-Noel-Baker correspondance, British Museum.
[2] Cited in Larus, ed., *From Collective Security to Preventive Diplomacy* (New York: John Wiley & Sons, Inc., 1965), p. 119.
[3] League Archives 1933-1940, Administrative Commissions, Danzig, 2B/7589/1579. Avenol said of Lester at this time:
"In searching among those whose services to the League were marked by great competence and devotion, the Secretary-General's attention was at once fixed on Mr. Lester, at present High Commissioner of the League in Danzig.
The eminent qualities displayed by him when he represented the Irish Free State on the Council had led to his appointment as High Commissioner.
During his three years in Danzig, the Members of the Council had themselves been able to appreciate the courage, dignity, self-sacrifice and political sense of Mr.

His purpose was threefold: appoint a qualified representative from a small power,[4] remove Lester as an irritant to the Nazis in Danzig, and eliminate the danger of personal harm to Lester. The Council quickly approved, although not before the British and French representatives (Eden and Delbos respectively) made the point that the promotion of the High Commissioner signified approval of his work, and that the appointment depended upon agreement on a successor who would also endeavor to protect the Constitution of the Free City.

In 1937 Lester began his term as Deputy to the Secretary-General, a term that was to last only until the fateful days of August, 1940, when Secretary-General Avenol finally decided to support Pétain and the Vichy regime by resigning his post and leaving Acting Secretary-General Lester to carry on. The position of Deputy Secretary-General was probably the least significant, until 1940, of the many capacities in which Lester served the League of Nations. Under Avenol, the Deputy was second-in-command, but from 1933 onward, the post had steadily diminished in importance.[5] Lester's assignment as head of liaison with member states gave some added significance to the position since for the first time a national from a small power was enabled to engage in political work from the vantage point of one of the principal officerships of the League Secretariat. But by 1937, of course, the extent of the League's political activity had declined drastically, and Lester's work remained primarily administrative.

Lester, and especially the sense of proportion which had enabled him to meet all the difficulties of a situation with which the Council was well acquainted".

[4] The circumstances in Danzig and in the League Secretariat combined to bring Lester in as Deputy Secretary-General. Pablo Azcaraté of Spain, Deputy Secretary-General since 1933, had resigned, and since his post had been created by virtue of the 1932 Assembly's decision that a Secretary-General from a major power should have as one of his two Deputies a national of a smaller power, the way was cleared for Lester.

[5] Avenol, when Deputy Secretary-General, worked under an arrangement which, according to the Noblemaire Report, left the Secretary-General and his Deputy "free to concentrate all the reins of policy in their hands". (Report of the Committee of Experts (Noblemaire Report), 7 May 1921, *Records of Second Assembly,* Minutes of Fourth Committee, Annex 2, p. 197.) As we have seen, this kind of top-level structure contributed in large measure to the German-Italian demands of 1928-1932 for changes in the highest echelon of the Secretariat. Azcaraté, however, after the 1932 settlement, was given charge of the Internal Administrative Services, and also of the Administrative Commissions and Minorities Questions Section. The consequence of this was, naturally enough, a lesser status for the Deputy. As Ranshofen-Wertheimer wrote:

By assuming administrative tasks the Deputy came more and more under the day-to-day jurisdiction of the Secretary-General. He accepted the Secretary-General's orders. He became a sort of glorified director. What he gained in direct administrative authority he lost in status and prestige. He ceased to be part of the Secretary-General's authority and his near-equal, and became a subordinate. (*The International Secretariat: A Great Experiment in International Administration* (Washington: Carnegie Endowment for International Peace, 1945), p. 56.)

Secretary-General Avenol's growing anti-British sentiment and his evident willingness to fit the League into what he believed would be a "new order" in Europe also contributed significantly to Lester's minor role between 1937 and 1940. While Avenol had been instrumental in making Lester one of his Deputies, as one former League official put it, "Avenol kept Lester out of things". Toward the end of the Secretariat crisis matters went much further. In line with what appeared to most observers and participants a deliberate attempt to rid the Secretariat of British and American influence, Avenol made his move to have Lester resign. A circular was prepared in the Secretariat permitting all members of the staff to offer their resignations as part of the general League retrenchment. As we have seen, Avenol evidently intended to retain only those staff members who might fit in with the "new order". But Lester had been informed of Avenol's purpose and decided at once to stay on.

Lester's role during the period immediately prior to Avenol's resignation is not completely known, but certain details may be pieced together from the Council documents pertaining to the resignation, as well as from communications with Arthur Sweetser. The atmosphere in which he worked in the first several months of 1940 was one of horror and frustration as the Second Word War engulfed Europe and the League of Nations began its final collapse. Sweetser, writing of his own leavetaking from Geneva in May, 1940, described the emptiness and pathos of the once proud League:

> The personnel was decreasing week by week. There had, of course, been the great decimation of the fall and early winter when some 300 permanent officials from the Secretariat alone had been mobilized, dismissed, or given leave. As the days wore on, others drifted off one by one, some to join their national forces, some to return home. The corridors became more and more empty...
> The Administration did all it could to encourage departures. In the Spring, it sent around a circular which practically invited everyone who desired to leave. Had I been a government representative, I should have had the feeling that, if officials were so unessential as they seemed by this circular to be, there was little need of my government continuing to subsidize the office. The dearth of leadership and inspiration was unbelievable; the office seemed without soul. One who had known the Secretariat in the old days of its glory would not have thought it could have sunk so low.[6]

Lester, without leadership from the Secretary-General, carried on as best he could. If Avenol had been doing little to save the League machinery, there were times when he at least spoke of the need "to save the institution".[7] Lester had suggested to his chief in early 1940 that it might be wise to make plans in the event of a real emergency, such as a German invasion of Switzerland. Avenol replied that "people were losing their heads", but that he would stand firm.[8] If this statement was inconsistent with his actions,

---

[6] Notes by Arthur Sweetser, May, 1940, entitled "Exit Geneva". Sweetser Papers.
[7] *Ibid.*
[8] *Ibid.* "One day I found Lester, Deputy Secretary-General, in deep distress. It seems that after much hesitation he had decided to suggest to Avenol that it would be wise to consider plans in case of emergency. Avenol became furious, said he did not

for Lester the problem was acute. The Secretariat Staff Committee were urging him to make plans for the safety of their wives and children; Secretariat officials wanted to know what would be done with their work and documents. Alexander Loveday asked Sweetser to take a set of photographic copies of his economic and financial records to the United States, but decided to take them himself to Princeton when Sweetser expressed fears for the safety of the records when he crossed into Italy on his trip from Geneva.[9]

The problems confronting Lester were those of a dying organization. Fear of invasion necessitated plans for the Secretariat staff and raised the issue of a possible transfer, at least in part, to Princeton. The inability of the League's political bodies to hold meetings, and Avenol's attitude resulted in Secretariat planning without an active leader, and with the support only of the Supervisory Commission. Financial planning became next to impossible as funds were scarce, and there were no political decisions to guide the League staff in its budget formulation. More general was the problem of deciding what work of a non-political nature should and could be kept going, and most basically, how the League idea could be kept alive after the League itself had failed to prevent another world war.

These, however, were questions for a Secretary-General to resolve with as much political help as could be obtained under the circumstances. For Lester, the only course was to resist Avenol's policy and to try to salvage what he could. At times caution was forced by Avenol's resistance to the Princeton transfer, and in early June, 1940, Lester had to ask Sweetser to slow down his investigation into the possibilities of sending some League sections to the United States.[10] At the same time, a note of desperation is evident in Lester's writings just before the fall of France:

As one sees opinion ["i.e. S.G." is handwritten in the margin] at the moment, division of the Secretariat is regarded as impossible and perhaps more particularly the transfer of any elements over the Ocean. We stand by here in Geneva until it becomes impossible; we may desire for urgent practical reasons to let an element of the Treasury and the Personnel side establish themselves in Vichy; but Vichy has rapidly declined in value; the center of France is being thronged with millions of regugees; the entry of Italy will lead to evacuations from the South Coast; if we go to Vichy in emergency, I have a horrible vision of us going as another bunch of regu
gees. Policy may change with events, but you will guess that salvage becomes more and more difficult. My own mind seems to be reconciling itself to what is at any rate a possibility: dissolution with dignity.[11]

Just one week later, on June 19, 1940, Lester wrote to Sweetser that "the German troops are marching along the Jura and may be in Bellegarde today. There seems to be absolutely no military or political reason now for

---

understand this state of panic, thought people were losing their heads; for himself, he would stand firm".

[9] *Ibid.*
[10] Letter from Sean Lester to Arthur Sweetser, June 12, 1940. Sweetser Papers.
[11] *Ibid.*

them to come into Switzerland and we may well be kept as an island... The world is crashing round our ears but [we] are keeping our heads up, if our hearts are broken..." [12]

The notion of dissolution was never seriously considered by Lester, however, and with the Princeton transfer finally accomplished, the Deputy Secretary-General was faced with perhaps the most delicate of the many issues he confronted before succeeding to the powers of the Secretary-General. He had to ensure adequate financing for the remaining League activities notwithstanding Avenol's argument for liquidation, and had to be certain that after Avenol resigned the powers of the Secretary-General would in reality be his.

There can be little question that Lester worked extraordinarily hard to salvage as much as possible of the League and that this ran directly in the face of Avenol's policy. Indeed, the friction between the two had grown so great that from the end of June, 1940, until the end of August, Lester and Avenol did not see one another, and had almost no contact. In a telephone message from Lester to Carl Hambro in New York City on August 27, 1940, Lester said he had not seen Avenol for two months, and that while Avenol had asserted that Lester was Acting Secretary-General from July 26 forward, he had not told Lester "anything about it". Arthur Sweetser's account of the message from Lester to Hambro continues as follows:

M. Avenol has now notified Mr. Lester by a telephone message that he [Avenol] will take up his functions again from August 28 to August 31.
Mr. Lester said he had had enough of this situation. He proposed to send a note to M. Avenol expressing all reserve for any action he may take, having already informed States Members that Mr. Lester is now responsible. Mr. Lester feels he cannot be publicly responsible for action which M. Avenol may take privately without his knowledge.[13]

It was Lester's judgment that Avenol, "in taking his [resignation] action at the request of this government did so reluctantly and with the *arrière pensée* of keeping control".[14]

Lester also attempted to obtain some kind of political support and guidance for what future work remained for the League. Failing the possibility of securing a quorum of the Supervisory Commission, he suggested a "meeting in sections" [15] to consider, among other items, the budget. He also proposed

[12] Letter from Lester to Sweetser, June 19, 1940. Lester continued:
"At the moment I have only two principles, or at any rate two immediate objectives: the first is that we should endeavour to keep a little bit of personal dignity whatever comes (an ideal, as I have little confidence in my own physical courage); and the other is that we should try to look after our staff who have been standing by us here, and especially those who are isolated, either from an invaded country or otherwise".
[13] Notes taken by Sweetser on August 27, 1940. Sweetser Papers.
[14] *Ibid.* See Chapter II, pp. 158-166, *supra.*
[15] Notes by Arthur Sweetser of telephone conversation between Lester and Sweetser (New York to Geneva), August 25, 1940. Sweetser Papers.

a system of cooption, or a meeting of the Presidents of the Assembly and the Council along with whatever members were available on the Supervisory Commission. The legality of decisions taken by such a group could obviously be questioned, but Lester considered that under the circumstances of the war, such a body "could issue an authoritative statement which would be accepted by the member states".[16] Seymour Jacklin of South Africa, the League Treasurer, agreed with this view, and felt that "any possible informality in cooption preferable to any informality in the budget".[17]

While Lester personally wanted to leave Geneva and return to Ireland, personal wishes meant less to him than the moral obligation and sense of responsibility he felt toward the League of Nations. His family had left Geneva in June, and with the war surrounding Switzerland, it soon became evident that if Lester stayed on, he would be separated from his family until the war ended. Yet Avenol's resignation had impelled him to remain in Geneva. On August 6th, 1940, he wrote:

I have been hoping that I might see a situation reached when the "element" which has been our chief problem disappeared and I could go. My family's interest and my own inclinations coincided in that hope, but now it seems to be impossible. We poor humans do get gripped in circumstances when we imagine we control them.[18]

There can be no doubt of the low esteem in which Lester held Joseph Avenol. Writing of the resignation, and the appeal to reconsider sent to Avenol by Hambro, Lester commented that he was first

rather pleased that the recipient should get such a telegram, in spite of everything; secondly that, knowing the sender, he had clearly been left without information (although I had endeavoured in a round-about way to see that it should not be so); thirdly, that if by any chance he *were* informed, I would feel morally released from continuing the efforts I had been making.[19]

One can only imagine the depths of Lester's antipathy for the man who had forced him into an unwanted position and did so while resisting attempts to save the little left of the League. On September 4, 1940, Lester wrote that after early July, when Avenol refused to see him

my main offence was in refusing tempting opportunities to go away. I should have many good marks somewhere for the restraint and forbearance I exercised, but I felt my personal interest, my inclinations having been sacrificed, I had to add an almost infinite tolerance. You will have to guess something of what we have endured. He [Avenol] has gone, undignified, indecent, and has done everything, literally everything he could to render any survival impossible. At the best, the problems would have been of the very greatest difficulty.[20]

---

16 *Ibid.*
17 Sweetser notes of telephone conversation between Lester and Carl Hambro (Geneva to New York), August 27, 1940. Sweetser Papers.
18 Letter from Lester to Sweetser, August 6, 1940. Sweetser Papers.
19 *Ibid.*
20 Letter from Lester to Sweetser, September 4, 1940. Sweetser Papers.

The problems of which Lester wrote were to preserve as far as possible the non-political activities of the League, to maintain the international character of the organization, and to do this with a greatly reduced budget. Securing funds became one of his chief preoccupations, as states withdrew from the Organization, and as the territories of many European Members were occupied by German forces.

All political work, naturally, was finished, and only a few technical activities remained possible. The Swiss Government was in an extremely difficult position. With German troops not far away, any political activity whatever by the League would have compelled Bern to demand its removal, and during the war this would probably have eventuated in its dissolution. The request to move never came, but the fear of such was never far from the forefront of Lester's worries. Extreme care had to be taken to prevent even the appearance of a political act of any kind, and it took comparatively little to constitute "a political act" in the eyes of the Swiss authorities.[21]

Since the League's political bodies were unable to meet during the war, decision making occured sporadically and without regularized procedures. The Supervisory Commission maintained its work during the 1940-1946 period under the emergency authority granted it by the 1939 Assembly. It will be recalled that the Commission was empowered to take, in agreement with the Secretary-General and the Director of the International Labour Office, any exceptional administrative or financial measures or decisions it thought necessary, and with the same authority as if the Assembly itself had taken the measures.

The League, of course, during this period was widely dispersed. The Secretariat, with Lester at its head, maintained its offices in the Palais des Nations in Geneva. Seymour Jacklin, the League Treasurer, headed the Treasury in London from early 1941 to the end of the war. With Great Britain remaining as the League's largest contributor, the arrangement had obvious advantages. The greater part of the Opium Supervisory Body and

[21] United States Consul Harold Tittmann telegraphed the United States Department of State on October 8, 1940 as follows:

"Aghnides told me this morning that the Secretariat has been seriously worried lately because of the attitude of the Swiss authorities toward the League of Nations whose presence on Swiss soil is apparently becoming increasingly embarrassing to them. The continued presence here of delegations of "phantom" countries has been especially criticized and also the expressions of support for the League received in reply to the telegram to member states announcing that the Acting Secretary-General had taken over his duties because these replies were regarded in some quarters as being indirectly a "plebiscite" in favor of Great Britain. Indirect but nevertheless persistent intimations suggest that the Swiss at the present time would prefer to have that instituion close down completely and the remaining members of the Secretariat leave Geneva. Aghnides said that is was improbable that the Secretariat would agree to liquidate on any grounds less direct than a formal request by the Swiss Government which the latter for obvious reasons is loath to make". (*National Archives,* 500.C/1054, Oct. 8, 1940)

the entire Office of the Permanent Central Opium Board moved to Washington, D.C. (the U.S. Government had cooperated in this area of League activity), and almost all of the Economic, Financial and Transit Department were sent "on mission" to Princeton, New Jersey, under the Directorship of Alexander Loveday. The International Labour Office had been at Montreal, Canada (with international status) since the middle of 1940, and remained there during the war under the guidance of Acting Director Edward Phelan, who succeeded J. G. Winant on February 15th, 1941. The High Commissioner for Refugees worked in London, and the President and Registrar of the Permanent Court of International Justice in Geneva.

The Supervisory Commission held its first post-Avenol meeting in Lisbon at the end of September, 1940, and met frequently during the war, mostly in the United States. Lester, of course, attended none of the meetings, and, until the autumn of 1944, did not leave Geneva at all. Seymour Jacklin took part in the meetings in the United States, and made several trips to Canada for purposes of handling the finances of the International Labour Office. But the Commission, under the leadership of its Chairman, Carl Hambro of Norway, kept in constant contact with Lester, Phelan, Jacklin, and Loveday, both by cable and letter.

The Lisbon meeting at the end of September, 1940, was of great importance, for the no-budget policy laid down by Avenol was reversed, and procedures for the future established. The Commmission decided that whenever it could not meet, decisions would be made on the basis of consultation (by whatever methods possible) between the several members and Chairman Hambro. The budget decision was a particularly happy one for Lester. On October 4th, 1940, he wrote to Hambro from Geneva:

We are very gratified indeed that a budget has been passed four weeks after it was the declared policy here that it neither should be nor could be; we have spared no efforts on this side and we will now face the problems of further economies as well as the greater ones affecting the future of the Secretariat and the League.[22]

---

[22] Letter from Lester to Carl Hambro, Octo:ber 4, 1940. Lester had intended to go to Lisbon for the September meeting of the Supervisory Commission, along with Jacklin and a few other League officials. The plan was to leave Aghnides in charge of the Secretariat in Geneva. The entire group, however, was turned back at the Spanish border and refused passage across Spain. The Madrid authorities had issued an order in August forbidding the entry into Spain of League personnel, and the Secretariat officials headed by Lester returned to Geneva.

Harold Tittmann, the United States Consul in Geneva at the time, telegraphed the United States Department of State on September 26, 1940, that Lester "was much upset by the action of the Spanish authorities in forbidding members of the League Secretariat to enter Spain. He felt not only that an affront to the dignity of the institution was implied by this action but also that an impossible situation involving the functioning of the League had been created. Lester seemed determined not to let the matter drop..." (*National Archives,* 500.C/1051, Sept. 26, 1940). However there was little the League could do, and the issue was in fact dropped.

The economies, naturally, were difficult, and in some cases, unpleasant for personal reasons. Officials in Geneva and the other cities housing portions of the League had to take cuts in salary and pension, and frequenty Lester had to break the news. He wrote: "I am feeling very sick at heart dealing with these matters and often 'wish to God' that some one else had to make the wretched calculations and to ignore other elements of such obvious importance".[23] Lester stressed repeatedly that while the value of the war-time Organization may have seemed problematical, he was thinking basically of the League idea, and that sacrifice for that idea was essential.

Lester himself was affected quite immediately by the financial cutback. As Acting Secretary-General, he lived at La Pelouse, but only in a small upstairs apartment. The entire downstairs was closed in an effort to economize and to emphasize the fact that Lester was not the Secretary-General, but rather the Acting Secretary-General.

The Supervisory Commission, with help from figures and estimates communicated by Lester and Jacklin, drew up a 1941 budget on the basis of expenditure which was 50% of the 1940 budget. While the actual expenditure turned out to be somewhat greater than 50%, the general drift was downward, and only slightly up again after the low point of 1942. Total League spending in 1939 was over twenty-eight million Swiss francs; in 1940 the figure was down to about thirteen million; and by 1941 the expenditure was just over eight million. Spending rose to almost ten million Swiss francs by 1945. For the years 1940-1945, the average percentage of collections from Member governments was 66%, and of that figure, Great Britain and the members of the Commonwealth contributed 74%.[24]

For Lester, the war years were busy, but at the same time quite lonely and sad. As described by some of his colleagues in Geneva, Lester was a quiet, introverted man who felt things deeply, but who did not give of himself easily, and apparently the enforced separation from his family affected his entire personality. He was never happy in Geneva during the war, and worked solely from a sense of responsibility to the League.

One associate described him as "straight-forward, with great common sense, and absolutely reliable. He had a great sense of duty and responsibility. He was not brilliant, but had a good feel for politics and administration". Carl Hambro was later to write that Lester "was a noble, selfless person" who "had a natural loathing of all publicity" and who "never spoke about himself".[25] Hambro touched on Lester's personal unhappiness in Geneva when he wrote that "what it cost Lester to hold the fort in Geneva

[23] Letter from Lester to Sweetser, November 29, 1940. Sweetser Papers.
[24] Report of the Supervisory Commission, League Document A.5.1946.X, 14 March 1946.
[25] Carl Hambro, "Sean Lester—The Man Who Remained True to His Ideals", *Aftenposten,* 25 July 1959. (Translation from the Norwegian.)

in a world which was falling apart cannot be easily measured today".[26] But for Hambro, and for many of his colleagues, Lester

was an endearing person, faithful both in the small things and the large, filled by what the English poets called the milk of human kindness. He was too wise to be naive in his judgment of people and conditions. But he was never unfriendly when talking of others. His goodness was a part of the moral strength which held him up and held a ramshackle organization up until it could be useful to and impart strength to a new world.[27]

Arthur Sweetser, who was very fond of Lester, described him "as a very friendly personality, but with a curious uncertainty which showed itself especially during and after his virtual imprisonment at Geneva during the war".[28]

Lester worked in the Palais des Nations with about thirty members of the professional staff, and perhaps one hundred officials altogether. He was at the office almost daily, maintaining his contacts with the League "outposts" as he called them, in London, Montreal, Washington, and Princeton, and trying to supervise the work everywhere. While German troops were stationed only ten walking minutes away, he prepared his annual reports on the League's work, and supervised the collection and dissemination of all kinds of statistics—financial, economic, transit, health, narcotic drugs, and others. He prepared the budget and decided upon allocations, after consultations with Hambro and other members of the Supervisory Commission, and oversaw the expenditure of funds. As he wrote from Geneva in October, 1945, "the framework of the League was maintained and the work was kept going in the heart of a continent virtually controlled by antagonistic forces. Within the shelter of the Swiss frontiers the difficulties were partly moral, partly political, and partly material".[29]

The most significant portion of the League's work during the war was in the area of economic, financial, and transit questions. As noted in the preceding Chapter, the 1939 Assembly had approved the Report of the Bruce Committee proposing the establishment of a Central Committee to unify under one direction the economic and social functions of the League. The war, of course, put an end to the plan. The Organising Committee appointed to start the machinery met once at the Hague in February, 1940 and planned to meet there again. But German troops then occupied the Netherlands, and not until the formal establishment of the United Nations Economic and Social Council was the Bruce Committee's plan finally implemented.

Lester was left with the task of reorienting the work during the war so as to achieve as nearly as possible the aims of the Committee's Report. With

[26] *Ibid.*
[27] *Ibid.*
[28] Letter to Jan-Gunnar Lindstrom, Oct. 2, 1961. Sweetser Papers.
[29] Report on the Work of the League During the War, *Introduction,* League Document A.6.1946, p. 11.

staff and financial resources greatly reduced, and with a much smaller volume of relevant statistical and other data, Lester and Loveday concentrated on the three most important publications of the Economic, Financial and Transit Department, i.e., the *World Economic Survey,* the *Monthly Bulletin of Statistics,* and the *Statistical Year-Book.* This work was supplemented by special studies on selected topics of importance. It was also decided to prepare a number of studies and analyses of the experience of the Economic and Financial Organization insofar as it dealt with major economic issues likely to be of decisive importance after the war.

The mission at Princeton turned out to be extremely valuable for the League's work in this area. Quite aside from the facilities for research and the ease of communication within the United States, the Princton mission provided a system for consultation with the economic advisers and experts of many nations stationed in or visiting the United States. Contact with other League bodies, such as the Opium Board in Washington or the International Labor Office in Montreal, was also facilitated.

The precise relationship between Lester in Geneva and subordinates in the United States was complicated. Loveday, while heading Economic, Finance and Transit at Princeton, was given powers, on behalf of Lester, over the Washington branch offices of the Opium Supervisory Body and the Permanent Central Opium Board. He was authorized to exercise all financial powers concerning the two Washington offices, subject only to "such reference to the Acting Secretary-General as circumstances may require". In addition, it was agreed that any decisions of an administrative or financial character taken by Loveday and applied to the Princeton group were to be communicated immediately to the other groups in the United States. Finally, while the Washington offices were permitted to communicate directly with the Acting Secretary-General, it was understood that all messages to and from Lester were to go through Loveday, who had full freedom to make whatever comments he wished.[30]

If the Princeton Mission was useful for liaison purposes with other League bodies separated from Geneva, it was also valuable as a base for establishing contacts with individuals in a position to assist the League, and as the central rallying point for those who wished to preserve the spirit of the Organization during the war. In April, 1941, Arthur Sweetser brought together at Princeton over one hundred Americans who had participated in the technical and non-political work associated with the League, the Labor Office and the Permanent Court of International Justice. The idea, said Sweetser at the time, was "to put them in touch with the present situation and the establishment of bits of the League here, and...to try to create

---

[30] League Archives, 1933-1940: Financial Administration, 17/40910/40910; also *Ibid.,* letter from Lester to Alexander Loveday, April 7, 1941. See Chapter II, pp. 157-158, *supra,* for the powers concerning the staff conferred on Loveday just prior to his leaving Geneva for Princeton.

homogeneity and a sense of common association amongst them".[31] The two-day meeting at Princeton was a great success. Henry Grady, Chairman of the Economic Committee was there, as were Dana Durand, Chairman of the Statistical Committee, Carter Goodrich, Chairman of the International Labor Office Governing Board, Manley Hudson, Judge on the Permanent Court, Frank Boudreau, of the Health Section in Geneva, and many others. Among the non-Americans present were the officials of the Princeton and Washington groups, Carl Hambro, who was at that time residing in Princeton, and Edward Phelan of the International Labor Office.

The personal contact, the business sessions at which twenty years of League work was reviewed, and the discussions of the Organization's position at that time and plans for the future, all had a deeply felt impact on those attending. Sweetser, in a letter to Lester in Geneva, wrote of the "big emotional pickup" provided by the conference. He added:

All of this, my dear Sean, despite its satisfaction and pickup, often seems small and unimportant against the lurid background of devastation and slaughter now encompassing such large parts of the world. Yet if only those who are better qualified than we in the art of conflict and battle can work out some satisfactory outcome to the present crisis, all this will have its very big importance in laying a foundation for the future. At the same time, it is my own very strong hope that the setting up of some such clear ideal and objective as we have envisioned here these past two days will have not only a future but a very real immediate value in creating that morale and sense of purpose which is essential to sustaining any great conflict... The little effort that we are making here, and that you are making in Geneva, is just to keep alive and ready as against the day, that little flame of enlightenment and hope which mankind needs to see ahead of him out of the blackness to guide him to something more worthy of the human race.[32]

There was not a little irony, noted by many, that the United States, which had dealt the League its first serious blow and had remained apart from the Organization for over twenty years, should now serve as host and provide substantial support for the League in its last years.

In any event, with a Secretariat staff of just over a hundred officials altogether, the League somehow carried on. In Geneva, the central concern was the more purely statistical studies, while the Princeton Mission prepared numerous descriptive and analytical volumes. Studies were produced dealing with reconstruction and relief, trade and trade policy, economic security, and demographic questions. Enormous care was taken to avoid anything that might be politically sensitive. Before publishing a demographic volume on the Soviet Union, for example, Loveday wrote to Lester that he had asked the Economic Committee in 1943 to

express its views on...whether it would be politically desirable for us to publish a special demographic volume relating to the Soviet Union. Such a volume has, in fact,

---

[31] Letter from Sweetser to Lester, April 23, 1941. Sweetser Papers.
[32] *Ibid.*

been prepared and I think it is very good and, on scientific grounds, would certainly like to publish it. However, the political issue is clearly an important one. So far as it was concerned—and I was only consulting the Committee off the record—it felt that the author of the volume should get in touch with the Soviet authorities in Washington and ascertain their view. As soon as I hear this I shall cable to you.[33]

The Economic and Financial Committees met a few times during the war in joint sessions, under the chairmanship of either Sir Frederick Leith-Ross of Great Britain, or Henry Grady of the United States. The issues studied and reported on included the general approach to post-war relief and reconstruction, monetary policy, and private foreign investment. The Fiscal Committee assisted in the organization of two tax conferences in Mexico, the object of both being the removal of tax barriers to trade and investment. The Economic, Financial, and Transit Department was often invited to send an observer or representative to the several war-time conferences, including sessions of the Council of the United Nations Relief and Rehabilitation Administration, the Bretton Woods Monetary and Financial Conference in 1944, the International Labor Office Conference at Philadelphia in 1944, and the Mexico City Inter-American Conference on Problems of War and Peace in early 1945.

The International Labor Office Conference in 1944 demonstrated quite clearly the complexities inherent in Lester's position, and the type of problem to which he was compelled to devote much of his time. The Acting Secretary-General was invited by Phelan to attend the Conference (although attendance was, of course, impossible for Lester in early 1944), or to appoint a representative. Lester appointed Jacklin and Loveday to represent him. The problem was the relatively simple one of the duties of the League Secretary-General under Article 19 of the Constitution of the International Labor Office. That Article requires all International Labor Office Conventions and Recommendations to be deposited with the Secretary-General of the League and for copies of the Conventions and Recommendations to be communicated by him to International Labor Office Members. Difficulty of communication to and from Geneva during the war years had already resulted in some delays, and the Conference adopted a resolution providing for communications through the International Labor Office Director "during periods of emergency".

Lester had opposed this procedure. He suggested that his representative in the United States act on his behalf in distributing certified copies to states more easily reached from America.[34] But Wilfred Jenks and Phelan argued that the Secretary-General's authority could be delegated in these matters only to the Director of the International Labor Office, rather than

[33] Letter from Loveday to Lester, December 9, 1943. League Archives: Economic Relations, 10A/42227/1778.
[34] League Archives 1933-1940: Legal, 3B/42296/904; cable from Lester to Edward Phelan.

to an official of the Secretariat. This view prevailed, and while constitutional procedures were technically left unchanged, the Acting Secretary-General's position and League authority were affected. As Martin Hill, of the Secretariat, stated in his notes on the Conference, "To a League official, the absence of the Secretary-General from the proceedings at Philadelphia was something of a tragedy".[35] Hill concluded that so long as the Secretary-General and the nucleus of the general services remain in Geneva, and so long as the representative organs of the League do not meet, then "new international work will tend to be assigned to the international bodies whose central staff are outside Europe and whose representative bodies can and do meet".[36]

The largely academic work of the League during the war on economic, financial and transit questions, generally supervised by Lester from Geneva and under the direct administration of Loveday at Princeton, was supplemented by a small measure of activity on questions of a social and humanitarian nature with which the world body had always dealt. These included health questions, drug traffic, assistance to refugees, mandates, intellectual cooperation, and a few legal questions.

Even during this period of emergency an occacional political issue had to be resolved. Perhaps the most important of these was the attempted withdrawal of France from the League. On April 19th, 1941, Jean-François Darlan, then Admiral of the Fleet and Secretary of State for Foreign Affairs in France, sent a cable from Vichy to Lester in Geneva stating that the French Government, "availing itself of the right which it is entitled to exercise under Article 1, Paragraph 3, of the Covenant, has decided to withdraw from the League of Nations".[37] Final withdrawal, according to the Covenant, was not effective until two years from the date of the withdrawal notice. Lester, therefore, simply acknowledged receipt and communicated the telegram to League Members.

On March 20, 1943, just one month prior to the expiration of the two year period, Lester brought the situation to the attention of Leland Harrison, the United States Minister in Bern, Switzerland.[38] Lester told Harrison that the Secretariat was not in a position to take any action, but that any government, whether a Member of the League or not, might feel free to act. Harrison forwarded the information and Lester's views to Washington, and the State Department reported the situation to Robert Murphy, one of its representatives then in North Africa. Murphy discussed the matter with General Henri Giraud, who was President, along with General Charles de Gaulle, of the French Committee of National Liberation.[39] Giraud was in

---

[35] *Ibid.*, notes prepared by Martin Hill on the I.L.O. Conference, May 22, 1944, p. 12.
[36] *Id.*, p. 13.
[37] League of Nations Document C.26.M.23.1941, April 21, 1941.
[38] Memorandum by Arthur Sweetser, dated April 1943.
[39] For further details, see *National Archives,* 500.C001/1525 (telegram from Leland

Algiers, and de Gaulle in London. On April 15, 1943, Giraud addressed a telegram to Carl Hambro, Chairman of the Supervisory Commission, although the message was sent to Geneva and received by Lester. Giraud stated that in agreement with General de Gaulle

I have the honour to inform you that the French at present free to express their will cannot regard as effective the notification which was made to you on April 19th 1941 when the French people deprived of the exercise of their sovereignty were not in a position to express through the medium of lawful representatives their views on the position of France in relation to the League of Nations. I accordingly request you to be good enough to consider that the said notification made under foreign pressure can have no effect and that consequently France continues to be a Member of the League of Nations.[40]

General de Gaulle in London dispatched the same message, addressed to the Secretary-General in Geneva, on April 16th. He added that the Committee of which he was a co-President had always considered "that France continued to be bound by her engagements and retained her prerogatives as a Member of the League of Nations".[41] He referred to the fact that Lester in Geneva had been kept informed of the measures taken by France under her mandates in the Middle East and in the territories of the Cameroons.

Lester informed Loveday and Jacklin at once, and the latter, on Lester's instructions, informed the members of the Supervisory Commission. There was no problem in accepting Giraud's and de Gaulle's refusal to permit France to leave the League. The Supervisory Commission asserted it was "conscious of the great value of France's membership of the League" and that it had taken note of the messages from Giraud and de Gaulle "with lively satisfaction".[42] France thus remained a Member of the League of Nations, largely because of the efforts of the United States State Department, acting on information from the Acting Secretary-General in Geneva.[43]

Generally, however, Lester and his remaining staff went very far to avoid

---

Harrison in Bern, Switzerland to Secretary of State Hull, dated March 20, 1943, and Hull's telegram instructions to Robert Murphy dated March 24, 1943); 500.C001/1526 (Murphy's response to Hull dated April 10, 1943); and 500.C001/1528 (telegram from Leland Harrison dated May 3, 1943).

[40] League of Nations Document C.8.M.8.1943, April 19, 1943.

[41] Ibid.

[42] League of Nations Document C.23.M.23.1943, September 20, 1943.

[43] The issue was of more than academic interest to France. On October 16, 1944, Georges Bidault, then the Minister for Foreign Affairs of the French Provisional Government, wrote to Lester concerning the functions in France of the League High Commissioner for Refugees. Bidault referred to the fact that an Agreement signed by France on March 11, 1929 (calling for certain services in France by the representative of the High Commissioner) was denounced on December 13, 1941 "by the de facto authority styling itself the Government of the French State". Bidault stated that the Provisional Government of the French Republic considered as null and void the denunciation, and the French Government would ensure the application of the Agreement. See League of Nations Document C.32.M.32.1944.

the impression of any League political action. The Acting Secretary-General insisted that his annual reports be almost totally descriptive and factual. He considered it impossible for him, "while holding headquarters here in Europe".[44] to write his reports in a fashion aimed at stirring popular interest or imagination. He felt that even had the Secretariat been removed entirely to the United States, or to any free atmosphere, there would have been a serious question whether any but a purely descriptive report was desirable.

The aim of his reports, wrote Lester in 1941, "had to be more or less in that of establishing in the Governments' minds that the organization functioned in spite of all its difficulties and that it wanted only a reviving touch of power to make it what they would".[45] He was satisfied that most of his reporting from Geneva "will seem humdrum matter-of-fact foot-pace stuff".[46] But he believed that if the reports gave the impression of an organization alive, working, and retaining its potentiality, enough would be achieved. Lester maintained this pattern in his reports, although in 1944 and after, there was a certain tendency to include a few "touches of eloquence and vision"[47] that he had earlier felt undesirable.

Similarly, Lester was extremely cautious concerning the nature and extent of publicity to be given the League during the war. He considered it essential to keep the idea of a League of Nations alive, and to portray an accurate picture of its activities in Geneva and elsewhere. He also attempted to demonstrate the past importance of the world organization, and the extent of its influence. But in large part because he recognized a growing interest in world organization in the United States, he wished to move ahead carefully.

He requested some of his former colleagues who were enthusiastic about reviving the League to emphasize that their ideas were their own, and not necessarily those of the Secretariat or of Lester. In 1941 he wrote that despite the fact that "the cauldron of ideas for the future is warming up", the time had not yet come "to crystallize and clarify the position for the future".[48] He was referring to a problem that would emerge to haunt him as plans for a new world organization began to take shape: the relationship between the League of Nations and the new United Nations Organization.

[44] Letter from Lester to Sweetser, August 1, 1941. Sweetser Papers.
[45] *Ibid.*
[46] *Ibid.*
[47] *Ibid.*
[48] Letter from Lester to Sweetser, September 22, 1941. Lester added that "I would not feel so sure on this point if we did not have the skeleton or foundation of the old organization still in existence and I hope likely to survive. The opinion I express in this paragraph may be subject to change within even six months according to developments, but I doubt if the moment has come when we should officially do more than encourage in every possible way interest and vigorous thought in discussing of the future".

Lester continued to underscore the work that had been maintained, rather than the enormous cutbacks in staff, activities, and budget. He didn't like the "deserted Palais des Nations" references that had become quite common, nor did he consider them accurate. While the Council Chamber was obviously deserted, he wanted this and similar reports to be "offset by a picture of quiet, steady work, actual services maintained and being rendered, readiness for the future".[49]

Caution on publicity followed from the League's financial position, and Lester felt strongly that the limited funds available should be utilized for what he perceived as the more essential tasks. He wrote in October, 1941, that Supervisory Commission discussions concerning publicity for the League seemed "extraordinary considering the difficulty I have to get enough money to carry on, in the most conservative economic way, vital technical activities".[50] He resented bitterly the fact of the League's meager financial resources, and observed that his enforced separation from Carl Hambro had made a difference:

The more efforts have been made for economies (and they have been tremendous) the more they [the Supervisory Commission] demand. Two entirely different standards have been applied to the ILO and the Secretariat: *they* are comparatively comfortable and well off, the Secretariat is chivvied; and the more reductions made the more are demanded; then a moment will come when I shall be calmly asked to provide staff and studies which may be impossible. I think a tremendous amount of difficulty has arisen from the separation between the S.C. and myself.[51]

Of the severe problems confronting Lester, however, perhaps none was more difficult than the dilemma of sustaining the League while making way for the United Nations, an issue that grew more acute as the war years unfolded, and as it became manifest that the League would be dissolved and superseded by a new world organization devoted to the same ends. The question was not simply academic, for by 1943 the Acting Secretary-General was faced with the difficulty of requests to League officials to begin work for United Nations agencies, and the resultant conflict of loyalties.

Lester's first recorded thoughts on the matter were set forth in early 1944. He wrote that the League should assist the new organizations in every way compatible with the League's own work, despite a growing governmental reluctance to mention or publish references to the Geneva Organization. Yet the nature of any future world body could not be known at that early date, and under the circumstances, Lester was clear that the League must be fully supported. "It is the positive policy of many Governments", he wrote, "that the League organisation should be kept alive and as active as possible, perhaps without prejudice to a still unpredictable future".[52]

[49] Letter from Lester to Sweetser, August 1, 1941. Sweetser Papers.
[50] Letter from Lester to Sweetser, October 4, 1941. Sweetser Papers.
[51] *Ibid.*
[52] Letter of February 24, 1944 from Lester to Dr. R. Gautier, a leading League health official, in response to a letter from Dr. Gautier. Dr. Gautier had written on

He stressed his belief in the essentiality of a general international organization, universal in its aim, and with most, if not all, of the principal technical activities coordinated with the political machinery. Changes would undoubtedly be made, although he thought that in the end, they would perhaps be surprisingly few. He cited what he perceived as "a somewhat pathetic passion at times for something new",[53] although he recognized that governments might have sound reasons to construct new organizations. New structures might generate some temporary confusion, but in the final analysis, the needed coordination and cohesion would be restored, and for Lester, the essential source of that cohesion was the League: "it is by no means sure that, in spite of certain current enthusiasms and certain practical needs, a plan for utilizing the League again as the central foundation for the reconstruction will not have substantial advantages".[54]

He also held that the attitude of the American Government was of vital importance in settling the issue of "League versus United Nations", but that Washington's strategy would probably not become entirely clear until after the 1944 Presidential election. Until then, the Government would "follow the line of least resistance building international cooperation piecemeal".[55]

Lester was apparently unaware of American planning for a new world organization, for by the time he recorded his thoughts on the matter, the State Department had published two draft plans for a new organization, and was shortly to publish three more.[56] Not one of these plans assumed the foundation of the new world organization to be the League of Nations. All of them envisaged the establishment of a new general structure for peace under a new constitution or charter. Yet it was also clear that while there was no general plan to revive the League, the new United Nations would

---

September 24, 1943 to Lester that "the time has come when the dilemma 'League of Nations or United Nations' must be faced. If we stick to the League, we will have to be satisfied with our present health activities, which may further disintegrate. If the United Nations card seems the right one, it should be played only if full use is being made of the League's experience and if continuity of action in certain domains is being secured...

This is the position as I see it; no possibilities under the League's auspices but large openings under the aegis of the United Nations. Perhaps the right policy would be to stay put, to wait and see, but the moment you are asked to place your experience at the disposal of a rival agency, you must know where you stand as loyalty is at stake. This is the difficulty I am facing".

[53] Letter from Lester to Dr. R. Gautier, February 24, 1944.
[54] *Ibid.*
[55] *Ibid.*
[56] The Department's Draft Constitution of International Organization was dated July 14, 1943, the Draft Charter of the United Nations was dated August 14, 1943, the Possible Plan for a General International Organization, April 29, 1944, the Tentative Proposals for a General International Organization came on July 18, 1944, and the Dumbarton Oaks Proposals were published on October 7, 1944.

be based almost entirely, in terms of both structure and function, upon the basic concepts underlying the League.

Lester finally left Geneva for London in late 1944 after the liberation of France, and at once became absorbed in preparations for the San Francisco Conference and for the final transfer to the United Nations Organization. His enforced four-year stay at the helm in Geneva had finally ended, and taking one last look back, he wrote in January, 1945, that "it was marvellous getting out to the free world again after my long vigil".[57] The loneliness was rendered tolerable by the activity in Geneva, expanded in great measure as senior colleagues departed, and by his conception that he was "holding a not unimportant part of the political front".[58]

Perhaps the importance of it is now diminished by the progress made towards the new League, though even so I think both a long and a short view will show that it was worth while, even apart from the survival and activity of certain important technical branches.[59]

For Lester personally, the most difficult part was the enforced separation from his family. But "it was not really difficult", he wrote, "to hold on and take the chances of invasion or whatever might come". One became accustomed after a time to German forces so near the Palais des Nations. "I do not take the slightest credit for loyalty in sticking to the post: those are normal things".[60]

In London Lester joined the League's treasurer, Jacklin, and together the two held several preliminary discussions with members of the Supervisory Commission on the numerous problems involved in transferring League services, archives, properties and personnel to what Lester called at the time "the new League". In the early spring of 1945, he returned to Geneva to supervise the work there, to write a final report on the activity of the Organization during the war years, and to prepare for the San Francisco Conference and for the final League Assembly.

It was clear that the League's position at the San Francisco Conference would not be strong. The League was a failure, and in any event, Washington still feared Senate opposition to the Organization. Shortly before President Roosevelt went to the Yalta Conference, he had a long talk with Arthur Sweetser at the White House in which he stressed the necessity of Senate approval for the United Nations and indicated his apprehensions that the country might link it with the League and thereby revive the old isolationist sentiment. Roosevelt was convinced that the most appropriate strategy was to establish an entirely new organization and of course this policy had formed the basis of the State Department's planning for the new United

[57] Letter from Lester to Sweetser, January 22, 1945. Sweetser Papers.
[58] *Ibid.*
[59] *Ibid.*
[60] *Ibid.*

Nations. The Soviet Union had its own reasons for supporting a new world organization. Moscow did not look kindly upon the Organization from which it had been expelled in 1939, and in addition, Lester and Phelan were citizens of Ireland, a country that remained neutral during the Second World War. In the Russian view, both the League and its leadership had been discredited.

Thus both the great superpowers wished to establish a new beginning, and with Soviet-American cooperation the keystone upon which the United Nations Organization was to be constructed, it was soon obvious that the men who held the League together during the war would have little influence at San Francisco.

Lester was aware of this, and fully realized that his own position at the Conference would be difficult. He wrote to Loveday in March, 1945 that if League officials were to be called upon seriously, he would need a strong group of advisers and assistants. Yet, he wrote, "it is pointed out to me... that it may be more a question of keeping in touch with the intention and spirit of the Conference in order to understand and cooperate more effectively later when the transition period opens and we obtain the necessary authority from our own Institution".[61]

Invitations to the League officials were formally issued by the State Department and approved by the Supervisory Commission. The League Secretariat group was headed by Lester, Loveday, and Jacklin. The International Labor Office was represented by Phelan, and the Permanent Court of International Justice by Julio Lopez Olivan, its Registrar, a citizen of Spain. The Soviet Union, alone among the Big Five, did not approve of the invitations initially, but relented on the State Department's assurances that the League, International Labor Office and Court officials would be invited by the United States "as host country" and only as "unofficial representatives" who might be available in San Francisco "for informal discussions".[62]

The welcome accorded Lester, Loveday, and Jacklin demonstrated clearly that the San Francisco Conference organizers were indeed most anxious to keep League officials in the background. They were assigned to a minor hotel, and seated in the next to last row of the top gallery in the Opera House where the Conference was being held.[63] The situation worsened further as the proceedings began. The State Department intimated to Lester and Loveday that some difficulties had arisen and it might be better if Lester were not present. Lester in turn insisted that he was not at San Francisco as an individual or as a citizen of the Irish Free State, but as the representative of the League of Nations. Alger Hiss, the

61 Letter from Lester to Alexander Loveday, March 2, 1945.
62 Memorandum by Arthur Sweetser, dated 12 May, 1945.
63 No seats on the main floor were available to them for a month, although from the start, all forty-two American private organizations at the Conference were seated on the main floor with all the delegates.

Secretary-General of the San Francisco Conference, also felt that Lester's presence would cause difficulties.[64]

An early compromise was reached. The International Labor Office authorities agreed that Phelan, who was still in Montreal, should not attend the Conference, and it was further agreed by the Court representatives that Lopez Olivan, who had already come from Geneva to San Francisco, would not be included in the League Delegation. Lester, however, after consultation with Carl Hambro and other members of the Supervisory Commission at the Conference, took the position that he must be recognized and continue as head of the League group, or the entire League Delegation would have to withdraw.

The matter was referred to the Steering Committee of the Conference, but this body simply sent the issue back to the various substantive committees for each one to decide for itself. The only invitation to Lester came from the Economic and Social Committee, and then only after much hesitation. Lester had informed the Committee that if he were invited, he would send Loveday as his representative, and at that point the invitation to Lester was sent out. The Acting Secretary-General of the League never appeared before any of the Committees at San Francisco, was never consulted by any of them, and was never asked to express his views on any topic. A little more than a month after he arrived at the Conference, Lester quietly went back to Geneva to continue preparations for the last League Assembly and for the final transfer to the United Nations.[65]

Loveday and Jacklin fared only slightly better. Loveday was invited to comment on details concerning League committee structure, and later he gave a long statement on the organization of the League Secretariat. His twenty-five years of experience with economic questions was largely ignored. Jacklin's detailed knowledge of budget questions was tapped only for the purpose of allowing him fifteen minutes on a recommendation for financing the United Nations during the interim period prior to its formal functioning.

The recognition due Sean Lester finally began to appear shortly after the San Francisco Conference. In the autumn of 1945, the Woodrow Wilson Foundation Directors voted to honor him with the Woodrow Wilson Award, citing him for 'distinguished service in maintaining throughout World War II the principles and the mechanism of the League of Nations which President Wilson was instrumental in creating after World War I".[66] The announcement continued:

---

[64] Sweetser Memorandum, *op. cit.*
[65] See *The New York Times,* June 23, 1945, pp. 1, 2.
[66] Letter from the President of the Woodrow Wilson Foundation to Lester, November 23, 1945.

The Directors wished by this action to recognize your steadfastness and loyalty in holding to a difficult post during six long war years when much other support was withdrawn; your success despite extreme obstacles in maintaining and operating such League services as were possible in war conditions; and, above all, your vision and generosity of spirit in making available to the new agency of the United Nations the rich experience and valuable facilities of the predecessor agency which had pointed out the way.[67]

Lester accepted the award "on behalf of all my colleagues wherever they served" in recognition of the loyalty of those who "would not yield their integrity nor allow force or the threat of force to mould their conduct".[68] He added:

In the Court of Honour of these great buildings in Geneva stands a monument to President Wilson. The League of Nations itself has been his greater monument and the world-wide services it has given during a quarter of a century are the fruits of his thought and judgment. The catastrophe of war, which could have been avoided by following Woodrow Wilson's sublimely commonsense vision, is his terrible and final justification.
The peoples are now rebuilding that which they destroyed by timidity or neglect.[69]

At the same time, Lester emphasized that the United Nations was, in his view, the best hope for peace, and that it "must get every possible support".[70] "It will have its growing pains", he wrote, but that the United States "was at last lining up" meant far more in terms of world peace "than some of the important elements in the Charter".[71]

Further recognition came at the last Assembly of the League of Nations, held in Geneva in April, 1946. Lester wrote to Hambro, who had been elected President of the Assembly, that "it is incumbent on me to take this occasion, the first which has offered, to place my post as Acting Secretary-General at the disposal of the Assembly".[72] The Assembly, on the recommendation of its General Committee, passed a resolution on April 18, 1946, stating that it "confirms Mr. Sean Lester as Secretary-General of the League of Nations as from September 1st, 1940". The delegates to the League's last Assembly, highly appreciative of Lester's work, bestowed much praise and approbation. Thanassis Aghnides, the former Under Secretary-General who remained with Lester in Geneva for part of the war period, spoke of his chief as having "held high the torch of that ideal to

[67] *Ibid.*
[68] Letter from Lester to the President of the Woodrow Wilson Foundation, December 4, 1945.
[69] *Ibid.*
[70] Letter from Lester to Sweetser, December 4, 1945. Sweetser Papers.
[71] *Ibid.*
[72] League of Nations Document A.17.1946, March 28, 1946. Lester added that when Avenol resigned in August, 1940, "a meeting of the Assembly to consider action under Article 6 (paragraph 2) of the Covenant was impracticable and the duties and responsibilities were therefore allotted to me. All Governments of Members of the League were fully and duly informed of the circumstances by the competent authorities".

which all of us without exception pay homage".[73] Carl Hambro, referring to the role of the Supervisory Commission during the war, and the necessity at that time for close cooperation between the Acting Secretary-General and other League officers, declared:

Much was demanded of Mr. Lester and Mr. Phelan, both initiative and resignation. Mr. Lester took over the functions of Secretary-General at a time of great confusion in the affairs of the Secretariat. How he took charge of the ship and enabled it to weather the storm is described throughout the pages of our annual reports. During the most difficult years he was obliged to stay in Geneva. We could communicate with him only by wire and sometimes by letter. And it is thanks to his loyalty and devotion and the mutual trust which inspired our work that no misunderstandings were allowed to disturb the work. He was a lonely man, exposed to many dangers and difficulties, and I pay the highest tribute to his spirit of loyalty and helpfulness.[74]

For Philip Noel-Baker, Sean Lester's position in Geneva brought to mind the words of Seneca: "With nothing to hope for, he despaired of nothing".[75] For Lester himself, the designation as Secretary-General was an honor. In a note reviewing the last League Assembly, Lester concluded by stating simply that "The Assembly...honoured me by giving me the post of Secretary-General, with retroactive effect from 1st September 1940, thus making me the third and last Secretary-General".[76]

All that remained for the League's last Secretary-General was the transfer to the United Nations of the assets and responsibilities of the Organization he represented. As early as September, 1945, Lester had been in close contact with Gladwyn Jebb of Great Britain, the Executive Secretary of the United Nations Preparatory Commission's Executive Committee, on the subject of the transfer of the League's activities. Jebb was requested by the Executive Committee to enlist Lester's cooperation so as to obtain information for the United Nations on all League activities, powers attributed to it by international treaties, and its assets and obligations. The information was supplied by Lester, both through written documents and oral discussions held between Lester, Jebb, and David Owen, then Jebb's assistant and later Executive Assistant and Assistant Secretary-General of the United Nations.[77]

Lester's greatest concern at this time was the transfer of the League Secretariat staff to the United Nations. He wrote a long note in November, 1945, examining various contingencies for the staff transfer, and suggesting means for the mitigation of hardships that might be entailed.[78] At the same

[73] League of Nations, *Official Journal*, Special Supplement No. 194, Records of the 21st Ordinary Session of the Assembly, Plenary, Fifth Meeting, April 12, 1946, p. 52.
[74] *Id.*, Second (Finance) Committee, First Meeting, April 8, 1946, p. 114.
[75] *Id.*, Plenary, Seventh Meeting, April 18, 1946, p. 64.
[76] Note by Sean Lester, April 25, 1946. Sweetser Papers.
[77] League Archives: General and Miscellaneous, 50/43298/4362.
[78] *Ibid.* In November, 1945, there were, according to Lester's note on transfer of Secretariat staff, 160 League Secretariat officials; of that number, 120 were in Geneva, 30 in the United States, 2 in New Delhi, and the remainder in London.

time, and throughout the entire next year, Lester, along with Jacklin, Henri Vigier, and a representative of the International Labor Office, took part in discussions with the Supervisory Commission, the newly-created Board of Liquidation (established by the last League Assembly in April, 1946), and the United Nations, on the many problems involved in the transfer.

The result of earlier discussions between a committee established by the United Nations Preparatory Commission and the Supervisory Commission was the "Common Plan" (approved by the United Nations in February, 1946 and by the League in April, 1946) for the transfer of League assets. Working under the Plan, Lester served with the League's Board of Liquidation and the United Nations committee, supervising the gradual transfer of assets, activities, and staff to the new world organization. The League, while formally dissolved in April, 1946, evidently continued to exist until September, 1947, through the Board of Liquidation and the Secretary-General, for the limited purpose of completing the transfer. Lester's work during this period included the power to bind the League by signing protocols transferring particular services, staff, and property, or by placing a valuation upon certain League assets.

The remaining League staff was progressively reduced, and in part transferred to the United Nations, until by the end of April, 1947, the League Secretariat consisted of only nineteen officials, most of whom stayed on to complete the liquidation.[79] The Board of Liquidation's final report, published at the end of July, 1947, revealed that more than two hundred former members of the League Secretariat had accepted employment with the United Nations or with Specialized Agencies. "The Board is glad to note", says the final report, "that the successor international organisations have thus secured the advantage of the experience gained by these officials during their service with the League Secretariat".[80]

The Board's figures, of course, did not include the considerable number of former League Secretariat members who had resigned prior to 1946 and were later taken on by the United Nations. The earliest available United Nations staff list (October 1947) shows that apart from language staff, some forty persons of member of section level or higher who at one time had worked in the League or International Labor Office were, by the middle of 1947, working at United Nations Headquarters at Lake Success.

Several of the League Secretariat's greatest names came over to the United Nations. Thanassis Aghnides became head of the UN's Advisory Committee on Administrative and Budgetary Questions. Arthur Sweetser, one of the key figures in the League's information program and one of the League's most important links to the United States, became a special adviser to Secretary-General Trygve Lie and later Director of the United Nations

[79] League of Nations Document C.4.M.4.1947, May 1, 1947 (at p. 6), being the fourth interim report of the League of Nations Board of Liquidation.
[80] League of Nations Document C.5.M.5.1947, 31 July 1947.

Washington Information Center. Today only two figures remain: Henri Vigier, one of the few to stay with Lester in Geneva, went on to become a senior officer in the United Nations Department of Political and Security Council Affairs, and later was appointed to the position of Chief Political Officer of the United Nations Truce Supervision Organization in Palestine. Martin Hill, who had worked with Loveday at Princeton, rose in the United Nations Department of Economic and Social Affairs to become a Deputy Under Secretary-General.

For Lester, however, the end of his work on the League's liquidation meant the end of his public responsibilities. The Board of Liquidation was dissolved after the issuance of its final report at the end of July, 1947, and all that remained was the distribution of non-transferable assets to United Nations Members entitled to participate. In August Lester communicated to those Members information on their shares, and in September he circulated as a League document Secretary-General Lie's reply, addressed to Secretary-General Lester.[81] Lester's work was completed, and he ceased to be the first official of the League of Nations.

He returned to Ireland to stay, and never again did he accept a position in public life. He had had enough, and wished to spend his remaining years in quiet seclusion with his family. Ireland offered him the positions of Ambassador to the United Nations or Minister in Washington. The United Nations itself approached Lester to discover whether he might be interested in the position of Principal Secretary and Representative of the Secretary-General in Kashmir, a position later taken by Eric Colban of Norway, another old League hand. He was also approached on the post of Principal Secretary of the Palestine Conciliation Commission, later taken by Pablo de Azcaraté.

Lester was determined, however, to avoid political responsibilities. He bought a fishing lodge on the edge of a large lake in County Galway in Ireland, and for the rest of his life his primary occupations were fishing, gardening, and reading on international politics. Public honor came again in 1947, with an honorary Doctor of Laws degree from the University of Dublin, and in 1948, with the same degree from the National University of Ireland. Lester also served as President of the Permanent Norwegian-Swiss Conciliation Commission, although this did not involve substantial public activity.

According to Carl Hambro, Lester had additional reasons for refusing to serve his country's government. Lester considered that his position as Secretary-General of the League of Nations was reason enough not to serve any one state, as Sir Eric Drummond had done after his resignation as Secretary-General, and in addition, according to Hambro, Lester's Irish Methodist views put him somewhat out of sympathy with de Valera's policy.

[81] League of Nations Document C.6.M.6.1947, September 9, 1947.

Most of the former League officials who knew Lester, however, are of the opinion that his primary reasons for retiring from public life were essentially personal. He was tired of the strains, affected and aged by the loneliness of his war-time Geneva experience, and obviously desirous of spending more time with his family. For almost twelve years, Sean Lester relaxed in his native Ireland. On June 13, 1959, he died at his home in County Galway.

Lester's death went almost unnoticed in the world press and in the United Nations. Arthur Breycha-Vauthier, League and United Nations Librarian in Geneva, wrote an article on Lester for the "U.N. Special" in Geneva, and another article appeared shortly thereafter in "La Tribune de Geneve". Carl Hambro also wrote an appreciation of Lester for a Norwegian journal.[82] Perhaps it was Breycha-Vauthier who best summed up Lester's position and contribution to the ideal of a world organization for peace: "It is difficult, if not impossible, for the new generation of international civil servants to realize what it all meant to be Secretary-General in the then central body of the world's Organization amidst the same world at war. Initiative and resignation were both equally needed for the wearing task which a lonely man carried out all those years with loyalty and devotion through which the bridge of confidence was strengthened between the semi-deserted Palais in Geneva and the free world at large".[83]

---

[82] Carl Hambro, "Sean Lester—The Man Who Remained True to His Ideals", *Aftenposten,* 25 July 1959. (Title translated from the Norwegian.)
[83] Breycha-Vauthier, "Sean Lester", *U.N. Special,* Vol. 9, No. 21, July 1959, pp. 1, 2.

CHAPTER IV

Trygve Lie
Secretary-General of the United Nations
1946-1953

To be the first Secretary-General during the formative years of the United Nations has been, indeed, a rare opportunity to be given any man for service in the cause of peace and for his fellow human beings. I thank the Governments of the Member States for giving me this opportunity. No man in this position could fail to make mistakes, and I have probably made my share... But there is a sense of satisfaction in knowing that you have done the best you could in the role that history has chosen for you, and that there are many others who will carry on the unfinished task of constructing a better and more peaceful world order. My share in the task has fallen in the founding and early testing period of the United Nations.
Trygve Lie, April 7, 1953

As the League of Nations gave way during the Second World War to the new United Nations Organization, the international system was remarkably transformed, with some of the differences from the League era auguring well for world order, and others indicating that international organizations devoted to the maintenance of peace faced a difficult and uncertain future.

On the one hand, the United Nations was to be a more nearly universal organization than the League, rather than a European-centered institution. The United States was determined not to revert to the isolation of the inter-war years, both because of its emergence from war as one of the greatest powers in the history of nations, and the crucial policy determinant of maintaining a decisive influence in the military decisions of post-war Europe. The Soviet Union as well, with powerful controls in Eastern Europe and world-wide interests, decided during the war to have an important role in world organization, and the nation that just a few years earlier had been expelled from the League now found itself a permanent member of the UN's Security Council, projected as the central organ of world-wide collective security. Until 1949 and the victory of the Communists in the Chinese civil war, each of the great powers was so represented, and the general membership approached very nearly the totality of independent states. The decay of colonial empires and the stirrings of Afro-Asian nationhood, along with the UN's commitment to freedom for non-self-governing peoples, further strengthened the global body in terms of breadth of membership.

The imminent collapse of colonialism and the agonies of Nazism also generated a substantial interest in the organized international community in economic and social development, as well as protection of basic human rights, and these themes were reflected in the UN Charter far more explicitly than in the League Covenant. World order strategies and the general issue of the maintenance of peace were perceived at San Francisco in 1945 as far more closely dependent upon economic and social variables than the statesmen at Versailles in 1919 were ready to admit. And notwithstanding extraordinary difficulties, these were issues upon which more solid agreement and accomplishment might be expected than in the contentious arenas of political and military influence and power.

Of great importance also was the enormous increase in communications capacity in the years since the founding of the League. Perhaps the most critical factor in the integration of political communities is the volume of transactions and communication, and surely these must be well developed if international institutions are to be established and maintained with any significant relevance for world politics. The United Nations has been the beneficiary, when measured against the League era, of an astonishing leap in technology and science that has considerably aided the UN in the performance of each of its basic functions.

Finally, the new world institution was the creation and embodiment of a very powerful idealism that was one of the central features of the international system just after the war. A world war can create an atmosphere of flux in which great changes become feasible, and when the war is fought against the tyranny of fascism and militarism, the devotion to peaceful change and progressive government predictably follow, and naturally find a place in a world structure for peace. The UN, much like the League, was a kind of pledge by the political elites of the international community to prevent still another conflagration of terror.

Yet most political analysts and decision-makers were not optimistic about the UN, for the realities of world power argued too strongly against any easy assumptions of a better world order. First, of course, the cold war conflict between the United States and the Soviet Union eliminated at once the possibility of implementing the new norms of collective security written into the UN Charter, and the great hostility between the superpowers rendered the Organization almost impotent as each side prepared to commit its security to immense weapons systems and regional military alliances. The UN was to have no real military or political power of its own, and the most likely prospect then was its utilization by the strong nations for diplomatic and propaganda purposes.

Further, competition between East and West and resultant mutual suspicions greatly weakened the Organization's promise even in areas not directly related to the security interests of Washington or Moscow, and certainly destroyed any capacity for UN action in the more sensitive questions of the time. The United States, fearful of Soviet expansionism, committed itself to the Truman Doctrine, the Marshall Plan, and a united

Western Europe, but its assistance was primarily bilateral rather than through the UN, and its military security planning was carried through without reference to world institution building. The atomic bomb generated enormous pressures in the Kremlin for an equal capacity to destroy, and atomic and conventional arms control seemed an impossible dream.

Limited successes appeared not unlikely in colonial and emerging nations, but essentially the United Nations Charter became obsolete in the most fundamental sense even before the Organization began to function, for the instrument of collective security had been changed into a weak and uncertain third party neutral intermediary at best, with East and West both clamoring to direct its behavior or at least use its forums to publish widely their favored views and programs. The threat of war, subversion, government takeover, and social and economic revolution confronted the Organization with challenges it was not equipped to handle adequately, and could not be, given the emnity between the gradual reformist and revolutionary perspectives of Washington and Moscow. Into this setting stepped Trygve Lie, the first Secretary-General of the United Nations, who, from his election in 1946 to a forced resignation in 1953, made a great contribution in terms of constructing and building an Organization and Office of Secretary-General, and seeing them through the early period of their harshest trials.

The central theme underlying the discussions at the San Francisco conference in 1945 was that the new United Nations Organization, while modeled after its League of Nations predecessor, would be more powerful than the League, more influential in world politics, and possessed of resources sufficient to construct a more rational and ethical world order than had theretofore prevailed. Among these resources, of course, was the Secretariat of the international organization, headed by a single Secretary-General empowered by the UN founding fathers with a very substantial political role in addition to the normal administrative capacity enjoyed by the League of Nations Secretary-General. San Francisco ratified what the League experience demonstrated was fact—that is, the head of the international civil service has the opportunity and resources, even without explicit constitutional prerogatives, to influence the course of decision-making in the international arena, and it was decided very early to legitimize that influence and if possible, carry it further by means of particular Charter norms.

Indeed, in one of its central position papers prior to the 1944 Dumbarton Oaks conversations among the Big Four, the United States State Department proposed a dual leadership for the Secretariat, composed of a President with primary political responsibility, and a Secretary-General for essentially internal administrative matters.[1] The plan was dropped, but the measure of

---

[1] This was the State Department's Possible Plan for a General International Organization, dated April 29, 1944. See *Postwar Foreign Policy Preparation 1939-1945*

political responsibility for the UN's chief officer did not disappear, as the Big Four early decided that the Secretary-General should combine political and administrative tasks, both to be recognized by the new Charter.

The San Francisco conference, in its construction of the new UN constitution, devoted Chapter XV to the Secretariat, including Articles 97 to 101. Article 7 of the Charter also mentions the Secretariat as one of the principal organs of the United Nations, apparently placing the Secretary-General on a par with the primary political bodies of the Organization, this also serving to strengthen the Secretary-General's political standing.

Under Article 97, the Secretary-General is listed as the chief administrative officer of the Organization, interpreted later by the Preparatory Commission of the United Nations as entailing general administrative and executive functions, technical and financial functions, and final responsibility for the organization and administration of the Secretariat.

Of greatest significance, however, was the insertion of Article 99 into the Charter, for here the international community was explicitly recognizing the political prerogatives of the Secretary-General, thereby clearly distinguishing his position from that of the League Secretary-General, and strengthening the independent executive capacity of the new global institution. Article 99 provides that "the Secretary-General may bring to the attention of the Security Council any matter which in his opinion may threaten the maintenance of international peace and security". The wording is important not so much for the specific authorization it provides the Secretary-General, but rather as a fundamental constitutional authorization of a political role for the executive head of the Secretariat, necessarily subsuming several political functions not mentioned specifically in the Charter. Thus, for example, it might be thought to follow logically that the Secretary-General has the legal capacity to undertake investigations on his own initiative for purposes of determining whether or not a threat to the peace exists, and indeed this construction has been borne out by subsequent practice of the Secretary-General. Political functions also entail processes of mediation and negotiation with representatives of member states, very much along the lines of behind-the-scenes discussions carried on by Sir Eric Drummond and Joseph Avenol during their administrations. A political role includes the right to draft proposals and resolutions for consideration by the UN's political organs, a prerogative much utilized by the three United Nations Secretaries-General. Further, given the legal parity of the Secretary-General with the main political organs of the UN, in addition to the key function prescribed by Article 99, it becomes clear that the Secretary-General alone symbolizes and speaks for the entire international community as represented by the UN.

(Washington: Department of State, Publication 3580; General Foreign Policy Series: 15, U.S. Government Printing Office, 1950), p. 590.

There were proposals at San Francisco for a further extension of the Secretary-General's political rights, including one suggestion enabling him to notify the General Assembly, as well as the Security Council, of any matter threatening international peace. Another recommendation was that the Secretary-General be enabled to bring before the Council any matter constituting a breach of basic Charter principles. Both were voted down, although there was very little discussion of the precise nature and proper limits of the Secretary-General's political functions, this being apparently due to an insufficient appreciation of the possibilities inherent in the Office and an implicit understanding that despite Article 99, the greater portion of the Secretary-General's labor would be in the administrative realm. The Preparatory Commission, however, indicated its more sweeping appreciation of community expectations concerning the political functions of the UN's first official:

The Secretary-General may have an important role to play as mediator and as an informal adviser of many governments, and will undoubtedly be called upon from time to time, in the exercise of his administrative duties, to take decisions which may justly be called political. Under Article 99 of the Charter, moreover, he has been given a quite special right which goes beyond any power previously accorded to the head of an international organization, viz: to bring to the attention of the Security Council any matter (not merely any dispute or situation) which, in his opinion, may threaten the maintenance of international peace and security. It is impossible to foresee how this Article will be applied; but the responsibility it confers upon the Secretary-General will require the exercise of the highest qualities of political judgment, tact and integrity.

The United Nations cannot prosper, nor can its aims be realized, without the active and steadfast support of the peoples of the world. The aims and activities of the General Assembly, the Security Council, the Economic and Social Council and the Trusteeship Council will, no doubt, be represented before the public primarily by the Chairman of these organs. But the Secretary-General, more than anyone else, will stand for the United Nations as a whole. In the eyes of the world, no less than in the eyes of his own staff, he must embody the principles and ideals of the Charter to which the Organization seeks to give effect.[2]

Article 98 of the Charter, while not generally considered to be of any great political significance at the San Francisco Conference, has evolved into still another constitutional authorization of wide-ranging political functions for the UN's chief executive. Under its provisions, the Secretary-General is to act in "that capacity" at all meetings of the Assembly and the Councils, "and shall perform such other functions as are entrusted to him by these organs. The Secretary-General shall make an annual report to the General Assembly on the work of the Organization". The "other functions" phrase generated no discussion at San Francisco, nor did Secretary-General Lie make extensive use of it for purposes of developing political prerogatives. Under Dag Hammarskjold, the phrase became a valuable instrument enabling the General Assembly and Security Council to entrust to the

[2] Preparatory Commission, *Report,* U.N. Doc. PC/20, 1945.

Secretary-General broadly-based mandates often governed by deliberately vaguely worded resolutions drafted in such fashion as to permit the Secretariat and Executive Office to perform the key decision-making role in the establishment and maintenance of international peacekeeping forces.

The Annual Report of the Secretary-General has clearly become a vital instrument in the movement toward more substantial political influence for the Secretary-General, as it has developed into a searching political and social analysis of the critical issues in world politics and UN involvement therein, frequently containing the Secretary-General's own recommendations for resolution of particular conflicts and pointing to directions in which the world organization might move in the achievement of its fundamental purposes.

The early planning for the Secretary-General's position also indicated general concern with the Office's political significance in the context of procedures for election, and the term of office. The Preparatory Commission stipulated, and the General Assembly later agreed, that the Security Council's nomination of a Secretary-General necessitated an affirmative vote of seven members, including the permanent members, and a majority of the General Assembly. The interest of the great powers in the identity of the Secretary-General was perhaps the best evidence that the Office was to have more than simple administrative functions to perform. It was also agreed that the first Secretary-General should be appointed for a five-year term, subject to renewal for another five-years. A relatively short term, combined with rotation in nationality, were important indicators of the perceived importance of the Office. Still further, the Preparatory Commission stated that only one candidate should be proffered for consideration by the Assembly, and that open debate should be avoided. A single figure representative of the Organization as a whole is less likely to be in a position to achieve significant results if his election has been preceded by disruptive debate in which his opponents make public their dissatisfaction.

Reflecting the experience of Sir Eric Drummond, the Preparatory Commission also recommended a clause governing the activity of the Secretary-General subsequent to his term of office: "Because a Secretary-General is a confidant of many governments, it is desirable that no Member should offer him, at any rate immediately on retirement, any governmental position in which his confidential information might be a source of embarrassment to other Members, and on his part a Secretary-General should refrain from accepting any such position".[3] The 1946 General Assembly session later provided that a retiring Secretary-General would receive a $ 10,000 pension for life—that is, a pension equal to one-half of the $ 20,000 salary recommended by the Preparatory Commission.

Quite important in the general scheme established at San Francisco is

[3] *Ibid.*

Article 100 of the Charter declaring that "In the performance of their duties the Secretary-General and the staff shall not seek or receive instructions from any government or from any other authority external to the Organization. They shall refrain from any action which might reflect on their position as international officials responsible only to the Organization". The second paragraph of Article 100 enjoins member nations to respect the international character of the Secretary-General's responsibilities as well as those of his staff, and obligates members to refrain from influencing the executive in the discharge of its responsibilities. This is a clear constitutional formulation of Sir Eric Drummond's initial notion of an international secretariat, one which is not stipulated in the League Covenant, but which he successfully established from the start of his administration in 1920. Drummond's conception of an international staff responsible only to the Organization it served was severely challenged by the Italian and German Under Secretaries-General toward the end of the League's first decade, and was to be challenged again during the United Nations era, but the general consensus of the world community in 1945, derived largely from the League experience, was that international service was practical and essential for furthering a movement toward rational world order. And this too could not help but strengthen the Secretary-General's political hand, for an independent and neutral civil service was far less likely to arouse, at least in the first instance, immediate suspicion from members who did not control the decision-making process at the top level of the Secretariat.

Whether in terms of administration, finance, or political responsibilities, the founding fathers at San Francisco constructed an Office of Secretary-General much like Drummond's model, but with enhanced and more meaningful tasks in international relations. Indeed, as noted, in Article 7 of the new Charter, the Secretariat (for which legal scholars and later Dag Hammarskjold read Secretary-General) is listed as one of the principal organs of the United Nations, along with the General Assembly, the Councils, and the World Court. The Charter was intended as a constitutional-type document, and of course everything depended upon its construction, which in turn would depend necessarily on the relationships among the world community, particularly the great powers. The instrument was there, as was agreement for the establishment of a chief executive serving the interests of the international community, and with powers unknown in the history of nations.

The Election of Trygve Lie as Secretary-General

Trygve Lie, born on July 16, 1896 in an Oslo suburb in Norway, was raised and trained in an atmosphere one would have thought hardly conducive to a career as Secretary-General of the United Nations. The Lie family was poor, and dependent entirely upon the father's small income as a carpenter. The elder Lie died when the son was a small boy, whereupon his mother established a boarding house to support the family. It was by means of the boarding house that Lie got his start in Norwegian Labour Party politics, for through the assistance of some of the boarders he was given a job as office boy and clerk at the Norwegian Labour Party National Headquarters in Oslo, a position that helped pave the way for his later career as an active member of the Labour Party.

When only sixteen years of age, Lie was elected President of the Organization's branch at Aker, a position he held concurrently with his office post at Party Headquarters until the completion of his law studies at the Oslo University in 1919. From that point, at age twenty-three, his rise in party politics and government position was rapid, the first responsible appointment being that of assistant to the Secretary of the Norwegian Labour Party from 1919 to 1922. By 1926 he was the Party's National Executive Secretary and from 1922 to 1935, he served as general counsel to the Norwegian Trades Unions Federation.

Lie's advance to national office in Norway came in 1935 when he was thirty-nine years old. He served as Minister of Justice in the Cabinet from 1935 to 1939, having been elected to the Parliament in 1935 and later re-elected in 1945. In 1939 he held the portfolio for trade, industry, shipping and fishing, as well as that of supply. With the invasion of Norway by the Nazis in 1940, Lie escaped to England with his government, but not without achieving substantial success for the Allied cause through his order to some 25,000 seamen to stay out of Norwegian ports, thus saving the Norwegian fleet, more than 3.5 million tons of shipping, from the Nazis. As a member of the Norwegian government-in-exile in London, Lie became acting Foreign Minister in 1940 and Foreign Minister in 1941. In April, 1945, he was appointed chairman of the Norwegian delegation to the United Nations Conference on International Organization at San Francisco, and while there, served as chairman of Commission III of the Conference, charged with drafting the articles of the Charter dealing with the Security Council. At the end of the war, Lie resigned as Foreign Minister, but was reappointed by the new Labour Government in October, 1945, and in his capacity as Foreign Minister, served as Chairman of the Norwegian delegation to the first UN General Assembly, held in London in 1946.

In January, 1946, one of the first significant political issues for the great powers at the London Assembly was the selection of the General Assembly's first president, a position to be held for just one year, but nevertheless deemed to be of importance, given the organizational responsibilities incumbent upon the first president, and of course the value inherent in the first indication of the new Organization's political leadership for the immediate post-war period.

Trygve Lie was both Washington's and Moscow's first choice for the post, and yet he was defeated by Paul-Henri Spaak, the Foreign Minister of Belgium. Cold war contention and confusion over the Assembly's rules of procedure were responsible for Lie's 28-23 defeat by Spaak, for the Soviets insisted on public nominations of Assembly presidents, a notion the United States disputed, and Soviet speeches on behalf of Lie's candidacy were met with silence by the American delegation, which felt the procedure to be harmful (it was later revised to prohibit public nominations) and that Moscow's warm support of Lie prevented Washington from taking a similar stance. The failure of the United States to speak out, and what was apparently viewed in some corners as Soviet "railroading",[4] convinced several smaller states that Spaak was the more appropriate choice. The United States had put no great pressure on its Latin American allies to vote for Lie, and the upshot was his defeat in a contest he wished to avoid but could not, given Norway's reluctance to evade the responsibility of the Assembly presidency after the initial declarations of American and Russian support. Had Moscow not insisted upon public nominations and supporting speeches in the Assembly, it is quite likely that Trygve Lie would have assumed the Assembly presidency, and thus of course been ineligible for the post of Secretary-General.

It seemed evident from the start that the first Secretary-General of the United Nations would have to be a national of one of the small powers, assuming increased political responsibilities and given the necessity for agreement by each of the Big Five on the Security Council prior to Assembly election. Nevertheless, among the several candidates mentioned as possibilities was Anthony Eden, who, as he later indicated, would not have rejected the nomination had it been offered to him.[5] His nomination was unacceptable to the new Labour Party Government, although many UN delegates, including Trygve Lie, regarded Eden as "an ideal choice".[6] Another suggestion for the post was General Dwight D. Eisenhower of the United States, certainly a popular choice for all but the Soviet Union, but quite impossible for that reason, as well as the projected location of the UN in the United States. The dominant powers of the League of Nations had provided that organi-

[4] Trygve Lie, *In the Cause of Peace* (New York: The Macmillan Company, 1954), p. 11. And as Lie noted further, "we both were Social Democratic Foreign Ministers of small Western European countries and in many cases equally unknown". (*Ibid.*)

[5] Eden later wrote in his memoirs: "For a time I was canvassed to be the first Secretary-General at the United Nations. Field-Marshall Smuts and Mr. Peter Fraser were active in this, while Mr. Paul-Boncour was a champion within the circle of the four great powers. The Russians, too, were said to be not unwilling. Mr. Trygve Lie was an enthusiastic protagonist on my behalf. ...I took no step to promote my candidature, but if this offer had been made to me, it could hardly have been refused". Anthony Eden, *The Memoirs of Anthony Eden: The Reckoning* (Boston, Houghton Mifflin Company, 1965), p. 642.

[6] Lie, *op. cit.*, p. 11. Lie states that Eden did not object to having the matter sounded out in London and Moscow.

zation with its first two Secretaries-General, but this was not to be for the new United Nations Organization.[7]

Trygve Lie's name appeared with some regularity in press accounts speculating on possibilities for the Secretaryship-General,[8] and on more than one occasion, he received indications of support from the United States and other nations. But Washington's first candidate for the post was Lester B. Pearson of Canada, an extraordinarily able diplomat who later went on to serve as President of the Seventh General Assembly, as Canada's Foreign Minister, and Prime Minister. The Soviet Union was very much opposed to the notion of a Secretary-General from North America, and particularly a nation so closely allied to the United States as Canada, and thus countered with Stanoje Simitch, at the time Yugoslavia's Ambassador to Washington. Simitch was never a serious contender, of course, but simply a name utilized to suggest to Washington the necessity for agreement upon a man more likely to be neutral as between East and West. Moscow had already opposed Spaak for the Assembly presidency because of his pro-Western views and tendency at the time to look favorably upon a Western alliance against the Soviet Union.

After Lie's defeat for the Assembly presidency, Washington placed him as number two man on its preferred list for the Secretaryship-General, and he was apparently third on Moscow's list, after Simitch and Wincenty Rzymowski, a journalist who was Foreign Minister of Poland. Under these circumstances, Lie's election seemed quite likely, and indeed, while Pearson was the choice of the majority, his unacceptability to the Soviet Union meant compromise was necessary, and on January 29, the Security Council met at Church House in London, and in short order unanimously recommended the nomination of Trygve Lie. The General Assembly elected Lie on February 1 by a vote of 46 to 3, and on February 2, 1946, he became the first Secretary-General of the United Nations. It was an encouraging sign of cooperation between the United States and the Soviet Union, coming as it did on the motion of U.S. representative Edward R. Stettinius, and after a very short period of political bargaining leading to the obvious compromise.

[7] The President of the organization envisaged by the Possible Plan of April 29, 1944 would have been, in Roosevelt's thinking, a statesman of international standing, thus reminiscent of the original thinking concerning the first League Secretary-General or "Chancellor". Eden and Eisenhower fit this category, but unlike the shift to Drummond in 1919, a lesser figure was necessary in 1945 because of the cold war divisions which made essential agreement on a national of a state more neutral between the superpowers. See also Andrew W. Cordier and Wilder Foote, eds., *Public Papers of the Secretaries-General of the United Nations: Volume I, Trygve Lie 1946-1953* (New York: Columbia University Press, 1969), pp. 3-8.

[8] Also mentioned as possibilities were Gladwyn Jebb of Great Britain, serving at the time as Executive Secretary of the Preparatory Commission, Eelco van Kleffens, Foreign Minister of the Netherlands, and Henri Bonnet of France, formerly a League Secretariat official and Director of the Institute of Intellectual Cooperation.

For Trygve Lie, it was a dramatic turn of events, for as he was later to state in his memoirs: "I had been nothing less than catapulted into the Secretary-Generalship of this new international organization... It was a challenge beyond my wildest dreams; but is was a nightmare as well. I hardly dared to think of the days ahead. Instead, I asked myself again and again, why had this awesome task fallen to a labor lawyer from Norway?" [9] In a solemn acceptance speech to the General Assembly on February 2, Lie thanked the delegates for their expression of confidence, and enunciated a minimalist approach to the role of the Secretary-General by declaring that he was not called upon to formulate policy but rather to implement decisions of the political organs.[10]

Secretary-General Lie quickly began the task of building a new Secretariat by making appointments to the top-level structure in accordance with agreements worked out earlier by the Big Five.[11] He had a "cabinet" of eight Assistant Secretaries-General, one to head each of the eight departments into which the Secretariat had been divided. The quality of the appointments at the beginning of Lie's administration was, through no fault of the Secretary-General's, not always of the same excellence as the early selections of Sir Eric Drummond. The Soviet Union, allowed the "portfolio" for Security Council affairs, proposed Arkady Sobolev for the position, and he was shortly thereafter appointed by the Secretary-General. Sobolev, a talented diplomat with extensive experience in international politics, received a post generally considered at the time to be the most important of the Assistant Secretaries. The United States, however, committed itself to the post of Assistant Secretary-General for Administrative and Financial Services, and submitted the name of John D. Hutson, an Under-Secretary of Agriculture in the Federal Government, and a man with no previous international affairs experience.

Perhaps the most critical, and certainly one of the best appointments made by Lie was that of Andrew Cordier as his Executive Assistant. Cordier, who worked as "second man" in the Secretariat until 1962, had taught political and social science in Indiana until 1944, and served as an expert on international security in the U.S. State Department from 1944 to 1946. He attended the San Francisco Conference as a member of the American

---

[9] Lie, *op. cit.*, p. 17.

[10] See pp. 256-261.

[11] In early 1946, after agreement was reached on Lie for the Secretaryship-General, the Big Five approved an agreement (never put in writing) in London apportioning the eight Assistant Secretary posts. The agreement specified that a Soviet national was to be appointed as Assistant Secretary-General for Political and Security Council Affairs, a position probably regarded at that time as the most politically sensitive and significant of the eight positions. The United States pre-empted the post of Assistant Secretary-General for Administrative and Financial Services; a national of the United Kingdom was given direction of the Department of Economic Affairs, while Social Affairs and Trusteeship were assigned to nationals of France and China, respectively.

delegation, was the chief of the Assembly section of the Preparatory Commission, and was an adviser to the Executive Secretary of the Commission. His post as the head of the Secretary-General's Executive Office was obviously of great importance, for if the Assistant Secretaries-General were to have basic responsibility for supervision of departments and services, then more broadly based responsibility would have to lie elsewhere, and the Executive Office seemed a convenient starting point. Indeed, as early as June, 1946, Secretary-General Lie stated that among the several functions of the Executive Office was that of assisting the head of the administration "in maintaining relationships with Members and with the organs of the United Nations" and that of chief responsibility for "liaison with diplomatic representatives".[12] From the outset, the Executive Office of the Secretary-General was the core of Secretariat political activity and decision-making, and Andrew Cordier remained at the center of that effort, particularly during the active years of the Hammarskjold era.

At the start of his administration, Secretary-General Lie clearly had no precise notion of how his role should be developed, nor a theory of the Office and its relationships with member nations and other United Nations organs. He wanted to expand upon Sir Eric Drummond's administrative conception, but he was very much aware of the limitations imposed upon his Office by the realities of world politics and the weaknesses of international organizations. As he was later to state, "it was clearly not the intention of the Charter that the limited concept of the office of Secretary-General which Sir Eric evolved in the League should be perpetuated in the United Nations".[13] It is perhaps true that Lie naturally under-estimated the potential inherent in the Office, for he spoke of the Secretary-General merely as a symbol of the international spirit, with his strategic position at the center of international affairs giving him a moral rather than a physical power:

The Secretary-General, it was said, should be more the general than the secretary—but where were his divisions? Thus I inclined, from the beginning, toward a middle-way—a pragmatic and open-minded approach. I would listen to all my advisors and be directed by none. I had no calculated plan for developing the political powers of the office of Secretary-General, but I was determined that the Secretary-General should

---

[12] "Report of the Secretary-General on the Work of the Organization", United Nations Doc. A/65, 26 June 1946. The Executive Office was also charged with maintaining relationships with specialized agencies and non-governmental organizations, with responsibility for protocol matters, handling of official communications to governments, agencies, and non-governmental organizations, and for the management of the agenda of the General Assembly. The Executive Office had the further responsibility of preparing the Secretary-General's annual and special reports, and the task of channelling to the proper Department or Service of the Secretariat the functions given to the Secretariat by General Assembly resolutions.

[13] Lie, *op. cit.*, pp. 41-42.

be a force for peace. How that force would be applied I would find out—in the light of developments.[14]

Lie's experience during the first days of the new United Nations was quite dissimilar from Drummond's at the start of the League, for significant conflict commenced at once for the UN, and Lie did not have sufficient time, as did Drummond, for constructing the most efficient Secretariat structure, nor could he avoid embroilment in cold war conflict that cast some doubt among one or more of the great powers as to his neutrality and impartiality. Yet the challenge had its advantage as well, for the Secretary-General not only had the benefit of the League experience, and a willingness by the international community to tolerate an independent politicized office of some consequence, but the opportunity to assume particular stances in issues of immediate significance to Washington and Moscow, thereby enhancing the importance of each of his political moves, and given the fact of great power involvement in the United Nations, Lie had the resources of a much more powerful organization than did Sir Eric Drummond. He could communicate with each of the great powers, whereas Drummond had only Britain, France and Italy during the first years, Germany only from 1926, and an international community that would not formally accept a large political role for international officials.

By the end of his administration, Lie still had no theory of the Secretary-General's role in world politics, but in fact he had constructed an Office that could no longer be ignored by UN members, including the great powers, even when vital interests were at stake and complex issues of diplomacy involved. Lie began by establishing the procedural prerogatives of the Secretary-General and concluded by legitimizing the right of the UN's first officer to take a position and help decide and shape policy affecting vital issues of world politics. The development was rather deliberate, pragmatic and realistic throughout, uninfluenced by ideological or theoretical notions, and for the most part generally acceptable to the community of nations.

The Iranian Issue

From the start, the Security Council of the new United Nations Organization served as a forum for bitter East-West propaganda exchanges, rather than as the key political body through which the great powers might construct a post-war collective security system as envisaged by the Charter, and the earliest Council debates reflected with great intensity the cold war divisions which were to weaken significantly the new Organization. Indeed, Trygve Lie's entire administrations coincided with the worst ravages of the cold war, and the UN's first Secretary-General had no political base from which

[14] *Id.*, p. 42.

to mediate the conflict beyond his own neutrality as an international civil servant and his skills as a practiced diplomat.

One of the Council's first problems was an Iranian complaint that Soviet troops stationed in Iran during the war remained there in clear violation of treaty commitments to withdraw by March 2, 1946. Soviet and British troops had been guarding lend-lease routes through Iran into the Soviet Union during the war, but the British withdrew within six months of the end of the hostilities, as stiplated by the 1942 Tripartite Treaty, while the Soviets stayed on in the province of Azerbaijan, and Iran naturally feared Soviet encouragement of an independence movement in the area.[15] Secretary-General Lie's first impulse was to press for direct and quiet negotiations between the parties, rather than a public Security Council debate that might only serve to harden positions and generate East-West charges certain to exaggerate cold war tension.

In fact, negotiations between the Soviet Union and Iran took place in March, and by the end of the month, Andrei Gromyko for the Soviet Union announced that troop withdrawals would be completed in five or six weeks, thereby eliminating any proper reason for placing the item on the Council's agenda. The United States disagreed, and the Security Council did discuss the problem, causing Gromyko to stage his first dramatic walkout. The Soviets continued to insist that their evacuation would be complete by May 6, and Iran responded by dropping its complaint before the Council. The United States, with a majority of Council members with it, agreed to defer the issue until May 6, but Moscow insisted that the charges should never have been brought in the first place, and demanded the item be dropped completely from the Council agenda. By April 15, Iran had formally withdrawn its complaint, and indeed, there seemed little for the Council to discuss unless the Soviets delayed still further the troop evacuation, but Washington, sensing the propaganda value of the item, and with eight Council members in support, argued just as strongly that the question be retained on the agenda, and at this point Secretary-General Lie made his first significant intervention at the United Nations.

The Secretary-General, with the assistance of Legal Counsel Abraham Feller, had prepared a legal memorandum essentially backing the Soviet viewpoint, and on April 16 he submitted it to the Council President. Lie argued that unless the Council voted an investigation, or recommended methods of adjustment, a request by both parties to a dispute for withdrawal of the complaint from the agenda should result in a Council decision automatically to drop the item in question.[16] The Soviet Union, along with Poland and France, supported both the substance of Lie's memorandum

---

[15] The Soviet Union was pressing for Azerbaijan's autonomy and for oil concessions. Quite aside from the propaganda value for Washington and London, there was also the important issue of Western oil interests in the area.
[16] SCOR: 1st year, 1st Series, 33rd mtg., 16 April, 1946.

and his right to intervene in the Security Council at his own initiative. The United States, along with eight other Council members, was displeased by the action, and naturally viewed the Secretary-General's maneuver as far beyond his authority as chief administrative officer, and as incorrect substantively. From Lie's perspective, the intervention was amply justified by Article 99 of the Charter, and indeed, the Secretary-General felt that the political significance of Article 99 enabled him to address the Council not only through legal memoranda, but through any written or oral communication and on any question before the Council.

The memorandum was submitted to the Council's Committee of Experts, whose final opinion mirrored the 8 to 3 political split in the Council itself, and thus on the substantive issue, Lie's views were overridden, and the item retained on the agenda. The Secretary-General stated later that he had never expected to alter the Council's action, but the move was important both in terms of the development of the Office, and for the Secretary-General's understanding of the nature of UN political debates in a cold war atmosphere.

The authority of the Secretary-General to intervene in this manner was questioned by the Council's President and by the delegate from China, who naturally stressed the basic administrative nature of the Secretary-General's position in the UN structure. The Soviet Union on the other hand, looking at Article 99, argued that the Secretary-General "has all the more right, and an even greater obligation, to make statements on various aspects of the questions considered by the Security Council".[17]

While Lie lost on the merits, he was the clear victor in the important procedural wrangle to follow, as the issue then focused on the problem of the Secretary-General's right to intervene at all in meetings of the UN's political organs. The Secretary-General pressed quietly for a rule enabling him to intervene in the Council's sessions as he wished, while the United States wanted a rule limiting his rights to speak or offer written presentations only upon the invitation of the Council's president. Moscow supported Lie, and after some hesitation, Great Britain shifted its position, and at that point the Council's Committee of Experts finally adopted the more liberal construction favored by the Secretary-General. The rule in the General Assembly was also changed to allow the Secretariat's chief officer to intervene at any time with oral or written statements, and thus Lie's first initiative was successful. The Organization and its members have long since become accustomed to participation by the Secretary-General in political debates, presenting his own position and viewpoints on even the most critical and controversial of issues. Lie had moved a long first step beyond the Drummond and Avenol tradition.

This seemingly minor issue was important for a few reasons. First, in terms

[17] *Ibid.*

of the constitutional development of the Office, Lie had gotten off to a quick start, for he was able to demonstrate that Article 99 in reality was far more than a mere procedural right. The Secretary-General was an important political figure and as such, entitled to certain political initiatives and an independent position in the world arena. Whatever later developments or refinements might bring, the Secretary-General of the UN was going to be more than an administrative officer, and if the first step in establishing his political role was a minor one, that it was a step in the direction of a strengthened chief executive for the global institution cannot be doubted.

Further, the Iranian issue was important in terms of the Soviet and American relationship with Secretary-General Lie. Washington was naturally suspicious, and tended to view Lie as slanted toward the communist position; American opposition to the Secretary-General was not long in coming, thus somewhat dampening Washington's relationship with the new Organization. Moscow, on the other hand, was greatly encouraged by Lie's first move, and at least for a time, was not at all adverse to an important role for the Secretary-General. In the final analysis, this was fortunate from the standpoint of the Office, for its first steps were undertaken with Soviet encouragement and support, and while Moscow was later to regret this, the precedent had been set and the Office launched in effect by the state that is today the most consistent exponent of the view that the executive's power must be restrained and controlled by the Security Council.

Finally, Lie's intervention was significant as an attempt by the Secretary-General to prevent the UN's political bodies from being turned into propaganda forums. "The United Nations... should aim to settle disputes", he later wrote, "not to enflame them".[18] There was already little question of the UN being used as an instrument of collective security, but perhaps at the least the Organization might be useful in terms of easing East-West conflict, and the Office of the Secretary-General might be important in terms of mediation efforts for outstanding issues between Moscow and Washington. In this Lie was not successful, for his Office and the few neutrals at the UN were certainly a fragile force between East and West, and his task in this regard was far more difficult than that subsequently faced by Hammarskjold and Thant. But Lie's use of legal principles was a sophisticated attempt to establish a political neutrality for the Organization as the only possible posture for a structure devoted to the maintenance of international peace. It followed from this, of course, that the UN had also to be used for quiet negotiations in which there was a substantial expectation of agreement. Merely airing a dispute publicly provided little assurance of peaceful settlement. "I believed then, and believe now", wrote Lie in 1954, "that open disagreements openly arrived at are not necessarily preferable to processes of diplomacy of a more discreet and effective character".[19] From the be-

18 Lie, *op. cit.*, p. 80.
19 *Id.*, p. 75.

ginning, the Secretary-General started on the read to "quiet diplomacy", as it came to be known under Dag Hammarskjold, and thus was a seemingly minor issue important in building an essential foundation for further development of the Secretary-General's prerogatives, and establishing the most useful procedures and functional attributes of the world organization. The opening round for the new Office of Secretary-General in the UN era was in effect a movement for mediation, neutrality, traditional diplomacy, and an independent and effective Secretary-General.

Palestine: 1947-1949

The position of Secretary-General Lie in the events surrounding the establishment of Israel in 1948 indicated perfectly the failure of the UN's collective security system and the near impotence of an international civil service working alone and without the assistance of an international armed force. The Middle East is an area in which a UN military presence may make a substantial difference (as was the case in the years between 1956 and 1967) and Lie appreciated this well before the establishment of Israel in May, 1948. Even with Moscow and Washington in agreement, without troops at his command the Secretary-General could do no more than mediate Arab-Jewish differences, attempt to legitimize the UN's decisions in the Middle East, and try to persuade member nations that those decisions should be enforced. Such functions were insignificant in comparison with the role played by the Secretary-General in later years, but the Office was still new in 1947, and Lie's willingness to take a strong public position on questions of great consequence to the parties most immediately concerned and to the superpowers was a further forward step in the development of the Secretary-General's political activity.

In April, 1947, a special session of the General Assembly was called to consider "the question of Palestine". Great Britain, the Mandatory power under the League of Nations since 1920, had been unable to mount a successful administration, for British interest in Arab friendship, the Suez Canal and Middle East oil conflicted with earlier promises of and wartime pressures for a Jewish state in Palestine. London could not concede the latter without sacrificing strategic resources and political influence in the area, and yet powerful political forces both in Britain and the United States were urging a partition of Palestine into Jewish and Arab states, and in the end Britain simply threw in the towel.

The Assembly's first step was to create the United Nations Special Committee on Palestine (UNSCOP), a political body charged with the obligation to make recommendations for the future of Palestine and to report by the autumn of 1947. The Committee, made up of representatives from Australia, Canada, Guatemala, India, Iran, the Netherlands, Peru, Sweden, Uruguay, and Yugoslavia, was divided on the critical issue. A majority of seven recommended the partition of Palestine into separate Arab and Jewish states, with an economic union between them, and a United Nations administration for Jerusalem, while a minority of three members (India, Iran, and Yugoslavia) voted for a single state administered by an Arab majority. Australia abstained altogether.

The real key to the Palestine issue was the attitude of the United States and Soviet Union, as each for very different reasons strongly supported the majority partition plan. The United States was fearful of antagonizing the Arab political élite, but was obviously sympathetic to the plight of Jewish refugees fleeing Europe and to the political claims pressed by its relatively large and influential Jewish population, while for the Soviet Union, the partition plan was easily the most effecient method for eliminating British influence from at least one part of the Middle Eastern area. Thus urged by both superpowers, the General Assembly, by a vote of 33 to 13 with 10 abstentions, adopted the partition plan on November 29, 1947, thereby legitimizing the establishment of a new Jewish state. The vote was marred by an Arab walkout and mounting violence, making it apparent that the state of Israel, essentially created by the organized international community, would be met by war.

Secretary-General Lie enthusiastically supported the partition plan even before its adoption by the General Assembly. Speaking of the special committee's majority plan for partition, the Secretary-General wrote in 1954:

What had emerged was a *clear victory for the principle of partition*. The international community, through its chosen representatives, had decided that two states should be created. As Secretary-General, I took the cue and, when approached by the delegations for advice, frankly recommended that they follow the majority plan.[20]

After the Assembly's official acceptance of partition, the Secretary-General's main concern was implementation. The resolution itself contained no provision for compliance by the parties, and Great Britain had given notice that it would force neither Arabs nor Jews to accept a plan not to their liking. The Assembly established a United Nations Commission to assume administrative authority from Britain no later than August 1, 1948, but the Commission, made up of representatives from Bolivia, Czechoslovakia, Denmark, Panama and the Philippines, could do little more than report to the Security Council that heavy fighting between Arabs and Jews had broken out, and indeed, that Britain, ever reluctant to antagonize the Arabs, refused even to allow its entry into Palestine until just prior to the Mandate's termination, now set for May 15, 1948. The UN Commission was rather forlornly known as the "five lonely pilgrams".

At the beginning of 1948, it was clear that if left to their own devices, Arabs and Jews could not achieve peaceful settlement, and would embroil

---

[20] *Id.*, p. 162.

the entire region in war. But despite their support for a Jewish state, neither of the superpowers was willing to commit resources to enforce partition, and thus Secretary-General Lie privately requested several smaller powers without immediate interest in the area to contribute troops to a Middle Eastern force under UN command, not so much to enforce a partition scheme as to prevent the outbreak of fighting. The Big Five were urged to reconsider. The Palestine Commission also called for external force to keep order after the termination of the Mandate in May, and with that in mind, Lie and Bunche together drafted a statement for presentation to the Security Council, described by the Secretary-General as follows:

As he and I worked it out with other advisers, it would have stressed that, despite the disagreement between East and West on providing the United Nations with armed forces, a sufficient degree of agreement had been reached for the establishment of a United Nations land force—an emergency international force composed of those minimum units which the Big Five were committed to placing at the Security Council's disposal. Such a force would be more than adequate to cope with the Palestine challenge.[21]

There was no question in Lie's mind that the Security Council possessed a legal capacity and an obligation to implement the General Assembly's partition plan.[22] Indeed, he had publicly said as much to the Palestine Commission at its opening meeting when he declared that the Commission was entitled to be confident that in the event it should prove necessary, the Security Council would assume its full measure of responsibility in terms of implementing the Assembly's resolution. "You have a right to assume, as I assume, that in such a situation the Security Council will not fail to exercise, *to the fullest, and without exception,* every necessary power entrusted to it by the Charter in order to assist you in fulfilling your mission".[23]

This was clearly an attempt by Lie to put some kind of pressure on the great powers, for he could have had no assurances at that time (early January, 1948) that the Council was disposed to use force to establish the new state of Israel. Indeed, Great Britain was generally uncooperative throughout, and in February, Representative Warren Austin of the United States announced before the Security Council that that body lacked the legal authority to enforce any political settlement for Palestine recommended by the General Assembly. The Secretary-General, viewing the matter as a Mandate problem handed to the United Nations by Britain as the original

---

[21] *Id.,* p. 166.

[22] Lie made public the memorandum drafted by the legal department in order to give expression to the views of the UN Secretariat on the matter, particularly with regard to the essentiality of an international armed force to keep peace subsequent to the transfer of authority from Great Britain as Mandatory Power to the Arab and Jewish authorities in the partioned state. See Cordier and Foote, *op. cit.,* pp. 105-115, and United Nations Doc. A/AC.21/13, 9 Feb. 1948. The Palestine Commission agreed that "an adequate non-Palestinian force" was necessary for the maintenance of peace.

[23] Stephen M. Schwebel, *The Secretary-General of the United Nations* (Cambridge: Harvard University Press, 1952), pp. 140-141; Cordier and Foote, *op. cit.,* p. 109.

Mandatory power, argued that "the Organization in these circumstances had full constitutional power not only to maintain order inside the territory but, even more, to resist any attempt from outside to overthrow its decision".[24] But his attempts to secure enforcement of partition suffered a further blow when in March, 1948, Austin announced that the necessities of peace required a temporary United Nations Trusteeship for Palestine. Washington, obviously fearful of its interests in the Arab states, and in nations with heavy Moslem populations, was now backing away rapidly from the notion of a Jewish state, and at this point Lie seriously considered resigning. From his perspective, "the American reversal was a blow to the United Nations and showed a profoundly disheartening disregard for its effectiveness and standing. I could not help asking myself what the future of the United Nations would be, if this was the measure of support it could expect from the United States".[25]

At the urging of both Washington and Moscow Lie stayed on, but it was clear that if Israel, having been created by the United Nations, was to maintain itself, it would be through its own efforts, and not those of other states or of the global organization. The General Assembly met once again in April, but after a month's debate, took no new significant action. The Assembly was not sympathetic to the temporary trusteeship proposal and would not go back on its November, 1947 partition scheme, but neither was there a rush to provide international armed force to prevent war. A UN Mediator was appointed to try his hand at bringing peace to the area, and as the Assembly ended its debate, the state of Israel was proclaimed on May 14, 1948. In still another policy change, Washington recognized the new government almost at once; the Soviet Union followed quickly, and the invasion of the new state by its Arab neighbors began.

Lie's efforts to implement the Organization's work resulted both from a profound sympathy for the notion of a Jewish state, and of course from a deep commitment to a prestigious world organization. His efforts having failed in fact, naturally the Organization's standing diminished commensurately, but the attempt tended to strengthen further the Office of the Secretary-General, for in this case, he had the clear support of the Soviet Union, and at least the sympathy, if not real backing, of the United States. Indeed, his only antagonists were the Arab states and nations with significant Moslem minorities, and given his own sympathies and interests as head of the Organization, the attempt to secure either great power support or an international armed force consisting of small power contingents followed quite naturally. Lie had demonstrated that at the least, the prestige of his Office could be used to legitimize one position or another, and that he had no hesitation to use it in that manner.

With the outbreak of fighting, the Secretary-General's public posture

[24] Lie, *op. cit.,* p. 167.
[25] *Id.,* p. 170.

and strategy changed little. Even with the invasion of Israel, the Security Council found itself unable to take action, and Lie then sent Assistant Secretary-General R. G. A. Jackson, of Australia, to London and Executive Assistant Andrew Cordier to Washington to present his view that failure to take action might well result in the demise of the United Nations. Lie also drafted a letter to each of the Security Council's permanent members, emphasizing the threat to peace in the Middle East, stating that the Security Council's consideration of the matter made unnecessary a formal invocation of Article 99, noting the danger of further intervention by outside powers, and the obvious injury to the United Nations that might result from failure to keep the peace in an area of intimate concern to the Organization.[26]

Toward the end of May, Great Britain was induced to support the position finally accepted by Washington, and pressed from the start of the war by United Nations headquarters. The Security Council demanded a four-week ceasefire with the threat of sanctions against any party refusing to comply, and requested Count Folke Bernadotte, recently appointed by the Council as UN mediator, to negotiate its precise terms and implementation. By June 11, the truce was in effect, a result primarily of Arab military weakness and the British policy shift.

The Secretariat and the Secretary-General were instrumental in assisting Bernadotte's mediation effort. Lie worked efficiently to get UN observers into the field, and ultimately some 750 UN personnel were stationed in the Middle East for purposes of observation, negotiation, truce supervision, and to act as a buffer between Arab and Israeli forces. This was the first large-scale UN truce observation effort, and the several hundred personnel constituted both an outstanding example of one of the Organization's primary functions as well as a forerunner of international forces to come. Lie also provided Bernadotte with United Nations Secretariat guards just a few days after they had been requested by the Mediator.

Relations between Bernadotte and Secretary-General Lie were very close, with the latter negotiating from Headquarters in attempts to achieve the ceasefire and political settlement. One student of the Secretary-General's Office has written that "It is in fact not too much to say that the United Nations' effort in Palestine was a joint field-headquarters endeavor in which the Mediator and the Secretary-General collaborated in an indispensably interdependent fashion, its successful results belonging as much to one as to the other".[27]

After the first truce agreement was reached, the Secretary-General, along with Bernadotte and Ralph Bunche, initiated serious efforts to arrange a lasting political settlement, but the month-long truce period was clearly insufficient and while the Israelis agreed to an extension, the Arab states refused, and renewed the warfare on July 9. Bernadotte and Bunche flew

[26] *Id.*, pp. 178-179; Cordier and Foote, *op. cit.*, pp. 116-117.
[27] Schwebel, *op. cit.*, p. 116.

back to their headquarters on the Greek Island of Rhodes to discuss their next move, but hardly had they reached the island when Bernadotte received an urgent message from King Abdullah of Jordan to come to Amman. Taking a plane from Rhodes at four in the morning, the two men found the King waiting for them on the porch of his palace. His first question to Bernadotte was: "Why did you let the ceasefire end?" Bernadotte answered: "I am surprised that you ask me that question. For a week I have pleaded with the Arabs to extend it, including your representative. In fact, he was one of the strongest in refusing". "Yes, I know that", replied Abdullah. "Then why", asked Bernadotte, "do you speak to me like that?" "You must force us", said Abdullah, to which Bernadotte replied: "I have no power to force you. I can only appeal to you".[28]

In fact, Jordan had only one week's ammunition left, and Abdullah was not adverse therefore to a legally binding UN order. Flying back to Rhodes, Bunche pointed out that the UN had never used the power of the Charter under Chapter VII, and probably would be reluctant to do so, but Berna-dotte said merely: "Let's try". On July 15th the Council invoked Chapter VII of the Charter for the first time in a resolution declaring "the situation in Palestine constitutes a threat to the peace within the meaning of Article 39 of the Charter". The Arab states and Israel were ordered to "desist from further military action" and Bernadotte was instructed to supervise the UN truce machinery. A second truce was now in effect, and the value of the Organization and the Secretary-General in terms of face-saving functions had been clearly demonstrated. The Security Council's binding order under Chapter VII was only one of two in the entire history of the Organization— the other being the compulsory economic sanctions against Rhodesia, order-ed by the Council in 1966.

Again Bernadotte went back to his mediation effort and while working to develop proposals acceptable to both sides, was assassinated in Jerusalem on September 17, 1948 by unidentified members of the Stern Group, an Israeli terrorist organization that believed he was favoring the Arab position.

Lie quickly appointed Ralph Bunche as Acting Mediator and this action was later ratified by the Security Council. With Bunche and Lie working in close harmony, and Israeli military successes in the field convincing the Arab states that a halt to military action was essential, months of hard work on Rhodes finally brought about the Israeli-Egyptian Armistice Agreement, signed on February 24, 1949. Later agreements were signed with Lebanon, Jordan and by the summer of 1949, with Syria. The truce in each case was supervised by the United Nations Truce Supervision Organization and Mixed Armistice Commissions through which the Israelis and Arabs

[28] Interview granted by UN Secretariat official to the author and Raymond B. Fosdick on April 13, 1966. Jordan's weak military position, including a desperate lack of am-munition, led King Abdullah to seek a UN binding order with which he could more easily comply.

negotiated particular problems as they arose. Ralph Bunche's skill, patience and dedication in carrying through the delicate negotiations brought him the satisfaction of achieving a structure for peace in the Middle East, a prominent role for international organization, and finally, in 1950, the Nobel Prize for Peace.

On July 7, 1949, Secretary-General Lie wrote in the *Introduction* to his Fourth Annual Report: "The establishment of the state of Israel and Palestine without a major war is one of the epic events of history, coming, as it does, at the end not merely of 30 years, but of 2,000 years of accumulated sorrows, bitterness and conflict. For Christian, Jew and Moslem alike Palestine symbolizes historic forces beside which the present ideological conflict appears to be a transitory phenomenon".[29] Of course, there was now no Arab Palestine nor international regime for Jerusalem, and these in addition to several hundred thousand Arab refugees were among the casualties of the failure to send an international armed force to the Middle East.

Writing in his memoirs in 1954, Lie again stressed his conviction that attacks by the Arab states on Israel were no less than violations of the United Nations Charter and attacks on the Organization itself. "I am proud of the United Nations' role in aiding the establishment of Israel", he wrote, "but I could be far prouder. The decision for partition, once taken by the United Nations, should have been resolutely upheld not only by some governments and the Secretary-General, but by all Members of the Organization". He added, "As Secretary-General, I stood by the early recommendation to partition Palestine, subsequently endorsed by the General Assembly, and I make no apologies for that".[30] The Secretary-General combined a very strong pro-Israeli sympathy to his essential role in protecting the interests of the UN, and within this context there was no alternative to strong support for Israel once it had been created by the community of nations. And of course, the Secretary-General's work on the Palestine issue was not only in defense of the new state and the Organization, but also served again to strengthen his Office.

Without troops his activity was necessarily marginal, but given the constraints of an international intermediary, Lie made the most of his opportunities for mediation, persuasion and good offices functions. The steps taken to strengthen his role were clearly important for the development of global institutions. For the Secretary-General, having earlier established essential procedural prerogatives and taken strong positions on critical substantive issues, was here demonstrating the capacity to act even in the midst of crisis, and on an issue of interest to both superpowers. He also ensured continued UN involvement in the Middle East through his efficient work in dispatching UN personnel and by the success of his cooperative relationship with the Mediator. The public call for an international armed

[29] GAOR: Fourth Sess., Supp. No. 1, United Nations Doc. A/930.
[30] Lie, *op. cit.*, p. 194.

force despite the breakdown of the Charter's collective security provisions helped make that notion acceptable perhaps a bit more quickly than would otherwise have been the case, thus laying the groundwork for expanded UN and Secretariat influence during the Hammarskjold administration. In this sense, the Palestine issue from 1947 to 1949 constituted a major opportunity for the political development of the Secretary-General's Office, and one grasped quickly and skillfully by Trygve Lie.

The United Nations Guard (Field Service)

As noted above, Lie was very much impressed by what he perceived as the usefulness of an international armed force in the Middle East, for here was an area of chronic conflict and of strategic importance; yet each of the powers in the area were weak, and while the great powers had substantial interest in the region, the British withdrawal now meant that some of the states primarily concerned were no longer within the sphere of influence of East or West. A neutral international armed force, therefore, might have serious value as buffer and mediator, but the United Nations had no armed forces at its disposal since the agreements required for such forces by Article 43 of the Charter had never been concluded. This in turn had been due primarily to the jockeying for strategic military advantage in Europe by both Moscow and Washington which resulted in the failure of negotiations for such forces by 1948.[31] In the years since, there has been no effort to provide the Organization with the military might required for a serious application of the Charter's collective security provisions.

The Secretary-General's thought was to establish a small armed force under the UN Secretariat with the Secretary-General as its commander, with contributions of contingents to be made primarily by small and neutral member nations. He called it the United Nations Guard, and publicly proposed it for the first time at a commencement address at Harvard University in June, 1948.[32] The Secretary-General had in mind a small army of some five to ten thousand men as a beginning, the message being that the

[31] The basic military disagreements concerned the size, location, and equality of contribution (from the great powers) for the Chapter VII forces. In general, the Soviet Union wanted a smaller UN army than Washington and with lesser amounts of equipment, and wanted national contingents based in their homelands, while the U.S. pressed for location in European base areas. Moscow also wanted equality of contribution in terms of troops and armaments, whereas Washington proposed that each state contribute comparably. See D. W. Bowett, *UN Forces* (London: Stevens & Sons, 1964), pp. 12-18. The military and technical squabbles were, of course, reflections of more fundamental political disagreements and suspicion. Each side suspected, correctly, that the other was seeking strategic advantage in Europe through its negotiating position.

[32] "It is possible that a beginning could be made now", Lie declared "through the establishment of a comparatively small guard force, as distinct from a striking force. Such a force could be recruited by the Secretary-General and placed at the disposal of

primary function of the United Nations was something different from the collective security system outlined in the Charter, and that the Organization's political influence depended upon a small armed force composed of neutral contingents acting to keep antagonists apart,[33] a conception that approached rather closely the notion of "preventive diplomacy" as articulated in later years by Secretary-General Dag Hammarskjold.

The proposal ran into stiff opposition, however, particularly from the Soviet Union, and Lie was forced to water down his recommendation from the start. Moscow insisted on Article 43 agreements for any force, and Washington, more interested in rearmament, had little faith in international forces. The assassination of Count Bernadotte had emphasized to Lie the significance of his planning here, but political resistance was too strong to be overridden, and Lie's first official proposal to the General Assembly, in September 1948, was a request for a much smaller force, and for narrower protective purposes.

Lie's report to the Assembly declared that UN missions in the field, such as those in the Balkans, Korea, Indonesia, India and Pakistan, as well as Palestine, made a guard force particularly useful. The Secretary-General now requested a body of just 800 officials working for the UN Secretariat, and of these only 300 would be permanent, with some 500 personnel in national sections available as reserve units. The guard was to protect the personnel of missions abroad and protect particular areas under truce arrangements or other UN intervention. Lie was at great pains to emphasize that the guard was in no way a substitute for the armed force contemplated by Article 43 of the Charter and was to have only "personal emergency defense weapons". It could only operate on a territory with the consent of the sovereign and its small size would insure that it could not be used in an aggressive manner.[34]

---

the Security Council. Such a force would have been extremely valuable to us in the past and it would undoubtedly be very valuable in the future".

"Even a small United Nations force would command respect, for it would have all the authority of the United Nations behind it. I do not think of a single case that has been dealt with by the Security Council so far in which a large force would have been needed to act for the United Nations, provided that a small United Nations guard force of some kind had been available for immediate duty at the proper time. I include Palestine". (Cordier and Foote, *op. cit.*, pp. 134-135).

[33] In his *Introduction* to the Third Annual Report of the Secretary-General, Lie stipulated a force of some 1,000 to 5,000 men, and suggested that such a force "could be used for guard duty with United Nations missions, in the conduct of plebiscites under the supervision of the United Nations and in the administration of truce terms. It could be used as a constabulary under the Security Council or the Trusteeship Council in cities like Jerusalem and Trieste during the establishment of international regimes. It might also be called upon for provisional measures to prevent the aggravation of a situation threatening the peace". (GAOR: Third Sess., Supp. No. 1, United Nations Doc. A/565, 5 July 1948)

[34] See Bowett, *op. cit.*, p. 1819; also Cordier and Foote, *op. cit.*, pp. 166-177. Lie now

The opposition persisted, however, and the proposal was further watered down in 1949 to the establishment of what came to be known as the United Nations Field Service, a small group of three hundred in the UN Secretariat, unarmed, but trained to carry out communications and transport services to UN missions in the field, and guard duties at Headquarters. This was a far cry from the five to ten thousand men originally suggested by Lie, but the first public recommendation by an official in a high position of international responsibility had been made. By 1956 a truly international UN army was established in the Middle East, a buffer force composed of contingents from small powers, and while there is no direct line of political influence from Lie to the United Nations Emergency Force in the Middle East, the acceptability of the 1956 force and the others that followed is due in some measure to the original conception and proposal by the UN's first Secretary-General. A UN force for other than enforcement purposes under Chapter VII was essentially the idea of Trygve Lie, an idea of crucial importance for the later active role of the UN in world politics.

The Berlin Blockade

The crisis caused by the Soviet Union's 1948 blockade of West Berlin was naturally not a matter in which the United Nations could play an important part, and indeed, the mediation efforts of the Organization and Secretary-General Lie were not particularly successful. In the final analysis the conflict was settled by direct negotiations between the superpowers, with an agreement reached quite apart from the diplomatic procedures of the UN, and even without reference to the face-saving devices forming the core of the world organization's recommendations for peaceful settlement.

Yet Lie's work in the Berlin crisis was significant, for it illustrated the value of the Secretaryship-General even in direct conflicts between Moscow and Washington. The Secretary-General served as a mediator in the dispute and for a substantial period was a key communication link between the antagonists. He also helped legitimize and articulate the compromise outlook favored by most members of the international community. Lie viewed the blockade as an illegal act, yet he did not assume a public posture of defender of the Charter, but rather remained the neutral international civil

---

emphasized the peaceful nature of the projected UN Guard, rather than "force" by eliminating from its functions anything in the area of maintenance of peace or order. The Soviet Union was the primary opponent of Lie's plan, fearing an independent military force not subject to the Security Council veto, and insisting on a constitutional interpretation under which any UN force could properly be established and maintained only by the Security Council. The Western powers were also not encouraging to Lie, concerned as they were with rearmament in the face of the perceived Soviet threat to the European area.

servant attempting to formulate mutually acceptable recommendations, or at the least, to induce the parties to negotiate directly. In fact, of course, the dispute was settled because of the dramatic Western airlift to West Berlin, a clear demonstration of the West's capacity to maintain its position in the city and to defend its legal rights there with military force if necessary, but the UN's mediation effort is an important example of the assistance the Organization has the capacity to provide in cases of serious East-West conflict.

The first attempts at settlement were carried on outside the United Nations, and seemed hopeful. An agreement reached in Moscow on August 30, 1948, provided for an end to the blockade, which had been completed by July 1, in return for the introduction of Soviet zone currency in West Berlin and the lifting of Western counter-measures taken against Soviet forces, these moves contingent upon an agreement in detail on financial and trade arrangements in the occupation zones. But Moscow refused to cooperate in implementing the August 30 agreement, and in September, the United States, Britain, and France appealed to the UN Security Council. According to Secretary-General Lie's account,[35] there were really two efforts at the UN. The first was led by Doctor Juan A. Bramuglia, the Foreign Minister of Argentina and spokesman for the Council's six "neutral members" (that is, the non-permanent members), while a second and parallel effort was headed by Secretary-General Lie with the assistance of the expert advice of his top aides, particularly Assistant Secretary-General Arkady Sobolev from the Soviet Union and legal aide Abraham Feller of the United States. Of great importance in Lie's contact with Washington was General Assembly delegate Philip Jessup, one of America's greatest international lawyers, and later a judge at the International Court of Justice.

Following a Soviet veto in October, 1948 of the six "neutrals" resolution calling for an end to the blockade and a meeting of the Berlin military governors to agree on currency matters,[36] Lie proposed to Jessup that it might be possible to plan for the simultaneous lifting of the blockade with the introduction of Soviet zone currency in Berlin. One of the key difficulties was, quite naturally, the United States' refusal to negotiate with the Soviet Union until the blockade was lifted; and given the success of the Western airlift, Washington was in no particular hurry to reach agreement. The Soviet move was not only illegal, but had failed in its purpose and the Western powers were obviously delighted to extract the maximum political value from the situation.

The Secretary-General, working quietly, wanted Assistant Secretary-General Sobolev and legal counsel Feller to negotiate with Moscow and

[35] See Lie, *op. cit.,* pp. 199-218.
[36] Moscow wanted the immediate introduction of the Soviet zone mark in Berlin in return for the lifting of the blockade. The "neutrals" had called only for a meeting of Berlin military governors on the matter.

Washington to reach agreement on a currency scheme. A detailed technical plan might be worked out by the Secretariat without any public knowledge that the Secretary-General and his top assistants had formulated the proposal, and by the end of October, Moscow was apparently willing to allow the Secretary-General and his staff to develop whatever possible solution they thought helpful. This marked a clear change from the previous Soviet attitude of reserve toward the UN's efforts in the matter—the Soviet Union had attacked Security Council consideration of the Berlin problem as unwarranted under the Charter. But with the Soviet Union now giving some encouragement to the Secretary-General's efforts, the Western powers (particularly Great Britain), began to hesitate, for the airlift was working remarkably well even in bad weather, and there was a disposition to demonstrate to Moscow that the city could be well supplied and supported even throughout the harsh winter. The United States was not anxious to permit the Russians a graceful withdrawal from an untentable situation. As President Truman was later to note, Washington wanted a settlement, but not one that required cooperation with Moscow.[37] By the beginning of November, Secretary-General Lie's compromise efforts seemed futile, and his only recourse was personal appeals to the great powers.

On November 13, Lie and Dr. Herbert Evatt of Australia, President of the General Assembly for 1948, sent a letter to the Big Four urging "immediate conversations and... all other necessary steps toward the solution of the Berlin question", support of the Security Council's neutral conciliation efforts, and backing for the currency studies conducted by the Secretary-General's Office.[38] The letter was resented in Western capitals as an indication of a left-leaning policy unwarranted in the context of an illegal blockade by the Soviet Union—for Washington there would be no negotiations until the blockade was lifted, and attempts at anything else by way of compromise were doomed to failure.

From this point forward, the Secretary-General's involvement in the UN efforts at peaceful settlement was distinctly marginal. He worked with the expert currency committee, appointed from the members of the Security Council's six neutrals at the initiative of Dr. Bramuglia, and appointed Gunnar Myrdal as a seventh representative to the committee. But not unexpectedly, the committee's report in February, 1949 was rejected by the United States, Washington remaining convinced it could get a settlement without agreement on currency control.

By the spring of 1949, the Soviet Union finally decided to concede. Stalin indicated Moscow's wish for a settlement, and did so without mentioning the currency problem, thus paving the way for talks between Jessup and Malik, and by May, final agreement. Secretary-General Lie did not take an active

---

[37] See Harry S. Truman, *Memoirs,* Vol. 2 (Garden City, N.Y.: Doubleday & Company, 1956), p. 130.
[38] For full text, see Cordier and Foote, *op. cit.,* pp. 180-182.

part in the Malik-Jessup conversations, although Lie reports that on one occasion they met in his home. By the middle of May, the blockade and the West's counter restrictions were lifted, and it was agreed that problems of Germany, including currency issues, would then be discussed by the deputies of the Council of Foreign Ministers of the Big Four. The settlement was reached outside the world organization and of course the Secretary-General's role had been severely circumscribed, for Washington's airlift response to the blockade had been carried out skillfully enough to avoid a wider conflict and to remain in Berlin while signifing Western determination to hold the city in the future. The United Nations had been successful only in making known to the general public the complex issues, including currency, raised by the blockade, and the negotiations in the Security Council and Secretariat were of some significance in terms of achieving a disposition to reach a peaceful settlement.

It is difficult to measure the UN's contribution in this kind of situation, but is is likely that some reduction of tension was achieved, as the Soviet Union was naturally quite willing to utilize the services of a third party neutral, and the United States, while less willing, was not disposed to thwart too patently the UN effort. In short, the Organization permitted some form of convenient negotiations and mediation proposals, however insubstantial, thus allowing time to elapse while each side tested the probable intention of the other and more rational approaches to conflict resolution. Secretary-General Lie was later to write that the total UN effort, including the work of the General Assembly, Security Council, Secretary-General, and neutrals' currency committee was important. "None of these efforts", he wrote, "brought immediate results, but their effect was greatly to moderate the tension, reduce the danger of war, and gain time for other factors tending to a settlement to make themselves felt".[39]

The effort was also important in the context of the Secretary-General's role as a mediator in world politics, for in the early days of his administration, every move made by Lie served as precedent for further development and indicated future directions for his Office. His attempt at mediation between Moscow and Washington on an issue of vital strategic importance, while not eminently successful, was nevertheless an important endeavor by Lie to strengthen his participation in UN affairs generally and in the entire arena of world politics. While his recommendations and approach were not favorably received by the Western powers, there was little disposition, with a few minor exceptions, to question his right to act as a neutral mediator in a critical East-West conflict, and as such, Lie's Berlin initiative constituted still another step forward in the progressive strengthening of the Office of the Secretary-General.

---

[39] *Id.,* p. 215.

The Peace Mission and Chinese Representation

By the end of 1949, the United Nations had reached its low point in terms of influence and great power consensus. The cold war had greatly weakened the Organization, as the essential security interests of the United States necessitated reliance upon regional military pacts, supplemented by a UN forum utilized for propaganda purposes. Notwithstanding a certain measure of success in the Balkans, Palestine, Kashmir, and Indonesia, the UN was clearly falling into disrepute primarily because of disuse by the superpowers. Further, the communist takeover in China in October, 1949 triggered a Soviet walkout from most UN bodies as a protest against continued representation of the Chinese Nationalist regime, and at the time, this move bade fair to destroy the struggling Organization.

For a period of six hectic months, Secretary-General Lie carried through what was to be his last serious attempt at bridging East-West differences. His famous "Peace Mission" and accompanying ten point memorandum (the basis of rather inconclusive negotitions in the Big Four capitals) constituted a bold attempt to save the United Nations from collapse and to stem the tide of the cold war by broaching several areas of possible negotiation between the Soviet Union and United States. The effort was spectacular enough, although strategically unsound in some respects, and certainly an initiative that was far far too little and too late. The simple encouragement by the Secretary-General of the United Nations was obviously insufficient to motivate Moscow and Washington to negotiate their strategic and political differences, for the issues Lie raised with the great powers were the problems of the cold war itself, rather than narrower questions upon which agreement was more likely. Lie was clearly aware, however, that serious East-West talks could not commence prior to a resolution of the Chinese representation issue, or in other terms, until the West was willing to grant legitimacy to the communist regime in Peking. While universality of membership constituted point five of the ten point memorandum, the core issue was Peking's right to speak for China in the council of nations.

Immediately following the Soviet walkout in January, 1950, Lie began an intensive campaign to seat the Peking regime, an effort consisting of several conversations with Security Council delegates in New York, the drafting of a legal memorandum based on principles that would have assured China's seat to the Peking government, and of course, a series of talks during his peace mission. The legal memorandum was simply an attempt to place neutral principles in the forefront, often an effective technique for masking political settlement. Each of the Secretaries-General has utilized principles of international law in just this manner, and in this case, it was policy of grave significance for the Secretary-General, as universality of membership to Lie was "fundamental to the fulfillment of the purposes of a *world* organization".[40] For Lie, there was little utility in the fiction that Chiang Kai-Shek's regime on Formosa represented the mainland and he felt the West to be most unwise in its attempts to isolate China.

The memorandum[41] drawn up by Lie's legal assistants Ivan Kerno of Czechoslovakia and Feller decried the distinction many UN members made between recognition of governments and representation in the United Nations. This was an unfortunate error in practical terms, they argued, and wrong in legal theory. The correct legal test was whether the government claiming to represent a state in the UN was "in a position to employ the resources and direct the people of the State in fulfillment of the obligations of membership". A proper principle of decision was based upon the analogous requirements of Article 4 of the Charter, requiring that applicants for UN membership be able and willing to carry out membership obligations. Given these criteria, there would have been no doubt as to the final decision taken. The United States, however, continued to justify its refusal to support the Peking regime upon the basis of its nonrecognition policy, and while the Secretary-General achieved a substantial measure of success with other members of the Security Council, the Korean War interrupted an effort that might otherwise have succeeded.

Even after the outbreak of the Korean conflict, Lie supported an objective test for UN representation. In July, 1950, in the *Introduction* to the Annual Report of the Secretary-General, he stated:

I have urged an inquiry to determine which Government has the power to employ the resources and direct the people of the State in fulfillment of the obligations of membership in the United Nations. I have expressed the opinion that the Government which has the power should represent China in the United Nations. Otherwise, the people of China are denied their fundamental constitutional right under the Charter to be represented in the United Nations at all times.[42]

During the course of the Korean War, however, Lie obviously changed his mind, for whereas theretofore the issue had been a relatively simple test of government control, he had clearly been influenced by Peking's intervention and now argued that no prospective UN member, and particularly a candidate for a permanent Council seat, could violate the basic precepts of the Charter. "The Peking government had become the enemy of the United Nations", he wrote, and "no one can attain membership or representation in the United Nations by menace".[43] Here was an essentially subjective test, in accordance with American policy, and if not altogether consistent with his previous effort, Lie's perspective at the time was very

---

[40] Lie, *op. cit.*, p. 254.
[41] SCOR: Fifth Year, Supp. for Jan-May 1950, United Nations Doc. S/1466, 8 March 1950.
[42] GAOR: Fifth Sess., Supp. No. 1, United Nations Doc. A/1287, 12 July 1950.
[43] Lie, *op. cit.*, p. 273.

much in accord with majority sentiment among the members of the organized world community.

The Secretary-General's peace mission in the spring of 1950 was, to be sure, an endeavor of greater significance than the single issue of collective legitimization of China's new regime. On his tour of Big Four capitals, the Secretary-General presented and discussed his now famous "Memorandum of Points for Consideration in the Development of a Twenty-Year Program for Achieving Peace Through the United Nations",[44] being a list of ten critical areas in which the Secretary-General perceived some chance of negotiation. None of the ten points were particularly original, but Lie was making a last and almost desperate attempt to avert the worse excesses of the cold war and perhaps to preserve world organization. The memorandum itself, not made public until after Lie's discussions with Truman, Attlee, Bidault, Stalin, and their Foreign ministers, included the following:

1. Inauguration of top level, periodic meetings of the Security Council, with further development of UN machinery for negotiation, mediation and conciliation of international disputes. Lie wanted the Security Council sessions to be held semi-annually and utilized for private conciliation away from the New York headquarters. He also argued that the great powers should seek agreement on veto limitation and the Security Council's pacific settlement procedures.

2. A new attempt to establish an international control system for atomic energy. The American atomic monopoly had by this time been broken by the Soviet Union, and the Baruch Plan, itself unacceptable to Moscow, was now totally irrelevant. Moscow, of course, had just begun its atomic program, and under these circumstances, serious negotiation with Washington on atomic energy control appeared rather remote.

3. A new approach to regulation of conventional armaments and other weapons of mass destruction. Lie did not outline the new approach he had in mind, but emphasized that negotiations should commence even without prior political settlement, on the supposition that any progress would help reduce cold war tensions.

---

[44] The peace mission began with a speech by the Secretary-General at a B'nai B'rith dinner in Washington, D.C. on 21 March 1950 in which he pleaded for serious negotiations between the great powers to reduce tensions, and declared that "What we need, what the world needs, is a twenty-year program to win peace through the United Nations". See Cordier and Foote, *op. cit.*, pp. 270-278. The tour itself began on April 20, 1950 and ended in Washington on May 29. For the text of the ten-point memorandum, see GAOR: Fifth Sess., Annexes II, agenda item 60, United Nations Doc. A/1304, 6 June 1950. Lie was much closer to success on the Chinese representation issue than is generally realized, for five Security Council members had recognized the Peking regime by the time of the peace mission, and only two votes more were needed. Peking has not been as close to membership in the last twenty years as she was during the first half of 1950.

4. A renewal of serious effort to reach agreement on the armed forces to be made available to the Security Council. Secretary-General Lie preferred armed forces under Article 43 of the Charter, but failing this, wanted a "small force sufficient to prevent or stop localized outbreaks threatening international peace". In essence this was a renewal of his prior call for a UN field force, deemed desirable in the absence of any realistic possibility for implementation of the Charter's collective security provisions.

5. Acceptance and application of the principle of universality of membership for the United Nations. The Secretary-General cited fourteen nations awaiting UN admission, and called for membership for Germany and Japan subsequent to the completion of the peace treaties. The real issue here, naturally, was representation of the Peking regime.

6. A sound and active program of technical assistance for economic development and encouragement of capital investment, using private, governmental and intergovernmental resources. The United Nations had been most successful in its economic and social programs, and the Secretary-General was here calling for further and renewed effort to raise living standards peacefully and to combat "the dangers and costs of the cold war".

7. More vigorous use by all Member Governments of the UN's Specialized Agencies. The primary point was to end the Soviet Union's isolation from several international activities in the economic and social area, both as a means of augmenting those programs and to add significantly to the measure of international cooperative efforts. Lie also called for expansion of world trade and the early ratification of the Charter of the ill-fated International Trade Organization.

8. Vigorous and continued development of the UN's work on human rights.

9. United Nations promotion by peaceful means of advancement for dependent, colonial or semi-colonial peoples toward a place of equality among nations.

10. Active use of Charter powers and UN machinery to speed development of international law toward an eventual enforceable world law for a universal world society. This would include ratification of the Genocide Convention, greater use of the International Court of Justice, and the systematic development and codification of international law.

It is apparent that there was little in the memorandum new to policy planners of the time, and indeed, many points were merely repetitive of obligations already undertaken by UN members under the Charter. What then was the Secretary-General trying to accomplish through the fairly spectacular diplomatic intervention of the first six months of 1950? In terms of his Office, progress was evident, for given the deep political divisions of the time, and the apparent incapacity of the organized world community to establish its importance in international affairs, Lie's *démarche* and the public receptions he received in the Big Four capitals evidenced the political nature of his work. His role from the beginning might be understood in this context, but the peace mission carried the process further along, for here was the UN's Secretary-General undertaking to mediate a series of outstanding questions between East and West and in some cases on the basis of recommendations clearly unacceptable to one of the superpowers. The most obvious examples here are, of course, the Secretary-General's insistence upon universality of membership, and the suggestion that agreement be reached on appropriate means to limit the Security Council veto. Given several instances of the Secretary-General's expression of opinion on outstanding issues between Moscow and Washington, the peace mission attempt to carry his views directly to the decision makers involved, and the willingness of the Big Four to permit the initiative, Lie was successful in carving out a political role unheard of for his League of Nations predecessors. If doubts still remained concerning the capacity and willingness of the UN's highest official to undertake political functions and to publish his political views, these were certainly put to rest by the 1950 diplomatic initiative. In short, the primary accomplishment was a strengthening of the Office.

Lie was less successful, however, in terms of progress on the ten substantive points outlined in his memorandum, and in initiating meaningful East-West negotiations. The entire project was scrapped, naturally, upon the outbreak of the Korean War in June, 1950, and until that time, Lie could show progress only on the Chinese representation issue, although this was the core upon which all else depended. The United States, obviously enough, was unhappy over Lie's position on China, and gave very little backing to a mission being carried out simultaneously with Western rearmament efforts. Criticism of Lie's mission appeared in the Western press, both as to substance and the secret tour of Big Four capitals that necessarily included discussions with Stalin. The West was in no mood for political compromise, and while the Soviet Union could not indicate as much, preparations and planning for the Korean War were most certainly in an advanced stage precisely at the time of the Secretary-General's mediation attempt. Lie could not have known this, to be sure, but Moscow was no more disposed then the West to make even the faintest beginning toward an accomodation, and the Secretary-General's efforts in this direction were therefore entirely futile.

Indeed, Lie's talks in the Big Four capitals indicate clearly that the UN's key members were not prepared to utilize the world organization even marginally as a center for peaceful settlement of cold war problems. The substance of the discussions, summarized by Lie in his Memoirs, presents a picture of the world community's principal decision-makers committed to the UN as an important forum for dissemination of their political views, but little more. While the Secretary-General was greeted in most instances with warmth and cordiality, he received only the vaguest expressions of support, and an insistence that the other side was really to blame for the apparent impasse. At no point was Lie really taken into the confidence of the heads of state and prime ministers he visited, and while a great outpouring of public support for the mission was manifest, it was insufficient for purposes of influencing governmental response. With the outbreak of war, nothing more was possible save for the passage of a General Assembly resolution commending the Secretary-General and passing the substantive points of his memorandum to the appropriate UN committees for further consideration.

Today, twenty years after the publication of the twenty-year plan for peace, certain substantive lines of progress are evident. The Security Council has again become an active force in UN politics, although the quiet periodic meetings recommended by Lie have yet to be held. While there is no overall system of atomic energy control, the last several years have witnessed successes by the international community in implementation of nuclear weapons limitations, such as the test ban treaty, nonproliferation agreement, and regional nuclear free zones. On the other hand, there has been no advance in terms of conventional arms control, nor is the United Nations any closer now than two decades ago to agreement on armed forces to be made available under Article 43 of the Charter.

Significant progress has been made in points five to ten outlined by Secretary-General Lie. While the Chinese representation issue has yet to be resolved, the UN is now very nearly a universal organization, and indeed, one of the key issues facing the world body is the vexing issue of membership for "mini-states", most of which are unable to participate fully in the Organization's affairs. The divided nations of Germany, Korea, and Vietnam also pose a serious East-West membership problem. In the past twenty years, the United Nations has made gains in technical assistance for economic development, and indeed, has done some of its best work in this area. And there has been a more vigorous use by member governments of the UN's specialized agencies, including more active participation by the Soviet Union. Further, the UN has supervised human rights work of great importance in the last several years, particularly in terms of legally binding treaties designed to implement the standard-setting provisions of the 1948 Universal Declaration of Human Rights. The recent covenants on political and civil rights, economic, social and cultural rights, as well as the covenant on the elimination of racial discrimination form part of the international legal fabric of our time.

As is obvious, the United Nations has been successful for the most part in channeling the movement toward independence of the colonial world within a peaceful framework, and while most of the critical issues before the world body are derived from the difficulties attendant upon colonialism's collapse in Africa and Asia, the transition has been peaceful in most instances, and the United Nations deserves a major portion of credit. Indeed, the Organization has in recent years become a forum for expression of anti-colonial viewpoints, and its resolutions have tended to legitimize the notion that non-self governing territories must achieve independence and consequently, that colonialism itself is in violation of international legal standards. Finally, while international law has been slow in its development, the International Law Commission of the General Assembly has done very significant work in codifying particular areas of law. The quasi-legislative output of the UN's political organs in itself is a development toward world law for a universal society, but progress along these lines has been much slower than social and political needs require.

Trygve Lie was clearly too optimistic in presenting his program as a twenty-year plan for peace, but nevertheless most of the directions to which he pointed are today likely of fruitful negotiation, and given the progress of the last twenty years, it is not unreasonable to expect that further advance in the next few decades along the lines indicated by the first Secretary-General may yet result in a meaningful peace for the international community.

The Korean War

In many ways the Korean War from 1950 to 1953 marked one of the great watersheds in the history of international organization. The United Nations committed itself to what was frequently described at the time as an effort to give meaning to the Charter's conception of collective security, and to resist aggression no matter where committed. In fact, the UN served as the legitimizing cover for the United States military response in Korea and as defender of the Charter against aggression, and in so doing, found itself opposed to the strategic policy of one of its key great-power members, the Soviet Union. The UN effort was thus not appropriately labelled a collective security operation, but after several years of limited activity, the Korean War marked the Organization's first large-scale military effort, a defensive operation undertaken on behalf of the UN-sponsored South Korean Government, and thus signifying the high point of Western domination of the world organization. This dominance would begin to change later in the 1950's, but at the beginning of the new decade, the world communty's structure for peace, including its Secretary-General, were enmeshed in violent confrontation between ideologically motivated rivals, and in a fashion which clearly served the interests of the West while defending the Charter and the essential conception of peaceful change.

For Trygve Lie, the Korean War thus marked the end of his acceptability to the Soviet Union, and the end of his active role as Secretary-General, for his position in the conflict was totally untenable. A neutral role, accompanied by mediation atempts, might have been acceptable to the Soviet

Union, but probably not to the United States.[45] And obviously, the strong
support given by Lie to the U.S. effort, necessitated in part by the UN's
sponsorship of the American defense in Korea, meant the end of his usefulness as a neutral international civil servant. To the Soviets, Lie's efforts
demonstrated with absolute clarity his subservience to the West and his
hostility toward the small Communist bloc in the UN.

In a very real sense, Secretary-General Lie did not have the powerful
political advantage derived from a large neutral Afro-Asian bloc of nations.
The third world in which each side competed for influence and favor in
1950 was small indeed, and provided almost no opportunity for a UN role
both active and at least ostensibly neutral. Faced with a likely loss of
acceptability to one of the two superpowers, Lie naturally came down
hard in defense of Charter principles which, he was convinced, had been
seriously undermined by the Korean invasion across the 38th parallel in
June, 1950. Informed of the North Korean attack both by the United States
and by the United Nations Commission on Korea, the Secretary-General
determined to take the strongest possible position before the UN Security
Council. As he later wrote:

I resolved to take up the Commission's suggestion [that the Secretary-General bring the
attack to the attention of the Council], not only because the United Nations organ most
immediately involved so advised, but because this to me was clear-cut aggression—
apparently well calculated, meticulously planned, and with all the elements of surprise
which reminded me of the Nazi invasion of Norway—because this was aggression
against a "creation" of the United Nations, and because the response of the Security
Council would be more certain and more in the spirit of the Organization as a whole
were the Secretary-General to take the lead.[46]

On the basis of advice and drafting assistance from Abraham Feller and
Andrew Cordier, and after discussions with several delegations at Lake

---

[45] Cordier and Foote are apparently of the view that Lie could have remained neutral
and still retained Washington's support. They wrote: "It was not necessary or expected
of him to speak first on that famous Sunday afternoon of June 25, 1950, and before the
Security Council had come to a decision. He had not done so on previous occasions
when the Council met to deal with outbreaks of armed conflict. Even when the Arab
States attacked in Palestine after the proclamation of Israel's independence he had
refrained from invoking Article 99 after first considering this step. Now the United
States had already acted to bring the Korean attack before the Council so that no
initiative by the Secretary-General was required for that purpose." (at page 20.) While
judgments on this point must necessarily remain speculative for some time, it does not
appear likely that a general posture of neutrality would have been satisfactory to
Washington. The success of the Communists in late 1949 in China, the new Soviet-
Chinese alliance, the breaking of the American atomic monopoly, and now clear-cut
aggression by Communist troops had generated enormous fear in the United States,
and President Truman's decision to resist the Korean attack with force met with widespread international approval. These factors, in addition to the general view of the
unjustified nature of the North Korean invasion made it difficult for Lie not to take
a strong public position with the West and most of the world community.
[46] Lie, *op. cit.*, pp. 328-329.

Success, Lie declared to the Security Council that the reports received by him from the Commission in Korea "make it plain that military actions have been undertaken by Northern Korean forces". The Secretary-General asserted that the military actions were a direct violation of the General Assembly resolution founding the UN-sponsored South Korean government as the nation's sole legitimate regime, and labeled the attack a "violation of the principles of the Charter". Without formally invoking Article 99 of the Charter, the Secretary-General asserted that the "present situation is a serious one and is a threat to international peace. The Security Council is, in my opinion, the competent organ to deal with it". He concluded by proclaiming it to be the "clear duty of the Security Council to take steps necessary to reestablish peace in that area".[47]

With this statement, the Secretary-General, with war raging, had clearly abandoned the customary role of administrative neutrality in international politics in favor of a strong political defense of Charter principles, for the North Koreans were publicly deemed by the UN's executive head to have violated fundamental Charter norms and created a serious threat to international peace. As both Lie in his Memoirs, and Stephen Schwebel in his outstanding study of the Secretary-General were later to point out, Lie's Security Council statement had the effect of associating himself and the Office with the international community's effort to give reality to principles of collective security.[48] This was not the San Francisco co:nception of collective security, but the UN was resisting an unjustified attack, and its Secretary-General supported that resistance publicly and with great vigor.

The Council was able to act only because of the Soviet boycott on the Chinese representation issue. On June 25, by 9 to 0 with Yugoslavia abstaining, the Council followed the Secretary-General's lead and on the motion of the United States, labelled the attack a breach of the peace, called for "the immediate cessation of hostilities" and directed North Korea to withdraw its troops to the 38th parallel. UN members were requested to render every assistance to the UN and to refrain from helping the North Korean authorities. The resolution was ignored by North Korea and the surprised South Korean troops were driven steadily back from their defensive positions. On the night of June 26th, the Secretary-General strengthened his argument and helped validate the forthcoming United States response by declaring on a radio program of the United Nations Correspondents Association that "If the Security Council had at its disposal military forces as mentioned in Article 43 of the Charter, I believe it could use those military forces in this situation if the order to cease-fire was not obeyed by the North Korean forces".[49]

[47] SCOR: 5th Year, 473rd mtg., 25 June 1950.
[48] Schwebel, op. cit., p. 105; Lie, op. cit., p. 330.
[49] Schwebel, op. cit., p. 105.

Even prior to the Council's explicit authorization of military assistance by UN members, President Truman had decided to send American troops to South Korea, justifing the move by reference to the Council call for members to render aid to the UN. American troops and naval forces sent to Korea came at first primarily from forward bases in Japan, and Truman simultaneously dispatched the U.S. Seventh Fleet to deter any possible Peking attack against Formosa. On the evening of June 27th, the Council requested UN members to "furnish such assistance to the Republic of Korea as may be necessary to repel the armed attack and to restore international peace and security in the area".

Once the United States' military action was under way, the Secretary-General tried to keep the UN in the picture in more substantial fashion than as a simple cover for American troops, but he was notably unsuccessful in the effort, primarily because General Douglas MacArthur of the United States, appointed UN Commander in Korea, wanted a free hand, and certainly would not tolerate direction from the United Nations in New York. For example, after cabling to UN member governments for information concerning the assistance they might be in a position to furnish, on July 3 the Secretary-General and his staff recommended a draft resolution requesting the United States to act as the UN agent in terms of directing the UN force, and suggested a committee on coordination to supervise contributions from member nations. Washington was quite unwilling to permit any kind of serious UN participation in military decision-making, however, and the Security Council's July 7 resolution simply established a Unified Command under United States direction, with the entire effort to be placed under the flag of the United Nations, and the command of Washington. General MacArthur was named by President Truman as UN Commander, and from this point forward, the United Nations' role in the Korean War became seriously circumscribed.

In theory the United States was the world community's agent in the defense against aggression, but in fact the United Nations had almost no influence over Korean War policy-making, and the Secretary-General supported American planning without any significant opportunity to supervise or direct an ostensibly UN-sponsored effort. Washington would not permit serious discussion in New York, and given the presence of Soviet Secretariat officials at Headquarters, it became necessary to channel offers of assistance to the UN only in the vaguest terms, with details to be worked out between the donor state and the Unified Command under General MacArthur. And naturally, the group of Secretariat officials dealing with Korean matters did not include Soviet Under Secretary-General Constantin Zinchenko. Indeed, all Lie could do was appoint a personal representative, Colonel Alfred G. Katzin, a South African veteran of the Second World War, to form weak liaison links with the UN Commission in Korea, the Unified Command, and the Government of South Korea. Katzin's reports to the Secretary-General were helpful in terms of keeping the United Nations well informed while simultaneously providing communications channels between Lie's Office and Command headquarters in Korea and Tokyo.

But if the Secretary-General was unsuccessful in establishing anything more than nominal control over General MacArthur, he was able to magnify the base of UN operations in Korea. He wanted the UN "response to aggression to be as genuinely international as possible and was determined that other Members should assume a meaningful proportion of the burden".[50] After close consultation with United States representatives Warren Austin and Ernest Gross, Lie sent cables to fifty-three nations that had supported the Security Council's resolutions on Korea. The Secretary-General requested military assistance, including combat forces, from the great majority of nations. The response was rather uneven, but with vigorous prodding from Lie, an international army of sorts began to take shape, and by the end of 1950, the United States and fourteen other Members of the United Nations were committed to the fighting, with the addition of a unit from Luxemburg in early 1951 raising the total to sixteen nations. The U.S. contribution was entirely dominant, for over fifty percent of the troops were Americans, while forty percent were South Koreans, and the remainder small units from Australia, Belgium, Canada, Colombia, Ethiopia, France, Greece, Luxemburg, the Netherlands, New Zealand, the Philippines, Thailand, Turkey, the Union of South Africa and the United Kingdom. The United States also contributed some eighty-six percent of the naval forces and over ninety-three percent of the air force. Given U.S. military dominance, and MacArthur's refusal to be bound by any UN control, there seemed little influence Secretary-General Lie could bring to bear, but his statements before the Security Council, his negotiations with members for purposes of assuring adequate military assistance to the UN command, and his almost total identification of the Secretary-General's Office with the United States involvement in Korea all combined to broaden the extent of international participation and to validate the defense against aggression as a United Nations endeavor.

It was clear, however, that Lie would pay a heavy price for his defense of basic Charter principles, for not only had he little power to influence the course of political decision-making, he naturally lost the last vestige of support from Moscow. Soviet representative Malik returned to the Council table in August, and from that point forward, the UN's primary peace-keeping organ could take no action. Lie was attacked by the Soviets as having come forth "against peace and in defense of an aggressive war" and as "the abettor of American aggression". He had destroyed his acceptability to one of the great powers, and for most practical purposes therefore, his utility as Secretary-General was gone. He remained useful to the United

[50] Lie, *op. cit.*, p. 336.

States, obviously, throughout the duration of the war, but henceforth, his capacity to deal with the Soviets was severely limited, and a natural effect was to weaken the Office.

Lie refused to accept the advice of those who would have him assume a neutral position as between East and West. "Rather", he wrote, "the duty of the Secretary-General is to uphold the principles of the Charter and the decisions of the Organization as objectively as he can. This is what I did in Korea".[51] As noted, the choice was in reality an impossible one, for failure to support the United States military action might well have resulted in a withdrawal of support from Washington, with very similar results. The fragility of the Secretary-General's status is obvious—any of the great powers has the capacity to destroy his effectiveness, and if any one of them insists upon making its continued favor dependent upon the perceived appropriateness of his response in any given case, his position will become extraordinarily precarious. In the case of Korea, there was no doubt that Lie's efforts shattered his political life at the United Nations.

In the meantime, the war continued, with the results of the first weeks dark indeed for the United Nations forces. And as the North Korean army drove deep into South Korea, it became apparent at once that a civilian operation of some size would have to be mounted. Hundreds of thousands of refugees were moving south and many needed assistance. On July 31, the Security Council adopted a resolution requesting the Unified Command to determine relief requirements and requested the Secretary-General, the Economic and Social Council, and other international and nongovernmental organizations to provide the necessary aid. Lie's representative, Colonel Katzin, was particularly helpful in this context. But for a time during the first weeks in July, there was some doubt that the UN forces would be able to remain in Korea at all. By the end of the month MacArthur reported he had a secure hold on the southern portion of the Korean peninsula around the port city of Pusan, and that UN forces would thenceforward be strengthened. The turning point was the famous Inchon landing of September 15 which caught the North Koreans by complete surprise. The almost desperate UN position was transformed into a complete rout of the North Korean army, and within two weeks, United States and South Korean troops reached the 38th parallel. At this point, Washington had to consider seriously what had been only contingency planning a few weeks before, that is, whether to move north of the 38th parallel, destroy the Communist regime in North Korea, and unify the country under United Nations auspices.

Secretary-General Lie was quite aware of the several complex considerations involved, strategic as well as legal issues. The Unified Command and the Secretary-General were agreed that the aggressor should not be permitted to regroup his forces for further attacks, and yet the risk of

[51] *Id., pp.* 342-343.

Chinese intervention could not be taken lightly. The opportunity to unify the country upon the basis of UN-sponsored elections would, of course, fulfill the original expectation of the international community in its Korean program. The question of legal authority for military action north of the 38th parallel was also at issue.

On September 30, Secretary-General Lie, after close consultation with Feller and Cordier, issued a working paper of "suggested terms of settlement of the Korean question" which provided one possible approach to a United Nations victory without further military operations. Lie's terms were certainly stringent enough from the North Korean perspective, for he recommended that the invading troops be withdrawn entirely beyond the 38th parallel, that they agree to a ceasefire and demilitarization, and that UN Commission and relief personnel enter North Korea for purposes of assuming international responsibility for the area. Free elections would be held in all of Korea within one year under auspices of the United Nations Commission, and until that date, the Communist regime would retain *de facto* jurisdiction and control north of the 38th parallel. The United Nations troops would not move north until after the election, but should Pyongyang refuse this proposal, the UN Command would be authorized by the General Assembly to move into North Korea, the objective being to overthrow the regime there and occupy the territory until all-Korean elections could be held.

But General MacArthur was in no mood even for this kind of arrangement, and given the brilliant success of the Inchon landing, his judgment was simply not open to question in Washington. Even while the Secretary-General was discussing his approach to a settlement, United States Ambassador Austin was arguing in the Assembly's first committee:

Today, the forces of the United Nations stand on the threshold of military victory. The operations authorized by the Security Council have been conducted with vigor and skill. The price paid has been high. The sacrifice in anxiety, sorrow, wounded, and dead must be abundantly requited. A living political, social, and spiritual monument to the achievement of the first enforcement of the United Nations peacemaking function must be erected.

The opportunities for new acts of aggression, of course, should be removed. Faithful adherence to the United Nations objective of restoring international peace and security in the area counsels the taking of appropriate steps to eliminate the power and ability of the North Korean aggressor to launch future attacks. The aggressor's forces should not be permitted to have refuge behind an imaginary line because that would recreate the threat to the peace of Korea and of the world...

The artificial barrier which has divided North and South Korea has no basis for existence either in law or in reason. Neither the United Nations, its Commission on Korea, nor the Republic of Korea recognizes such a line. Now, the North Koreans by armed attack upon the Republic of Korea, have denied the reality of any such line.

Whatever ephemeral separation of Korea there was for purposes relating to the surrender of the Japanese was so volatile that nobody recognizes it. Let us not, at this critical hour and on this grave event erect such a boundary. Rather, let us get up standards and means, principles and policies, according to the Charter, by which all Koreans can hereafter live in peace among themselves and with their neighbors.[52]

At the initiative and urging of the United States, the General Assembly adopted on October 7 a resolution supporting a UN move north of the 38th parallel. The Assembly called for appropriate steps to insure conditions of stability throughout Korea, for all constituent acts, including elections under UN auspices, for the establishment of a unified, independent, and democratic government of Korea, and for UN troops to remain in North Korea only for purposes of implementing those objectives. The Assembly assumed, rather than explicitly authorized, the movement of UN forces into the North. It was further provided that all necessary steps be taken for the economic rehabilitation of the nation, including the establishment of a UN Commission for the Unification and Rehabilitation of Korea. Aside from the Soviet bloc, there was some opposition to the resolution from Yugoslavia, India, and a few Arab states, but given the repeated North Korean characterization of its retreat as temporary and strategic, the Secretary-General supported the resolution, and indeed, it fit rather well with his own recommended settlement.

The day following the passage of the Assembly resolution, General MacArthur issued an ultimatum to North Korea, calling for a total cessation of hostilities and cooperation with the United Nations in establishing a unified government, and he declared that in lieu of an immediate response the United Nations would take appropriate military action to enforce the resolution. The ultimatum was not issued, to be sure, with any serious thought or hope of North Korean compliance, and shortly thereafter, UN forces moved across the 38th parallel and began a drive to the Yalu River on the border of China. Given the risk of Chinese intervention, the Unified Command undertook certain minimum precautions. On September 27, the American Joint Chiefs of Staff had issued a directive to General MacArthur stating that under no circumstances should his troops enter into Manchurian or Soviet territory, and that for obvious policy reasons, no non-Korean combat units be used in the northeast provinces bordering the Soviet Union or in areas adjacent to the Manchurian border. The directive is itself evidence of Washington's policy-making well before the Assembly's October 7 resolution.

But in short order, United Nations troops were meeting resistance from Chinese "volunteer" forces in Korea, and by October 24, General MacArthur in effect lifted the restrictions on the use of non-Korean troops, justifying the move as a matter of military necessity. This was accepted in Washington, but there were other limits imposed upon MacArthur's freedom of action, as the United States attempted to limit its military operation so as not to provoke a serious Chinese intervention. Bilateral contacts and

[52] See Leland M. Goodrich, *Korea: A Study of U.S. Policy in the United Nations* (New York: Council on Foreign Relations, 1956), pp. 130-131.

negotiations at the United Nations, including resolutions proposed by the Security Council, tried to reassure the Chinese that their border with Korea would be held inviolate and their interests in the frontier zone protected. But now Peking was in no mood for compromise, and refusing even an invitation to take part in a Council discussion on the matter, mounted a massive attack from Manchuria at the end of November, and the United Nations effort which had seemed so remarkably close to success now suffered an enormous reverse. The Yalu River had been reached, but the American and South Korean troops were driven back rapidly below the 38th parallel and again a total UN defeat did not seem unlikely.

For the Secretary-General of the United Nations, it was indeed a dark hour, for the risks of world war mushroomed, and the fate of the five-year-old international organization devoted to preventing that war was in doubt. Lie now grasped at any opportunity to mediate and to utilize whatever political influence he might have had with the Chinese, and given Peking's desire at that time for international favor and a place in the UN, it did not seem unreasonable to hope that the Secretary-General might be granted a certain courtesy by the Chinese, and perhaps a considerable receptivity to his thinking. While China would not publicly discuss her intervention in Korea, she had sent a delegation to Lake Success to participate in the Council discussions of her complaint concerning an alleged American "armed invasion of Taiwan", and the Secretary General began talks with the chairman of the delegation, General Wu Hsiu-chuan, on December 1st.

Given the absence of direct contact between Washington and Peking, Lie served as a mediator between the antagonists, working with the United Nations and the Chinese delegation simultaneously. The outcome of his conversations was disappointing, and apparently the result of rigid instructions from which the Chinese delegation would not waver in the slightest. Lie had been seeking serious negotiations on a ceasefire, to be agreed upon quite apart from Peking's political demands for UN admission and US withdrawal from Formosa. The Secretary-General invited the delegation to his home, where they met with representatives to the UN from Britain, India, Pakistan, Sweden, and Israel. "My purpose", wrote Lie, "was to bring the Chinese into amiable contact with the United Nations world".[53] The talks with the Chinese took a favorable turn on December 9, when, according to the Secretary-General, General Wu stated his government's wish for a ceasefire without mentioning UN representation or sovereignty over Formosa. According to Lie, Wu wanted the Secretary-General's assistance in learning the ceasefire terms acceptable to Washington and the UN command, but within a few days the Chinese delegation reverted to the more rigid posture. "A sudden change", wrote Lie, "seemed to have come over the Chinese delegation. I suspected that they had been talking to Mr.

[53] Lie, *op. cit.*, p. 353.

Vyshinsky or had received a rebuke from Moscow by way of Peking".[54]
The Secretary-General later met with the Cease Fire Committee established
by the General Assembly, where he learned the Unified Command's ceasefire conditions.

But the Chinese delegation no longer seemed interested in UN peace
terms, and insisted upon leaving New York by December 19. The Secretary-
General tried his best to persuade the delegation to remain a few days longer,
or at least to hear the UN terms, but General Wu insisted that Peking's
instructions would not be varied. Lie had failed, but through no fault of his
own, for the Chinese would not halt the fighting with UN troops reeling
backward. The peace terms, which were in fact cabled to Peking, envisaged
a ceasefire and a demilitarized zone with its southern border on the 38th
parallel. This was a far cry from the victory-flushed days of late September
and early October when the UN was calling for a unified, independent
Korea with nation-wide elections, but now Peking sought total victory, and
the war continued through the winter of 1950-51.

The General Assembly labeled the Chinese invasion of "volunteers" an
act of aggression, but at the same time efforts ware made by the Assembly's
Cease-Fire Group and Good Offices Committee throughout the winter to
reach agreement on a ceasefire formula. Yet so long as the Chinese forces
were achieving significant military victories in the field, these endeavors
were of little consequence. By March, 1951, however, when UN troops
began to drive Chinese units back to the 38th parallel, hope grew for a compromise agreement based on a stabilized ceasefire line at or near the original
demarcation between North and South Korea.

During this period, Secretary-General Lie called publicly for a ceasefire
along the 38th parallel, declaring that should this be accomplished, the
crucial goal of UN action in defending against aggression would have been
fulfilled.[55] There now seemed little fear that Communist forces would regroup in the North to mount still another attack at a later date, and in June,
1951, Lie distributed privately a memorandum recommending that the
military commanders in Korea attempt to arrange a ceasefire without regard
to political questions of any kind. The hope was that recent United Nations
successes in the field would induce Peking to eliminate for the time being
the political conditions it had attached to the ceasefire discussions.

---

[54] *Id.,* p. 354.

[55] At a press conference at Lake Success on 6 April 1951, Lie clearly separated the UN
objectives of repelling aggression and unifying Korea under a free, democratic, and
independent regime. Much as the Chinese attached political conditions to their military negotiating position, so too the UN had made the unification of Korea under
UN auspices one of the main goals, along with military success. Lie now divided the
two UN aims, the second to be achieved "by the peaceful means of negotiation, conciliation, and economic assistance". He stressed that "these two objectives—and the
fundamental difference in the means to reach them—should be clearly understood by
all concerned". (UN Press Release, SG/151, 6 April 1951)

The Secretary-General's initiative in the matter was very much in line with United States policy, and with the general consensus of opinion in the United Nations. President Truman's description [56] of the National Security Council's recommendation of May, 1951 indicates the extent to which American planning had deviated from the original conception of total success in Korea. Washington now wanted a ceasefire agreement permitting reestablishment of South Korean authority "over all of Korea south of a northern boundary line suitable for defense and administration and not substantially below the 38th parallel". Both Washington and the Secretary-General were willing to distinguish quite clearly the military objective of repelling the aggression from the political aim envisaging an independent Korea united under a democratic government chosen by a free election process. There was no hope of achieving the latter, and the primary emphasis, quite naturally, was upon the compromise military stance now accepted in Washington and publicly recommended by the Secretary-General.

The turning point came on June 23, when Jacob Malik, still the permanent representative of the Soviet Union to the UN, declared that "discussions should be started between the belligerents for a ceasefire and an armistice providing for mutual withdrawal from the 38th parallel".[57] Two days later, an editorial in the People's Daily of Peking endorsed the suggestion, calling for the withdrawal of all foreign troops from Korea, and on June 27th Foreign Minister Gromyko declared the ceasefire should be strictly military in nature, separated from a discussion of political problems.

Talks were scheduled to begin on July 10, and prior to that date Secretary-General Lie was busy in the preparation of several documents felt desirable on the UN side. At the end of June, he circulated a legal memorandum prepared by Abraham Feller, the essential point being that the United Nations had the right to conclude a ceasefire or armistice without additional authorization from the Security Council or Assembly, but that this right was restricted to military questions, political authorization being necessary for discussion of political issues. A few days later, Lie distributed an *aide mémoire* that constituted a UN admonition to the North Korean and Chinese governments concerning continued willingness of UN troops to fight. He indicated doubt whether proposed ceasefire negotiations would lead to the end of hostilities and appropriate armistice arrangements, and implied that the talks might be utilized by the invading troops for further strengthening their military position. He urged member governments to declare themselves satisfied that a ceasefire seemed feasible, but requested them at the same time to give evidence of their readiness to furnish ground troops in the event that a ceasefire and satisfactory armistice were not arranged. The *aide mémoire* was circulated to the sixteen nations providing

---

56 Truman, *op. cit.*, pp. 455-456.
57 Lie, *op. cit.*, p. 363.

troops, but Washington decided there was no advantage in a general circulation, particularly since the Unified Command had never been content with the military problems generated by the large number of small units from around the world.

The Secretary-General made one last effort to strengthen the UN position in Korea by suggesting that the UN Commission for the Unification and Rehabilitation of Korea be dissolved and in its place a UN mediator or representative appointed to supervise truce arrangements and negotiate the key political questions of unification of Korea, elections, and the nature of the post-war government. In the event, the recommendation seemed quite irrelevant as the ceasefire and general military negotiations dragged on for a period of two years, and Lie had no opportunity to work with the North Korean authorities on the question of UN-sponsored elections followed by the establishment of a unified and independent Korea.

The Secretary-General was quiet during the course of the tortuous negotiations at Panmunjom, and there were no new initiatives from his Office. During this time he was gradually being driven from the Secretary-ship-General by the Soviet Union's insistance that his action during the conflict and his support of the West branded him an accomplice of aggression, and Moscow's refusal to recognize him as Secretary-General or deal with him in any way severely limited his usefulness to the Organization. Lie's final notice of resignation came in the autumn of 1952, and he was succeeded in April, 1953 by Dag Hammarskjold. In July of that year, the armistice agreements were finally signed and the Korean War came to an end. There was no political settlement, of course, and a line near the 38th parallel became essentially the permanent boundary between two Koreas.

For Trygve Lie, as for many observers of the time, the United Nations action in Korea constituted an attempt to enforce a system of collective security against a clear-cut case of aggression. The original expectation had been that UN collective action would occur only upon agreement of the permanent members of the Security Council, with armed force utilized only subsequent to the conclusion of agreements under Charter Article 43. The notion at San Francisco had been that the United Nations would serve primarily as an instrument of conciliation and mediation, and there was certainly no disposition to permit measures of a military nature against the real or perceived interests of any of the great powers. But the label "collective security" was applied to the Korean case, and among those who made the phrase fashionable was certainly the Secretary-General, who repeatedly emphasized his conviction that the failure of the UN to act would have had as a consequence the demise of the Organization itself. "Though the price was high and the waiting long", he wrote, "Korea was not permitted to become another Manchuria".[58] In the *Introduction* to the Secretary-General's

[58] *Id.*, p. 366.

Annual Report for 1951-1952, one of Lie's last official political statements to the international community, he declared that:

[A]ll the evidence of the past, and especially the history of the 1930's, indicate that failure to act against aggression in Korea would have undermined faith in collective security everywhere, reduced the military significance and deterrent power of regional treaties, and encouraged further adventures in armed aggression elsewhere.

The United Nations resistence to aggression in Korea, on the other hand, has increased the security of all nations which desire to live in peace, both by the act of collective resistence itself and by the increase in deterrent military power against the threat of future armed aggression that has resulted.

The present dangerous divisions and conflicts in the world make the need for effective world-wide collective security against armed aggression all the more urgent. But we need clearer and more affirmative definitions of policy from Governments in support of this principle, and further advance planning and preparation for the effective mobilization of collective force to prevent any future Koreas.

At the same time, it should be made clear that the development of United Nations collective security is not aimed at the security or peaceful aspirations of any nation or group of nations. We seek only to prevent and oppose armed aggression from whatever source it springs.[59]

This kind of stance was of obvious significance for realizing maximum political benefit from the UN sponsorship of a United States decision to resist attack in Korea, and there seems little doubt that this was Lie's essential purpose. Even if his role in the Korean War entailed the sacrifice of his personal position, he deemed it desirable in terms of the Organization's interests and world peace. If no defense had been made in Korea, or if the United Nations had not associated itself with Washington's effort then surely the Organization would have suffered, for in either case it would have been of no importance to the crucial political and military issue of its time, the failing above all else that determined the fate of the League of Nations. There was risk, of course, that the United Nations would lose in its military effort, but in that eventuality, the result would likely be no worse than total inaction. Further, even if the Office of Secretary-General were weakened by Lie's initiative and political role, this was certainly preferable to a weakening of the entire Organization. In the early 1950's, this kind of thinking was probably correct, although the rise to prominence in the UN of the Afro-Asian nations a few years later rendered much of the analysis irrelevant. The Office then became a factor of much greater significance in influencing the direction of the world body itself, and a failure by the Secretary-General to observe principles of neutrality as between East and West might well have rendered the UN incapable of action in a particular case. But in the early 1950's, the conception of the Organization acting as a serious instrument of conciliation and preventive diplomacy between the superpowers was not nearly so well developed, and it clearly had little

[59] GAOR: Seventh Sess., Supp. No. 1A, United Nations Doc. A/2141/Add.1, 30 Sept. 1952.

application within the context of a military confrontation between Communist forces and the West.

Lie's role in the Korean War does raise some important questions, however, concerning the Secretaryship-General. It may well be argued that no matter what Lie's response in this case, his personal position would have been destroyed, yet the critical issue was not Lie's personal future, but rather the capacity of the Office. Until Korea, the Secretary-General had made strenuous efforts to present at least the appearance of neutrality in East-West conflicts even if, as in the case of the Chinese representation issue, the appeerence was rather transparent. Lie's switch in the Korean War was highly significant for the future of the Office, for the alienation of the Soviet Union resulted in an attitude the full expression of which we are now witnessing.

When Moscow agreed to the selection of Dag Hammarskjold in 1953 as the UN's second Secretary-General, it did so in the mistaken belief that he would not function as a significant actor in the international arena, would not have an important political role, and would serve essentially administrative and clerk functions in the quiet manner of the Drummond tradition. Moscow was in serious error, and the result is that the current Secretary-General is under the most severe limitation on the exercise of powers normally associated with the Office, the Soviet Union insisting that the UN's first official possess only very limited discretionary power. The Soviet perspective on the Office is essentially traceable to the warmth with which Trygve Lie embraced the Western position during the Korean War. Perhaps the Soviet attitude by the 1960's would have been the same in any case, but had Lie maintained the neutral posture of his first few years in office, it is unlikely that Moscow would so soon have urged an administrative-clerk Secretary-General, and Washington, while it naturally would have been displeased, would also have been in no position to attribute his neutrality to a superfluity of executive power.

From the vantage point of the 1970's and given the experience of Dag Hammarskjold and U Thant, Lie's Korean War role may reasonably be judged to have commenced the period of serious Soviet disenchantment and distrust of an international executive of any capacity in world politics. As noted, this consideration had to be of lesser importance for Lie, even assuming it was thought to be at all relevant, for in 1950 it could not have been foreseen that the effectiveness of the world organization might one day turn on the capacity of its Secretary-General. A weakening of the Office must surely have appeared at the time a worthwhile price to pay for the strengthening of the UN's position in world politics and thus Lie's decision to abandon political neutrality in favor of a strong defense of Charter principles was probably correct, given the limited nature at that time of UN executive power.

Whether Lie's abandonment of neutrality was justified in terms of the political and legal posture deemed appropriate for a Secretary-General is a difficult question. It is naturally one of the primary functions of the Secretariat's first official to execute as fully as the limitations of the Office allow the political decisions and directives of the Security Council, Assembly and other political bodies of the Organization. But this is frequently impossible to square with non-partisanship, and perhaps even impossible to operationalize given an armed attack that the organized community deems in serious violation of basic Charter principles.

Yet it might appear that the true difficulties involved here were not so much matters of conflicting substantive obligations as a matter of style and procedure. There have been frequent cases throughout the history of the United Nations when the institution has taken decisions clearly contrary to the wishes of a great power, and it would seem that the Secretary-General is perfectly capable of associating himself with such decisions in a manner calculated to maintain rather than diminish his political support. Perhaps it is simply a matter of the right words, or avoiding particular formulations that must necessarily result in alienation. Secretaries-General Hammarskjold and Thant have both demonstrated significant capacity to assume positions quite contrary to the stated policy of one or more of the great powers, without this resulting in a loss of support. On the other hand, it may well be argued that the very existence of a large Afro-Asian bloc of nations in the UN has made this significantly easier—Trygve Lie had only the most fragile of neutral bloc structures with which to work. Thus it would probably be incorrect to judge Lie's role in the Korean War as having seriously weakened the neutrality of the Secretary-General.

There has also been much debate on the question whether the Korean initiatives strengthened the Office at least as of the early 1950's. Schwebel, for example, argues that "the strength and influence of the Secretary-General were immeasurably enhanced by the Korean initiative",[60] and while this is later qualified by reference to Lie's close identification with the Western effort in Korea, the general judgment is left standing. As noted above, it is more likely that the long term effect of Lie's role was to weaken the Office while strengthening the UN position, but there can be no doubt that the Secretary-General continued his disposition to politicize the Office far beyond the limits conceived proper by his League of Nations predecessors. The Secretary-General's willingness to make judgments concerning the rights and wrongs of the Korean episode, and his close identification with the Western military response, particularly concerning the movement north of the 38th parallel and the retrenchment in war aims subsequent to the Chinese intervention, all stamped the effort with an unmistakable political cast that helped shift the common conception of the Secretary-General away from the administrative-clerk image to a more important political figure.

The judgment, then, that Lie weakened the Office to save the Organization must be qualified by the statement that his deliberate politicization of

[60] Schwebel, *op. cit.*, p. 110.

the Secretaryship-General allowed for opportunity to utilize that Office as never before in world politics, carrying with it the assumption that active political intervention might be reconciled and made consistent with principles of neutral action. The latter assumption could not be validated in Lie's time, but under Hammarskjold and Thant, the consonance between the two became the only rational basis for United Nations action. In this sense then, Lie had cleared the way for further development of the Office he headed, and had set the stage for a strengthened United Nations, given the right nexus of conditions that was to arise with the influx of Afro-Asian members and the resultant opportunity for UN action as a neutral third party intermediary with the primary purpose of keeping East and West apart in local conflicts isolated from the disputes of the cold war.

The Issue of American Communists in the UN Secretariat

In 1952 and 1953, during the McCarthy era in the United States, Secretary-General Lie confronted one of the most difficult political and administrative decisions of his career, for the McCarthy search for Communist influence in every corner of the American government had reached into the United Nations Secretariat as well. United States citizens engaged in foreign service of any kind were particularly susceptible to the gigantic hunt for Communists and fellow travelers which obsessed the American people for nearly two years, a search that came close to paralyzing the State Department and the far weaker structure of the United Nations Secretariat.

Trygve Lie had never obtained meaningful cooperation from the American government in the complex task of buiding a Secretariat staff. From the beginning, the UN was compelled to provide its own screening of candidates for Secretariat staff positions, and given the needs of a rapid buildup in the early years, the process naturally allowed into UN service a number of individuals whom the Secretary-General would not otherwise have hired. Lie never feared that American Communists in the Secretariat posed any substantial threat either to the security of the United States government or to the UN itself, for the public nature of UN activities precluded the Organization from serving as an efficient espionage center for Communists, nor were there many individuals whose total unsuitability for international civil service work was not apparent during the first years of UN activity.

Yet Lie emphasized his wish to eliminate American Communist party members from the international civil service, notwithstanding that every Secretariat member has full freedom of personal political conviction provided his obligations as an international servant are met. Lie wrote:

I would never knowingly have employed a member of the American Communist party in the Secretariat. First of all, an American Communist is not a representative American citizen. Although the Communist Party had not been directly outlawed in the

United States, many laws and regulations, in effect, labeled it as a subversive organization dedicated to the overthrow of the government of the United States by force and violence. With the Permanent Headquarters in the United States, it was plain common sense not to want any American Communists in the Secretariat... If there was even one American Communist in the Secretariat I wished to get rid of him.[61]

The nightmare began with a federal grand jury investigation of alleged communist activity in the New York City area, including an examination of Americans employed by the UN Secretariat. No indictments were handed down by the grand jury, but without naming individuals, a finding was made of "infiltration into the United Nations of an overwhelmingly large group of disloyal United States citizens".[62] The proceedings before the jury caused an enormous outcry in the press and from the United States Congress, generating attacks directed at the integrity of the Secretariat and for the most part originating from sources with a history of antagonism to the United Nations. In October, 1952, the Internal Security Subcommittee of the United States Senate Judiciary Committee held a set of hearings in New York City, during which it called to give testimony eighteen American staff members (out of some 1800) on possible past Communist associations. On the advice of legal counsel, both before the Senate Committee and the federal grand jury, the UN civil servants refused to testify, pleading as grounds the Fifth Amendment of the U.S. Constitution which provides that a person shall not be compelled in any criminal case to be a witness against himself.

The first question for the Secretary-General was his response to the refusal to testify. Apparently it was Lie's strong conviction that the invocation of the privilege against self-incrimination was inconsistent with the obligations of an international civil servant, for he insisted that UN officials had frequently to waive particular constitutional rights upon becoming members of the UN staff, and he was later to write that the witnesses' attitude before the federal grand jury and Senate subcommittee tended to "discredit the Secretariat as a whole, to cast suspicion on all the staff—and, still more serious, it imperiled the position of the Organization in the host country".[63] Quite apart from public outcry, Trygve Lie was convinced that as a matter of rational policy for an international organization, staff members who refused to testify before the proper authorities of their own nation concerning past activities had fallen short of required standards in

---

[61] Lie, *op. cit.*, p. 388.

[62] Cordier and Foote, *op. cit.*, p. 487.

[63] Lie, *op. cit.*, p. 397. The Secretary-General added that "The impression that the Secretariat harbored those subversives of American institutions was heightened by the practice of the Internal Security Subcommittee in generally calling only those staff members to testify in *open* session who earlier had refused in closed session to answer questions about Communist party membership, or who had admitted past membership. Although these witnesses were about one in a hundred of the Americans employed by the United Nations, the impression conveyed to the public was that of a parade of Americans working for the United Nations who were Communists, former Communists, or at least had something to hide". (*Ibid*).

the regulations governing staff conduct, and that the failing required immediate dismissal. His first step was to fire those holding temporary fixed-term contracts.

The question of staff members holding permanent contracts, however, was more complex, as dismissal here was appropriate under the regulations only for reasons of misconduct, unsatisfactory service, physical incapacity, or the abolition of the post in question. Abraham Feller and the Secretary-General agreed that the best strategy would be the establishment of an international Commission of Jurists to advise upon the question whether refusal to testify on grounds of the self-incrimination clause of the Constitution amounted to a breach of Secretariat staff regulations. Lie was unable to persuade several distinguished attorneys from the United States, Britain and other nations to serve, but after some difficulty, a three-man panel [64] was brought together for its first meeting on November 14, 1952.

One day before the Commission met, and just three days after Lie submitted his resignation as Secretary-General, Feller committed suicide. This was an enormous shock for both Lie and the entire United Nations, for Feller had been one of the Secretary-General's closest advisers during the entire seven years of the Lie administration, and had been at the center of decision-making in the Secretary-General's Office for every one of the critical political and legal issues confronted by the world organization since 1946. Most observers at the time, including the Secretary-General, attributed his death to the overwhelming strain connected with the attack upon the Secretariat by the federal grand jury and the United States Senate Internal Security Subcommittee. "He has worked tirelessly day and night under my direction", stated Lie, "to uphold due process of law and justice in the investigations against indiscriminate smears and exaggerated charges. This placed him under a prolonged and serious strain. This terrible tragedy of his death today is the result".[65] Feller's death was the occasion for a general tribute to his service and indirectly a statement of confidence in the United Nations by many United States government officials and representatives of foreign nations. Among the many in the American government who attended his funeral was U.S. Secretary of State Dean Acheson.

Nevertheless, powerful pressure continued to be exerted against Secretary-General Lie and the Secretariat, with the core of this effort in the United States led by Senators McCarthy, McCarran and Eastland, aided by encouragement from the extreme right wing press. At the end of November, the Commission of Jurists published an opinion with which the Secretary-General found himself in fundamental agreement. Refusal to testify on the basis of the self-incrimination clause was considered by the jurists a breach

---

[64] The Commission was made up of three outstanding attorneys—William Mitchell, former Attorney General of the United States, Sir Edwin Herbert, an English solicitor, and Paul Veldekens, a law professor in Belgium at the Catholic University of Louvain.
[65] UN Press Release SG/268, 12 Nov. 1952.

of the Secretariat staff regulations, and they recommended that Lie dismiss the nine staff members on permanent contract who had so refused to testify. The Secretary-General allowed the offending members to withdraw the plea, which they refused to do, and then dismissed them, as was expected. Lie was criticized by many members, particularly from Western Europe, for having deferred to American right wing pressure, and it was not surprising that criticism from the right was unabated for what appeared to be his hesitation in removing the offending members in the first place, and permitting them a second chance before final dismissal.

But the worst part of what Dag Hammarskjold was later to call a "short nightmare" was yet to come. On January 9, 1953, President Truman issued an executive order calling for FBI investigation of American staff Secretariat officials and of candidates for Secretariat positions, with the information to be transmitted to the Secretary-General for use as he saw fit. The procedure decided upon involved the filling out of forms and fingerprinting by FBI and civil service agents in UN headquarters itself, and the Secretary-General was thus faced with the decision whether to allow the U.S. government agents to enter the premises or not.

Once again under heavy political pressure, the Secretary-General gave way, later contending that the Americans on the staff were not opposed to his decision, the bulk of protests coming from staff personnel uninvolved in the proceedings. No American on the staff was exempt from the investigation, and with this the United Nations Secretariat clearly reached its lowest point. Twenty-five years earlier the League of Nations Secretariat had undergone a similar experience, as the Fascist government of Italy insisted upon government clearance for Italians, the idea being to prevent opponents of Mussolini from serving as staff members. And in 1952, the charges against Americans reached into the highest levels, as even the distinguished Ralph Bunche was accused by the American right of communist associations. He was examined by the Senate subcommittee and the international employees loyalty board, and after three lays of screaming press headlines, was publicly acquitted. Bunche and the Secretary-General were agreed that the entire episode had seriously affected the morale of the Secretariat, much as the McCarthy atmosphere had injured the American State Department.

If the Secretary-General's response to political pressure in this case was of doubtful wisdom, it can only be understood within the context of the early 1950's atmosphere in the United States, and the power of McCarthyism throughtout the nation. On March 10, 1953, less than one month before Dag Hammarskjold succeeded him, Lie presented to the General Assembly a long statement in defense of himself and his personnel policy, maintaining the correctness of his actions and of the basic policies concerning dismissal of staff members pleading the Fifth Amendment, and allowing United States government officials from the FBI and civil service to enter UN

Headquarters for investigative purposes. Never before had Lie been subjected to such powerful criticism from friendly delegates to the UN and his position was somewhat defensive. "Permit me", stated Lie, "to say simply that I have done the best I could in political circumstances that were not of my making. I have done my best to maintain the Charter inviolate and to uphold the basic principles of an independent, international Secretariat... It is for the representatives now to decide whether I have been right or wrong and to take the responsibility for whatever decision they may come to".[66] Lie was generally supported in the Assembly, but it was an unfortunate conclusion to his seven years as Secretary-General. It was obvious throughout that he was most unhappy over the pressure exerted by the US government and conservative political circles in the United States, and his decisions were clearly taken with much reluctance. He later wrote:

It remains true that the world struggle to sustain freedom, which America has led abroad, still has its home front. Although the Secretariat of the United Nations cannot fight the battle which is properly to be left to the American liberal tradition, it must stand guard against the assaults which continue to be made against its international integrity and ideal.[67]

The problem gradually faded away under the administration of Dag Hammarskjold. The new Secretary-General ordered the FBI agents off UN premises, feeling their presence to be an intolerable challenge to the international character of the Secretariat, and he was successful in establishing a judicial process for staff members against whom allegations had been brought by the U.S. government. This tended to remove the immediate glare of press publicity until the issue lost interest for the American public. He also insisted upon substantive and procedural safeguards for the judicial process, including substantial evidence concerning unsuitability for staff membership. Hammarskjold later proposed staff regulations amendments making more explicit the prohibition on political activities of Secretariat staff members, and strengthening his own power to dismiss officials on

[66] GAOR: Seventh Sess., Plenary, 413th mtg., 10 March 1953. Lie discussed the many factors that helped explain and defend his actions, among them the exposed position of the Secretary-General as the only UN organ with exclusively international responsibilities, cold-war conflict, the UN location in New York, varying notions among members of the status of a civil service, rapid staff recruitment in 1946-1947, and the necessity of seeking the assistance of Members in checking on possible appointments. But the Secretary-General reaffirmed his conviction that Secretariat staff members had the "clear obligation, under the Charter and the Staff regulations, to take no part in any activity, either open or secret, aimed at subverting or overthrowing the Government of a Member State". Further, no American Communist Party member "who is, thereby, barred from employment in the service of his own Government, should, as a matter of policy, be employed in the Secretariat". Finally, for a UN staff member to refuse to testify was to "draw upon himself grave suspicion of being a danger to the security of a Member State" and as such, "a grave breach of the staff regulations concerning the conduct required of staff members".
[67] Lie, *op. cit.*, p. 405.

permanent contract. The United States government seemed perfectly satisfied with this approach. Hammarskjold wrote that his administration

was only prepared to accept information from governments concerning suitability for
employment, including information that might be relevant to political considerations
such as activity which would be regarded as inconsistent with the obligation of international civil servants. It was recognized that there should be a relationship of mutual
confidence and trust between international officials and the governments of Member
States. At the same time, the Secretary-General took a strong position that the dismissal of a staff member on the basis of the mere suspicion of a government of a
Member State or a bare conclusion arrived at by that government on evidence which is
denied the Secretary-General would amount to receiving instructions in violation of
his obligation under Article 100, paragraph 1, of the Charter "not to receive in the
performance of his duties instructions from any government".[68]

It has generally been considered that the problem of American Communists in the Secretariat was handled much more satisfactorily by Hammarskjold than by Trygve Lie. Yet it was clearly a more difficult issue for
Lie, as the pressures were more intense, the publicity in the United States
and elsewhere greater, and it was the UN's first attempt to handle the
problem on a large scale. Hammarskjold had the advantage of hindsight,
Lie's experience, and an American public more accustomed to the issue. Lie
was caught in an unfortunate crossfire of pressures from the Korean War,
McCarthyism, and as he generously described the problem in his memoirs,
the relative newness of America's involved relationship with the rest of the
world, including hostile nations and a superpower with the capacity to
destroy it. Lie was quite right in pointing to the 1927 Italian measures as a
precedent for the American action of 1952, and in equating it with Soviet
attacks against the integrity of the Secretariat. Fortunately, however, the
situation was righted with relatively little damage done, and the international
community has learned much from Lie's experience. The Soviet Union was
also unsuccessful with its "troika" attack in 1960, and given the rise of the
Afro-Asian group of nations, there is reason for hope that the incentive for
broadside attacks against the Secretariat which tend to degrade its impartiality and integrity will not emerge again. It was a great misfortune, however,
that Secretary-General Lie did not have sufficient strength to withstand
political pressures which, if permitted to go unchecked, might well have
destroyed the international civil service.

Lie's Views on His Office and United Nations Political Functions

The public statements and speeches of Secretary-General Lie on the role of
world organization are in one sense strikingly similar to those of his League
of Nations counterparts, while in some respects they show marked differ-

[68] Wilder Foote, ed., *Dag Hammarskjold: Servant of Peace* (New York: Harper & Row,
1962), p. 340.

ences. Much like Sir Eric Drummond and Joseph Avenol, Lie was not given to theoretical pronouncements concerning the role of the Secretary-General or the world organization he headed. In the manner of his predecessors, Lie devoted many of his public speeches to rather straightforward analyses of the UN structure and processes, naturally concentrating on its successes, explaining failures by reference to cold war conflicts, generally calling for greater cooperation among the great powers, and extolling the United Nations as the best hope for world peace. Lie did initiate the now accepted practice of writing a more thoughtful *Introduction* to the Secretary-General's Annual Report, this addition to past practice being carried to its most useful form by Dag Hammarskjold. Lie's introductions were at a generally higher level than the public speeches (directed as they were to mass opinion), but still there was very little of a theoretical or doctrinal nature. In this respect, he was not of a cast of mind that found such pronouncements desirable, and of course he found it congenial to follow the practice of his League predecessors.

On the other hand, as noted many times, Lie was not at all hesitant to express his political views in the strongest terms, even on the most controversial of international issues, and this very significant departure from League practice obviously helped politicize the Office, legitimate its political functions, and combined with Lie's active role as negotiator and mediator in several disputes, constituted a substantial enlargement of the powers of the Secretaryship-General. In terms of the Office itself, Lie enunciated few meaningful statements regarding its powers, and while there exist some scattered references to his thoughts throughout the body of the public statements, these in no way form a cohesive analysis, and it is only by inference from actions in particular cases that one is able to construct a notion of Lie's perspective on the Office.

At the start of his administration, Lie was naturally quite cautious. "Your Secretary-General is not called upon to formulate the policy of the United Nations", he stated. "The lines of that policy are laid down in the Charter and determined by decisions of the different relevant organs of the United Nations. The task of the Secretariat will be to assist all those organs of the United Nations in preparing and carrying out all decisions taken by them in order to make the policy program of the Charter a living reality".[69] This amounted to a straightforward statement of generally accepted views, and was certainly in accord with the League conception of executive responsibility, but while Lie never changed his conviction on the point, as he became involved in international politics his emphasis certainly broadened the scope of his initial understanding, and grew far more positive in tone. Indeed, Lie rather quickly came to understand the Secretary-General not as a formulator of policy, but rather one who deeply influenced the decision-

---

[69] GAOR: First Sess., Part I, Plenary, 22nd mtg., 2 Feb. 1946.

making process and helped shape UN policy through independent investigation and mediation attempts, including countless discussions with state representatives and delegates, and through public statements. As early as 1946, Lie stated before the Security Council his view that Article 99 of the Charter implied lesser powers of investigation. In September of that year, the United States had proposed a Council investigation commission to inquire into border violations along the Greek frontier of Albania, Bulgaria, and Yugoslavia. The Soviet Union opposed the plan, but Lie declared before the vote that this would not deter his own rights of investigation:

Just a few words to make clear my own position as Secretary-General and the rights of this office under the Charter. Should the proposal of the United States representative not be carried, I hope that the Council will understand that the Secretary-General must reserve his right to make such enquiries or investigations as he may think necessary, in order to determine whether or not he should consider bringing any aspect of this matter up to the attention of the Council under the provisions of the Charter.[70]

As noted, Lie's first steps in developing the Office were within the context of the right to make statements to the Security Council and General Assembly, both written and oral presentations, and at his own initiative, rather than upon invitation of the President. Procedural capacity to take part in public debates complemented by the right to carry out the independent investigation implied by Article 99 would permit significant opportunity for the Secretary-General to shape and influence UN policy making. This was further augmented by Lie's use of the Introduction to the Annual Report from 1948 onward, and naturally by the several public addresses and press conferences that enabled him to utilize large audiences and mass media to communicate his views of world politics and the possible role of the United Nations.

Lie also used his Office for purposes of guardianship of the interests (real and ostensible) of the world organization. All the UN Secretaries-General have used neutral legal principles in the perceived interest of the Organization, as a kind of cover for political expression, and as a means of influencing the outcome of particular policy disputes. As we have seen, Lie was particularly fond of the legal memorandum as a technique for pressing his own political convictions, and not infrequently he served as spokesman for the Organization in order to achieve precisely the same goal. In 1948, Lie wrote:

As Secretary-General of the United Nations I am responsible to the collectivity of the Member States. It is not my business as Secretary-General to assess the rights or the wrongs between the two sides [East and West] in this conflict. The collective judgment of world public opinion can be trusted to do that. But it is my recognized duty to speak for the organization—which includes everybody—when I believe the United Nations to be in danger.[71]

---

[70] SCOR: First Year, 70th mtg., 20 Sept. 1946.
[71] Cordier and Foote, op. cit., p. 124.

This was a statement of Lie's position during the Korean War—that is to say, the interests of the Organization and the sense of the Charter principles compelled him to associate himself and his Office with the Western military effort, and while this amounted to passing judgment upon the merits of a particular dispute involving East-West conflict, he understood anything less on his part to be detrimental to the Organization, and this a Secretary-General could not permit. In his acceptance speech to the General Assembly subsequent to its extension of his term of office on November 1, 1950, and speaking against the background of Soviet opposition to his Korean War stand and refusal to support him for another term, Lie commented:

> I have tried, in all sincerity and with all the energy in my command, to carry out that pledge [oath of office of the Secretary-General] in letter and in spirit, to uphold the Charter of the United Nations, to act in accordance with the decisions of all its organs, and to use the influence of my office always in support of peace and the authority of the Organization.
>
> The United Nations can not function effectively unless the Secretariat acts in loyal conformity with the decisions and recommendations of the organs of the United Nations. The United Nations cannot function effectively unless the Secretariat acts in the collective interest of the United Nations as a whole, and in the collective interest only.[72]

And as shall be noted in the next section, Lie's decision to agree to an extended term was taken notwithstanding a personal preference to return to Norway. "There were some principles involved", he stated, "and I could not fail to take up the duty and responsibility which I was called upon to take up".[73]

In short, while the Secretary-General did not formulate policy, Lie was explicit in asserting that he assisted UN decision-making by exerting influence in many ways within the limits of the structure and process circumscribing his actions. There was always some question as to how frequently the Secretary-General should intervene to help shape policy, and the only consistent response framed by Lie was again the necessity for speaking out when the interests of the United Nations itself were at stake. Thus in 1949, in an address to the American Association for the United Nations, he argued that within the limits of the resources at his disposal, the Secretary-General had to exert influence primarily in two ways:

> He can act privately by direct discussion with representatives of Member Governments on questions at issue. Or he can act publicly, either in an open meeting of an Organ, or in a report, or in a speech. In this case, he takes a public position and appeals to the Member Governments and to world public opinion to support that position.
>
> I have been criticized by some people who are good friends of the United Nations for not intervening often enough in political issues before the United Nations. I have been criticized by others, who are equally good friends, I am sure, for intervening

---

[72] GAOR: Fifth Sess., Plenary, 299th mtg., 1 Nov. 1950.
[73] UN Press Release SG/135, 21 Dec. 1950.

at all. Between these two extremes I have tried to take a common-sense middle course, conscious always of my responsibility to stand only for the interests of the United Nations as a whole.

It is necessary for the Secretary-General to act with full realization of the consequences of taking public positions on matters closely affecting the peace of the world. At the same time, there have been and will be issues that affect the well-being and even perhaps the very life itself of the United Nations. On such occasions, I believe with all my heart and soul that it is necessary for the Secretary-General to speak out for what he believes to be right...[74]

The UN Secretaries-General have strongly supported not only the position that the Secretariat's highest official is in effect a guardian for the interests of the Organization, but that political issues directly affecting the interests of the UN as a whole necessitate an initiative or a political role for the Secretary-General notwithstanding serious risk of alienation of one or more of the great powers, and even at the price of weakening the Secretary-General's Office. As noted above, in the Korean War context, Lie was quite willing to sacrifice himself and perhaps weaken the Office in return for a strengthened and active Organization. This was possible during his administration, as a weak executive branch at that time meant that the two were not as likely to come into conflict as in later years under Hammarskjold and Thant.

Perhaps it is fortunate that Lie did not attempt to spell out a clearly defined or consistent theory of the Secretary-General, for his administration was essentially involved in building a foundation for UN participation in world politics, and that process naturally necessitated flexibility in constitutional construction. It was far more difficult during the early days than it is now to perceive patterns of response generated by particular initiatives undertaken by the Secretary-General, and the overall framework for action that evolved in the beginning of Lie's tenure was essentially the result of free accommodation and flexible maneuver, a process not as likely to have been successful within a rigid and *a priori* framework. Lie was obligated to find his way, so to speak, and procedures of trial and error were crucial. The general thrust was always in the direction of expanding his power, much as it was under Hammarskjold, the effort being rewarded on some occasions and disputed and frustrated on others. There was little guidance precisely because Member Nations realized full well the potential significance of an important actor at the top level of the UN Secretariat, and they wished to make decisions concerning the full extent of his proper capacity only when forced to do so.

This is not to say, of course, that Lie himself did not wish more precise guidance. Schwebel quotes Lie as having said unofficially that "I think the office of Secretary-General should be clearly defined... The Charter should actually say that he is more than the chief administrator. I think the experience gained now, the Secretary-General's right to state his opinion,

74 UN Press Release SG/22, 29 Sept. 1949.

should be clearly stated in the Charter. Article 99 should be detailed, its implications written out... Article 99 is an atomic bomb, or at least a 32 inch gun... Why can't I use the smaller rifles? Why just on world peace?" [75] While the desire for more precision in outlining functions is understandable, it is probably neither necessary nor desirable, given the Charter articles dealing with the Secretary-General as vague outlines of power to be inter- preted by each incumbent. A more clearly delineated authority might run the risk of restraining further development, and there is always the chance, especially at present, that particular proposals will be turned down, thus justifying further restrictions upon the Secretary-General's discretionary power. Hammarskjold was later able to demonstrate that Articles 98 and 99 of the Charter provide more than sufficient foundation for an extension of responsibility, and given U Thant's experience with Soviet and French resistance to any significant authority on his part, Lie's desire for greater clarification seems, from the perspective of the 1970's, somewhat misplaced.

The narrow range of UN possibilities in a world dominated by East-West conflict was also reflected in Lie's thought on the wider issues of the proper role of international organization. Thus in the *Introduction* to his First Annual Report, Lie began a seven-year emphasis on the necessity for great power cooperation: "The United Nations was not designed to perform the functions of a Peace Conference nor was it equipped to act as a referee between the great powers. It was founded upon the basic assumption that there would be agreement among the permanent members of the Security Council upon major issues. ... I should be failing in my duty, in presenting this report, if I did not emphasize the absolute necessity that the powers should seek agreement among themselves, in a spirit of mutual under-standing and a will to compromise, and not to abandon their efforts until such agreement has been reached".[76]

Essentially, this was the central theme of Trygve Lie's entire administration, for all the Secretary-General could do under the circumstances of the cold war was plead for greater cooperation, and try to depict the Organization as the structure best suited for a process of diplomacy that might point toward a more rational and ethically based world order. As time elapsed it soon became apparent that the United Nations was able to exert a certain influence for peaceful agreement in conflicts outside the area of immediate interest to the great powers and even, as the Berlin dispute demonstrated, within a context of critical significance to the postwar European settlements. By 1949, the Secretary-General could cite UN successes in the colonial cases of Palestine, Kashmir, and Indonesia, and the settlement of the Berlin crisis:

In these disputes, as in the Great Power conflict itself, the United Nations has de-

---

[75] Schwebel, *op. cit.*, p. 205.
[76] GAOR: First Sess., Supp., United Nations Doc. A/65, 26 June 1946.

monstrated that it can exert powerful influences for conciliation and mediation. Nothing better illustrates this than a comparison of the relationship between the Great Powers before and after the Berlin dispute was brought to the United Nations...[77]

As noted above, UN Berlin efforts were not themselves successful, but at least they provided time for rational discussion between the parties to the dispute.

The United Nations had certainly not been conceived as a political force with sufficient capacity to serve peacemaking functions in cases of dispute between Moscow and Washington, and lacking agreements under Article 43 of Chapter VII, the UN was reduced to essential buffer functions and third party neutral intermediary roles, although not just for purposes of isolating particular conflicts from the cold war, but also, as Berlin demonstrated, to assist in the resolution of cold war disagreements. Secretary-General Lie recognized the significance of this in his 1949 Report, citing the peaceful settlement techniques of Chapter VI of the Charter in the context of great power disputes.[78] And while he conceded that "regional security arrangements may sometimes redress the balance of power in the world", he was generally suspicious of regional military arrangements, such as the North Atlantic Treaty Organization, asserting flatly that "it is impossible to obtain lasting security from war by any arrangement that leaves out any of the Great Powers".[79] If the global organization could not act as an instrument of collective security, and was reduced to buffer functions, then these could be undertaken even in case of sharp dispute between the superpowers, but the Secretary-General was clear that enforcement action against a great power would mean war at a level of destruction leaving "neither victors nor vanquished".[80]

Yet Lie's thinking underwent a marked change during the Korean War, for now the UN was in a position of implementing an enforcement action against a communist state directly supported by the Soviet Union. The Secretary-General was still concerned to utilize the UN forum for East-West negotiation, but he perceived the Korean attack as a challenge to the integrity and even the existence of the Organization, and under these circumstances, initial conceptions concerning global action in the face of a great power split were easily cast aside in favor of a liberal Charter construction enabling the world body to respond to unjustified military provocation.

Lie thus found it possible to write in the *Introduction* to his Sixth Annual Report in September, 1951, that "the founding of the United Nations was motivated by a far more fundamental and lasting concept concerning the world than a passing war-time alliance of Great Powers".[81] The Secretary-

[77] GAOR: Fourth Sess., Supp. No. 1, United Nations Doc. A/930, 7 July 1949.
[78] *Ibid.*
[79] *Ibid.*
[80] *Ibid.*
[81] GAOR: Sixth Sess., Supp. No. 1A, United Nations Doc. A/1844/Add. 1, 20 Sept. 1951.

General's argument now was that the founding fathers wanted a world organization "through which the Member Nations could over a period of time develop adequate means for controlling unlawful international conduct on the part of *any* government..."[82] He emphasized the point by concluding that "armed aggression anywhere, or the threat of armed conflict anywhere, is, in fact as well as in theory, becoming more and more the concern of nations everywhere". And this was correct even "in a case directly involving the Great Powers conflict".[83]

This official validation of the UN as an instrument of defense against illegal acts regardless of source has not been generally accepted for obvious reasons. Perhaps at the time of Korea, the necessity of injecting life into an Organization in serious risk of premature demise was sufficient justification for associating the UN with a defensive effort that would have taken place in any event. Surely, however, had the armed struggle been taken directly against the Soviet Union, Lie's security pronouncements would not likely have been so enthusiastic, and of course, a sweeping extension of the Korean response into a doctrine embracing international military defense against aggression even by great powers is a notion that Lie himself had rejected very shortly before Korea. Lie's Korean doctrine must be taken much as the conflict itself was in terms of international organization capacities—that is, an aberration unlikely to be repeated in the foreseeable future.

Secretary-General Lie pressed hard throughout his administration for a conception of global organization as an instrument for progressive economic and social change, including a rapid end to colonial domination, racism, particularly in southern Africa, and a redistribution of wealth accompanied by human rights programs that in the final analysis constituted the critical foundation of a rational world order system. In this regard, his outlook was in accordance with the views of a great number of Afro-Asian states that began to enter the Organization in the mid-1950's, and in many ways he helped shape the third world orientation of the global body. Dag Hammarskjold and U Thant were later to enunciate many of the themes originally pronounced by Trygve Lie. The ten point memorandum is perhaps a better testament to the Secretary-General's thoughts on world organization than public statements attended by polemic whenever cold war issues were directly involved.

For a time Lie argued persuasively against regional security organizations as insufficient responses to global challenges, and while he tried with not insignificant skill to ease East-West tensions through personal discussion and mediation, he deemed it desirable to use the Organization in a partisan manner subsequent to the Korean attack. If this was felt essential to strengthen the Organization, it also served to isolate China from the international community and to deepen the split between Moscow and Washing-

[82] *Ibid.,* italics added.
[83] *Ibid.*

ton in a fashion that rendered cooperation impossible for several years. But the Organization remained a functioning structure, and this was the essence of Lie's contribution to world organization. He was not a man given to introspection and analysis, but he possessed the capacity to build the structure, basic processes, and essential attributes of the organized international community. The fundamental meaning of Lie's administration was not theory, but construction, and in this sense he served well the nations of the world.

The Extension of Lie's Term and His Final Resignation

Secretary-General Lie's original intention had been to retire at the end of his first five-year term. By the end of 1949 the cold war had destroyed any hope of a world organization serving in a meaningful capacity to enforce peace, but at least the Organization had survived, there had been no large-scale warfare, and the UN had been successful in moderating and assisting to final resolution several conflicts in former colonial areas; and in this process, the Secretary-General had been instrumental, both in terms of conflict management and in establishing the essential prerogatives of an international secretariat. Until the Korean War, Lie had been able to maintain excellent relationships with both Moscow and Washington, even while expanding the political influence of his Office, and notwithstanding certain doubts on both sides concerning his impartiality in East-West disputes. And for Lie this was enough. At a press conference on December 16, 1949, he announced he was not a candidate for reappointment, a position for which he offered no explanation and from which he never waivered until the Korean War. He later wrote that "As Secretary-General, my overriding objective had been to establish a record of complete fairness and impartiality, and now I had evidence of backing by both the opposing camps. An active Secretary-General could not hope for a better voucher for personal integrity after five years in such an international maelstrom. It was time to go home".[84] Lie had been willing to consider the possibility of staying on for perhaps an extra year or two "only if events made it clear that the interests of the United Nations really required it".[85] He had general great power backing, except for Nationalist China, naturally unhappy over his support of the Peking regime.

The Korean War, of course, changed the picture entirely, for resignation under the pressure of Soviet attack might well have compromised the integrity of the Office and the cause of a Secretary-General who viewed his role in large part as defender of basic Charter principles. Given implacable Soviet opposition to Lie's reappointment, the issue quickly emerged whether

[84] Lie, *op. cit.*, p. 369.
[85] *Ibid.*

the Western powers should nevertheless insist on a renewed term for the Secretary-General, or whether the Organization would be better served by a Security Council recommendation of a candidate upon whom each of the great powers could agree. Given the general assumption of a Soviet veto of Lie's renomination, there was considerable speculation concerning the possibility of a General Assembly extension of the Secretary-General's term, a maneuver with uncertain legal sanction, but one allowing a vote of confidence in Lie from the overwhelming majority of nations while avoiding the Soviet veto.

After considerable delay, and hesitation in private discussions even by Britain and France to support Lie at all cost, the Security Council began its consideration of the Secretaryship-General on October 9, 1950, and within three days, the Soviet Union had vetoed his renomination.[86] The Council then voted to turn to the Assembly, where the United States was prepared to back an extension of Lie's term, but the Soviet Union, through Foreign Minister Vyshinsky, had just begun its Security Council battle to remove Lie from office. Moscow was willing to join in the recommendation of almost anyone but Trygve Lie, and it exterted enormous pressure to convince Britain, France and other members of the Council that the proper functioning of the Organization necessitated great power agreement on its executive head. The issue was fought out in the Council until the end of October, when Vyshinsky's veto of Lie and a United States threat to veto anyone but Lie provided the final impasse that brought the question to the General Assembly. The Soviet strategy, however, came very close to success, for the alternative candidates it suggested were palatable to most members of the Council, even including the United States. Those in contention were Charles Malik of Lebanon, Luis Padilla Nervo from Mexico, Sir Benegal Rau of India, and General Carlos P. Romulo of the Philippines, each supported by the Soviet Union.

The Council rejected an Indian plan for nomination of two candidates by each Council member with the permanent members permitted to delete any name that might result in a veto. This was a technique for quiet consultation without political debate to agree upon a list of candidates each of whom might have achieved election, but it would clearly have eliminated Lie from the race, and was thus unacceptable to the United States. The Council then asked its permanent members to consult privately, but it was apparent that chances of agreement were minimal, given American insistence upon Lie's reappointment or continued service under an extension of his initial term, an insistence backed by Washington's first threatened veto.

It is somewhat difficult to tell whether U.S. Representative Austin's veto threat was necessary, although there is evidence in the case of Padilla Nervo

---

[86] Lie's name was placed in nomination by Yugoslavia, the Soviet Union countering with Zygmunt Modzelewski, Poland's Foreign Minister. The vote on the Yugoslav recommendation was 9 to 1, with China abstaining.

to indicate that France was induced to shift its support for Nervo given the futility of his candidacy under the circumstances of United States strategy in the matter. Nervo had the support of the Soviet Union, India, China, Egypt, Cuba and Ecuador, and since France evidently preferred a normally functioning Secretariat with an executive head supported by each of the big powers, it might well be the case that Nervo's withdrawal from the race resulted only from France's desire not to force Washington to utilize the the veto as threatened. Sir Benegal Rau also withdrew and Malik and Romulo received only four affirmative votes. Nervo had come within one vote of the United Nations Secretaryship-General. His failure was a result solely of Washington's insistence that Lie's Korean War stand could not be punished by Moscow, and that his reappointment was essential as legitimization of UN action in Korea and of Lie's pro-Western stand, all this despite the risk of destroying the Secretary-General's capacity to act in cases involving the interests of the Soviet Union. Before the Assembly voted Moscow served notice that it would refuse to consider him Secretary-General of the United Nations should his term be extended by the Assembly.

On November 1, 1950, the General Assembly voted by 46-5-8 to extend Lie's term for a three year period. Only the Soviet bloc opposed, with Australia abstaining on legal grounds, Nationalist China abstaining because of Lie's stance on the Peking regime, and the Arab bloc abstaining due to his strong support of Israel. Lie accepted the vote as a statement of confidence in him, and called it "a reaffirmation by the General Assembly of the independence and integrity of the office of Secretary-General of the United Nations".[87]

While there are serious doubts concerning the legal validity of the Assembly's action, it is apparent that the strategy did serve to strengthen the Office, for the clear message to the Soviet Union was that the Secretary-General would in the future take strong positions on political questions, notwithstanding great power opposition, and particularly in the face of grave challenge to the integrity of the Organization, such as aggression across international frontiers. It is true that the Soviet refusal to recognize Lie after his term expired in February, 1951 reduced markedly his effectiveness as an international civil servant, and led to his resignation prior to the termination of the extended term, although the Communist issue in the Secretariat and the drawn-out negotiations in Korea did nothing to help a beleagered Trygve Lie. The Soviet boycott finally gained its objective, but as Lie himself later stated, "the immediate political objectives had been won",[88] and it was the immediate goals that were of primary importance to the continued functioning of the Organization and Office, for the independence of the international administration had been maintained and UN action generally validated by the international community.

[87] GAOR: Fifth Sess., Plenary, 299th mtg., 1 Nov. 1950.
[88] Lie, *op. cit.*, p. 385.

Had Lie been dismissed, the message to the world community would have been equally clear—that is to say, the Secretary-General's attempt to establish himself as an important actor in world affairs had failed, leaving the Secretary-General unable to defend Charter principles in the face of opposition from any of the Council's permanent members. The crucial immediate objectives having been won, however, Lie's resignation under Soviet boycott pressure indicated only a temporary defeat to be subsequently repaired, rather than submission and deference to Soviet opposition. And yet the debates surrounding Lie's extended term, as well as the entire Korean War experience, indicate clearly the essentiality of superpower restraint in areas concerning fundamental Charter norms, for the organized international community cannot endure many cases of aggression as authoritatively judged by the Assembly of nations. Korea was an aberration for UN peacekeeping processes, and fortunately so, since such challenges to the integrity of the Organization might well end in its destruction. It was in large measure due to Lie's personal strength that the UN and the Secretaryship-General were maintained as independent institutions with a vital political role to play in international politics.

But if the Western powers and Lie were successful in maintaining the basic Charter principles of peaceful settlement and an independent Secretary-General, certainly the Soviet Union won its struggle to remove Lie, for the political and social boycott finally forced the Secretary-General to relinquish his office prior to the completion of his extended term. The decision to resign was made during the summer of 1952, though only a very few close colleagues in the Secretariat and government representatives were informed prior to Lie's resignation speech to the Assembly. The British and French were informed of the decision in September, but not until November 5 was Secretary of State Dean Acheson told, and of course by this date it was far too late to induce Lie to reverse his position. The Secretary-General's short statement to the Assembly outlined in concise terms why a resignation at this point was desirable. He had wished to resign in 1950, he said, but the Korean War obligated him to stay on, although the situation now differed from 1950 as the UN had "thrown back aggression in Korea". He alluded briefly to his difficulty as Secretary-General without unanimous great power support, declaring that he "would not want the position of Secretary-General to hinder in the slightest degree any hope of reaching a new understanding that would prevent world disaster".[89]

As Lie makes clear in his memoirs, there was a mixture of public and private reasons underlying his wish to retire. The new permanent headquarter facilities had been completed, and the Secretariat established and maintained in efficient fashion. Lie also admits to a certain irritation at his untenable position, the point being that there was little satisfaction to be

[89] GAOR: Seventh Sess., Plenary, 392nd mtg., 10 Nov. 1952.

derived from a post unable to accomplish anything without the cooperation of the Soviet Union. Lie had had enough, and seemed anxious to get home to Norway. The Soviet boycott naturally played a very large role in the decision to resign, as Lie was to reveal in his major address on personnel in March, 1953. He cited his desire to strengthen the Secretary-General's political role, adding that in every case but that of the Soviet Union, UN member nations respected his right as Secretary-General to speak and act as he did. For Lie, the boycott constituted "by far the most serious violation of Article 100 of the Charter that has occurred" and was "a policy of the crudest form of pressure, not only against me but against any future Secretary-General who may incur the displeasure of the Soviet Union for doing his duty as he sees it under the Charter".[90] The Secretary-General asserted that he had the personal strength to bear the attacks made upon him, but there were other and more significant considerations:

I want the office of Secretary-General to be in a position to wield its constitutional powers with the greatest possible degree of influence and prestige. When the Secretary-General speaks or acts for peace and freedom in some future crisis, he should have behind him, not only the weight of his constitutional authority, but the weight of political influence conferred upon him by the fact that he is in office by the affirmative votes of all five Permanent Members of the Security Council and is recognized as Secretary-General by all the Member States.

Thus, although some may say that my resignation constitutes in one respect a yielding to U.S.S.R. pressure upon me personally, I regard it as an act to strengthen, for the critical times ahead, the office of Secretary-General in the framework of the United Nations and to enhance its influence for peace in the world. That, my friends, has always been my first consideration in everything—not for myself personally, but for my office and my staff.[91]

The Soviet Union naturally depicted the resignation as a victory for the boycott strategy, as perhaps it was after a fashion, but this was far from the dramatic confrontation between Foreign Minister Vyshinsky and Secretary-General Lie during the 1950 battle over the extended term, and only the Soviet bloc viewed the final resignation as vindication for its initial Korean policy. Lie stayed on until the first week in April, 1953, when Dag Hammarskjold of Sweden was finally elected to succeed him, and on May 8, Lie left New York City for Norway.

Lie was never happy with the choice of Hammarskjold, fearing that the quiet Swedish civil servant would weaken the political role of the Office by returning to the quiet behind-the-scenes Drummond manner, and he made known his personal preference for Lester Pearson of Canada. Lie later expressed his apprehensions in his memoirs, citing his meeting with Hammarskjold at Idlewild Airport in April, 1953, at which he declared that "the task of the Secretary-General is the most impossible job on earth". Lie wrote in 1954 that "Any Secretary-General will find it so if he tries to

---

[90] GAOR: Seventh Sess., Plenary, 413th mtg., 10 March 1953.
[91] *Ibid.*

be the kind of officer that I think the San Francisco Charter envisaged. Should his conception be the same as mine, he will find it impossible to avoid the displeasure of one or more of the greater or smaller states during the years to come. He will be the target of criticism from right, left, and center".[92]

Lie's last statement to the General Assembly, on April 7, 1953, was a brief and emotional summing up of his administrative accomplishments, and a note of welcome to Dag Hammarskjold. The formative years of the United Nations were over and an era in the Secretariat and Organization had come to an end, for the bitterness of war was receding, and Stalin's death and the soon-to-be concluded Korean negotiations augured well for world peace and the future of global institutions. A new administration had come to office in Washington as well, and the rapid influx of Afro-Asian nations into the United Nations was just a few years off. Dag Hammarskjold inherited an administrative mechanism and world organization fashioned into an instrument well equipped to serve an international community in need of third party neutal intermediaries and instruments of preventive diplomacy between East and West. Trygve Lie had helped create the UN, and then saved the Organization from disaster during the period of its greatest challenge, enabling his successor in office to use the world body as a creative instrument for the maintenance of international peace and security.

The years after the Secretaryship-General were relatively quiet for Trygve Lie, as he held a series of important but relatively nonpolitical positions in Norway, in sharp contrast to the appointment of Sir Eric Drummond as Ambassador to Italy after his resignation as first League of Nations Secretary-General. In 1955, Lie was appointed Governor of Oslo and Akershus, a position he held until 1963, and from 1959 to 1963, he was also Chairman of the Foreign Industry Committee, with the primary function of obtaining foreign investment for Norway. He was Minister of Industries from 1963 to 1964, and Minister of Commerce in 1964-1965. His only venture into international diplomacy was an unsuccessful attempt in 1959 to resolve the long-simmering border conflict between Ethiopia and Italian Somaliland. Between 1953 and 1958, Lie also found time to publish four volumes of memoirs, the first being *In the Cause of Peace* in 1954, followed by *Live or Die, Norway at War,* 1955, a work on his term as Foreign Minister of Norway. In 1956 he published *With England In the Front Line, A History of the War Years,* and finally in 1958, came *Homeward Bound,* memoirs devoted to his native Norway. He died in Norway on December 30, 1968, at the age of 72.

---

[92] Lie, *op. cit.,* p. 417.

CHAPTER V

Dag Hammarskjold
Secretary-General of the United Nations
1953-1961

Hammarskjold was one of the greatest servants the community of nations ever had—a brilliant mind, a brave and compassionate spirit. I doubt if any man has done more to further the search for a world in which men solve their problems by peaceful means and not by force than this gallant friend of us all.
Adlai Stevenson

While 1953 signalled a fresh beginning in international politics, with new administrations in the United States and the Soviet Union, the end of the Korean conflict, and the early emergence of the Afro-Asian world to temper the harsh rigidities of the cold war, it was as well a period of great difficulty for the United Nations. The UN had been successful in thwarting aggression in Korea, but Soviet alienation was at a peak, rendering the Organization's future role in international politics rather obscure. The institution had for several years avoided significant intervention unless accompanied by East-West agreement, but Korea, of course, committed the UN to military force even without the support of one of the super-powers, a commitment formalized through Trygve Lie's wholehearted advocacy of the Western position.

The result for the Office of the Secretary-General was devastating. Lie was driven from his post and the newly reconstructed Office stood in severe danger of collapse. The experiment begun in 1920 was still new, and the League's experience not so encouraging as to permit a serious regression. Sir Eric Drummond's work had been successful, but the period between June, 1933 and January, 1946 was a long stretch without an effective executive head. Now after only five years of reconstruction and expansion of the Office and its role in world politics, Lie was attacked bitterly by the Soviet Union, finally driven from Office in late 1952, and under circumstances that suggested a narrower set of functions for the Secretary-General. There were no assurances in early 1953 that the Organization's chief executive would continue the active public role so well established by Lie, and in the person of Dag Hammarskjold of Sweden, the impression of withdrawal and retreat seemed at first to be substantiated.

Hammarskjold's training and temperament seemed well suited to the quiet and unobtrusive civil servant model of the Drummond era, and indeed, Lie was unhappy with his selection for precisely that reason. In fact, Hammarskjold not only maintained the powers of the Office as initially

271

constructed by Lie, but expanded its role far beyond the limits dreamed possible by the Organization's founding fathers. He benefited greatly from the newly emergent third world and the resultant emphasis on preventive diplomacy, for these were the chief factors, along with the decided shift in decision-making capabilities to the General Assembly, necessitating an executive role in UN peacekeeping. His diplomatic talents were essential, however, in rescuing the Office from the low point of the early 1950's, and in so doing, making a reality of the UN's new tasks as third party neutral intermediary.

In 1960, Hammarskjold finally confronted the same kind of envenomed conflict with the Soviet Union that had driven Lie from office, and once again the Secretary-General's standing in the world community was severely damaged and the Office's future rendered inauspicious. Yet Hammarskjold's administration had constituted a continuous education for the world community in the value and possibilities of the Secretaryship-General. His conception of the proper role for the Office was attacked by the Soviet Union at every fundamental point, and is still debated today, but the choice for nations was never so clearly posed. Lie had been unacceptable because of his Korean War stand; Hammarskjold's actions in the Congo were the immediate trigger of Soviet discontent, but the objections ran far deeper. Dag Hammarskjold was the first Secretary-General to illustrate the capacity of world organization for independent behavior, and the first to impart to the Office a life and influence akin to that of important individual actors in the international arena. His contribution to the construction of world order institutions was thus enormous, and while his notions have not been accepted by the entire community, they have been perceived as raising the relevant questions for debate. Hammarskjold indicated a path toward a stronger system of international government and made us aware, as never before, of the institutional choices open to nation-states in their long search for peace.

Dag Hammarskjold was born in Jönköping, Sweden on July 29, 1905, the youngest of four boys. His childhood home was in Uppsala, an old university town, where his father, Hjalmar Hammarskjold, had been appointed Provincial Governor in 1907.

The Hammarskjolds had a long tradition of public service, continued in full by Dag's father and brothers. In 1914, when Dag was nine years old, his father was appointed Prime Minister of Sweden. He resolutely maintained the nation's neutrality during the war, although under the stress of food shortages caused by a British blockade, he resigned in 1917 and returned to his old post as Governor at Uppsala. The oldest son Bo (fourteen years older than Dag) also served as Governor of a province and in retirement is known as one of Sweden's outstanding elder statesmen. The second brother, Ake, was appointed Registrar of the Permanent Court of International Justice at age twenty-nine, and subsequently served as a judge until his death at forty-four. Sten was a novelist and journalist.

Dag graduated from the University of Uppsala in 1925 with a reputation as a brilliant scholar—particularly in literature, philosophy, and French. He received further degrees in philosophy in 1928, law in 1930, and his doctorate in economics in 1933, after which he taught economics at the University of Stockholm for a short time. The student days were happy for the young Hammarskjold. In an address in 1954 upon the occasion of his succession to his father's membership in the Swedish Academy, he recalled that the "strange brief idyll which burgeoned all over Europe between two crises and two wars had a reflection all its own in Uppsala".[1]

In 1930, having just received his law degree and begun preparation for his doctorate, Hammarskjold was appointed Secretary of the Royal Commission on Unemployment, a post he held until 1934. He so impressed his superiors with the quality of his work for the Commission that in 1936, at age thirty-one, Hammarskjold was appointed Under-Secretary in the Ministry of Finance, the youngest man ever to hold so high an office in Sweden. He remained with the Ministry until 1945. From 1941 to 1945 he served also as Chairman of the Board of Governors of the Bank of Sweden. Hammarskjold never joined a political party.

In 1947 began the experience in international affairs that was to lead to his election as Secretary-General only six years later. He was first selected as Sweden's chief delegate to the Paris conferences preparing the way for European cooperation that Washington had decreed as a prerequisite to Marshall Plan assistance, and served as Sweden's representative to the Organization for European Economic Cooperation. He was a member of the OEEC Executive Committee, and a delegate to the new Council of Europe.

Hammarskjold's appointments in Sweden reflected the addition of international affairs to his domestic economic interests. After working as a special adviser on economic and financial problems for the Swedish Cabinet from 1945 to 1947, he was selected as Under-Secretary in the Foreign Office with primary responsibility for the international economic issues confronting Sweden, including foreign trade and international cooperation. In 1949 he was made Secretary-General of the Foreign Office, and by 1951 was appointed Vice-Minister of Foreign Affairs with cabinet status. In 1952 he served with the Swedish Delegation to the United Nations.[2]

[1] Wilder Foote, ed., *Dag Hammarskjold—Servant of Peace* (New York: Harper & Row, 1962), pp. 77-78.
[2] There is a larger body of literature on Hammarskjold, including his background and career as Secretary-General, than any of the League or United Nations chief executives. The key book-length works on Hammarskjold are Joseph Lash, *Dag Hammarskjold* (Garden City, N.Y.: Doubleday, 1961); Richard Miller, *Dag Hammarskjold and Crisis Diplomacy* (New York: Oceana Press, 1961); Emery Kelen, *Hammarskjold* (New York: G. P. Putnam's Sons, 1966); Wilder Foote, ed., *Dag Hammarskjold—Servant of Peace*

The resignation of Trygve Lie in November, 1952 raised once again the problem of the kind of Secretary-General the international community might find appropriate. For Britain, France, and particularly the Soviet Union, the preferred arrangement was a Secretary-General more in the Drummond model—quiet, working without publicity and behind the scenes, and without seeking to develop the political importance of the Office. Dag Hammarskjold, the economic technician and administrator, seemed to meet those requirements.

Between November 1952 and March 1953, many names were proposed and discussed in New York, but consensus developed slowly. Most of the familiar personalities were considered anew—Carlos P. Romulo of the Philippines, Padilla Nervo of Mexico, Lester Pearson of Canada, Spaak of Belgium, to name but a few. The Security Council finally met on March 11, but with scant hope of agreement. The United States wanted Romulo and the Soviet Union backed one Stanislaw Skrzeszewski of Poland. The only serious candidate was Lester Pearson, officially nominated by Denmark, but clearly with American support. Pearson was vetoed by the Soviet Union, although his nine affirmative Council votes indicated widespread recognition of his capacity for the Secretaryship-General.

The search suddenly ended on March 31 with Hammarskjold's nomination by France, seconded by Great Britain, and without objection from the United States or the Soviet Union. Washington knew little about Hammarskjold. Some State Department officers had worked with him on the Marshall Plan, and more details were filled in by British and French negotiators on OEEC matters. Soviet Foreign Minister Vyshinsky found the quiet economic technician from neutral Sweden quite acceptable. The only opposition appeared to be Trygve Lie's, as the former Secretary-General feared a stagnation in the development of the Office, and was evidently unhappy when the first signs of deadlock in the search for his successor did not result in a movement for his own renomination. The Assembly approved the Council's choice on April 7, and Dag Hammarskjold took the oath of office on April 10.

Arriving in New York to assume responsibility for what Trygve Lie had just called "the most impossible job in the world",[3] Hammarskjold told the press that his task was to "analyze and learn to understand fully the forces at work and the interests at stake, so that he will be able to give the right

(New York: Harper & Row, 1962). There is a large body of material on Hammarskjold in Leon Gordenker, *The UN Secretary-General and the Maintenance of Peace* (New York: Columbia University Press, 1967). The publication of Hammarskjold's diary *Markings* (New York: Alfred A. Knopf, 1964), led to works by Henry P. van Dusen, *Dag Hammarskjold: The Statesman and His Faith* (New York: Harper & Row, 1967) and Sven Stolpe, *Dag Hammarskjold: A Spiritual Portrait* (New York: Charles Scribner's Sons, 1966).

[3] Trygve Lie, *In the Cause of Peace* (New York: Macmillan Company, 1954), p. 417.

advice when the situation calls for it".[4] The unobtrusive civil servant apparently viewed his work, at least initially, very much in the fashion of Sir Eric Drummond. It is significant that in this first statement, Hammarskjold stressed administrative tasks as well as the political: "Irrespective of the political responsibilities of the Secretary-General to which I have just referred, he has an important, indeed an overwhelming job as chief administrator of the UN Secretariat. To me it seems a challenging task to try and develop the UN administrative organization into the most efficient instrument possible".[5]

If the world knew little of the public life of Dag Hammarskjold, it appreciated far less of the essential inner person. He was without question the greatest intellect to serve as Secretary-General and one of the most brilliant men ever to work in the public service of his nation and the world community. At the same time he was an intensely shy and lonely man, never married, and devoted totally to his public responsibilities and intellectual development. Loneliness and sacrifice were perhaps the two key themes of Hammarskjold's view of himself, as revealed in the now famous *Markings,* his private diary first published in Sweden in 1963.

The range of his interests and knowledge was truly remarkable. There were few fields of human endeavor that did not hold an enormous fascination for Hammarskjold. He loved literature and collecting books, and at his death owned a private library of several thousand works. He read widely in history and philosophy, as well as theology. He retained a great love of nature from his youth in Sweden, including hiking, bicycling, skiing, and mountain-climbing. He was a photographer of some note, and had his pictures of Mount Everest printed in *The National Geographic Magazine* in January, 1961. Even as Secretary-General he maintained his membership in the Swedish Tourist Association, serving as its vice-president.[6]

Hammarskjold's love of literature led directly to his translation of particular works into Swedish. In 1960, Djurna Barnes' *Antiphon* was presented in Stockholm in Swedish, with the translation by Dag Hammarskjold.[7] During his last days in September, 1961, he was engaged in a translation of Martin Buber's *I and Thou.* Even at the height of the Congo crisis in 1960, he was at work translating a volume of poems by Saint-John Perse. Indeed, W. H. Auden said of Hammarskjold, in the foreword to the English edition of *Markings,* that "His knowledge and understanding of

[4] Foote, *op. cit.,* p. 27.
[5] *Id.,* pp. 27-28.
[6] Plans had been made for him to become president of the Association after his retirement as Secretary-General.
[7] See Van Dusen, *op. cit.,* p. 115.

poetry, the only field in which I was competent to judge the quality of his mind, were extraordinary..."[8]

His knowledge of modern art was phenomenal, once causing the Director of the Museum of Modern Art in New York to ask whether Hammarskjold was the Director of the Swedish Royal Museum. In 1954, on the New York museum's twenty-fifth anniversary, Hammarskjold was the guest speaker, presenting his own analysis of the meaning of modern art. He had a vast knowledge of music, preferring classical works to contemporary, and he personally supervised the concerts at the United Nations, even on one occasion presenting his own interpretation of Beethoven's Ninth Symphony.

While he found the social life and endless cocktail parties at the United Nations rather unattractive, he frequently invited eminent personalities to his Park Avenue apartment for intellectual and serious interchanges that usually added to the understanding of the topic under consideration. Andrew Cordier has written of Hammarskjold's "complete social identification with like-minded people and inspiring conversation, often binding the group on elevated levels of understanding and inspiration on the topics of discussion. Guests always went away from his home delighted, inspired and enlightened".[9] Cordier comments upon the occasion of a luncheon Hammarskjold had in his apartment for Pablo Casals, Fritz Kreisler, Leonard Bernstein, and their wives: "I regret to this day that I do not have a record of the table conversation. Without monopolizing the conversation, Hammarskjold, through comments and subtle questions, produced an exciting and informative interchange on great events in the field of music and on the concert stage ranging from the days of Queen Victoria to the present".[10]

Hammarskjold's statements and addresses on the United Nations were numerous, in the manner of Trygve Lie, but were often highly elaborate interpretations of the role of world organization and the Office of the Secretary-General.[11] He was not an outstanding speaker, but his addresses were all beautifully written, often by himself, and in some cases were of great significance in terms of postulating new understandings and interpretations of the UN's functions. The several Introductions to the Annual Report were utilized by Hammarskjold to expound his general philosophical position on many crucial issues of world politics and the possible contribution of the Organization. These statements and several of his formal addresses are the source of a very substantial portion of the theoretical pronouncements that helped assist understanding of the proper role of the UN and the Secretary-General.

He did not view the press conference as an ideal forum for political dis-

[8] *Markings,* op. cit., p. xi.
[9] Andrew W. Cordier and Kenneth Maxwell, eds., *Paths to World Order* (New York: Columbia University Press, 1967), p. 7.
[10] *Id.,* p. 8.
[11] See pp. 327-339, *infra.*

cussion with the international community, and except for general explanations of past statements or perhaps an occasional action he had taken, he tended to be unresponsive to reporters' questions. His answers were frequently abstruse and somewhat remote or inapplicable.

Hammarskjold viewed the UN as a modest but important step forward in the development of world order. In the Introduction to his first Annual Report in 1953 he wrote: "The work of the United Nations should always be viewed as a continuing process over a long period of time in which there is constant change and development. It is difficult to measure the significance of results in the perspective of any single year. Often the unspectacular or the unnoticed may prove to be a significant forward step on the long road toward peace... The United Nations is a positive response by the world community to the fundamental needs of our time. Its record should be judged against this background".[12] He did not necessarily view the UN as an embryonic world government, but it did point "more directly towards the ideal of a true constitutional framework for world-wide international cooperation".[13]

For Hammarskjold, there were "three great challenges of our times: ... first, the relationship of the peoples of Asia and Africa with the peoples of western traditions; second, economic development for that majority of mankind which has so far shared so little in the fruits of the industrial age; third, the unresolved conflict between the ideologies that divide the world. Because the United Nations is now becoming more widely representative, its capacity to serve as an influence for peace and constructive progress in meeting these great challenges, has been increased".[14]

Hammarskjold's administration witnessed the great influx of new African and Asian members into the United Nations, and he naturally placed a great deal of emphasis on their importance in world politics. In 1960 he wrote:

The fifteen years which have passed since the founding of the United Nations have witnessed... a split among the permanent members (of the Security Council) which, in fact, has created the major war risk of today and considerably hampers the development of the Organization. But, further, we have experienced a growth into independence of the majority of the States of two great continents, with other interests, other traditions and other concepts of international politics than those of the countries of Europe and the Americas. Who can deny that today the countries of Asia or the countries of Africa, acting in a common spirit, represent powerful elements in the international community, in their ways as important as any of the big Powers, although lacking in their military and economic potential? [15]

---

[12] GAOR: 8th Sess., Supp. No. 1 (A/2404), *Introduction* to the Annual Report of the Secretary-General on the Work of the Organization, 15 July 1953, p. xi.
[13] Foote, *op. cit.*, p. 255.
[14] GAOR: 11th Sess., Supp. No. 1A (A/3137/Add. 1), *Introduction* to the Annual Report, 4 October 1956, p. 1.
[15] GAOR: 15th Sess., Supp. No. 1A (A/4390/Add. 1), *Introduction* to the Annual Report, 31 August 1960, p. 8.

He also proclaimed a UN responsibility for supporting independence for colonial peoples, and his conception here went well beyond the legal obligations found in the Charter. Speaking of Africa, the Secretary-General declared that the UN "must further and support policies aiming at independence, not only in the constitutional sense but in every sense of the word, protecting the possibilities of the African people to choose their own way without undue influence being exercised and without attempts to abuse the situation. This must be true in all fields—the political, the economic, as well as the ideological—if independence is to have a real meaning".[16]

It followed naturally, and here he was following closely the perceptions of his predecessors, that global institutions had basic obligations for the economic development of poorer nations. Indeed, for Hammarskjold, in the final analysis the UN would be judged for its achievements in this area, and of course the basic issue was how to create a disposition on the part of decision makers in wealthy countries to share more of their riches with the lesser developed members. He wanted the UN to have a primary role here, and went so far as to call for "a harmonization of national economic development policies within the United Nations".[17] He was particularly concerned that economic grants be channelled through the UN, and once again, Africa was uppermost in his thoughts, for UN development programs would best promote their political independence and place in the international system:

The United Nations is now, or will be, their Organization. The United Nations can give them a framework for their young national life which gives a deeper sense and a greater weight to independence. The United Nations has not had a past in any of these regions in the sense that any one country necessarily has had. The United Nations, for these reasons, without pushing, without, so to say, becoming a party in their development, can through proper means, even on the basis of fairly small amounts of money, come into the picture in such a way as to help considerably in the framing of their political life after independence and in the building up of the national state.[18]

As with each of the Secretaries-General, Hammarskjold frequently stressed the inadequacy of economic assistance, and viewed savings from arms budgets as the most likely source of funds: "The world's potential capacity for promoting social and economic welfare is far from being fully exploited. It is unfortunately true that the volume of resources which is absorbed each year in military uses considerably exceeds the total resources available for economic development".[19]

Hammarskjold's greatest contributions to the doctrines of international organization concerned the role of the UN in world politics, and the political

---

16 *Id.,* p. 2.
17 *Id.,* p. 6.
18 Foote, *op. cit.,* p. 240.
19 GAOR: 13th Sess., Supp. No. 1A(A/3844/Add. 1) *Introduction* to the Annual Report, 25 August 1958, p. 3.

tasks and development of the Office of the Secretary-General. These will be discussed in later pages.[20]

Hammarskjold at Peking

During the first twenty months of his administration, Secretary-General Hammarskjold acted very much in the tradition of the quiet administrative head exemplified by the service of Sir Eric Drummond. There were a few fairly obvious reasons for this. Aside from his own temperament, Hammarskjold had had little prior United Nations experience, and naturally took some time to become acquained with the workings of the UN system and its complex processes of diplomacy. Simultaneously, he was concerned with the structure of the Secretariat, and spent substantial periods of time organizing and fashioning the top level of the administrative staff to suit his own notions of organization efficiency.[21]

Perhaps most important in this context, however, was the unusual state of flux apparent in the international arena. Stalin was dead, and a new era was beginning in the Soviet Union; the Eisenhower administration had just taken office in Washington; an Armistice had ratified the stalemate in Korea; and tensions between the U.S. and China remained high because of conflicting commitments on Taiwan and the Taiwan Straits. At the same time, France was withdrawing from Indochina, and both Moscow and Peking were initiating efforts to gain friendship and influence in the growing Afro-Asian world of poor, primarily non-white peoples.

In December, 1954, Hammarskjold was given his first significant political assignment by the United Nations. During the course of talks between the United States and Nationalist China on a mutual defense treaty, the Peking radio announced that in January, 1953 a UN aircraft manned by eleven American pilots had been shot down over China, and that the crew had been sentenced to long prison terms as espionage agents. The announcement itself was taken as evidence that China intended to release the prisoners (and four others captured at different times) but wanted something in return.

---

[20] See pp. 327-339, *infra*.

[21] Hammarskjold recommended and supervised a reorganization of the Secretariat's top-level staff. Instead of the eight Assistant Secretaries-General under Trygve Lie, there were to be sixteen posts at the supervisory level, comprising seven Under-Secretaries, five Heads of Offices, and four Deputy Under-Secretaries, all having the same status. The Departments were to deal with matters involving a specific substantive field or area of UN work (such as Trusteeship), while the Offices would handle the coordination of administrative or legal matters affecting all units of the world organization. There were also two Under-Secretaries without portfolio, to "have assignments predominantly of a political character which also cut across the competence of several departments". (GAOR: 9th Sess., Annexes, Agenda item 53 (A/2731, para. 14)).

For Washington, the case was covered by the Korean Armistice Agreement, which called for the repatriation of all prisoners of war. China, however, argued that the matter was really one of internal espionage, and as such not covered by the prisoner of war agreement, which in any case did not bind Peking as a non-party to the accord.

Direct negotiation with China seemed out of the question. It might have implied a degree of recognition Washington was unwilling to grant, and since no diplomatic exchange existed between the two nations, special arrangements would have been necessary, thus emphasizing the significance of the issue and perhaps raising any price the United States might have to pay.

Faced with severe Congressional pressures for military retaliation, the Eisenhower administration decided to use the UN as a possible instrument for negotiation with China. At that time, the world organization was still of great interest to the Communist regime, and cooperation by Peking with the international body did not seem an unreasonable assumption.

At the prodding and initiative of the United States, the General Assembly, in December, 1954, passed a resolution that met Washington's requirements, but was hardly conducive to a rapidly negotiated settlement. The Assembly condemned the measures taken against the UN fliers, and then requested the Secretary-General to seek their release through "continuing and unremitting efforts" and "by the means most appropriate in his judgment".[22] This was the first instance of the "leave it to Dag" phenomenon and one of the earliest substantial steps toward the growth of discretionary executive powers that would make of the Office of Secretary-General an international actor of some import in world politics.

Hammarskjold had decided even prior to the passage of the resolution to go to Peking himself to discuss the matter with Premier Chou En-lai, but there were obvious diplomatic difficulties. The Assembly resolution condemning China's actions while simultaneously requesting Peking to negotiate the issue did not strike Hammarskjold as an auspicious basis for settlement. Further, Chou had made it clear, in separate cables to Hammarskjold, that while he was willing to discuss with the Secretary-General pertinent questions of international peace, the UN was not justified in seeking to interfere "in an internal matter such as the conviction of spies by a Chinese court".[23] Finally, of course, Communist China had been barred from the UN, and it was possible that Peking would not willingly cooperate with its Secretary-General. Yet if Chou valued a UN seat at all, it would be hardly to his advantage to turn away the neutral Hammarskjold.

The Secretary-General's response was a clever diplomatic maneuver that later came to be known as the "Peking formula".[24] Hammarskjold rejected the Assembly resolution as the basis of his mission, and relied instead upon

[22] G. A. Res. 906 (IX), 10 December 1954.
[23] Quoted in the *United Nations Review,* February, 1955, p. 3.
[24] See pp. 337-338, *infra.*

his general authority under the UN Charter. The problem of the Assembly's condemnation of Peking was avoided, as was the issue of Peking's refusal to recognize UN competence over what it considered to be an internal matter. Further, of course, if Chou wanted to discuss other issues relating to international peace, the Assembly resolution was too confining, and the "Peking formula" was the perfect answer. Hammarskjold never even forwarded to Chou the Assembly's resolution, knowing full well that such a step would have been self-defeating.

The China mission was of great importance, for it tended to break the isolation in which the Peking regime found itself, and to thwart strong American pressure for military confrontation. Early in January, 1955, the Secretary-General arrived in Peking, where he and his party were received with great cordiality by Chou En-lai. The party included Doctor Ahmed Bokhari of Pakistan, the Under-Secretary for Public Information, accompanying the Secretary-General as a political adviser, and Professor Humphrey Waldock of Great Britain, who advised on international legal problems. Formal conversations between Hammarskjold and Chou in the Hall of Western Flowers occupied four days, and the communiqué issued at the end of the discussions was, characteristicly, very brief. It said merely that the talks had been useful, and that the parties hoped "to be able to continue the contact established in these meetings".

The Secretary-General returned to New York urging restraint, and while he had no pledge of immediate results, his understanding was that the airmen would apparently be released over a period of several months, perhaps a few at a time. Hammarskjold had recommended to Washington that it allow the families of the fliers to visit them, thus providing Peking with a convenient device for releasing the prisoners. This was quickly rejected by Secretary of State Dulles. President Eisenhower, however, also urged calm notwithstanding the Secretary-General's failure to secure the immediate release of the airmen, and he supported the notion of a UN ceasefire in the Formosan Straits, thus assuring Peking that the United States was not about to back a Nationalist invasion of mainland China. But this step was rejected by Peking, and Eisenhower's simultaneous request to Congress for authorization to use U.S. troops to defend Formosa and the Pescadore Islands increased tensions once again.

By April, 1955, a change for the better seemed apparent. Perhaps under the influence of the Bandung Conference, and the perceived need on both sides to build influence in the emerging Afro-Asian world, both Peking and Washington indicated a desire to negotiate a settlement of the Formosa crisis. On May 30th, Peking made the first concession on the prisoner issue by releasing four airmen shortly after a ten-day visit to Peking by Krishna Menon of India.

The final break came in late July, 1955, as Washington and Peking announced their intention to begin talks in Geneva, Switzerland at the

Ambassadorial level. The Conference actually began on July 31, and the next day, August 1, the Chinese government announced that the remaining eleven American fliers would be released in a few days. On August 4 the eleven men left Communist China, and Hammarskjold's mission had successfully ended.

Peking was clearly anxious to create a favorable atmosphere for the Geneva talks, but the August 1 announcement came only two days after the Secretary-General's birthday, which thus seemed to constitute the convenient device Hammarskjold had felt all along Chou En-lai needed before releasing the airmen. Indeed, Peking's birthday message to Hammarskjold stated that the fliers would be released not in deference to the United Nations itself, but rather for purposes of maintaining friendship with the Secretary-General. They sent him their warm congratulations on his birthday.

The release of the American pilots constituted an important success for the Secretary-General, for while one may argue over the influence of India in the matter, and the critical factor of both sides' determination to avoid military confrontation over the Formosa Straits issue, it was Hammarskjold who made the first contact with Peking, doing so in the face of strong U.S. pressure for military action. UN intervention had succeeded, indicating to the international community the value inherent in the Office of the Secretary-General as a potential go-between for parties who might not otherwise communicate with each other at all. This strenghtened the Office and led to many more significant grants of power by UN political organs to the Secretary-General.

Essentially, Hammarskjold performed what might be called communications and mediation functions.[25] He served as a kind of substitute for diplomatic relations between Washington and Peking by passing messages and information between the two parties and of course by outlining various bases and possible solutions himself. His diplomatic handling of the problem was superb, as he refrained from commenting of the validity of the legal charges and made no public recommendations for settlement beyond his constant stress on the humanitarian aspects of the problem and the need for peaceful settlement.

His availability as an alternative to the military pressures in the United States was significant in terms of easing the tensions of the moment, and for the first time since the founding of the United Nations it seemed apparent that the Organization had within its structure an executive office quite capable of effective and *independent* utilization in the international arena. Hammarskjold had demonstrated his capacity to deal in the complexities of international diplomacy and the creative possibilities of a third party neutral intermediary in a position to negotiate quietly and without polemics of any kind.

[25] See pp. 441-442; 451-452, *infra*.

As Trygve Lie had essentially established the new Office of Secretary-General, made sure of its prerogatives before the political bodies of the Organization, and made of it a greater force than the League Secretary-General, so Dag Hammarskjold fashioned an Office that was to become an international actor in its own right, depending for its success upon the diplomatic skills and ingenuity of its incumbent. The accomplishment took only a few years, beginning with successful diplomacy in Peking in early 1955. By 1960 Hammarskjold was to become a world leader of outstanding distinction, and a Secretary-General without parallel in the history of the Office.

Crisis in the Middle East: 1956-1957

One of the great pivotal points in the development of the Office came in late 1956 and early 1957, as the organized international community once again turned to Hammarskjold for assistance in helping to resolve peacefully the protracted conflict in the Middle East. Nasserism had come to power recently in Egypt, and the nationalist drive to rid the area of colonial influence and what was perceived to be alien aggression was directed against the state of Israel. The Soviet Union sympathized deeply with Arab interests in the Middle East in order to serve its own advantage in terms of political influence and military presence. The United States, for its part, had generally supported Israel, and great power claims of support tended to degrade the slim structure of peace that now hung solely by the fragile thread of the 1949 Armistice Agreements.

Indeed, one of the central problems of peacekeeping in the Middle East was precisely the fact that the United Nations presence was far too slender to prevent a serious military confrontation. The United Nations Truce Supervision Organization had merely 120 members, and more important, was simply an observation force incapable of performing a serious buffer function. There was scant incentive for either side to scale down its military preparations or for Egypt to halt the series of fedayeen raids into Israeli territory. The superpowers quite naturally supported their clients, but were hardly able to restrain them.

In the early months of 1956, tension rose substantially as each side prepared for war.[26] The UN's response, voiced in the form of a Security Council resolution on April 4, was once again to turn to its Secretary-General. The Council requested Hammarskjold to survey the various aspects of compliance with the Armistice agreements and to arrange "any measures" that

[26] Border raids by Arab guerrilla forces and sharp Israeli reprisals in late 1955 and early 1956 sent Hammarskjold off to Cairo and Jerusalem for consultations with President Nasser and Prime Minister Ben Gurion.

might reduce tension in the area.[27] To underscore the fact that Hammarskjold was the Council's agent in the matter, however, it was stipulated that he report back within a month. The agency theory was essential for purposes of making the resolution acceptable to the Soviet Union and to the Arab states, although Hammarskjold insisted that the nature of his Office provided him with broader authority. As agent of the Council, his duties were very strictly limited, but Article 99 of the Charter provided the Secretary-General with greater areas of competence in the context of peace and security, and allowed him to discuss a broad spectrum of issues with the parties.[28]

Using Beirut, Lebanon as his headquarters, Hammarskjold spent the month between April 6 and May 6 establishing contacts in the region, finding some underlying grounds for peaceful settlement and, of course, evolving some strategy for a resolution of the conflict. After talks in Israel, Egypt, Syria, Lebanon, and Jordan, Hammarskjold returned to New York with the agreement of both sides to comply with the overriding ceasefire obligation of the 1949 Armistice Agreements.

He had insisted upon, and got assurances of, compliance by both sides with the ceasefire clause whether or not other obligations or agreements were violated. For Hammarskjold,

the very logic of the Armistice agreements show that infringements of other articles cannot serve as justification for an infringement of the ceasefire article. If that were not recognized, it would mean that any one of such infringements might not only nullify the Armistice regime, but in fact put in jeopardy the ceasefire itself. For that reason alone, it is clear that compliance with the said article can be conditioned only by similar compliance of the other party.[29]

This was really no more than a statement of the parties' obligations under the UN Charter, and thus the Secretary-General also noted each side's right to the Charter's Article 51 self-defense privileges. This proviso was annexed to each party's acceptance of the independent ceasefire obligations. The ceasefire was the key to full compliance with each of the other obligations of the Armistice Agreements, and most of the Secretary-General's effort was devoted to that point.

Indeed, despite his original insistence upon a kind of reserve power for the Secretary-General, Hammarskjold stated in his May 9 report that he had "stayed strictly within the scope of my mandate".[30] He had been forced to leave aside "those fundamental issues which so deeply influence the

[27] United Nations Doc. S/3575, 4 April 1956.
[28] Hammarskjold remarked in the Council that "The specific responsibility which this request puts on the Secretary-General is entirely in line with the character and obligations of his office. It is obvious that this request neither detracts from nor adds to the authority of the Secretary-General under the Charter". (SCOR: 722nd mtg., 4 April 1956).
[29] SCOR: 11th year, Supp. for April-June, 1956, Doc. S/3596, 9 May 1956, p. 35.
[30] *Id.*, p. 55.

present situation".[31] Yet hopes were raised as raids and counterattacks diminished and as the propaganda output from each of the countries in the area grew less venomous and hostile. He drew the praise of Council members who again had "left it to Dag" and saw their strategy rewarded. The French representative noted that "Mr. Hammarskjold's stature has been increased by the test to which we subjected him, and the same applies to the prestige—which I know to be dearer to him than his own prestige—of his office".[32]

But the subsequent Council debates and voting showed that the path toward peaceful solution was far from clear. The Arab states would not accept Israel's borders as then defined, for they extended far beyond the original partition plan voted by the General Assembly in 1947. All the Council could do was request Hammarskjold to carry on his efforts to secure full compliance with the Armistice Agreements, and once again he was limited to a mandate which excluded an effort to mediate fundamental differences. Hammarskjold was, as ever, optimistic, but there was little will to make a lasting peace or to restrict preparations for war.

On July 26, 1956, came the tragic turning point. For on that date Secretary of State John Foster Dulles suddenly cancelled the American offer to help build the Aswan High Dam in Egypt and in retaliation, Nasser nationalized the Suez Canal. For the next three months, as the drift toward war continued and the ceasefire obligations staggered under a series of violent incidents, the Canal became the primary subject for negotiation. On August 21, the representatives of the eighteen governments whose shipping accounted for almost all of the Canal's tonnage recommended a set of proposals that would have placed the Canal management under the supervision of an international board. Essentially, given their trade and shipping requirements, the British and French were attempting to undo the nationalization by maintaining control of an international governing body. Nasser naturally rejected the proposals, and the problem was brought to the Security Council for what was to be the last attempt at peaceful settlement.

The Council meetings were quickly turned into private discussions in Secretary-General Hammarskjold's office between the foreign ministers of Britain, France, and Egypt. Hammarskjold, of course, was present throughout, and it is likely that his participation in the talks, even limited as it was to precise formulation of ideas upon which agreement seemed likely, was a factor adding to the meaningfulness of the discussions. It is frequently the case that the mere presence of a third party neutral, particularly one with general support, will induce parties to the negotiations to work seriously towards mutually acceptable accommodation. This seemed to be the case with the Suez Canal issue in the first weeks of October, 1956.

The outcome of the negotiations in Hammarskjold's office was agreement

[31] *Ibid.*
[32] SCOR: 11th year, 723rd mtg., 29 May 1956, p. 10.

on six basic requirements necessary for any permanent settlement of the Suez question. Precise implementation of the principles was to be the subject of further negotiation. The requirements included free and open transit through the Canal without discrimination, overt or covert, respect for the sovereignty of Egypt, and the insulation of the Canal from the politics of any country.[33] The critical problem was that in terms of operationalization, the last two were inconsistent with each other. At the time, however, the principles were accepted by the Security Council as the first part of an Ango-French draft resolution. The second part of the draft, calling for international mangement, was objected to by the Arab states and vetoed by the Soviet Union.

Despite the expected rejection of the international management proposal, it was generally agreed by those present that an optimistic mood prevailed, and that negotiations would continue on the basis of the six accepted requirements. Indeed, Hammarskjold proposed still further discussions between himself and foreign ministers Lloyd, Pineau and Fawzi in Geneva. Even the date for the talks was agreed upon—October 29. What was not known by Hammarskjold and what could not have been foreseen was that the failure of the international management proposal had resulted in a decision by Anthony Eden and Guy Mollet to use force at Suez to regain control of the Canal.

On October 29, Israeli troops swept across the Sinai Peninsula with the stated objective of destroying fedayeen bases in the area. The United States quickly called for a Security Council meeting, and introduced a strong draft resolution calling for Israel to withdraw its armed forces behind the armistice lines and asking for a halt to military, economic or financial aid to Israel until it complied with the 1949 Armistice agreements. But it was evident that more than another Middle East outbreak was involved as the British and French both vetoed the U.S. resolution and reported to the Council their ultimatum to Israel and Egypt to end hostilities within twelve hours or have British and French troops intervene to occupy the Canal area.

The United States was staggered at the British and French move. Washington had not been consulted beforehand and given the rise of Soviet influence in the Middle East, along with the rapid increase in the membership of the Afro-Asian bloc at the UN, it was hardly likely that the U.S. response would be to the liking of London and Paris. By the end of the first day after their attack, Israeli troops were moving rapidly across the Sinai Peninsula, and Egypt had rejected the twelve hour ultimatum. The next day, October 31, reports came in that the British and French were bombing

[33] The other requirements included agreement between Egypt and the other users on the manner of setting tolls and charges, a reasonable proportion of the dues to be allocated to Canal development, and arbitration in cases of unresolved disputes between the Egyptian Government and the Canal Company.

Egyptian airfields in the Canal Zone and that troops from the two nations were on their way.

Hammarskjold was equally stunned. At the Council meeting that after-noon he stated that had not the Council been called into session by the United States, he would have called a meeting himself, thus announcing his view of the nature of the crisis and his willingness to invoke Article 99 of the Charter as a result. He then went on to make one of his most famous statements:

The principles of the Charter are, by far, greater than the Organization in which they are embodied, and the aims that they are to safeguard are holier than the policies of any single nation or people. As a servant of the Organization, the Secretary-General has the duty to maintain his usefulness by avoiding public stands on conflicts between member nations unless and until such an action might help to resolve the conflict. How-ever, the dicretion and impartiality thus imposed on the Secretary-General by the char-acter of his immediate task, may not degenerate into a policy of expediency. He must also be a servant of the principles of the Charter, and its aims must ultimately deter-mine what for him is right and wrong. For that he must stand. A Secretary-General cannot serve on any other assumption than that—within the necessary limits of human frailty and honest differences of opinion—all Member nations honor their pledge to observe all articles of the Charter. He should also be able to assume that those organs which are charged with the task of upholding the Charter, will be in a position to fulfill their tasks.

The bearing of what I have just said must be obvious to all without any elaboration from my side. Were the members to consider that another view of the duties of the Secretary-General than the one here stated would better serve the interests of the Organization, it is their obvious right to act accordingly.[34]

The last part of Hammarskjold's statement was intended as a challenge or perhaps even a threat to resign, and was followed by an immediate de-monstration of support by most of the Council delegates, including the Soviet Union, protesting their complete confidence in the integrity of the Secretary-General. Nevertheless, British and French resistance prevented the Council from taking action, and at the initiative of the United States, Yugoslavia called for an emergency special session of the Assembly, acting under the Uniting for Peace Resolution. At this point, Israel had captured the Gaza Strip, from which many of the fedayeen raids had come, and was facing only token resistence in the rest of the Peninsula. British and French bombers were taking their toll in the Suez Canal Zone.

The Assembly met on November 1 and in the early hours of the next morning adopted a ceasefire resolution introduced by Secretary of State Dulles for the United States.[35] The resolution was milder than the Council draft (there was no call for a halt to aid to Israel) but the key points were satisfactory to the great majority of UN members, including its now power-ful neutral group. The U.S. demanded a ceasefire and withdrawal behind the Armistice lines, a halt to the intrusion of troops and arms into the

[34] SCOR: 11th year, 751st mtg., 31 October 1956, p. 2.
[35] G. A. Res. 997 (ES-I), 2 Nov. 1956.

area, and scrupulous observance of the 1949 Armistice agreement. The U.S. draft called further for the re-opening of the Suez Canal and a restoration of freedom of navigation. Hammarskjold was requested to observe the implementation of the resolution and report on its compliance to the Council and Assembly.

While this was a significant expression of the world community's judgment on the matter, no mechanism was provided to insure compliance, nor was any incentive provided to the parties. It was therefore of great interest to the UN when Lester D. Pearson of Canada, in explanation of his delegation's abstention on the Assembly's vote, proposed publicly for the first time the establishment of a truly international peacekeeping force to serve as a buffer between the contending parties. Pearson was not thinking of a UN force under Article 43 of the Charter, the original intention of the San Francisco founding fathers. Rather he wanted a resolution "authorizing the Secretary-General to begin to make arrangements with Member States for a United Nations force large enough to keep these borders at peace while a political settlement is being worked out".[36] Dulles stated in the Assembly that he agreed with Pearson's suggestion, and since Sir Pierson Dixon of Great Britain had already explained his country's willingness to withdraw its troops if the UN would assume responsibility for peace in the region, there seemed a reasonable basis for a quick halt to the hostilities.

Pearson's first notion had been that the force would consist primarily of British and French troops flying the UN flag and authorized to act by UN resolution. But this was totally unacceptable to the Egyptians and to the great majority of neutrals in the Organization, and Pearson's thinking soon turned to an international force composed of troops from small nations—deliberately excluding the great powers—and thus providing a face-saving device for the British and French while preventing the Soviet Union from gaining a foothold in the Middle East. Apparently Hammarskjold was doubtful at first that such a force was feasible under the crisis conditions of the Middle East hostilities, but at separate conferences with Henry Cabot Lodge, the U.S. Ambassador, Pearson and Andrew Cordier, his Executive Assistant, the Secretary-General was soon convinced.

In the early morning hours of November 4, the General Assembly approved an Indian draft resolution calling for a ceasefire and withdrawal of all forces behind the Armistice lines, and passed by a vote of 57-0-19 Pearson's proposal, And once again, the world body turned to Hammarskjold. He was asked to submit "within forty-eight hours a plan for the setting up, with the consent of the nations concerned, of an emergency international United Nations Force to secure and supervise the cessation of hostilities in accordance with all the terms of the aforementioned (November 2) Resolution".[37]

[36] GAOR: First Emergency Special Session, Plenary, 562 mtg., 1 November 1956, p. 36.
[37] G. A. Res. 998 (ES-I), 4 November 1956.

The idea, of course, was to set up an international peacekeeping mission, not under Chapter VII of the United Nations Charter, but rather under the authority of the General Assembly, with the Commander responsible to the Secretary-General. It was a crucial turning point for the UN, as a clear indication that the Organization's primary function in world politics was not to keep the peace by the combined military strength of the great powers, but to serve as a neutral third party keeping the peace by placing itself between belligerent nations. As Hammarskjold left the General Assembly Hall, he turned to Ralph Bunche and said "now, Corporal" (a nickname the Secretary-General used for Bunche), "go get me a force". Said Bunche later: "We had so many offers we were embarrassed...from twenty-three or twenty-four countries. We couldn't use even half of what had been offered".[38]

At the same time, Soviet troops and tanks were invading Hungary and once again Washington offered a withdrawal resolution to the Security Council, only to have it vetoed, but this time, naturally, by the Soviet Union. Hammarskjold cited the statement he had made to the Council on his understanding of the Secretary-General's duties, but it made little difference. There was no hope that the UN could deal with the situation in Budapest as it could with the Middle East crisis.

Hammarskjold had been given forty-eight hours to submit a plan for a Middle East international force, but in something less than seven hours he had a preliminary statement prepared. Never was Hammarskjold's brilliance appreciated more than at this point, for the problems involved were profoundly difficult. There were no precedents upon which the UN could draw, nor were there even any academic plans that considered the issues here, not to speak of serious contingency planning. Under the circumstances, it was impossible to inform possible contributor states of the precise obligations they were to undertake. As Hammarskjold understated the matter: "We had to work under heavy pressure, at great speed and with a considerable risk of making mistakes or running into misunderstandings".[39]

Hammarskjold's preliminary report[40] called for a United Nations command under General E. L. M. Burns of Canada, the UNTSO Chief of Staff. The Secretary-General stipulated that none of the officers or troops of the UN force should be nationals of the great powers. This was approved by the General Assembly and the international community had thus created the first international peacekeeping force in its history. The UN command concept was in sharp contrast to the Korean case, in which the U.S. acted in theory as the agent of the Security Council and General Assembly. Further, the Assembly simply left it to the Secretary-General to establish the force and at least in the first instance to decide upon the principles underlying its structure, nature and functions. Hammarskjold, the key

38 Interview with the author and Raymond Fosdick, April 13, 1966.
39 United Nations Press Release, SG/742, 5 November 1958.
40 United Nations Doc. A/3289, 4 November 1956.

members of his Executive Office, and Ralph Bunche met continuously with military officers, representatives of possible contributors, and delegates from interested states in order to work out the multitude of issues connected with the establishment of the force.

But agreement on the principles of an international armed force did nothing to constrain the British and French from implementing their invasion plans. Paratroopers began to land in the Canal Zone early in the morning of November 5, causing Premier Bulganin of the Soviet Union to threaten intervention while suggesting that the United States and Soviet armed forces join for purposes of "ending the aggression". There was no chance that such a proposal would be adopted by the Security Council, but the threat of Soviet intervention in the Middle East, coming as it did on top of the invasion of Hungary, could not be taken lightly in Western capitals.

Pressure from Washington for acceptance of the UN ceasefire resolution of November 2 was intense, and on the night of November 5, Hammarskjold was able to report that both France and Great Britain had agreed to cease all military action upon condition of the acceptance by Israel and Egypt of the UN force to take the place of the invading troops. He reported further that Egypt had already accepted the ceasefire resolution and the principle of the UN force, and that Israel had also confirmed its readiness to a ceasefire. Everything seemed to turn then on the successful establishment of the force by Hammarskjold and the adoption by the Assembly of the principles upon which the first international army would be based.

By the morning of November 6, Hammarskjold was ready with his second and final report. He was still not able to set down with any precision the size or organization of the force, nor could he recommend an exact plan for financing. But the basic question of principle and functioning of the United Nations Emergency Force (UNEF), as it came to be known, were fashioned in a manner which won the overwhelming approval of the Assembly the next day. For Hammarskjold, the emergency force

would be more than an observers corps but in no way a military force temporarily controlling the territory in which it is stationed; nor, moreover, should the Force have military functions exceeding those necessary to secure peaceful conditions on the assumption that the parties to the conflict take all necessary steps for compliance with the recommendations of the General Assembly.[41]

The Secretary-General was asserting that UNEF would serve as a buffer, and while it would "secure" peaceful conditions, this would not mean an enforcement of the peace, but rather a supervision based on the voluntary compliance with the ceasefire resolution by the parties themselves.

Further, according to the Secretary-General, the Assembly intended that the force "should be of a temporary nature" the length of its assignment determined in essence by the needs of the particular conflict. However,

[41] United Nations Doc. A/3302, 6 November 1956.

Hammarskjold stated that the Assembly "wished to reserve for itself the full determination of the task of this emergency Force, and of the legal basis on which it must function in fulfillment of its mission".[42] But the force was clearly established under authority of the Assembly, and as such, required the consent of the parties concerned for the stationing and operation of troops. UNEF was not an enforcement action directed against anyone, and while it was a para-military organization, it was "not a force with military objectives". It followed that there was no intent to influence the military balance in the Middle East and thereby the political balance of forces in the region.

Hammarskjold also called for a small advisory committee of the General Assembly to assist the Secretary-General, and he called for discretionary powers for himself:

time is vital, and this is some excuse not only for the lack of detail in this first approach but also for decisions by the General Assembly reached in more general terms than is customary. If the Force is to come into being with all the speed indispensable to its success, a margin of confidence must be left to those who will carry the responsibility for putting the decisions of the General Assembly into effect.[43]

Finally, the Secretary-General attached to his report written statements from Canada, Colombia, Denmark, Finland, Norway and Pakistan, promising to contribute contingents. Without precedent of any kind, it was a feat of brilliant inprovisation, and was so regarded when the Assembly met on November 7. Hammarskjold's recommendations were approved and for the first time there was a feeling of confidence.

The Assembly requested General Burns to proceed with the organization of UNEF, set up an advisory committee to assist the Secretary-General, and authorized Hammarskjold to issue the necessary regulations and instructions for the force and "to take all other necessary administrative and executive actions".[44] It was an enormous vote of confidence in Hammarskjold, and marked at that time the pinnacle of power reached by the Secretary-General in world politics. While the original conception of the emergency force was not his, Hammarskjold was clearly the chief agent in its construction and the formulation of its basic principles, and was of course its primary administrative officer as well.

The critical work, however, was just beginning, for now the UN had to insure the real establishment of UNEF, its deployment in the Canal area, the withdrawal of the British, French, and Israeli troops, and the clearing of the Suez Canal itself, which had been blocked by Egypt at the commencement of the hostilities.

The Secretary-General's initial move was to send a small contingent of UNEF to a staging area at Capodichino airport in Naples, Italy. By Novem-

---

[42] *Ibid.*
[43] *Ibid.*
[44] G. A. Res. 1001 (ES-I), 7 November 1956.

ber 10, one hundred Danes and Norwegians had arrived, and UNEF was quickly becoming visible, a key point in the Secretary-General's strategy. But it was a full week after the passage by the Assembly of Hammarskjold's second report on UNEF before Egypt finally agreed, on November 14, to permit the entry onto her territory of the troops now rapidly arriving in southern Italy.

During that week, an intense series of negotiations between Britain, France, Israel, Egypt and the Secretary-General finally hammered out agreement on precisely how many troops would enter Egypt, where they would be deployed, and their functions. Whether or not UNEF would be an instrument to "vacate the aggression" only, or would remain in Egypt pending a final settlement in the Middle East was one of the critical issues underlying the talks. This touched directly on the length of stay projected for the force, and the precise conditions under which the host country might justifiably request its withdrawal. On November 15, ninety-five UN troops from Denmark and Norway were permitted to enter Egypt, but difficulties were still apparent.

Hammarskjold flew to Egypt for talks with President Nasser and Foreign Minister Fawzi and was apparently able to convince them of the importance of allowing UNEF troops to enter the country quickly, and of enabling the General Assembly to play a role in any final decision as to when the tasks of UNEF were completed. Egypt declared it would be "guided in good faith" by the Assembly resolution of November 5 which established the UN command. Hammarskjold also wrote an *aide mémoire* which set out his understanding of the talks between himself and President Nasser concerning the precise role of the Assembly. This document, never published or deposited in the UN archives, became one of the critical issues in the final withdrawal of UNEF from the Middle East in May, 1967.[45]

The Secretary-General was also in a position to assure President Nasser that UNEF troops would not be stationed along the Suez Canal, despite the policy preferences of London and Paris in the matter, and that he would not support Canal clearance until after British and French troops had withdrawn. London and Paris were insistent upon getting some kind of concession from Egypt, even one limited to an influential role in the clearance of the Canal, but this was contrary to the overwhelming sentiment of the international community, and given strong support from the United States and the Soviet Union, the Secretary-General resisted the demands.

Finally, it was agreed that Canal clearance would begin as soon as British and French troops had left. The last of the invasion force departed from Egypt on December 27, just short of seven weeks from the day it had landed. Port Fuad was now in the hands of UN troops and two days later UN salvage teams began to clear the Canal of the several ships and two

[45] See pp. 393-400, *infra*.

destroyed bridges that were blocking its passage. Ultimately, UNEF was to consist of 6,000 men from ten countries, under the command of General Burns. The Force was at once the international community's symbol of its opposition to the British and French invasion of Egypt, and a convenient face-saving device enabling the invaders to withdraw gracefully. It also served as an agent of "preventive diplomacy",[46] as it has come to be known through Hammarskjold's writings, as its establishment and functions made the likelihood of any United States or Soviet intervention rather remote. The Soviet Union was never enthusiastic about UNEF, but was not disposed to resist Nasser's wishes on the issue.

Clearance of the Canal was the result of an extraordinarily efficient UN operation. With Cordier as his chief aide on the problem, the Secretary-General persuaded Lieutenant General Raymond A. Wheeler, retired Chief of the United States Army Corps of Engineers, to accept the assignment. Hammarskjold also succeeded in assembling a salvage fleet from Belgium, Denmark, Sweden, the Netherlands, Italy, Yugoslavia and Germany, and while Great Britain looked on rather contemptuously, the hastily summoned and extemporized fleet succeeded in clearing the Canal in record time. The work was finished by April, 1957.

In terms of the original issue of Canal control, Egypt clearly emerged the winner. For despite continued pressure from the Western powers, and advice from India to accept some measure of international supervision, Egypt retained total control of the Canal. Cairo promised compensation to the former owners, and gave assurances of freedom of navigation. This did not mean, however, freedom of navigation for Israeli shipping, which was totally barred from the waterway.

The most difficult problem was inducing the Israelis to withdraw. Israel did not begin to pull back until the British and French made the final announcement of their intended departure, and it was not until the middle of January that most of the Sinai Peninsula was evacuated. Even then, however, Israel held its positions at the Gulf of Aqaba and the Gaza Strip. The objective was to insure that its ships might freely pass through the Straits of Tiran toward the port of Elath, and that the Gaza Strip would not continue as a base area for the fedayeen.

Once again, the question was essentially whether the United Nations would be used to supervise Israeli withdrawal only, or whether it would help to implement a basic settlement of outstanding issues. Israel, of course, pressed for the latter, but the majority sentiment in the UN was for an unconditional withdrawal. Hammarskjold tried to sidestep the conflict by focusing once again on the legal requirements of the 1949 Armistice agreements, despite the Israeli declaration that in her view, these agreements had no further validity. From Hammarskjold's perspective, strict compliance

[46] See pp. 331-333, *infra*.

with the Armistice agreements would have satisfied Israel's primary concerns, for the agreements barred force of any kind, and appeared to bar the belligerency that Egypt relied upon to justify in international legal terms its blockade of Aqaba. But Israel wanted more substantial guarantees than the Armistice agreements were able to provide. And so discussions between Hammarskjold and Abba Eban, Israel's representative to the UN, made little progress.

The talks were subsequently continued between Eban and Secretary of State Dulles, and a compromise formula was finally worked out. There would be no General Assembly resolution, but the understanding was that United Nations troops would enter the Gaza Strip and Sharm El-Sheikh. While both areas would remain Egyptian, and without a formal internationalization, Israel would have assurances of no fedayeen raids from the Gaza Strip, and of free rights of passage through the Gulf of Aqaba. By the end of March, 1957, UN troops were stationed on the Egyptian-Israel Armistice demarcation line, and the last foreign troops, other than those of the UN command, had now left Egypt. The UN was able to keep the peace in the Middle East for a period of eleven years, until May, 1967, when it was forced to withdraw and war broke out once again.

For the Office of the Secretary-General, the Middle Eastern crisis was a striking turning point. For the first time in the history of the Office, the Secretary-General had delegated to him discretionary power over the organization and administration of an international armed force, thus initiating a development which was to establish the Office as a significant factor in international diplomacy. Essentially, Hammarskjold had turned the United Nations away from the impossible concept of collective security, the discredited foundation upon which its Charter still rests, and turned it forcefully toward the notion of a third party neutral intermediary that could serve as a buffer keeping hostile states apart while simultaneously insuring that great power intervention did not create a meaningful threat of world war. Given the conflict between the United States and the Soviet Union, Hammarskjold implemented new procedures and wrote new principles upon which international forces are still based, and he imparted a sense of direction to the UN that retains its validity today.

And once again, at the critical time, Hammarskjold had succeeded. For he was able to construct a force quickly and move it to a nearby staging point for maximum pressure value upon a reluctant host government. He was able to outline its functions, structure, processes and location in a manner satisfactory to each of the contending parties and again, was able to do it quickly. He was the focal point for the process of international bargaining that went on throughout the period of crisis and was able to press particular positions and formulations not altogether pleasing to any of the parties, but without at any time losing their confidence. It at times he took refuge in legal postures, this was not for lack of political sensitivity, but precisely the opposite. Many a political settlement is deeply imbedded in a legal formulation, and many compromises are possible by reference to neutral principles of law. It was not pedantry, but rather political wisdom that impelled the Secretary-General to utilize law as a path toward mutually acceptable peaceful settlement. And through it all, the Secretary-General maintained an extraordinary composure under the stress of events and indeed, made some of his best decisions under the heaviest pressure.

Above all, Dag Hammarskjold had opened new vistas in the life of the United Nations and made an enormous contribution to the development of his Office. While the full implications of his work at the time were not fully appreciated, the Secretary-General was not long in articulating what is now a crucial subject of debate in the councils of the world body. If the UN is to be a meaningful instrument for the peaceful settlement of international conflict, it must have some independent rights and power of its own, and must be able to take certain initiatives in conflict situations even without the full support of each of the great powers. This was the essence of Hammarskjold's message as it comes down to us from the Middle Eastern crisis of 1956-1957, and it was Hammarskjold who helped give that perception the shape and vitality essential for the goals of world order.

The Hungarian Revolution

While the United Nations struggled slowly but surely, and finally successfully with the Middle Eastern crisis of 1956, a spontaneous and popularly-based revolution shook the formerly passive Soviet satellite state of Hungary in 1956 and threatened to destroy the theretofore seemingly invincible Russian hegemony in Eastern Europe. Soviet military repression of the uprising constituted an enormous tragedy for Hungary, but the rest of the world and the United Nations could do no more than watch helplessly. The United States was certainly not about to risk world war over the fate of a nation that it and the international community recognized to be within the Soviet economic and military sphere.

Sparked by several demands of university students in Budapest, the upheaval in Hungary was essentially an outgrowth of the de-Stalinization process that had begun with the denunciation of the former Soviet autocrat by Premier Khrushchev early in 1956. Stalinism had continued unabated in Hungary, causing great numbers of students to demand a relaxation of controls, a new place of equality in the Soviet Eastern European system, and a renewed emphasis upon Hungarian nationalism. But political leadership in Hungary was totally unresponsive to the demands, and students had difficulty in making known their several points. Peaceful demonstrations soon turned violent when the political police fired on a crowd at the Budapest radio station on the night of October 23, and by the morning of October 25,

Soviet tanks and troops were in Budapest. Hungarian resistance was fero-
cious, and found the Soviet military intervention insufficient. Indeed, a
Soviet withdrawal began on October 29, the fighting stopped the next day,
and for a few days, Hungary was free. But by the night of November 4,
massive Soviet intervention began again, and by November 8, the uprising
had been totally suppressed. The Soviet Union had successfully held its
power in Eastern Europe without a significant challenge from anyone
beyond Hungary's borders.

Clearly, there was never a substantial opportunity for the United Nations
to intervene in any meaningful way, and it followed that there was no
important role for the Secretary-General. During the first week of the
revolution, Hammarskjold was silent. It was clear from the outset that at
best, the West would be able to score some propaganda points in the UN
forum, and that there was no chance whatever of reversing the occupation.
Further, this was an East-West dispute in which any significant intervention
by the Secretary-General would simply threaten his acceptability to one or
the other of the superpowers.

There was also a delicate strategic consideration of some importance.
During the first few days, it appeared that the revolutionists might succeed,
and so long as there was any reasonable hope of this outcome, the Western
powers were anxious not to provoke the Soviet Union through strong UN
action. And there was the obvious multi-crisis problem. The Secretary-
General and his staff were working extraordinarily long hours on the Suez
issue. The Middle East was naturally an item of higher priority as chances
of success in the area were clearly greater than in Eastern Europe. There
was little time and energy left for strong steps in Hungary, and in any event,
no hope of an important role to play.

In the early morning hours of November 4, the second Soviet intervention
commenced with the entrance into Budapest of Soviet tanks and troops in
great numbers. The Security Council met again with great urgency, but
naturally, the Soviet Union vetoed the American draft resolution condemning the intervention. For the first time Hammarskjold made a statement,
but confined himself to a citation of the Security Council declaration he
made four days earlier in connection with the British and French invasion
of the Suez Canal zone. Hammarskjold was indirectly, but clearly condemning the Soviet intervention as he had earlier censured the surprise
attack on Egypt. The careful wording of the statement could not possibly
be offensive to the vast majority of UN members, nor to the Soviet Union
itself, but the basic meaning was apparent to all.

With the Soviet veto, however, the focus of attention then shifted to the
General Assembly, which in its helplessness simply condemned the invasion
and asked the Secretary-General to do his best. Actually, Hammarskjold
was given several tasks to perform, only a few of which were possible. He
was requested to "investigate the situation" and to "observe directly through

representatives named by him" and to inquire into the needs of the Hungarian people for food, medicine, and other similar supplies.[47]

On November 8, the final day of the Soviet repression of the uprising, Hammarskjold requested the Hungarian government to allow observers designated by him to enter the country, to travel freely within its borders, and to report their findings. This was turned down at once by Hungary, but Hammarskjold persisted, citing the general consensus of opinion in the international community.[48] Budapest replied on November 16 that Hungarian representatives would be glad to meet Hammarskjold in Rome, but this was rejected out of hand by the Secretary-General.

In early December, there was a flurry of excitement when the Hungarian representative to the UN announced that his government was "ready to discuss with the Secretary-General" arrangements for his projected visit to Budapest. Shortly thereafter, Hammarskjold informed the Assembly that arrangements had been completed for his visit to Hungary on December 16, 17, and 18. The next day, however, the Budapest radio announced that his visit would be "unsuitable" at that time.[49] While the revolutionary surge was by then quite spent, evidence of destruction was rather widespread, and there was no disposition to concede international competence. In terms of negotiating a peaceful settlement however, it was far too late. On December 12, the General Assembly, reflecting the impotence of the Organization, condemned the Soviet Union anew and requested the Secretary-General "to take any initiative that he deemed helpful".[50] On its face, the resolution appeared to delegate to the Secretary-General more latitude for action than ever, but under all the circumstances, the gesture was meaningless.

The United Nations served as a propaganda forum for the Western powers, and was able to make public the evidence derived from the hearings held by a special fact-finding committee in Geneva, Rome, Vienna, London, and at the UN headquarters in New York. Much of the testimony was from refugees who had fled the country. The committee's findings were generally in line with the Western view, and one that was accepted by most members of the international community. The uprising was found to be spontaneous and essentially a demand for a form of democratic socialism, somewhat along the lines of Western socialist movements. The committee rejected the view that the revolution was caused by "reactionary circles" who wanted to restore either bourgeois or Fascist systems of government in the country. The United Nations was also successful in helping to assist the 190,000

---

[47] G. A. Res. 1004 (ES-II), 4 November 1956.
[48] See Richard I. Miller, *Dag Hammarskjold and Crisis Diplomacy* (Oceana, 1961), pp. 143-144.
[49] *Id.*, pp. 146-147.
[50] G. A. Res. 424, 12 December 1956.

Hungarians who fled the country. That figure represented about two percent of the entire population.

In a very real sense, the Secretary-General's frustration in the Hungarian crisis only served to underscore the wisdom of his policy planning in the Middle Eastern situation. For the UN obviously has no role where its action is perceived by one of the superpowers as contrary to its vital interests, and indeed, this is the assumption upon which the Charter itself is based. In the Middle East, UN intervention was both possible and highly desirable in terms of forestalling a subsequent great power intervention. Here the Secretary-General could function effectively as an international statesman of great reputation and acceptability. In the Hungarian case, there was little to do. The Soviet Union had made abundantly clear its willingness to absorb short run political losses for the substantial benefits to be derived from keeping Hungary within the Soviet bloc. The performance of the United Nations and its Secretary General was as effective as the circumstances dictated.

Lebanon

In 1958 the attention of the United Nations and Secretary-General Hammarskjold once again turned to the Middle East. The issue in this instance was not the hostile relations between Israel and her neighbors, but rather Arab rivalries derived from the perception of Nasser's intent to dominate the Arab states in the region. Egypt and Syria had joined in February, 1958, thereby establishing the United Arab Republic and strengthening Cairo's claim to be the center of Arab nationalism. Iraq and Jordan resisted Nasser's approach to national development and international collaboration with the Soviet Union, and indeed formed their own union at the same time, known as the Arab Federation.

Arab rivalries, fanned by support from the superpowers, was dangerous enough in terms of the chronic instability of Middle Eastern politics. But the situation worsened markedly in the spring of 1958 as conflict intensified between Moslems and Christians in Lebanon, primarily on the issue of the presidency of the nation. The Cairo radio had been calling for the overthrow of pro-Western governments in Lebanon, Jordan and Iraq.

And indeed, by April, Lebanon was faced with a serious insurrection as rebels began to take control of areas near the Syrian border. There was fighting in the capital city of Beirut in May upon the discovery of a carload of weapons and ammunition being smuggled into Lebanon from Syria. At the same time, President Camille Chamoun, a close ally of the United States, did nothing to discourage a movement to amend the constitution in a manner that would enable him to run for a second six-year term. The Moslem opposition, assuming that they were now in the majority in the country, and influenced by the rising tide of Nasserism throughout the Middle East, were not disposed to allow Chamoun another term. The United States rushed to bolster the Lebanese government, and Premier Khrushchev of the Soviet Union offered strong verbal support to President Nasser. Within Lebanon, full scale civil war seemed not unlikely, aggravated somewhat by a rather insubstantial infiltration of men and arms from Syria. During the last week in May, Lebanon formally complained to the Security Council of intervention in the internal affairs of the country by the United Arab Republic and declared that the situation was likely to endanger the maintenance of international peace.

It has always been impossible to establish with any precision the extent to which Lebanon's difficulties were the result of foreign intervention. The public postures assumed by each of the contending parties naturally differed widely. For Lebanon, it was a problem of "massive illegal and unprovoked intervention" and for the United Arab Republic, Lebanon's representatives were fabricating for purposes of masking their own domestic troubles caused by the nation's dependence upon western imperialism. It was difficult for an authoritative judgment to be made by the United Nations without additional information, but from the beginning of the crisis, the general appreciation was that Lebanon's basic problem was internal, reflecting the religious division between Moslems and Christians, the ideological issue of dependence upon the United States and the acceptance by Lebanon of the "Eisenhower Doctrine", and the extent to which the country should be influenced by Nasser's approach to Arab politics.

From the time the issue was handed to the United Nations, the situation in Lebanon took a sharp turn for the better. On June 5th, President Chamoun announced that parliament would meet in July to select a new president, thus conceding to the Moslem opposition one of its key demands. In the UN Security Council, meanwhile, Sweden, after consultation with Secretary-General Hammarskjold, introduced a resolution directing Hammarskjold to "dispatch urgently an Observation Group to proceed to Lebanon so as to insure that there is no illegal infiltration of personnel or supply of arms or other material across the Lebanese borders".[51]

Omar Loutfi, the UAR representative, feeling confident of the findings of such a group, and noting that it would be stationed within Lebanon's borders, had no objection, and thus the Soviet Union refrained from casting a veto, but abstained on the ground that the Security Council passed no judgment whatever on the merits of the issue brought before it. The resolution [52] was passed by the Council on June 11, and Hammarskjold set directly to work to get the United Nations Observation Group in Lebanon (UNOGIL) into the country. For Charles Malik, the Lebanese representative, and for the United States Secretary of State Dulles, this was to be a

[51] SCOR: 13th year, 825th mtg., 11 June 1958, p. 7.
[52] *Ibid.*

critical test of the UN's capacity to handle "indirect aggression". For the UAR, this was the perfect mechanism to demonstrate conclusively the correctness of President Nasser's position and the non-existence of massive intervention or infiltration, and to place the onus upon what he viewed as a repressive and unresponsive pro-western regime.

The differing outlooks on the conflict gave rise to an immediate controversy over the proper size and functioning of UNOGIL. Hammarskjold stressed the fact that UNOGIL was not a peacekeeping force in the UNEF sense, but rather an ordinary observation team of which there had been several in the UN's history. Despite the wording of the authorizing resolution, the proper function of the group was simply to observe whether or not massive infiltration, as charged by Malik, was occuring. Dulles and Malik preferred a large group of observers, and indeed wished for something on the order of UNEF to prevent infiltration. But the Council, being unable to agree on the point, once again permitted the Secretary-General the discretion to make his own interpretation. Hammarskjold had never been convinced that the Lebanese charges were accurate, and thus his construction of the June 11 resolution was narrow. His June 16 report to the Security Council spoke of increasing the number of observers in Lebanon to 100.[53]

Once again, the Secretary-General was heavily engaged in the process of constructing an international team. He established the legal status of the observation group through an exchange of letters with Malik, appointed a three-man executive group to supervise th operations in the field, negotiated with several countries for qualified personnel, and arranged for equipment, such as aircraft, helicopters and jeep transports needed by the observers.

While UNOGIL began its operations and tried to extend its effectiveness to areas controlled by rebels along the Syrian border, the dispute between the Secretary-General on one side and Lebanon and the United States on the other continued. Secretary of State Dulles insisted that the United States would send troops to Lebanon if his government felt this essential to protect the independence of the country. From Hammarskjold's point of view, however, a neutral Lebanon in a neutral Middle East isolated as far as possible from the cold war was the most rational approach to peacemaking in the area. And he remained unconvinced that Lebanon's basic problem was anything but internal. The Secretary-General's impressions were reinforced by his talks in several Middle Eastern capitals in the days immediately following the authorization of UNOGIL. His position was further bolstered by UNOGIL's first report, made public on July 4. Conceding that substantial border areas were rebel controlled and not open to UNOGIL, and that night observation had not been attempted, the report nevertheless offered no support to the Lebanese charges. The value of the conclusions was naturally disputed by the Western powers, but the first evidence in

53 United Nations Doc. S/4029, 16 June 1958.

was that indeed Lebanon's difficulties were those of civil conflict rather than foreign intervention.

At this point, with Hammarskjold hopeful that quiet negotiations would eventually settle the conflict in Lebanon, the Middle East was shaken by a military *coup d'état* which overthrew the government in Iraq, killing King Faisal. President Chamoun immediately called Washington for troops to protect his government, and within a few hours the United States responded affirmatively. On July 15, the first contingent of several thousand American marines arrived in Lebanon, the United States indicating clearly to the Soviet Union that it would keep Lebanon afloat and would preserve its influence as far as possible in the entire Middle Eastern region. Some 15,000 American marines were dispatched to Lebanon, a force larger than the entire Lebanese army. And shortly thereafter, British paratroopers landed in Jordan after an appeal from King Hussein. US representative Henry Cabot Lodge insisted that U.S. forces would be withdrawn as soon as the United Nations was able to "take the steps necessary to protect the independence and political integrity of Lebanon".[54] But the threat of war came closer as the Soviet Union announced large scale maneuvers near Turkey and Iran.

The Secretary-General, while never publicly objecting to Washington's intervention, was known to be displeased and irritated at the action. He felt it to be unnecessary, even from the point of view of Western interests in the area, and could serve only to encourage Soviet intervention in support of Egypt and Syria. In the Security Council the Secretary-General reported success in arrangements for UNOGIL inspection along the entire Lebanese border and stated that the observation group was "fully equipped to play the part envisaged for it".[55] An agreement just the day before by Lebanese political parties to elect General Fuad Chehab, a Maronite Christian and Commander of the Army, as President, indicated that the constitutional crisis in the country was coming to an end. From Hammarskjold's perspective, the United States intervention had come at a time when the problem was in fact easing.

Ambassador Lodge, however, continued to request the dispatch of a peacekeeping force to Lebanon as a condition for the withdrawal of United States troops. He stressed the necessity of a United Nations capacity to deal with indirect aggression and failing in this, the likelihood of the Organization's collapse. The Soviet Union promptly vetoed Lodge's resolution, but the representative of Japan suggested the Council compromise by authorizing Hammarskjold to strengthen UNOGIL in order to make United States withdrawal possible. The Secretary-General backed a strengthened observation group in Lebanon, but maintained his position that a peacekeeping force, as proposed by Ambassador Lodge, could not be read into the

[54] SCOR: 827th mtg., 15 July 1958, p. 22.
[55] *Id.*, 829th mtg., Doc. S/PV.829, 16 July 1958, p. 2.

Japanese proposal. The Soviet Union vetoed the Japanese resolution as well, not because of opposition to the enlargement of UNOGIL, but on the sole ground that the wording of the proposal did not include a demand for the immediate withdrawal of United States' troops from Lebanon.

The veto of the Japanese resolution, however, did not deter Secretary-General Hammarskjold. His talks with Security Council members had persuaded him that there was no opposition whatever to enlarging UNOGIL, and he proceeded to do precisely that. To justify his position, the Secretary-General cited his liberal conception of the Secretary-General's powers, including the view first expressed the year before, that he should be expected to act without specific guidance "should this appear to him necessary in order to help in filling any vacuum that may appear in the systems which the Charter and traditional diplomacy provides for the safeguarding of peace and security".[56] The Secretary-General also referred to general Charter principles, knowing full well that he had the agreement of the Council and that at the moment his prestige was never higher. UNOGIL was enlarged, and finally was able to achieve full border inspection, both during the day and at night.

Hammarskjold stood at the peak of his power. Just three days prior to his decision to implement the vetoed Japanese resolution, he had been invited by Premier Khrushchev of the Soviet Union to take part in a summit conference of the United States, the Soviet Union, Great Britain, France, and India. The United States responded by suggesting a summit meeting within the Security Council framework, and this was accepted immediately by Khrushchev. The plan fell through, however, after the Soviet leader made a quick visit to Peking. China opposed the meeting, and the Soviet Union thus raised a last minute objection of Western domination of the Council and withdrew altogether. Nevertheless, the outlook was still bright as General Fuad Chehab was formally elected President of Lebanon at the end of July. The immediate cause of the crisis had evidently been settled, and there was by this time a greater acceptance of the Secretary-General's view that the problem was not one of external aggression. Yet the issue of domination by Cairo still persisted, and of course the problem of troop withdrawals once more occupied the attention of the Secretary-General and his staff.

On August 8, Hammarskjold presented to the third emergency session of the General Assembly a five point plan originally intended for presentation to the summit conference. The Secretary-General called first for continued observation by UNOGIL, pending the establishment of another form of UN presence in the area to help maintain Lebanon's independence. Second, particular attention to the essential role of Jordan in the Middle East, with special measures appropriate for the situation in that country. Third, a re-

[56] Foote, *op. cit.*, p. 150.

affirmation by the several Arab states of the basic principles underlying the Arab League's charter, including "mutual respect for each other's territories, integrity and sovereignty, of non-aggression, of non-interference in each other's internal affairs, and of equality and mutual benefit". Fourth, a pledge by the superpowers to avoid intervention in the area, thus allowing the people of the region to "shape their own destiny". Fifth, cooperation by the Arab states, with the assistance of the UN, for purposes of regional economic development.[57]

Hammarskjold's initiative in publicly announcing a political program in a sensitive region of the world was generally well taken, and very clearly influenced the speech made by President Eisenhower to the General Assembly a few days later. The Soviet Union continued to hit hard on the necessity for immediate American and British withdrawal from Lebanon and Jordan, but quiet negotiations in which the Secretary-General participated indicated that something along the lines of a general settlement was wanted by the majority of the foreign ministers present, including those of the powers most directly concerned.

After several days of backstage negotiation, a turning point came on August 20 when the ten Arab nations, in a highly unusual display of unity, proposed a resolution unanimously adopted by the Assembly the following day. Known as the "Good Neighbor Resolution", the Arab compromise stressed the principles of the Arab League charter, called upon all UN members to respect such obligations, requested the Secretary-General to examine the possibilities of UN assistance for an Arab economic development scheme, and asked Hammarskjold to make "such practical arrangements as would adequately help in upholding the purposes and principles of the Charter in relation to Lebanon and Jordan in the present circumstances, and thereby facilitate the early withdrawal of the foreign troops from the two countries".[58]

Neither Dulles for the United States nor Andrei Gromyko for the Soviet Union were entirely satisfied with the Arab states' compromise formulation, but given the clear evidence of at least temporary Arab unity on the point, neither argued strongly against the resolution. Dulles had wanted a UNEF type police force to insure protection against "indirect aggression" and Gromyko had pressed hard for an immediate withdrawal of U.S. and British troops. Hammarskjold recommended a middle position, and this was essentially adopted by the Arab states. The Secretary-General preferred a withdrawal, but not a powerful UN presence in the area. He was in effect asking Dulles to go along with the evidence that Arab cooperation would not dissipate into a struggle between Nasser and the more conservative Middle Eastern leaders.

[57] GAOR: Third Emergency Special Session, Plenary, 732nd mtg., 8 August 1958, pp. 4-5.
[58] G. A. Res. 1237 (ES-III), 21 August 1958.

Having succeeded in getting his compromise through the Assembly, the Secretary-General then took off for still another Middle Eastern tour of Arab capitals. The crisis in Lebanon had abated significantly, so that by September United States troops began to leave. And by November, the United Nations Observation Group had little work, for the evidence adduced by the observers indicated to everyone's satisfaction that external intervention and infiltration were minimal. The Observation Group completed its task some six months after it began work. Hammarskjold's primary purpose in undertaking another round of negotiations in the Middle East was to establish some kind of United Nations presence in Jordan, which still felt threatened by the revolt in Iraq and by Nasserist pressures.

After a long series of negotiations with most of the governments in the region, the Secretary-General was able to announce in September the essentials of an agreed plan. The UN "presence" in Jordan would be a special representative of the Secretary-General, Pier Spinelli, director of the UN European Office in Geneva. Plans were also made for liaison offices in Lebanon and Syria, although Hammarskjold later felt these to be superfluous, and in fact they never functioned. Iraq and the UAR did not accept even this kind of limited UN presence. The Secretary-General also planned for a senior diplomatic representative stationed at UN headquarters in New York but in a position to visit the Arab capitals to insure implementation of the Good Neighbor Resolution of August 21. The representative was not appointed as his functions also appeared unnecessary in the light of better relationships in the Middle East. By early September, British troops had departed from Jordan, and a substantial portion of the economic blockade imposed upon Jordan by Egypt and Syria was lifted.

Secretary-General Hammarskjold emerged from a crisis of serious proportions with enhanced prestige and a more powerful position for the Office. He had not accomplished all his aims, which were certainly ambitious and in fact constituted something close to a permanent settlement for the region. He was not successful in establishing regional cooperative institutions for economic development, and the "radio truce" and "radio disarmament" he sought never materialized under conditions of continuing hostility between President Nasser and his more conservative Arab colleagues in Jordan. Neither the Soviet Union nor the United States diminished their attempts to gain influence in the Middle East, including in their efforts a continuous supply of arms and equipment to the region. Neutralization of the area and its removal from the cold war was one of Hammarskjold's basic conceptions, as the strategic advantages to be gained by continuing penetration into the Middle Eastern arena were quite obviously too tempting for the great powers to refrain from continuing the same strategy that helped to precipitate the original crisis. Given the nature of the superpower drive into the area, the problem was difficult, but Hammarskjold had room for maneuver because the intervention was never complete.

There was no desire for military confrontation, and under these circumstances, the Secretary-General, as a third party neutral, had much to contribute.

Essentially, Hammarskjold's office was the focal point upon which all of the parties converged in their search for a reasonable compromise. National interests, public stances, and political necessities at home all dictated that the creative work of compromise diplomacy devolve upon an imaginative third party. Again, the UN presence symbolized the interest of the world community in isolating the region from East-West ideological conflict. The UN was successfully protecting the newly won independence of the peoples in the Middle East, and the shield the Organization offered, while a thin one, was perceived by the states primarily concerned as beneficent. And for the foreign offices of those states, there was never any doubt that the essence of the UN presence was the Office of the United Nations Secretary-General.

The Laotian Crisis

The isolated Kingdom of Laos became a focal point of world attention in 1959 as the United Nations sought to demonstrate anew its ability to influence the course of political conflict subsequent to the collapse of western colonial domination. The 1954 Geneva Agreements, which formally ratified French inability to reestablish its hegemony in Indochina after the Second World War, divided the area into the three independent states of Vietnam, Cambodia, and Laos. The expectation in 1954 was that Laos would remain neutral in East-West disputes, but domestic instability was almost assured when failure to agree upon an internal settlement forced the negotiators at Geneva to give control of two northeastern provinces in the country to the Communist dominated Pathet Lao movement.

As was to be expected, conflict in Laos developed over the issues of royal Laotian government control in the two provinces, and over the integration of the Pathet Lao forces and political leaders into the army and government of Laos. An agreement in November, 1957 between the government and the Pathet Lao ostensibly settled these matters, but the election held in May, 1958 resulted in substantial communist gains, and the governing coalition faltered.

Prince Souvanna Phouma tried his best to maintain a viable regime that included the Pathet Lao, but he was thwarted by contrary pressures from the United States, which feared an eventual communist take over. Souvanna Phouma was succeeded by Phoui Sananikone, a conservative politician who had the full backing of Washington. With the Soviet Union, China, and North Vietnam providing material and political support to the Pathet Lao, the stage was thus set for a classical case of international struggle in a former colonial nation, each side being aided by its superpower sponsor. The government declared itself no longer bound by the Geneva accords of 1954, and United States military assistance quickly picked up. Fighting began in the spring of 1959.

Secretary-General Hammarskjold became involved in the Laotian crisis comparatively early, and completely on his own initiative. He made an official visit to the Kingdom in March, 1959, during which he spent several days in talks with King Savang Vathana. While there is no record of the substance of the discussions, it is rather likely, given the King's and Hammarskjold's attitudes on the neutrality of the area, that agreement on the isolation of the country from the cold war threat formed a significant part of the discussions.

By the summer, however, the Laotian government was calling for an "observer team" from the United Nations as a means of warding off "aggression" from North Vietnam. Hammarskjold's response was exceedingly cautious.

If it were a case of one of these fairly newfangled iniatives of the Secretary-General acting without authorization or without a formal decision of any of the other organs, he can never permit himself to act, so to say, in a legally ambiguous way.[59]

The Secretary-General was naturally thinking of the continued validity of the 1954 Geneva Agreements and of the peacemaking potential inherent in a system of neutrality for the region, the basic policy premise underlying the Agreements. Notwithstanding the powers implied by Article 99, the Geneva Agreements would have to be taken into account, and the Secretary-General "could not override them on the basis of the Charter and he should not do so".[60] Yet the Laotian government was insisting upon some kind of UN presence in the country. Hammarskjold considered this, as well as a plan for observers from Great Britain and the Soviet Union, the two co-chairmen of the Geneva Conference. The Soviets, however, supported the North Vietnamese insistence that UN intervention was uncalled for, and that the International Control Commission remained the proper supervisory body for the 1954 Agreements.

In early September, the Laotian government became alarmed at the increased communist activity in the northern regions of the country, and sent a request directly to Hammarskjold, asking him for an emergency force to "halt aggression". A Security Council meeting was called, but the threat of a Soviet veto resulted in a United States proposal for the establishment of a Council fact-finding committee to investigate the Laotian charges. The legal complexities of the matter were familiar ground for old UN hands. The Soviet Union naturally considered its vote against the proposal a veto, but for the United States, a fact finding sub-committee is a procedural matter and thus not subject to the veto. The fact finding group, composed of

[59] United Nations, O.P.I., Note No. 2020, 13 August 1959.
[60] *Ibid.*

representatives from Argentina, Italy, Japan and Tunisia, spent almost four weeks in Laos in September and October, but found no evidence of a North Vietnamese invasion. There was clearly external support for the Pathet Lao movement, primarily through the channeling of military supplies and equipment.

Even prior to the publication of the sub-committee's report, however, Hammarskjold had decided to take a new initiative. In the face of Soviet opposition to any UN presence in Laos, and despite United States resistance to the notion of neutralization for the region, the Secretary-General decided to make a personal trip to the country and to leave behind a personal representative. It is most unlikely that Hammarskjold undertook the trip without at least the private approval of both the superpowers, but at least for the public record, the Soviet Union was very much irritated by the move. For the Secretary-General, however, this kind of initiative followed quite naturally from his powers as Secretary-General under Article 99. If he was to invoke the procedures of the Security Council for purposes of discussing and possibly settling a threat to international peace and security, it was essential for him to have adequate data at his disposal, and this was quite apart from particular tasks assigned to him by the political organs of the United Nations.[61]

The Secretary-General's approach to the Laotian crisis was based upon his recommendation that the country follow a strict neutrality in the cold war. Hammarskjold was not at all hesitant to proclaim his interest in a basic shift in the theretofore pro-Western nature of the government's policy. Neutrality, he felt, would stave off further great power intervention in the region, and if buttressed by internal conciliation, most likely in the form of a coalition regime, and by substantial economic development assistance from the UN, the cause of peace would be served. A UN presence, neutrality in East-West conflicts, and initiation of both by a series of talks between Laotian government leaders and the Secretary-General held far more promise than the cold war maneuvering of a fact finding sub-committee opposed by the Soviet Union.

Even while Hammarskjold was still in Laos, he called in Sakaari Tuomioja, of Finland, Executive Secretary of the UN Economic Commission for Europe, to make recommendations for economic development with UN assistance. Tuomioja's mission, while resulting in several costly economic suggestions, also served as a cover for continued negotiations between the government and the Pathet Lao. Hammarskjold's public posture was unassailable, while the private and more significant purpose was to keep the UN presence intact, press for a compromise between East and West, and attempt to effect a change in great power insistence upon drawing Laos into areas of political influence.

[61] See pp. 336-337, *infra.*

After Tuomioja had left Laos in early 1960, he was succeeded there by Roberto M. Heurtematte, UN commissioner for Technical Assistance, whose primary task was to coordinate the work of the various UN specialized agencies in Laos. Finally, the Secretary-General sent a small technical assistance team to the country under Edouard Zellweger of Switzerland. Zellweger, whose background was more political and legal than economic, was evidently the special representative serving political purposes that the Secretary-General had originally in mind. Ostensibly, his work was economic, but political functions predominated.

As the Secretary-General worked slowly toward neutral status for the region, opposition emerged from the Laotian right. In early January, 1960, a group of conservative generals overthrew the regime of Premier Sananikone, primarily on the basis of the correct assessment that the Premier was gradually shifting toward a neutral status in accordance with the Hammarskjold formula. The Secretary-General, who was in the Congo Republic at the time, immediately sent a message to King Savang Vathana, in which he expressed the hope "that the line of independent neutrality and democratic effort for the economic progress and the integration of the population be firmly maintained".[62] In Lebanon, the Secretary-General had outlined a policy program for a region, and now only a year later, he was essentially interfering in the domestic affairs of a single nation, and without generating public opposition from the Organization's members.

But Hammarskjold did not actively intervene again in Laos, despite another *coup d'état* and continued fighting with the Pathet Lao, further assistance from both the Soviet Union and the United States, and the threat of internal collapse. For Hammarskjold there were now other issues. He was heavily engaged in the Congo crisis, and the reconvened Geneva Conference of 1961 had taken the initiative away from the United Nations. Further, of course, by 1960 the Soviet Union was trying seriously to constrict the role the Secretary-General had created for himself in world politics.

Moscow had not resisted Hammarskjold's move during the Lebanon crisis in 1958, but was not happy with the notion of an international civil servant acting in a manner more appropriate for national decision makers. Soviet suspicions were confirmed by Hammarskjold's role in the Laotian crisis. His diplomatic activity had more than once conflicted with Soviet pronouncements, and now the Russians began to object strongly to the principle of a Secretary-General acting without the positive backing of the great powers as expressed through Security Council authorization. Further, Hammarskjold not only initiated new policy, but in the case of Laos, tended to change the previous expectation derived from the Geneva Agreements of 1954, and again without the unanimous agreement of the primary parties in interest.

[62] Quoted in Joseph P. Lash, *Dag Hammarskjold: Custodian of the Brush-Fire Peace* (New York: Doubleday, 1961), p. 145.

The Secretary-General had demonstrated still another of the many functions of his Office. He was in a position to avoid the Soviet veto in the Security Council, as well as the clumsiness of a General Assembly attempt to establish policy lines for the internal development of a member nation, by undertaking negotiations and asserting a thin UN presence in Laos solely for the purpose of directing the country toward a neutral posture. He was arguing, by implication, the essentiality of UN intervention even in domestic civil conflict if it involved a significant risk of intervention by either side in the cold war.

If the General Assembly was too awkward an instrument, and the Security Council hindered by the veto, then the Office of the Secretary-General could accomplish more. This was correct, and was precisely what the Soviet Union feared most about the Organization, although it took the Congo crisis to bring about the final Soviet break with Hammarskjold. In a sense, however, his work was rewarded when the newly installed Kennedy administration in 1961 shifted U.S. policy toward the pro-neutral stance the Secretary-General had so long been advocating and working for. The Geneva Conference results of 1962 were similar, reflecting clearly the judgment of the international community that the Secretary-General had been correct all along.

The Congo

The crisis in the Congo was for Hammarskjold the most severe that ever challenged him and the Organization, and the last he faced as Secretary-General. In 1960 he had made a six-weeks' trip through Africa—a journey which took him through 24 African territories. Calling it one of the most important experiences of his life, the Secretary-General returned with the conviction that massive economic assistance channeled through the United Nations was absolutely essential for the peaceful development of former colonial empires in Africa. The sums he had in mind for immediate action were necessarily modest, but he hoped to trigger large outflows of capital and insofar as possible, to work through global institutions for economic development.

The Congo, one of the countries Hammarskjold had particularly in mind, had vast natural resources, primarily in the province of Katanga—copper, uranium, cobalt, and other minerals—exploited largely by a private corporation known as the Union Minière du Haut-Katanga, owned chiefly by Belgian and French interests, with smaller British holdings. But for the United Nations, and for Secretary-General Hammarskjold, the Congo was far more than a difficult problem of economic and social development. The stakes were high in this central African country recently granted its freedom by the Belgians, and the capacity of the UN to resolve the critical issues facing the Congolese community and its relationship with Africa and the superpowers was questionable at best.

For the UN, the first problem was maintaining order immediately subsequent to a rapid withdrawal by a colonial power that had done little to prepare its colony for independence. In the Congo, the Organization had to act in a nation torn not by one, but by two simultaneous civil wars. And since one of the internal conflicts revolved about the secession of the wealthy Katanga province, the whole spectrum of issues raised by tribalism, distribution of wealth, and the unity of African nations torn by artificially drawn colonial lines was handed to the organized international community.

The United Nations was also forced to work within a cold war context, resulting in the classical pattern of outside support for international clients. In the case of the Congo, this meant actual intervention by the colonial power wanting to maintain economic influence for itself, threatened intervention by the Soviet Union, desirous of gaining a political foothold in the heart of Africa, and an American policy of working through the UN to maintain a pro-Western government in Leopoldville.

Independence day for the 13.5 million inhabitants of the Congo came on June 30, 1960. In the entire nation there were just a handful of university graduates and just one lawyer. There were no doctors, no judges, no engineers or technicians, and no courts of justice. The Congolese army had not one Congolese officer. There were no top level Congolese in the civil service. Belgian officials controlled the political structure of the nation, and in granting independence to the Congo, had given up none of the economic control or power they enjoyed as colonial master.

Within a week, the Congolese army staged a mutiny in Thysville against its Belgian officers, and the result was panic among the European settlers in the capital city of Leopoldville. Belgian reaction was not long in coming. On July 11, Katanga Province declared its secession from the Congo, and the next day Belgian paratroopers began to enter the country to protect Belgian citizens and property and to restore order. The appearance of the Belgians was vigorously resisted by the Congolese Government as a violation of its sovereignty. The Government was challenged, however, by Moise Tshombe, political head of Katanga and a Belgian puppet, who quickly proclaimed Katanga's independence and demanded still more Belgian troops.

The UN's thinking shifted steadily upward in its evaluation of the Congo's basic need for assistance. Before independence it was assumed that the UN's technical assistance program would constitute the major part of the Organization's effort in the country. When the mutiny broke out, the Secretary-General, after consultation with Ralph Bunche, who had been in the Congo for the independence day ceremonies, decided that the Organization could properly and usefully send military experts to help the Congolese Government reorganize and train the army. This would be in addition to a more general technical aid program.

But the re-entry of Belgian troops on July 12th changed the situation entirely. The Leopoldville Government first appealed for military assistance to the United States, but was directed to the UN. Premier Lumumba and President Joseph Kasavubu then cabled Secretary-General Hammarskjold, asking him for military assistance to protect the Congo against "the present external aggression which is a threat to international peace".[63] While no Security Council session had been requested by the government, Hammarskjold decided that a Council session was vital, for now it was obvious that a good deal more than simple technical assistance, even to military authorities, was involved. For the first time in the history of the Office of the Secretary-General, Article 99 of the UN Charter was formally invoked. This underscored the solemnity of Hammarskjold's evaluation of the quickening crisis, and the UN's interest in resolving the issues, which meant isolation of the Congo from the cold war, and avoidance of the manifest threat to peace and newly won independence posed by military intervention.

The Secretary-General had already been hard at work lining up support for what was to become the largest international peacekeeping force in the history of world organization. And the Security Council's response on July 14, 1960, was to adhere quite closely to Hammarskjold's recommendations. The Secretary-General had argued that Belgian military intervention was unacceptable as a "stop-gap arrangement" and that UN aid would permit the troops to withdraw. Most Security Council members agreed, and despite Soviet hesitance to delegate further discretionary power to Hammarskjold, the Congolese government request, backed as it was by the Afro-Asian nations, resulted in a Soviet decision not to oppose the resolution. The Council rejected a Soviet suggestion to condemn the "armed aggression" by Belgium, but called for a withdrawal of foreign troops from the Congo, and authorized the Secretary-General to:

take the necessary steps, in consultation with the Government of the Republic of the Congo, to provide the Government with such military assistance as may be necessary, until, through the efforts of the Congolese Government with the technical assistance of the United Nations, the national security forces may be able, in the opinion of the Government, to meet fully their tasks.[64]

The resolution was passed, although three of the five permanent Council members abstained. They were China, France, and the United Kingdom, and this in itself was an indication that the tasks ahead for the Organization would not be easy. Even Moscow went along only because of intense African pressure, as it wished to avoid being grouped with the three Western powers who were not anxious to initiate UN action in the Congo.

Immediately after the Council meeting, three key officials of what later came to be known as the "Congo Club" in the Secretariat, that is Hammarskjold, his Executive Assistant Andrew Cordier, and Heinrich Wiesch-

[63] SCOR: 15th year, 873 mtg., Doc. S/4382, 13 July 1960, p. 21.
[64] Security Council Res. S/4387, 14 July 1960.

hoff, an African expert in the trusteeship section, began to put together the Congo force. It would be known as ONUC, the French initials for Force de l'organisation des Nations Unies au Congo.

The Secretary-General moved quickly to set down the basic principles upon which the force would be established. Drawing heavily upon the UNEF experience, Hammarskjold insisted upon exclusive UN control over the force, again in sharp contrast to the Korean case, and this meant command by the Secretary-General under rather loose control of the Security Council. Since it was not a Chapter VII force, ONUC would not interfere in the internal affairs of the host state, whose consent was needed for the presence of the force in Congolese territory. ONUC would remain neutral in all domestic conflicts, would not help any faction or become a party to any internal conflict, and would limit its armed action to self-defense. It was, however, to have complete freedom of movement throughout the entire nation. Finally, there would be an emphasis on troop contributions from African nations, but the force would be universal in its make up except for the complete exclusion of troops from the great powers.[65]

The UN force in the Congo ultimately was to number, at its height, about 20,000 men, and of these, the first few thousand arrived within a few weeks. The first contingents, coming from Tunisia, reached the Congo within forty-eight hours after the passage of the Security Council's authorizing resolution. By July 18, there were 3500 troops in the country, including 460 Ethiopians, 770 Ghanaians, 1250 Moroccans, and 1020 Tunisians.

The first steps looked hopeful, but the threat of internal civil war was imminent. Katanga was acting the role of an independent state, and on July 14, the very day of the first Security Council resolution authorizing ONUC, Tshombe declared that UN troops would be denied entry into Kantanga, and that Belgian troops had to remain to prevent the anarchy and chaos spreading throughout the rest of the Congo.

The Security Council, meanwhile, met again on July 20 and two days later passed a resolution[66] commending Hammarskjold for his action in setting up the Congo force, and calling upon Belgium to withdraw its troops at once. Since UN soldiers had begun to arrive in the Congo, Leopoldville envisaged an immediate Belgian withdrawal and had already threatened to appeal to the Soviet Union for assistance. Hammarskjold had Belgium's promise to withdraw as soon as UN troops could assure the maintenance of order, but Tshombe's recalcitrant attitude made UN entry into Katanga province a doubtful proposition, and obvious economic interest provided little incentive for Brussels to support anything but an independent Katanga.

Nevertheless, Belgium did begin a withdrawal of troops, and for at least a few weeks the government of President Kasavubu and Premier Lumumba seemed to be satisfied with the UN operation. Toward the end of the month,

[65] United Nations Doc. S/4389, 18 July 1960.
[66] Security Council Res. S/4405, 22 July 1960.

Lumumba and Hammarskjold held discussions in New York on the issue of technical assistance to the Congo and the overall pattern of economic aid that the international organization might provide.

For the first two weeks following the Security Council's initial authorization of ONUC, all had gone fairly smoothly. But the critical issue of Katanga's secession was about to break. And the key here was the set of demands made upon the UN and Secretary-General Hammarskjold by Premier Lumumba. Evidently unhappy with Washington's and Canada's response to his appeal for economic assistance, Lumumba began to criticize the UN operation and to move quite perceptibly to the left. He allied himself frequently with the Soviet Union, which naturally backed him as the best opportunity for increased Soviet influence in the country.

Lumumba demanded that the UN operation be placed at the disposal of the central government in Leopoldville, or at least, be ordered to enter Katanga, using force if necessary, to achieve re-integration with the Congo. Hammarskjold's view, as set down in his basic principles for the force, was that the UN could not be a party to any internal conflict, and would not be used to impose a settlement. If military force were to be used, this would necessitate a decision under Chapter VII by the Security Council, and in the absence of such authorization, ONUC was a peacekeeping force that fired only in self-defense. Hammarskjold dispatched Ralph Bunche to talk with Tshombe on the UN entry issue, and Bunche advised the Secretary-General that Kantaga was prepared to fight.

Hammarskjold thought he had paved the way for a peaceful entry. He had emphasized to Tshombe and to Belgium his insistence that ONUC would not be used to force Katanga into submission. Wieschhoff, who had been sent to Belgium to discuss the matter, had foreseen no difficulties. But Tshombe assured Bunche that UN troops would be met with force. Hammarskjold backed away because above all else, he wanted to avoid bloodshed. As he said to Soviet representative Kuznetsov during an August Council meeting: "I do not believe that we help the Congolese people by actions in which Africans kill Africans or Congolese kill Congolese, and that will remain my guiding principle for the future".[67] The Secretary-General strongly resisted Soviet demands that the UN shoot its way into Katanga if necessary.

The Security Council, on the initiative of Tunisia and Ceylon, acting with the agreement of the African bloc, passed a resolution very much along the lines of what Hammarskjold wanted. The Council declared that the entry of the UN force into Katanga was necessary, but that ONUC would not be a party to or in any way intervene or be used to influence the outcome of internal conflict in the Congo. The Council once again demanded that Belgium immediately withdraw her troops, and requested the Secretary-

[67] SCOR: 15th year, 885th mtg., 8 August 1960, p. 23.

General "to implement this resolution", and to report back to the Council. The resolution [68] was passed on August 9 by 9-0-2 (France and Italy abstained) and so far an open break with the Soviet Union had been avoided.

The Council directive also gave Hammarskjold a strong bargaining position with Tshombe. On August 12, the Secretary-General arrived in Katanga with a few companies of Swedish troops assigned to ONUC. Tshombe relented after an initial refusal to permit the troops to land and the Secretary-General was soon shaking hands with the Katangese leader, although he pointedly refused to recognize the "independence" of Katanga by refusing Tshombe's invitation to inspect the honor guard. Swedish troops took over the airport and a few days later more than 2,000 UN soldiers were spread throughout Katanga province.

Hammarskjold's success was generally taken as a positive step forward, but Lumumba could not be placated. In three scathing letters, he accused the Secretary-General of unjustified interpretations of the Council's July 14 resolution and demanded that the UN force be placed at the disposal of his government. He wanted all airports turned over to Congo troops and police, and UN aircraft made available to transport Congolese army forces wherever necessary. He asserted that his government had in fact lost confidence in the Secretary-General. And indeed, fearing that he was losing power in the country, Lumumba directed an anti-UN effort designed in the final analysis to drive ONUC out altogether.

Once again the Security Council met, and again the Secretary-General was supported in his interpretation of the Congo mandate. No formal resolution was forthcoming, but neither was there any question that aside from the Soviet Union, Hammarskjold had general support. Having been given no specific guidance by the political bodies of the Organization, he had had to interpret the vaguely worded mandates himself, and when callenged, submitted the issues in question to the Council. Receiving no rebuke from that body, he felt justified in continuing to interpret his assignment along the lines of the basic principles earlier laid down. He welcomed the support granted him by the Council, but the lack of clear directives simultaneously allowed him discretionary power and left him vulnerable to further criticism. As Hammarskjold stated later to the General Assembly:

Sometimes one gets the impression that the Congo operation is looked at as being in the hands of the Secretary-General, as somehow distinct from the United Nations. No: this is your operation, gentlemen... It is for you to indicate what you want to have done. As the agent of the Organization I am grateful for any positive advice, but if no such positive advice is forthcoming—as happened in the Security Council on

---

[68] Security Council Res. S/4426, 9 Aug. 1960. The resolution's first operative clause is a strong Council endorsement of Hammarskjold's work. It "Confirms the authority given to the Secretary-General by the Security Council resolutions of 14 July and 22 July 1960 and requests him to continue to carry out the responsibility placed on him thereby".

21 August, when my line of implementation had been challenged from outside—then I have no choice but to follow my own conviction, guided by the principles to which I have just referred.[69]

The Secretary-General did, however, make several concessions to the Lumumba viewpoint. He replaced Ralph Bunche as his personal representative in the Congo with Rajeshwar Dayal of India, and suggested the establishment of an advisory committee of states contributing troops to the Congo operation, much on the model of the UNEF advisory group. But Belgian troops remained in the Congo, Lumumba was completely alienated, and the Soviet Union, viewing Lumumba as the most likely stepping stone to increased Soviet influence, was moving further away from the Secretary-General.

If the Katanga conflict had been the occasion for renewed Belgian intervention, the Kasavuba-Lumumba split and the internal cleavages it symbolized provided the gateway for Soviet maneuvers in the Congo. With Belgium refusing to remove that portion of its personnel it characterized as "technical assistants", the Soviet Union refused to remain a quiet member of the UN consensus. Moscow had already been contributing food to the central government directly, rather than through UN channels, and six weeks after the initial Security Council resolution of July 14, the Soviets were dispatching transport planes, trucks and technicians for Lumumba's use. The Secretary-General's inquiries concerning the planes were met with the acid reply that the Soviet Union had every right to aid the Lumumba government as it wished. At the same time, Belgium was pouring weapons and supplies into Katanga and Hammarskjold could merely protest.

On September 5 began the tragic comedy marking the disintegration of Leopoldville's governing structure. President Kasavubu announced the dismissal of Lumumba and was almost immediately ousted in turn by the Premier. Both moves were invalidated by the chamber of representatives, and a few days later the army chief of staff, Colonel Joseph Mobutu, announced the assumption of power by the army and the closing of Parliament. On September 20, Mobutu, strongly supported by both Belgium and the United States, announced the formation of a new governing body, the Collège des Universitaires.

Even prior to these maneuvers, the Soviet position in the Congo had been greatly weakened. For Andrew Cordier and Major General Carl von Horn of Sweden (ONUC's commander), acting to prevent civil war between the Lumumba and Kasavuba factions, shut down the radio station in Leopoldville and closed the airports to all incoming planes. The action was taken without the prior authorization of the Secretary-General, but was later endorsed strongly by him. This was the critical turning point, however, for Patrice Lumumba, and it was the real end of any meaningful cooperation between the Soviet Union and Hammarskjold.

[69] Quoted in Foote, *op. cit.,* pp. 316-317.

On its face, Cordier's and von Horn's act was a neutral and impartial attempt to prevent civil war, but the effect was to give a rather substantial assist to those trying to eliminate Lumumba from the political life of the country. Kasavubu was able to use the Brazzaville radio across the river, and Tshombe controlled communications facilities in Elisabethville. Only Lumumba was hurt. Further, obviously, the influx of Soviet supplies was halted. The result was unintended, but Western forces were strengthened in the country, and Moscow was outraged. Almost simultaneously, Lumumba's staff was arrested by the central government and President Kasavubu named Joseph Ileo as the new Premier. Mobutu remained the "strong man" in charge of the army, and without much prodding from the West, the new government ordered the Russian and Czech ambassadors and technical staffs out of the country. Soviet intervention had been successfully thwarted by a combination of UN actions and Western pressure. The Western powers were naturally rather pleased with the turn of events, but for Secretary-General Hammarskjold it was the beginning of the end.

Still again the Security Council met to give some expression of policy and direction to the rapidly deteriorating crisis in the Congo. The Soviet Union blasted the Secretary-General for siding with the United States and its NATO allies in seeking to undermine the Lumumba government, and it vetoed a resolution submitted by Tunisia and Ceylon which stipulated "that no assistance for military purposes be sent to the Congo except as part of the United Nations action".[70] The Afro-Asian bloc had supported the resolution, and the extent of Soviet alienation was indicated clearly by their willingness to risk a split with the majority of new members in the UN. The United States immediately called for an emergency special session of the General Assembly to begin on the evening of September 17.

The emergency Assembly voted a strong motion of confidence in the Secretary-General and did essentially what the vetoed Security Council resolution would have done. It called upon all states to "refrain from the direct and indirect provision of arms or other materials of war and military personnel... except upon the request of the United Nations through the Secretary-General..."[71] The vote was 70 to 0 with eleven absentions (the Soviet bloc nations, South Africa and France).

On September 19, 1960, began the fifteenth session of the General Assembly, perhaps the most famous in the history of the parliamentary body. More heads of state and prime ministers attended than ever in the Assembly's history, and the lines were drawn for the confrontation between Premier Khrushchev of the Soviet Union and Secretary-General Hammarskjold. This was the Assembly of the shoe pounding, the troika, the strong Soviet bid for the friendship of sixteen new African states, and the bid by Khrushchev to demonstrate to Peking and the rest of the Communist world

[70] SCOR: 15th year, 906th mtg., 17 Sept. p. 18.
[71] G.A. A/Res/1474/Rev. 1 (ES-IV), 20 Sept. 1960.

that here indeed was a revolutionary Communist who could bend even Western dominated international organizations to suit his will. The Soviets were infuriated by their near miss in the Congo, and their response was to saddle Hammarskjold with most of the blame.

For Premier Khrushchev and the Soviet Union, the Secretariat of the United Nations did not reflect the division of the international arena into capitalist, socialist and neutral camps. As was evident from Hammarskjold's work in the Congo, and by Western domination of the "Congo Club", the Secretary-General had sided with the colonialists in implementing Security Council resolutions on the Congo, and that was not a surprising development. For the Soviets, there were no neutral men, and the Secretary-General, being a Westerner, must necessarily reflect that fact in his actions and perceptions. It was only natural that the Congo operation should be utilized to carry through Western interests in Africa, but clearly this had to be corrected. Khrushchev formally proposed that the office of Secretary-General be abolished, and replaced by a "collective executive body" of three persons, representing the Western powers, the socialist states, and the neutralist countries.[72]

Given the weakness of the Soviet position in the UN, the "troika" proposal, as it came to be known, was an obvious response. As noted, Germany and Italy, taking part in an interwar League of Nations dominated by the British and French, had formally proposed an advisory board to limit the powers of the League Secretary-General.[73] The Soviet maneuver was much the same. The UN had been dominated by the United States from the beginning, but the growing plurality of Afro-Asian states gave the Soviet Union at least a measure of influence in the Organization it might not otherwise have had.

Khrushchev felt able to make a move which might be appealing to some African and Asian states who were also dissatisfied with the rate of UN progress in the Congo, and at the same time increase Soviet influence in the Secretariat. Moscow was attempting to avoid the unpleasant consequences of the growing power of the Assembly and Secretary-General, both of which tended to erase its veto power in the Security Council, by establishing a veto over the workings of the Secretariat. It was a stunned General Assembly and Secretary-General that heard Khrushchev's words, for while Soviet displeasure with Hammarskjold had been manifest, the proposal here was to abolish the Office altogether. The scheme would clearly have slowed UN peacekeeping operations to a crawl, for Khrushchev later indicated that all three Secretaries would have to agree before a particular decision could be implemented.

Hammarskjold's response was the only one possible. The UN arena had

[72] See GAOR: 15th Sess., 869th, 882nd, and 904th Plenary mtgs., 23 September, 3 October, and 13 October 1960.
[73] See pp. 39-43, *supra*.

become witness to an enormous and unequal struggle between a superpower and a Secretary-General, and the latter's strategy was to appeal openly to the great majority of small nations in the Organization, particularly those of Africa and Asia. The hope was that the new nations would view the Congo operation as basically in their interests, and the Organization itself as the best instrument for preservation of their neutrality. For Hammarskjold:

> this is a question not of a man but an institution. Use whatever words you like, independence, impartiality, objectivity—they all describe essential aspects of what, without exception, must be the attitude of the Secretary-General. Such an attitude... may at any stage become an obstacle for those who work for certain political aims which would be better served or more easily achieved if the Secretary-General compromised with this attitude. But if he did how gravely he would then betray the trust of all those for whom the strict maintenance of such an attitude is their best protection in the world-wide fight for power and influence. Thus, if the office of the Secretary-General becomes a stumbling block for anyone, be it an individual, a group or a government, because the incumbent stands by the basic principle which must guide his whole activity, and if, for that reason, he comes under criticism, such criticism strikes at the very office and the concepts on which it is based. I would rather see that office break on strict adherence to the principle of independence, impartiality and objectivity than drift on the basis of compromise. That is the choice daily facing the Secretary-General.[74]

In Hammarskjold's view, that choice was also facing the General Assembly, and "all those whose interests are safeguarded by the United Nations will realize that the choice is not one of the convenience of the moment but one which is decisive for the future, their future".[75] A sweeping ovation accorded Hammarskjold by the Assembly indicated the Organization's confidence in him, but the debate had not yet ended.

Premier Khrushchev pushed his demand for an Assembly vote of no confidence in the Secretary-General. Asia and Africa, as well as the Communist bloc, he argued, were not given sufficient representation in the Secretariat, and the head of the Organization "has always upheld the interests of the U.S. and other countries of monopoly capital". A new structure was needed, but even without this, Hammarskjold had to go. "I want to reaffirm", declared Khrushchev, "that we do not trust Mr. Hammarskjold and cannot trust him. If he himself does not muster up enough courage to resign, so to say, in a chivalrous manner, then we shall draw the necessary conclusions from the situation obtaining".[76]

Hammarskjold's reply,[77] perhaps one of his most famous, appealed even more openly to the new nations. "The man does not count", said Hammarskjold, "the institution does". A weak executive "would no longer be able to serve as an effective instrument for active protection of the interests of those many Members who need such protection". For Hammarskjold the

[74] Foote, *op. cit.*, p. 316.
[75] *Ibid.*
[76] GAOR: 15th Sess., 882nd mtg., 3 October 1960.
[77] *Ibid.*

only criterion to be applied was whether or not the incumbent of the Office would strengthen the executive branch. If so, he should remain; if not he should resign.

Hammarskjold stated that the Soviet opposition to him seemed to provide a strong reason for his resignation. However, since the Soviet plan involved the abolition of the Office of Secretary-General and its replacement by an arrangement which would weaken the executive, he would have to stay on. To do otherwise would be tantamount to throwing the Organization "to the winds", an impossible step because of his responsibility to those states for which the Organization was of "decisive importance".

It is not the Soviet Union or, indeed, any other big Power who need the United Nations for their protection; it is all the others. In this sense the Organization is first of all *their* organization, and I deeply believe in the wisdom with which they will be able to use it and guide it. I shall remain in my post during the term of my office as a servant of the Organization in the interests of all those other nations, as long as *they* wish me to do so.[78]

As the Secretary-General uttered the words "I shall remain in my post", there was a tremendous wave of applause from the General Assembly. Hammarskjold was intensely proud of that moment. Not long after, he and his close friend Bo Beskow, listened to a recording of the speech. As the phrase was spoken and the applause broke out, the Secretary-General paced nervously about the room exclaiming excitedly, "listen to that, listen to that".

Hammarskjold had his vote of confidence, and was thus permitted to continue his work in the Congo, but the Soviet attack had severely damaged his position. He became an object of great hostility in the Soviet Union and other Communist bloc countries, and throughout some of the more militant left-African countries. His prestige and acceptability had deteriotated substantially, and his ability to mediate between East and West or to undertake any significant action was greatly circumscribed. The constraints under which he labored grew worse in February, 1961, when the Soviet Union officially withdrew its recognition of him as Secretary-General immediately subsequent to the death of Premier Patrice Lumumba.

While the "troika" attack generated no significant structural changes in the Secretariat, it did result in the resignation of Andrew Cordier, in June, 1961, as Hammarskjold's Executive Assistant. The man who had been closer to Hammarskjold than anyone else gave up his post to allow greater African and Asian participation in the Secretariat's upper echelon. Cordier was replaced by C.V. Narasimhan of India, but retained his responsibilities as Under Secretary-General for General Assembly Affairs. Cordier stayed on until 1962, several months after Hammarskjold's death.[79]

[78] *Ibid.*

[79] Cordier became Dean of Columbia University's School of International Affairs in 1962; in 1968 he was named Acting President of Columbia, and he became the University's permanent President in August, 1969.

In the meantime, events within the Congo provided little hope for a successful outcome of the UN operation. For despite the withdrawal of Belgian troops from Katanga province, Belgian police officers and members of the Katanga gendarmerie remained, and several hundred Belgian nationals returned to Katanga in political and administrative capacities. By the beginning of 1961, Tshombe was hiring white mercenaries to provide the military power essential for the successful maintenance of the secession. The UN was in Katanga, but evidently powerless to induce a change.

The Organization struggled vainly to find a government in Leopoldville it could support. The split between Colonel Mobutu and President Kasavubu on the one hand, and the supporters of Patrice Lumumba on the other, was reflected by a collapse in the general consensus at the UN among the Afro-Asian group. With Lumumba under house arrest in Leopoldville, Kasavubu consolidated his strength in the Western provinces of the Congo, while Antoine Gizenga took effective control of Kivu and Oriental provinces. The Soviet Union strongly supported Gizenga, while the West naturally preferred a strong central government under Kasavubu and Mobutu. The UN's position, espoused both by Hammarskjold and representative Dayal, was a neutralized Congolese government of national reconciliation, including all of the chief factions. A government could be built around the office of the Chief of State and Parliament, the two remaining governmental institutions retaining any kind of legitimacy.

Kasavubu and Mobutu, supported by the West, wanted the UN force to suppress Gizenga, but this was rejected by Hammarskjold and Dayal, thus generating great hostility towards the UN operation, the Secretary-General and his representative. And eventually, under pressure from Washington, both during the remaining days of the Eisenhower administration and even from the newly installed Kennedy administration, Dayal was forced from his job. Each side had wanted the UN to move against the other, while the UN insisted on neutrality. The result was impasse, and meetings of the Security Council and General Assembly in December and in January, 1961, produced no clarification of policy, no enforcement of Hammarskjold's mandate in the Congo, and indeed, merely reflected serious divisions of opinion which were undermining still further the Secretary-General's already weakened position.

A critical turning point came in February with the announcement from Elisabethville that Patrice Lumumba was dead. Lumumba, whose arrest had once been thwarted by ONUC, had voluntarily left UN protection in November and was arrested by the Congolese army. He was held for several weeks at a prison near Thysville, but in January was moved to Katanga. On February 13, the Katanga government announced that Lumumba had been killed by hostile villagers during an attempted escape, and while no definitive proof has been forthcoming, it has been generally assumed that Lumumba was murdered at the direction of Katangese authorities. The Soviet Union immediately withdrew its recognition from Hammarskjold as Secretary-General, labeling him "an accomplice and organizer of the murder"[80] of the ex-premier. The Afro-Asian response was less violent, but the sense of shock was enormous, and it seemed clear now that the UN position was the only meaningful alternative.

The Security Council met again, and on the basis of a report from a UN conciliation commission in the Congo, and taking Lumumba's death as a spur to action, the Council in effect called for a stronger UN position in Katanga, and a government of national conciliation at Leopoldville. For the first time, the use of force by UN troops in the Congo was publicly sanctioned by the Council, although in a rather moderate form. The UN was urged to take all appropriate measures for the prevention of civil war in the Congo, including "the use of force, if necessary, in the last resort".[81] The Council also urged that "measures" be taken for the evacuation of Belgian and other foreign military and paramilitary personnel, as well as mercenaries and political advisers not under UN command. The use of force in Katanga, therefore, was not specified, but taking two sections of the resolution together, if the secession of Katanga posed a significant threat of civil war, it followed, at least to some observers, that force in Katanga itself was justified.

The Council also took the first steps toward the establishment of a new government of national reconciliation, urging the convening of Parliament and the reorganization of the Congolese armed forces "with a view to the elimination of any possibility of interference by such units and personnel in the political life of the Congo".[82] Neutrality of the army, obviously, would necessitate peaceful negotiation by each of the main factions attempting to form a coalition regime.

In April, the General Assembly indicated its support of the Security Council approach (amid signs of its own restoration of unity) by passing three separate resolutions embodying the same dual approach previously accepted by the Council. A central factor, said the Assembly, was the continued intervention of Belgian and other foreign military and paramilitary personnel, and these had to be totally withdrawn. Concerning the struggle for power in Leopoldville, the Assembly also urged the Congo government not to attempt a military solution, and called for the release of political prisoners and the convening of Parliament.[83]

Meanwhile, conferences at Tananarive, in the Malagasy Republic and at

---

[80] *The New York Times*, 15 February 1961, p. 1.
[81] See D. W. Bowett *et al.*, *United Nations Forces* (London: Stevens & Sons, 1964) p. 165.
[82] *Ibid.*
[83] The Assembly's actions also constituted an endorsement of the Secretary-General's approach after the Soviet split with Hammarskjold had become complete.

Coquilhatville in the Congo helped to pave the way for political agreement among the contending factions. The first conference called for a confederation of the Congo with Joseph Kasavubu as president. The second attempted to work out in greater detail the relationship between the central government and the provinces, but faltered on Tshombe's insistence upon auto·nomous provinces under a rather weak central government. Indeed, Tshombe's opposition resulted in his detention by the Leopoldville government, although by June he had agreed verbally with President Kasavubu on the convening of Parliament and the integration of Katanga. The UN Secretariat's good offices were helpful in arranging meetings between Leopoldville and Stanleyville representatives in June that led finally to agreement to convene Parliament.

Kasavubu, Gizenga, and Tshombe had all committed themselves to peaceful settlement, and thus the three most powerful political groupings in the nation were represented in the July-August meeting of Parliament at the University of Louvanium. From these sessions there emerged in the Congo a government of "national unity and political reconciliation" under Prime Minister Cyrille Adoula, and on August 13, 1961, Secretary-General Hammarskjold confirmed to Adoula that thereafter the UN would deal exclusively with his government.

With the problem of authority in Leopoldville apparently solved for the time being, the UN was able to turn its full attention to Katanga province. And at this point began the series of controversial and then tragic events leading directly to the death of Dag Hammarskjold. The problem in Katanga was clearly the mercenaries that Tshombe had been hiring since the beginning of 1961. Aside from a group of Belgian army officers and other soldiers training his gendarmerie, Katanga had recruited Europeans from Belgium, France, South Africa, and Southern Rhodesia. Hammarskjold wanted to move against the mercenaries, but notwithstanding the Security Council's February resolution, felt he had no authority to use force in the first instance.

On August 23, 1961, Hammarskjold cabled to Mahmoud Khiary, chief of UN civilian operations in the Congo, suggesting to him that the Adoula government should "immediately issue an order, the terms of which should declare as 'undesirable' all the non-Congolese officers and mercenaries serving in the Katangese forces" and that the government should demand their immediate exit from the Congo.[84] The very next day, the Congo issued a decree, called Ordinance 70, carrying out Hammarskjold's recommendation, and on August 28, ONUC troops in Katanga, acting under the Security Council's February resolution and the new decree, carried out Operation Rumpunch, a surprise maneuver that ended in the capture of 338 mer-

[84] Ernest W. Lefever, *Uncertain Mandate* (Baltimore: The Johns Hopkins Press, 1967), p. 229.

cenaries.[85] The remaining 104 were not interned because of political pressure from Belgium and a promise from Brussels to repatriate immediately all prohibited personnel.

But the Belgian promise did not materialize, and UN officials began immediately to plan a follow-up to Operation Rumpunch. The next step, to be known as Operation Morthor, called for the arrest of the remaining mercenaries in Katanga and the arrest of the key figures in the Tshombe government. The Katanga gendarmerie would also be disarmed and the central government would assume control in the province. To this end, UN forces planned the capture of strategic positions in Katanga's urban centers.

Apparently, most of the planning for the second operation was undertaken by Khiary and Conor Cruise O'Brien, the UN civilian representative in Elisabethville. It was generally expected by UN officials in Katanga that the operation would be peaceful, as Operation Rumpunch had been, and there is evidence that the entire course of UN planning was approved by Hammarskjold. Lefever states in his account of the UN Congo operation that Sture Linner, the UN officer-in-charge in the Congo at the time, "cabled details of the plan to Hammarskjold and received his approval in principle for putting it into effect if the situation remained as described. The Secretary-General left the timing to his subordinates in the Congo".[86]

But this time Tshombe was prepared for the UN action, and the result was a bloody eight-day fight that left about fifty Katanga troops and eleven UN soldiers dead. Secretary-General Hammarskjold was due to arrive in Leopoldville on September 13, and O'Brien originally estimated that the operation which began in the early hours of that morning would be completed by mid-afternoon. In fact, by the evening UN troops had captured only the post office and radio station in Elisabethville after bloody fighting, and just one high official of the Katangese government had been captured. Tshombe had escaped to Northern Rhodesia. On the night of September 13, O'Brien announced that the secession of Katanga was ended and that he had acted in accordance with the February 21 resolution. In reality the fighting continued, and the United Nations was being heavily criticized in many Western states for attempting a violent repression of the secession. Hammarskjold was subjected to immediate pressure, primarily by the British, to end the operation at once. The Secretary-General was obviously upset at the decision to use force to implement a plan which he had understood to be a peaceful operation.

In defense of himself and of the entire UN action in Katanga, Hammarskjold issued on September 14 a public statement [87] that minimized as

---

[85] See Conor Cruise O'Brien, *To Katanga and Back* (New York: Simon & Schuster, 1962).
[86] Lefever, *op. cit.*, pp. 54-55.
[87] *Id.*, pp. 58-59.

far as possible the significance of Operation Morthor. It was depicted as a simple continuation of Rumpunch and as completely defensive in nature. According to the Secretary-General, a critical event was a fire in a UN garage. UN troops proceeding to extinguish the fire were shot at from a building housing the Belgian Consulate and from other houses where non-African residents were staying. There was, of course, far more to the operation than that. Morthor was to have been the final settling of accounts with Katanga province, and the ultimate UN effort to reintegrate the area into the Congo. The Secretary-General made no comment on the plans to seize strategic centers in Elisabethville, or the arrest of key ministers in the Tshombe government, nor did he attempt to answer questions concerning his own authorization and approval of the actions taken.

On September 17, Secretary-General Hammarskjold took off from Leopoldville to meet with Tshombe at Ndola in Northern Rhodesia to negotiate a ceasefire between UN forces and Katanga. The UN plane carrying the Secretary-General and several of his aides crashed in a forest near the airport. The only survivor was a UN security officer, and he too died after a short time.[88] A few days later, a ceasefire agreement was reached between Tshombe and Khiary at Ndola, resulting in a victory for the Katanga leader. There was a prisoner exchange and return of all the strategic points held by the UN forces. For the UN this did not imply a recognition of the regime in Elisabethville, but in fact its independence was maintained, buttressed throughout by white mercenaries fighting for an independent and wealthy Katanga.

The death of Dag Hammarskjold brought to a sudden and dramatic end a vital era in the history of world organization. For while crisis in the Congo continued unabated, and the UN had still to solve the complexities of a disintegrating post-colonial African nation, the development of an independent role for global institutions, symbolized so magnificently by Hammarskjold, would henceforth be questioned and restrained, and it appeared unlikely that the Secretary-General's successor would be permitted the freedom to strengthen executive capacities.

Further, it now seemed questionable whether the UN would again, at least in the foreseeable future, involve itself in a situation requiring so much in the way of governmental resources. The Congo operation would be completed, and under U Thant the UN would wield more power and the Secretariat maneuver with substantial independence. But again, political constraints were forcing a reevaluation, and future large-scale operations seemed unlikely.

In a very real sense, the Congo marked the peak of UN activity in its short history, and clearly the high point in the first four decades of the

[88] See Arthur Gavshon, *The Mysterious Death of Dag Hammarskjold* (New York: Walker, 1962).

organized international community. For the UN in the Congo and the Secretariat under Hammarskjold had tried to deal with many of the great issues of world politics. East-West confrontation, colonial withdrawal and influence, African societal disintegration based on economic interest and tribal lines, and the pacifying and neutral role of the UN intermediary were the crucial themes of the drama played out in Leopoldville and Katanga.

The Congo tragedy also marked the first failure of Dag Hammarskjold in his more than eight years as Secretary-General. There were perhaps two basic errors. The first was his failure to give a more rapid institutional expression to the rising influence and strength of the Afro-Asian members of the Organization. The "Congo club" was Western, and even American dominated, and the result was a Secretary-General vulnerable to Soviet charges of imperialist bias. When events in the Congo did not suit Soviet interests, it was an easy matter for Moscow to blame Hammarskjold, greatly weaken his influence, and attempt to destroy the Office altogether. Trygve Lie had had a similar problem, but for Lie there was no powerful Afro-Asian bloc, and he was caught between East and West with no recourse save the principles of the Charter and the resultant sacrifice of his political position. Hammarskjold had sufficient opportunity to built a third-world wedge in the Secretariat, but he was slow to take advantage of it, and the result was his own political downfall.

The second error was the greater tragedy, leading directly to Hammarskjold's death. The Secretary-General had relied very heavily upon the UNEF experience in drawing up the guiding principles for ONUC, and above all, under pressure from the West, this meant a no-force policy by the UN in Katanga. Yet most of the Afro-Asian states were not adverse to a stronger role for ONUC against the Tshombe regime and the foreign mercenaries. Further, the logic of the UN's position and Tshombe's commitment to an independence supported almost entirely by foreign white soldiers meant that ridding the province of outside interference (and this was the UN mission) indicated that armed force in some degree would be extremely difficult to avoid. Tshombe had little price to pay by holding on to the mercenaries, and that being the case, the UN would have to try sanctions or fail in its mission. But Hammarskjold insisted on peaceful resolution.

The Secretary-General wanted complete freedom of movement for his troops throughout the Congo, including Katanga, but was unwilling to view Tshombe's refusal to grant freedom of movement as a justification for force used in self defense. Nor was he willing to fight when foreign mercenaries fired at UN troops trying to arrest them. And when Operation Morthor brought bloodshed, Hammarskjold quickly agreed to negotiate a ceasefire enabling Tshombe to maintain an independent Katanga. He died on the way to negotiate the agreement.

Yet Hammarskjold had shouldered an enormous burden. Subject to intense political pressure from East and West, he fought hard for neutral principles, for an independent Secretariat, for a dynamic United Nations with interests and authority of its own, and for a peaceful settlement of the Katanga conflict when it seemed just barely possible that peaceful negotiations might succeed. It should be noted here that U Thant tried for still another year to negotiate with Tshombe before more forceful measures were used.

Working with incredible energy and his usual diplomatic skill, Hammarskjold had put together the largest international army ever assembled and successfully prevented great power intervention with the accompanying spectre of larger conflict. He had supervised the beginning of UN efforts to hold a new African state together, while allowing the colonial power to begin its withdrawal. Once more he had indicated with his typical clarity the most useful functions of the world organization, and he had asked the right questions concerning an independent role for international institutions. Several years after that fateful crash at Ndola, the questions he asked have still to be answered by the world community, but above all, the choices we confront and the implications for peace they bear are understood as well as they are because of the work of Dag Hammarskjold.

The news of the Secretary-General's death came as an enormous shock to the entire world. At the General Assembly on September 19, the delegates and most of the Secretariat staff stood in a minute of silent prayer. The President of the Assembly, Frederick Boland, of Ireland, a close associate of Hammarskjold's, stood next to Andrew Cordier. The Secretary-General's chair was empty. As one observer expressed it, "never was a minute so long, or silence so silent or a chair so empty".[89]

The New York Times said in an editorial "he carried our aspirations with him on all his perilous enterprises, including that last journey when his plane plunged into an African forest. How can the power of this irreplaceable man be analyzed? It rose from patience, from an inherited wisdom, from a profound experience, from the ability to detach himself from the deep traditions of his native land and to be first of all an international statesman... The man himself is dead, but... his voice can still be heard, and in men's memories... it will be heard for many a long year".[90]

The lonely years were over. Dag Hammarskjold had built the Organization he served and the Office of Secretary-General to a pinnacle of power unmatched in the history of international organization. He had suffered much during his years as Secretary-General, but at the same time he had made an enormous impact on the history and events of his time. The devotion and skill with which he worked for peace marked Hammarskjold as one of the great statesmen of our era, and assured for him an honored place

[89] Emery Kelen, *Hammarskjold* (New York: G. P. Putnam's Sons, 1966), p. 15.
[90] *The New York Times,* 24 September 1961.

in the history of world civilization. The movement toward a peaceful world community was slow and painful, and yet this one man had made a re-markable contribution, for

no matter how deep the shadows may be, how sharp the conflicts, how tense the mistrust reflected in what is said and done in our world of today...we are not per-mitted to forget that we have too much in common, to great a sharing of interests and too much that we might lose together, for ourselves and for succeeding generations, never to weaken in our efforts to surmount the difficulties and not to turn the simple human values, which are our common heritage, into the firm foundation on which we may unite our strength and live together in peace.[91]

Hammarskjold's View of the UN and the Office of Secretary-General

There is no question that of the six Secretaries-General, Dag Hammarskjold was by far the most articulate in defining the proper role in world politics of the Secretary-General and the primary functions of the United Nations itself. This was due in part to the changing nature of the international arena in which the United Nations operated, and the resultant opportunity for self-conscious introspection at the UN.

The weakness of the UN's position in the Korean War indicated the essentiality of new directions for the world organization if it were to survive at all as a meaningful factor in international affairs. The Charter concept of collective security had been destroyed by the cold war, and the Korean conflict, often taken as an instance of a UN-supervised collective security operation, was of course nothing of the kind. A military struggle in which each of the superpowers supports a different side was not what the framers of the Charter had in mind by collective security.

But the death of Stalin and the emergence of the Afro-Asian world gave new life to the United Nations. The Organization was now able to intervene primarily for the purpose of isolating local conflicts from the overriding East-West struggle for power and influence. This radical departure from original expectations enabled students and those who fashion policy to con-struct new theoretical formulations appropriate to the changed dynamics of international peacekeeping. Given his natural bent for theoretical con-structs, Secretary-General Hammarskjold was very much disposed to take advantage of the changed circumstances to make such pronouncements. He made great efforts to extract the most meaningful principles from the UN's experience and did so in a manner that naturally emphasized, and perhaps exaggerated, the potential contribution to international peace of the global institution he headed.

Throughout the nearly eight and one-half years of his tenure as Secretary-General, he stressed a few themes of overriding importance. In the final

---

[91] Foote, *op. cit.*, p. 380.

analysis, there are perhaps three basic concepts we now associate particularly with Dag Hammarskjold. The first is the notion of "quiet diplomacy", essentially an appeal to the international community to utilize the structure of the UN for private behind-the-scenes discussion of all outstanding issues. Despite Woodrow Wilson's "open covenants", Hammarskjold saw in global institutions the kind of structure that facilitated secret, and by implication, fruitful negotiation. Public diplomacy had its part, but the critical work had to be done quietly. Second, Hammarskjold is generally credited with legitimizing the notion of "preventive diplomacy", or the idea that the UN's essential justification in world politics is its ability to intervene quickly in local disputes to minimize chances of violent conflict while simultaneously reducing the likelihood of superpower intervention. For the UN to succeed here, its "presence" would be crucial in many cases, and this necessitated an activist role for the Organization, rather than a passive conference machinery.

Finally, Hammarskjold never missed an opportunity to strengthen his own Office, both in terms of political initiative undertaken on behalf of the UN's political organs, or in terms of theoretical abstractions designed both to justify past activity and to enable him to push further toward a strong chief executive for the international community. Thus Hammarskjold's insistence upon his general autonomy under the Charter, in contrast to his more limited scope for action as an agent of the political organs, and the insistence that the Secretariat's highest official had every right to initiate action even without the guidance of the Council or Assembly if such a course were essential for the maintenance of international peace and security.

At the same time, the Secretary-General was cognizant of the extraordinary fragility of the institution he served, and of the superpowers' natural propensity to utilize structures and processes outside the Organization for purposes of serving their essential security interests. But he perceived the UN as one more instrument, albeit all too frequently a tool of marginal importance, for the amelioration of disputes outside the ken of the great powers' direct arenas of influence. And he was quite aware that his own strength as Secretary-General depended rather heavily upon his capacity to maintain friendly relationships with both the United States and the Soviet Union.

Within the frequently harsh and constricting limits imposed by the political realities of his time, however, Hammarskjold worked relentlessly to refine the techniques of international conciliation in which he was engaged. He was a man of great intelligence who possessed the will and energy to comprehend in all their complexities the political problems confronting the United Nations. His ability to fashion responses acceptable to parties with enormous diversity of interest and commitment has established Hammarskjold as one of the great international statesmen of our era.

He made more of the Office of Secretary-General than any of the other incumbents because his extraordinary intellectual capacity was combined with the changing and developing role of the Organization. His personal attributes were truly remarkable. As Wilder Foote aptly phrased it, Hammarskjold had a "brilliant, orderly, pragmatic and subtle mind, capable of lightning speed in both comprehension and construction, yet certainly disciplined".[92] His purely intellectual abilities, when joined with his monumental physical energy, profound learning and general life style produced "that most rare of persons in human affairs—a man of true inner greatness in a position of high leadership".[93]

His first public statement after his election as Secretary-General in 1953 indicated a rather restricted and conservative view of the Secretary-General's functions. The UN's chief executive was

there in order to assist, so to say from the inside, those who make the decisions which frame history. He should—as I see it—listen, analyze and learn to understand fully the forces at work and the interests at stake, so that he will be able to give the right advice when the situation calls for it. Don't think that he—in following this line of personal policy—takes but a passive part in the development. It is a most active one. But he is active as an instrument, a catalyst, perhaps an inspirer—he serves.[94]

The Secretary-General serves, and thus has an active role, but only within the context of providing advice and serving as an inspiration. In a few years, Hammarskjold was to assert a very different position, primarily on the basis of a more active role for the United Nations.

The real turning point for Hammarskjold's conception of the proper role of the Secretary-General and the UN was the Suez crisis of 1956-57 and his re-election in 1957. Until that time, his addresses and statements on the UN had been in a rather conservative vein, differing little from his predecessors' presentations. And while he had insistently stressed the difference between his authority as agent of the UN political organs, and his general scope for action under Article 99 of the Charter, this was never developed systematically, and certainly was not accompanied by any particular action other than the Peking mission in 1955. The *Introduction* to Hammarskjold's Annual Report for 1955-1956, issued early in October, 1956, says nothing very remarkable about the UN and stresses its uses an "an instrument for negotiation of settlements, as distinct from the mere debate of issues".[95] Here was the emphasis on "quiet diplomacy", but not much more.

It is also clear that until 1957, Hammarskjold had no very extensive notion of an activist role for the Secretariat. Indeed, it might well be argued that he said less than he might. In 1955 for example, he asserted that the Secretariat "has creative capacity. It can introduce new ideas. It can in

[92] *Id.,* pp. 13-14.
[93] *Id.,* p. 13.
[94] *Id.,* p. 27; see Joseph P. Lash, "Dag Hammarskjold's Conception of his Office," XVI *International Organization* (No. 3., Summer, 1962), pp. 542-543.
[95] GAOR: 11th Sess., Supp. No. 1A (A/3137/Add. 1), *Introduction* to the Annual Report, 4 October 1956, p. 2.

proper form take initiatives. It can put before the Member Governments new findings which will influence their actions".[96] These notions were certainly correct, but gave little indication of the independent actions taken by high Secretariat officials just a year after these words were written. The stress on quiet diplomacy, fast becoming Hammarskjold's hallmark, was applied as well to the Secretariat's political work. Thus, in a 1955 address at the University of California at Berkeley, he warned of the "propaganda" and "rigidity" introduced into United Nations debates, and suggested a better balance 'between conference diplomacy and quiet diplomacy".[97] And certainly the Secretary-General's work demanded the secrecy of behind-the-scenes discussion. In a statement that brings to mind Sir Eric Drummond, Hammarskjold asserted that even in the context of Article 99 initiatives, the role was best performed quietly:

Even this last function of the Secretariat—and by necessity especially of the Secretary-General personally—is and should be unspectacular. The very rules of the game, and the specific position of the Secretariat inside the system, force the Secretariat in its activities as representative of the organization as a whole to apply what is now often called quiet diplomacy. Such an activity, in fact, comes very close to that of a Foreign Office, working along classical lines as a servant of the Government and of the people —with a discretion and integrity rendered necessary by the fact that none of the interests it is there to safeguard and none of the confidences that it may be privileged to enjoy, is its own property but something entrusted to it by its master, the people.[98]

Beginning with his re-election to a second term in September, 1957, Hammarskjold began to expand rather liberally on the meaning of his Office and that of the United Nations. His statement to the Assembly upon his re-election reflected his experience with the establishment of UNEF in 1956, and his general activity in the Middle East. Hammarskjold declared he did not believe the Secretary-General should be requested to act without guidance either in the Charter or in the decisions of the UN political organs. Within those limits, however, it was the Secretary-General's duty to use his Office and the UN machinery as fully as circumstances would permit. Thus, "On the other hand, I believe that it is in keeping with the philosophy of the Charter that the Secretary-General should be expected to act also without such guidance, should this appear to him necessary in order to help in filling any vacuum that may appear in the systems which the Charter and traditional diplomacy provide for the safeguarding of peace and security".[99]

For the first time, the Secretary-General had enunciated a doctrine endowing his Office with a capacity to act in international affairs in a manner independent of the great powers, assuming that to be essential for the maintenance of peace. Never before in the history of the Office had a Secretary-General publicly stated a similar view. Without great explication, Ham-

[96] Foote, *op. cit.*, p. 94.
[97] *Id.*, p. 95.
[98] *Id.*, p. 94-95.
[99] *Id.*, p. 150.

marskjold was justifying his own role in the Middle Eastern crisis and simultaneously establishing an authoritative rationale for the independent activity of the Secretary-General in world politics. The statement was of enormous significance for the development of the Office and of the executive capacity of the United Nations itself, for it reflected the first dim outline of the global institution as a structure with its own interests and capacity standing ever so slightly apart from the separate members and constituents. This was of historic importance, for it coincided in real world terms with Hammarskjold's conception that the United Nations itself was indicative of a slow but perceptible movement toward "higher forms of an international society".[100]

For all its weaknesses, the United Nations pointed "more directly towards the idea of a true constitutional framework for worldwide international cooperation" and while it was an effort experimental in nature, that effort "seems already to have been carried so far that we have conquered essential new ground for our work in the future. This would remain true in all circumstances and even if political complications were one day to force us to a wholly new start".[101]

Not long after his re-election, Hammarskjold began to speak of United Nations work in the area of "preventive diplomacy" and of the accompanying notion of a "UN presence", usually utilizing these notions within the context of a discussion on the growing independence of the Secretary-General. Hammarskjold had not originally spoken of "preventive diplomacy" in the Middle Eastern crisis in 1956-1957, but his later statements made manifest its application there just as well. The key to the notion of preventive diplomacy was the independent position of the Organization and the Secretary-General:

What I should like to call active preventive diplomacy...may be conducted by the United Nations, through the Secretary-General or in other forms, in many situations where no government or group of governments and no regional organization would be able to act in the same way. That such interventions are possible for the United Nations is explained by the fact that...the organization has begun to gain a certain independent position, and that this tendency had led to the acceptance of an independent political and diplomatic activity on the part of the Secretary-General as the "neutral" representative of the Organization.[102]

The independent position of the Secretary-General was vital because it enabled the UN to maneuver without the same necessity for public debate that in many cases could be quite damaging. The neutral Secretary-General could negotiate quietly within the framework of the Charter and with far greater flexibility than usually resulted from public discussion. A good example was Hammarskjold's dispatch of a representative, Johan Beck-

100 *Id.,* p. 255.
101 *Ibid.*
102 *Id.,* p. 210.

Friis of Sweden, to Southeast Asia to mediate a relatively minor conflict between Thailand and Cambodia. As Hammarskjold put it, "the parties agreed not to raise the issue in the Security Council but, anticipating a possible outcome, to direct parallel invitations, as it were, to the Secretary-General to send someone to assist them in getting over the difficulty. Without in any way making this a precedent, I responded to the invitations and a representative was sent there, with the acquiescense of members of the Security Council. You can see how much more effective and smooth-working such a technique is than the regular one, which involves all the meetings and debates, and so on".[103]

But the essential compass of preventive diplomacy, made possible by the independent position of the Secretary-General and the growing acceptance of the UN presence idea, was to remove particular local conflicts from the cold war. For Hammarskjold this notion defines "the main field of useful activity" of the organization in its efforts to maintain peace and security.

Experience indicates that the preventive diplomacy, to which the efforts of the United Nations must thus to a large extent be directed, is of special significance in cases where the original conflict may be said either to be the result of, or to imply risks for, the creation of a power vacuum between the main blocs. Preventive action in such cases must in the first place aim at filling the vacuum so that it will not provoke action from any of the major parties, the initiative for which might be taken for preventive purposes but might in turn lead to counter-action from the other side. The ways in which a vacuum can be filled by the United Nations so as to forestall such initiatives differ from case to case, but they have this in common: temporarily, and pending the filling of a vacuum by normal means, the United Nations enters the picture on the basis of its non-commitment to any power bloc, so as to provide to the extent possible a guarantee in relation to all parties against initiatives from others.

The special need and the special possibilities for what I here call preventive United Nations diplomacy have been demonstrated in several recent cases, such as Suez and Gaza, Lebanon and Jordan, Laos and the Congo.[104]

For Hammarskjold, the UN's preventive diplomacy functions also had an important, albeit indirect influence upon East-West conflicts, since the Organization's activities outside the spheres of influence of the great powers tended to stabilize areas of potential dispute and possibly even to reduce the areas in which bloc differences became relevant. Generally speaking, the Secretary-General was reversing almost totally the original conception upon which the Organization was based. The notion of collective security by the great powers was now eliminated even in theoretical terms as a useful function for the world organization, and in its place was substituted the notion of the UN as a third-party neutral acting primarily to localize conflict and keep the great powers apart. This more modest conception, however, went far beyond the "conventional thinking which sees in the Organi-

[103] *Id.*, p. 264.
[104] GAOR: 15th Sess., Supp. No. 1A (A/4390/Add. 1), *Introduction* to the Annual Report, 31 August 1960, p. 4.

zation only, or mainly, a machinery for negotiation"[105] and as such, constituted at once a more realistic appreciation of the UN's possible contribution in world politics, and a vision of the future in which international structures played a prominent part in constructing a better world order.

Soviet attacks on Hammarskjold's role in the Congo crisis resulted in two of the Secretary-General's most famous statements, taking still further his thought on executive discretion and UN functions. The first was a lecture delivered at Oxford University in May, 1961, entitled *The International Civil Servant in Law and in Fact.*[106] The second was Hammarskjold's last *Introduction* to the Annual Report 1960-1961,[107] published in August, 1961. The Oxford speech was a summary history of the development of the international civil service from the League days, and a statement of the Charter principles upon which the current UN Secretariat is based. Hammarskjold reviewed several of the traditional problems facing an international civil service, and then touched on the critical issue of the independent political role for the Secretary-General.

Not surprisingly, Hammarskjold took refuge in the law. He reviewed the problem involved should the political organs of the UN, having once entrusted a specific mandate to the Secretary-General, subsequently find themselves unable to agree on a particular line of action, or divided concerning a particular clarification sought by the Secretary-General. The choice is open to the executive: he can implement the original resolution as he sees fit, running the risk of alienating one or more member nations, or he might refuse to implement the resolution altogether, thereby avoiding criticism and charges of partiality.

For Hammarskjold, the choice was clear. Refusing to move further would not be compatible with the legal responsibilities placed upon the Secretary-General by the United Nations Charter:

> The answers seem clear enough in law; the responsibilities of the Secretary-General under the Charter cannot be laid aside merely because the execution of decisions by him is likely to be politically controversial. The Secretary-General remains under the obligation to carry out the policies as adopted by the organs; the essential requirement is that he does this on the basis of his exclusively international responsibility and not in the interest of any particular State or groups of States.[108]

But a crucial problem remained. For if the Secretary-General insisted upon acting without guidance from political organs if this were necessary for the maintenance of peace, what criteria were to be selected by him to guide his actions. The Secretary-General naturally pointed to the principles and purposes of the Charter, the general body of international law and UN

---

[105] See GAOR: 16th Sess., Supp. No. 1A (A/4800/Add. 1), *Introduction* to the Annual Report, 17 August 1961.
[106] Foote, *op. cit.,* pp. 329-349.
[107] See footnote 105, *supra.*
[108] Foote, *op. cit.,* p. 346.

resolutions, and more broadly, political advice from the permanent missions to the UN and advisory committees, the latter two essential for purposes of "reducing the element of purely personal judgment".[109] Nevertheless, if the Charter principles and international law are insufficient, and if political advice is conflicting, then the Secretary-General must "move within an area inside which personal judgment must come into play". This, for Hammarskjold, was a question of integrity or of conscience. There was no simple answer, but basically the idea was to prevent personal notions from influencing action:

The international civil servant must keep himself under the strictest observation. He is not requested to be a neuter in the sense that he has to have no sympathies or antipathies, that there are to be no interests which are close to him in his personal capacity or that he is to have no ideas or ideals that matter for him. However, he is required to be fully aware of these human reactions and meticulously check himself so that they are not permitted to influence his actions. This is nothing unique. Is not every judge professionally under the same obligation? [110]

In the final analysis, it was a question of integrity, of respect for law and truth, and if this were to drive the Secretary-General into conflict with particular interests, then "that conflict is a sign of his neutrality and not his failure to observe neutrality—then it is in line, not in conflict, with his duties as an international civil servant".[111] Thus the personal discretion of the Secretary-General was to be reduced as far as possible, but if genuinely meaningful world order were to evolve than international cooperation would necessitate effective international structures, including a civil service, making an independent Secretary-General a key element in global peace.

Secretary-General Hammarskjold's last testament was the *Introduction* to the Annual Report for 1960-1961, issued just one month prior to his death. In this document, the Secretary-General depicted with great clarity and perception the essential choice facing the international community concerning the role of the United Nations. The statement was basically a strong response to the Soviet challenge to his Office and to the UN operation in the Congo. Hammarskjold asserted that certain UN members looked upon the Organization "as a static conference machinery for resolving conflicts of interests and ideologies with a view to peaceful coexistence" serviced by a Secretariat not truly international but "representing within its ranks those very interests and ideologies". On the other side were members who perceived of the UN as primarily "a dynamic instrument of governments" designed to seek reconciliation of conflicts but through which members also attempted "to develop forms of executive action, undertaken on behalf of all Members" in an organization that itself aimed at forestalling conflicts and

---

109 *Id.*, p. 347.
110 *Id.*, p. 348.
111 *Ibid.*

resolving them in accordance with the principles and purposes of the Charter.[112]

The choice naturally was reflected in members' views of international executive action and the role of the Secretary-General. An organization regarded as a standing diplomatic conference does not need a truly international Secretariat, but a United Nations as a dynamic instrument of governments "cannot be satisfied with anything less than a Secretariat of an exclusively international character, and thus cannot be reconciled with a Secretariat composed on parties lines and on the assumption that the interests represented in the main organs in this manner should be represented and advocated also within the Secretariat".[113] Geographical distribution was essential, but ideological distribution was another matter. The key was the spirit in which the Secretariat worked in isolation from outside influence, as required by Article 100 [114] of the Charter. "While it may be said that no man is neutral in the sense that he is without opinions or ideals", wrote Hammarskjold, "it is just as true that, in spite of this, a neutral Secretariat is possible".[115] Any man of integrity, notwithstanding his own views, can act in an exclusively international spirit "and can be guided in his actions on behalf of the Organization solely by its interests and principles, and by the instructions of its organs".[116]

The Secretary-General made no attempt to clarify how one defines the interests of the United Nations, nor did he refer here to the personal judgment that must inevitably come into play when the Secretary-General can find no sufficient guidance from the political organs nor from the Charter or principles of international law. This was perhaps an easier statement of the problem, but by referring to "anyone of integrity" the Secretary-General was still insisting that diverse political factions in the world arena must allow some discretion to international civil servants who can be relied upon to act in good faith. If their decisions run contrary to the perceived interests of particular nations, then the short run loss must be taken and weighed against the longer run gains.

In most rational terms, there was little to quibble with in this formulation, but as an appeal to the great powers, it remained more of a normative state-

[112] GAOR: 16th Sess., Supp. No. 1A (A/4800/Add. 1), *Introduction* to the Annual Report, 17 August 1961, p. 1.
[113] *Id.*, p. 6.
[114] Article 100 provides as follows:
1. In the performance of their duties the Secretary-General and the staff shall not seek or receive instructions from any government or from any other authority external to the Organization. They shall refrain from any action which might reflect on their position as international officials responsible only to the Organization.
2. Each Member of the United Nations undertakes to respect the exclusively international character of the responsibilities of the Secretary-General and the staff and not to seek to influence them in the discharge of their responsibilities.
[115] *Introduction* to the Annual Report, 1961 *op. cit.*, p. 6.
[116] *Ibid.*

ment than an expression of real world politics. Despite the eloquence of his presentation, it seemed rather unlikely that Hammarskjold could persuade the Soviet Union, to take but one example, as a member of an international organization controlled by others, that short run interests had sometimes to be sacrificed for purposes of world peace. Most nations in the international community have agreed strongly with the Secretary-General, but the great powers have not, and the debate on the issue presented with such clarity by Hammarskjold still rages today.

The Secretary-General also provided a legal defense for Secretariat action in establishing observer missions or peacekeeping forces. He emphasized the importance of Article 98 in conjunction with Article 99:

As these, or many of these, arrangements require centralized administration measures, which cannot be performed by the Council or the General Assembly, Members have to a large extent used the possibility to request the Secretary-General to perform special functions by instructing him to take the necessary executive steps for implementation of the action decided upon. This has been done under Article 98 ... and has represented a development in practice of the duties of the Secretary-General under Article 97. The character of the mandates has, in many cases, been such that in carrying out his functions the Secretary-General has found himself forced also to interpret the decisions in the light of the Charter, United Nations precedents and the aims and intentions expressed by the Members. When that has been the case, the Secretary-General has been under the obligation to seek guidance, to all possible extent, from the main organs; but when such guidance has not been forthcoming, developments have sometimes led to situations in which he has had to shoulder responsibility for certain limited political functions, which may be considered to be in line with the spirit of Article 99 but which legally have been based on decisions of the main organs themselves, under Article 98, and thus the exclusive responsibility of Member States acting through these organs. Naturally, in carrying out such functions the Secretariat has remained fully subject to the decisions of the political bodies.[117]

Hammarskjold combined the agency theory of Article 98 with the more generalized political responsibilities inherent in Article 99. Adding these to Article 7 of the Charter, which places the Secretariat on a par with the main political organs of the UN, and defending the resultant independent executive role he projected by reference to the neutrality principles of Article 100 of the Charter, Hammarskjold fashioned a persuasive theoretical justification for an independent role for the Secretary-General. The limited functions he shouldered by reason of disagreement in the political organs was within the spirit of Article 99 of the Charter, although legally his actions in this regard were based on decisions (however vague) under Article 98. Article 99 gave a meaning to Article 98 never intended by the framers of the Charter.

For Hammarskjold, Article 99 was the heart of the Secretary-General's authority to undertake political responsibilities, including tasks independent of formal delegations of power by the Security Council or General Assembly. He insisted that Article 99 gave him the right to engage in fact-finding and

[117] Foote, *op. cit.,* pp. 366-367.

other diplomatic activity on his own initiative. In the Oxford address, Hammarskjold asserted that Article 99 necessarily implies "a broad discretion to conduct inquiries and to engage in informal diplomatic activity in regard to matters which 'may threaten the maintenance of international peace and security'." [118] This was the justification for his action in the Laotian question. If the Secretary-General had the legal capacity to initiate Security Council discussions under Chapter VII, then surely he could take the lesser step of discovering whether there was in fact a threat to the peace. He had remarked in 1960: "In the case of Laos I said it may be a threat to peace and security but how can I know? If I am to take the very serious action of putting into motion Chapter VII, I must know. Therefore, in a potential case of 99 I can send observers". [119]

From Hammarskjold's perspective, the Office of the Secretary-General had a competence and standing of its own, and was not completely dependent upon the decisions of member governments. The first articulation of this viewpoint was the construction of the "Peking Formula" utilized for the trip to China in 1954-1955 and again in 1960 for a negotiating mission to South Africa. Peking and Pretoria recognized his authority as Secretary-General, but not the competence of the political organs that had requested him to act. Thus, the Peking Formula "meant that if an organ of the UN asks the Secretary-General to do something and does so without delegating its authority, he has only the authority vested in him under the Charter. The resolution is only an instruction to him to use the authority he has under the Charter, although he is, of course, guided by the resolution". [120] While Hammarskjold never developed the implications of this analysis, at the least it justified quiet negotiations by the Secretary-General on his own initiative. As a primary organ of the United Nations system under Article 7, there was much he could do without political direction or authorization. Article 7 provided Hammarskjold with an enormous leeway, although aside from missions to Peking, Pretoria, and the early 1956 trip to the Middle East to shore up the Armistice Agreements, he relied on Article 99 to establish an independent source of power.

In the *Introduction* to his Annual Report for 1959, Hammarskjold again enunciated his views on an independent authority for the Secretary-General, but without reference to particular Charter authorization:

It should also be noted that in some recent cases of international conflict or other difficulties involving Member States the Secretary-General has dispatched personal representatives with the task of assisting the governments in their efforts. This may be regarded as a further development of actions of a "good offices" nature, with which the Secretary-General is now frequently charged. The steps to which I refer here have, been taken with the consent or at the invitation of governments concerned, but without

---

118 *Id.*, p. 335.
119 Lash, "Hammarskjold's Conception of his Office", *op. cit.*, p. 551.
120 *Id.*, p. 548.

formal decisions of other organs of the United Nations. Such actions by the Secretary-General fall within the competence of his office and are, in my view, in other respects also in strict accordance with the Charter, when they serve its purpose. As a matter of course, the members of the appropriate organ of the United Nations have been informed about the action planned by the Secretary-General and were given an opportunity to express views on it. These cases also should not be considered as setting precedents, especially as it always remains open to the appropriate organs to request that such an action, before being taken by the Secretary-General, be submitted to them for formal decision. However, in these cases too, what has been tried may provide experiences on which, later, stable and agreed practices may usefully be developed.[121]

Hammarskjold later commented that these statements were derived from his interpretation of Article 99, and declared that "I am sure the founding fathers would be extremely surprised to find 99 has developed chapter and verse".[122]

In sum, given the fundamental political value of the United Nations as an agent of preventive diplomacy, and the attendant executive role for the Secretary-General, Hammarskjold found his justification as an active figure in the Charter and the processes of the Organization. Article 7 made the Office a primary organ along with the Assembly and the Councils, thus justifying some independent political activity. Article 98 provided agency authority which, when combined with the spirit of Article 99, warranted substantial diplomatic work with the delegation of power leading to certain discretionary initiatives. Article 99 also provided legitimization for independent investigative and negotiatory roles. In any of these cases, the political organs were kept well informed and had the capacity to prevent such activity if they wished, and of course, the Article 100 requirements of the neutral international civil service constituted necessary protection. But Hammarskjold reserved the right to act unless there was a specific prohibition or decision to the contrary, acting "as a spokesman of the Organization in its capacity as an independent opinion factor" and as the chief executive of an institution that indicated a gradual evolution of "higher forms of an international society".

Too few years have passed to permit prediction as to whether Hammarskjold's conception of his Office and his role in world politics will be of lasting significance. His successor has committed himself to Hammarskjold's pronouncements, but has been severely constrained in his actions by Soviet resistance to independent authority for the Secretary-General.

Nevertheless, Hammarskjold put the important issues squarely before the international community. If there is to be movement toward more highly developed forms of world-wide cooperation, then some independent authority for central executive branches of international government becomes essential. If the main political actors wish to remain where they are in terms of sovereign capacities in a limited institution of nations, then Hammar-

---

[121] Foote, *op. cit.*, pp. 226-227.
[122] Lash, *op. cit.*, p. 553.

skjold's conception may well be rejected. At the present time, the choice has yet to be made. But for world order to have any real meaning, the theory and practice of Secretary-General Hammarskjold must be studied closely as of enormous importance. He blazed a new path. Whether the organized international community will follow it may be one of the crucial questions facing our civilization.

From the perspective of the 1970's, it would appear that Dag Hammarskjold's contribution to world order was as fundamentally important as Sir Eric Drummond's. Drummond had constructed the first international civil service, maintained it against strong attack, played a significant political role, and left as his legacy all of this and the remarkable virtues that made him a truly great Secretary-General. Hammarskjold performed a vital service in 1960 by his powerful defense of the Drummond world civil service model, and he carried out his functions in a manner that recalled Sir Eric. Hammarskjold was quick, extraordinarily hard-working, remarkably imaginative in formulating proposals so as to maximize possibilities of agreement, and above all, in the Drummond manner, was knowledgable. Nothing of any importance at the United Nations escaped his attention. He had opinions and valuable advice on a multitude of questions, political, economic, and administrative. As in the Drummond era, delegates and governments trusted him and constantly sought his views, thereby endowing his Office with an enormous moral authority and influence. The Drummond virtues were also Hammarskjold's.

Dag Hammarskjold's most significant contribution by far, however, was the demonstration that the United Nations could perform as an independent actor in world politics while maintaining the general support of the superpowers and the states primarily concerned in a given conflict. If the words of the UN Charter had been too brave, still the global organization could take on a life of its own, primarily through the Secretariat and the Secretary-General's Office, as a neutral intermediary. This demonstration, and its legitimization through action and theoretical construction, constitute the unique legacy of Dag Hammarskjold. He took us further along the road toward world order than any of the Secretaries-General in these first fifty years of the Office. His contributions, along with those of Sir Eric Drummond, have thus been of vital importance in man's long search for peace.

It is important to note here that Hammarskjold had the advantage of serving as Secretary-General in an international system significantly changed from the largely bi-polar system that so restricted the capacity of the UN during the Lie administration. The emergence of the Afro-Asian world made an enormous difference. Hammarskjold's assertion that the UN is "*their* organization" is meaningful not only in the sense originally intended—that is, protection of small power interests—but also in larger system terms. The UN could do little in a world dominated by harsh

Soviet-American rivalry; but a third world has imparted strength to the UN and enabled the Organization to stand between the superpowers in some critical cases. During the Lie years, the UN could mediate and plead, or align itself with the West. Hammarskjold was quick to grasp the opportunities offered by a rapidly changing world system in the 1950's, and he made the most of them. The Soviet Union refrained from vetoing the initial authorization by the Security Council of the Congo mission, for example, not only because of African preferences, but also because the Assembly would itself have authorized ONUC, leaving even less influence and control in Soviet hands. The third world had altered the international system, and this was quickly reflected in the UN system.

This understanding of Dag Hammarskjold's contribution to the UN and the development of the Secretary-General's Office must be tempered by an appreciation of the serious reversals that occurred in 1960 and 1961. Soviet resistance to Hammarskjold's later work in the Congo, the swing back to the Security Council in the 1960's, and continued Soviet opposition to further development of the Office, have rendered the permanency of Hammarskjold's construction somewhat doubtful. Indeed, in late 1960 and throughout 1961, the Office itself was in danger of destruction. Secretary-General Thant has been able to consolidate some, but certainly not all of the Hammarskjold gains.

Yet it remains true that Hammarskjold's vision of a global institution stepping between parties in conflict, both to maintain the peace and to isolate inter-state and internal wars from great power influence and intervention, represented at once a more realistic perception than the Charter indicates of UN possibilities in a divided world, and a constructive drive toward stronger structures of international government. The wisdom of his teachings has now been debated for over ten years, and still the question has yet to be resolved. For Dag Hammarskjold, however, it would have been enough to know that he succeeded in having the world community confront the right question.

CHAPTER VI

U Thant
Secretary-General of the United Nations
1961-

Most of my colleagues present in this Hall know me personally. They know that I come from a relatively small country in Asia. They also know that my country has steadfastly pursued over the years a policy of nonalignment, and friendship for all other nations whatever their ideologies. In my new role, I shall continue to maintain this attitude of objectivity, and to pursue the ideal of universal friendship.
U Thant, on his election to a full term as Secretary-General, November 3, 1961.

September, 1961 marked another historic turning point for the Office of the Secretary-General and its role in world politics. In many significant ways, the world organization had changed from the Western-dominated structure of the late 1940's and early 1950's to a larger and unwieldy group strongly influenced by the insistent neutralism and anticolonialism of the growing number of new nations from Asia and Africa.

Yet while the original membership of 50 states had jumped to 103, resulting in drastically reduced influence for the United States and its western allies, the leadership of the Secretariat had changed but slowly. Trygve Lie and Dag Hammarskjold had been essentially men of the western world, and consciously or not, this was reflected in the tone and style of their leadership. Even under the hammer blows of the Soviet Union's troika proposal, Hammarskjold kept as his two closest aides Ralph Bunche and Andrew Cordier, both Americans. And while few would question this small "triumvirate's" devotion to the neutral principles of the international civil service, it is not difficult to understand why many wanted to change the narrow base of the Secretariat's top-level direction.

Now Hammarskjold was dead, and accurately reflecting the shift in influence within the Organization, the United Nations turned to U Thant of Burma to head the Secretariat. Thant was from a nation that had known both colonial domination and foreign military occupation, and both he and Burma were avowedly neutralist in the cold war, strongly anti-colonialist, and acutely aware of the desperate need for economic and social development in the countries of the southern hemisphere. The crash of the plane at Ndola that dark night of September 17, 1961 brought to world attention a man who would more clearly than ever make the Organization an instrument for the articulation of "third world" interests and who would himself serve as a leading spokesman for those interests.

U Thant was born on January 22, 1909 at Pantanaw, Burma, a small town not far from the capital city of Rangoon in the flat delta region. He was the first son of a moderately wealthy land owner who introduced his children to English, and indeed, Thant's predilection for English language and literature led him to try his own hand at writing and translations. He was educated at the National High School in Pantanaw, and then prepared for a career in journalism.[1]

His father's death in 1923 and the loss of several family properties, however, limited Thant's attendance at Rangoon University to two years, rather than the full four, and in 1928, at age nineteen, he returned from Rangoon and began to teach at Pantanaw High School to earn money for his family. His subjects were English, history, mathematics, and civics, and in the meantime he won several translation prizes in local publications. In 1931, Thant was appointed headmaster of the Pantanaw School after earning the highest grade in the country in the Secondary Teachership Examination, and his life from then until 1947 was essentially that of educator and writer. In 1933 he published a translated work on the League of Nations, and in 1946 published a book stemming from recommendations he had made during the war for educational reforms in Burma. He also devoted some effort to freelance journalism during this period.

Thant left Pantanaw for good in 1947, moving to Rangoon in order to found a magazine, but an old college friend, Prime Minister U Nu, asked him to serve as the nation's Press Director. Thant accepted, and from that point forward advanced swiftly, first in Burmese politics, and later at the United Nations. Teaching and journalism faded rapidly, although in 1952, he published still another work on education. In 1948, Thant became Director of Broadcasting, and in 1949, at age forty, was appointed Secretary in the Ministry of Information. These were significant posts in the newly independent Burma, and gave him his first training in politics. In 1953 he became Secretary for Projects in the Prime Minister's Office and in 1955 added to that burden the duties of Executive Secretary of Burma's Economic and Social Board.

Experience in foreign affairs began in 1951 with appointments to Burmese good-will missions to Thailand and Indonesia. In 1952 Thant came to New York for the first time, as a member of Burma's delegation to the United Nations, and by 1955, his most important work was in international affairs. He served on many occasions as an adviser to Prime Minister Nu, at the first two Colombo Prime Ministers' Conferences, and at the Asian-African Conference in Bandung, Indonesia, in 1955. Thant was one of the key figures in the planning of the Bandung Conference. He was also an adviser to Prime Minister U Ba Swe at the third Colombo Prime Ministers'

---

[1] For a good biography of Thant, see June Bingham, *U Thant: the Search for Peace* (New York: Alfred A. Knopf, 1966).

Conference in 1956, and at the Asian Socialist Conference in Bombay the same year.

In 1957, Thant assumed the post of Burma's Representative to the United Nations with the rank of Ambassador, and served as Chairman of the Burmese delegation to the General Assembly from 1957 to November, 1961, when he became Acting Secretary-General. In 1959 he was one of the Assembly's Vice-Presidents, and in 1961 was appointed Chairman of the United Nations Congo Conciliation Commission and Chairman of the Committee on a United Nations Development Fund. He also found time to publish in 1961 a two-volume history of post-war Burma.

Thant is the first Secretary-General from Asia, and the first Buddhist to hold the office. He gives the impression of a mild-mannered and soft-spoken politician who enjoys his responsibilities with good humor. There is a serenity of approach significantly different from the Lie or Hammarskjold methods, and perhaps ironically for a Buddhist, none of the mysticism apparent in the Christian Hammarskjold. Thant is a pragmatist more in the Lie and Drummond tradition, although without the technical bent and training of either Drummond or Hammarskjold.

Notwithstanding several years of administrative experience in the Burmese Government, Thant does not particularly enjoy the technical details of Secretariat administration, and much like Lie, has largely delegated his authority in this area to subordinates. In this he is at the other end of the spectrum from Drummond and Hammarskjold. Indeed, since Hammarskjold's death, the authority of the Under Secretaries-General, and the frequency with which they initiate proposals, even of a political nature, has grown substantially.

Despite a generally mild and diplomatically correct style, Thant has on several occasions spoken out quite frankly on important issues, and has not always masked his displeasure at particular aspects of member states' policy. Both Moscow and Washington have at times been angered by his words, and other powers have sometimes thought him rather outspoken in more than one instance. Thant recalls to many the bluntness of Trygve Lie, and indeed the predilection for sharp words is in marked contrast to the more restrained manner of Drummond, Avenol, and Hammarskjold. It may be that the present Secretary-General can more easily afford to speak his mind because of his support based on the Asian, African, and to a lesser extent, Latin-American membership. He is less dependent upon the great powers than any of his predecessors.

As for the development of the Office, Thant's administration since 1961 has essentially been a period of consolidation. He has not been able to expand the importance of the Office beyond the point at which Hammarskjold left it, and indeed, has not been permitted even to hold the line. This is not a phenomenon due in any large measure to Thant's leadership capacity, for both the Soviet Union and France have strongly resisted further development of the discretionary powers of the Secretary-General. Whether Thant would havee been a more powerful Secretary-General in the absence of such resistance must remain purely speculative. He has succeeded in reducing enormously the controversy swirling about the Office at the end of Hammarskjold's administration. Thant has not articulated intricate theoretical propositions concerning the structure and processes of the Office as did Hammarskjold. He has supported Hammarskjold's theory, but has not insisted on a strong application; nor has he any desire to construct a limiting theory. The result has been a marked absence of abstract pronouncements, and a concentration on pragmatism very much in the vein of Drummond, Avenol, and Lie. In terms of articulating the nature, role, and goals of the Secretary-General, Thant has left the field to Hammarskjold.

To a substantial degree, this is exactly what was expected of him from the beginning. The need to diminish or eliminate the pressures threatening the Office in 1960 and 1961 were obvious when Thant assumed the Secretariat leadership. A period of quiet and calm was essential, at least until the Soviet Union could regain some assurance that executive discretion at the UN would not threaten its interests, and that the decision-making apparatus and process at the top level of the Secretariat was more sensitive to non-western concerns. This has been provided by Thant, at times at the price of needed forceful leadership. But to date the quiet teacher and writer from Burma has maintained the confidence of the great powers, and most of the smaller powers of the world, for more than eight years.

The Election of U Thant

When the delegates to the United Nations Sixteenth General Assembly gathered in New York in September, 1961, international tensions were at a high level. Of greatest importance were the Bay of Pigs disaster the preceding April and the Soviet resumption of nuclear tests after a three-year voluntary moratorium by both sides. There was a new Berlin crisis. And of course, there was the Congo. Katanga's secession was still a reality, the United Nations still hesitated to use force to drive foreign advisers and mercenaries from the province, and Moscow was demanding a troika to replace the Office of Secretary-General. Hammarskjold was faced with the same kind of Soviet boycott that had driven Trygve Lie from office, despite support from a large majority of the membership.

With many questioning whether Hammarskjold could long remain as an effective Secretary-General, or worrying whether an attempt to do so might result in the permanent structural weakening of the Office (perhaps in the form of a troika or "sub-troika"), word came on September 18 that Hammarskjold had died in a plane crash while en route to arrange a ceasefire with Tshombe. Andrei Gromyko quickly informed Dean Rusk that the Soviet Union would insist on the troika plan. This would have required a Charter amendment, and Washington let it be known at once that if necessary, it would use the veto for the first time to prevent its adoption. However, the American strategy quickly became one of avoiding the Security Council altogether.

Secretary of State Rusk, in a speech to the Foreign Press Association in New York, recommended that the General Assembly immediately choose "an outstanding world leader" to serve as head of the Secretariat on an interim basis. This, he argued, would defeat the Soviet attempt to "paralyze" the world organization.[2] The idea was to have the Assembly by-pass the Security Council by naming an Acting Secretary-General to serve the remainder of Hammarskjold's term, that is, until April, 1963. Avoiding the Security Council was of doubtful legality, but Hammarskjold's death had removed one of the West's strong bargaining points. Had Hammarskjold lived, then the West, looking to the Lie precedent, could have threatened to keep him in office after 1963 if the Soviet Union vetoed a successor Washington found acceptable. With Hammarskjold gone a successor had to be found under the guns of the Soviet's troika plan, and an Acting Secretary-General appointed by the Assembly seemed the natural way out. But just as clearly, the Soviet Union was strongly opposed to a temporary appointment made by the Assembly.

The decision rested in large measure with the neutralist countries of Africa and Asia, of which there were now forty-seven at the United Nations. This alone was probably sufficient to ensure that a successor to Hammarskjold would be a neutralist from the Afro-Asian group, and indeed, most of the earlier contenders were non-Europeans. Among them were General Assembly President Mongi Slim of Tunisia; Brij Kumar Nehru, a cousin of Prime Minister Nehru of India and the new Indian Ambassador to the United States; and U Thant of Burma. Another name mentioned was Frederick H. Boland of Ireland, President of the Fifteenth Assembly.

As noted in Chapter V,[3] the neutral states did not support the troika proposal, for if the Organization was to be an active instrument of preventive diplomacy, helping to shield developing countries from the cold war, an effective Secretariat was essential, and that meant one-man leadership. Thus the response to Washington's plan for an Acting Secretary-General to complete Hammarskjold's term was favorable, but not by means of an Assembly vote. To avoid the Security Council would have meant antagonizing the Soviet Union and might well have ended in a Secretary-General without any support from one of the great powers, leading to total ineffectiveness. The Lie precedent could not be ignored.

Washington dropped the idea of a General Assembly appointment, and

[2] Quoted in *The New York Times,* 24 September 1961, Section IV, p. 1.
[3] See pp. 317-319, *supra.*

the Soviets, not wishing to incur the hostility of the Afro-Asian group, had to give up the troika proposal. The United States relented fairly quickly. Boland, one of its favorite candidates, had no real chance for success, and Slim did not favor appointment by the General Assembly alone. Quite naturally, he insisted on support from the Security Council before taking even an interim appointment. Furthermore, France did not want Slim. The United States found Thant acceptable, and since the Soviet Union had no objection, he seemed to be in a perfect position.

But Moscow backed away slowly from the troika, and began the now famous "numbers game" in October, 1961. The first Soviet move was to press for a variant of the troika under which there would be four Under Secretaries-General, one of whom would be elected by the other three to serve as the executive head of the Organization. Each of the four would have a veto, and each would take his turn as head of the administration. Of the four, all to be elected by the Security Council, two would be nationals of neutralist nations, one would be from the West and one from the Soviet bloc. This was later revised to include five Under Secretaries, adding one from Latin America. Giving each the veto meant an enlarged troika, and neither the West nor the neutralists could accept it. The Soviets finally dropped the idea, and all future discussions were based on the assumption that a single Secretary-General would be retained.

Moscow then turned to what came to be known as the "sub-troika" plan —a Secretary-General with three deputies, all four officials to be named by the General Assembly on the recommendation of the Security Council. There would be no veto, but the Secretary-General would have to "maintain daily cooperation with his deputies and the deputies with him, and... seek to achieve mutual agreement with them on the major questions of the work of the Secretariat".[4] The United States rejected this as well. The Western powers preferred four or five Assistant Secretaries, and wanted public assurances that the Acting Secretary-General would be free to consult them as he saw fit, without the necessity of agreement.

The Soviet Union retreated further to a position under which the number of assistants might vary, but each would have to be consulted on all important matters. The precise number of assistants varied from four to eight, depending upon the geographical areas from which they were to be drawn. This was a far cry from the ideological representation of the troika. Thant himself, now assumed to be the next Secretary-General, entered the talks with proposals of his own, but he opposed restrictions on his right to appoint subordinates as he wished.

[4] See *The New York Times,* 3 October 1961, pp. 1, 2. The three deputies the Soviet Union had in mind were Ralph Bunche, Georgi P. Arkadev, and Chakravarthi V. Narasimhan. Moscow also indicated that it would not oppose the appointment of a fourth deputy from Africa. This plan, unlike the "troika" or its variants, did not require a Charter amendment, and was thus a practical possibility.

The break came on October 13, 1961, as the Soviet Union made another concession. At a news conference, Valerian A. Zorin, a Soviet Deputy Foreign Minister, stated for the first time that the Russians would accept an Acting Secretary-General who could consult with his aides at his convenience, and without the need for mutual agreement. His comments were very much in line with dominant thought on the responsibility of the Secretary-General. "If his views differ", he said, "he is in the last analysis the one responsible and he can act as he feels necessary". In replying to reporters' questions, Zorin stated that there was "no question" of polling his subordinates or treating them as "a cabinet". "He is the one to make the decision and nobody else", he said.[5]

At the beginning of November, 1961, the United States and the Soviet Union finally agreed that Thant should decide how many assistants he wanted, but that he should work with them in "a spirit of mutual understanding". Zorin had apparently not retreated completely, and the latter phrase was inserted in a statement read by Thant to the General Assembly after his election.[6] On November 3, 1961, U Thant became Acting Secretary-General of the United Nations, his mandate as interim head of the Secretariat to expire on April 10, 1963.

In his acceptance speech, he emphasized at once his commitment to the Afro-Asian conception of neutrality that he had pursued as head of the Burmese delegation to the General Assembly:

Most of my colleagues present in this Hall know me personally. They know that I come from a relatively small country in Asia. They also know that my country has steadfastly pursued over the years a policy of nonalignment, and friendship for all other nations whatever their ideologies. In my new role, I shall continue to maintain this attitude of objectivity, and to pursue the ideal of universal friendship.[7]

The next year witnessed a generally cautious approach by the Acting Secretary-General. His election to a full term as Secretary-General, if it were to come at all, would occur at the seventeenth session of the General Assembly in the autumn of 1962. This necessitated approval by the great powers, which meant that the Soviet Union would have to drop or postpone still further the troika proposal.

There were two key organizational issues Thant had to face in 1962—the continuing dispute between the West and the Soviet Union over the UN role

---

[5] *Id.*, 13 October 1951, p. 2.
[6] Thant designated eight "principal advisers", to be consulted "individually, collectively, or otherwise, as the occasion demands, on important questions pertaining to the performance of functions entrusted to the Secretary-General by the Charter". The institution of the eight "principal advisers" has achieved no institutional significance whatever. Thant's chef de cabinet, C. V. Narasimhan, of India, has noted that the Secretary-General has been eager to dispel the notion that there is any kind of hierarchy of Under-Secretaries. ("Administrative Changes in the Secretariat", *Annual Review of United Nations Affairs 1961-62* (1963), pp. 3, 4.)
[7] GAOR: 16th Sess., 1946th Plenary Mtg., 3 Nov. 1961.

in bringing Katanga's secession to an end, and the UN financial crisis, brought on by the refusal of the Soviet Union and France to pay their assessed shares for the Congo operation. Moscow refused to help pay for UNEF as well. Thant was extremely circumspect on the financial issue, and since the General Assembly had referred legal aspects of the matter to the International Court of Justice, there was no need until July (when the decision came down) for Thant to take a stand. He naturally stood by the Opinion, as did the General Assembly. But he carefully avoided intervening in the continuing financial crisis—this was an area to be left to political agreement between the United States and the Soviet Union.

The Congo was the more critical issue, particularly since the Soviet Union had broken with Hammarskjold over his insistence upon peaceful settlement, and while Thant was given (in November, 1961) a clear mandate for ONUC to use force in Katanga against the foreign advisers and mercenaries, he did not use it until December, 1962. For almost the entire year, he tried, as had Hammarskjold, for a peaceful solution, and again, Moscow was not pleased. But the Afro-Asian members of the United Nations were split on the issue of drastic action against Tshombe's support in Katanga, and the group as a whole was not willing to criticize Thant on the point. That being the case, the Soviet Union was also in no position to withdraw support. It was far easier to attack the Swedish Hammarskjold for following a moderate policy than the Burmese Thant. Further, Thant had pleased the great majority of neutralists and the Soviet bloc on his role in the negotiations on the West New Guinea dispute, resolved essentially in favor of Indonesia. The Netherlands handed the area to the UN for a temporary administration prior to the final transfer to Indonesia.

Thant received United States backing for election as Secretary-General very early. By May, 1962, U.S. Representative Adlai E. Stevenson announced Washington's hopes for a full five-year term for Thant. Several Western European states followed suit a few months later, and there was never much doubt concerning the great majority of the huge Afro-Asian group, nor even the Latin American states. The only serious question was the attitude of the Soviet Union.

Thant himself, while insisting during this period that he had not yet decided whether to seek re-election, acted very much like a candidate. The summer of 1962 was given to travel in Europe, Latin America, and the Soviet Union, conferring with government leaders, making speeches, and answering reporters' questions at a series of press conferences. He received a warm welcome in Moscow, but later insisted he had not sought Russian backing and that the issue of his re-election had never been raised.

Indeed, during his five-day visit to the Soviet Union, Thant made one of his more famous pronouncements that could not help but antagonize his host. He stated in a talk recorded for use by the Moscow radio (but apparently not broadcast on the home service) that "the Russian people do not fully understand the true character of the Congo problem" and this was "probably due to the absence of the presentation of the other side of the coin". Thant said that if Russians only had "the means of knowing all the facets of the problem they will certainly revise their opinion of the nature of the United Nations involvement in the Congo".[8] The Soviet press during this period raised the troika proposal again, but it was never certain that Moscow was prepared to insist on its adoption. The seventeenth session of the General Assembly began in September, 1962, with the Soviets giving no hint of their final stand on the Secretaryship-General.

As of October, 1962, Thant's position was strong, with only some question as to the support of the Communist bloc. Remaining doubts were quickly dispelled by his role in the Cuban missile crisis in October and November. While the total UN role in the crisis was certainly no more than marginal, the Organization and the Acting Secretary-General had intervened in a manner permitting the Soviet Union to back down without a totally damaging loss of face and prestige through the appearance of bowing to UN appeals. Premier Khrushchev was appreciative of Thant's efforts. He thanked the Acting Secretary-General for his work in the crisis, and stated in a letter to Thant that "your efforts to insure world peace will always meet with understanding and support on our part".[9] The general feeling among UN delegates now was that Moscow would support Thant as Secretary-General for a full term.

At first the Russians resisted somewhat, arguing that the missile crisis had to be settled first, but on November 28, 1962, Stevenson and Anastas I. Mikoyan, a Soviet First Deputy Premier, reached agreement, and it was clear that the Cuban crisis had tipped the scales. Zorin for the Soviet Union, speaking in the Assembly, argued that the troika was still the "most fruitful and correct" decision for the world organization, but in view of the Acting Secretary-General's previous work and the "active contribution of U Thant to a peaceful solution of the dangerous consequences in the Caribbean",[10] Moscow had decided to support him.

On November 30, 1962, the Security Council approved the nomination, and the General Assembly unanimously elected Thant as Secretary-General of the United Nations for a term lasting until November 3, 1966. In accordance with Thant's wishes, the term was to run for five years starting from his initial selection as Acting Secretary-General in November, 1961. The word "Acting" was dropped from his title, and Thant looked forward to at least four more years as Secretary-General. He had done well during his tenure as Acting head of the Secretariat. The West New Guinea problem and Cuban crisis had been settled peacefully, and while the Congo still perplexed the United Nations, Thant's position as spokesman for the Afro-Asian group

---

[8] United Nations Press Release SG/1307, 30 Aug. 1962, p. 1.
[9] United Nations Press Release SG/1357, 26 Oct. 1962, p. 2.
[10] See *The New York Times,* 1 Dec. 1962, pp. 1-2.

shielded him from Soviet and left-African criticism. And as the year 1962 drew to a close, it seemed evident that the UN was going to move forcefully in Katanga, with the obvious approval of the Secretary-General. His prestige was high, and prospects for a successful administration encouraging.

The Congo Crisis

The first great test of Acting Secretary-General Thant's capacities in world politics was, of course, the Congo. The seemingly intractable problem of Katanga's secession brought innumerable and often irreconciliable pressures on "Dag Hammarskjold's successor", as Thant was often labelled in the earliest days of his administration. Essentially, the question was what degree of coercion or persuasion should be used by the United Nations against Moise Tshombe's regime, supported by foreign advisers, mercenaries, the Union Minière du Haut-Katanga, and powerful financial interests in Belgium, Great Britain, France, and West Germany.

The first round of fighting between ONUC and the Katangese forces in September, 1961 resulted in defeat for the United Nations. A provisional ceasefire was agreed upon a few days after Hammarskjold's death and under a protocol of October 13, the UN surrendered all the key points it had captured during the September offensive.

But the ceasefire meant little as clashes continued sporadically between Katangese and Central Government troops, and once again the Security Council met to consider the mandate under which ONUC was working. The Council gave to the newly-elected Acting Secretary-General a far clearer sanction for the use of force in Katanga than had been available to Hammarskjold. On November 24, 1961, Thant was authorized to

take vigorous action, including the use of requisite measures of force, if necessary, for the immediate apprehension...of all foreign military and paramilitary personnel and political advisers not under the United Nations command, and mercenaries...[11]

Thant welcomed the new mandate, announcing he would carry out the Council's wishes with "determination and vigor", but he voiced the dominant Western view in stating that the UN would "continue and even redouble its attempts to achieve reconciliation, by peaceful means, of course, of the sharp differences which now seriously endanger the unity of the country".[12]

The Soviet Union, as expected, pressed Thant hard to use force in Katanga. At the beginning of December, 1961, the Soviet UN delegation demanded that ONUC ignore the "illegal" ceasefire agreement (illegal as not negotiated by the Security Council) and take military action against the

[11] S/5502, 24 Nov. 1961. The resolution was adopted by a vote of 9-0-2 (France and the United Kingdom abstaining).
[12] United Nations Doc. S/PV. 982, 24 Nov. 1961, pp. 71-75.

Katanga Government. Many of Thant's Secretariat advisers agreed that force should be used, and the Council resolution of November 24 seemed sufficient authorization, but the Western powers held back. Peaceful settlement was yet possible, they argued, and should be pursued further.

The response from Katanga was not long in coming. In the first few days of December, rioting Katangese troops and paracommandoes fired on and seized UN personnel, set up roadblocks, and fired on UN helicopters and other aircraft. Thant ordered his commanders to take any air or ground action necessary to restore ONUC's position in Elisabethville, while insisting that the fighting was for the limited purpose of restoring "freedom of movement" in Elisabethville for UN forces. He repeatedly stressed that the operation was not intended to carry out the November 24 resolution.[13]

Despite these protestations, UN troops fought hard, and this time with substantial military power. Fifteen jet fighter planes were now at ONUC's disposal, and the number of troops had risen to over 15,000. By the second week in December, the UN asserted it had gained possession of Katangese plans for defense of the province, which were said to include the demolition of Union Minière's installations. This aroused Western fears of a total UN takeover, and again the Acting Secretary-General insisted that the total secession problem would be settled peacefully.

The conflicting pressures were intense. The Soviet Union and at first even the United States backed ONUC's military action in this second round. United States Assistant Secretary of State George Ball said his Government opposed another ceasefire in Katanga until the UN had achieved its minimum objectives, and he warned against a repetition of the events of September. But Great Britain and France, and of course Belgium, felt differently. On December 8, the Earl of Home, British Foreign Secretary, told the House of Lords that he did "not want to see a situation in which the Secretariat of the United Nations, for want of patience, indulge in activities and take force beyond policing".[14] Two days later Home formally requested Thant to order another ceasefire. The Quai d'Orsay issued a statement asserting that ONUC's action was not in accordance with the UN Charter, and that the Congo's internal affairs should be left to the Congolese.

Thant was distinctly cool to the request for a ceasefire. UN forces were militarily far stronger this time, and by December 16 were in almost complete control of Elisabethville, the capital of Katanga. Camp Massart, the principal Katangese military base in Elisabethville, was under UN control and prospects for a complete military victory in Katanga thus seemed bright. Round two, however, was to end with another ceasefire, followed by one full year of inconclusive negotiations.

Pressure from the British, French, and Belgians, combined with rising opposition in the United States Congress, finally induced Washington to

[13] *The New York Times,* 8 December 1961, p. 4.
[14] *Id.,* 9 Dec. 1961, p. 6.

change its position. Tshombe had requested President Kennedy to intervene to stop the fighting, and the State Department announced that if Tshombe left Elisabethville for an agreed meeting place with Premier Cyrille Adoula of the Central Government, the fighting might be "suspended".[15] Thant was not happy with Kennedy's move but every one of the great powers except the Soviet Union urged that course on him, and on December 18, the Acting Secretary-General ordered his commanders in Katanga to agree to a temporary and conditional ceasefire. The conditions were that ONUC achieve its immediate military objectives in Katanga (the Presidential Palace and a Union Minière installation) and that "firm arrangements" be made for Tshombe to fly to Kitona, in Leopoldville Province, to confer with Premier Adoula. Kitona was one of the major military bases available to the Central Government and to the United Nations.

It seemed clear that the main impetus for the halt in the fighting had come from the United States. Tshombe was accompanied to Kitona by Edmund A. Gullion, the United States Ambassador to the Congo and President Kennedy's personal representative at the Kitona talks. He remained in the background, but was "at the disposal" of the conference throughout the negotiations.

After more than fifteen hours of uninterrupted discussion at Kitona, Tshombe agreed to the "Kitona Declaration", a pledge to recognize the "indivisible unity" of the Congo, to accept the *Loi fondamentale* (the Congo's provisional constitution of May 19, 1960), and to put the Katanga Army under President Joseph Kasavubu's control. Kasavubu was to be recognized as chief of state. Tshombe also promised to send Katanga representatives to the National Parliament and to a Government commission scheduled to work out a new constitution. He committed himself further to "facilitate" UN resolutions that, among other things, called for the withdrawal of foreign mercenaries from Katanga.

Had the Kitona Declaration been taken seriously by Tshombe or by the government in Katanga, the secession obviously would have ended quickly. But negotiations on implementation dragged on without agreement, and in January, 1962, Moscow called for a Security Council meeting to deal with the problem. The Soviets insisted that Washington had demanded the Kitona talks simply to keep Tshombe in office, and that the ceasefire ending round two was just as illegal as that for round one. There was little support for the Russian move, however, and the talks continued.

After several months it was clear that agreement was impossible, and on June 26, 1962, the discussions were halted. Tshombe left for Elisabethville to be out of Leopoldville when the Congo's independence was celebrated, and to be in Elisabethville to celebrate Katanga's secession on July 11. Six months after the Kitona Declaration, the Katanga problem was unresolved,

---

[15] *Id.*, 16 Dec. 1961, p. 2.

and the reality of a separate state was becoming more significant with each passing day. Thus ended the "Kitona" phase, and the Acting Secretary-General turned to economic sanctions as a possible technique for integrating secessionist Katanga.

Despite the Security Council resolution of November 24, 1961, authorizing the use of force "if necessary", the major powers other than the Soviet Union continued to oppose a UN military takeover. Critical factors were the precedent value of the world organization's use of force in what was essentially a civil conflict, the threat of destruction to the Union Minière installations, and the irreparable damage that such destruction could do to the Congolese economy and European financial interests. The Acting Secretary-General was given little room for maneuver. In July, 1962, Thant emphasized that the United Nations had not been authorized to commence military operations and would not do so.

At the same time, he was bitter over the continued intransigence of Katanga's key governmental figures, and his language was blunt. In Helsinki, Finland, during his European trip in July, 1962, Thant made one of his most famous, if perhaps most unfortunate public characterizations of his opponents:

Mr. Tshombe is a very unstable man, he is a very unpredictable man. The same can be said of his two colleagues, Mr. (Godefroid) Munongo, who pretends to be the Interior Minister of Katanga, and Mr. (Evariste) Kimba, who pretends to be the Foreign Minister. I have tried to get Mr. Tshombe and the Central Government to negotiate but without any results.
I don't know what I can do with such a bunch of clowns.[16]

By the end of July, Washington and the UN Secretariat were cooperating in designing a program of progressive economic sanctions against Katanga, in an attempt to secure compliance with UN directives without resort to military force. But again, Britain, France and Belgium were opposed. For those states, the financial question remained paramount. For the Kennedy Administration, the reintegration of Katanga meant the strengthening of the moderate Adoula regime in Leopoldville against possible Soviet attempts to gain a foothold in the Congo, as had been attempted in 1960. It seemed clear in Washington, at any rate, that Adoula could not maintain his Government without a successful resolution of the Katanga issue, and the Kennedy Administration perceived that the fall of Adoula would ensure a shift to the left at best, and at worst, an unacceptable degree of Soviet influence in the heart of Africa.

[16] *Id.*, 21 July 1962, p. 1. Thant's remarks drew a sharp riposte from the Katanga President: "Just yesterday Mr. Gardiner [Robert K. A. Gardiner of Ghana, successor to Sture Linner of Sweden as Chief of the UN Congo Operation], a high United Nations official, proposed to me that I become Vice President of the Congo—me, the clown". (*Id.*, 22 July 1962, p. 9)

The financial interests at stake were substantial. France and Belgium were the principal buyers of copper from Katanga, and while Great Britain bought very little copper, British investors were believed to own about forty percent of the stock of Union Minière. West Germany was another large purchaser of copper, and the United States was the main buyer of Katanga's cobalt, used in space vehicles and jet aircraft. Most of the second half of 1962 constituted the sanctions phase of the UN effort. In August Thant published a Plan of National Reconciliation, based largely upon proposals submitted earlier to him by the United States, after consultation with Britain, France, Belgium and West Germany. Essentially, the idea was integration of Katanga under threat of economic pressures. Washington had agreed with Thant's basic approach, then worked out in detail the steps of the plan, and the Acting Secretary-General made some modifications and published it as the Plan of National Reconciliation.

The Plan called first for the drafting of a federal constitution for the Congo, a step already in motion as the Acting Secretary-General, in response to a request from Premier Adoula, had appointed constitutional law experts from Canada, India, Nigeria and Switzerland to help draw up a basic law. Time needed for drafting and the requirements for approval by the Congolese Parliament meant that Thant was delaying any showdown between ONUC and Katanga until at the least some time in October.

Thant suggested that until the Constitution was completed and approved, the Central Government and Katanga should agree on an equal division of all revenue. He also called for the unification of the Congo's currencies, and integration and unification of all military, paramilitary, or gendarmerie units into a national army and gendarmerie structure within a period of three months. The Plan recommended a general amnesty for all political prisoners, and the representation of all political and provincial groups in the Central Government. Premier Adoula had already made offers along these lines. Thant emphasized the need for all UN members to prohibit unauthorized movements of men, arms or war material to the Congo. This was a call to the great powers to stay out, and to permit the UN to function effectively as an interpositonary force, and a plea to Katanga's allies in Southern Rhodesia, Angola, and South Africa not to aid the secessionist province.

Thant did not himself set a deadline, but stated that Robert Gardiner, Chief of the UN operation in the Congo, was authorized to propose a time-table for compliance. Gardiner gave Tshombe (and formally Adouda) ten days to reply, not unreasonably short in light of the secessionist leader's previous delaying strategy. At the same time, the United Nations emphasized that the Plan was not negotiable and "must be accepted as a whole".

True to form, on September 3, the last day of the ten-day period set by Gardiner, Tshombe gave his formal approval to the Thant Plan, and hopes were lifted once again. The Katanga leader's acceptance was in principle, and he proposed commissions to be set up to work out details on revenue sharing and armed forces unification. But the first hopeful response quickly faded into more delaying tactics. Indeed, shortly after Tshombe's acquiescense, two Katangese gendarmes were killed in a skirmish with ONUC troops, and Tshombe labelled the incident as "proof" of the UN's bad faith and called Thant's Plan an "enormous bluff".[17] The talks with financial, currency and military experts got under way, however, amid reports of more fighting, and the downing of a low-flying UN reconnaissance plane. By the end of September, 1962, the Thant Plan was still accepted in principle, and continued to be the primary focus of negotiations in Elisabethville, but at the same time, Gardiner publicly charged that Katanga was maintaining its recruitment of mercenaries and stockpiling of arms.

During October, just one week before the beginning of the Cuban missile crisis, Thant's outlook seemed to change significantly. He was still trying to line up support for economic sanctions, but only the United States and West Germany appeared willing to comply, and the Acting Secretary-General began to supplement ONUC's military power. He spoke privately to delegates on the issue of placing ONUC troops in the interior of Katanga to protect Union Minière installations from Tshombe's long threatened "scorched-earth" policy.

The Acting Secretary-General also informed his Congo Advisory Committee that additional troops would be needed if Tshombe resorted to widespread destruction, and further talks were held with representatives of states in a position to offer contingents. Thant made efforts to obtain more jet fighter planes. Time was beginning to run out in the Congo, and the Acting Secretary-General supervised the drawing up by his staff of plans for the use of military force by UN troops. At the same time, he gave Katanga until November 15 to accept the new constitution that had been drafted, but this was just one more deadline that meant little to the province's leaders.

In the meantime, Washington worked feverishly to reach a peaceful accomodation. George C. McGhee, Under Secretary of State for Political Affairs, urged Thant to "go slow" on military action while he attempted to get Adoula and Tshombe to agree on the new constitution.[18] McGhee failed in this, but he worked out another plan for Katanga's integration that would have had outside experts, supplied if possible by the International Monetary Fund, determine what percentage the Central Government should retain of the taxes and foreign exchange being paid exclusively to Katanga by Union Minière. This would have given Tshombe some hope for a better division than the fifty-fifty split proposed by Thant. McGhee also recommended that Thant request Adoula to modify the proposed constitution to give Katanga

17 *Id.*, 23 September 1962, Section IV, p. 4.
18 *Id.*, 18 November 1962, Section IV, p. 11.

and other provinces still more authority under the Federal Government.

Lining up support for an economic boycott proved extremely difficult. France made it clear from the start she would not participate and Britain was hesitant as well. West Germany was persuaded, and Belgium "agreed" on two conditions: that it could be shown that Tshombe was in fact recalcitrant, and that there was reason to believe that economic sanctions would be effective even without Britain and France. Not since the Suez Canal crisis of 1956 had the United States and its major allies been so far apart on a major issue. And since Britain, France and Belgium had given solid support to the Kennedy Administration during the Cuban missile crisis, Washington was reluctant to emphasize their differences over the Congo. This was particularly so since the Berlin question was not far from the first thoughts of the NATO alliance. If Moscow wished to force another showdown over Berlin, Western solidarity would be more important than ever.

At the end of November, 1962, the United States and Belgium formally threatened Katanga with "severe economic measures" if progress toward unification did not become evident in a short time. President Kennedy and Paul-Henri Spaak, the Belgian Foreign Minister, issued the statement in an attempt to bolster the sagging Adoula regime, and to announce full support for the Thant Plan. Shortly thereafter Adoula barely survived a confidence test in the Congolese Parliament, and his position continued to weaken.

It seemed clear that little time was left for the UN effort. Adoula could not keep his government in power without success in Katanga, and his downfall was Washington's primary anxiety. Further, some members with contingents in ONUC were threatening to withdraw their troops if no decisive action appeared imminent. India, particularly, whose contingent numbered 5500 of ONUC's then 18,000 man force, was worried over Chinese attacks in her border regions. Moreover, the UN financial crisis, caused largely by the refusal of the Soviet Union and France to pay the share of ONUC's costs assessed against them by the General Assembly, greatly weakened the UN's position. ONUC was authorized only to December 31, 1962, and there appeared little prospect for Thant to secure a renewal unless some success in Katanga seemed likely.

From the beginning of December, the UN's program for economic sanctions began to merge more clearly with military planning. Gardiner warned Tshombe on December 10 that the UN was prepared to impose economic pressures, including a suspension of international postal and telecommunications with Katanga, a boycott of Katangese copper and cobalt, and a blockade of all imports and exports. The blockade was to be imposed by cutting rail lines into the province, and this appeared unlikely without heavy fighting. Two days later, Belgian Foreign Minister Spaak characterized Tshombe as a "rebel" and said that Belgium would back the Central Government if it fought in Katanga. He announced one last diplomatic attempt to persuade Tshombe to bring Katanga back into the

Congo, and said if it failed, Thant would obtain the power to impose sanctions that would surely entail military action.

In the meantime, Thant made his first important moves to impose economic pressure on Katanga. He requested a boycott by key minerals purchasers unless duties were paid to the Adoula Government at Leopoldville. He asked South Africa, British Rhodesia and Portuguese Angola to prevent the transit of goods on which duties had not been paid to Leopoldville, and he appealed to Brussels to freeze all foreign exchange earnings of the Union Minière. The Secretary-General warned that ONUC might set up roadblocks, as well as cut rail lines, to stop all exports, and that if Katangese gendarmes tried to prevent this by force, ONUC troops would fight. Economic sanctions and military action were no longer distinguishable. The UN would fight to impose economic penalties for failure to comply with the provisions of the Thant Plan.[19]

By mid-December, it became evident that the third round of fighting between ONUC troops and Katangese gendarmes and mercenaries was imminent. Reports had apparently come to Washington that the Soviet Ambassador in Leopoldville had been offering military assistance to several Congolese politicians.[20] Valid or not, President Kennedy ordered a United States military team led by Lieut. General Louis W. Truman to consult with Thant on ONUC's military requirements, and to fly to the Congo to examine UN needs on the spot. Thant wanted mostly transport aircraft, helicopters and jeeps from the United States, although he was simultaneously getting more than twenty jet fighter planes from Sweden, Italy, and the Philippines, some 1500 Indonesian troops, and a Norwegian anti-aircraft battery.

The Truman mission caused an uproar among opposition groups in the Congo, and triggered an avalanche of criticism from the Soviet Union and some African states who charged United States interference in the Congo. The State Department played down the mission, gave it little publicity, and insisted that Washington was working within the framework of the Thant Plan. Thant himself viewed the Truman mission primarily as an attempt to strengthen ONUC and thus induce Tshombe to carry out a recent offer to turn over foreign exchange earned by Union Minière to Leopoldville's Monetary Council.[21]

---

[19] Thant was unsuccessful in his attempt to prevent Katanga's copper and cobalt from leaving the province. Portugal, British Rhodesia, and South Africa clearly had little sympathy for the UN action in the Congo, and having received an enormous amount of criticism over the years for their colonial and racial policies, were not disposed to cooperate against Katanga. Many key purchasers of copper and cobalt from other nations complied with Thant's appeal, although France, which at the time bought approximately one-third of Katanga's copper output, refused to join the boycott.

[20] See *The New York Times,* 19 December 1962, p. 1.

[21] This offer was contingent upon a return to the mining concern of funds sufficient for its business needs, with the remainder to be divided equally between the Central Government and Katanga.

If nothing else, the Truman mission demonstrated rather plainly that the United States was now inclined to have ONUC use force to unify the Congo and thus maintain the Adoula regime. The only question appeared to be precisely when the Organization would make its move. If fact, the Katangese gendarmes answered the question themselves. On December 24, they shot down a UN helicopter, killing an Indian lieutenant serving with ONUC. There was also a heavy exchange of gunfire near a Union Minière installation in Elisabethville. The next two days were quiet, although tensions were rising rapidly in Elisabethville, and on December 27, the gendarmerie began firing on ONUC positions in three parts of the city, presenting the appearance of a well-planned attack.

Tshombe tried to stop the fighting, but with no success. In the presence of Eliud Mathu, the UN's representative in Elisabethville, he telephoned his gendarmerie commander and ordered all roadblocks removed to give ONUC complete freedom of movement, and commanded his gendarmes to cease fire. But Tshombe had lost control and the third round of fighting between the UN and Katanga was under way.

The first orders from headquarters were to clear all roadblocks in and around Elisabethville and to establish freedom of movement for ONUC. At the beginning of the action there was little indication how far the UN would proceed against the Katanga government. Thant was silent, and Gardiner said that decisions would be made depending upon the success of the roadblock clearing. The operation was so successful that in short time ONUC had virtual control of Elisabethville, including the headquarters of the Katangese gendarmerie. The tone coming from UN headquarters in Leopoldville then echoed the feeling of many diplomats that this was the end of the line for independent Katanga. "We are not going to make the mistake this time of stopping short", said Gardiner in Leopoldville. "This is going to be as decisive as we can make it".[22] The tone coming from the UN headquarters in New York was somewhat different. Thant congratulated Gardiner on the successful completion of the roadblock action, described the UN action as defensive, and regretted the necessity to use force.[23]

But UN troops quickly occupied all of Elisabethville and Kaminaville and by January 3, 1963, with very few casualties and almost no resistance, captured Jadotville, a key mining center. Thant rejected the expected call from Tshombe for a ceasefire and new negotiations (described by one diplomat as an attempt to get "another Kitona"), but at the same time there were signs of dispute between New York and Leopoldville on the actions taken by ONUC. While the reports are somewhat conflicting, it appears that

[22] Quoted in *The New York Times,* 31 December 1962, p. 1.
[23] *Id.,* p. 2. Britain called for still another ceasefire, evidently concerned with British financial interests in Katanga, the role of the UN in settling the conflict through force, and the implications of all this for the Rhodesian federation.

Thant had sent orders to Leopoldville not to capture Jadotville "at this time" and that the orders, while relayed from Gardiner to ONUC forces in Katanga, either did not reach the commanders there, or were misunderstood. There were also reports in Leopoldville that Gardiner had threatened to resign if the military operation, called Operation Grandslam, halted short of total victory.[24] In any event, Thant subsequently ordered ONUC contingents to remain at Jadotville, and not to move against Kolwezi, the last remaining strongpoint for Tshombe. The order was obeyed.

The UN had been completely successful militarily, and Thant's only worry was destruction of installations by Katangese gendarmes in Kolwezi, but the political pressure on the Secretary-General to halt the fighting was very strong, particularly from London and Brussels. Thant's position was that the UN would deal with Tshombe only if he gave up the scorched-earth policy, opened Kolwezi to ONUC, and granted complete freedom of movement to the UN throughout Katanga. After some hesitation, Tshombe acceded to all of Thant's demands, and on January 21, 1963, the UN took Kolwezi without a shot fired. ONUC now controlled all the major population and communication centers in Katanga, and Tshombe was at last cooperating.

Two weeks later, the Secretary-General reported to the Security Council that the UN mandate in the Congo was "largely fulfilled". The UN had been able to maintain the Congo's territorial integrity and political independence, had prevented the occurrence of civil war, and had "for all practical purposes" removed all foreign military and paramilitary and advisory personnel not under the United Nations Command.[25] For the first time since July, 1960, there was a sense of relief about the Congo. The country had been held together, destruction and loss of life were minimal, and while enormous problems remained, the UN membership looked to the rapid scaling down and eventual conclusion of the largest and most expensive and divisive peacekeeping operation in the history of the international organization.

The only remaining issue for Thant was how quickly ONUC should be withdrawn, and again, there was little consensus on the issue. The Soviet Union and France wanted the force withdrawn as quickly as possible, as did a number of African states. The United States and other Western UN members preferred a few thousand UN troops to remain in the Congo at least until the end of June, 1964. Thant recommended a total withdrawal by December 31, 1963. He was preoccupied with the financial crisis and the political strains on the world organization caused by continuing disagreement on the nature, needed authorization, and role of peacekeeping

---

[24] *Id.,* 4 January 1963, pp. 1, 3; 5 January 1963, p. 3.
[25] See United Nations Doc. S/5240, 4 February 1963, the Report by the Secretary-General on the Implementation of the Security Council Resolutions of 14 July 1960, 21 February and 24 November 1961.

operations. Washington was worried about the slow pace of retraining the Congolese armed forces, and feared new outbreaks of violence unless the UN stayed on. Many Africans felt the Organization was spending far too much to keep one moderate pro-Western Government in power, and were incensed when Adoula asked several NATO powers and Israel for help in training his army.

The Western view prevailed, and it was not until June 30, 1964, that the last of the UN troops left the Congo. For the first time since July 15, 1960, which was just two weeks after the Belgian Congo became an independent nation, there were no UN troops in the country. Thirty-four UN members had provided personnel for the military and civilian operation in the Congo, of whom 126 were killed in action, 75 died as a result of accident, and 34 died from natural causes. The cost of the military side of the UN presence was set at $ 381.5 million. The economic and technical assistance program brought the bill as of the end of 1964 to well over half a billion dollars, many times the size of the world organization's regular yearly budget.

The economic aid program has continued in the Congo, and so has the instability that plagued the country from the beginning. Notwithstanding his wish to withdraw ONUC quickly, Thant was rather gloomy in 1964 on the Congo's future. He stressed the need for training and reorganization of the national army, particularly training for a large officer corps, the desperate need for national reconciliation among the many political factions in the country, and the essentiality of continuing UN economic, social, and technical assistance. Premier Adoula resigned as the UN left, and ten days later, in one of the great ironic footnotes to the UN involvement in the Congo, Moise Tshombe became Premier of the Central Government.

The successful conclusion of the Congo operation in early 1963 has so far marked the zenith of UN influence in world politics. The Organization came rather close at times to behaving as an independent actor with the Secretariat as its executive head. This was particularly so just prior to and during the course of each of the three rounds of fighting, when the great powers each urged different operating policies on the Secretary-General. Many of the essential decisions were in the hands of Thant, rather than the foreign ministries of UN members; and indeed, even the Secretary-General was unable at one point (the capture of Jadotville on January 3, 1963) to control the military outcome as completely as he wished. There was more substantial discretion in the UN force and its executive head and thus more independence than ever before for a world body never intended to have a policy of its own.

The Secretary-General's orders inevitably had political effects and it was never clear that any of these were agreed upon by all the great powers. There was a continual competition among them to influence Thant and his top aides. Because of the inability of the Security Council to utilize the power it had called for in November, 1961, Thant was necessarily left with more authority than a Secretary-General has had before or since. The Soviet Union and France, ever hostile to any significant independence for the United Nations or the Office of Secretary-General, have subsequently tried to limit further development of autonomy through a rigid insistence that peacekeeping operations be created, administered, and financed solely by the Security Council.

It must be emphasized, however, that Thant was never in a position to fashion substantive policy of his own. If he was able to take particular steps, including some of extraordinary military and political import, without the concurrence of the great powers, he had to find some common ground for action and could never move too far from the stated position of the key Security Council members. In fact, it seems clear that the essential lines of UN action in the Congo followed rather closely the Kennedy Administration's policy.

Washington's position was somewhere between the Soviet demands for force, on the one hand, and British and French preferences for peaceful settlement on the other. The United States, after the Kitona phase, pressed for economic sanctions, as did Thant. Toward the end of 1962, Washington indicated, through the Truman mission, that military power might be the only method for maintaining Western influence, and the UN then moved rapidly in that direction. Thant's sympathies may or may not have been to the left of the United States' position, but his public utterances and actions were clearly in line with dominant sentiment in Washington. The halt to the fighting in the second round of hostilities in December, 1961 would probably not have been ordered without the demand from Washington; the Thant Plan of August, 1962 was based largely upon detailed recommendations drawn up in the State Department; and the final use of force was backed by the United States.

Clearly, the Secretary-General could not please all the great powers at any given moment, but his trump card was Afro-Asian backing. As UN action suited the majority of the neutralist states, it was difficult for either the Soviet Union or United States to press a strong attack. Following Washington's lead as a middle ground in addition to Afro-Asian support certainly made it awkward for the Soviet Union to complain more than occasionally of insufficient UN effort. The British and French were disenchanted, but isolated, and Thant survived the Congo crisis with heightened prestige and a mandate to continue as Secretary-General.

Throughout the crisis, Thant demonstrated repeatedly the leadership traits that have characterized his administration ever since. He did a good deal more following than Hammarskjold, and left more discretion and initiative to his subordinates in the Secretariat, and to member states. He did not travel at all to the Congo (Hammarskjold made two important trips, on the second of which he was killed) and did not take the initiative in formulating possible lines of action as did Hammarskjold. Perhaps most important in terms of the Office, however, Thant was able to still the storm raging about the Secretary-General during the latter part of Hammarskjold's administration. His actions were applauded, not just defended, and his quiet and easy manner reassured many state representatives who did not care for the distant and complex maneuverings of Hammarskjold. Thant seemed more truly interested in advice than his predecessor, and more willing to reconcile conflicting points of view. He surrounded himself with more Afro-Asians in the Secretariat, and greatly weakened the partly justified charge of pro-Western dominance levelled at the "Congo Club".

Thant also had the advantage of coming later to the crisis than Hammarskjold. By the autumn of 1961, the complicated issues of the Congo were far better understood, and the civil conflict in Leopoldville, while not entirely resolved, was not at the same critical level. Hammarskjold had to deal with two civil wars at once—Thant only one. Thant also had a clear mandate from the Security Council to use force, while until he died, Hammarskjold carried the impossible burden of implementing vague directives that masked disagreement.

Thus it was that the "weaker" Secretary-General was able to accomplish more than the stronger, that the more passive Thant succeeded, and the forceful Hammarskjold failed. It will probably be many years, if ever, before the United Nations is able to launch and sustain a substantial peace-keeping operation without solid agreement on policy by the great powers. Thant's role in the Congo crisis from 1961 to 1964 marked a key turning point for the development of the Office. At least for the foreseeable future, the only possible repetition of a truly powerful role for the Secretary-General in peacekeeping is a Congo-type case in which there is consensus among the great powers upon the establishment of a peacekeeping operation, but dissent among them during the course of its operation. The alternatives would be its abandonment or immobilization or direction by the Secretary-General as the executive agent of a larger political body, such as the General Assembly. In such a case, the experience of the Secretary-General in the Congo crisis will loom large, and his role studied with care.

West New Guinea

The dispute between the Netherlands and Indonesia over West New Guinea (West Irian) at the eastern tip of the Republic of Indonesia presented the United Nations with still another opportunity to aid in the decolonization process—this time by functioning primarily and essentially as a face-saving agency for the Netherlands.

In accordance with the terms of the 1949 Charter of the Transfer of Sovereignty, the Dutch had conveyed full sovereign title over the islands to the new Republic of Indonesia, but no agreement was reached on the status of West New Guinea. The Charter states, rather vaguely, that "the *status quo* of the [Dutch] residency" was to be preserved, with negotiations to settle the final status of the territory. From the Dutch viewpoint, legal sovereignty over West New Guinea had not been transferred, but the Indonesians argued that the Netherlands had retained only administrative control pending the final outcome of the negotiations, and that Indonesia was sovereign there as elsewhere in the Republic.

Discussions over the years proved fruitless, and Indonesia turned down repeated suggestions that the issue be submitted to the International Court of Justice. The question was placed before the General Assembly on several occasions, but Indonesia was unable to persuade a two-thirds majority to accept its position.

The Organization's composition changed dramatically, however, in the late 1950's and it was patent to the Dutch that the Assembly would in short order be adopting a posture akin to that of their adversaries. This was particularly obvious after the 1960 Declaration on the granting of independence to colonial countries and peoples. Furthermore, President Sukarno was stepping up pressure (with threats of force latent throughout) as were the great majority of Afro-Asian powers. Western members were growing restive with continually worsening propaganda defeats over a small territory of no immediate significance to anyone but Indonesia. Even the Dutch had no powerful motivation to maintain their grip on the area. The West New Guinea balance of trade had withered rapidly from the middle of the 1950's, and oil production had been discontinued completely.

At the sixteenth session of the General Assembly in 1961, the Netherlands suggested it was prepared to implement the 1960 Declaration and to transfer sovereignty as soon as possible. However, the Dutch insisted upon the application of the self-determination principle stressed so often by the Afro-Asian group in the Assembly, and this notwithstanding the primitive nature of the great majority of the 750,000 Papuans living in the territory. The Netherlands recommended the establishment of a United Nations Commission to determine the opinions of the inhabitants, to look into the possibility of a UN plebiscite "to register the wishes of the population" and of a possible temporary United Nations administration. The idea of a UN Commission was generally regarded as a device to stave off what many members felt was an inevitable outcome. There was substantial support, however, for the idea of further negotiations looking to a transfer, a plebiscite, and an interim UN administration. But a two-thirds vote was still not forthcoming, and with no solution in sight, President Sukarno announced, in December, 1961, his intention of seizing the region by force.

Neither side wanted a major confrontation, but each was willing to risk precisely that by taking relatively minor steps. In January, 1962, Dutch destroyers sank two Indonesian torpedo boats and drove off a third, each of them apparently headed for West New Guinea. Later in the spring, several hundred Indonesian paratroopers were dropped on the territory, and a group of infiltrators landed by boat.

From the early part of 1962, and for the next several months, negotiations were carried on seriously. Acting Secretary-General Thant's role was marginal, but he was in a position to perform essentially intermediary functions. As expected, he made the usual appeals for a peaceful settlement, and at the start, both the Netherlands and Indonesian Governments communicated with each other through his Office. Thant had requested both sides, on January 17, 1962, to undertake discussions with him, and both agreed. Washington was an interested party from an early date—the State Department was anxious to achieve a settlement, but without becoming directly involved in the negotiations. President Kennedy praised Thant's efforts at a news conference in January, and it was reported shortly thereafter that Thant was "Washington's candidate" to mediate the dispute.[26]

On the suggestion of the United States, accepted by both sides and the Acting Secretary-General, retired U.S. diplomat Ellsworth Bunker began a series of talks with the parties as Thant's formal representative. The Acting Secretary-General's role throughout this period was minimal, and never publicly involved the substance of the problems involved. His public functions were limited to appeals to the parties to resume negotiations, after the talks were broken off in the spring following an increase in Indonesian military pressure. The Executive Office followed the talks quite closely, however, and for several months was the only segment of the UN system directly involved in the dispute. The issue was not put to the political organs again until the seventeenth session of the General Assembly in the autumn of 1962.

Agreement was finally reached on August 15, 1962.[27] For the first time in its history, the United Nations was to assume direct responsibility for the administration of a territory. The Agreement, based largely on a plan submitted by Ambassador Bunker, called for a temporary transfer of West New Guinea to a United Nations Temporary Executive Authority (UNTEA), to be established by and under the jurisdiction of the Acting Secretary-General. UNTEA was to be assisted by a security force (UNSF), and was to administer the territory for a period of several months from the time of its authorization by the General Assembly. The administration lasted from October 1, 1962 to May 1, 1963 at which time the United Nations formally handed the territory over to the Republic of Indonesia.

Another key feature of the Agreement was the provision for a plebiscite, scheduled to be held before the end of 1969, allowing the inhabitants of

---

[26] See *The New York Times,* 17 January 1962.
[27] The text of the August 15 agreement may be found in United Nations Doc. A/5170, Annex, pp. 1-21. See also Paul W. van der Veur, "The United Nations in West Irian: A Critique", XVIII *International Organization* (No. 1, Winter, 1964), p. 53.

West New Guinea to decide whether they wished to remain with Indonesia, or to sever ties with the Republic. President Sukarno was never happy with this pledge, although the Suharto regime later promised to fulfill it.

On September 21, 1962, the General Assembly acknowledged the role conferred upon the Acting Secretary-General in the Agreement, and authorized Thant to carry out the tasks entrusted to him. Despite the debate (at the height of the Congo crisis) on the issue of the Secretary-General's independent authority in the administration of peacekeeping operations, the Assembly gave Thant a general authorization over UNTEA, which in turn was to administer West New Guinea. The Acting Secretary-General had no financial worries as well, since it had been agreed that the costs of the operation would be divided between the Netherlands and Indonesia.

Thant's first task, after the conclusion of the August 15 Agreement, was to arrange for the total cessation of hostilities between Dutch and Indonesian forces. The ceasefire came into force on August 18, under the general direction of Brigadier-General Indar Jit Rikhye of India, the Military Adviser to the Acting Secretary-General. Brazil, Ceylon, India, Ireland, Nigeria and Sweden also provided a group of twenty-one military observers to supervise the ceasefire arrangements. Their task was completed within a few days, and Thant turned to the transfer of administration of the territory to UNTEA. José Rolz-Bennett, Thant's deputy chef de cabinet, was sent to West New Guinea to confer with Dutch officials and to draft plans for the transfer to take place on October 1st.[28] Rolz-Bennett, named Temporary Administrator, worked hurriedly to establish a UN administration as Dutch officials and technicians began to leave.

Thant had been authorized to establish a United Nations Security Force (UNSF) for UNTEA, and upon his request, Pakistan dispatched a contingent of 1500 men, with supporting aircraft and crews from the United States and Canada. The UNSF was in position by October 5, and all Indonesian forces still in the area were grouped under the UN observers' supervision. Rolz-Bennett also had under his authority the remaining Dutch troops who had not yet returned to the Netherlands, the Papuan Volunteer Corps, and the civil police. On October 22, Thant appointed Dr. Djalal Abdoh, of Iran, as UN Administrator. Dr. Abdoh served until the UN withdrawal on May 1, 1963.

Essentially, UNTEA's primary function was to serve as the government of West New Guinea until the final transfer to Indonesia. Under Thant's general authority, the Administrator had full authority to appoint government officials and members of the local councils, and to publish legislation for the territory; the Administrator had power to issue travel documents to

---

[28] On October 1st, 1962, the flags of the United Nations and the Netherlands flew side by side over West New Guinea. Thant had previously agreed to an Indonesian demand that the Indonesian flag fly over the territory by New Years' Day, 1963, and the Dutch then insisted upon their flag flying from October 1st to January 1st.

local inhabitants for overseas travel; and he was responsible for UNTEA's tasks in protecting the civil liberties and property rights of the Papuans. UNTEA had obligations to maintain the economy of the territory, and its public health and education programs.

The Secretary-General relied heavily throughout the seven-month administration upon Abdoh and his staff. There were few political questions of any significance requiring Thant's personal attention, and his role remained marginal and behind the scenes for most of UNTEA's tenure. Perhaps the key issue faced by Thant was how far the United Nations should comply with insistent Indonesian pressure to shorten the period of administration, thus allowing Indonesia to take control prior to May 1, 1963.

The issue was complex because the August 15th Agreement was vague on the terminal date of the UN mission. The Agreement refers to the "first phase" of UNTEA's administration to be completed by May 1, 1963, and a "second phase" (of indefinite duration) during which the Administrator was to "have discretion to transfer all or part of the administration" to the Republic of Indonesia "at any time" after the execution of the first phase. Thant was caught between the conflicting pressures of Indonesian demands and Dutch insistence that UNTEA carry out its work at least until May 1, 1963, and he responded with a compromise that proved successful. He argued that he could not shorten the duration of UNTEA's administration without the consent of the General Assembly and both parties to the dispute. At the same time, however, he sent his chef de cabinet, C. V. Narasimhan, to West New Guinea to work out a formula for UNTEA's earliest possible departure.

On February 9, 1963, after a series of consultations between Narasimhan, Abdoh, and Dutch and Indonesian officials, UNTEA announced that the final transfer would take place on May 1. Narasimhan also revealed that the replacement of Dutch officials by Indonesians would be "accelerated". In early April, the Pakistani troops comprising the UNSF began to leave their positions, and by May 1, they were all in Biak waiting to be returned to Pakistan. Indonesian units began to replace them by April 14.

Narasimhan argued that the second phase was shortened to a few hours on the recommendation of Dr. Abdoh. In fact, the UN was tactfully bowing to Indonesian pressure. For Thant, the curtailment of UNTEA's mission and the rapid entry of Indonesian officials served "to ensure the continuity and expansion of all essential services, especially those concerning the welfare of the people, and also to help as far as possible to accelerate plans for development of the territory".[29]

On May 1, 1963, the United Nations flag was lowered, and Indonesia formally assumed control over West New Guinea. The few remaining Dutch officials had already left the territory, and had been replaced by Indonesians.

[29] GAOR: 18th Sess., Supp. No. 1 (A/5501), *Annual Report of the Secretary-General on the Work of the Organization,* 1963, p. 39.

While Thant may have had private doubts on the significance of the UN's essentially face-saving role in West New Guinea, he pleaded eloquently in public for a favorable view of the mission. He asserted that UNTEA was a unique experience that had succeeded in carrying out its mandate for a peaceful change of administration, accompanied by maintenance of essential public services and utilities, and continuity in employment.

At the completion of the mission, Thant established a United Nations Development Fund to finance pre-investment and investment projects in the territory. At the same time, he announced the appointment of a few United Nations personnel to advise and assist in the preparations for the plebiscite provisions of the August 15 Agreement, stating he was "confident that the Republic of Indonesia would scrupulously observe the terms of the Agreement concluded on 15 August 1962 and would ensure the exercise by the population of the territory of their right to express their wishes as to their future".[30]

The final phase came in the summer of 1969. Thant's Representative, Fernando Ortiz-Sanz of Bolivia, had suggested to Indonesia that the act of free choice be conducted on a "one-man, one vote" basis in the developed coastal regions of the territory, and through a system of collective consultation in the jungle and mountain areas. Jakarta rejected this primarily because of the primitive state of a majority of the West Irianese, and insisted on consultation with representatives of the population. Between July 14 and August 5, eight councils composed of 1,075 delegates decided to retain West Irian's ties to Indonesia, thus formally implementing the August 15, 1962 Agreement, and ending any further Indonesian responsibilities to the United Nations on the issue. The process was not taken as seriously by Jakarta as had initially been intended by the UN. "We are going through the motions of the act of free choice because of our obligation under the New York Agreement of 1962", stated an Indonesian member of Parliament, "but West Irian is Indonesian and must remain Indonesian. We cannot accept any alternative".[31]

The Organization and the Secretary-General performed several important functions in the West New Guinea dispute. The UN served as an aid to diplomacy between the Dutch and the Indonesians, and by interposing itself in the territory, was valuable as a buffer force as well. Intervention by the interested states was made far less likely by the UN presence. Primarily, to be sure, UNTEA served as a convenient face-saving device for the Netherlands. The territory was lost to the Dutch in any event, and the only issue was how to hand over without the appearance of capitulation before a show of superior military might. Since the territory had little more than symbolic value to the Netherlands, the United Nations was the ideal instrument for

---

[30] *Id.,* p. 40.
[31] *The New York Times,* 7 July 1969.

face-saving, and was utilized throughout by the Dutch for that purpose. Simultaneously, of course, UNTEA's mission added strength to the anti-colonial direction of most UN undertakings, and further developed the growing rule against the legitimacy of colonial domination. UNTEA's primary mandate was to facilitate a smooth transfer from colonial status to an act of self-determination. It was a mechanism embodying an anti-colonial policy, and it seemed almost natural for Thant's and Narasimhan's interpretations of its mandate to be more akin to Indonesia's world outlook than to the Netherlands'. Finally, UNTEA provided the Organization and its members with some experience in the direct administration of a political system and territory. It is conceivable that the world body might be of similar assistance in the future in areas where a particular territory is in dispute.

Thant's role in the West New Guinea question was marginal throughout. His functions were essentially the same as those of the Organization itself, although in addition, his personal involvement was useful in terms of procedural arrangements. The Secretary-General was concerned not so much with the substance of the dispute (which had, for most purposes, been settled by the parties themselves), as with the modalities of agreement. He was able to provide the forum for discussion, the means of international intervention, and, when necessary, the effort at mediation that accompanies almost every United Nations force in the field. The UN administration was too limited and of short duration to permit any growth of independent power in Secretariat officials or in the Secretary-General, but UNTEA does stand as a precedent for future development in international administration, and as such, is important in the history of the Office of the Secretary-General.

The Cuban Missile Crisis

On October 14, 1962 began the most dramatic and gravest crisis to face mankind since the darkest days of World War II. The United States Government, through the instrumentality of U-2 reconnaissance planes, had discovered incontrovertible proof of what had been feared in Washington for many months—the Soviet Union had begun to place medium and inter-mediate-range missiles in Cuba, thus securing a strategic base in the Caribbean from which an attack against the United States became feasible.[32]

For a full week a small group, later known as the Executive Committee of the United States National Security Council, debated in almost total secrecy the American response. There was little agreement within the Kennedy Administration as to the military significance of the missiles, although there was consensus that the balance in the Western Hemisphere

[32] For an excellent account and analysis of the crisis, see Elie Abel, *The Missile Crisis* (New York: Bantam Books), 1966.

had been affected, and that at the very least, the Soviet Union would reap an enormous political and psychological advantage were the missiles, the sites, and the long-range bombers also sent in allowed to remain. After a week of painstaking review of possible alternatives and likely Soviet replies, the debate in Washington boiled down to a discussion of two initial responses: an air strike against the sites, or a naval blockade to prevent more missiles from entering Cuba.

By Saturday, October 20, the Administration, still without any knowledge on the part of other governments or the public, had made its decision. A naval blockade or "quarantine" would be instituted to ensure no further delivery of missiles or other "offensive" weapons to Cuba, and if negotiations did not result in the prompt removal of the missiles already on the island, options including a more inclusive contraband list and an air strike would be considered.

The United States position permitted the Soviet Union a minimum of time within which to back down, or face the dominant power of American military might in the area. The Kennedy Administration would try to avoid a confrontation necessitating the use of force against the in-coming Soviet ships, but in the final analysis, Moscow would have to capitulate entirely without a period of negotiation if the attempt were to be successful. Thus the great risk of war, or perhaps a Soviet counter-move in Berlin or elsewhere. Clearly, the issue was for settlement by the superpowers themselves.

Even so, Washington's response did leave some room for the United Nations and Acting Secretary-General Thant to play a part. On October 22, President Kennedy informed the nation and the world of the deceptive entry of Soviet missiles into Cuba, and of the "quarantine" he had decided upon. This was to be authorized by the Organization of American States the next day, and by the morning of October 24, the blockade was in effect. Kennedy also called for a Security Council meeting to approve a resolution requiring the Soviet Union to dismantle and remove all offensive weapons from Cuba before the quarantine would be lifted. U.S. Representative Adlai Stevenson introduced a draft resolution authorizing Acting Secretary-General Thant to send a United Nations Observer Corps to Cuba to ensure the removal of all offensive weapons.

On October 23, the Security Council met to consider the American draft, Stevenson declaring that Premier Castro had turned Cuba "over to the Soviet Union for a long-range missile launching base" and had carried "the Soviet program for aggression into the heart of the Americas". For Stevenson, "the day of forebearance" was past.[33] Valerian Zorin rejected the accusations, and introduced his own draft condemning the actions of the United States as a violation of the Carter. The Cuban delegate, Mario Garcia Inchaustegui also censured the United States and declared

[33] SCOR: (17th year), 1022nd mtg., 23 Oct. 1962, p. 15.

that his Government would never accept United Nations inspection teams.

That night, a group of more than 40 unaligned nations, led by Algeria and other members of the "Casablanca group" in the UN (Ghana, Guinea, Mali, Morocco, and the United Arab Republic), requested Acting Secretary-General Thant to appeal to the United States and the Soviet Union and Cuba to take no steps to aggravate the crisis. The next day, October 24, Thant intervened for the first time. His initial step was to send identical letters to President Kennedy and Chairman Khrushchev, appealing for a halt to the blockade by the United States, and to arms shipments by the Soviet Union, for a period of two or three weeks. Thant noted in his letter that his appeal had been made upon request of a great number of member governments, and that in their view it was important to gain time to allow for negotiations leading to a peaceful settlement. The Acting Secretary-General wrote that a voluntary suspension of the blockade and of all arms shipments to Cuba would "greatly ease the situation and give time to the parties concerned to meet and discuss with a view to finding a peaceful solution of the problem". He added that he would gladly make himself available "to all parties for whatever services I may be able to perform".[34] Thant also appealed to Cuban President Osvaldo Dorticos-Torrado and Premier Fidel Castro to help find "some common ground" in the present "impasse". He urged them to suspend the construction and development of military facilities during the negotiations.

On the night of October 24, Thant made his first public statement on the crisis in a short address to the Security Council.

Today the United Nations faces a moment of grave responsibility. What is at stake is not just the interest of the parties directly involved, nor just the interests of all member states, but the very fate of mankind. If today the United Nations should prove itself ineffective, it may have proved itself so for all time.

In the circumstances, not only as Acting Secretary-General of the United Nations, but as a human being, I would be failing in my duty if I did not express my profound hope and conviction that cooperation, self-restraint and good sense will prevail over all other considerations.[35]

Thant went on to cite what he perceived as a common will to negotiate rather than fight, mentioned his appeals to Kennedy and Khrushchev, and repeated a solemn plea for talks. The Acting Secretary-General made only one brief comment on the merits of the crisis. He stated that some of the measures the Council was called upon to approve were "very unusual, and I might say extraordinary, except in wartime". This was generally assumed to be a statement of disapproval of the naval blockade. He also cited, and thereby associated himself with, Dag Hammarskjold's famous statement to the Security Council in 1956 at the beginning of the Suez crisis:

[34] See The New York Times, 25 Oct., 1962, pp. 1, 23; also Abel, op. cit., p. 131.
[35] See United Nations Review, Nov. 1962, pp. 7-8.

The principles of the Charter are, by far, greater than the organization in which they are embodied, and the aims which they are to safeguard are holier than the policies of any single nation, or people.

The discretion and impartiality ... imposed on the Secretary-General by the character of his immediate task may not degenerate into a policy of expedience ... A Secretary-General cannot serve on any other assumption than that—within the necessary limits of human frailty and honest differences of opinion—all member nations honor their pledge to observe all articles of the Charter ...[36]

But by the end of the day of October 24, there were no clear indications of Moscow's response, and Soviet merchant ships moved closer to the blockade area. In the afternoon, twelve of the twenty-five ships en route to Cuba appeared to stop or change direction, and this was taken as the first flicker of reassurance that war might be avoided. Early the next morning, October 25, a Soviet oil tanker and an East German passenger ship passed through the blockade without being halted.

Later in the day came President Kennedy's and Premier Khrushchev's replies to Thant's appeals. Kennedy agreed to "preliminary talks", but there was no mention in his letter of Thant's request for a suspension of the blockade. The U.S. Government felt strongly that the apparent symmetry of Thant's appeal in fact left the advantage with Moscow. The President thus reiterated the basis of American policy by declaring that "the existing threat was created by the secret introduction of offensive weapons into Cuba, and the answer lies in the removal of such weapons".[37] Chairman Khrushchev's response was naturally more affirmative. He announced his welcome of Thant's initiative, declared his agreement with the proposal made by the Acting Secretary-General, and stated briefly that it "accords with the interests of peace".[38] The Soviet Union was already beginning to yield, as word came on October 25 that a dozen Soviet vessels had turned back, and Khrushchev needed the best face-saving device available. At the time, this was the United Nations, in the person of the Secretary-General.

Despite the announcement from Washington that several Russian ships headed for Cuba had reversed course, Thant made another appeal to Kennedy and Khrushchev on October 25. This was done on the advice of U.S. Under Secretary of State George Ball, acting through Representative Stevenson. Thant asked Kennedy to issue instructions to American vessels in the Caribbean "to do everything possible to avoid direct confrontation with Soviet ships in the next few days in order to minimize the risk of any untoward incident".[39] There had been some indications of worry in Washington that the naval commanders on blockade duty might not do "everything possible" to avoid such confrontation.

Thant's message to Khrushchev requested orders for Soviet ships "al-

---

[36] *Ibid.*
[37] Abel, *op. cit.,* p. 148.
[38] *Ibid.*
[39] United Nations Press Release SG/1358, 26 Oct. 1962, p. 2.

ready on their way to Cuba to stay away from the interception area for a limited time only, in order to permit discussions of the modalities of a possible agreement..."[40] Khrushchev's reply the next day, October 26, accepted Thant's suggestion. The Soviet Chairman attacked the "piratical measures" taken by the United States, but acceded to the proposal "in the hope that the other side will understand that such a situation, in which we keep vessels immobilized on the high seas, must be a purely temporary one; the period cannot under any circumstances be of long duration".[41] Once again, however, it seemed clear that the Soviet Union was happy to utilize the UN for face-saving purposes. Khrushchev's response to Thant was laudatory: "I thank you for your efforts and wish you success in your noble task. Your efforts to ensure world peace will always meet with understanding and support on our part". Kennedy's reply to Thant's second appeal was also approving and assured the Acting Secretary-General that the United States would accept and abide by his request if the Soviets agreed to avoid the interception area.

That day, the Security Council met again for the last time during the crisis period. This was the famous session of the dramatic confrontation between Stevenson and Zorin, the latter refusing to answer Stevenson's insistent questioning whether the USSR had placed and was placing medium and intermediate-range missiles in Cuba. Stevenson used enlarged photographs taken by U.S. reconnaissance planes to show the missiles and their sites, leaving no doubt whatever that the evidence was trustworthy. From the end of the session, which was adjourned that evening to give time to Thant to hold discussions in his 38th floor Secretariat offices with U.S., Soviet and Cuban representatives, the role of the United Nations was channeled exclusively through the Acting Secretary-General. He was naturally at the center of discussions directed to the question of UN inspection of the sites in Cuba to ensure removal of the missiles.

But at the beginning of the next day, October 26, an agreed settlement was still not discernible. Early in the morning a Soviet freighter was stopped and searched, and permitted to pass through the blockade line of destroyers. There was no Soviet opposition and this was another hopeful sign, but in the meantime the missile site construction was continuing apace, and Washington feared the missiles would soon be operational. If the quarantine did not succeed in short order, the pressure for an air strike to destroy the sites would increase substantially.

Early in the evening of October 26, Khrushchev sent another letter, not to Acting Secretary-General Thant, but directly to Kennedy.[42] It was a long and rambling defense of Soviet policy in installing missile sites in Cuba, and the heart of the matter was that the Soviet Union would promise to

[40] *Id.*, SG/1357, 26 Oct. 1962, p. 1.
[41] *Id.*, p. 2.
[42] See Abel, *op. cit.*, pp. 158-162.

bring in no weapons of any kind if Kennedy would pledge not to invade Cuba or to support anyone who might be planning to invade. This letter, read together with earlier private proposals made that day for dismantling the sites and shipping them back to the Soviet Union under United Nations supervision, added up to a reasonable compromise, and a peaceful settlement began to take shape.

The next day, October 27, witnessed a serious turn for the worse. There was an evident change in the Kremlin's thinking, and the price for removal of the missile sites was raised. The United States would have to remove its missile bases and rockets from Turkey. For Washington the Jupiter bases in Turkey were totally irrelevant to the problem of Soviet intervention in the Caribbean, and the Kennedy Administration's response gave scant attention to issues beyond the Cuban crisis.

Kennedy's reply was simply to recommend what appeared might be acceptable on the basis of the mélange of Soviet communiqués. The Soviet Union would remove the missile systems from Cuba under UN supervision and would halt the further introduction of offensive missile systems. The United States would end the quarantine, and would "give assurances" against an invasion of Cuba. This agreement, declared Kennedy, would enable the two countries to discuss other matters, such as armaments and a détente between NATO and the Warsaw Pact. At the same time, the President quietly let it be known to Moscow that time was running out, and that the Cuban sites would be bombed in a few days unless progress was made quickly on their removal.[43]

On the same day, October 27, Premier Fidel Castro invited Thant to visit Cuba "with a view to direct discussions on the present crisis, prompted by our common purpose of freeing mankind from the dangers of war".[44] To many in New York and Washington, this appeared to indicate that should Moscow decide to withdraw its missiles, there might be less opposition than was at first believed to UN inspection teams.

The critical juncture for the Soviet Union, however, had now arrived. If Kennedy's terms were accepted, the Russian capitulation would seem complete; if they were turned down, or decision delayed, bombing in Cuba would begin shortly and the risk of war increase substantially. The decision must have been extraordinarily difficult for the Soviet leadership, but the realities of America's strategic dominance in the region left little room for real choice. On the morning of October 28, Moscow announced it would dismantle the missile systems it had constructed, and return them to the Soviet Union. Kennedy would make a no-invasion pledge, and the United Nations would verify the dismantling of the sites. The Soviet Union had accepted *in toto* Washington's terms, and the Cuban missile crisis was nearing its end.

[43] *Id.*, pp. 176-179.
[44] *The New York Times,* 28 October 1962, p. 31.

There still remained, however, the complex issue of the missiles already in Cuba, and the verification procedures. American and Soviet agreement on UN inspection of the dismantling was of course not binding on Premier Castro, and indeed, the Cuban leader refused to accept international inspection teams. In form, he imposed several "conditions" before the United Nations could enter the country. These included a U.S. withdrawal from Guantanamo Bay and the ending of all economic pressures. The United States, obviously, felt no need to make concessions, as Castro well knew, but combined Soviet, American and United Nations attempts at persuasion made no difference. There would be no international inspection.

Acting Secretary-General Thant had had plans drawn up in the Secretariat for UN verification of the dismantling. He had intended to rely on aerial photographs supplied by the United States to find the missiles, and to utilize some fifty military officers from states that had diplomatic relations with Cuba. In Latin America, this would have meant inspectors from Brazil, Bolivia, Chile, Mexico, and Uruguay. Other states Thant was likely to request assistance from included Ethiopia, Sweden, and Switzerland. He wanted a heavy representation from neutral nations, although Canada was also mentioned as one of the likely possibilities.

Before embarking on his Cuban journey, Thant requested the United States to make one gesture of symbolic value—a suspension of the quarantine for a short period. He believed this might help emphasize the easing of the crisis, and perhaps aid him in the forthcoming talks with Castro. Washington lifted the blockade for a two-day period, although maintaining surveillance of Cuba, primarily by means of aerial reconnaissance.

Thant's trip to Cuba and his discussions with Castro were totally futile. UN inspection was not his only recommendation. Moscow had agreed before his trip to Havana that the Red Cross, or even a group of inspectors taken from the diplomatic corps would be acceptable, and the United States entered no objections. But the Cuban Government, still infuriated and feeling betrayed, would not permit any international presence. Thant evidently had not expected to be turned down. His invitation had been viewed as an indication of diminishing Cuban opposition to inspection. The Acting Secretary-General took with him several top aides, including his military adviser, Brigadier Rikhye of India, Omar Loutfi of the United Arab Republic, his Under-Secretary for Special Political Affairs, and Hernane Tavares de Sá of Brazil, the ranking Latin-American official in the Secretariat and Under-Secretary of Public Information. Thant had also intended to leave twelve members of his party in Havana to begin implementation of the inspection agreement, but on returning, he brought the entire group back to New York. Castro had rejected inspection by the UN (even by air), the Red Cross, and the diplomatic corps in Havana. Possibilities such as UN examination of Soviet ships at sea and Red Cross monitoring of ships in Cuban ports (earlier agreed to by the Soviet Union) were also turned down.

Anastas I. Mikoyan, a Soviet First Deputy Premier, subsequently tried his hand with Premier Castro, but with the same result.

The final outcome was unilateral inspection by continued United States aerial reconnaissance, and naval checks on the high seas. Washington was satisfied with the pace of the dismantling and the return of the missile systems to the Soviet Union, although one difficulty was the presence in Cuba of Ilyushin-28 long-range mombers. It was not until November 20 that Khrushchev announced his willingness to remove them as well, and Kennedy then ordered the end of the naval blockade. By December 6, the last of the bombers left for the Soviet Union, and the crisis was over. In early January, 1963, the United States and the Soviet Union thanked Thant for his assistance, and declared that the matter no longer need occupy the attention of the Security Council.[45]

The Acting Secretary-General had been useful to the great powers in one of the most critical confrontations of power since the Second World War, but obviously his role was of secondary importance. It is always open to the Secretary-General to make appeals to states, and the willingness of the Soviet Union to respond made it clear that at least one side in the dispute was utilizing the Organization as a face-saving agency. But the key discussions and communications in the Cuban crisis were bilateral, and were not channeled through New York.

The Acting Secretary-General was useful, as he almost always is, as the center of the UN diplomatic system. Each side, as well as the majority of neutral nations, was able to press its claims, if it wished, through Thant's office, and in the Cuban case, the neutral members made ample use of the Secretariat's 38th floor. He was valuable as a source of information and as an appraiser of likely responses to particular proposals. He carried on a continuous stream of conversations with members' representatives and other government officials. His diplomatic functions had made him a serviceable, if not essential, instrument—even in a case of direct East-West conflict. Thant was also in a position to implement any agreed-upon system of inspection, and of course, he made many suggestions for verification of the dismantling. This is important, naturally, not only within the context of the Cuban missile crisis itself, but in the broader sense of world organization intervention or interposition between the superpowers in crisis-level conflict.

The Yemen Observation Mission

The civil conflict in Yemen, touched off in September, 1962, was the occasion for the establishment by the Secretary-General of another UN

45 See United Nations Doc. S/5229, 9 January 1963 for this message and Thant's brief reply of thanks.

observation team, known as the United Nations Yemen Observation Mission (UNYOM). The internal war between the modernizing republican regime of Colonel Abdullah Al Sallal and the overthrown royalist government of Imam Mohammed Al-Badr, the Yemeni monarch, triggered very substantial intervention by traditionalist Saudi Arabi and the United Arab Republic. Saudi arms and money were channeled to the royalists, while Cairo sent up to 28,000 troops to aid the republicans.

Through the parallel efforts of Secretary-General Thant, Ralph Bunche, and Ellsworth Bunker, a disengagement agreement [46] was worked out requiring complete withdrawal by the intervenors and a demilitarized zone on each side of the Saudi-Yemeni border with UN observers in the zone to check each sides' compliance with the agreement. Thant ordered Major General Carl Carlsson von Horn of Sweden, Chief of Staff of the UN Truce Supervision Organization in Jerusalem, to make arrangements for the observers. On the basis of von Horn's recommendations, Thant called for some two hundred observers with the requisite equipment to enter the zone. There was a small civilian staff, 114 Yugoslavs from UNEF to serve as a reconnaissance unit, and an air unit of fifty men from the Royal Canadian Air Force. In accordance with the agreement, UNYOM's functions were strictly limited to observation and reporting.

The Mission was ready to begin work by the first week in June, 1963, but while Thant encountered little opposition to the notion of an observation force, the Soviet Union naturally contested the propriety of a mission established by the Secretary-General without Security Council authorization. The Soviet delegate, Nikolai T. Fedorenko, demanded a Council session to authorize UNYOM, a two-month time limit on the force, and the detailing of financial arrangements in the authorizing resolution's operative paragraphs. Each side had agreed to finance the force, but initially for a period of only two months, and this effectively constituted the time limit Moscow wanted. The Council set no formal limit, inserted the financial disposition in the preambular paragraphs, and noted Thant's promise to report back to the Council in advance should two months' observation work prove insufficient. On June 11, 1963, by a vote of 10-0-1 (the Soviet Union) the Council authorized Thant "to establish the observation operation as defined by him" and to report back to the Council.[47] In substance the Secretary-General had created still another UN force to act as an observation team, and the Soviet Union maintained its formal insistance on Security Council authorization.

The efforts of UNYOM were entirely futile, for while the Secretary-General found evidence of Saudi compliance with the disengagement agreement, the UAR withdrew at most only 6,000 of the 28,000 troops it had sent to Yemen. Repeated extensions of UNYOM's mandate through Sep-

[46] United Nations Doc. S/5298, 29 April 1963.
[47] United Nations Doc. S/5331, 11 June 1963.

tember, 1964 had no effect, and finally Saudi Arabi declined to share the expenses of the mission beyond the final two-month extension ending on September 4. Thant decried the narrow mandate assigned to UNYOM,[48] but the parties to the conflict could not agree on broader functions and the Congo experience dictated caution on large-scale peace-keeping operations. The Secretary-General tried to strengthen the UN's political presence by appointing Pier P. Spinelli of Italy, Under-Secretary and Director of the UN European Office, as his Special Representative and head of UNYOM. The idea was to initiate talks between the two intervening states under UN auspices, but this too achieved no results.

Thant asserted that during the fourteen months of its work, UNYOM had "greatly diminished" the threat to world peace posed by the conflict, and had "exercised an important restraining influence on hostile activities" in Yemen.[49] He emphasized that only negotiations at the highest level would result in progress toward disengagement.

The mission did little to develop the political power of the Organization or the Secretary-General. Thant had made no strenuous public effort to enlarge the scope of UNYOM's activities or the size of its field staff, nor did he make an issue of Moscow's successful attempt to involve the Security Council as the proper authorizing agent for the force. The civil war in Yemen marked one of the first clear indications that Thant would be unable to maintain the precedents established by Hammarskjold for the independent functioning of the Secretary-General.

The Federation of Malaysia

The United Nations is very rarely used for purposes of arbitration in a dispute between nations, and only once has the role of arbitrator been assigned to the Secretary-General. In the Malaysian Federation issue, a critical part of which was handed to Thant for both fact-finding and political judgment, the parties agreed that his findings and conclusions would be binding, thus making him essentially an arbitrator. Indeed, the Secretary-General accepted his mandate only on condition that his word be in fact

---

48 United Nations Doc. S/5447, 28 Oct. 1963. Thant stated: "In the course of my consultation with the parties I have made clear my own dissatisfaction with the mandate of UNYOM as now defined. That mandate, set forth in the disengagement agreement, is so limiting and restrictive as to make it virtually impossible for UNYOM to play a really helpful and constructive role in Yemen. Indeed, given the nature of the situation and of the terrain, it is not possible for UNYOM with its present personnel, or for that matter, with a much expanded establishment, to observe fully, let alone to certify to the satisfaction of both parties, what specifically is being done in the way of disengagement. I frankly see little prospect that the disengagement agreement could be so amended as to correct this deficiency". (*Id.*, p. 8)
49 United Nations Doc. S/5927, 2 Sept. 1964, p. 4.

binding, and did so without authorization from the General Assembly or Security Council.

The Federation of Malaysia was originally intended to include Malaya, Singapore, North Borneo, Sarawak, and the British Sultanate of Brunei. The latter withdrew, and questions were raised with regard to North Borneo and Sarawak by the Philippines and Indonesia. The Philippines to this day claim sovereignty over North Borneo. Indonesia objected generally to the Federation as neocolonialist and as a clear attempt to maintain British influence in the area. The Philippines couched the issue in legal terms, but for Indonesia the problem was one of self-determination and independence from colonial domination.

In June, 1963, the foreign ministers of Indonesia, the Philippines and Malaya signed the Manila Accord, which welcomed the establishment of Malaysia "provided the support of the people of the Borneo territories is ascertained by an Independent and Impartial Authority, the Secretary-General of the United Nations or his representative".[50] On July 9, before the accord was formally approved by the three governments, Malaya and Britain signed an agreement to create the Federation, and this was without reference to opinion on the issue in North Borneo and Sarawak. Malaysia was to be born on August 31, 1963.

Tensions were raised by Malaya's apparent disregard for the spirit of the Manila Accord, and at the end of July, Prince Abdul Rahman, the Prime Minister of Malaya, President Sukarno of Indonesia, and President Macapagal of the Philippines met in Manila for another attempt to resolve the conflict peacefully. Shortly thereafter, the three nations requested Secretary-General Thant to help resolve the dispute by ascertaining whether the 1,200,000 inhabitants of the two territories wished to join the new Federation of Malaysia. Prince Rahman stated at the time that "We are bound completely by whatever the Secretary-General says. We cannot wiggle out of that".[51]

The method for determining the wishes of the people of North Borneo and Sarawak was, however, a question of some difficulty. Britain and Malaya preferred not to delay the transfer of sovereignty beyond the August 31 date previously agreed upon, and yet it appeared impossible for Thant to test opinion in any meaningful way in the short time left. The Secretary-General was reported to have declared that the United Nations could not hold a referendum on the issue by August 31,[52] and he asked Indonesia, Malaya and the Philippines to state what method they preferred for ascertaining the inhabitants' views.

A referendum was one possible arrangement. Another was to test senti-

[50] Manila Accord, 11 June 1963, in "Three Basic Documents" (Republic of Indonesia Mission to the UN, New York), para. 10.
[51] Quoted in *The New York Times,* 1 Aug. 1963, p. 3.
[52] *Ibid.*

ment by referring to elections recently held in North Borneo and Sarawak. The latter approach was chosen, and on August 5, the three heads of government cabled Secretary-General Thant a request to make a "fresh approach" to the issue. The terms of reference [53] in the request were complex, and required Thant to make findings of fact and reach political judgments, both of which would be binding on the three nations. The Secretary-General was to examine, in his analysis of the recent elections of North Borneo and Sarawak, whether (a) the proposed Federation was a major issue, if not the major issue; (b) the electoral registers were properly compiled; (c) the elections were free and without coercion; (d) the votes were properly polled and counted; and (e) the opinion of those who could not vote in the recent elections because of their detention for political activities or absence from the territories would have made a difference. But this was not all. Secretary-General Thant had to make his findings "within the context" of a previous General Assembly resolution that provided, *inter alia,* that a non-self-governing territory integrating with an independent state should have attained an advanced stage of self-government with free political institutions. Finally, he had to use a method which, in his opinion, was "necessary to ensure complete compliance with the principle of self-determination". [54]

Thant accepted the task without authorization of any of the United Nations political organs, and did so just one month prior to the convening of the General Assembly. There was no Soviet opposition. He made it clear, however, that his acceptance was subject to British approval, which was forthcoming. Thant insisted that his decisions were to be final and binding, that his investigating teams were to be responsible only to him, and neither their reports nor his conclusions would be subject to ratification or confirmation by anyone. The three countries directly concerned agreed to share the costs of the mission.

The Secretary-General had thus publicly insisted upon a position of fact-finder and arbitrator, and without any backing from United Nations organs. This was somewhat risky, for if any of the parties refused to comply with what constituted his "award", his prestige would have suffered. It was the first time a Secretary-General had gone beyond simple mediation to the role of arbitrator, and within a context of strongly conflicting claims in which it was not at all clear that any of the parties were willing to lose. President Sukarno of Indonesia had threatened to "crush" Malaysia, and the feeling was widespread at the time that he would reject an unfavorable finding by Thant. Some UN diplomats felt, however, that Sukarno was willing to use the UN effort as a face-saving device to terminate his campaign for North Borneo and Sarawak.

The Secretary-General sent a nine-man team to the area, headed by Laurence V. Michelmore of the United States, at the time the Deputy

---

[53] See United Nations *Yearbook,* 1963, p. 41.
[54] *Ibid.*

Director of Personnel in the Secretariat. He was assisted by George V. Janecek of Czechoslovakia, an official in the Secretariat's Office of Public Information. The mission arrived in Sarawak on August 16, and remained there and in North Borneo until September 5. The work could not be completed before August 31, and the inauguration date for the Federation was pushed back to September 16.

By September 14, Thant's conclusions were made public.[55] He reported a "sizeable majority" of the inhabitants of North Borneo and Sarawak wished to join the Federation, and "while more time might have enabled the mission to obtain more copious documentation and other evidence, it would not have affected the conclusions to any significant extent". The work had been carried out by "consultations with the population, through the elected representatives of the people, leaders of political parties and other groups and organizations and with all persons who were willing to express their views". Thant asserted that every effort had been made to ascertain the views of those in detention or in exile for political reasons. He concluded that if all exiles and those in detention had been able to vote, there would have been no significant difference in the results. Thant agreed with the commission that meaningful acts of self-determination had been carried out, and that the territories had reached an advanced stage of self-government with free political institutions enabling the inhabitants to make a responsible choice.

It is difficult to evaluate the impact of the Secretary-General's report. It is possible that additional opposition to the western-oriented Federation did not develop in some part because of Thant's findings. Yet the report had seemingly very little effect upon Malaya and Britain. An announcement of the official decision to establish the Federation came on August 29, and on September 16, just two days after Thant's report, the Federation of Malaysia was officially inaugurated. The Secretary-General noted that some of the resentment of Indonesia and the Philippines might have been avoided had the official announcement come after his report.

At this point, and despite Sukarno's policy of "confrontation" that resulted in several armed clashes with Malaysia, the United Nations role came to an end. Indonesia, at least while Sukarno held power, never really accepted Thant's conclusions, and the Philippines still insists that it possesses sovereignty over Sabah (North Borneo). But Malaysia survived as a Federation that included Sabah and Sarawak, and remained allied with Great Britain.

Thant's role was valuable as an accomodation device for Indonesia, for if Sukarno was either unwilling or unable to crush Malaysia as he threatened, the Secretary-General's conclusions on self-determination served as a useful tool. And it would have been politically quite difficult for the Philippines or

[55] *United Nations Review,* Oct. 1963, pp. 14-15.

Malaya to resist the investigation. Arbitration is a role, however, that will only rarely be assigned to the Secretary-General. States are not often willing to lose international disputes, and when they are, in some few cases, disposed to risk loss, the issues are frequently narrow, susceptible of legal treatment, and submitted to the International Court. The Secretary-General will not frequently be called upon to decide the merits of a conflict between states.

Peacekeeping in Cyprus

The largest and most important peacekeeping force to have been established during Secretary-General Thant's administration is the United Nations Force in Cyprus (UNFICYP), a buffer between hostile Greek and Turkish Cypriots on the island, and to date a successful instrument for preventing external intervention by either Greece or Turkey.

The immediate cause of the increasing tension that erupted in violence in December, 1963 was the Cypriot Constitution of 1960, the year Cyprus gained its independence from Great Britain. The Constitution incorporates a number of agreements reached at Zurich in 1959 between Great Britain, Greece, Turkey and representatives of the Greek and Turkish Cypriots.[56] The 1959 agreements contain provisions designed essentially to protect the Turkish minority (20 percent of a total population of about 600,000) on Cyprus. There are precise ratios for Greeks and Turks in the Government, and perhaps most important internally, the President and Vice-President of the Republic (the former must be Greek and the latter Turkish) each have a veto over important governmental questions, including foreign relations. Further, interventionary rights are provided for, essentially to enforce Cyprus' pledges to ban the partition of Cyprus or union with any country. The latter was aimed at *enosis,* or union with Greece. Should breach of this obligation occur, Greece, Turkey and Great Britain are entitled "to take action with the sole aim of re-establishing the state of affairs" created by the Treaty of Guarantee of 1959. The interventionary privileges were strengthened by the right given to Greek and Turkish army contingents to remain in Cyprus and for Britain to maintain two sovereign base areas.

The trigger for violence was a set of proposed constitutional amendments put forward in November, 1963, by Archbishop Makarios, leader of the Greek Cypriots and President of Cyprus. Makarios had never been satisfied with the extraordinary constitutional arrangements, but accepted them in 1959 as part of the price for an independent Cyprus. Now a few years later, as head of a sovereign nation, Makarios felt strong enough to make a move toward what he perceived as more rational structures and processes of

[56] See *American Foreign Policy, Current Documents, 1959* (Washington: U.S. Government Printing Office, 1963), pp. 765-775.

Government. Most significant among the proposed changes were the elimination of the veto power of both the President and Vice-President, and the reduction of Turkish representation in the civil service, armed forces and police. The Turkish response was entirely predictable, and violence soon flared. The United Nations concern was based upon the built-in interventionary privileges of Britain, Greece, and Turkey, which presaged a significant threat to international peace. The first response of the three guarantor powers was to establish their own interpositionary force under British command, and while peace was being restored, Britain organized a conference in London in January, 1964 for purposes of arriving at a long-term political solution.

Makarios turned down Britain's proposals at the London Conference. He was not opposed to an international force, but wanted it responsible to the United Nations. The Archbishop also called for a clear statement of Cyprus' territorial integrity in order to cast doubt on the validity of the Treaty of Guarantee allowing for external intervention in Cyprus. He made little headway in London with these points, and the Security Council then became the focus for debate. Secretary-General Thant had in the meantime kept a close watch on the conflict and the negotiations. The UN was kept informed and ready precisely because it was feared that the London talks might fail. At the request of the parties, Thant sent Lieut. Gen. P. S.Gyani of India as United Nations observer of the ceasefire on Cyprus, and he dispatched José Rolz-Bennett to London to confer with the delegates there.

The Security Council debate of February-March, 1964 culminated in the establishment of still another international peacekeeping force, and once again, the Secretary-General was assigned important responsibilities. The Council, in a resolution unanimously adopted on March 4, 1964,[57] recommended the creation of a UN force in Cyprus, and left the composition, size and command of the force to Secretary-General Thant, in consultation with Cyprus, Greece, Turkey, and Great Britain. He was obligated to report to the Council on the operation of the force. The chronic financial crisis was reflected in a provision of the resolution stipulating payment of costs by countries providing contingents and by Cyprus. Thant was also authorized to accept voluntary contributions.

The issue of discretionary responsibilities for the Secretary-General was resolved without much difficulty, although the Soviet Union and France made their points, and compromises were evident in the final decisions. First, it was the Security Council that established the force, or at least issued the primary authorization for the Secretary-General to do so. Second, the order to Thant to report periodically to the Council was conceived as a method for indicating and assuring Council supremacy. Finally, while the Soviet Union and France voted for the resolution as a whole, those two states and Czecho-

---

[57] Security Council Res. 186, United Nations Doc. S/5575, 4 March 1964.

slovakia abstained from voting on the paragraph entrusting Thant to decide on the size, composition and command of the force. The French delegate complained that the Council was "divesting itself of responsibilities" and that it was "really going very far indeed in the direction of the delegation of powers to grant them in this way to a single individual".[58]

The Secretary-General went ahead quickly to establish UNFICYP. He indicated a force of some 7000 troops, based on Britain's offer to match contributions from other nations up to a total of 3500. He had difficulties in securing the necessary contingents, and certainly not the least part of his problem here was the financial issue. Assurances of contributions from Britain and the United States finally provided the necessary leverage, and UNFICYP was operational by March 27, 1964. In another month, the force was virtually complete, with troops from Austria, Canada, Finland, Ireland, Sweden, and the United Kingdom. This was the first time that great power troops were included in a UN peacekeeping force.

The negotiations carried out by Thant and his aides with possible contributors of military contingents were complex. Financial problems were evident, and it was incumbent upon the Secretary-General to explain the structure of the force, its functions and status, and probable duration of its stay in Cyprus. Some of these questions were unanswerable at the beginning, some had to await the completion of further agreements, and issues such as duration to this day have no more elucidation than in 1964. Thant was going through a process now familiar after the work of Dag Hammarskjold in establishing UNEF in the Middle East and ONUC in the Congo.

Even before negotiations for contingents had been completed, the Secretary-General appointed Gyani as Commander of the force. He also selected deputy chef de cabinet José Rolz-Bennett as mediator, but this choice being unacceptable to Turkey, the Secretary-General appointed Finland's Ambassador to Sweden, Sakari S. Tuomioja. Tuomioja served until August, 1964, when he was taken ill, and after his death in September, Galo Plaza, formerly President of Ecuador, assumed the post.

The Secretary-General, acting on behalf of the United Nations, concluded a "Status of Force Agreement" with Cyprus at the end of March by means of an exchange of letters with the Cypriot Foreign Minister.[59] Once again, the pattern of UNEF and ONUC was followed and relied upon rather heavily. The agreement, which constitutes an international treaty between the United Nations and Cyprus, covered problems such as the status of UNFICYP, criminal and civil jurisdiction, privileges and immunities of the force and its members, taxation and fiscal regulations, currency, supplies and services, settlement of claims and disputes, and many related matters.

---

[58] SCOR: (19th year), 1102nd mtg., 4 March 1964.
[59] United Nations Doc. S/5634, 31 March 1964.

Thant also published, on April 11, 1964, an *aide-mémoire* [60] setting out the primary functions of the force, and depicting in great detail the guiding principles essential for its functioning. This document, again following Hammarskjold's practice, established without challenge from member states the Secretary-General's interpretation of the role to be played by UNFICYP and the basic norms governing its behavior. UNFICYP's efforts were to be directed to prevention of violence, maintenance and restoration of law and order, and a return to normal conditions. But this was to be accomplished without influence over Cypriot politics. The familar principle of non-intervention in domestic affairs was stressed much as it had been in the Congo. The Secretary-General underlined his responsibility for establishing the force and for its direction. The Soviet Union could not have agreed with his formulation; but Moscow did not publicly object. UNFICYP was under exclusive UN control and command, and the Secretary-General was in turn responsible to the Security Council for its conduct. Further, UNFICYP would act with force only in self-defense, and the concept of self-defense was given the most detailed definition and analysis in the history of UN peacekeeping forces.

The Status of Force Agreement and the *aide-mémoire* setting forth basic guiding principles for UNFICYP were essential constitutional documents, but at the end of April, 1964, Thant went further by publishing a "conprehensive programme of action" for UNFICYP.[61] He offered detailed prescriptions for objectives designed to implement its mandate, including freedom of movement throughout Cyprus for all communities, removal of fortified positions, negotiations of measures for the reintegration of the police, disarming of civilians, the formulation of amnesty arrangements, security measures, and the return of Turkish Cypriots to their civil service posts. The Secretary-General, in looking forward to a general resumption of governmental services, also recommended the use of UNFICYP good offices to improve unacceptable living conditions, particularly through resumption of essential public utilities. He stopped just short of suggesting UNFICYP's use as a mechanism of government.

UNFICYP has been generally succesful over the past several years, both in military and non-military undertakings, but the underlying political and social conflict between Greeks and Turks on Cyprus persists, and the United Nations has not been able to assist in achieving a political settlement. A succession of mediators and personal representatives, and several extensions of UNFICYP's original three-month mandate have maintained the UN's position as a buffer, but little more. Much of the Secretary-General's effort since 1964 has consisted of appeals for financial contributions and for further extensions of UNFICYP's mandate. Reports issued to the Council,

[60] United Nations Doc. S/5653, 11 April 1964.
[61] United Nations Doc. S/5671, 29 April 1964, Annex 1, pp. 1-3.

and appeals for calm and restraint after outbreaks of fighting have also been frequent exercises for Thant.

The conflict on the embattled island remains enormously complex. The Turks have withdrawn into armed enclaves, the largest of which is in, and to the north of, the capital city of Nicosia. Officially they are still demanding "taksim", or partition, just as "enosis", or union with Greece is still the official Greek Cypriot position. Both are forbidden by the 1960 Constitution. The Greek Cypriots could easily force their will on the Turks on Cyprus, but Turkey, which is far stronger militarily than Greece, is just adjacent to the island, and is capable of supporting the Turks there. The situation is complicated by Soviet and United States foreign policy interests. Washington is very much interested in a settlement between its NATO allies, and particularly since the Soviet Union has moved into the eastern Mediterranean following the June, 1967 war between Israel and the Arab states. There are also the British bases on Cyprus to consider, for since Britain's withdrawal from Aden, these are the last large Western bases in the eastern Mediterranean.

Pending settlement of the conflict, the United Nations has been able to maintain an uneasy quiet on Cyprus. Perhaps the most serious outbreak and threat of full-scale war between Greece and Turkey came in the autumn of 1967. This was triggered by a heavy Cypriot Government attack against two villages where Turkish Cypriots had fired on two policemen patrolling the area. Turkey was prepared to intervene, and a massive diplomatic effort was mounted. President Johnson sent Cyprus R. Vance, a former deputy Secretary of Defense, to the area; Thant dispatched Rolz-Bennett, and even Mario Brosio, NATO's Secretary-General, tried his hand at peacemaking. The outcome was a temporary settlement of the immediate dispute, but without a long-range solution.

Secretary-General Thant, in November and December, 1967, issued three separate appeals for restraint, and made known his plan for the eventual withdrawal of all non-Cypriot armed forces other than UNFICYP, as a step towards demilitarization of Cyprus. He also called for a broadening of UNFICYP's mandate, a step subject to Security Council action, and offered his good offices to the parties and to the Council. The Council supported the Secretary-General but a new series of negotiations produced few results. An agreement at the end of 1967, worked out essentially by Cyrus Vance, called for an end to threats, a reference to the already agreed upon dismantling of Turkey's invasion force, and for the withdrawal of Greek and Turkish troops illegally infiltrated into Cyprus. No mention was made of Turkey's demand for the disbanding of the Greek Cypriot National Guard. UNFICYP itself, having been gradually reduced to 4500 troops over the past few years, has not been enlarged, nor has its mandate been broadened. The Secretary-General has tried to assist in settling the basic conflict, but even his authority in that context has been subject to question. Greece and

Cyprus want him to work toward a general settlement, while Turkey has preferred that his efforts be limited to easing immediate tensions stemming from the 1967 outbreak.

Thant has not been able to establish a significant role for the Office in the larger conflict. He has performed the functions of chief administrator of UNFICYP, and his appeals for peace during intermittent periods of violence have been convenient to the parties, particularly in 1967. But the fundamental problem appears intractable. The United States has sent some of its ablest diplomats to the area, but for experienced negotiators such as Dean Acheson, George Ball, and Cyrus Vance, the Cyprus tangle has proved too much. Thant's quiet mediation efforts and his attempts at providing good offices to the parties have borne little fruit. His effective leadership in securing an early United Nations intervention in Cyprus has substantially decreased the likelihood of external intercession, and in that sense, the Organization and its Secretary-General have played an important role in the maintenance of peace in the area.

The Kashmir Question

The disputed area of Kashmir, a largely Moslem territory some two-thirds of which is ruled by India and the remainder by Pakistan, has been one of the hardy perennials before the United Nations. The issue has been discussed by the world organization since India achieved her independence from Great Britain and the subcontinent was divided largely along communal lines between India and Pakistan. At the time of the partition in 1947, both nations claimed the 84,000 square miles of Kashmir. Pakistan's claim was based primarily upon the preponderance of Moslems in Kashmir; India's more legalistic argument was that Kashmir's Hindu Maharajah had, through a letter of succession, made his state part of India. In the armed conflict that followed, India maintained her grip over some two-thirds of the territory, and integrated it into the Indian Union. Pakistan has been calling for a plebiscite ever since, but without result. In 1949, the United Nations established a ceasefire line, patrolled by the United Nations Military Observation Group in India and Pakistan (UNMOGIP) and appointed a representative, Dr. Frank Graham of the United States, to try to work out a long-range agreement. To date, the situation remains essentially unchanged —each side controls the same portion of the area, there is still a ceasefire line, and no political settlement is likely.

The renewal of fighting in August, 1965 in Kashmir, triggered by the infiltration of armed Pakistanis in civilian clothing cross the ceasefire line, brought undeclared war to the subcontinent. It was a war none of the great powers wished to see spread, and as the external military assistance to both sides terminated, the fighting ground to a halt. Military exhaustion, rather than a will to peace, was the salient factor.

The United Nations role revolved around the Security Council (which was forced to pass five resolutions demanding a halt to the fighting), the Secretary-General, and UN observers in the area. Thant issued several appeals of his own, and was requested by the Council, in a resolution of September 6, 1965,[62] to exert every possible effort to give effect to the Council's call for a ceasefire, and to take all measures possible to strengthen UNMOGIP. Thant's reports to the Council, based on information supplied to him by Lieutenant-General Robert H. Nimmo of Australia, the head of UNMOGIP, were invaluable sources of data for the Council.

The Secretary-General left on September 7 for a nine-day visit to the subcontinent and talks with Prime Minister Lal Bahadur Shastri of India, President Ayub Khan of Pakistan, and other top government officials of the two nations. This indicated Thant's sense of urgency on the matter, as did the fact that a few days before, he became the first Secretary-General in the seventeen years of debate on Kashmir to present a personal report thereon to the Council. Thant was not very successful in his mission. India agreed to a ceasefire, but only after Pakistan withdrew its armed infiltrators, and of course, India was resolved to maintain its sovereignty over Kashmir. Pakistan also agreed to a ceasefire, but only if it included a self-executing arrangement leading to a final settlement of the Kashmir issue. This meant a UN sponsored Afro-Asian force to maintain order in the area, and a plebiscite within three months. Thant could only report that each side had attached conditions rendering a ceasefire impossible.

On September 17, the Secretary-General submitted an oral report to the Council in which he recommended action under Chapter VII of the United Nations Charter. He suggested an order for a ceasefire under the provisional measures clause of Article 40, with a failure to comply to be regarded by the Council as a breach of the peace within the meaning of Article 39. This is the prerequisite for Council-imposed sanctions, and it was clearly economic sanctions the Secretary-General had in mind. This was probably put forward at the suggestion of the United States, following a Senate speech recommending sanctions by Senate majority leader Mansfield of Montana.[63] Thant also recommended a meeting between Shastri and Khan, and reported on measures being taken to strengthen the military observer group in the area. The Council, on September 20, adopted a resolution demanding a ceasefire (although no mention of sanctions or

[62] Security Council Res. 210, United Nations Doc. S/6662. 6 September 1965.
[63] See *The New York Times,* 10 September 1965, pp. 1, 4; 18-19 September (International Edition), pp. 1, 3. The United States wanted a quick end to the fighting, and was prepared to threaten and apply sanctions for that purpose, but not alone. Working through the Security Council would help commit the Soviet Union to the same course, and thereby avert possible damage to Western interests in India or Pakistan.

Chapter VII of the Charter was made) and requested Thant to provide the necessary assistance to ensure supervision.[64] By September 22, a ceasefire was agreed to, but violations persisted, and even after both sides had little military strength left for protracted conflict, armed battles continued in Kashmir until early January, 1966.

The next step for the Secretary-General was to send more military observers to the area. He increased UNMOGIP's strength from 45 to 102 and provided 90 observers for a new mission to be known as the United Nations India-Pakistan Observation Mission (UNIPOM). Whereas the first group would continue to operate along the original ceasefire line in Kashmir, the second mission was to work in areas outside Kashmir where fighting had occurred. Funding came from Thant's emergency sum of up to $ 2 million per year authorized by the General Assembly for unforeseen peacekeeping expenses. Major-General B. F. MacDonald of Canada was appointed Chief Officer of UNIPOM.

It took the Soviet Union over a month to protest publicly Thant's work in organizing a new observer mission, but the attack was sharp when it finally came:

The Soviet delegation considers it necessary to draw the Council's attention to the fact that the action taken by the Secretary-General with regard to the United Nations observers in India and Pakistan...is at variance with the provisions of the Charter, under which only the Security Council is competent to take the necessary decisions on all specific matters connected with United Nations observers, namely, their functions, number, command, the financing of their activities and so on. Meanwhile, all these questions were being settled outside the Security Council, whose members are merely informed about measures that have already been taken. This situation is, of course, abnormal and, as we have noted, at variance with the Charter.[65]

The Soviets also complained that the comand posts were "being assigned mainly to senior NATO officers". Britain and the United States gave strong support to the Secretary-General, but France backed the Soviet position. Moscow did not object to more observers *per se,* nor to their work in the area of conflict; but the Soviets could not accept the principle of UN missions established, commanded, and financed by the Secretary-General.

More observers, however, did not halt the fighting. At the suggestion of the Secretary-General, and agreed to in principle by India and Pakistan, the Council, in a resolution of November 5, 1965, demanded that each country send envoys to meet with Thant's representatives in order to formulate a plan and schedule for troop withdrawal.[66] On November 25, Thant selected Brigadier-General Tulio Marambio of Chile as his representative. At the end of the year, negotiations were still in progress, but ceasefire violations persisted at many points.

[64] Security Council Res. 211, United Nations Doc. S/6694, 20 September 1965.
[65] SCOR: (20th year), 1247th mtg., 28 Oct. 1965.
[66] Security Council Res. 215, United Nations Doc. S/6876, 5 November 1965.

The formal indication of both sides' willingness to end the fighting, if not the overall dispute regarding Kashmir, came on January 10, 1966, when India and Pakistan signed what is known as the Tashkent Declaration. After a series of meeting at Tashkent, in the Soviet Union, the two nations agreed to restore peaceful relations and to withdraw their armed personnel to positions held before the fighting began in August, 1965. The Declaration signalled the end of the latest phase of the Kashmir dispute, and while it was not intended to imply final settlement of the Kashmir question, it was generally regarded as an important diplomatic achievement for Premier Aleksei N. Kosygin of the Soviet Union.[67] It was the Soviet Union's first attempt to end a conflict between non-Communist countries.

From this point forward, troop withdrawals went smoothly, as Marambio and both India's and Pakistan's military leaders agreed in late Janauary on a plan and schedule of withdrawal which was carried out by the agreed deadline of February 25. The Secretary-General disbanded UNIPOM in March, 1966, and reduced UNMOGIP to some 50 observers along the original ceasefire line. The Parties were back where they started in August, 1965.

If military exhaustion was the key factor in terminating hostilities, most of the diplomatic effort involved in the world community's response was through the United Nations, entailing an important role for the Secretary-General. Thant acted as spokesman for the Organization, and at the same time, was able to negotiate almost on behalf of the great powers. He had their support for his several appeals to the parties, and during the mission to India and Pakistan. His representatives and observer missions in the area were, of course, able to provide disinterested information, and the core of the administrative mechanism essential to the success of the final withdrawal agreements. Perhaps most important, given the backing of the superpowers, and his built-in advantage as a third party neutral in close contact with the contestants, Thant was able to recommend to the great powers what United Nations policy should be, and most often, his suggestions were accepted. The Secretary-General functioned as an effective policy-maker in the Kashmir case, in addition to his more routine tasks of fact-finding.

Thant's executive capacities were not enlarged by the crisis, as his action in strengthening the observation mission in the area was based on many precedents and was on a small scale. While his activity involved interpretation of Security Council resolutions, he had little leeway beyond dispatching more observers, although even here the Soviet Union and France entered the familiar objection that the Secretary-General had exceeded his mandate. The complaint was for the record, as the Council backed his work as executive agent for the world community's diplomatic effort to restore peace to the Indian subcontinent.

[67] See *The New York Times,* 11 January 1966, p. 1.

Secretary-General Thant's Re-election

As the year 1966 opened, the last year of the Secretary-General's five-year term, Thant began to cast doubt on his availability for reappointment. The years since Hammarskjold's death had not fulfilled expectations for the United Nations or the Secretary-General. The membership was divided on critical issues of responsibility for peacekeeping forces and their financing, and on the problem of the discretionary authority and responsibilities of the Secretary-General. These reduced, in the final analysis, to the willingness of member states to be bound by collective community decisions with which they sometimes disagreed. The long and agonizing financial crisis was a reflection of the dislike of nations, particularly the Soviet Union and France, for international institutions that tended to inhibit in any meaningful way their ability to influence the course of world politics. Secretary-General Thant had carried the main burden of this attitude, as his powers were frequently restricted, or hedged in whenever possible. He could make no attempts to widen the authority of the Office, and indeed, was unable to maintain its powers at the point at which Hammarskjold had left it. He could develop no theory of the Secretary-General's role, as his predecessor had done. Thant was also unhappy over the painfully slow growth of the UN's economic development programs, the slow pace of progress in disarmament, and the failure to achieve universality of membership.

The gravest of the political problems confronting the Organization was the war in Vietnam, a war in which the UN played no part. Indeed, the world body's entire effort to influence the course of events in Southeast Asia centered on the Secretary-General, whose continuous endeavors failed to stem the relentless intensification of the combat. Vietnam overshadowed the UN's successful efforts in the many cases of conflict with which Thant had dealt, and was the central factor in his apparent decision to resign.

There were personal reasons as well. His wife was not particularly happy in New York City, and this added significantly to the increasing burdens. Ties to his native Burma had also to be considered, although prospects for important governmental work there appeared rather dim, given the ouster of his close friend and associate, U Nu.

Yet the Secretary-General had many successes to his credit. The Congo crisis was past, and while the government there remained unstable, there was no longer the same threat of external intervention and war. The Cuban missile crisis was peacefully resolved, even given the marginal role of the United Nations. West New Guinea had been transferred to Indonesia without extensive conflict, and the Malaysian Federation launched with the assistance of Thant's arbitration efforts. In Yemen, the Secretary-General had failed, and in Cyprus, the peace was tenuous, but the UN could count the Kashmir settlement on the credit side of the ledger. Perhaps most important, Thant had been able to maintain good relationships with both the

United States and the Soviet Union, and had calmed, if not eliminated much of the controversy over the Office of the Secretary-General. Disagreement concerning independent powers persisted, of course, but no longer did the Soviets threaten to destroy the Office by replacing it with a "trioka" arrangement.

The Secretary-General continually delayed his final decision, all the while issuing stronger statements of his impending retirement, but leaving the door always ajar. He first proposed June, 1966 as a suitable time for decision, then September 1st. He gave the impression of being sincerely anxious to resign, but unable to withstand the intense pressure to remain from almost the entire UN membership. "My feeling is", he declared, "that nobody should aspire to be Secretary-General of the United Nations for more than one term. Knowing the functions of the office as I do, I think it is a very killing job, if I may say so, and from time to time it is a very frustrating job".[68]

There was no question of general support. His trips to Europe, Latin America and the Soviet Union in the summer of 1966 resulted in renewed expressions of almost universal backing. Declarations and appeals came from many quarters, including the twenty-three nation Western European group in the General Assembly, and the 61 member African-Asian bloc. In August, 177 United States Congressmen signed a telegram asking Thant to stay on for five more years.

On September 1, Thant issued what was generally taken as a statement of resignation:

It is my belief, as I have said more than once in the past, that a Secretary-General of the United Nations should not normally serve for more than one term. I have similarly made it known that I do not believe in the concept of indispensability of any particular person for any particular job. In the circumstances the conclusion I have reached will, I hope, be understood by all my friends and colleagues: I have decided not to offer myself for a second term as Secretary-General, and to leave the Security Council unfettered in its recommendation to the General Assembly with regard to the next Secretary-General.[69]

Thant's term was to end on November 3, and his statement, which stressed Vietnam and the other reasons mentioned above for his dissatisfaction at the UN, thus gave the Council two months to find a successor. It also left open the possibility of a draft, and the result was merely to increase the pressure to stay on. A widely held view was that by coupling an emphasis on the war in Vietnam with a resignation statement that did not bar a draft, the Secretary-General was using what leverage he had to get concessions from the great powers on Vietnam, or increased authority as Secretary-General, or both. Intended or not, Thant was setting a price for remaining at his post.

The Secretary-General urged the Security Council to find a successor,

---

[68] Quoted in *The New York Times,* 30 April 1966, p. 1.
[69] United Nations Press Release SG/SM/557, 1 Sept. 1966, p. 4.

but declared his willingness, on September 19, to continue in office until the end of the General Assembly's twenty-first session, scheduled for December 20. The price-tag for re-election cropped up again, as Thant complained that he

found it increasingly difficult to function as Secretary-General in the manner in which I wish to function, and secondly, I do not subscribe to the view that the Secretary-General should be just a chief administrative officer, or, in other words, that the Secretary-General should be a glorified clerk.[70]

There was never a serious search for a successor. The diplomatic effort was directed to persuading Thant to remain, and it was soon rewarded by signs that the Secretary-General had indeed reconsidered. On November 1, the General Assembly endorsed a Security Council recommendation extending his term to the end of the twenty-first session. In a brief statement, Thant referred to his "final decision" as coming sometime in the future, indicating that the September 1st "resignation" had not been his final word on the matter.

On December 2, 1966, the General Assembly unanimously elected Thant to a second term as Secretary-General after receiving an unchallenged recommendation by the Security Council. The term was set to expire on December 31, 1971. It is not known what understandings, if any, were reached concerning the Secretary-General's role, peacekeeping activities, or the financial crisis, but the Council appeared to agree on a wider and more positive role for the UN's chief executive. In a statement issued on December 2, the Council declared that its members

fully respect his position and his action in bringing basic issues confronting the organization and disturbing developments in many parts of the world to their notice, as he has done in his statement of 1 September 1966, to which they accord their closest attention.[71]

It has never been clear precisely what this statement was intended to accomplish. The Secretary-General already has the right, under Article 99 of the Charter, to bring to the attention of the Council any matter which in his opinion may threaten the maintenance of international peace and security. Thant presumably now has the same right when, in his view, there are "basic issues confronting the organization" or "disturbing developments". A Council discussion on such matters is not, of course, guaranteed. To this day, there has been no Council debate on the war in Vietnam. The statement on its face would appear to do little in terms of enhancing the Secretary-General's role, and indeed, his powers and activities have remained very much what they were prior to the re-election.

Thant himself appeared sensitive to this, for his acceptance speech to the General Assembly indicated little had changed: "I would like to make

[70] United Nations Press Release SG/SM/567, 19 Sept. 1966, p. 4.
[71] SCOR: (21st year), 1329th mtg., 2 Dec. 1966.

it clear that my present decision is not based on any new element which has developed in recent weeks or on any fond hope for the forseeable future".[72] He noted with appreciation the Council's statement, but declared that the problems outlined in his September 1st statement were still his primary concerns. He had decided to serve another term as he felt compelled to accept the overwhelming weight of opinion that his continuance as Secretary-General "would best serve the higher interests of the organization".[73]

The members of the organized international community had pressed Thant to accept a second term because he had succeeded in maintaining something akin to universal confidence. The United Nations was confronted with sufficient divisive issues without the additional and it appeared unnecessary burden of reaching agreement on a new and lesser known chief executive. The price paid, in the form of a Council statement implying greater freedom of action for the Secretary-General, appeared to be minimal at the time, and in fact has been of little significance. Yet the great outpouring of respect and the homage paid to Thant from nearly every quarter could not help but augment the prestige of his Office. From the days of the "troika" plan and the near destruction of the Office just five years before, to a unanimous Council and Assembly pleading with Thant to remain at the head of the Secretariat was a remarkable distance. For Thant it was a personal honor and tribute; for the Office of Secretary-General it was an essential path toward the reconstruction of an effective role in world politics for the UN's chief executive.

The Arab-Israeli War and the Withdrawal of UNEF: 1967

Perhaps the most stunning reverse for the UN's peacekeeping role and capacities, and a failure that generated more adverse criticism of Secretary-General Thant than ever before, was the rapid withdrawal of the United Nations Emergency Force from the Middle East in May, 1967, and the week-long "June War" between Israel and its Arab neighbors. The renewal of violent conflict and the impotence of the Organization demonstrated strikingly the fragile nature of UN peace-keeping forces, the necessity of greater international effort at peace-making as well as peace-keeping, and the need to clarify relationships between UN missions, the host state, the political organs of the UN, and the Secretary-General.

While UNEF had done well since 1956 in keeping the peace between Israel and the United Arab Republic, the small mission was being speedily outflanked by a growing rivalry between the UAR and Syria for leadership of the more militant Arab countries. Increasingly frequent raids by members

---

[72] United Nations Press Release SG/SM/619, GA/3290, 2 Dec. 1966, p. 2.
[73] *Id.,* p. 1.

of the Syria-backed Al Fatah organization, carried out from the territories of Syria and Jordan, prompted Israel to respond with greater force against both countries. President Nasser was accused, particularly by Syria, of hiding behind UNEF while the brunt of military activity was carried by others. And the burden of attack as well, for in November, 1966, Israel mounted a massive raid against Jordanian villages, and in early April, 1967, bombarded Syrian positions in the demilitarized zone south of the Sea of Galilee.

There were further incidents in April 1967, involving Israel and Syria, and on May 11, Israeli Prime Minister Levi Eshkol declared that Israel viewed the Syrian Government as responsible for the raids. Statements from several quarters in the Israeli Government were harsh, and on May 13, Eshkol declared that Israel did "not recognize the limitations [the Syrians] endeavor to impose upon our acts of response".[74] This was never intended as a threat of massive invasion, but Syria charged just that. The UAR declared its intelligence reports indicated that Israel was planning to invade Syria in three days, and Nasser placed his armed forces in a state of readiness and began to move them across the Sinai Peninsula toward Israel. The UN Truce Supervision Organization found no evidence that Israeli troops were massing for attack,[75] nor could newsmen at the scene find any, but tensions mounted as the Arabs and Israelis prepared for war.

The beginning of UNEF's collapse, and of Secretary-General Thant's much criticized role therein, came on May 16, 1967, when General Mohamed Fawzi, the UAR's Chief of Staff, requested UNEF's Commander Indar Jit Rikhye of India, to withdraw "all UN troops which install OP's [observation posts] along our borders".[76] The original intent of the UAR apparently was to move UNEF away from certain strategic positions to be occupied by Egyptian forces. Fawzi was asking the UN to move over—not to leave altogether. Rikhye cabled the request back to Thant in New York, and the Secretary-General called in the UAR's permanent representative to the UN, Mohamed Awad El Kony, for clarification. El Kony knew nothing of the matter, and Thant requested the Ambassador to communicate with Cairo, and to transmit the Secretary-General's own views on the question. Thant's position, reported to Cairo by El Kony, was that UNEF could not be asked "to stand aside in order to enable the two sides to resume fighting". However the UAR was entitled to withdraw the consent it gave in 1956 for the

[74] Quoted in Theodore Draper, "Israel and World Politics", *Commentary*, August 1967 (Vol. 44, No. 2), p. 31.
[75] Secretary-General Thant, in a report dated 19 May 1967, stated that "Reports from UNTSO Observers have confirmed the absence of troop concentrations and significant troop movements on both sides of the [Syrian] line". United Nations Doc. S/7896, 19 May 1967, p. 2. For a convenient collection of the relevant United Nations documents covering the withdrawal of UNEF and the June, 1967 war in the Middle East, see *International Legal Materials*, May-June 1967 (Vol. VI, No. 3) pp. 557-642.
[76] United Nations Doc. A/6730/Add. 3, 26 June 1967, p. 3.

stationing of UNEF in its territory, and "on receipt of such a request, the Secretary-General would order the withdrawal of all UNEF troops from Gaza and Sinai, simultaneously informing the General Assembly of what he was doing and why".[77] Thant then instructed Rikhye to maintain all UNEF positions pending further instructions. The Secretary-General had, perhaps prematurely, in terms of retaining UN influence in the conflict, assured President Nasser that UNEF would be withdrawn for the asking—there would be no delay, no debate or discussion, and no referral to political bodies. The UN would leave "on receipt of such a request".

On May 17, UAR troops began to take over the UN positions without final word from Cairo to New York, and Thant protested later that day that UNEF could not remain in the field under such conditions. He declared that if the orders to the UAR troops were maintained, he would "have no choice but to order the withdrawal of UNEF from Gaza and Sinai as expeditiously as possible".[78] UNEF troops already found themselves behind UAR units in several areas.

On the afternoon of May 17, Thant met with representatives of the countries that contributed troops to UNEF—Brazil, Canada, Denmark, India, Norway, Sweden, and Yugoslavia. He had already learned that India and Yugoslavia intended to withdraw their troops from UNEF no matter what the UN's position should be if Nasser so requested. Brazil and Canada, it was reported, urged Thant to discuss the matter with Nasser before Cairo made a final demand for UNEF's recall. Apparently, however, El Kony informed Thant after the meeting that any such approach to Nasser by Thant would be viewed as a hostile act in Cairo, and no discussions were held before the UAR's final withdrawal message was received.

The formal request to the Secretary-General for a total withdrawal of UNEF was communicated from Cairo on May 18. It stipulated that the withdrawal be accomplished "as soon as possible",[79] but Thant perceived no advantage in that phrase. He convened the UNEF Advisory Committee and informed the members he had no choice in the matter—UNEF had to be withdrawn. Despite some disagreement in the Committee, no General Assembly meeting was demanded, and Thant informed El Kony that UNEF would depart without delay. The Secretary-General's official reply to Cairo stated his misgivings as well, but his fears for peace in the area were stated after he complied with Cairo's demand, and could not be utilized in negotiation aimed at maintaining UNEF's position.

Four days later, on May 22, Thant left New York for consultations with President Nasser, but it seemed apparent that the Secretary-General had just relinquished his most significant source of influence in the Middle East, and that his negotiating hand would be weak. This was confirmed when it

[77] United Nations Doc. A/6669, 18 May 1967, pp. 4, 5.
[78] *Id.*, p. 6.
[79] *Id.*, p. 1.

was announced by Cairo, while the Secretary-General was still en route to the UAR, that President Nasser had decided to reinstitute the blockade against Israel in the Straits of Tiran. Thant cut short his visit as it became obvious that discussions designed to avoid hostilities were fruitless, as were any attempts to persuade President Nasser to lift the blockade. President Johnson's public statement at the time that Thant had been requested by Washington to appeal to Nasser on the blockade issue evidently rendered it politically impossible for the UAR President to back down, even had he wished to do so.

The United States tried to gather support for a declaration and perhaps international action to open the Gulf of Aqaba. Most maritime powers agreed that Israel should have shipping rights in what they regarded as an international waterway, but they refused to test the UAR's blockade, and war seemed unavoidable. On May 30, the Jordanian army was placed under the command of a UAR general, and on June 1, a new government in Israel promoted the 1956 Sinai campaign hero, Moshe Dayan, to the post of Minister of Defense.

War came to the Middle East on June 5, 1967 as Israel attacked several airfields in the surrounding Arab countries, destroying most of the Arab aircraft on the ground, thereby achieving aerial supremacy for the duration of the week-long conflict. By June 12, Israel's armies had captured all of Jerusalem and the entire West Bank of the Jordan River, taken Sharm el-Sheikh, thus breaking the blockade of Aqaba, and taken control of the Gaza Strip, the entire Sinai peninsula, and the Golan Heights in Syria. The rout of the UAR, Jordan, and Syria was complete and swift, and for the United Nations there was no role save repeated demands by the Security Council for a ceasefire. Beyond that point of agreement, the Soviet Union and United States were not prepared to cooperate on a settlement, as in 1956, with the result that the UN's deliberative organs had extreme difficulty in formulating even an initial response.

While Secretary-General Thant was successful in sending UNTSO observers to the Suez Canal dividing line between UAR and Israeli forces (and did so without Council authorization, notwithstanding the Soviet Union's preferences), the Council and Assembly could reach no agreement on a Middle East resolution. The central issue was whether Israel should withdraw her forces prior to a settlement of outstanding issues, or whether withdrawal and settlement should be linked. There were majorities for both approaches, but not the required two-thirds, and the Assembly's emergency session in July had to content itself with resolutions declaring Israel's unification of Jerusalem illegal and calling for humanitarian assistance in the area.[80]

[80] General Assembly Res. A/RES/2254 (ES-V), 14 July 1967; A/RES/2256 (ES-V), 21 July 1967.

Not until November 22, 1967, was the Council able to pass a substantive resolution,[81] one based on a British draft. It called for withdrawal of Israeli armed forces, termination of belligerency, and acknowledgement of the sovereignty, territorial integrity and political independence of every State in the area, and their right to live in peace within secure and recognized boundaries free from threats of force. This appeared to link withdrawal with political settlement by the Arabs, although which comes first is still subject to debate. The Council cited the necessity for freedom of navigation through international waterways, a just settlement of the refugee problem, and guarantees of independence by such measures as demilitarized zones. Finally, the Council requested the Secretary-General to designate a Special Representative for the area to establish contacts and assist in achieving a peaceful settlement. On November 23, Thant appointed Gunnar Jarring, the Swedish Ambassador to the Soviet Union, as his Special Representative.

In the period since the June war, there has been a progressively increasing number of violent outbreaks along the Suez Canal and in the West Bank area, as well as terrorist incidents in Israel. But Israeli military forces have maintained a firm grip on the captured areas, and given Jerusalem's demand for direct negotiations, which the Arab states refuse to grant, the likelihood for peaceful settlement is dim indeed. Ambassador Jarring's efforts have been entirely futile to date, while Big Four and Big Two attempts throughout 1969 to reach a common ground have been equally unavailing. In a special report to the Security Council in early July, 1969, Secretary-General Thant warned that "open warfare" had been resumed along the Suez Canal area. Egyptian artillery firings had increased in frequency and intensity, prompting Israeli reprisals, including bombing of selected military targets deep inside the UAR. Similar reprisals were directed against Jordan. As the year ended, there was no prospect of meaningful negotiations looking toward a political settlement.

For the Secretary-General, the critical period of involvement was, of course, the few days in May, 1967 just prior to UNEF's withdrawal. There are three salient issues: first, was Thant authorized to withdraw UNEF on his own initiative without authorization from a UN political organ; second, assuming such authority, was he wise in acceding so quickly to Cairo's demand; and third, what are the implications for the Secretary-General's role in peacekeeping operations.

The question of the Secretary-General's initiative in withdrawing UNEF produced a curious reversal in the now traditional positions assumed by the United States and Soviet Union. For the United States, a strong exponent of an independent role, was critical of Thant for not seeking advice from a more representative political body than the UNEF Advisory Committee. The Soviet Union and France, on the other hand, long opposed to inde-

81 Security Council Res. 242, 22 November 1967.

pendent initiatives by the Secretary-General, said not a word in protest as he withdrew UNEF.

More narrowly, the question arises of the original terms negotiated by Dag Hammarskjold in 1956 with President Nasser for the entry of UNEF into Egypt. UNEF's establishment by the Secretary-General on recommendation of the General Assembly necessarily implied, since Chapter VII of the Charter was not applicable, that the consent of the host state was required for its presence. Hammarskjold naturally was anxious lest consent be withdrawn before UNEF's tasks had been completed. Egypt had pledged itself to be guided "in good faith", when exercising its sovereign rights on any matter concerning UNEF, by its acceptance of the Assembly resolutions defining UNEF's tasks. But Hammarskjold wanted more.

The Secretary-General had a series of talks on the matter in November, 1956, with Fawzi and Nasser, and subsequently drafted an *aide-mémoire* of his understanding of the agreements reached. The memorandum was never made an official document or published in any form until June, 1967.[82] Hammarskjold had given a copy of the memorandum to his private attorney in New York, Ernest A. Gross, who had the document published just after Thant withdrew UNEF. Given its significance it is somewhat mysterious why Hammarskjold chose not to reveal the content of the memorandum nor to refer to it in any manner in his reports on UNEF.

The main thrust of Hammarskjold's interpretation of his talks in Cairo, as set out in his private memorandum, was that Egypt would not request withdrawal of UNEF until its tasks had been completed; if there were a question as to whether the tasks had been completed, the issue would go to the General Assembly for public discussion and attempt to reach agreement. In the final analysis, the host state's wish would be controlling. But according to Hammarskjold, Egypt had agreed to submit the matter to public discussion, and to try to reach agreement on the question of completion of tasks.

Secretary-General Thant did not, of course, refer the issue of completion of tasks to the Assembly in 1967, nor did he allude to Hammarskjold's *aide-mémoire*. Indeed, there is some question whether he had heard of it prior to its publication after UNEF's withdrawal. In any event, Thant did not perceive that Hammarskjold's private memorandum necessitated any restraint upon his independent authority to withdraw UNEF at the UAR's request. He asserted that it was not an official document and that the UAR Government "knew nothing about it and was in no way bound by it".[83] Further, the UNEF Advisory Committee had not called for an Assembly meeting on the issue, although it was entitled to do so. Thant stressed the legal necessity of consent to peacekeeping operations by the host state and he argued

[82] See *International Legal Materials, op. cit.,* pp. 595-602. The memorandum was also published in *The New York Times* on June 19, 1967, p. 12.
[83] Quoted in *The New York Times,* 20 June 1967, p. 19.

further that the tasks assigned to UNEF were greatly broadened in early 1957, well after Hammarskjold's talks with Nasser. In November 1956 the task of UNEF was "to secure and supervise the cessation of hostilities". In 1957 the Assembly widened the task by calling on UNEF to oversee the "scrupulous maintenance of the armistice agreement". According to Thant, Hammarskjold did not have the 1957 tasks in mind when he negotiated the "good faith" accord with Nasser.

Thant's legal argument rests on both the invalidity of the private memorandum, and on its inapplicability. He assumes, in defense of himself, that without the restraints imposed by the wording of the memorandum, he was perfectly free to withdraw the force on his own authority. Assuming the legal propriety of Thant's move, there is a question of the political and strategic wisdom of prompt compliance with Cairo's request. It has been argued that at least some delay and discussion of the matter might have induced greater rationality and thus helped to avoid the war. The Secretary-General replied that delay could not have changed the result. Cairo had warned him prior to withdrawal that appeals for UNEF's remaining would be taken as a hostile act. In addition, with India and Yugoslavia determined to withdraw their contingents regardless of Thant's actions, UNEF might well have collapsed by itself. Further, the Secretary-General argued that since Israel refused to take the UNEF contingents on her side of the line, and with Egyptian troops already having destroyed UNEF's effectiveness, delay might well have endangered the safety of the UN forces. In any event, once the UAR decided UNEF had to leave, there was no practical task the force could accomplish—it was now valueless, and delay in ordering retreat would have accomplished nothing.

It was unfortunate that the Secretary-General's action should have put him in a defensive position. Particularly in the West, Thant's role was viewed as vulnerable to attack, and the several reports issued by his Office explaining and defending the action were taken as further evidence of the weakness of his position. At the least, the episode was a serious blow to the prestige of the Secretary-General, as he was not only involved with, but also, to his critics, constituted one of the central reasons for the UN's impotence and the ensuing war. Even for those who defended the action, or who were unwilling to pass judgment, the rapid withdrawal of UNEF demonstrated the absolute necessity for clarification of the Secretary-General's authority in peacekeeping missions, and his legal responsibilities to the political organs of the UN in any given case. Even if Thant possessed the legal authority to withdraw UNEF on his own initiative, he would have been better advised to encourage discussion of the matter in the Assembly. Had the result been the same, the burden of defense would not have rested with the Secretary-General.

If the powers involved in a conflict want war, then obviously the UN and the Secretary-General are powerless to prevent it. It was never certain prior to UNEF's withdrawal, however, that the states concerned did prefer war, and thus the need for even the most marginal of possible restraints. The Secretary-General is obligated in any crisis to work to persuade the parties that peaceful settlement is preferable to violent change, but persuasion implies influence, and the shortcoming in Thant's response to Cairo was that he worked at peace-making only after he had been deprived of his best source of influence.

The ultimate instruction to be derived from the UN's failure is the essential need for the Organization to devote far greater effort and resources to the functions of peace-making, as well as peace-keeping. This implies a greater use of the traditional diplomatic skills of mediation and negotiation by the Secretary-General. The UN should have been continually at work between 1956 and 1967 in the Middle East in terms of long-range settlement, rather than mere passive interposition. Perhaps here lies a fruitful path to development of the powers of the UN's chief executive.

The War in Vietnam

One of the greatest frustrations for the United Nations and its Secretary-General since 1946 has been the war in Vietnam, for the combination in that country of civil conflict and external intervention has produced a large-scale regional war and a grave threat to world peace, and yet for the UN there has been no active role, little influence, and no attempt even to debate the issues. The world organization's efforts at peace-making have been channeled to date through the Office of the Secretary-General, although in the years since 1963, when Thant first began his endeavors to bring peace to Vietnam, the results have been meager. There has never been a serious opportunity for the UN political organs to become involved with the war. First, any meaningful agreement was most unlikely. Second, neither North nor South Vietnam are members of the Organization, and of course, the continued exclusion of Communist China indicates that any settlement reached will be in forums outside the UN. Thus the Geneva Conferences of 1954 and 1962, and the Paris talks begun in 1969. The failure of the UN to achieve universality of membership also connotes an inability to intervene at all in the early stages of international conflict involving a non-member. This is crucial, for once intervention is large-scale, particularly by a great power, the UN's capacity for peace-making or peace-keeping is reduced substantially.

The Secretary-General acted to fill the void prior to the initiation of full-scale negotiations in early 1969 by trying to bring the parties together and by indicating possible bases for settlement and conditions for talks. It was not a happy experience for Thant—more than once he incurred the hostility of both sides in the war, but his increasingly outspoken remarks and important initiatives represented the preferences of the great majority of UN members. Yet his recommendations were long unheeded, and even the threatened resignation in 1966 made no difference.

Thant's general position on Vietnam has been essentially opposed to the United States' involvement in the conflict. He has always disputed the American view of the war as a case of Communist aggression—for Thant the war has been a struggle for national independence, with nationalism, and not communist ideology as such, the motivating force. The Secretary-General's perspective has resulted in policy formulations unacceptable to Washington, but his world-wide support finally forced the United States to give him public backing for his efforts, even while ignoring his proposals, and this created a great deal of tension between Thant and the U.S. State Department.

The Secretary-General's efforts began in 1963, while the American role in South Vietnam was on a comparatively small scale. In January, 1963, the Secretary-General declared at a press conference that "If one says that the presence of Soviet technicians on Cuban soil constitutes a threat to peace in the area, other may say—they are actually saying it—that the presence of the American troops in South-Vietnam also constitutes a threat to peace in that particular area".[84] Thant pleaded for UN intervention in the conflict, but that was not to be. He made few public comments that year, and his concern was primarily with the dispute between the Diem government in Saigon and the Buddhists who strongly opposed the regime. Thant was asked to intervene in the dispute by fifty-six African and Asian nations, and the Secretary-General appealed to Diem at the end of August, 1963 to settle the Buddhist crisis in accordance with the principles of the Universal Declaration of Human Rights. On September 12, Thant publicly criticized the internal policy of South Vietnam, asserting that Diem relied upon force rather than persuasion, and given Saigon's inability to change government by constitutional process, it was apparent, he charged, that two key virtues of a democracy were lacking in the country. Thant also suggested to Washington, after the fall of the Diem Government in November, 1963, that the U.S. support a coalition government that would include a number of political exiles who favored the neutralization of South Vietnam. The idea was not accepted. For the most part, in 1963, the Secretary-General made no important attempts to bring about negotiations, nor did he comment on the substantive issues of the war or on any possible UN role.

During the following year, the Secretary-General developed many of the themes he expressed throughout the period of escalation. First, there was no effective role for the United Nations, as key parties to the conflict were not members, and the matter was a "cold war" issue—meaning that Security Council or Assembly debates would be sterile and for propaganda purposes

[84] Quoted in Mario Rossi, "U Thant and Vietnam: The Untold Story", *The New York Review of Books,* 17 Nov. 1966, p. 8.

only. The UN might be used, he felt, to ensure that the terms of any agreement reached were properly observed. Second, there could be no military solution to the conflict, as neither side was strong enough to prevail by force of arms over the other. Thus political and diplomatic methods toward a settlement had to be utilized. Third, the best forum for negotiation was a reconvened 1954 Geneva Conference, with a recommitment to the terms of the 1954 accords that formally ended the French colonial struggle in Indochina.

In August, 1964 began Thant's now famous initiative for peace in Vietnam.[85] On August 6, during a visit to the White House, the Secretary-General broached the idea of private talks between U.S. and North Vietnamese representatives. Secretary of State Dean Rusk evidently said nothing to discourage Thant, who then requested a Russian staff member in the Secretariat to have the Soviet UN Mission inquire whether Hanoi would be interested in private talks with U.S. representatives. According to information currently available, toward the end of September Hanoi's response through the Soviet Government was positive—they were interested. Thant informed Adlai Stevenson, the U.S. Representative at the UN, who relayed the message to the State Department. In October, 1964, Stevenson indicated to Secretary-General Thant that it would be better to wait until after the November Presidential election.

After the election, Thant was informed that according to Washington's information, Hanoi was not interested in negotiation. On December 1, Soviet Foreign Minister Andrei Gromyko assured Thant that they were interested, and the latter advised Stevenson to inquire again in Washington. Stevenson made no progress but suggested to Thant that a meeting place be selected. On January 18, 1965, the Burmese Government notified the Secretary-General that Rangoon was acceptable as a site for private talks. But on January 30, Washington's final reply was that the U.S. could not take part. What Thant could not have known was that American participation in the war was about to be stepped up. The bombing of North Vietnam began in February, 1965, and American troops began to pour into the south shortly thereafter until the total reached over half a million men. Later that year, President Johnson advised Thant that he had not heard of his initiative in the autumn of 1964. In October, 1966, Rusk told Thant that Stevenson, who had died in July, 1965, was not authorized to reject the Secretary-General's peace initiative.

It was a tragic end to a promising opportunity to negotiate a relatively early end to the war. It seems difficult to believe that Stevenson acted on his own in saying no to Hanoi's offer, and at best it was a misfortune for President Johnson not to have been informed of Thant's initiative. Essen-

---

[85] Accounts of Thant's first important initiative are found in Rossi, *op. cit.*, and in David Kraslow and Stuart H. Loory, *The Secret Search for Peace in Vietnam* (New York: Vintage Books), 1968.

tially, the Secretary-General's attempt was simply ill-timed, although he could not have been aware of it. The United States wanted desperately to improve Saigon's extremely weak military position, and once the bombing of North Vietnam began in earnest, Washington then appeared anxious to talk. From the North Vietnamese perspective, however, negotiations became impossible until the bombing of the North stopped entirely. Thant was angry, and at a press conference on February 24, while declaring his respect for President Johnson "whose wisdom, moderation and sensitivity to world public opinion are well known", added

I am sure that the great American people, if only they know the true facts and the background to the developments in South Vietnam, will agree with me that further bloodshed is unnecessary. The political and diplomatic method of discussions and negotiations alone can create conditions which will enable the United States to withdraw gracefully from that part of the world. As you know, in times of war and of hostilities, the first casualty is truth.[86]

But the Secretary-General maintained his efforts. In February he proposed a seven-power conference, to include the United States, Soviet Union, Britain, France, Communist China, and North and South Vietnam. Messages were sent to all but China. Washington and Saigon turned down the idea, and it was reported that North Vietnam was indicating "a less positive attitude" than it did during Thant's 1964 attempts.

In April hopes were raised again. A speech on March 31 by Harlan Cleveland, U.S. Assistant Secretary of State for International Organization Affairs, was the first indication that Washington would support a role for the Secretary-General in the Vietnam conflict, and on April 7, President Johnson declared he was ready for "unconditional discussions". Thant sounded out Communist China's views through the Algerian Government after several neutral delegations to the UN suggested that he go to Hanoi and Peking. China was hostile to any UN effort, and the Secretary-General was rebuffed once again. He warned that the UN was in serious danger of being undermined as an agency for the maintenance of peace, and that while he was sensitive to his rights under Article 99 of the Charter, the powers of the Secretary-General "must not be frittered or thrown away in useless dramatic gestures".[87] They must be "husbanded" to be used to best advantage when the situation demanded it. Thant was saying he had no power or influence in the situation, and his formal Charter powers were thus meaningless.

He kept up his contacts, however, and was even thanked for his efforts by the United States, but escalation of the military effort was relentless. There were several peace feelers toward the end of 1965 but none materialized as diplomats reported that North Vietnam was considerably more influenced by Peking's intransigent attitude in 1965 under the impact of the bombing

86 Quoted in *The New York Times,* 25 Feb. 1965, p. 1.
87 United Nations Press Release SG/SM/304, SG/T/59, 21 May 1965, p. 3.

than it had been in 1964. Hanoi now evinced no interest in indirect soundings by Thant concerning the possibility of talks, and the Secretary-General simply asked for major concessions by both sides and "perhaps 10 years too late" the implementation of the Geneva accords.

In 1966, Thant strengthened his opposition to the American perspective on the war:

As the war worsens, its justification in terms of confrontation of ideologies is becoming more and more misleading. For democratic principles, which both sides consider to be at stake in Vietnam, are already falling a victim to the war itself.

In Vietnam there is growing evidence that the so called "fight for democracy" is no longer relevant to the realities of the situation. Twenty years of outside intervention and the presence of a succession of foreign armies have so profoundly affected Vietnamese political life that it seems illusory to represent it as a mere contest between Communism and liberal democracy.

Indeed, events have shown that the passion for national identity, perhaps one should say national survival, is the only ideology that may be left to a growing number of Vietnamese.

Thus, the increasing intervention by outside powers in the conflict—involving their armies, their armaments and, above all, their prestige—has tended to alienate the people of Vietnam from their own destiny. And if therefore the issue in Vietnam is not a struggle between two different views of democracy, what is really at stake, unless an early end to the hostilities is brought about, is the independence, the identity and survival of the country itself.[88]

The Secretary-General, in denouncing the Vietnam conflict as "one of the most barbarous wars in history",[89] adduced three basic points as necessary for a conference looking to a peaceful settlement. They were the cessation of the bombing of North Vietnam, the scaling down of all military activities in South Vietnam, and the willingness of all sides to enter into discussions with those who are "actually fighting". The latter would include the Vietcong. The Secretary-General was convinced, and repeated frequently, that the United States would have to take the first step and unconditionally cease the bombing of the North. Without this concession, there could be no negotiated settlement. The Secretary-General's three points remained a basic theme throughout 1966, along with a condemnation of the notion that the Vietnam conflict was a kind of "holy war between two powerful political ideologies".[90]

In September, 1966, the United States appeared to accept Thant's three-point plan, but with one key difference. The Johnson administration demanded assurances of a reduction in military activity by North Vietnam as the price of a halt to the bombing. The American thirty-seven day bombing pause in late December, 1965 and all of January, 1966 had not brought about talks, nor had there been any decrease in the level of violence in the

[88] United Nations Press Release SG/SM/510, 24 May 1966, pp. 10-11.
[89] United Nations Press Release SG/SM/524, 20 June 1966, p. 4.
[90] GAOR: 21st Sess., Supp. No. 1A (A/6301/Add. 1), *Introduction to the Annual Report of the Secretary-General on the Work of the Organization*, 1966, p. 13.

South. Washington's demand now became reciprocal restraint, or at least some minimum price for a bombing halt. Hanoi derided the United States' position, but remained silent on the Secretary-General's original three points for several months.

In October, 1966, Hanoi accepted the first and the third of Thant's suggestions, but not the second. The North Vietnamese declared that a scaling down of military activity by both sides in the South was tantamount to a demand by the Secretary-General that the Vietnamese people "should curb its struggle for independence and freedom".[91] A few days later, President Johnson emphatically rejected the first of Thant's three points, and the two sides seemed at an impasse. Thant had the support of the great majority of Asian and African UN members, and even quiet backing from some nations closely allied with the United States, but the general consensus had little impact.

Still the UN's chief executive continued his efforts. At the end of 1966, the Secretary-General apparently gained some leverage for action from his threatened resignation. On December 19, seventeen days after his re-appointment, Thant was requested to make a new attempt by U.S. Ambassador Arthur Goldberg:

We turn to you . . . with the hope and the request that you will take whatever steps you consider necessary to bring about the necessary discussions which could lead to . . . a cease-fire. I can assure you that the Government of the United States will cooperate fully with you in getting such discussions started promptly and in bringing them to a successful completion.[92]

Washington's request to Thant was a long way from its response to the Secretary-General's first important initiative in the autumn of 1964.

Nevertheless, Thant's contacts with Hanoi in the early months of 1967 added no new hope for peace talks. The Secretary-General insisted that the United States would have to cease the bombing unconditionally for negotiations to begin, and he continued to stress his differences with the U.S. over the meaning of the war. At a news conference in January, he declared that the N.L.F. was not a "stooge" of Hanoi, that the "so-called domino theory" was invalid, and that South Vietnam was not "strategically vital to Western interests and Western security".[93] He continued to advocate non-alignment for all of Vietnam.

In March, 1967, the Secretary-General, perhaps discouraged by the negative response to his original three-point plan, tried another tack. While maintaining that his original plan remained the most useful, he suggested another three points: first, a general standstill truce; second, preliminary talks; and third, reconvening the Geneva Conference. Washington accorded the new plan a qualified endorsement, and Hanoi naturally rejected it. For

91 Quoted in *The New York Times,* 11 Oct. 1966, p. 5.
92 *Id.,* 20 Dec. 1966, p. 4.
93 *Id.,* 11 Jan. 1967, p. 4.

a time it seemed to some observers, particularly in Washington, that Thant had accepted the American demand for reciprocity, but given Hanoi's rebuff the Secretary-General reverted at once to his original three points, and insisted throughout the remainder of the year that only an unconditional halt to the bombing would result in negotiations.

During the first few months of 1968 there were more contacts with North Vietnam, including a conference in Paris in February with Hanoi's chief representative in Europe, but the outcome was the same—further appeals to the United States. Thant tried hard to bridge the gap between Hanoi's stand and President Johnson's "San Antonio formula" (a halt in the bombing if this would bring productive discussions and if Hanoi would not "take advantage" of the cessation during the talks) by urging the U.S. to assume North Vietnam's "good faith" on the issue of ground fighting in the South. Thant's talks in New Delhi, Moscow, and London in early 1968 produced no change in his assessment of the war or in his policy stand.

The turning point came finally on March 31, 1968. That night President Johnson announced he would not seek re-election, and reported his decision to limit the bombing of North Vietnam to zones with no heavy population concentrations (the bombing continued in North Vietnam up to the 19th parallel). Within three days Washington and Hanoi agreed to talks of a preliminary nature. Johnson's plan was given to the Secretary-General just two hours before the President went on the air, and it was reported that Thant was "irritated with Washington over his exclusion from any part of the diplomatic soundings" [94] preceding the March 31 announcement. There were also reports, however, of diplomats congratulating Thant, evidently on the theory that the agreement to start negotiations was a victory for his efforts and viewpoint.

After preliminary talks between Washington and Hanoi began in May, 1968, the Secretary-General continued to stress his original three-point plan and his opposition to American policy in Southeast Asia. With the parties deadlocked over the issue of an unconditional cessation of all bombing or a halt in return for some restraint by the North Vietnamese, Thant declared (just after the talks began) that the bombing only "hardened the determination of the North to prosecute the war, and not to negotiate under duress".[95] He asserted that the bombing was of "questionable morality and doubtful legality".[96] In a news conference in June he stated that while the United States had reduced the bombing area in the North, it had simultaneously increased the number of sorties, and he predicted a long deadlock in the talks, the essential obstacle being the erroneous belief by both sides that military victory was possible.[97]

[94] *Id.*, 8 April 1968, p. 7.
[95] Quoted in the UN *Monthly Chronicle,* June 1968 (Vol. V, No. 6), p. 112.
[96] *Ibid.*
[97] *Id.*, July 1968 (Vol. V, No. 7) pp. 64-72.

The United States took the next step to extricate itself from the Vietnam conflict in the autumn of 1968. On October 31, President Johnson announced that as of the next day, November 1, all bombing of North Vietnam would be halted. The statement gave no indication of reciprocal undertakings by the North. At the same time, a long series of discussions on procedural matters began at the Paris talks, and by January 18, 1969, full-scale substantive negotiations were initiated between representatives of the United States, North Vietnam, the Vietcong and the Saigon regime. Secretary-General Thant praised the decision to cease all bombing in the North as "a first and essential step towards peace which I and many others have been urging for nearly three years in the conviction that it could lead to further steps towards achievement of a just and peaceful settlement of the prolonged and increasingly tragic and dangerous war in Viet-Nam".[98] At a press conference on January 28, 1969, the Secretary-General asserted that "Out of my three proposals, two points have been met, at least technically. From all available accounts, there is now a cessation of the bombing of North Viet-Nam, and, secondly, discussions have started involving all the parties involved in the fighting. So, I must say that the prospects for peace in Viet-Nam today are brighter than at any time in the past".[99]

While public accounts of the Paris talks indicated no significant advances throughout 1969, there were some signs of progress in the field. On June 8, President Nixon announced that 25,000 American troops would be withdrawn from Vietnam before the end of August, and as the withdrawals began, battlefield lulls over the summer months raised hopes of a more general stand-down. By the end of 1969, American ground combat forces had been reduced to about 472,000, and the Nixon administration announced its hope of bringing that figure down to about 275,000 by the end of 1970.

As the Paris talks dragged on without progress throughout 1969 and into the early months of 1970, Secretary-General Thant began to publicize his views on what he characterized as "the priorities for peace". For Thant a simple ceasefire was impracticable since there were no clearly demarcated lines or boundaries and some villages were occupied by Government forces in the day and by "forces of the other side" at night. This made it "impossible to supervise any ceasefire arrangements". Proposals for elections were equally unrealistic: "In the very messy situation prevailing in South Vietnam today, free and fair elections are out of the question". The Secretary-General urged a coalition government as the first priority:

The first priority for peace should be the emergence of a broad-based national Government in South Vietnam which has the confidence and trust and allegiance of most, if not all factions in South Vietnam. Of course, I cannot say that of any other Government, but, because of the peculiar situation of South Vietnam, and because of the very important repercussions generated by the Vietnamese war on the international scene,

---

[98] UN *Monthly Chronicle,* Vol. V, No. 10, November 1968, p. 29.
[99] *Id.,* Vol. VI, No. 2, February 1969, p. 37.

408

I believe that I am quite justified in coming out publicly with this priority item number one. [99a]

Thant expressed optimism at the end of 1969, despite the Paris stalemate and the apparent downgrading of the talks by the resignation of the chief U.S. representative, Henry Cabot Lodge, and the Administration's failure to replace him with a negotiator of comparable standing. The Secretary-General, without explication, asserted that "the chances of the people of Vietnam fashioning their own future are brighter now than ever before".[99b]

Secretary-General Thant's efforts since 1963 to bring peace to Vietnam were far more often than not thwarted or minimized, but there is little doubt that his role was important. He served as the spokesman for a growing consensus concerning the basic significance and meaning of the war, and how best to end it. His views were not accepted in Washington or Hanoi, but they summarized well the position of a majority of the UN's membership, and tended to legitimize that viewpoint. He retained his support in Washington, despite strained relations with Secretary of State Rusk and a position that was probably more consistently critical of a great power's policy than any in the history of the Office, and one reason was precisely because he was speaking for a majority of nations. The legitimizing role was of great importance, for that segment of the American poplation opposed to U.S. involvement in Southeast Asia frequently referred to Thant's perspective on the war and his policy recommendations to buttress their positions. In this sense, it was not uncommon to see references to the Secretary-General and the Pope in the same sentence. There is little question that Thant weakened support for American intervention, and strengthened the opposition thereto. He helped build a world-wide public opinion on the issue.

The Secretary-General was extremely useful as a diplomatic contact able to learn the positions and likely responses of all the parties involved in the conflict. Since Washington has no diplomatic relations with Hanoi or Peking, or with the Vietcong, it was a matter of considerable convenience to utilize the Office of the Secretary-General as one source among many for reliable data concerning attitudes and policy formulations. Thant was both a messenger and an active agent in seeking out responses, much as he is in nearly every case of international conflict. This was a role of considerable importance, for authoritative information is difficult to secure under the best of circumstances, and is certainly not assured within a context of relative isolation of the parties. The Secretary-General frequently acted as a kind of substitute for diplomatic relations among the concerned governments. His contacts were often indirect (e.g., through the Algerian Government) and sporadic, but he was able to serve both sides as an additional source of dependable communication. Finally, he made many suggestions of possible

[99a] *Id.*, Vol. VII, No. 1, January 1970, p. 185.
[99b] *Id.*, p. 184.

approaches preliminary to serious substantive negotiations on ending the war, acting as a mediator for the parties.

The Secretary-General strived mightily to fill the huge gaps left by the UN's failure to achieve universality of membership and to intervene at an early stage in Southeast Asia. The two are related, of course, as mentioned above, since interposition is most unlikely without the adherence to the Organization of all interested parties. Once the United States and North Vietnam began to intervene in South Vietnam, there was little hope for a meaningful UN role. Thant served as the primary channel for the Organization's limited effort in Vietnam, and if he was not totally successful, he was certainly useful.

The years of Thant's administration have not been easy ones for the United Nations. The chronic conflict over finances has forced the Secretary-General all too often into the position of money-collector dependent upon voluntary contributions for peacekeeping operations, such as UNFICYP. He has decried the necessity for *ad hoc* arrangements, but given the Soviet Union's insistence that only the Security Council is empowered under the Charter to arrange for the financing of peacekeeping missions, Thant has had little choice. At the end of 1961, on the suggestion of the United States, he formally recommended a $ 200 million bond issue to cover the deficits from the UNEF and ONUC forces. The scheme was adopted over the violent objection of the Soviet Union, and voluntary contributions in combination with payments by the parties primarily concerned has been the norm ever since.

At the same time, and closely related thereto, have been the critical questions of authorization for peacekeeping or observation missions, and the role of the Secretary-General. Once again, the Soviet Union has fought hard to maintain Security Council control, and to limit the Secretary-General to administrative functions and the implementation of precise Security Council directives. This move has not been completely successful, but there is no question that Thant's discretionary powers have been limited.

He has indicated a strong preference for the United States' view on authorization for peacekeeping operations and on an independent role for the Secretary-General. Perhaps his strongest expression of his notion of a role for the Assembly in peacekeeping matters came in his address to the "Pacem In Terris" Convocation in 1965:

... the writers of the Charter envisioned complete agreement among the five permanent members of the Security Council, who would be collectively responsible for keeping the peace by supplying arms and men, in certain contemplated situations. These situations, however, did not come about. History took a new turn; the Security Council could not act in the manner it was intended to act, and the General Assembly assumed, or had to assume, certain functions not originally contemplated in the Charter.

We are now witnessing the beginning of the great debate—whether the big Powers in unison, through the agency of the Security Council, should take exclusive responsibility for maintaining international peace and security while the General Assembly functions as a glorified debating society in political matters, or whether an attempt should be made to secure a fair, equitable, and clearly defined distribution of functions of the two principal organs, in the light of the changing circumstances, and, particularly, bearing in mind the increase in the membership of the Organization, from 50 in 1945 to 114 in 1965. Account will have to be taken of the fact that in the General Assembly are represented, in addition to the big Powers, all the other States, the smaller Powers, whose understanding, assistance and cooperation are nevertheless essential in regard to decisions involving issues of international peace and security.[100]

As noted, Thant has built no theory of the Office, as did Hammarskjold before him, and indeed, has relied quite heavily on Hammarskjold's conception of the Secretary-General's role, although this has been demonstrated not by performance, but through isolated pronouncements. The threatened resignation in 1966 presented an opportunity for comment on his position. "I have found it increasingly difficult", he stated, "to function as Secretary-General in the manner in which I wish to function, and secondly, I do not subscribe to the view that the Secretary-General should be just a chief administrative officer, or, in other words, that the Secretary-General should be a glorified clerk. I do not accept this concept of the Secretary-General. As I have said repeatedly on previous occasions, besides the functions of administration, the Secretary-General must take the necessary initiatives in the political and diplomatic fields. These political and diplomatic initiatives, in my view, are an essential part of the functions of the Secretary-General".[101] He added that he had "experienced increasing restrictions on the legitimate prerogatives of the Secretary-General".[102]

Thant has not been completely consistent in his declarations concerning an independent role for the Secretary-General. In 1964, in a routine address on the United Nations, he asserted that "the Secretary-General is very much a servant of the Organization and can act only within the mandates given to him in a particular situation by the Security Council or the General Assembly and in close and continuous consultation with the Members of the Organization and with the Governments particularly concerned in a given problem. Should this cease to be the case, the position of the Secretary-General would very rapidly become so exposed as to be untenable".[103]

In 1965, however, under the impact of the rapid escalation of the war in Vietnam, Thant sounded a substantially different note:

Two simple considerations are inescapable. First, the Secretary-General must always be prepared to take an initiative, no matter what the consequences to him or his office may be, if he sincerely believes that it might mean the difference between peace and war. In such a situation the personal prestige of a Secretary-General—and even the

---

[100] United Nations Press Release SG/SM/254, 19 Feb. 1965, p. 6.
[101] United Nations Press Release SG/SM/567, 19 Sept. 1966, p. 4.
[102] *Id.*, p. 8.
[103] United Nations Press Release SG/SM/51, 3 April 1964, pp. 11-12.

position of his office—must be considered to be expendable. The second cardinal consideration must be the maintenance of the Secretary-General's independent position, which alone can give him the freedom to act, without fear or favour in the interests of world peace. Such an independence does not imply any disrespect of the wishes or opinions of Member Governments. On the contrary, his independence is an insurance that the Secretary-General will be able to serve the long-term interest in peace of *all* the Members of the Organization in full accordance with his oath of office.[104]

It should be noted that Thant has more commonly acted in accordance with the 1964 dictum, rather than the 1965 statement, with the exception of the Vietnam war. And certainly he has not claimed an executive position totally divorced from the strategies of the great powers. Yet while he has not explicitly formulated a doctrine of "filling vacuums" in the Hammarskjold sense, he accepts the propriety of executive action even without precise instructions from the Security Council or General Assembly. This assumes, of course, a place for the United Nations as an important actor in international politics. He has affirmed his view that a Secretary-General should be impartial, but not neutral on questions "involving moral issues".[105] He has spoken approvingly of President Roosevelt's 1944 description of the UN's Chief Executive Officer as the "Moderator".

The Secretary-General agrees with his predecessor's characterization of the job as lonely and adds: "It is not only the lonelist job in the world; in my view, it is sometimes the most frustrating job in the world".[106] He credits his traditional Buddhist environment in Burma with assisting him to find the strength for the discharge of his responsibilities as Secretary-General.

Thant has left no doubt that he envisages a growing role for the Organization with a developing stature as an independent force possessing a will and interests of its own. Indeed, he has gone so far as to declare that "the United Nations must ultimately develop in the same way as sovereign States have done, and... if it is to have a future, it must eventually assume some of the attributes of a State. It must have the right, the power and the means to keep the peace. We are only in the beginning and the process will surely take several generations. But the peace-keeping operations already conducted by the United Nations provide the hope that we are on the road to these essential developments".[107]

In the meantime, Thant shares with his predecessors a view of the UN as devoted essentially to mediatory and conciliatory tasks, with peace-keeping operations designed to keep hostile parties from engaging in violent conflict. The Secretary-General has also placed some stress on a largely negative function of the United Nations, but one that is extremely valuable in an

104 United Nations Press Release SG/SM/304, SG/T/59, 21 May 1965, p. 3.
105 United Nations Press Release SG/SM/493, 30 April 1963, p. 12.
106 *Id.*, p. 13.
107 United Nations Press Release SG/1477, 30 April 1963, p. 5.

international system in which the primary actors are powerful nation-states:

In certain situations the United Nations and the Office of the Secretary-General can provide a useful middle ground on which the parties may meet without any loss of face or prestige, and accommodate their differences in a civilized and dignified manner. I like to think that the United Nations played a useful role of this kind in the resolution of the Cuban crisis...[108]

The face-saving function of the United Nations and of its Secretary-General has been useful in a great number of disputes, and is likely to remain one of the most useful roles for the Organization for many years.

Thant, like Lie and Hammarskjold, has of course spoken out frequently in other key areas of concern to the United Nations. He has, for example, helped to legitimize the view that the wealthy industrialized nations of the Northern hemisphere have an obligation to do more for the poor nations in the South, and that the United Nations should be a primary instrument for the redistribution of wealth. For Thant,

...one of the central tasks of statesmanship must be to bring about in the industrialized nations a more profound recognition of the dangers to the security and well-being of all nations which are inherent in the present slow rate of economic growth in the developing countries. Whatever other pressing problems and responsibilities fall upon the leaders of the industrialized countries, those leaders cannot safely postpone bringing their people to face—morally, intellectually and financially—the fact that the future of the world will be largely determined by the extent of their effort to promote progress and to defeat despair in the developing nations.[109]

Colonialism is naturally one of the prime concerns of a Secretary-General from once dependent Burma, and given the Charter norm of eventual independence for colonial territories, Thant has been quite willing to denounce colonial domination and the strong disinclination of some administering powers to relinquish their possessions. In this he has the strong support, of course, of the Afro-Asian majority in the United Nations. Thant's appeal is uncomplicated:

It is my earnest hope that all Member States, and in particular the administering powers, would do their utmost to bring about the final end of colonialism without further delay. In this context I appeal to those administering powers which have so far refused to co-operate with the Organization in respect to territories under their administration to reconsider their position and to adopt policies which are in keeping with the objectives of the Charter.[110]

The Secretary-General has often noted that the great majority of political conflicts confronting the United Nations since 1946, including several he dealt with in his own administration, were the legacy of European colonialism and its collapse. Further, racial discrimination, such as that practiced in Southern Africa, is "inherent" in colonial problems, and is an "evil weed"

[108] *Id.*, p. 4.
[109] GAOR: 21st Sess., Supp. No. 1A (A/6301/Add. 1), *Introduction to the Annual Report of the Secretary-General on the Work of the Organization,* 1966, p. 13.
[110] UN *Monthly Chronicle,* Oct. 1967 (Vol. IV, No. 9), p. 126.

capable of surviving even in advanced and prosperous societies.[111] The equation of colonialism and racial discrimination is a developing theme at the UN, and it obviously has the support of Secretary-General Thant.

Economic disparities and racial tensions are viewed by Thant as far more serious potential threats to international peace and stability than current ideological conflicts, which the Secretary-General views as passing phenomena. He frequently emphasizes the collapse of the bipolar international system and is suspicious of military alliance structures as retrogressive. He speaks of a great "synthesis" in the context of East-West ideological conflict, but is plainly worried that the rapidly growing economic gulf between North and South might block progress toward world order and lead to violent conflict. Thant pleads for universality of membership in the UN, thus hoping to expand the Organization's influence as an agent of conciliation and as a third-party neutral intermediary. He is basically optimistic that the United Nations will gain in its capacity to influence world politics.

In making his viewpoint known to the world, Secretary-General Thant has utilized various media very much as Lie and Hammarskjold did before him. He has travelled a great deal every year, for purposes of engaging in substantive discussions with various national leaders, attending a multitude of conferences, and of formal speechmaking devoted to general matters of concern to the United Nations. His speeches, written reports, various messages, *Introductions* to his Annual Report, and press conference performances have provided him with ample opportunity to present his positions outside of formal UN debates. His writings and statements are closer to Lie's than to Hammarskjold's in terms of intellectual complexity and doctrinal content. He is less given to justifying actions in legal nomenclature than was Hammarskjold, and far more likely to give a simple and direct response to a question. His blunt and often outspoken declarations recall Lie far more often than Hammarskjold, and while Thant is given to abstract propositions more frequently than Lie, he has made no attempts, as did Hammarskjold, to utilize public forums for developing theoretical constructs concerning the role of the UN and the Secretary-General.

Thant does not possess the same extraordinary skill in diplomacy enjoyed by Hammarskjold, and even given the restraints imposed upon him by the Soviet Union and France, has perhaps not pushed as hard as he might have to expand his own role or that of the Organization. As there are "strong" and "weak" Presidents and Premiers, so too will there be Secretaries-General who more or less help to shape the course of events around them. In terms of developing the powers of his Office, Thant might have accomplished more, although in the context of public pronouncements and attitude formation, Thant has gone further than either Lie or Hammarskjold, and of course beyond the wildest dreams of the three League Secretaries-

[111] United Nations Press Release SG/SM/488, 3 May 1966, p. 8.

General. His administration has served as a period of consolidation for the Office, all the while maintaining excellent relations with the great powers and causing the harsh Soviet attacks on the Secretary-General to recede far into the background. If Thant has not been permitted to retain the gains made by Hammarskjold, he has been an activist and committed to a stronger role for the UN's chief executive.

Thant is a perfect reflection of the forces that now dominate the United Nations. As a spokesman for Afro-Asian interests, he is also building what may be called a "constituency" upon which he relies for support, particularly when he has antagonized either of the superpowers. He has helped to move the Organization to a neutral posture in East-West conflicts, and has strengthened its endeavor to terminate colonialism and promote rapid social change and economic development throughout the poor regions of the world. He has regained for his Office the prestige that was significantly diminished by the Soviet attacks on Hammarskjold in 1960 and 1961. This is important for the majority of small nations in the UN, particularly if the Secretary-General is to serve as their spokesman on many of the great issues of world politics. Above all, Thant has intervened in several serious international conflicts that were of interest to the great powers, and in no case has he undermined his own position or (with the possible exception of the 1967 Middle East conflict) weakened the United Nations. Both Lie and Hammarskjold, after years of successful construction, came perilously close to weakening severely the Office of the Secretary-General. Thant has been an activist Secretary-General who has maintained, if not strengthened the Office, and this remains his greatest accomplishment.

CHAPTER VII

The Secretary-General in World Politics
Resources and Functions

A review of the Secretary-General's activity in world politics during the first fifty years of international organization reveals a gradual development of his role in the international system. As noted in the Introduction, the historical record contains many gaps, and in some respects the available data provides but the slightest trace of the Secretary-General's techniques in cases of organizational intervention in inter-state conflicts. Yet while complete historical analyses must await the opening of national archives, enough information is known to begin the difficult task of constructing propositions to assist in understanding the nature of the Office of the Secretary-General, and its value in the contemporary world arena.

Developed hypotheses are certainly not possible at the present time. Among many other items, serious work on the United Nations at a relatively high level of abstraction is in its very early stages, and clearly no meaningful theory of the Secretary-General can be established without link-up to the larger context of the UN, international organization in general, and the role of third parties in world politics. Even within the narrower scope of the Office itself, the resources and functions of the Secretary-General cannot yet be analysed in a fashion productive of serious theory. Ultimately, we want to know how much weight should properly be attached to the several resources, capabilities, and functions of the Office, and their relationships.

The purpose of this chapter is to formulate another perspective by elucidating, primarily on the basis of the data set forth in the preceding chapters, a number of considerations relevant to the resources and political functions of the Secretary-General, how they have developed over the first fifty years, and the likely power position of the Office in the near future. The object is to work at what might be called a middle level of abstraction, higher than the traditional analyses that concentrate in detail on diverse aspects of peacekeeping,[1] but lower than an Eastonian framework,[2] for example, applicable to any political system, but perhaps difficult in terms of further specified research for that very reason.[3]

---

[1] Cf. Leon Gordenker, *The UN Secretary-General and the Maintenance of Peace* (New York: Columbia University Press, 1967).
[2] See David Easton, *A Systems Analysis of Political Life* (New York: Wiley, 1965).
[3] Work in this area has been done by Oran Young in *The Intermediaries: Third Parties in International Crises* (Princeton: Princeton University Press, 1967), particularly in chapters 7 and 8. Young presents an analysis of the Secretary-General's resources and

A study of the resources at the command of the Secretary-General involves a rather artificial dissection of his base of authority into several discrete assets, but this may be helpful for conceptual purposes and comparative analysis. A primary purpose here is to discover why states find the head of the international secretariat a useful tool for diplomacy. Why have they turned to him for assistance with great frequency in the past fifty years? The Secretary-General has no military power, only a recently developed embryo of a political constituency, and just the smallest of staffs to provide essential expertise. What then does he have to offer? His authority and power have developed quite significantly since 1920, and most decidedly since the years of the Hammarskjold administration. This has been due in part to rapid advances in communication arts, in part to the changing nature of the international system, and to the successes of the Secretary-General himself.

Perhaps the most critical asset at the disposal of the Secretary-General is his *neutrality,* and thus his accompanying acceptability to competing powers in the international arena. Members of the world community have generally been assured, from 1920 to the present, that the Secretariat and its leadership do not usually favor one side in any given conflict or dispute, and as a result, state representatives have been willing to seek advice from the Secretary-General, and to include him in their bargaining sessions. Nations have at times been willing to accede to requests made by him, and adopt his thinking on an issue simply because it came from a friendly, or at least not antagonistic source. States have also worked to legitimize their positions through the Secretary-General's Office because acceptance by a leading neutral figure in international affairs carries with it a special sanction of integrity and rectitude.

Neutrality has not always meant, however, a simple posture somewhere between two antagonists. It is possible for a Secretary-General to remain neutral in a dispute by standing on Charter principles, rather than between the narrowly defined political or military interests of the parties, but Charter principles may support one side or another, and of course, may always be interpreted to give a desired result. The Secretary-General is much more likely to rest his case on ostensibly neutral provisions of the Charter if the competing states are small, and there is no obvious great power interest of relevance. This is a technique for taking sides without appearing to do so, and is generally considered acceptable by the international community. A blatant favoring of one side even in a minor issue would antagonize the great powers upon whom the Secretary-General must rely for support, for the precedent value would be substantial. Such action is still beyond the bounds

---

functions within the context of international crises, particularly involving high-level conflict between the United States and the Soviet Union.

of acceptable behavior by a Secretary-General, no matter how inclined he might be to develop the powers of the Office.

Neutrality will also weaken if the entire community of nations is more or less agreed on a position against one or a small number of powers. It is easier to abandon neutrality if the Secretary-General finds himself in agreement with both Washington and Moscow, or with a solid majority of nations, providing neither the United States nor the Soviet Union has any strong objection. Certainly U Thant is not neutral in the dispute over *apartheid* between the UN and South Africa, nor was Trygve Lie particularly even-handed in his treatment of the Palestine issue in 1947-1948. In the *apartheid* case, Thant can certainly refer to the Charter and the burgeoning structure of human rights law, but he is not required to do so—it is open to him to remain silent, although in this case the abandonment of neutrality is in accord with the stated policy of almost every nation in the world, and costs the Secretary-General little even while it adds somewhat to the moral posture of the Office and the illegitimacy of racial discrimination. In the Palestine problem, Lie was less disposed to find refuge in the Charter—it was far more a matter of deep-rooted sympathy for Israel, even if at the felt expense of the Arab nations.

Occasionally a Secretary-General will abandon absolute neutrality in favor of Charter principles that clearly favor one side even if a great power is involved, as with Lie and the Korean War. If the issue is important enough, this might well mean the end of the Secretary-General's effectiveness, as the power might withdraw its backing in retaliation, but the stand on the Charter has always been considered more important even than the survival of the Office itself. Another example is Drummond's work in the Sino-Japanese conflict, for despite charges that he too willingly tolerated compromise with the Japanese, his support of the Covenant seemed unswerving. This has traditionally been viewed as essential for preservation of the Organization, even if at the price of loss of effectiveness for the incumbent or a weakening of the Secretary-General's powers.

Finally, in matters of great importance to the structure of the Organization, the Secretary-General will usually take a strong position. An example of this is universality of membership, an issue that has prompted each of the UN Secretaries-General to push for the representation in the Organization of the Communist regime in China, to the displeasure of the United States. Dag Hammarskjold fought the troika scheme to maintain the integrity of his Office, and would surely have done so even had he not already lost Soviet backing, for here was a dispute in which neutrality would have been meaningless for himself, and destructive of the Office.

But despite these tendencies, and notwithstanding a new development in the neutrality concept under U Thant,[4] the customary impartiality of the

---

[4] See pp. 420, 431-433, *infra*.

Secretary-General has been an asset of enormous importance since 1920. The accompanying acceptability has provided the Secretary-General with a flexibility of maneuver and influence in international negotiation quite out of proportion to what might be expected of any political figure with no military power or popular support. That lack of real power is confining is obvious: the unusual and striking aspect is how much weight can be brought to bear by international officials who are accorded great respect precisely because they are peace-makers concerned with a rational world order system and as such clearly outside the normal competitive arena of inter-state claims and responses. A Secretary-General is rarely a threat, and may well be a source of information and imaginative thought on problem solving even in the most complex of cases.

It is clear, of course, that neutrality standing alone is insufficient as a source of influence in international politics. There are many persons, governmental and private, who might be impartial in a given conflict and yet do not possess the authority of a Secretary-General. Neutrality in con-junction with the several other resources of the Office, however, is of great importance, for the resulting acceptability to key actors in the world arena is the foundation stone for an active political role.

The two most difficult problems in this setting are first, the perception of impartiality by states, and second, the occasional insistence by particular nations that the Secretary-General take a position in their favor despite the certainty of alienating other powers. Both have caused a great deal of trouble during the first fifty years of the Office.

State perceptions naturally fluctuate in accordance with the importance of the issue and the extent and scope of the Secretary-General's role. The more significant the political intervention by the Secretary-General, the more likely are the interested actors to perceive the action as something less than perfect neutrality. In many cases this constitutes an inherent limitation on the neutrality resource, particularly if the great powers are involved, but it clearly need not inhibit the Secretary-General every time, for even serious interventions, such as the 1962 Cuba crisis, do not always generate perceptions of bias. It may be argued that the nature of the issue was the more significant variable in the Cuba case, rather than the scope of the intervention, for in grave crisis situations involving a real threat of nuclear war, it is perhaps rather likely that any action by the Secretary-General tending to reduce tension will be acceptable to the parties. In lesser cases, involving political influence, rather than survival, the inhibiting factor may become important.

Insistence by parties that the Secretary-General adopt a particular position and abandon neutrality is rare, and is likely to be masked by reliance upon neutral principles of law or the Charter. It may also be the case that simple political pressure, with no reference to the law, may result in the abandonment of impartiality. This kind of phenomenon is almost always the result of great power influence exerted in conflicts deemed to be of overriding significance in terms of political independence or integrity. Such cases may prove decisive, for critical questions dividing the great powers are precisely the kind in which third party neutrals may become most useful.

The administrations of Drummond, Avenol, Lie, and Hammarskjold all demonstrate these difficulties, while Thant's has been somewhat easier essentially because of the Afro-Asian influence. For Sir Eric Drummond, neutrality constituted a very substantial portion of what he could offer during his tenure. As we have seen, a neutral international civil service was his creation, marking a crucial departure from the previous practice of national secondment. His impartiality was all the more notable in the early years of world organization, given his British nationality and the complex divisions between *status quo* and revisionist powers. Neutrality was the foundation upon which he was able to establish a very substantial feeling that he was a man to be trusted, talked to, and relied upon for meaningful substantive and procedural advice. It is significant, however, that his most extensive political activity in a grave international crisis (the Sino-Japanese conflict) generated a perception in many quarters that the Secretary-General had departed from the totally correct posture of previous years, and this has been the case with every succeeding Secretary-General.

It is widely agreed that Avenol was not only a weak Secretary-General, but also totally committed to the appeasement strategy as dictated by the Quai d'Orsay and the British Foreign Office, the result being the near total destruction of the key resource so carefully constructed by Drummond. In fact, Avenol's position was impossible, for the most basic norms underlying the structure of the League of Nations and its Covenant were under attack, and his choice was limited to support of the Covenant at the expense of the Axis powers, or a compromise with Fascism and militarism at the expense of the League. Avenol chose the latter, and has been rightly castigated for so doing, but this was clearly not a free-willed derogation from the neutral principles of an international civil service.

Indeed, Secretary-General Trygve Lie had a rather similar problem, although within the context of a totally different international system. Upon the outbreak of the Korean War, Lie's choice was to withhold judgment while attempting mediation, or to take a strong stance in defense of Charter principles, thus lending the prestige of his Office to the UN-covered American response. Either way, Lie's support was gone, for the United States was not likely to have accepted a neutral position from Lie, and the Soviet Union would have nothing less. The Secretary-General's crucial asset had been destroyed by the parties, and his role as a possible neutral intermediary between East and West reduced to a nullity.

Dag Hammarskjold's neutrality was generally unquestioned until the Congo crisis of 1960-1961 but the Soviet view of Western bias, inferred

from his work in the Congo, as well as the American-dominated "Congo Club", ruined the Secretary-General's theretofore correct working relationship with the Soviet Union. Hammarskjold's appeal to "third world" members of the United Nations might well have succeeded, although chances of success had been markedly reduced by its coming subsequent to, rather than before, the open Soviet attack.

The rather constant backing of the neutral groupings at the United Nations has enabled Secretary-General Thant to establish and maintain a very different concept of neutrality, for the current Secretary-General is in the enviable position of having strong support from the great majority of United Nations members, most of whom wish very much to stand aside from East-West conflicts. So long as Thant continues to receive backing from the Asian, African, and to a lesser extent Latin American states, he has less reason to fear alienating either the United States or the Soviet Union than did Lie and Hammarskjold. Thus Thant's views of the United States' involvement in Vietnam has not lost him the support of Washington, nor did Moscow react to his public denunciation of the Soviet occupation of Czechoslovakia in August, 1968.

Soviet-American competition for influence in the third world, in addition to the majority status in the United Nations of the neutral states, has somewhat changed the nature of the neutrality expected of the Secretary-General and has significantly enlarged the breath of his acceptability to the major powers. Neutrality is still a crucial asset in the repertoire of resources available to the Secretary-General, but it is a far more positive tool today than during the administrations of Thant's predecessors, for it now permits greater flexibility. Yet as Thant's experience has indicated, this does not necessarily generate a forward development in discretionary powers. The Soviets have been quite willing to risk disagreement with the Afro-Asian states in order to prevent the establishment of an uncontrolled and possibly significant new actor in the international arena. Nevertheless, for the foreseeable future, the Secretary-General's Afro-Asian based neutrality is likely to enhance his already considerable capacity to influence world politics, and might prove important in a gradual but perceptible evolution of his executive power.

One of the key resources at the disposal of the Secretary-General is *political information,* primarily in the form of information on members' policies. The Secretary-General presides over one of the focal points of international bargaining and diplomacy, and assuming a substantial degree of impartiality and independence, is in an excellent position to acquire important data regarding the political views of member nations, claims and counterclaims being pressed, and likely responses to proposed courses of action.

The information resource has been a function of both the personal qualities of the Secretary-General, and the support facilities in the Secretariat for data gathering and evaluation. In terms of the Secretary-General himself, there is little question that Drummond and Hammarskjold were the most knowledgable of the six. As we have seen, it was perhaps the essential merit of the League Secretariat's first dozen years that its executive head kept himself remarkably well-informed of the politics and policies of that Organization's members, and of course this contributed very heavily to his political influence. And the Drummond model was followed closely by Dag Hammarskjold, who had a truly great command of the entire range of issues confronting the United Nations, enabling him to engage in a creative and important diplomacy during the eight years of his administration.

In terms of support facilities, the advantage has been entirely with the United Nations Secretaries-General. A larger secretariat, and greater numbers of officials in the Executive Office have made far more efficient and rapid the process of data gathering and evaluation, not to speak of the enormous improvement in communications facilities. The many permanent missions of member states located in New York have also added to the information-gathering capacity, for they have made liaison with national governments relatively efficient and have added an absolutely essential supplement to national "representation" of the great powers in the Secretariat's top-level structure.

Perhaps the gravest deficiency in the information resource is the almost total absence of data concerning military and strategic planning by the more important members, resulting in a complete lack of contingency planning for crises beyond a comparatively shallow effort to accumulate relevant materials on peace-keeping forces and observer missions. Oran Young has argued persuasively that the Secretariat has a pressing need to acquire far more military and strategic expertise, and to engage in serious contingency planning for possible use in future crises.[5] It is true that the United Nations Secretary-General now has a Military Adviser, but his office is quite small, engages in no planning for serious crisis or conflict, and the range of data relevant for his work does not encompass even a fraction of the military and strategic structures, processes, and plans of any of the principal members of the United Nations. The Secretariat itself has argued against further development of contingency planning, citing the special nature and particular features in any given case, although perhaps the real point is political acceptability. As Secretary-General Thant stated in the *Introduction* to his Annual Report for 1967:

It is all too obvious that contingency military planning by the Secretariat for specified future operations would be, to put it mildly, politically unacceptable. Apart from anything else, such planning would depend upon the gathering of political intelligence which would be out of the question for the United Nations to attempt.

It has been said also that the preparation of all sorts of standing operational proce-

---

[5] Young, *op. cit.*, pp. 284-294.

dures would greatly improve the quality of United Nations peacekeeping performance. The fact is that such procedures do exist and have been compiled routinely for each peacekeeping operation. These are used as a basis when a new operation is mounted, but experience has shown that instructions and procedures have to be adapted specifically to each operation since, so far at any rate, the various peacekeeping operations have differed widely in scope, nature, composition and function.[6]

Thant is no doubt right in warning of the political impossibility of establishing anything that resesmbles a United Nations-sponsored intelligence agency. But much more can be done along these lines, for without great expenditure, the Military Adviser's office could be expanded, outside strategists brought in, and surely it would not be politically unacceptable to make greater use of published data and theory that might be useful in future United Nations' operations. The fact that such missions have differed widely in scope and nature in the past, and will continue to do so in the future is an argument in favor of more contingency planning rather than the reverse, for the very diversity of possible future conflicts and the normal range of possible United Nations undertakings argue strongly for an attempt to impose a limited but rational ordering of categories and types, so far as possible, and to think out credible responses in any even remotely likely future crisis. This cannot be less fruitful than abandoning such planning on the notion that the complexities involved are simply beyond human capacities. We have come a long way from the years since Sir Eric Drummond established the utility of his Office by making procedural and substantive recommendations on the basis of hundreds of conversations held with League representatives, and within the general context of the information and knowledge available to the highest official of the United Nations, there is no persuasive reason why we cannot go further.

Perhaps the most variable of the Secretary-General's assets is *diplomatic skill* and capacity to exercise influence based primarily on imagination, intelligence, and capacity to fashion proposals and timely recommendations acceptable to the parties concerned, even when what might be called vital national interests are at stake and irreconcilable bargaining positions adopted. Timing, drafting skill, imaginative use of available data, and ability to foster and maintain good personal relationships are perhaps the key elements. Drummond and Hammarskjold were again brilliant in every respect, whereas Avenol, Lie, and Thant, while demonstrating not inconsiderable diplomatic capability, have also indicated certain shortcomings. Avenol's training was almost exclusively in economics and finance, and only rarely was he able to exercise any significant influence in the conflicts facing the League of Nations in the 1930's—he ranks rather low in all of the variables. Trygve Lie, on the other hand, was perhaps the strongest politician of the six Secretaries-General, but this did not necessarily entail a great deal of the more subtle diplomatic requisites. Lie fought hard and well

---

[6] Quoted in *UN Monthly Chronicle*, Vol. IV, No. 9, October, 1967, p. 102.

for his prerogatives as Secretary-General during the first years of his administration, established a solid foundation for the Office and made it clear that the quiet, behind-the-scenes role of former days was gone. But his blustering style did not lend itself to diplomatic practice and niceties, and it is not generally considered by those who knew and worked closely with Lie and Hammarskjold that Lie's diplomatic adeptness matched that of his successor. U Thant has been more circumspect and discreet than was Lie, notwithstanding that many of his statements have matched Lie's in terms of strength and general frankness, but Thant has perhaps not been as apt nor as imaginative at formulating acceptable recommendations as Hammarskjold.

In the most meaningful sense, diplomatic excellence is apparently to be the most critical asset in the future development of the Office. Assuming the continued functioning of the Secretary-General in world politics, most of his other resources have been accepted as part of the international system, and have achieved a quasi-independent existence, but diplomatic facility depends upon personal characteristics, and is most subject to variation from one Secretary-General to another. Drummond and Hammarskjold, operating in far different systems, and with enormous variance in supporting mechanisms, achieved more than the others in large part because of their own skills in diplomacy. In contemporary politics, this is of crucial importance, for it is still the case that most of the Secretary-General's sources of influence are intangible, and without military power at his command, his intelligence and diplomatic deftness remain the most likely source of influence.

The lesson for the future is clear enough. One of the key issues still to be resolved is the extent of the Secretary-General's discretionary power and influence, particularly in conflict situations. The Soviet Union's insistence upon the strictest limitations on the Office's power is the challenge of the next several years, and one not easily met. In 1953 the Soviets approved Hammarskjold because in part they perceived a quiet administrator, somewhat in the Drummond mode, who apparently had neither the temperament nor inclination to become a commanding political figure as had Trygve Lie. The error was striking, precisely because even the quiet Drummond had a great political influence, and of course, it was not long before Hammarskjold was also to be a strong figure. Given the requirement of agreement among the permanent Security Council members, it is open to Moscow to withhold its approval until a figure without significant skills in diplomacy can be agreed upon. From the Soviet perspective, the ideal choice would appear to be the quiet administrator content to work unobtrusively without public fanfare, and one who lacks any conspicuous imaginative capacities. Until the Soviet Union has some assurances that the Secretary-General will not take action or intervene in a fashion deemed by Moscow to be contrary to its interests, it may seek a Secretary-General with neither political nor diplomatic ability. Since such assurances are not likely to be forthcoming, the Office may well be facing the gravest challenge of its first fifty years.

A resource of growing importance is the *prestige* and respect accorded the Secretary-General, a source of power and influence naturally dependent upon the first three assets and the successes fairly attributable to the efforts of the Secretary-General and his Office. As the practice of intervention by international organization has gained legitimacy in the world community, and as nations have become accustomed to an executive role for the Secretary-General, his prestige has developed slowly but perceptibly, with expected ebbs and flows, and with the greater growth during the United Nations years. U Thant, for example, is far more likely to be able, through his international prestige, to help shape attitudes toward the war in Vietnam than was say, Sir Eric Drummond in a position to influence opinion during the Sino-Japanese crisis in the early 1930's.

It is important to distinguish here between prestige in the various foreign offices and authoritative decision-making units throughout the world, and preeminence or esteem among the many publics of the international community. The primary difference between League and UN Secretary-General in this context is that in the first case, respect was limited to government representatives and diplomats, whereas in the latter, distinction and fame have developed also among larger masses of people, although concededly any serious impact has been among the relatively small number of persons concerned with foreign affairs. Whether the Secretary-General's limited popular support is capable of generating any kind of governmental response has yet to be determined, although states unhappy with a particular action naturally prefer that it be accomplished as quietly as possible.

The important point for the Secretary-General is that he be accepted by government decision-makers as a natural component of the international system of diplomacy. This is far more likely to be the case with small powers in the contemporary system, not only because they tend to support the Organization with greater fervor than the superpowers, but also for the obvious reason that international organizations are more likely to be seriously involved in disputes between relatively weak states. UN activity in cases such as the Berlin crisis of 1948-49, the Korean War, or the 1962 Cuba missile crisis was distinctly marginal. Yet even in these instances of comparatively high level conflict, the Secretary-General was included in the negotiating sessions, not solely because he symbolized the Organization and the interest of the world community in peaceful settlement, but also for the informed recommendations he might make. Drummond's work in the Sino-Japanese case or Hammarskjold's role in the Middle East or Congo were taken for granted by statesmen, and publics as well in the Hammarskjold era. The greater the respect accorded the Secretary-General, the easier is the assumption of national decision-makers that he has an important contribution to make to the resolution of conflict.

Given the higher level of prestige enjoyed by Drummond and Hammarskjold, it would appear that diplomatic proficiency is a vital element in explaining a rather elusive concept. Certainly in the case of the League Secretary-General, such prestige as was accorded Sir Eric in the foreign offices of the world was a direct function of his negotiating aptitude, for as noted, he gave few addresses, did not hold press conferences, and given the nature of his work behind the scenes, was almost totally unknown to the general public. Even as the League began its decline in the early 1930's, his reputation among decision-makers remained undiminished. During the Avenol administration, as we have seen, the power of the Office collapsed almost entirely, and indeed, the League's second Secretary-General was only slightly better known among the statesmen of his time than he was to the public at large. From the very start of his tenure. Avenol indicated little interest in several League political programs and there was no question of imaginative mediation. The adverse affect upon his standing in the international community was immediate.

The Secretary-General of the United Nations has had an easier time in establishing some standing and eminence, for factors beyond diplomatic capacity have assumed greater importance, such as the continuous participation of the United States and the Soviet Union in the world organization, and the deliberate attempt by the founders of the UN to create a more meaningful role for the Secretariat's first official. Expanded communications facilities and the successful effort by Trygve Lie to capitalize on his position as a potential mediator at the center of the system of parliamentary diplomacy have also contributed. Dag Hammarskjold's dazzling diplomatic adroitness was aided by an extra-constitutional shift at the UN away from the Security Council to the Assembly in the processes of international peace-keeping, generating an increased executive role for the Secretariat, and in turn a more substantial influence for the Secretary-General. Governments and publics alike indicated a growing awareness of, and sensitivity to the Secretary-General, reflected by, among other things, a great outpouring of literature in the 1950's and 1960's on the Office and the Secretariat.

U Thant has been able to take the process a step further still, for while he has not been able to demonstrate the diplomatic talent of a Hammarskjold, he has been in office during the early development of a "constituency" based on the numerically superior neutral nations. As general spokesman for the most basic claims of the Asian and African states—that is to say, political independence, rapid economic and social development, and neutrality in ideologically based East-West conflicts, Thant has been able to establish perhaps an outsized reputation among his supporters. Once again, Soviet and American competition for influence in the developing nations has given him a measure of influence and prestige he might not otherwise enjoy. Thant also has the advantage of serving as Secretary-

General during a period of a relative loosening of previously tight alliance and bloc structures, permitting a receptivity to certain of his initiatives that might not have been forthcoming in another system.

A closely related factor here is the Secretary-General's *structural position* as the focal point of the Organization and thus his status as one of the central figures of the international system. The contemporary Secretary-General symbolizes the Organization, serves as its spokesman, and as defender of its interests and involvement in international politics. The relative prominence and visibility of the Office have changed over the years. Drummond's, Avenol's and naturally Lester's post did not enjoy the salient position of the current Office, and to this day, we are apt to identify particular statesmen, such as Briand or Eden, with the League of Nations. Since the earliest days of the UN, we tend to think of the Organization as dominated at a particular period by the work of its Secretary-General rather than by the preeminence of the personalities who have appeared in its forums.

The current Secretary-General and his staff are the only international officials in a position to marshal rapidly the resources essential for effective implementation of Assembly or Council peacekeeping directives, thereby adding to the UN's executive power in shaping the means and strategy of third-party intervention. His central location provides an outstanding opportunity to acquire relevant information of interest to representatives, and enables the Secretary-General to perform the role of advisor or mediator. States may turn to him for face-saving recommendations acceptable from a neutral international civil servant, but not from a hostile party, and of course, the Secretary-General's structural position makes liaison with member states relatively easy, particularly through the several permanent missions.

The Secretary-General's place at the center of the organized international community has been a key asset in terms of the development of his discretionary powers, for if unwieldly political bodies were forced to delegate certain powers to the UN's executive branch, he quite naturally became obligated to assume further responsibilities. The Germans and Italians in 1930 and the Soviet Union in 1960 were in reality attacking the Secretary-General's privileged post at the center by blunting his capacity through an attempted collectivization of staff decision-making.

Current Soviet insistence that the Security Council is the proper forum for the planning, establishment and direction of all UN forces is an argument directed against the centrality of the Secretary-General's place in world diplomacy and an interpretation severely limiting the basic constitutional significance of Articles 98 and 99 of the Charter while resurrecting the Council not merely as the primary organ for peacekeeping, but as the sole agent of third-party intervention by the UN. One of the great questions for international organization after its first fifty years is whether the Secretary-

General will be permitted to retain the salient position he has enjoyed in world politics.

This raises the issue of the *constitutional theory,* prescribed or customary, of the Secretary-General's role and the functions properly attributed to his Office. This is a resource, naturally, to the extent that liberal constructionist views thereon are accepted by principal members of the Organization, for this is essentially a matter of the rules of the game by which the Secretary-General operates and the acceptability of those rules to national actors. While the questions raised in this context are a matter of emphasis and degree, the focus is upon the capacity and willingness of the Secretary-General to serve in an independent fashion rather than as a strictly accountable agent of the Organization, to serve publicly as well as privately and behind the scenes, to work critically rather than in an accomodating manner, and to be generally active rather than passive in world politics.

There is no question that Dag Hammarskjold did most to fashion in an explicit manner a relatively liberal set of rules, and to take advantage of the lack of serious opposition thereto. Of the six Secretaries-General, only Avenol and Lester made no attempts to expand the political role and influence of the Office—Avenol because of personal limitations and narrow political views, and Lester because of the caretaker nature of League operations during the war.

Drummond, as we have seen, while only rarely articulating his conception of the role of the Secretary-General, acted on the assumption that his executive obligations were to be consistent with the accomodating "private secretary" theory of the Office. Drummond was certainly not passive, but he took no public initiatives of any consequence whatever, served at the Council's whim, and worked quietly with the full knowledge and acquiesence of the League's primary members. Nevertheless, due essentially to his remarkable abilities and contribution within the extraordinarily confining parameters of the Office in the 1920's and early 1930's, and the value of his position to member nations, the UN founding fathers inserted Article 99 into the Charter, thus explicitly changing the rules and enlarging the potential scope of the Secretary-General's influence. The addition of Article 99 was of great assistance to Trygve Lie in his attempts to fashion a meaningful place for the Office, particularly in terms of speaking out on critical issues and in lending his prestige to one or another of the demands and claims pressed by members of the international community.

Lie added a whole new dimension to the Drummond model, for not only was he an active Secretary-General, as was Sir Eric, but he successfully and rapidly established the practice of working publicly as well as privately, and doing so in a manner critical of states and their programs. The development of meaningful discretionary authority had to await a new international system in the 1950's, a transfer of power from the Security Council to the General Assembly, and the opportunity for international peacekeeping operations. But Lie's contribution was important for he had gained general acceptance of an advanced position on the scale of interpretation of the Secretary-General's constitutional position. If we draw a line running from private to public activity, then to delegated powers, and finally to independent field actions, it is clear that Drummond took the first step and Lie succeeded in equaling that and taking the next one. It remained for Hammarskjold to make the final advance toward an independant role for the Secretary-General.

As noted, Hammarskjold was the only Secretary-General to develop an explicit theory of his functions, and naturally enough, his Charter interpretations were liberal. He insisted on the right to take certain field actions even without authorization. He relied only in part on Article 99, and gave a great deal more prominence to Articles 7 and 98 than had theretofore been generally accepted by students and statesmen. His marked tendency to equate the Secretariat with the main political organs of the UN constituted an enormous change in the rules of the game and allowed for a flexibility of maneuver unparalleled in the history of the Office. Hammarskjold's constructions were accepted passively, rather than enthusiastically, probably indicating an incomplete appreciation of the full implications of the rules change, although awareness was made manifest during the Congo crisis, when the acceptability of his constitutional position was nearly dissipated.

Secretary-General Thant has been in a difficult position ever since. He has tried to emulate Hammarskjold's maximalist approach, but has formulated no theory of his own, and as we have seen, has been severely hedged in (primarily by the Soviet Union and France) on the matter of discretionary executive functions. Thant has been able to enlarge the scope of the Secretary-General's ability to speak out on various issues, even in a manner highly critical of the United States and Soviet Union, but his power to influence peacekeeping operations without authorization by the great powers has been challenged, and this has already served to retract to more modest dimensions the constitutional framework within which the Secretary-General now operates. There can be no doubt that the Secretary-General's ability to write his own rules in the Hammarskjold manner has been severely weakened, at least for a period extending well into the foreseeable future. Further, Soviet resistance has reduced the importance of the Office so that in constitutional terms, the position in 1970 is more akin to that of the early 1950's. Thant has not been able to maintain the Hammarskjold line, although his political role appears today somewhat more advanced than Lie's.

A related intangible resource available to the Secretary-General in the past (it is close to inoperative today) is his own *record* in the international arena. To the extent he succeeds in any given case, he is more likely to expand his authority and influence in subsequent issues, while a record of failure naturally tends to contract the scope of his power. An output that "works" tends to feed back and become a resource or potential resource upon which the Secretary-General may later draw. If the performance is deemed unsatisfactory or too displeasing to the great powers, the output may well have a kind of negative feedback effect, and serve to reduce his influence. Output in the sense of the Secretary-General's work product thus becomes a contingent and potential resource.

Examined in this light, there are marked divergencies among the six Secretaries-General. Drummond's record was a continuous asset to him, even during the worst moments of the Sino-Japanese crisis. His contribution was valuable and impartial, and generally perceived as such throughout his administration. Avenol's performance was commonly regarded as unsatisfactory, and his authority shrank accordingly. Lester, as we have seen, had no political output at all, given the inability of the League of Nations to function during the war except in the most non-controversial economic and technical areas.

Lie and Hammarskjold generally benefitted from their records by rewards of increased authority until their work in the Korean and Congo cases, respectively, greatly impaired their capacity to act further. In the case of Lie and the Korean War, the problem was one of irreconcilable American and Soviet demands either of which standing alone, and certainly when taken in combination, were sufficient to undermine the Office. He could not remain passive in the face of aggression; yet a stand in defense of the Charter meant Soviet alienation. The United Nations itself was successful in Korea, but the political pressures upon Lie were simply inconsistent with the nature of the Office, and resulted in his demise as an effective international official.

Hammarskjold's failure in the Congo was essentially a system failure to respond and adapt adequately to changes in the environment. He lost the support of the Soviet Union because, among other reasons, he seemed to be resisting the rapidly growing influence of the Afro-Asian states in the organization. The no-force doctrine in Katanga province combined with the significant role of the Western-dominated "Congo Club" in the secretariat made somewhat believable for third-world states the Soviet perception that Hammarskjold was aligning himself too closely with Western interests. Hammarskjold's general record during the 1950's constituted one of the great resources at his disposal at the beginning of the 1960's, and indicated to the international community the enormous value of the Office, but perceived failure to adapt resulted in a near-collapse of his powers, and has left his successor in a greatly weakened condition.

U Thant thus serves as Secretary-General during a time of an artificially debilitated Office. The Soviet Union and France have been loathe to utilize the post to the full extent of its proven capabilities, and the result has been that any given output for Thant does not have the same feedback value it might have had for preceeding Secretaries-General. Thant can have no general expectation that present success will be rewarded by future grants of power. The building block approach so skillfully utilized by Hammar-skjold is not available to Thant, and it is highly problematic whether successful performance will generate further power in the foreseeable future.

A closely related factor here is the capacity of international organization to act at all in world politics. The Office of the Secretary-General is a subsystem within the larger system represented by the League or United Nations, and the capabilities of the larger unit determines in large measure the power of the Secretary-General. There is, to be sure, interaction here, as the Secretary-General's position and the use he makes of it are important in determining the potential value of the larger organization.

Needless to say, the United Nations is still a marginal factor in world politics, although it has demonstrated a far greater capacity for action than the League and this is reflected in the development of the Office of Secretary-General. The League was primarily a European-based organization, with limited interests in Asia, Africa, and Latin America, and was riven by desperate conflicts between the totalitarian powers and the western democracies, the former being only too willing to fight, and the latter too weak to resist until war was thrust upon them. There was only a very small group of neutrals, without the highly motivated competition for influence among them between the major contestants that governs in the present international system. Unlimited warfare was quite thinkable, and the absence of weapons of mass destruction provided scant incentive for recourse to limited hostilities for limited ends. Under these circumstances, it was something of a wonder that the League of Nations tried at all to intervene in the Sino-Japanese conflict of the early 1930's, and close to miraculous that the Organization attempted to force a policy change on the government of Italy during the Italian-Ethiopian crisis of 1935-1936. The failure of sanctions meant the effective end of the League's political role and this of course signalled the demise of the Secretary-General as a factor of any importance.

The United Nations has had an enormous advantage over the League in that the international system developing since the early 1950's has been far more conducive to a significant role for global institutions. A great power split has, as noted many times, destroyed the original concept of collective security upon which the UN was originally based, and indeed, the resultant weakness of the Security Council came very close to paralyzing the Organization during its formative years. The Korean conflict marked a resurgence of the UN, though only as a legitimizing cover for the United States response to the military attack. But after the Korean War, and the death of Stalin, and subsequent to the rapid influx of Asian and African members, the Organization found itself able to act with some frequency and flexibility. The neutral nations, primarily interested in rapid economic and social development, naturally wished to avoid involvement in East-West military conflict, and if this meant UN interposition, then the Soviets and the

Americans, both wishing to find favor in the third world, could not readily object. The result was a growth in influence for the world body, and a subsequent development of the Secretary-General's political role. The irony is that the fullest development of his influence came prior to the emergence into statehood of the great mass of Asian and African countries. And while the United Nations has now achieved near universality in membership, with a heavy concentration of neutral nations, the influence of the Secretary-General has been narrowed by reason of Soviet and French opposition.

Nevertheless, the future role of the UN, and by turn the power of the Secretary-General, is not totally unpromising. It has become a commonplace to speak of the North-South conflict, with a kind of East-West overlay based primarily on ideological and economic competition for influence in the South. This pattern assumes the absence of nuclear warfare and the persistence of limited (and commonly internal) conflict in areas where colonial disputes of the past have yet to be resolved, or where there is significant dispute over the most appropriate means to modernization and social change. Given the aversion of most third world nations for serving as the arena for large-scale warfare, and given the desire of Moscow and Washington to maintain or expand their power in the third world, UN intervention in areas outside of the superpowers' immediate spheres of influence appears a likely prospect for some time to come. It will necessarily require a certain amount of discretionary power for the Secretary-General to organize and maintain UN peacekeeping or observation forces, despite contrary pressure that will certainly continue to be exerted by the Soviet Union. The power of the Organization (and therefore that of the chief executive) to act in international affairs is likely to be maintained at least at its current level.

The early development of a *political constituency* for the Secretary-General has been a factor of considerable importance in contemporary politics. As a resource, this has meaning only for the current holder of the Office, at least in terms of providing a base enabling him to engage in a process of flexible independent diplomatic maneuver between East and West. As noted, Thant's position as spokesman for, and to a certain extent representative of the Asian-African group of nations at the UN has been of substantial assistance to him.

There was nothing comparable for the other Secretaries-General. Drummond and Avenol had the advantage of British and French support but this obviously did not serve to enhance their acceptability to Germany and Italy. The League Secretary-General's independence was made far more difficult by reason of national affiliation than has been the case with the United Nations' three executive heads. The Norwegian Lie was certainly in a better position to assume a posture of neutrality between the great powers than Drummond or Avenol. Yet, Lie's central position between Moscow and

Washington was clearly fragile, for while he had the open blessing of the Scandinavian nations, there were very few Asian and African UN members throughout the seven years of his tenure, and his independence thus depended far more on his wits than anything else. The situation was markedly different for Dag Hammarskjold only during the last few years of his administration.

The changed nature of the system has become abundantly clear during the 1960's administration of U Thant, for the Organization's current roster of members includes a majority of third world states forming the central core of support for the Secretary-General, whether in matters of inter-state conflict, economic and social development, colonialism, or human rights. Without alienation of the superpowers, Thant may utilize his embryonic "constituency" as a base of authority and influence, assuming a continued competition for power by Moscow and Washington in the Afro-Asian world. At the least he has a certain measure of flexibility, in terms of public statement and recommendation, beyond the more confining parameters of the Lie and Hammarskjold years.

His September, 1968 press conference statement in which he suggested the General Assembly would approve a resolution calling for a cessation of U.S. bombing in North Vietnam could not have been made without prior assurance of support from his backers. It has been commonly supposed that lack of a constituency enhanced the Secretary-General's freedom of expression by permitting him to avoid confining political obligations, but the precise opposite is probably correct. So long as the Secretary-General is forced into a position of neutrality between the dominant opposed powers of the Organization, and so long as the majority of nations adopt a position of independence between those great powers, the Secretary-General will find his freedom of expression enhanced. Thant's strong statements either criticizing the U.S. on Vietnam, or recommending policy known to be unacceptable to Washington, his views on the Soviet invasion of Czechoslovakia in the summer of 1968, and his outspoken words on economic development and expanded assistance from wealthy to poor nations are a result of that freedom that is the more secure for its political base.

Yet the notion of "constituency", and its potential as a source of authority for the Secretary-General should not be exaggerated. There are certainly limits to what any Secretary-General may publicly assert in criticism of the nations whose positive support he must have to remain an effective figure. If the issue is deemed crucial enough, the superpowers will not hesitate to withdraw their backing, even despite a substantial risk of third-world disaffection. The Soviet response to Hammarskjold's role in the Congo is an example of Moscow's willingness to tolerate serious disenchantment from the Afro-Asian group in order to destroy a clearly perceived antagonist. Washington protested Thant's Vietnam's statement in September, 1968, and has been quite unhappy over the general tenor and substance of his

Vietnam declarations, making withdrawal of support a restraining force for the Secretary-General.

Further, the Afro-Asian states do not in fact vote or act as a bloc on several of the key issues before the world body, and Thant can properly look to them for uniform guidance on only a few, if admittedly important problems. Even such similarity as can be found in third world conceptions and Thant's own thinking is more likely than not to be expressed in very general terms acceptable to almost the entire range of UN membership. It is more a matter of emphasis, tone, and style that serves to characterize Thant as a representative of large groups of African and Asian states in international diplomacy, rather than his bringing influence to bear on particular political problems.

Perhaps most important, even assuming a uniform posture on any given question, and a resultant enlargement of the Secretary-General's freedom of expression, this does not necessarily result in an expansion of his independent powers, particularly in the all important area of peacekeeping and general third-party intervention in cases of crisis or high-level conflict. As noted, the Soviet Union is quite willing to risk alienation to prevent this development, and its resistance is likely to continue well into the foreseeable future. In a particular case in which Moscow wishes to maintain close relations and the pressure for a UN presence is quite strong, it is likely that the Secretary-General will be permitted to organize an intervention through the Secretariat with the informal guidance of the Council or Assembly, but this will not occur frequently. Further, as the Organization develops, it is not out of the question for the United States to adopt a similar stance, depending, of course, upon the real strength the Afro-Asian states and to some extent Latin America, can give to a neutralist Secretary-General. The constituency of the Secretariat's first officer should be understood as a limited source of power.

Following closely upon the notion of a constituency for the Secretary-General, resources of great importance for him are particular *authorizations or grants of power,* emanating either from the political organs of the global body or more informally, from particular nations or groups acting quietly. It is necessary to distinguish formal parliamentary delegations of power and specific Council or Assembly directives from the informal message to the Secretary-General authorizing him to undertake a mission of some kind, engage in diplomatic bargaining sessions, or make public statements. For the League Secretary-General, grants of power were made only informally, except in the most narrow administrative areas. Drummond and Avenol were never directed by the Council or Assembly to undertake a political action of any kind, although in Sir Eric's case, there were clearly many informal delegations made behind the scenes, involving requests to take part in negotiations, and to share the benefit of his information and wisdom with the states most directly concerned in any given question. In many cases,

Drummond utilized the general authorization of the Secretariat to prepare papers on questions before the League to inform himself and then take part in discussions quite naturally and without even informal warrant of any kind—the authority was by implication, and Sir Eric made the most of it for fourteen years. But he had a clear understanding of the political limitations upon his capabilities for initiating political action, and suggestions for procedures or terms of settlement were never made without thoroughly preparing the way. Avenol, as we have seen, was more willing to act on his own initiative, and did so without political support or authority in some instances, but his apparent disposition to compromise at the expense of the League resulted in a debilitated Office.

Formal assignments of authority in political matters did not become a meaningful phenomenon at the United Nations until the Dag Hammarskjold era, beginning with the issue of the UN flyers in China in late 1954. In that case, the delegation of authority was a last resort measure, as the United States had no diplomatic relations with Peking and preferred an attempt by the global institution to the alternative of unilateral intervention. The more important delegations of authority resulted from the shift of effective decision-making power over peacekeeping from the Security Council to the General Assembly, necessitating an executive capability to manage the field operations deemed desirable at the time. Hammarskjold was the recipient of delegated authority in a number of critical cases, particularly the Suez crisis of 1956 and the Congo in 1960. His work in the Congo, as well as that of Thant after September, 1961, marked the zenith of the Secretary-General's independent powers and the fullest development to date of his role in world politics.

Formal grants of power, however, are not an unmixed blessing for the Secretary-General, for very much depends upon the motivation and character of the authorizing directives. Precisely-worded resolutions render his tasks simpler and provide a reasonable understanding of the limits of his authority. But they may have an inhibiting effect as well, and the most recent tendency has been to limit the Secretary-General's options by formulating in comparatively narrow fashion the boundaries of his action. Vaguely phrased mandates naturally permit greater room for maneuver, but all too often they simply mask underlying political disputes whose resolution is delayed by allowing the Secretary-General to try his hand. The political risks inherent in this process are obvious enough.

Perhaps the key point in delegating authority to the Secretary-General is the motivation, for if, as in the Suez case and the early days of the Congo crisis, the assignment is one primarily of convenience, there is little risk of alienation. The Secretary-General is chosen as the most efficient and convenient instrument to establish and maintain a peace observation force, for example, or even a peacekeeping operation, and his authority flows from a political consensus on the desirability of the operation and its direction by the international staff. Questions deemed by the Secretary-General as beyond the scope of his initial authorization may be resolved by reference to political representatives of the states concerned, and assuming a continued reliance on his discretion flowing from political agreement, there is little occasion for difficulties in the relations between staff and principal powers.

The more disturbing question for the Secretary-General is how to respond to delegations of authority made by the Council or Assembly only because there is no fundamental agreement on a question upon which rapid action is necessary. This was the Hammarskjold dilemma in the Congo—his discretionary powers after the initial authorization resulted from conflict, and the burden of decision was placed in the Office with the hope that a successful resolution might be developed, or if not, one side or the other was in position to apportion blame. The decision to use force in Katanga Province was left in his hands, with the obvious risk of seriously provoking the resentment and even animosity of the Soviet Union or the West. The Secretary-General was placed in a position from which the Office has not yet recovered.

What seems to have evolved during the Thant administration is a kind of working compromise. The pattern has been to continue to grant the Secretary-General particular administrative powers in the formation of peacekeeping forces, even though these may have some political significance, but to keep the reins tight and permit almost no independent power in the substantive direction of such operations. The Secretary-General is also the recipient of many requests from member nations to undertake a particular task requiring his independent action, such as Washington's request that Thant make contact with the North Vietnamese regime for purposes of sounding out Hanoi's real demands for political settlement of the war in Vietnam. It is not at all likely that the Security Council or Assembly will revert in the near future to the Hammarskjold era of broad delegations of authority, whether for reasons of administrative convenience or to mask substantive disagreement, for the Soviet Union and France will exert enormous pressure to prevent it. Further, if the motivation appears bad to the Secretary-General, he also may demand further attempts to reach consensus prior to the passage of broadly-worded directives that might later endanger his position.

As noted, the political role of the Secretary-General does not depend entirely upon delegations of authority, no matter what the motivation. Articles 7 and 99 of the Charter, taken together, have in the past provided sufficient constitutional justification for "filling vacuums" or acting without directives from the UN's political organs. Indeed, such independent action has been to date the highest manifestation of the Secretary-General's diplomatic activity in the current international system. The problem for the contemporary Office, of course, is to preserve as much independent authority and delegated power as is politically feasible.

Turning to resources within the Secretariat, the first item of importance is the availability of *skilled personnel,* including both permanent staff and outside experts whose services are utilized for a particular problem. This is of great consequence at the top, or decision-making level of the Secretariat. The Secretary-General's output is naturally affected in large measure by the capabilities of his most immediate assistants, particularly in the demanding cases of threatened or actual inter-state conflict. Top second men have been indispensable, including Frank Walters under Drummond, Abraham Feller and Andrew Cordier in the Lie administration, Cordier with Hammarskjold, and C. V. Narasimham in the Thant era. As noted previously, the real need for the contemporary Office is not so much politically skilled personnel as it is for greater numbers of staff trained in matters of military and strategic importance, for here the top-level Secretariat structure has been woefully undermanned.

The Secretary-General's closest assistants have a large range of political responsibilities. They help prepare speeches, reports, documents, the annual report, all communications from the Office, and assist in negotiations and the establishment and administration of field forces. Indeed, high-level personnel perform very much the same set of functions as the Secretary-General, although most frequently without the visibility and public knowledge usually associated with their chief's many tasks. This is particularly true of the few dozen or so officials in the Executive Office, many of whom are among the most capable Secretariat officials, and with the more interesting and significant assignments.

The general level of competence of the staff closest to the Secretary-General has been relatively high over the years, although never so outstanding as during the administration of Sir Eric Drummond. He was surrounded by a group of truly gifted men, small in number though they were, who made it possible to turn the League Secretariat into a first-rate international institution. There were, to be sure, problems of universality and shrinking size. After it became clear that the United States would not join the League, and Raymond Fosdick resigned his post as the American Under Secretary-General, the United States had no one at the "cabinet" level of the Secretariat until the United Nations era. Further, the Soviet Union was not a member of the League at all until the 1930's, and then only for a short period. There was also the troublesome issue of the national role played by the Italian and German Under Secretaries during their tenure. And naturally, under the stress of war in the 1930s, the Secretariat began to shrink as the number of withdrawals mounted, and this was reflected in the size of the top level structure. During the war years under Sean Lester, the Secretariat was a shell of its former self.

Notwithstanding the difficulties, the general level of performance of the existing high-level staff during the 1920's was extraordinarily high. And given the nature of the "British system" Drummond imported into the

Secretariat, top officials were permitted a good deal of initiative even in politically significant matters. As we have seen, while Avenol utilized the "French system" of administration, ostensibly necessitating a lesser role for the cabinet, he nevertheless permitted a good deal of personal responsibility for each of his closest aides, primarily because of lack of interest and will on his own part.

Trygve Lie relied heavily on the advice of his most immediate assistants in the Executive Office and upon the Department heads. While each of Lie's eight Assistant Secretries-General administered a department in the Secretriat, diplomatic work assumed progressively added importance along with the increased political role for Lie.[7] This finally brought about a weakening of administrative responsibilities of some of the more skillfull staff, such as Ralph Bunche, who were simply too important in political negotiations to be saddled with extensive bureaucratic work. It also entailed bringing in personnel from outside the Secretariat for particular tasks.

Hammarskjold doubled the size of the "cabinet", in recognization of the growing Secretariat and the need for greater specialization in the administration of several departments, but at the same time he created two Under Secretaries for Special Political Affairs without portfolio, a clear institutional recognition of the fact that top level officials were playing an important political role. The Executive Office was also expanded and an enormous amount of responsibility entrusted to Andrew Cordier. Yet Hammarskjold generally centralized the administration as never before, and greatly decreased the initiative and responsibility originating from lower levels. He did not like to delegate authority, in marked contrast to Lie and Thant, although as the years passed and his own responsibilities expanded, the number of top level Secretariat officals whose primary responsibility was political grew apace. By the end of his administration, Hammarskjold formally proposed a new top level structure that would have included five Assistant Secretaries-General with diplomatic and political tasks and without substantial administrative duties. Hammarskjold also made extensive use of outside personnel, as has Thant. In terms of reliance upon his immediate assistants, Thant is very much more in the tradition of Trygve Lie, as officers such as Narasimham and Bunche have a far greater opportunity to take initiatives than was the case under Hammarskjold.

The UN Secretariat has had certain difficulties in terms of the competence of its top-level officials, and for a number of reasons. The requirement of a wide geographical distribution (which, contrary to the terms of the Charter, has taken precedence over technical competence) has at times resulted in

[7] Once source of difficulty was that the Soviet Assistant Secretary-General, who occupied the post for Security Council affairs, soon adopted the practice of reporting anything he deemed of potential interest to Moscow back to the Soviet UN Mission, resulting in a diversion of sensitive questions elsewhere, particularly to the Executive Office.

the placing of persons without adequate training and background in positions of responsibility. The insistence of some nations on a policy of short-
term secondment has also had its effect. A growing percentage of the Secretariat staff is on short-term contract, and while this has certain advantages in
terms of national civil service training and exposure to global institutions,
it adds little to the common fund of knowledge and experience of the staff
as a whole. It cannot be demonstrated that officials on short-term loan from
their governments are any the less dedicated to the international interests
of the UN than career staff, but the tendency to withdraw an officer after
two or three years of training in New York deprives the Organization of
services that have just begun to be valuable.

Perhaps most important, however, is the reluctance by a number of the
Organization's key members, particularly during the formative years, to
place their most highly skilled officers in the UN service. The United States,
for example, having taken the lead in establishing the United Nations, has
done relatively little to make its Secretariat a first-rate structure. Indeed,
one scholar in the field has written:

> ...unlike many other governments, the United States has never encouraged such
> service as an honor, or, in the case of government officials, as a basis for continued
> advancement in the national service. Even though the number of positions open to
> Americans is limited and becoming more so as the membership increases, service with
> the United Nations should be made a matter of both professional honor and national
> interest rather than, as it is now, tacitly if not openly stigmatized.[8]

This has changed somewhat for the better over the years since 1946, although there is still much room for improvement.

A serious personnel problem is the kind of training higher level officials
receive prior to entering the Secretariat, and the expertise they are prepared
to offer. As noted, military and strategic knowledge, and contingency
planning capabilities are not widely shared resources of the Secretariat at
the present time, and this clearly has an inhibiting effect on the potential
functions of the Secretary-General, and constitutes as well a real limitation
on the value of the current tasks he is capable of performing. The problem
has become aggravated since the mid-1950's, when the world body began
to utilize peacekeeping operations on a relatively large scale as an instrument
of Hammarskjold's "preventive diplomacy". As discussed, the problem
does not appear insurmountable, although the Secretariat itself has not perceived a need for substantial change in this area.

The Secretary-General's more *tangible* physical resources suitable for
political tasks, including intervention with UN missions, are severely limited.
In terms of equipment and materiel, there is almost nothing, except a few
facilities that may be shifted from one operation to another, and the result
is a total dependence upon a relatively few member states to provide

---

[8] Lincoln P. Bloomfield, *The United Nations and U.S. Foreign Policy* (Boston: Little,
Brown and Company, 1967 edition), p. 177.

essential supplies, particularly expensive transportation equipment. Lie's Field Force proposals would have remedied this to some extent, but the rejection of his plans, and the resistance to a standing UN army of any size by Hammarskjold and Thant (not to speak of the powerful opposition of the Soviet Union) has meant that an independent and effective source of power for the Secretary-General has been eliminated. Once an operation is closed out, as was say the Congo operation in 1964, or UNEF in 1967, the Secretary-General loses his troops.

It is important to give due weight to *communications facilities* as one of the Secretary-General's valuable tangible resources. The UN has its own radio, television, telegraph, telephone, press, and documentary services enabling the Organization to communicate efficiently internally, with missions abroad, and with member nations, either through the several representative offices in New York or with their home governments. The Secretary-General has access to all of these, of course, in addition to the normal commercial communications channels. While the UN's own resources would probably prove inadequate in a severe crisis, they have generally been sufficient and workable for most UN operations, including the larger peacekeeping forces.

In sum, analysis of the Secretary-General's sources of authority and power must necessarily concentrate upon the several intangible items that provide him with the marginal influence he currently possesses in world politics. And given the abstract and insubstantial nature of the assets available, it seems clear from the perspective of the 1970's that while the Office of the Secretary-General is certainly dependent upon and shaped by its past history and practice, it is also what each chief executive makes of it. Clearly, a successful Secretary-General must be capable of maximizing most of the intangible assets, and while some are beyond his immediate control, such action in itself necessitates a rather impressive diplomatic talent. As noted, in future appointments of a Secretary-General, nations opposed to the development of the Office may seek an official who is not of the highest caliber, for this is at once the easiest variable to limit before the appointment, and the keystone upon which much of the remaining structure depends. This may well be the most efficient method to degrade the Office, and it should not be discounted lightly, for the ability of the Office to thrive, or even survive, may well turn in large measure upon the intelligence and diplomatic dexterity of the incumbent.

As with the rest of the Secretariat staff, the selection of a Secretary-General is bedeviled by the conflict between the requirement of broad geographic distribution on the one hand and technical competence on the other. While the Charter insists that primary deference be accorded to individual capacity, in fact geography and ideological suitability have been far more important. Yet for the Secretary-General, most members of his Executive Office, and other top-level staff, it is of absolutely critical importance to find and attract the most skilled personnel available. The periods of greatest gain for the Secretary-General have been during the administrations of Sir Eric Drummond and Dag Hammarskjold, the two most highly talented in the art of international diplomacy. And given the general nature of the contemporary global system and the essentiality of interventionary and intermediary functions for the world body, it is probably the case that in very large measure the success of the Organization turns on the abilities of its Secretary-General. The organized international community must find first-rate men if the United Nations is ever to play more than the most marginal of roles in world politics.

Turning to the substantive political functions of the Secretary-General, the primary concern is with those activities and tasks that bear directly upon the international political process. As will be seen, the political functions of the Secretary-General, as depicted in the following analysis, are at different levels of abstraction, result from differing motivations, and result both in international system maintenance and system change. The interest here in political functions entails analysis of roles and tasks primarily intended, manifest, and designed to assist the dominant actors in the international system to carry on diplomatic intercourse and reach peaceful settlement of disputes. The Secretary-General has always functioned as an aide to states in maintaining any given balance of power, but always within a context of peaceful change. The attempt here is to gain further understanding of the several reasons why nations find the Office of the Secretary-General a useful supplement to the normal workings of their foreign policy processes. Most of the functions attributed to the Secretary-General may certainly be performed by other actors, in some cases simultaneously, in others as an alternative. As previously noted, a useful hypothesis of the Secretary-General would entail assigning weights to the diverse functions and establishing their relationships to each other, the resources from which they flow, and the rest of the global organization and system. The more modest analysis below is set forth in the hopes of making a start toward theory by shedding light on the functions themselves.[9]

The reasons why nations utilize the Office (perceive its value or functions) given its manifest weaknesses in the arena of power conflict, are diverse and certainly at different levels of behavioral regularity and of abstraction. This should be clearly understood. Nation-states have been interested in world organization from many perspectives, and an informal analysis is

[9] The term "functions" here is used only in the context of the Secretary-General's perceived value to national actors, and not in any formal relation to the approaches of functionalism or structural-functionalism. As Merton points out, "the large assembly of terms used indifferently and almost synonymously with 'function' presently include use, utility, purpose, motive, intention, aim, consequence". (Robert K. Merton, *Social Theory and Social Structure* (Glencoe, Ill.: The Free Press, 1957 edition), p. 23.)

justified provided it is further appreciated that certain "functions" are intended and others unintended, some are manifest, while others are latent, and that any given task of the Secretary-General has a direct relationship to the maintenance or development of any given international system, past or present.

An inquiry into the Secretary-General's tasks naturally entails an understanding of his work in every substantive area of concern to global institutions. General diplomatic functions, for example, are carried on within the context of any of the Organization's activities. But the stress here will be on those tasks and roles with the most consequential political impact, and functions of greatest value to nation-states. It is difficult to categorize the several services performed by the Secretary-General, and perhaps the most efficient method is to analyze them under the functional headings commonly associated with world organization itself. Given the concentration upon political tasks, the larger categories are (1) diplomatic functions; (2) conflict management functions; (3) integration functions.

Diplomatic functions obviously touch not just politics, but economic and social development, colonialism, the development of international law, and so on. But they clearly are critical for the general political processes of world organization, and thus their inclusion here. One of the most important tasks of the Secretary-General over the years since 1920 has been *communication*. Given the political information and data to which the Secretary-General has constant access, and given his structural position at the focal point of the League or UN system and as a central pivot for the process of international diplomacy, the executive head is in an excellent position to communicate with states, both members and non-members of the Organization, on any matter in which they might be interested.

There are many facets to the communications work of the Office. It has been convenient for nations to supplement more normal channels of diplomacy through recourse to the international Secretariat. This has happened not infrequently during the League and United Nations era. The National Archives of the United States, for example, are filled with documents indicating a request by the Secretary of State to his representative in Geneva to seek or pass on some information through Sir Eric Drummond and later, to a lesser extent, through Joseph Avenol. Nations have often been able to communicate information, seek a reply to a given questtion, discover likely responses to projected programs, and generally deal indirectly with authoritative decision-makers of other countries through the Office of the Secretary-General.

The Secretary-General is also in a position to communicate on his own initiative undistorted information and relatively disinterested interpretations of particular facts, problems, and responses. The disinterested and impartial quality of such communication naturally has a great bearing in terms of acceptability to nations that might otherwise be distrustful, and this could be of extreme importance in case of a severe international crisis. Here the resources of independence (and accompanying acceptability) in addition to the Secretary-General's structural position in the total system allow for the effective operation of the communication function. The Secretary-General may also facilitate direct communication between other nations through the use of what has been called "good offices". This refers essentially to the requisite psychological assistance the Secretary-General might offer to parties in conflict should a spur be needed to begin negotiations.

The nature of the communications function has not changed in any remarkable way since the founding of the League of Nations. Communication was one of the most important areas of Drummond's work, and while the task itself continued unabated during the Avenol years, communications flows were more likely during that period to move through other top-level offices in the Secretariat. The process has picked up in speed and intensity during the UN years, primarily as a result of increased capacities and the growing scope of the international bargaining process. The communications work of the Office has served the UN membership well during most of the conflicts in which the Organization has had a role to play, and even in cases in which the UN has not been directly involved. Examples of the latter are Thant's role in the Cuban missile crisis in 1962 and his early service in the Vietnam conflict as a kind of limited substitute for direct diplomatic dealings between the United States and North Vietnam.

The process depends in large measure upon the size of the Secretary-General's staff and the skills of its members. Should the Military Adviser's staff be expanded, this would provide a big assist not only in terms of military and contingency planning, but also in the communications process. The sending of messages concerning military positions, structures, processes and intentions might be of great importance in future international conflicts.

The second of the Secretary-General's diplomatic functions may be characterized as the *articulation and aggregation* of interests, tasks not commonly associated with the Office, but nevertheless a very important part of its activity. Articulation is closely related to the legitimacy function discussed below.[10] The Secretary-General does press hard, in private negotiations particularly, and even in public forums on occasion, for particular programs, ideas, structures, and processes that coincide with the interests and claims expressed in the Organization by many of its members. Most frequently, of course, these are generally accepted by the majority of nations, although not necessarily by most of the key national actors, and much depends upon the precision of formulation. The Secretary-General may speak and write without difficulty of the need for more rapid economic development in the poorer nations and even perhaps about the underlying obligation of wealthy states to provide greater assistance. Particular trade patterns,

10 See pp. 445-447, *infra.*

capital flows and bilateral or multi-lateral aid programs, however, is quite another matter. The Secretary-General may, and often does, argue with particularity in this context, but almost always in private, utilizing public media of communication for more general formulations.

Similarly, in the area of peacekeeping, the Secretary-General has frequently spoken in favor of a strengthened UN role in intermediary-type missions while not depicting precise objectives he feels should be met by the United States and Soviet Union in their running disagreement over peacekeeping forces. Or he may cite obligations to grant political independence to the remaining non-self-governing territories, but without detailed prescription.

The Secretary-General thus publicly articulates interests at a level of acceptable generality while shaping the nature and scope of his value judgments and expressions in accordance with the wishes of the predominant viewpoint of the international community on a given issue. His private work naturally entails greater particularity, but the task remains essentially the same. While the conception of interest articulation is commonly described and analyzed in terms of public activities of particular groupings, whether interest groups, political parties, or other units in a political setting, the Secretary-General and his Executive Office have frequently through the years expressed through private communications and messages the perceived interests of groups of states or individual states. Indeed, it may be argued that the greater precision and specificity of formulation permitted by behind-the-scenes discussion with authoritative decision-makers makes the function ever so much more valuable, for it is likely to be a more accurate rendition of the exact demand in question. Even public statements by representatives frequently reflect in their diffuseness an aggregation or compromise process. "Corridor" bargaining is likely to be frank, and the Secretary-General is constantly engaged in that kind of negotiation.

It may even be the case in forums such as an international Assembly that the only possibility of serious interest articulation on certain issues is in private negotiation. The war in Vietnam, for example, has never been the subject of meaningful debate in UN public forums and yet exchanges of views and pressures on the United States have been common enough in private discussions there. The Secretary-General has assumed almost the entire burden of publicly expressing a UN viewpoint on the issue, and has served as the key mechanism for quiet statements of majority sentiment to American representatives and government officials. Perhaps the outstanding case of private interest articulation was the work of Dag Hammarskjold in implementing what he characterized as "quiet diplomacy", in which the Secretary-General and his top aides, particularly in cases of conflict, expressed to the states concerned the views of the majority with greater exactness than was possible in public.

It is true, to be sure, that simply expressing a viewpoint held by another state is not the same thing as interest articulation. If the Secretary-General states a claim in the sense of pressing a demand for political action, he is performing the function of interest articulation. On many an occasion, it is a matter of interpretation, for the expression of an interest may be manifest or latent, much as the Secretary-General's entire range of functions. And of course, diffuseness may frequently be a deliberate mask for something quite specific.

It may also be the case that the Secretary-General, as an international civil servant, articulates interests of his own, or of the Organization. Certainly Drummond's defense of the Office in 1930 and Hammarskjold's in 1960 against proposed systems for degrading its central position and influence were expressions of institutional interest and to some extent, even personal claims.

In the League years, most of the Secretariat work of public expression went no further than the interests of the Organization itself, and this most frequently took the form of public speeches devoted to the structure and activities of the League. Beyond that were the many appeals for peace couched in the most general of terms, and not likely to be offensive to anyone. Arms control, economic and social development, colonialism, and human rights were naturally primary issues of the day, along with peaceful settlement, but the League Secretaries-General were in no position to express publicly the interests of the smaller nations on these questions, nor would they dare criticize the great powers in the Organization. In the UN era, both private and public interest articulation have become commonplace, with the essential difference between them being that the private aspect is more likely to be specific rather than diffuse, and manifest rather than latent. The public rhetoric of the United Nations Secretaries-General has been directed primarily to asserting claims of the smaller nations in the Organization, and this has become more acute under the Thant administration. Through his style, tone, and the nature of his work, it is not difficult to perceive the clear expression of interests on behalf of third-world nations, most notably in the areas of economic development, colonialism, and human rights.

Throughout the first fifty years of world organization, the Secretariat has played an important role in this process through its staff of experts who have contributed the knowledge and data necessary to articulate demands and claims in an intelligent fashion, and of course, the work of drafting resolutions, reports, and programs for consideration by the Assembly and Councils has had a significant impact on the entire organizational input of interest articulation. The Secretariat is certainly not the only institutional interest group in the organized international community, but it has always been one of the most important sub-groups in shaping raw claims and sometimes vague formulations of interest from the huge assortment of national and regional interests throughout the world.

The Secretary-General and the Executive Office thus play a significant role in *aggregating* the diverse and conflicting claims made by national actors. The primary functional channels here are, obviously, the main voting groups in the Assembly and the Councils, but the Secretary-General's Office has been crucial in the bargaining and compromise procedures that are the essence of the aggregation process. The Secretary-General and his staff have long been of assistance in quasi-legislative practices by privately and quietly recommending draft resolutions and approaches to most of the issues before the Organization. Many of the Secretary-General's statements, speeches, and reports are a distillation of conflicting claims and counterclaims and are thus valuable as an accurate indication and barometer of acceptable formulations of policy. In this sense, the Secretary-General helps to reflect and shape the bargaining process.

The communication role is of vital significance here, for the Office acts as a kind of clearing house or gateway through which the interests of the Organization's members may be, and often are expressed. The Office is equipped to inform representatives and delegates of member nations what demands are acceptable and what modifications, adaptions and compromises should be made in order to reach agreement. Face to face bargaining in the Assembly and other political organs is the central process required for aggregation of interests, but with a very solid assist from the Secretary-General.

Closely related to the interest articulation and communication functions of the Secretary-General is his *legitimization* role. The League of Nations and United Nations have long been utilized by states for purposes of having one or another political organ bestow approval or disapproval upon a particular action, program, idea, or claim by one or more of the members or other nations.[11] The Organization may even be used to bestow legitimacy upon the status of a state, as Israel in 1949, or a great number of African nations in the 1950's and 1960's. The United Nations Secretary-General has played an important part in this process, although such a function was impossible for the League Secretary-General, given the limited nature of that Office, the narrow role assigned to the international Secretariat, and the unobtrusive work pattern established by Drummond.

The more eminent position of the UN Secretary-General, however, has made his bestowal of approval or disapproval rather important to member states. A positive expression of policy by the Secretary-General, whether one of politics, economic development, human rights, or international law, can usually be taken as a statement of predominant sentiment among the community of nations, and one that generates an aura of righteousness and legitimacy. The Secretary-General's expressed opinion may also help to create consensus on a given matter, and may assist in shaping

11 See Inis Claude, Jr., *The Changing United Nations* (New York: Random House, 1967), pp. 73-103.

the outcome of parliamentary processes in the General Assembly or Security Council.

The process is closely related to interest articulation and resembles it in most respects, the key difference being that legitimization is essentially the final goal of interest articulation—that is, it signifies the formal approval of the organized international community, and as such, is highly prized by most states. Another difference is that the Secretary-General's legitimization function is almost entirely confined to his public statements, whereas interest articulation may be either private or public. The formal seal of approbation by its nature can have little impact unless in the form of public statement, whether through Assembly or Council resolution or a speech or statement by the Secretary-General. Beyond these distinctions, the process is very much the same. Legitimization by the Secretary-General may be manifest or latent, and of course, given the public nature of the process, tends to be diffuse and general rather than specific and particular. For example, he is more likely to validate the notion that colonialism is no longer justifiable than the more specific recommendation that Great Britain grant independence at once to a particular non-self-governing territory. The Secretary-General may well, in defending the interests of the Organization or his Office, attempt to legitimize a higher status in world politics for those institutions.

There are countless examples of the Secretary-General's work in legitimizing important general conceptions, such as the invalidity of colonialism, the necessity for greater economic development assistance from the wealthy nations, the unjustifiable nature of *apartheid* or separate development, and on some of these issues, there are conflicts with major powers. There have also been a few instances of the legitimization process in critically important areas of war and peace. Of great consequence was Trygve Lie's support of Communist Chinese representation in the UN, and his backing of the United States response to the North Korean attack in 1950. In the first instance, Lie did not succeed in winning general acceptance for the proposition that the Organization should be a universal body, but his backing of that principle helped generate further support. And not surprisingly, governments, political leaders, and private persons and institutions wishing to change the present exclusionary conception have frequently cited all three UN Secretaries-General. Lie's support for the United States' role in Korea was clearly intended to legitimize that action, as was his backing for the more controversial step of sending UN troops north of the thirty-eighth parallel. Simultaneously, of course, his actions tended to cast disapprobation upon the policies of North Korea, China and the Soviet Union. This is the reverse side of the coin of legitimization, demonstrated anew by Dag Hammarskjold in 1956 through his statements expressing disapproval of the British and French attack at Suez and the quashing of the Hungarian uprising by Soviet intervention. Important here also are U Thant's expressions of displeasure with United States bombing in the Vietnam war, as well as Soviet repression in Czechoslovakia in 1968.

In terms of method, the Secretary-General naturally relies upon the public media open to him, particularly the press conference, public addresses, special reports, and the annual report. The latter is perhaps the most meaningful of the several formats, for the careful preparation of the annual reports and the tradition associated with them since Dag Hammarskjold have given their words a solemnity and moral weight generally considered to be of great consequence, and with the resultant widespread publicity. The preparation of draft resolutions for consideration by the Assembly and Council is also important, as they help shape the thinking of the political organs and indicate the Secretariat's position as well.

The Secretary-General rarely voices a public opinion on a controversial matter, and then only if he is certain of the encouragement of a majority in the world community. This is essential if he is to maintain his acceptability to member nations. If a great power disagrees, the more discreet course is to avoid commitment or comment in most instances, unless there is an overwhelming support from the community, as there was in the cases cited.

It is not difficult for nations to perceive the present Secretary-General as a spokesman for Asian and African interests rather than a representative of the entire world arena, and this tends to degrade somewhat his legitimization role. The point, however, should not be taken too far. Thant's role as a spokesman for his embryonic constituency has generally been careful and responsible, and given the lack of unanimity among third-world nations on several critical issues, the Secretary-General has not been in a position to enunciate majority sentiment with any great frequency. Further, in the actual exercise of his powers, limited though they may be, the Secretary-General has been strongly influenced by the views of the dominant members, particularly the United States, as seen most clearly in his handling of the Congo case in the early 1960's.

Finally, the Secretary-General's diplomatic tasks of communication, interest articulation, aggregation, and legitimization, all play a part in what might be characterized as his *rule-making* function. The Secretary-General's role in the process of shaping many of the resolutions passed by the Organization's political bodies contributes to the formulation of recommendations and of international law. On occasion the rule-making authority may be specifically delegated, with a reserved approval by the political organs, or frequently the Secretary-General will take the initiative and suggest particular formulations that the Assembly or Councils may or may not adopt, or modify as they wish. While final directives come from political organs in all cases, the Secretary-General, aided by a large staff of expert civil servants, assists in the rule-creation process through precise statements of demands and claims made by interested states. As with large governmental structures everywhere, the rule-making function is not limited to legislatures or judiciary bodies, but is performed very frequently by the executive as well, particularly in cases of some technical complexity.

In political matters, the Secretary-General's rule-making tasks became most visible and important in the establishment and maintenance of peace-keeping operations, for the Secretariat has become the primary instrument for their governance. Dag Hammarskjold, as noted, wrote the basic principles and regulations (later approved by political organs) governing the composition and tasks of UNEF and ONUC, and U Thant has done the same for UNFICYP. The Secretariat has been the primary agent in establishing the accepted rules for all UN presences, including the observation teams that have gone into the field since the 1940's.

The Secretariat's data collection process and research are important here, for many of the Organization's committees are dependent upon the international staff for the basic information that determines in large measure the nature and direction of particular resolutions. This is particularly the case with questions of primary concern to the smaller and poorer nations, such as colonialism and economic development, for their own bureaucracies have insufficient resources to provide essential data, and heavy reliance is therefore placed upon the Secretariat. Since Assembly majorities can be made up by the lesser developed member states, the Secretariat's role in rule-making has expended, and the essentiality of accurate and thorough data collection seems obvious enough.

The diplomatic functions of communication, interest articulation, aggregation, legitimization, and rule-making are highly inter-related and dependent upon each other, as the Secretary-General's activity in any of these areas will have some impact upon the others. A speech or a news conference statement may serve all of these roles at once, although the final effect may be of greater consequence in one area than another. As discussed above, the League Secretary-General, because of his behind-the-scenes work, had almost no legitimization function, although he was quite important in each of the remaining diplomatic roles. The UN Secretaries-General have performed the several diplomatic tasks from the inception of the Organization in 1946, with the peak perhaps reached from 1956 to 1963 during the era of large-scale peacekeeping operations. Needless to say, the efficiency of the Secretary-General's diplomatic performance is dependent upon the information at his disposal, which brings into focus a system of thorough information gathering and processing. The current system is hardly sufficient even at the present level of activity, and is clearly in need of expansion if the Organization is to be of assistance in cases of severe crisis.

The Secretary-General's *conflict management* functions turn the analysis to narrower political tasks crucial to peaceful settlement. While several of the functions discussed below are important in areas other than interstate conflict, they are included here because of their rather frequent connection and association with political matters. In a sense, the phrase "conflict management" is somewhat presumptuous, for global institutions cannot deal with interstate disputes with any likelihood of peaceful resolution without great power unanimity, and even then there is little assurance of success. But they do have a role to play, and in the years since 1920, the Secretary-General has been a vital part of world institutional attempts to displace the course of international contention into channels of peaceful settlement, performing several functions as a third-party neutral in pursuance of those efforts.

Conflict management functions include all the diplomatic tasks of communication, interest articulation and aggregation, legitimization, and rule-making. Communication and rule-making are of particular importance in this setting, for the neutral intervenor's capacity to send messages containing undistorted data, to establish a channel through which important communications may pass, and to set rules for settlement, including norms governing peacekeeping or observation forces, are clearly of enormous consequence in the general area of conflict resolution and management.

Beyond the diplomatic roles identified in previous pages, however, conflict management functions include a number of *additional diplomatic tasks* particularly relevant to settlement of interstate disputes. These are categorized in the ensuing analysis as participation, mediation, arbitration, and accommodation. These tasks are to be distinguished from a number of *independent executive functions* under the conflict management rubric, discussed here as mobilization of resources, policy planning, field operation, and interposition.

These categories are helpful for analytic and conceptual purposes in attempting to understand the contribution made by the Office to peaceful settlement, but again, the separation is artificial in terms of real-world functioning. An intervention by the Secretary-General may have utility in any one or several of these roles, and there is a large overlap in actual practice. Further, a few of the categories, particularly participation and field operation, include several subfunctions listed here at a lower level of significance, but any one of which might be crucial in a given case.

Participation by the Secretary-General in the international bargaining process is included as a discrete function because the mere presence of the chief executive in any serious negotiating setting has utility. The bargainers have some indication of the expectations of the world community, as well as incentive to act more responsibly and reasonably in the presence of a third party neutral. Both aspects are important in conflict management. The parties may value whatever information and suggestions the Secretary-General has to offer, and while they naturally rely heavily upon their own national sources for data and policy prescriptions, the centrally-placed Secretariat staff may serve as a useful supplement. While the UN archives are not yet available to reveal the Secretary-General's utility in this context of participation in negotiations between others, the information now open on the League of Nations indicates the very solid contribution made by Sir Eric Drummond in negotiating sessions between representatives of states in conflict.

There is no acceptable method of demonstrating that the Secretary-General's presence at negotiating sessions has produced more reasonable and flexible behavior by the participating state representatives, although there is evidence that such is the case in labor relations bargaining [12] and arguments have been made to that effect in international politics as well. [13]

The participation role is important for a number of reasons, but the task of initiating international discussion has received the most attention, particularly within the context of the UN Charter's Article 99. The Secretary-General of the United Nations has the authority to initiate on his own motion international debate at the highest level, and then to take part in the actual bargaining sessions. The League Secretary-General needed the authorization of a member before he could call the Council into formal session. The Secretary-General has had an extensive part in initiating negotiations throughout the League and UN periods. The most likely forum, however, is his own office, where private talks may be held between the chief executive and state representatives, singly or in groups. UN peacekeeping missions have provided a great many opportunities for the initiation of talks, particularly with advisory committees for the Middle East and the Congo, or simply with concerned member states. Representatives of states contributing observers or contingents for a peacekeeping force are frequently called in by the Secretary-General. Initiation of discussions is an accepted part of the chief executive's tasks in any substantive area of concern to world organization, although it has a greater saliency in the more restricted field of conflict management.

It is important to note that participation may be directed at a great variety of purposes, and in that sense, identification of a participation function for the Secretary-General is useful as a comprehensive task embracing numerous possibilities. Briefly, the Secretary-General may wish merely to encourage the participants to engage in face-to-face negotiations, or he may want to stress the significance of particular issues, or frame the alternatives in a certain manner, or perhaps simply emphasize the critical nature of the problems and warn of the implications of failure. He may be able to communicate disinterested information, interpretations, and analyses that might clear up misunderstandings and the kinds of distortions common to international conflict. His presence might be necessary just to allow negotiations to go forward, or he may establish the agenda for discussion, including or separating particular issues and arranging them in such fashion as to facilitate the highest level of agreement. The Secretary-General may sense the utility of a face-saving device for any one or more of the parties,

[12] See sources cited in Young, *op. cit.,* pp. 36-37.
[13] *Id.,* pp. 37-39.

and may even wish to take on the responsibility himself for a given phase of the settlement. These are common functions for any third-party neutral intermediary, including the Secretary-General, and have been a major part of his activity since 1920.

There are rather severe time and geographic limitations upon the Secretary-General's participation capabilities, although Drummond did take part in most serious negotiation sessions in Geneva, and even several in Paris, while the UN Secretaries-General have been frequent intervenors in New York. If time or geographic considerations preclude the Secretary-General's personal participation, he may well appoint a representative. Ralph Bunche, for example, was sent to the Greek Island of Rhodes in 1948 to assist in the talks between Israel and Arab negotiatiors. Any conflict prolonged over time, or one requiring a field operation, such as UNEF, ONUC, or UNFICYP, will naturally necessitate a representative, although the Secretary-General may personally intervene at crucial stages. Dag Hammarskjold was particularly active in this setting, assuming a large burden of travel and negotiation in the protracted disputes in the Middle East and the Congo.

The functional utility of the Secretary-General's personal participation is quite high in terms of preventive diplomacy, for threatened intervention by any of the great powers may necessitate an active role for the Organization that can be asserted successfully only by the neutral executive. If the Secretary-General can quickly and forcefully move to formalize a general preference for non-intervention, he may succeed in forestalling great power initiatives that would render peaceful settlement far more difficult. In the context of internal war in modernizing societies, this is a consideration of great consequence, and as Vietnam indicates, perhaps the most critical problem of contemporary world politics.[14] It is of greater significance before international intervention in the form of peacekeeping operations, for once the interposition is complete, external intervention becomes much less likely.

One of the Secretary-General's best-known conflict management functions is *mediation,* a task performed by each of the Secretariat's chief executives in the years since 1920. This role is closely related to each of the diplomatic functions, and certainly includes each within its scope, as well as the several possibilities identified under the analysis of participation. But it goes further in the sense that mediation entails positive recommendations of substance or procedure made by the Secretary-General to the parties, either privately or publicly, and in general or specific terms. Such recommendations may also serve interest articulation or aggregation purposes, and may well be intended to legitimize a particular conception or rule, but the primary goal of all mediation effort is to assist the parties to reach a peaceful resolution with gain to both sides if at all possible, and with as much symmetry as the situation permits.

[14] See Richard Falk, *Legal Order in a Violent World* (Princeton: Princeton University Press, 1968).

Mediation usually includes a mix of the several tasks mentioned under the participation role, and is frequently at the procedural level, although this always has certain substantive implications. Quite often mediation involves a certain face-saving aspect for one or more of the parties, as it is usually easier to accept recommendations from a neutral Secretary-General than from an antagonist, even in cases of high-intensity conflict, such as the Cuban missile crisis of 1962. The entire process may be quite formal, entailing an invitation to the Secretary-General to take part in official talks, or may be little more than informal discussions between the Secretary-General and state representatives.

The requirements of a successful mediation effort include most of the resources identified earlier in this chapter, but there is a particular need for independence, full and accurate information, and an imaginative capacity enabling the Secretary-General to fashion proposals with dexterity, good timing and resourcefulness. Even if he is not successful in persuading the parties to accept his proposals, he might have sufficient influence to shape the output of political bodies along the lines of his own thinking. The historical record reveals Sir Eric Drummond's persuasiveness for the League Council, whether in the Aland Islands conflict in 1920, or the Sino-Japanese crisis in 1931-1933. Mediation efforts may thus be important in framing a response by the entire organized international community to a given dispute.

The Secretary-General's mediation function is crucial in cases of protracted conflict involving peacekeeping operations in the field. The executive direction of such missions necessarily entails a constant stream of recommendations and informal suggestions from the Secretariat, at times from Headquarters in New York and more frequently from the field. The issue may be an important policy question, an attempt to halt an outbreak of violence, or simply a matter of procedure for the Organization's forces. Peacekeeping missions, essentially at the mercy of the host state whose consent may be shaped in a narrow manner, or withdrawn altogether, necessitate a steady interplay between the government and the Secretariat, much of which is in the form of recommendation by the Secretary-General or his representatives.

The mediation function is more likely to provide the Secretary-General with a comparatively authoritative and influential role so long as he retains command of a force, for he usually has some discretion over its movements and activities, and this naturally tends to add to the persuasiveness of his proposals. As noted in the last chapter, it was perhaps the tragedy of Thant's work in 1967 in the Middle East that the high card of UN interposition was thrown away with nothing in return, for it clearly reduced whatever mediation power the Secretary-General might have exercised.

The related function of *arbitration,* which implies the legally binding nature of the terms of settlement, has very rarely been entrusted to the

Secretary-General, for states have never been disposed to consign politically important issues to the arbitration process. Given a narrowly defined and precise legal question, or a comparatively unimportant issue, states are more willing to take a loss and arbitration or judicial settlement becomes feasible, but the appropriate arena in such circumstances has customarily been a court or panel of arbitrators. Except for the Malaysian dispute, essentially arbitrated by Thant, there has been no instance of a real arbitration role for the Secretary-General.

Yet the possibility should not be ruled out entirely, for once again, an unpleasant decision is more easily accepted if rendered by an international and presumably disinterested neutral third party. And experience with international arbitration indicates that the final result is almost always cast in the form of a compromise, giving each side something of what it wants. Further, the procedures are more flexible than the open and public processes of courts or formally constituted arbitration panels might suggest, for working through the Secretary-General's Office, it is possible to arrange an arbitration process quietly, without fanfare, and with assistance from the parties in shaping the final settlement. This might bring it somewhat closer to the normal mediation and participation functions of the Secretary-General. It is not foreseen that such processes would be useful for any but small powers intent upon the peaceful resolution of relatively minor conflicts.

At quite another level, but still within the category of diplomatic aspects of conflict management roles is a task that might be classified as *accomodation,* a function with a number of important features, all of which are directed toward relieving states of unpleasant diplomatic burdens, either through the taking of a particular decision, or an assumption of responsibility. One of the most significant aspects of the accomodation function may be characterized as face-saving—an important role for the Secretary-General and the entire Organization throughout the five decades of League and United Nations history. Face-saving is desirable to states that occasionally find it necessary to back down gracefully without significantly weakening their political position. The Secretary-General or his representatives have been especially useful in those conflict situations in which considerations of national pride and prestige have weighed heavily. An example from the League era was Drummond's successful effort to induce Tokyo to accept a mission in the Far East during the Sino-Japanese crisis. Japan wished to ward off the possibility of something more severe and gain the benefit of delay while appearing to make a concession to the League rather than any of the great powers.

In the UN period, the Middle East conflict is an important example demonstrating the utility of the Secretary-General's accomodation role. Lie's representative Ralph Bunche was the third party making it possible for the Arabs to negotiate with Israel without appearing to do so directly, thus saving face and leading to the 1949 Armistice Agreements. Ambassador Jarring performed a similar task for U Thant after the 1967 war. And of course, a substantial portion of Hammarskjold's effort after the 1956 Suez crisis was aimed at facilitating the withdrawal of British, French, and Israeli troops through UN interposition arranged in large part because of the assistance he provided. The UNEF operation was designed in part as a face-saving device for the occupying states. In the 1962 Cuban missile crisis, Premier Khrushchev responded positively to Thant's appeals as a means of backing away from a confrontation with the United States. Face-saving was also important in the West New Guinea dispute as the Dutch used Thant's personal representative, Ambassador Ellsworth Bunker, to withdraw gracefully from an untenable position. Indonesia was happy to avoid serious confrontation with Malaysia in 1963, and utilized the Secretary-General's arbitration as a face-saving device.

The availability of international organization to states that wish to become involved in a particular case without the appearance of unilateral action provides the Secretary-General with further opportunities for accomodation activity. For example, the United States has frequently wished to influence the outcome of a dispute without intervening directly, or appearing to put unilateral pressure upon the interested parties. In recent years this has been important to Washington, as it has hesitated to intervene in certain areas particularly sensitive to colonial influence. Thus in the Congo case of 1960-1963, the State Department deferred to the UN even when requested by the Leopoldville government to send military aid. Nations are in a position to influence events from the sidelines, so to speak, by working through the United Nations or even the Office of the Secretary-General. This is not often perceived as an alternative to unilateral intervention, but rather as a complement to the more traditional tools of international diplomacy. Suez, Lebanon in 1958, the Congo, and Cyprus in 1964 are cases in which the western big powers utilized the UN, including the Secretary-General, as a means of multilateral intervention through which more subtle and indirect influence might be exercised.

On occasion, states will call upon the Secretary-General for assistance simply because there are few attractive alternatives, as was the case with Washington's request to Hammarskjold in 1954 to seek the release of the imprisoned UN pilots from China. At times there are problems apparently too difficult for one state to handle alone successfully, and thus Great Britain handed the Palestine Mandate issue to the UN in 1947, resulting in a prominent role for Lie in legitimizing the new state of Israel. It is also possible to perceive a grouping of these accomodation roles in any given case, such as the work of Sir Eric Drummond in the Aland Islands question in 1920.

The Secretary-General may have an active role thrust upon him by default, particularly if the states concerned in a conflict do not submit it to

the Organization because there is no realistic expectation of a fruitful outcome. An example of this is the war in Vietnam, which has generated a role
for the UN only in the narrow framework of the Secretary-General's Office.
Small states that might have wished to discuss the matter publicly have
refrained from raising the issue in the Assembly because of Soviet and
American opposition, and the Secretary-General has assumed a role in the
absence of activity by the political organs, partly in response to third-world
pressures.

Accomodation has been important in peacekeeping operations as well,
with perhaps the outstanding example being the work of Hammarskjold in
the Congo in interpreting resolutions deliberately left vague by parties in
disagreement. The hope was that his interpretations would be satisfactory,
and while he was unhappy with this kind of delegated power, Hammarskjold
did not refuse the task. The Secretary-General thus conciously made himself
a target for criticism if events evolved in a manner deemed unsatisfactory
by one or more of the parties. Accomodation here was in the form of
assuming a burden the parties themselves were unwilling to shoulder, and
bearing the weight of blame if things turned out poorly.

The Secretary-General's *independent executive functions* (within the
conflict management category) have been important in the United Nations
period, and within the context of the establishment and direction of observation and peacekeeping missions. The peak of activity, 1956 to 1963,
was in the Middle East and Congo. Yet the Secretary-General has retained
enough power in this area to render conceptually accurate an analysis of
such functions as part of the current repetoire of practice, and certainly to
include them as a portion of a Secretary-General's likely or possible tasks.
Again, it is unrealistic to assume that his independent executive functions
can be separated in practice from each other, or from the conflict management and diplomatic roles discussed above.

The executive functions here include *mobilization of resources* for the
several UN observation and peacekeeping forces. The administrative and
political decision-making and planning involved have to be accomplished
extraordinarily quickly, and under the tensions of comparatively severe conflict. The Secretary-General must negotiate agreements with states willing
to send contingents, while simultaneously ascertaining whether his proposals are acceptable to the host state. He must spell out in detail the mandate
of the force and the general principles upon which it is based, and must
supervise organizational arrangements, staffing matters, finance and the
distribution of proper supplies and materials to the force in the field.
Naturally he is assisted and at times limited by political advice and demands
made by concerned parties, but a very substantial portion of the mobilization
work is accomplished through the independent executive powers of the
Secretary-General and his staff.

His dealings with the host state may have very serious political implications. Hammarskjold's discussions with President Nasser in 1956 and 1957, for example, dealt essentially with the conditions under which UNEF would be permitted to enter Egypt and the limitations, if any, on the host state's right to demand withdrawal of the force. The Secretary-General's *aide mémoire* on his 1956 negotiations concerning withdrawal of consent indicates the extraordinary discretion accorded Hammarskjold in creating the force. He threatened more than once to withdraw UNEF until Egypt agreed to make any retraction of its consent to the mission dependent upon the completion of UNEF's tasks.

The Secretary-General's power to establish a field force is naturally limited by particular claims of the states concerned and the general policy conceptions underlying the original political decision to create a force (observation or peacekeeping). But he shapes the force in the first instance. His views are bound to be influential as the initial statement is essentially his, and all else is in the form of amendment. The imprint, in terms of size, composition, functions, structure, command, materials, and guiding principles is largely that of the chief executive, with the remainder of the world community reacting only if displeased by a particular item. In the context of observation teams, the discretionary power is likely to be greater, as the Secretary-General has on occasion acted even without formal authorization, and at least in one case, that of Lebanon in 1958, in the face of inhibiting Security Council action. The Secretary-General's appointments to the command structure may also engender political results of some consequence, and at the beginning of an operation they may be of great importance to the processes of large-scale peacekeeping forces. An obvious example is Hammarskjold's decision to send Cordier to the Congo as his representative in the early days of the ONUC mission.

The Secretary-General's *policy planning* function for UN observation or peacekeeping missions is a natural extension of his role in mobilizing the resources for such forces, and of course, the two tend to shade into each other. The Secretary-General has been extremely important in the authoritative policy planning and governance of field forces. On occasion, if there is sharp division in the political community, he may have such power delegated to him by default, or, in moments of crisis, his representatives in the field may be forced to take critical decisions without authorization or instruction. Even with comparatively straightforward and specific standards to guide him, however, the ultimate interpretations must be made by the Secretary-General and the field commanders, and with great impact on the functioning of the force. So long as the chief executive retains the final authority (rather than the Security Council), and the more difficult the problem, whether in terms of political complexity, time limitations, or severe crisis, the more likely is his influence to be significant. Thant's decision to withdraw UNEF in May, 1967 with no attempt to defer to political decision-making by the Security Council or General Assembly is an example of all these factors resulting in a vital decision by the Secretary-General.

Indeed, as the UN is presently constituted, the Secretariat is the only body capable of day-to-day direction of field forces. It is the only organ large enough to include the essential expertise required, and of course, it is the only segment of the UN system to work continuously. The flow of cables and messages coming in from field operations frequently require replies giving detailed instructions, and on occasion this requires political decision-making by the Secretary-General and the top members of his Executive Office. If difficult questions are raised, and time permits, authorization and instructions from political advisory committees or the main political bodies will certainly be sought, although as we have seen, even this might not be sufficient for the Secretary-General to avoid taking his own decisions. If the Secretary-General is to be severely limited in his policy planning capabilities for peacekeeping and observation missions, then the future outlook for such activity appears dim, for no matter how strict the political limits, there must remain an area of discretion falling naturally within the authority of the chief executive.

The policy planning role is performed by the Secretary-General not only in case of emergency, divided opinion, or through an irreducible discretion, but in the normal course of his duties as well. His input in the policy-making process for field forces is fashioned through each of his several other diplomatic and conflict management functions. Information coming through his Office from the field is frequently the most thorough and accurate in terms of specific UN problems, and this gives his evaluations a saliency that renders him quite influential in shaping policy. His recommendations on force movements, activities, and general role in a given area have been effective in persuading the Council and Assembly to adopt a specific course of action or set a general framework for an operation. Draft resolutions on field forces from the Executive Office have been of great consequence in the final decisions taken by political bodies.

The *field operation* role includes numerous tasks performed by small international forces, usually observer groups reporting to the Secretary-General, and frequently authorized by him to carry out a number of responsibilities important for conflict management. Fact-finding is one of the key functions for any UN presence, whether an individual representative of the Secretary-General, a formal observation mission, or a large peace-keeping force. Data collection and processing has always been an important feature of the Secretary-General's work, even in the League era, but while the chief executive's role throughout the years has been somewhat passive, Hammarskjold insisted on the right to initiate fact-finding missions without specific and formal political authorization. The more normal procedure is for the Secretary-General to secure a political decision authorizing a representative to serve as the UN "presence" in an area, and to have him serve in part as a reliable fact-finder for the Organization. Larger missions are always utilized for this purpose, with Secretariat personnel sending back data through the Executive Office.

The Secretary-General's field operation function involves inspection, verification and supervision tasks assigned to international missions. Observers may be called upon to verify a cessation of hostilities in the form of a truce or ceasefire, and to patrol demarcation lines. The UN Truce Supervision Organization (UNTSO) in the Middle East has been engaged in these tasks for many years. Verifying compliance with international legal obligations such as these, or supervising the maintenance of a demilitarized or buffer zone may involve Secretariat responsibility.

Political tasks have included the verification of democratic elections, the transfer of territory, and even the supervision of particular areas. Important examples of the latter are the Port Said area in 1956, the Congo, and West New Guinea (UNTEA). The West New Guinea case entailed the direct international supervision of a territory followed by its transfer, and necessitated Secretariat responsibility for the total government and social welfare provisions in the territory for a period of several months. In the Congo, the Secretary-General had more field authority than at any time in the history of the Office, and more than is likely to be authorized again for a period well into the foreseeable future.

Finally, the Secretary-General's conflict management functions include, at the most abstract level, what may be characterized as *interposition,* the natural task of a third-party neutral intermediary in stepping between parties to a conflict and attempting to achieve a peaceful resolution. This has been the heart and real meaning of the work of the Secretary-General and his staff since 1920, although the manifestations have been far more obvious in the UN period.

For Drummond and Avenol, interposition was entirely diplomatic in nature, and given the framework of private negotiations with no public role of any kind, it tended to serve as a supplement to the efforts of national actors. There was very little of an independent executive activity. In the years since 1946, the Secretaries-General, through public statements, diplomatic work, and field operations, have created an interpositionary function that symbolizes the primary value of the Organization itself. In the preventive diplomacy setting, the Secretary-General has frequently been selected as the instrument for interposition, and at times, has initiated such action himself. Peak effectiveness was reached during the Hammarskjold administration, in the sense of both maximum political impact of the Secretary-General's intermediary diplomatic efforts and the strength of physical intervention through observation and peacekeeping missions.

While the interposition role of the Secretary-General is not likely to be of substantial value in cases of very severe international crises, it has been extremely helpful in several conflicts at a lower level of intensity. In terms of physical intervention, the Secretary-General's activity in the Middle East,

Cyprus, Yemen, and even Kashmir have been significant in imposing restraints. But the notion of interposition should not be confined to activities in the field. Diplomatic work has been important as well in the hope of influencing antagonists. Thant's activity in the 1962 Cuban missile crisis is an example at a comparatively high crisis level, and each of the other cases of real UN intervention have entailed diplomatic work for the Secretary-General of an interpositionary nature. Whatever impact the chief executive may have in any given case, in the most fundamental sense it is aimed at peaceful settlement through separation of parties in conflict and the adoption of a neutral posture somewhere between the claims of each side. This has very little relation with initial expectations of collective security, but it is far closer to world organization's capabilities. If it also bears a striking resemblance to the League of Nations' role in the international system of its time, it is certainly at a more advanced level in terms of diplomatic and physical effect. Current attempts to roll back the Secretary-General's powers and to undo the value of precedents set by Hammarskjold and Thant (in his administration's early years) will necessarily restrict the overarching interpositonary function upon which all else is based.

Integration functions have been identified as the final, and perhaps most fundamental, of the Secretary-General's tasks in the international arena. In a basic sense, the entire system of international organization created in 1920 has been devoted to the achievement of a more substantial level of integration in the world setting, not for purposes of consolidating the community of nations into one world state, but to reach that level of world order and integration indicated by the peaceful settlement of conflict. Global institutions have been struggling to create what Karl Deutsch has characterized as a "pluralistic security community".[15] While such organizations have had only a marginal impact to date, a large portion of their effort has been the fostering of a minimum enmeshing of national and global decision-making systems consistent with the requirements of peaceful change and the maintenance of separate states.

The Secretary-General has been a part of this effort, and even while his integration activity has touched on matters far from the arena of political dispute, the direction and effect are potentially of great political consequence. Whether he has had any significant integrative impact is quite another question, and one that is currently impossible to answer with any assurance of accuracy. The total organizational effort appears to have been of marginal utility in generating an integrative process and the Secretary-General's functions are but a part of that effort. Yet his activities touch on some of the relevant variables essential to political integration, and if impact

[15] Karl W. Deutsch, et. al., *Political Community and the North Atlantic Area* (Princeton: Princeton University Press, 1957), p. 6.

cannot presently be measured, analysis of the integration-related activity is nevertheless important for an understanding of the Office.

There are, of course, a great number of variables requiring study in any serious consideration of the integration process taken as a whole, but for purposes of analyzing the part played by the Secretary-General in the slow movement toward world order, it is necessary only to take into account those factors in which his work appears relevant. Further, it is obvious that the international arena has a long road ahead to reach the lowest level of integration worthy of the name. Peaceful resolution of conflict among nation-states is naturally the primary aim of world organization, meaning that the threshold of integration among independent actors is the ultimate goal directing organizational activity. In this the Secretary-General plays some part, and if his functions as chief executive touch only a fraction of the relevant variables, certainly his work relates to some of the most crucial among them.

One of the key factors here is compatability of values, particularly those major values bearing most directly upon a nation's inclination to resort to violence rather than utilize mechanisms of peaceful change. Privately and publicly, the Secretary-General has strived mightily to create a disposition to comply with norms of international law and organization, and to create a pool of common values on peace, independence, economic and social change, and basic human rights. His public statements have naturally been directed to the general public and his private work to authoritative decision-makers and élites of various kinds, but the common thread of an educative role for the Secretary-General may be traced throughout the first fifty years of the Office.

While progress in terms of world-wide sharing of values in any of these areas has not been overwhelming, nevertheless in 1970 there is a greater compatibility of thought on issues of colonialism, redistribution of wealth, human rights, and even the norms of peaceful change than was the case in 1920. How much of this may properly be attributed to global institutions, including the activities of the Secretary-General, is impossible to state. Yet there are a few indirect and rather general indications of a certain impact. The expansion of executive powers over the years implies growing trust and confidence, and while there have been ebbs, the general direction has been toward increased influence. Development of responsibility is not likely to follow for an institution or office devoid of impact upon behavior or thought. For example, Dag Hammarskjold was instrumental in legitimizing the conception of "preventive diplomacy" among decision-makers, and was a primary beneficiary of the notion that the UN can be a valuable instrument for intervention designed in part to impede great power involvement.

Certainly, repeated reliance upon the Secretary-General's Office for the performance of certain tasks in conflict management involves an appreciation of organizational norms and rules of the game fostered and in some measure developed by the Secretary-General himself. This is the roughest of gauges for deciding whether he has had any impact, and measurement is even more difficult in areas such as economics, self determination, and human rights, but it remains likely that general task expansion of the Office is a reflection in some part of the Office's effect upon certain major values in the world arena. At the very least, the Secretary-General has been among those few actively working to increase consensus and to establish a set of shared values, certainly among decision-makers and élites, conducive to peaceful settlement.

Closely related to the variable of shared major values is the notion of responsiveness and predictability of behavior. Nations may be more inclined to settle disputes peacefully if there is a bond of confidence and trust toward other nations with whom they have dealings, derived primarily from familiarity and a capability to predict (based on shared values) general behavior patterns and likely responses. If states demonstrate responsiveness to the felt needs and claims of others, and do so frequently enough to establish mutual capacities for predicting behavior, then there is more likely to be an integrative process at work rather than the reverse. Both responsiveness and predictibility are the key variables.

It seems fairly certain that the Secretary-General has had some effect here, for his diplomatic and conflict management roles have been important in facilitating knowledge and awareness among states of the claims of others, and this alone tends to encourage responsiveness. His communication role has been designed and carried out since 1920 with these utilities in mind, and the record indicates the importance of his work at least in terms of awareness, and perhaps in the context of responsiveness as well. For example, given the authoritative nature of his communications, U Thant's insistence that a full bombing halt by the United States in North Vietnam would result in full-scale substantive negotiations between the two sides in the war was probably relevant to the United States as a judgment supplementing other sources of information, and one to which Washington of course responded.

As discussed in previous pages, the Secretary-General's position in the system permits him to gather great quantities of useful data, and to the extent that he is well informed, states may be expected to rely upon his judgment in making recommendations. In the context of observation and peace-keeping missions, nations have deliberately relied upon the Office to provide them with information essential to their own decision process. As for responsiveness, the Secretary-General has made strenuous efforts over the years, and again, while his impact cannot be measured, task expansion gives some evidence of probable effect. In recent years, the Secretary-General has directed substantial effort toward the legitimization of self-determination concepts and redistribution of wealth, and in both areas has directed a rapid growth of international institutional efforts.

Another factor of importance in the integration process has been identified as a broadening of élites, and in the case of global organization, growth by means of recruitment and socialization of political élites throughout the world. The Secretary-General, through his executive responsibilities for the administration of the Secretariat, has been a key actor in one of the Organization's more manifest contributions to integration. The Secretariat has been an active training ground for diplomats from many nations, particularly several of the newer African and Asian states, and has assisted in the socializaiton of authoritative decision makers from throughout the world through exposure to the essential values of the Organization as well as those of their colleagues. Socialization through work in global organizations has helped expand the political élite structure in many of the world community's poorer nations, for frequently Secretariat employment is among the best kind of training available. In terms of integration potential, it has the further advantage of reinforcing commitments to mutual values in several key areas, including the substantive matters previously adduced.

Naturally, the United Nations Secretary-General has been more influential in this setting than his League counterpart, who headed a Secretariat staff largely of European nationality, reflecting the preponderant weight of the membership. The UN Secretariat, much like the Organization itself, is more nearly representative of the entire international community, and therefore far better suited to socialization and (given the large number of third-world and underdeveloped nations) to recruitment resulting in an expansion of élite structures. Assuming the Secretary-General's continued emphasis upon a widespread geographic distribution, even if on occason at the expense of technical competence and expertise, and the developing practice (in which he has acquiesced) of granting short-term contracts, socialization and recruitment through the Secretariat are likely to perpetuate the broadening of political élite structures in most of the world's developing nations.

One of the crucial variables in the integration process is the scope and rate of transaction flows across political units, including international trade, capital flows, communications, mobility of persons, and the creation of institutions to manage an orderly flow. The Secretary-General's work here has been primarily educative and persuasive, through public and private statements urging a progressive weakening and ultimate disappearance of trade barriers and increased liquidity and capital flows. The League and United Nations have also been instrumental in promoting the development of world-wide functional interests, through particular agencies devoted to economic, social and technical problems. The Secretaries-General have strongly supported these efforts and the institutional structures designed for their governance.

Perhaps the greatest contributions in this area have been made by Avenol and Thant. As noted in Chapter II, Avenol was responsible for the concept of central administration of League economic and social programs, an advance not only in institutional and structural terms, but also as encouragement and added strength to one of the more successful areas of League activity. The central institutions planned by Avenol were given life during the Lie and Hammarskjold administrations, and Thant has supervised the establishment of new agencies, such as UNCTAD, whose primary purpose is to fashion programs of more substantial and rapid economic aid by the wealthy nations. This is as much a matter of responsiveness by the developed countries as it is a question of increased transactions across national boundaries, but each necessitates the other. The Secretary-General's effectiveness in this setting has so far been slight, but his persistence in seeking expanded transactions may have potential significance if the international community is ever to approach the threshold of integration.

A final variable relevant for the Secretary-General's activity is government effectiveness, and in the context of world organization, the expansion of tasks by international institutions. An expanding governmental structure is both an indication of and contributor to an integrative pattern. At the international level, of course, institutions are not being developed for purposes of maintaining order or to control the distribution of power and wealth. Expectations and planning are at a much lower level, and hopes confined to the ultimate establishment of many more cooperative relationships and a greater intermingling of national processes of government and decision-making with those of global institutions. In this sense, the Secretary-General's work has been important, for particularly in the United Nations period the Office and its tasks have expanded to embrace a large set of peacekeeping functions that have indeed helped establish a more significant intermingling of national and international processes. This has had some effect in terms of creating a predisposition by governments to utilize the world organization as a neutral third-party intermediary.

It is a far cry from governmental effectiveness as the phrase is commonly understood at national or local levels, but does constitute a step in the direction of institutional power and influence absolutely essential in shaping the integrative process. The Secretary-General has been instrumental in enlarging upon the tasks of the Organization itself, and its capabilities in the peaceful settlement of disputes. Indeed, his activity has been more important in enlarging upon conflict resolution tasks than any other substantive area of interest to international organization. The path, obviously, has not been consistently upward, and since the end of the Congo operation, there has been a retraction in the peacekeeping power of the Office and the Organization. Further, in the first fifty years, the threshold of integration marked by a general pattern of peaceful settlement has never been approached. Yet the overall trend appears to be, from the perspective of five decades, in the direction of expanded capabilities for the Office and world organization, and therefore the slow development of a cooperative system of world order.

Select Bibliography

The following is a listing of leading books and articles dealing directly or at some length with the Secretary-General and Secretariat of the League of Nations and United Nations. The references here are to published secondary sources, and do not include the invaluable material found in national archives and private collections.

Aghnides, Thanassis, "The standards of conduct of the international civil servant", *Intl. Rev. of Adm. Sci.* (1953), pp. 179-187.

Alexandrowicz, D. H., "The Secretary-General of the UN", 11 *International and Comparative Law Quarterly* (1962), pp. 1109-1130.

Anglin, Douglas G., "Lester Pearson and the Office of Secretary-General", 17 *International Journal* (1962), pp. 145-150.

Bailey, Sydney D., *The Secretariat of the United Nations,* New York: Carnegie Endowment for International Peace, 1962 (U.N. Studies, No. 11).

Bailey, Sydney D., "The Troika and the Future of the United Nations", *International Conciliation,* No. 538, 1962.

Barros, James, *Betrayal From Within.* New Haven: Yale University Press, 1969.

Bingham, June, *U Thant—The Search for Peace.* New York: Alfred A. Knopf, 1966.

Bowett, D. W., *United Nations Forces.* London: Stevens & Sons, 1964.

Boyd, Andrew, *United Nations: Piety, Myth, and Truth.* Great Britain: Penguin Books, 1962.

Calderwood, Howard B., *The Higher Direction of the League Secretariat.* Dallas: Southern Methodist University, 1937.

Carnegie Endowment for International Peace, *Proceedings of Conference on Experience in International Administration.* Washington: C.E.I.P., 1943.

Carnegie Endowment for International Peace, *Proceedings of Exploratory Conference on the League of Nations Secretariat.*

Carnegie Endowment for International Peace, *The United Natoins Secretariat.* New York: CEIP, 1950 (U.N. Studies, No. 4).

Chamberlin, Waldo, "Administrative Matters", *Annual Review of UN Affairs: 1955-1956.* New York: New York University Press, 1957.

Claude, Inis L., *Swords Into Plowshares,* 3rd rev. New York: Random House, 1964.

Cohen, Maxwell, "The United Nations Secretariat—some constitutional and administrative developments", 49 *American Journal of International Law* (1955), pp. 259-319.

Commission to Study the Organization of Peace, *The United Nations Secretary-General; his role in world politics.* 14th Report, 1962.

Commission to Study the Organization of Peace, *The Secretary-General and the Secretariat.* 9th Report, 1955.

Cordier, Andrew W., "The Role of the Secretary-General", *Annual Review of UN Affairs, 1960-61.* New York: New York University Press, 1962.

Cordier, Andrew W., and Foote, Wilder, eds., *Public Papers of the Secretaries-General of the United Nations* Vol. I Trygve Lie. New York: Columbia University Press, 1969.

Cox, Robert, "The Executive Head: An Essay on Leadership in International Organization", XXIII *International Organization* (1969), pp. 205-230.

Crocker, W. R., "Some Notes on the United Nations Secretariat", IV *International Organization* (1950), pp. 598-613.

Davies, Jack, G. W., "The Work of the Secretariat", *Annual Review of UN Affairs: 1952.* New York: New York University Press, 1953.

Department of State. *Postwar Foreign Policy Preparation: 1939-1945.* Washington, D.C.: U.S. Government Printing Office, 1950.

Dworkis, Martin B., "Administrative Matters", *Annual Review of UN Affairs: 1954.* New York: New York University Press, 1955, pp. 174-208.

Egger, Rowland, "Road to Gethsemane", 6 *Public Administration Review* (Winter 1946), p. 71.

Erven, L., "The question of the Secretary-General", *Review of International Affairs* (Yugoslav), 20 Oct. 1961.

Foote, Wilder, ed., *Dag Hammarskjold—Servant of Peace: A Selection of his Speeches and Statements.* New York: Harper & Row, 1962.

Friedmann, W., "The United Nations and National Loyalties", 8 *International Journal* (Toronto), 1952-1953, p. 17.

Gavshon, Arthur L., *The Mysterious Death of Dag Hammarskjold.* New York: Walter, 1962.

Goodrich, Leland M., "The Political Role of the Secretary-General", XVI *International Organization* (1962), pp. 720-735.

Goodrich, Leland M., "Geographical Distribution of the Staff of the U.N. Secretariat", XVI *International Organization* (1962), pp. 465-482.

Goodrich, Leland M., *The United Nations.* New York: Thomas Y. Crowell Co., 1959, pp. 130-142.

Gordenker, Leon, *The UN Secretary-General and the Maintenance of Peace.* New York: Columbia University Press, 1967.

Hamilton, Thomas, "The U.N. and Trygve Lie", 29 *Foreign Affairs* (1950), pp. 67-77.

Hammarskjold, Dag., *Markings.* New York: Alfred A. Knopf, 1966.

Hammarskjold, Dag., *The International Civil Servant in Law and in Fact,* A Lecture delivered to Congregation on 30 May 1961. Oxford: Clarendon Press, 1961.

Honig, F., "The International Civil Service: basic problems and contemporary difficulties", *Int'l Affairs,* April 1954, pp. 175-185.

Howard-Ellis, C., *The Origin, Structure & Working of the League of Nations.* London: George Allen & Unwin, 1928 (Chapter VII).

Jackson, Elmore, "Constitutional Development of the United Nations: the Growth of its Executive Capacity", American Society of International Law *Proceedings,* 55, 1961. Pages 78-88.

Jackson, Elmore, "The Developing Role of the Secretary-General", VII *International Organization* (1957), pp. 431-445.

James, A. M., "The Role of the Secretary-General of the United Nations", 1 *Intl. Relations* (1959), pp. 620-638.

Jenks, Wilfred, "Some Problems of an International Civil Service", III *Public Administration Review* (1943), pp. 93-105.

Jessup, P. H., "The International Civil Servant and his Loyalties", IX *Journal of International Affairs* (1955), pp. 55-61.

Joyce, James Avery, "Strength of U Thant", 80 *Christian Century* (28 August 1963), pp. 1047-1050.

Kaplan, Robert, "Some Problems in the Administration of an International Secretariat", 2 *Columbia Journal of International Affairs,* No. 2 (Spring, 1948).

Kay, David A., "Secondment in the United Nations Secretariat: An Alternative View", XX *International Organization* (1966), pp. 63-75.

Kelen, Emery, *Hammarskjold.* New York: G. P. Putman's Sons, 1966.

Kraslow, David & Loory, Stuart, *The Secret Search for Peace in Vietnam.* New York: Vintage Books, 1968.

Kunz, Josef, "The Legal Position of the Secretary-General of the United Nations", 40 *American Journal of International Law* (1946), pp. 786-792.

Langenhove, Fernand Van, *Le Rôle Proéminent du Secrétaire Général dans L'Opération des Nations Unies au Congo*. Bruxelles: Institut Royal des Relations Internationales, 1964.

Langrod, Georges, *The International Civil Service*. Leiden: Sijthoff, 1963.

Lash, Joseph P., *Dag Hammarskjold: Custodian of the Brush-Fire Peace*. New York: Doubleday, 1961.

Lash, Joseph P., "Dag Hammarskjold's Conception of his Office", XVI *International Organization* (1962), pp. 542-566.

Laves, Walter H., and Stone, Dnald C., "The United Nations Secretariat", XXII *Foreign Policy Reports*, No. 15, Oct. 15, 1956.

Lengyel, Peter, "Some Trends in the International Civil Service", XIII *International Organization* (1959), pp. 520-537.

Lie, Trygve, *In the Cause of Peace*. London: Macmillan, 1954.

Loveday, Alexander, *Reflections on International Administration*. Oxford: Clarendon Press, 1956.

Malkin, Lawrence, "Battle for the Independence of the UN Secretariat", *Reporter*, Sept. 27, 1962, pp. 29-32.

Mannes, Marya, "Visit with U Thant", *New Republic*, Jan. 8, 1966, pp. 10-12.

Masland, John W., "The Secretariat of the United Nations", *Public Administration Review*, vol. 5 (Autumn 1945), p. 365.

Miller, David Hunter, *The Drafting of the Covenant*. New York: G. P. Putman's Sons, 1928.

Miller, Richard, *Dag Hammarskjold and Crisis Diplomacy*. New York: Oceana, 1961.

Moore, Bernard, "The Secretariat: Role and Functions", *Annual Review of UN Affairs 1949*. New York: New York University Press, 1950. pp. 21-31.

Morley, Felix, *The Society of Nations*. Washington: The Brookings Institution, 1932.

Narasimhan, C. V., "Administrative Changes in the Secretariat", *Annual Review of UN Affairs: 1961-1962*. New York: New York University Press, 1963.

O'Brien, Conor Cruise, *To Katanga and Back*. New York: Simon and Schuster, 1962.

Pelt, Adrian, "Peculiar Characteristics of an International Administration", *Public Administration Review* (Spring 1946), pp. 108-115.

Phelan, E. J., *Yes and Albert Thomas*. London: The Cresset Press, Ltd., 1936.

Purves, Chester, *The Internal Administration of an International Secretariat*. London: The Royal Institute of International Affairs, 1945.

Ranshofen-Wertheimer, Egon F., *The International Secretariat: A Great Experiment in International Administrative*. New York: Carnegie Endowment for International Peace, 1945.

Reymond, Henri, "The Staffing of the United Nations Secretariat: A Continuing Discussion", XXI *International Organization* (1967), pp. 751-767.

The Royal Institute of International Affairs, *The International Secretariat of the Future*. London: Oxford University Press, 1944.

Russell, Ruth B., *A History of the United Nations Charter*. Washington, D.C.: The Brookings Institution, 1958.

Schachter, Oscar, "Dag Hammarskjold and the Relation of Law to Politics", XVI *American Journal of International Law* (1962), pp. 1-8.

Schwebel, Stephen M., *The Secretary-General of the United Nations—his Political Powers and Practice*. Cambridge: Harvard University Press, 1952.

Schwebel, Stephen M., "Origins and Development of Article 99 of the Charter; powers of the Secretary-General of the United Nations", 28 *British Yearbook of International Law* (1951), pp. 371-382.

Schwebel, Stephen M., "The International Character of the Secretariat of the United Nations", XXX *British Yearbook of International Law* (1953), pp. 71-115.

Scott, F. R., "The World's Civil Service", *International Conciliation,* No. 496 (January 1954).

Settel, T. S., ed., *The Light and the Rock—The Vision of Dag Hammarskjold.* New York: E. P. Dutton & Co., 1966.

Sharp, Walter, "Trends in U.N. Administration", XV *International Organization* (1961), pp. 393-407.

Simmonds, K. R., " 'Good Offices' and the Secretary-General", *Nordisk Tidsskrift for International Ret,* vol. 29, pp. 330-345, 1959.

Siotis, Jean, *Essai Sur Le Secrétariat International.* Geneva: Librairie Droz, 1963.

Stein, Eric, "Mr. Hammarskjold, the Charter Law and the Future of the United Nations Secretary-General", LVI *American Journal of International Law* (1962), pp. 9-32.

Stolpe, Sven, *Dag Hammarskjold—A Spiritual Portrait.* New York: Charles Scribner's Sons, 1966.

Stone, Donald C., "Organizing the United Nations", *Public Administration Review* (Spring 1946), pp. 116-129.

Swift, Richard N., "Personnel Problems in the United Nations Secretariat", *International Organization* (1957), pp. 228-247.

Tandon, Yashpal, "UNEF, The Secretary-General, and International Diplomacy in the Third Arab-Israeli War", XXII *International Organization* (1968), pp. 529-556.

Tead, Ordway, "The Importance of Administration in International Action", *International Conciliation,* No. 407, January, 1945.

Turner, Bruce, "The Secretariat", *Annual Review of UN Affairs: 1950.* New York: New York University Press, 1951. pp. 159-177.

U.S. Senate Committee on Foreign Relations, Subcommittee on the UN Charter. *The Status and Role of the Secretariat of the United Nations.* Staff Study No. 12, 1954.

U Thant, *Toward World Peace—Speeches and Public Statements 1957-1963.* New York: Thomas Yoseloff, 1964.

Van Dusen, Henry P., *Dag Hammarskjold: The Statesman and his Faith.* New York: Harper & Row, 1967.

Virally, Michael, "La Role Politique du Secrétaire-Général des Nations Unies", *L'Annuaire Français de Droit International,* IV (1958).

Von Horn, Carl, *Soldiering for Peace.* New York: David McKay Company, 1967.

Walters, Frank P., *A History of the League of Nations.* London: Oxford University Press, 1952.

Walters, Frank P., *Administrative Problems of International Organization,* Barnett House Papers, No. 24, London: Oxford University Press, 1941.

Williams, David C., "Dag Hammarskjold—Lonely Leader of the U.N.", *The Progressive,* Dec. 1958, pp. 22-24.

Winchmore, Charles, "The Secretariat: Retrospect and Prospect", XIX *International Organization* (1965).

Young, Oran, *The Intermediaries: Third Parties in International Crises.* Princeton: Princeton University Press, 1967.

Zacher, Mark W., "The Secretary-General and the United Nations' Function of Peaceful Settlement", XX *International Organization* (1966), pp. 724-749.

Zacher, Mark W., *Dag Hammarskjold's United Nations.* New York: Columbia University Press (1970).

Index

A

Abdoh, Djal, 365, 366
Abdullah, King, 222, 222n
Abyssinia, *see* Ethiopia *and*
    Italo-Ethiòpian conflict
accomodation function, 380, 412, 449,
    453-455
Acheson, Dean, 253, 267, 386
Adacti, Baron Minéitciro, 78
Addis Ababa, 127, 130, 131
Aden, 385
Adoula, Cyrille, 322, 352-358, 360
Africa
    colonialism, 235
    Congo crisis, 310, 325, 353, 360
        fifteenth General Assembly, 316
        troika proposal, 317, 318
        troops, 312
    Hammarskjold journey 1960, 309
    Hammarskjold views on, 277, 278
    Italo-Ethiopian conflict, 127, 137
    League of Nations, and, 18
    legitimization function, and, 445
    record of Secretary-General, and, 430
    support for Thant, 343
    Thant election, and, 345, 346n
    UN change in 1960's, 341
Afro-Asian group
    attacks on Secretariat, 256
    Congo crisis, 311, 316-318, 320, 321,
        325, 361, 362
    constituency for SG, 431-433
    Hammarskjold administration, 269, 271
    Hammarskjold in Middle East, and,
        286
    Hammarskjold at Peking, and, 279, 281
    Hammarskjold views on, 277
    integration function, and, 462
    legitimization function, and, 447
    Lie views on, 263
    neutrality of SG, and, 419, 420
    prestige of SG, and, 425
    record of SG, and, 429-431
    support for Lie, 237, 250
    support for Thant, 412, 414,419,425,
        431-433
    Thant election as Acting SG, and,
        345-347

    Thant election as SG, and, 348, 349
    Thant reelection, 391
    UN action, and, 248, 251, 327
    UN peacekeeping forces, and, 53
    UN universality, and, 201
    Vietnam War, and, 401, 405
    West New Guinea, and, 363
aggregation function, 445, 447-449, 451
Aghnides, Thanassis
    Avenol resignation, and, 159, 164
    expulsion of Soviet Union, and, 149,
        152n
    Greco-Bulgarian crisis, 71
    Lester period, 180n, 181n, 195, 197
    Princeton University, and, 153, 154
    Secretariat crisis 1938-39, and, 142,
        143, 146
Akershus, Norway, 269
Al-Badr, Mohammed, 376
Al-Fatah, 394
Al-Sallal, Abdullah, 376
Aland Islands question 1920-21, 53,
    54-60, 68, 454
    Commission of Enquiry, 57, 58
    Commission of Jurists, 57-59
    mediation of SG, 452
Albania, 68, 258
Algeria, 370, 403, 408
Algiers, 188
Aloisi, Baron Pompeo, 125, 126, 126n,
    128, 129, 131, 132
American Association for the United
    Nations, 259
American Communists in UN Secretariat,
    251-256, 266
    Commission of Jurists, 253, 253n, 254
    Federal Bureau of Investigation, 254,
        255
    Feller, Abraham, 253
    Hammarskjold, Dag, and, 254-256
    United States Constitution, 252-254
    United States Senate Judiciary
        Committee, 252
        Internal Security Subcommittee,
        252-254
Ames, Sir Herbert, 49
Amman, Jordan, 222
Angola, 354, 357

Annual Report of Secretary-General,
see UN SG
Antiphon, 275
Anzilotti, Dionisio, 35
apartheid. 417, 446
appeasement policy, 105, 121, 124, 135,
141, 143n, 152, 171, 419
Aqaba, Gulf of, 293, 294, 396
Arab Federation, 298
Arab-Israeli War 1967, 385, 393-400,
414, 454
General Assembly, 395, 396, 398, 399
Hammarskjold *aide mémoire,* 398, 399
Nasser, Gamal, 394-396, 398, 399
Syria, 393-396
United Arab Republic, 393-396, 398,
399
UNEF, 393-400
Arab League, 303
Arab refugees, 223, 397
Arab states
Korean War, 243
Lebanon 1958, and, 298, 303
Middle East 1956-57, 283-286
Palestine 1947-49, 217-224, 237, 266,
451, 453
arbitration, 69, 72, 74, 76, 126, 286n
function of SG, 449, 452, 453
Italo Ethiopian conflict, 126, 127
Malaysian dispute, 377, 379, 381, 453,
454
Argentina, 66, 67, 73, 74, 140, 227, 307
Arkadev, Georgi P., 346n
Armistice Agreements for Palestine 1949
1956 crisis, 283, 288
1967 war, 399
accomodation function of SG, 454
Article 7 of UN Charter, and, 337
conclusion of, 222
Israeli withdrawal 1957, 293, 294
arms control, 203, 232, 235, 444
articulation function, 226, 442-449, 451
Asia, 235, 277, 318, 341, 345, 347, 430
Asian Socialist Conference 1956, 343
Asquith, Herbert H., 20, 58
Aswan High Dam, 285
Athens, Greece, 71
Atlee, Clement, 232
atomic bomb, 203, 232, 237n
atomic energy control, 232, 235
Auden, W. H., 275
Austin, Warren, 219, 220, 240, 242, 265
Australia, 147, 217, 218, 221, 228, 240,
266, 387

Austria, 106, 128, 137, 383
Avenol, Joseph
analysis, 169-172
background, 106, 107
Bruce Report, 146-149
communication function, 441, 442
compared with Drummond, 31, 107,
112-115, 137, 168-172
compared with Lie, 215, 257
compared with Thant, 343, 344
consituency, 431
constitutional theory of, 427
Deputy SG, as, 71, 83, 83n, 117, 118
diplomatic skills, 422
Drummond contribution, and, 101, 102
expulsion of Soviet Union, and,
149-152
functions, 171
grants of power, and, 433, 434
integration, and, 462, 463
interposition, and, 458
Italo-Ethiopian conflict, 124-137
later years, 166-169
Lester, and, 174-179
neutrality, and, 419
prestige of, 425
Princeton transfer, 152-158, 159, 160
record, and, 429
resignation of, 158-166, 176, 179, 195n
attempt to shut down League,
161-165, 178, 181
"null and void" affair, 163-164, 165
Secretariat crisis 1938-39, and, 141-146
Secretariat debate 1928-32, and, 39-41,
43
Secretariat staff, and, 32, 37n, 113-115
selection as SG, 96, 98, 99, 108-112
Sino-Japanese conflict and Japanese
withdrawal, 94, 116-124, 135, 136
skilled personnel, and, 436
structural position, 426
UN founding, and, 204
views on League, 115-116, 137-141
Axis powers, 139, 419
Aydelotte, Frank, 155n
Azcaraté, Pablo de, 111-114, 146, 175n,
198
Azerbaijan, 214, 214n

B

Ba Swe, U, 342
Baker, Newton, 109
Balfour, Sir Arthur, 20-22, 58, 106, 108

Balfour Report and principles, 36, 38-40, 42, 101
Balkans, the, 71, 225, 230
Ball, Goerge, 351, 371, 386
Baltic Commission, 55
Bandung Conference 1955, 281, 342
Bank of France, 106
Barnes, Djurna, 275
Barros, James, 54n, 69n, 71n
Baruch Plan, 232
Bassett, R., 94n
Bay of Pigs, 344
Beck-Friis, Johan, 331, 332
Bedford Gramar School, 19
Beer, George, 60
Beirut, Lebanon, 284, 298
Belfast, Ireland, 173
Belgium, 21, 33, 59, 93, 109n, 139, 144n, 147n, 152, 209, 240, 253n, 274, 293
    Congo crisis (Hammarskjold), 309-313, 315, 320-323; (Thant), 350, 351, 353, 354, 356, 357, 359
Bellegarde, France, 173, 177
Ben-Gurion, David, 283n
Benes, Edvard, 109n
Berlin blockade 1948, 226-229, 261, 262, 344, 356, 424
Bern, Switzerland, 71, 72
    Avenol resignation, and, 159, 160
    Bruce Report, and, 148
    expulsion of Soviet Union, 151
    Lester period, and, 180, 187, 188n
    Princeton University, 153, 155
    Secretariat crisis 1938-39, 145
Bernadotte, Count Folke, 221, 222, 225
Bernstein, Leonard, 276
Beskow, Bo, 319
Biak, West New Guinea, 366
Bidault, Georges, 188n, 232
Big Five, 193, 209, 211, 211n, 219
Big Four, 203, 204, 228-230, 232-234, 397
B'nai B'rith, 232n
Board of Liquidation, *see* League of Nations
Bokhari, Ahmed, 281
Boland, Frederick, 326, 345, 346
Bolivia, 174, 218, 367, 374
    Avenol resignation, 162
    Gran Chaco conflict, 72-75
Bombay, India, 343
bond issue 1961, 409
Bonnet, Georges, 142
Bonnet, Henri, 210n

Borah, William, 61, 65
Boudreau, Frank, 149n, 185
Bourgeois, Léon, 57, 58, 63
Bourquin, Maurice, 147n
Bova-Scoppa, Renato, 128
Bramuglia, Juan A., 227, 228
Brazil, 33, 66, 67, 74-77, 365, 374, 395
Brazzaville (Congo), 316
Bretton Woods Monetary and Financial Conference 1944, 186
Breycha-Vauthier, Arthur, 199, 199n
Briand, Aristide, 44, 72, 80-82, 84, 85, 426
British Civil Service, 114, 169
British Foreign Office, 99, 114, 116
    Aland Islands question, 57
    Drummond, and, 20-22, 32, 43
    Italo-Ethiopian conflict, 129
    neutrality of SG, and, 419
    Sino-Japanese conflict, and, 87
Brosio, Mario, 385
Brouckère, Louis, 109n
Bruce, Stanley M., 147
    Bruce Committee, 147, 147n, 183, 184
    Bruce Report, 146-149, 162, 169, 171, 184
Brunei, 378
Brussels, Belgium, 57, 62
Brussels Financial Conference, 106
Buber, Martin, 275
Bucknell, Howard, 142, 143, 143n
Budapest, Hungary, 289, 295-297
buffer functions, 18, 221, 224, 226, 262, 283, 288, 290, 294, 367, 381, 384
Bulganin, Nikolai, 290
Bulgaria, 71, 72, 107, 258
Bullitt, William, 149, 150n, 152n
Bunche, Ralph, 341, 346, 437, 451
    American Communists in Secretariat, 254
    Congo crisis, 310, 313, 315
    Middle East 1956-57, 289, 290
    Palestine 1947-49, 219, 221-223, 451, 453
    Yemen, 376
Bunker, Ellsworth, 364, 376, 454
Burma, 341-345, 390, 402, 411, 412
Burns, E.L.M., 289, 291, 293
Butler, Harold, 108, 147n

298, 302

University of, 330

Calonder, Felix, 58

Cambodia, 305, 332

Cambridge University, 138

Cameroons, the, 188

Camp Massart (Katanga), 351

Canada
Congo crisis, 313, 354
Cuban missile crisis, 374
Hammarskjold election, 268, 274
ILO during war, 181
Korean War, 240
Lie election, 210
UNEF, 288, 289, 291, 395
UNFICYP, 383
UNIPOM, 388
UNSCOP, 217
West New Guinea, 365

Capodichino, Italy, 291

Carnegie Endowment for International
Peace, 113n

Casablanca group, 3170

Casals, Pablo, 276

Castle, William R., 82

Castro, Fidel, 369, 370, 373-375

Cecil, Sir Robert (Lord Cecil), 22, 24,
24n, 28n, 29n, 86, 87, 174

Central Committee for Economie and
Social Questions, 148

Ceylon, 313, 316, 365

Chamoun, Camille, 298, 299, 301

Chancellor, proposed, 22-24, 27, 48,
210n

Charron, René, 154, 159

Charter of the Transfer of
Sovereignty 1949, 362, 363

Chatham House, 116n

Chehab, Fuad, 301, 302

Chi Tsai, Victor Hoo, 122-124

Chiang Kai-Shek, 231

Chile, 67, 74, 374, 388

China, 211n, 215, 237n, 263, 302, 305,
316, 356
civil war, 201
Hammarskjold at Peking, 279-283,
337, 434, 454
Korean War, 241, 243-246, 250, 446
Nationalist Government, 92, 117,
230, 264-266, 279, 281, 311
Sino-Japanese conflict 1931-33,
77-96, 116-124, 136, 137, 170,

417, 419, 424, 429, 430, 446, 452,
453
technical aid (League), 117, 119-121
UN representation, 230-232, 234,
235, 249, 417, 446
Vietnam War, 400, 403, 408

Chinchow, China, 80

Chou En-lai, 280, 281-282

Church House, 210

Ciano, Galeazzo, 132, 133, 135

Clemenceau, Georges, 62

Clémentel, Etienne, 58

Cleveland, Harlan, 403

Codding, George, 113n

Cohen, Armand, 126n, 127n

Colban, Erik, 34, 54, 55, 109n, 198

cold war conflict
American Communists in Secretariat,
255n
Chinese representation, 230
Congo crisis, 310, 311, 325
extension of Lie's term, 264
Hammarskjold views on, 332
Iranian issue, and, 213-216
Laos, and, 306, 307, 309
Lebanon, and, 300, 304
Lie defeat for Assembly
Presidency, 209
Lie election as SG, 210n, 213
Peace Mission 1950, 230, 232-234
Thant election, 345
UN opportunities, 202, 251, 261-263,
271, 327
Vietnam War, 401

collective security, 201-203, 213, 216,
217, 224, 233, 262, 294, 327, 332, 459
Korean War, 236, 238, 247, 248
record of SG, 430

Collège de la Rochelle, 106

Collège des Universitaires (Congo), 315

Colombia, 67, 72-77, 173, 240, 291

Colombo, Ceylon, 342

Colombo Prime Ministers Conferences,
342-343

colonialism, 201, 203, 233-236, 261-264,
278, 283, 305
1960 Declaration on, 363
articulation, and, 444
Congo crisis, 309, 310, 325
constituency of SG, and, 432
diplomatic functions, and, 441
legitimization function, and, 446
Malaysia dispute, 378
record of SG, 431

rule-making function, 448
Thant, and views on, 341, 412-414
West New Guinea, 362, 363, 368
Columbia University, 319
Comert, Pierre, 111, 111n
Commission of Inquiry to the Far East,
see Lytton Commission
Commission of Jurists, *see* American
Communists in UN Secretatiat
Committee of Eighteen, *see* Italo-
Ethiopian conflict
Committee of Enquiry (Committee of
Thirteen), *see* League of Nations
Committee of Five, *see* Italo-
Ethiopian conflict
Committee of Nineteen, *see* Sino-
Japanese conflict
Committee on Organization of the
League of Nations, *see* League of
Nations
Common Plan, 197
communications functions and
capacities, 102, 171, 202, 226, 282
functions, 441, 442, 445, 447-449
integration, 461
resource, 421, 425, 439
communism, 47, 92, 106, 201, 251-256,
305, 401, 404; *and see* American
Communists in UN Secretariat
communist bloc, 237, 243, 266, 628,
316-319, 346
compatability of values, 460
Conference of Ambassadors 1923, 68,
69
Delimitation Commission, 68
conference diplomacy, 330, 334, 335
Conference for the Reduction and
Limitation of Armaments, *see*
Disarmament Conference
conflict management, 448, 449, 460, 461
Congo crisis 1960-64, 272, 275, 308,
309-327, 332-334, 344, 350-362, 365,
383, 384, 390, 434, 455
accomodation function, and, 454, 455
Adoula Government, 321-322
background, 309, 310
Bunche, Ralph, and, 310, 313, 315
Congo Club, 311, 317, 325, 362, 420,
429
Congo Conciliation Commission, 343
constituency, 432
constitutional theory, 428
Cordier, Andrew, 311, 315, 316, 319,
319n, 456

effect on SG Office, 324-327
field operation function, 458
financial crisis, and, 348
grants of power to SG, and, 434, 435
Hammarskjold death, 324
integration function, 463
Kitona phase, 352-353
legitimization function, 447
Lumumba alienation, 313-316
Lumumba death, 320-321
mobilization function, 456
neutrality of SG, 419, 420
ONUC establishment, 311-313
ONUC withdrawal, 359-360
participation function, 451
prestige of SG, 424
record of SG, 429
Round Three, 357-359
Round Two, 350-352
Rumpunch and Morthor, 322-324
sanctions phase, 353-356
Soviet opposition, 316-319
Thant election as SG, and, 348-349
Tshombe, Moise, *passim*
Union Minière du Haut-Katanga,
309, 350-355, 357, 358
consent of host state for UN force, 291,
312, 398, 452, 456
constituency for SG, 414, 416, 425,
431-433
constitutional theory as SG resource,
427, 428
contingency planning, 421, 422, 438, 442
Coquilhatville, Congo, 322
Cordier, Andrew, 211, 212, 341, 436,
437
Congo crisis, 311, 315, 316, 319,
319n, 326, 456
Hammarskjold background, 276
Korean War, 237, 237n, 242
Middle East 1956-57, 288, 293
Palestine, 221
Corfu crisis 1923, 37, 68-71
committee of jurists, 70-71
Costa du Rels, Adolfo, 162-165
Costa Rica, 65, 66, 66n
Council of Europe, 273
Cricton-Stuart, Lord Colum, 35
Cruise O'Brien, Conor, 323
Cuba, 47, 67, 73, 266, 401
missile crisis 1962, 349, 355, 368-375,
390
accomodation, 454
communication function, 442

interposition function, 459
mediation, 452
neutrality of SG, 418
prestige of SG, 424
UN inspection, proposed, 372-374
Curzon, Lord, 56
Cyprus, 381-386, 390, 454, 459
1960 Constitution, 381-182
Greece, 381-382, 385
London Conference 1964, 382
Makarios, Archbishop, 381, 382
Turkey, 381, 382, 385, 386
UNFICYP, 381-386
UN Security Council, 382-385
Czechoslovakia, 24, 57, 109n, 128, 137, 218, 231, 316, 380, 382, 383
Thant and Soviet occupation 1968, 420, 432, 447

D

Danzig, 54, 146, 147, 174n, 175, 175n
League High Commissioner, 146, 147, 174, 174n, 175
Darlan, Jean-François, 187
Davis, Norman, 79, 109
Dayal, Rajeshwar, 315, 320
Dayan, Moshe, 396
de Gaulle, Charles, 187, 188
de Valera, Eamon, 97, 198
Delbos, Yves, 134, 135, 175
Denmark, 109n, 152, 218, 274, 291-293, 395
Deutsch, Karl, 459
Diem Government, 401
diplomatic functions, 202, 375, 441 ff.
diplomatic mission, 70
diplomatic skills, 214, 272, 283, 422-424, 425
disarmament, 17, 60, 64, 77, 97, 116, 133, 138, 390
Disarmament Conference, 77, 83, 87, 88, 95, 96
discretionary power of international secretariat and SG, 101, 141, 204, 249, 261, 280, 291, 294, 297, 300, 334, 335, 344, 390, 409
Congo crisis, 311, 314, 360, 361
constitutional theory resource, 427, 428
diplomatic skills, 423
grants of power to SG, 435
mobilization function, 456
neutrality of SG, 420

policy planning, 457
record of SG, 431
structural position of SG, 426
distribution of nationalities, see League of Nations Secretariat
Dixon, Sir Pierson, 288
Djibuti-Addis Ababa railroad, 128
Dodds, Harold W., 155n, 157
Dominion Governments, 155
Donner, Ossian, 55, 56
Dorticos-Torrado, Osvaldo, 370
Draft Charter of the United Nations 1943, 191n
Draft Constitution of International Organization 1943, 191n
Drummond Castle, 19
Drummond, James, 20
Drummond, James Eric
accomodation function, 454
addressing Assembly and Council, 30-31
Aland Island question, 54-60, 452
articulation function 444
Avenol appointment as Deputy, 106
Avenol selection as SG, 110-112
British Foreign Office, and, 20-22, 32, 43
background of, and appointment as SG, 19-27
calling Council meetings, 28
character of, 24-27
communications function, 29, 30, 53, 441, 442
compared with Avenol, 31, 107, 112-115, 137, 168-172
compared with Hammarskjold, 44, 53, 102, 249, 268, 274, 275, 279, 330
compared with Lie, 53, 102, 211-213, 215, 257
compared with Thant, 343, 344
compared with Thomas, Albert, 26-27
constituency, 431
constitutional theory, 427, 428
construction of League systems, 32-33
contribution to world order, 100-103, 271
Corfu case, 68-71
debate of 1928-32, 38-43, 317
destruction of papers, 52, 68
diplomatic skills, 422, 423, 440
establishment of international civil service, 33-43
face-saving function, 453
functions, 27-33

Gran Chaco conflict, 72-75
grants of power to, 433, 434
information resource, 421, 422
interposition, 458
investigation functions, 28, 29
later career, 99-100, 198, 269
Latin-American relations, 64-67
legitimization function, 445
Leticia Trapeze conflict, 75-77
Lie election, 210n
mediation and negotiation, 29, 452
neutrality, 417, 419
parliamentary and staff functions,
    31-32
participation functions, 450, 451
political role, 51-77
    apparent lack thereof, 51-54
prestige, 424, 425
quoted, 17
record, 429
resignation, 42, 51, 74, 77, 94, 96-99,
    108, 110, 118, 170
salary, 28n
Sino-Japanese conflict, 77-96, 118,
    118n, 136, 429, 452, 453
skilled personnel, 436
Special War Mission, 20-22
structural position, 426
UN founding, and, 204, 206, 207
U.S. membership, and, 60-64
Versailles, and, 22-24
views on League and Secretariat,
    43-51
Drummond, Lady, 25
Dublin, 173
    University of, 198
Duillier sur Nyon, Switzerland, 167
Dulles, John Foster, 281, 285, 287, 288,
    294, 299, 300, 303
Dumbarton Oaks Proposals 1944, 191n,
    203
Durand, Dana, 185

E

Eastern Europe, 139, 201, 295, 296
Eastland, James, 253
Easton, David, 415
Eban, Abba, 294
Economic Commission for Europe, 307
economic depression
    Avenol election and early years, 105,
        112
    Drummond contribution, 103

Drummond resignation, 96
League prospects, 18, 46, 170
Sino-Japanese conflict, 77, 80, 86,
    93n, 95
U.S. membership, 62
Economic and Social Council, *see*
    United Nations
Economic, Social and Cultural Rights,
    Covenant on, 235
economic and social development, 17,
    19, 64, 100, 116, 146-149, 202, 233,
    235, 263, 277, 278, 303, 304, 307, 309,
    341, 390, 414
    articulation, 442, 444
    constituency, 432
    diplomatic functions, 441
    integration, 460, 461
    legitimization, 445, 446
    prestige, 425
    record, 430
    rule-making, 448
Ecuador, 266, 383
Eden, Anthony, 168, 175, 209, 209n,
    210n, 426
    Italo-Ethiopian conflict, 124-126, 128,
        131, 134, 135
    Middle East 1956-57, 286
Egger, Rowland, 38n
Egypt, 117, 222, 266
    Lebanon 1958, and, 298, 301, 304
    Middle East 1956-57, 283-296, 456
Ehrensvard, Count Albert, 59
Eisenhower, Dwight D., 209, 210n, 281,
    303
    Eisenhower Administration, 279, 280,
        320
    Eisenhower Doctrine, 299
Ekstrand, Erik, 109n
El Kony, Mohamed Awad, 394, 395
Elath, 293
Elimination of Racial Discrimination,
    Covenant on, 235
Elisabethville, 316, 320, 323, 324, 351,
    352, 355, 358
embargo, 74, 76, 77
Enckell, Carl, 59
English system, *see* League Secretariat
enosis, 381
Eshkol, Levi, 394
Estonia, 107
Ethiopia, 124-137, 138, 240, 269, 312,
    374
Eton, 19
Europe

Avenol analysis, and, 170-172
Avenol background and election, 105, 107, 109, 109n, 110
Avenol later years, 166-168
Avenol views, 116, 138-140, 160, 166-168
Bruce Report, 146
cold war, and, 203
Corfu case, and, 68
decline of League, and, 138-140
Drummond functions, and, 67
Drummond political role, and, 52, 75
Drummond resignation, 99
Drummond views, and, 46
Italo-Ethiopian conflict, and, 129, 133, 135-137
League as institution, and, 18
Lester period, 176, 180, 187, 189
Palestine, and, 218
Princeton transfer, and, 152, 157
Sino-Japanese conflict, and, 83, 84
UN, and, 201
UN Guard, and, 224, 224n
U.S. League membership, 61, 62
Western Hemisphere, 72
L'Europe Silencieuse, 167
Evatt, Herbert, 228
Executive Assistant, *see* UN SG

F

face-saving function, 222, 226, 288, 293, 362, 412, 426
Cuba missile crisis 1962, 371, 372, 375
SG function, 453, 454
West New Guinea, 367, 368
Faisal, King, 301
Far East, 99, 117-121, 453
fascism, 202, 297, 419
Fawzi, Mohamed, 286, 292, 394, 398
fedayeen, 283, 286, 287, 293, 294
Federal Bureau of Investigation, 254, 255
Federenko, Nikolai T.,376
Feller, Abraham, 214, 227, 231, 237, 242, 246, 253, 436
field operation functions, 449, 457, 458
financial crisis, 348, 356, 359, 382, 383, 390, 409
financial reconstruction, 106
Finland, 291, 307, 353, 383
Aland Islands question, 54-60
expulsion of Soviet Union, 113, 149-152

Fitzmaurice, Lord, 20
Foote, Wilder, 237n, 273n, 329
force short of war, 68-71
Foreign Press Association, 345
Formosa, 231, 239, 244, 279, 281
Formosa Straits, 281, 282
Fosdick, Raymond B., 33, 35, 44, 44n, 114n, 222n, 289n
U.S. membership in League, 60-63, 63n, 436
France
Aland Islands question, 55, 58, 59
Arab-Israeli War 1967, 397
Avenol analysis, and, 170, 171
Avenol background and appointment as SG, 105-110
Avenol resignation and later years, 159, 160, 166, 167, 168
Avenol and staff, and, 113, 113n
Avenol views, and, 139
Berlin blockade 1948, 227
Bruce Report, and, 147n
Congo crisis, 309, 311, 314, 316, 322, 350, 350n, 351, 353, 354, 356
constituency, 431
construction of League Secretariat, and, 33, 35, 37
Corfu crisis, 69
Cyprus, 382, 383
debate of 1928-32 on League Secretariat, 38, 39, 41
Drummond political role, and, 52
Drummond resignation, and, 98
Drummond selection, and, 21
Drummond views on League, and, 45
expulsion of Soviet Union, 149, 150n, 151n
financial crisis, and, 348, 356, 390
Gran Chaco conflict, 74
Greco-Bulgarian conflict, 71, 72
Hammarskjold election, and, 274
Hammarskjold at Peking, 279
Iranian issue,214
Italo-Ethiopian conflict, 124-130,132, 134-137
Kashmir, and, 388, 389
Korean War, and, 240
Laos, 305
Latin-American relations, and, 65
League Secretariat crisis 1938-39, and, 142,-144 144n, 146
Lebanon 1958, and, 302
Lester period, 175, 177, 187, 188, 188n, 192

Lie's election and early years, 211n, 213
Lie's extension of term, 265, 266
Lie's resignation, 267
Middle East 1956-57, 285-293, 296, 446, 454
participation function, and, 451
pressures for limited SG Office, 261, 343, 361, 413, 428, 429, 431, 435
Princeton University, and, 152, 153, 158
Sino-Japanese conflict, and, 80, 83, 85, 88, 93n, 94, 118, 118n, 120, 123
Thant election as Acting SG, 346
U.S. membership in League, and, 62
Vietnam war, and, 402, 403
Franco, Francisco, 135
Fraser, Peter, 209
French Committee of National Liberation, 187, 188
French-Italian, entente 1935, 127
French system, *see* League Secretariat
French Treasury, 106
functionalism, 440, 440n, 441

G

Galilee, Sea of, 394
Gardiner, Robert K. A., 353n, 354-356, 358, 359
Gautier, R., 190n, 191n
Gaza Strip, 287, 293, 294, 332, 395, 396
General Assembly, *see* United Nations
Geneva, Switzerland, 18, 33, 35, 36, 48, 52, 62, 107n, 109, 113-115, 137, 167, 170
Avenol resignation, and, 159, 161, 163-165, 176
communication function, 441
Drummond resignation, 98
expulsion of Soviet Union, 149-151
Greco-Bulgarian conflict, 71
Hammarskjold at Peking, and, 281, 282
Hungarian revolution 1956, and, 297
Italo-Ethiopian conflict, and, 125, 127, 130-135
League Secretariat crisis 1938-39, and, 142, 145
Lebanon 1958, and, 304
Lester period, and 173, 178n, 179-189, 192, 194-197, 199
Middle East 1956-57, and, 286
participation function, and, 451

Princeton University, and, 153-158, 177
Sino-Japanese conflict, 78, 79, 81, 85, 88, 119, 120, 122, 123
Geneva Accords 1954, 305, 306, 308, 402, 404
Geneva Conference, 306, 308, 309, 400 402, 405
Geneva Protocol 1924, 138
Geneva, University of, 147n
Genocide Convention 1948, 233
geographical distribution, *see* UN Secretariat
Germany
admission to League, 30, 67
Aland Islands question, and, 58
Avenol background and selection as SG, 105, 107-111
Avenol resignation and later years, and, 159, 160, 167, 168
Avenol views on League, and, 116
Bruce Report, and, 148
constituency for SG, 431
Cuba missile crisis, and, 369
decline of League, and, 137
Drummond background, and, 19-21
Drummond later years, and, 99
Drummond political role and views of League, 46, 52, 213
expulsion of Soviet Union, and, 151-152
Italo-Ethiopian conflict, and, 124, 128, 129, 136
League Secretariat crisis 1938-39, and, 142, 143, 143n, 145
League Secretariat debate 1928-32, and, 38-43, 101, 317
Lie Peace Mission, and, 233, 235
Middle East 1956-57, and, 293
Princeton University, and, 153,-154, 157
Sino-Japanese conflict, and, 92n
structural position of SG, and, 426
Thant election, and, 344
treaty revision, and, 139
Weimar Republic, 83
Ghana, 312, 370
Gilbert, Prentiss
Avenol election, 109, 110
Italo-Ethiopian conflict, 130, 133, 134
Sino-Japanese conflict, 80-81, 92, 92n, 97, 119-121, 123
Gilchrist, Huntington, 60, 61, 64, 114, 114n

Giraud, Henri, 187, 188
Gizenga, Antoine, 320, 322
Golan Heights, Syria, 396
Goldberg, Arthur, 405
Good Neighbor Resolution 1958, 303, 304
good offices, 73, 223, 322, 337, 384-386, 442
Goodrich, Carter, 144n, 185
Gordenker, Leon, 274n, 415n
government effectiveness, 463
Grady, Henry, 185, 186
Graham, Frank, 386
Gran Chaco conflict, 72-75, 173
Grandi, Dino, 81
grants of power as SG resource, 433-435
Great Britain
    accomodation function, and, 454
    Aland Islands question, and, 55-58
    American Communists in
        Secretariat, and, 253, 253n
    Arab-Israeli War 1967, and, 397
    Avenol analysis, and, 171
    Avenol background and election as
        SG, 105-109, 111n, 112, 113
    Avenol resignation, and, 160, 166
    Berlin blockade, and, 227, 228
    Bruce Report, and, 147n
    Congo crisis, and, 309, 311, 323, 350-351, 353-354, 356, 358n, 359, 361
    constituency for SG, and, 431
    construction of League Secretariat,
        and, 35-37
    Corfu crisis, and, 69
    Cyprus, 381-383, 385
    decline of League, and, 139
    Drummond later career, 99, 100
    Drummond political role, and, 52
    Drummond resignation, and, 97
    Drummond selection, and, 23, 24
    Drummond views on League, 45, 46, 48, 50
    expulsion of Soviet Union, and, 151
    Gran Chaco conflict, and, 74
    Greco-Bulgarian conflict, and 71, 72
    Hammarskjold background and
        election, and, 272, 274
    Hammarskjold Peking mission, and, 281
    Hungarian Revolution, and, 297
    Irianian issue, and, 214, 214n, 215
    Italo-Ethiopian conflict, 124, 125, 127-132, 134-137
    Kashmir, and, 386, 388

    Korean War, and, 240, 244
    Laos, and, 306
    League Secretariat crisis 1938-39,
        and, 142-144, 144n, 146
    League Secretariat debate 1928-32,
        and, 38-43
    Lebanon 1958, and, 301-304
    legitimization, and, 446
    Lester period, and, 175, 176, 180-183, 186, 188, 192, 196, 196n
    Leticia Trapeze, and, 77
    Lie background, election, and early
        period, 208-210, 210n, 211n, 213
    Lie's term extension, and 265
    Lie's resignation, and 267
    Malaysia, and, 378-380
    Middle East 1956-57, and, 285-288, 290-293, 296, 446, 454
    Palestine 1947-49, and 217-219, 219n, 221, 224
    Princeton University, and, 153, 155, 156-158
    Sino-Japanese conflict, and, 80, 84-88, 90, 93n, 94, 103, 120, 121, 123
    U.S. League membership, and 60-62
    Vietnam war, and, 403, 406
Greco-Bulgarian conflict 1925, 71-72
Greece, 24, 33, 107, 109n, 142, 146, 147n, 240,258
    Corfu case, 68-71
    Greco-Bulgarian conflict, 71-72
Cyprus case, 381, 382, 385
Grenoble, 113n, 118n, 123n, 130n, 132n, 147n, 158
Grey, Sir.Edward, 20, 21n
Gromyko, Andrei, 214, 246, 303, 345, 402
Gross, Ernest A., 240, 398
Guantanamo Bay, 374
Guatemala, 217
Guinea, 370
Gullion, Edmund A., 352
Gyani, P. S., 382, 383

H

Haas, Robert, 111, 111n
Hague, The, 82, 183
Halifax, Canada, 20
Hambro, Carl J., 38, 1440n, 147n, 178
    Avenol resignation, 161, 163-165, 165n, 179, 179n
    Lester period, 181-183, 185, 188, 190, 194-196, 198, 199, 199n

Princeton University, 155-157
Hammarskjold, Ake, 97, 272, 273
Hammarskjold, Bo, 272
Hammarskjold, Dag
  accomodation function, and, 454, 455
  Ake Hammarskjold, and, 97
  American Communists in Secretariat,
    and, 254-256
  articulation function, and, 443, 444
  background, 271-273, 275,276
  compared with Drummond, 44, 53,
    102, 249, 268, 274, 275, 279, 330
  compared with Lie, 216, 217, 225,
    249-251, 260-261, 263, 276, 279n,
    283, 325, 341, 343-344
  compared with Thant, 216, 341, 343-
    344, 361-362, 383-384, 410
  Congo crisis, and, 309-327, 348, 350,
    432, 434-435, 451, 455-456
  constituency, 432
  constitutional theory as resource,
    427, 428
  diplomatic skills, and, 422, 423, 440
  election as SG, 247, 268-269, 274-275
  field operation function, 457
  grants of power, and, 434-435
  Hungarian Revolution, and, 295-298,
    446
  information resource, and, 421
  integration, and, 460, 463
  interposition, and, 458-459
  Laos, and, 305-309
  Lebanon 1958, and, 298-305
  legitimization function, and, 446
  Middle East 1956-57, and, 183-295,
    370, 398-399, 434, 446, 451, 456
  mobilization of resources, and, 456
  neutrality, and, 417, 419-420
  participation function, and, 451
  Peking mission, 279-283, 454
  prestige, and, 424-425
  record, 429, 430
  resources, 416
  rule-making, and, 448
  skilled personnel, 436-438
  tangible resources, and, 439
  Thant election, and, 341, 345
  troika proposal, and, 43, 256, 316-
    319, 341, 344, 417
  views of Charter, 302, 328, 330-331,
    333-338
  views of UN and SG Office, 205, 207,
    276-278, 301, 327-339, 410-414
Hammarskjold, Hjalmar, 272

Hammarskjold, Sten, 273
Hankey, Maurice, 24, 98
Harding Administration, 63
Hardinge, Lord, 57
Harrison, Leland, 187, 187n, 188n
Harvard University, 224
Haute Direction, *see* League Secretariat
Haute-Savoie, 167
Havana, Cuba, 374
Helsinki, Finland, 150n, 350
Herbert, Sir Edwin, 253
Heurtematte, Roberto M., 308
Hill, Martin, 187, 187n, 198
Hiss, Alger, 193, 194
Hitler, Adolf, 18, 105, 135, 137, 160
Hoare, Sir Samuel, 128, 130
Hoare-Laval Plans, *see* Italo-Ethiopian
  conflict
Hoden, Marcel, 141-143
Holma, Harri, 151
Home, Earl of, 351
Hotel National, Geneva, 35
House, Colonel Edward M. 20-24, 60
House-Drummond Memorandum, 21
House of Lords, 99, 351
Howard-Ellis, C., 27n, 28n
Hudson, Manley, 60, 64, 185
Hughes, Charles Evans, 63
Hull, Cordell, 130, 146-147, 156, 188n
human rights, 202, 233, 235, 263, 417,
  432, 444-445, 460-461
Hungary, 107
  Hungarian Revolution, 289-290,
    295-298, 446
Hurst, Sir Cecil, 23, 24
Hussein, King, 301
Hutson, John D., 211
Hymans, Paul, 93

I

I and Thou, 275
Ileo, Joseph, 316
Ilyushin-28 bombers, 375
Inchaustegui, Mario Garcia, 369
Inchon landing, 241, 242; *see* Korean War
India
  Arab-Israeli War 1967, 394-395, 399
  Congo crisis, and, 315, 319, 354, 356,
    358
  Cuba missile crisis, 374
  Cyprus case, 382
  Hammarskjold Peking mission, and,
    281-282

480

Kashmir, 386-389
Korean War, 243, 244
Lebanon, and, 302
Lie term extension, and, 265-266
Middle East 1956-57, and, 288, 293
Thant election, 345, 347n
UN Guard, 225
UNSCOP, 217, 218
West New Guinea, 365
Indiana, University, 211
Indochina, 279, 305, 402
Indonesia, 225, 230, 261, 324, 3248, 357, 390
Malaysia, 378, 380, 454
West New Guinea, 362-368
information resource, 420-422, 441
Ingram, Edward, 132
inspection, 458
Institute of Intellectual Cooperation, 210n
Inter-American Conference on Problems of War and Peace 1945, 186
Interallied Commission for Reconstruction, 106
internal war
Congo crisis, 310, 312, 315-316, 321, 353, 359, 362
Laos, 309
Lebanon, 283-295
participation function, 451
record of SG, 431
Vietnam, 400
Yemen, 375-377
International Control Commission (Indochina), 306
International Court of Justice, see United Nations
international integration, 101, 172, 202, 459-463
International Labor Organization, 26, 39, 50, 60, 108, 112n, 114, 131, 135, 143n, 144n, 147n, 158, 170, 180-181, 184-185, 190, 193-194, 197
ILO Conference, 26, 60, 186, 187n
ILO Constitution, 186
international law, 70, 76, 115, 140, 230, 233, 235-236, 333- 335, 441, 445, 447, 460
International Law Commission, 236
International Monetary Fund, 355
International Trade Organization, 233
international system, 18, 201-202, 413, 419, 426-427, 430, 435, 440-441, 459
interposition, 400, 449, 454, 458-459

investigation, 28-29, 204, 258, 337-338, 457
Investigation Committee (Shanghai), 89
Iquitos, Peru, 77
Iran, 214, 217-218, 301, 365
Iranian issue 1946, 213-217
legal memorandum, 214-216
Lie presentations to Council and Assembly, 215-216
Iraq, 298, 301, 304
Ireland, 112n, 146, 173, 174n, 193, 198-199, 326, 345, 365, 383
National University of, 198
Ishii, Viscount, 70
Israel
Arab-Israeli War 1967, 385, 393-400
Congo crisis, and, 360
Korean War, and, 244
Lebanon 1958, and, 298
legitimization function, and 445, 454
Middle East 1956-57, 283-287, 290-294, 454
Palestine 1947-49, 217-223, 237n, 266, 451, 453
Italian Somaliland, 125n, 269
Italo-Ethiopian conflict, 18, 113, 123, 124-137
Aloisi, Baron Pompeo, 125, 126, 126n, 128, 129, 131, 132
Avenol trip to Rome, 132-135
Committee of Eighteen, 129-130
Committee of Five, 129
direct negotiations, 124-127, 131
Eden, Anthony, 124-126, 128, 131, 134, 135
Hoare-Laval Plans, 130, 131
Italo-Ethiopian Treaty of Amity, Conciliation and Arbitration 1928, 126-127
Mussolini, Benito, 124-126, 128-129, 131-133, 135, 138
sanctions, 129-132, 135-138
Tripartite Pact 1906, 127, 127n, 128
Wal-Wal incident, 125, 125n, 128
Italy
Avenol appointment, and, 108-111
Avenol resignation, and, 159-160
Avenol views, and, 105, 138-139, 167-168
Bruce Report, and, 148
Congo crisis, and, 314, 357
constituency, 431
construction of League Secretariat, and, 35, 37

Corfu case, 68-71
Drummond, ambassador to Rome,
99, 269
Drummond background, and, 21
Drummond functions, and, 30
Drummond political role, and, 52,
60, 213
Drummond views on League, and, 45
expulsion of Soviet Union, and, 149
Fascist law regarding Italians in
Secretariat, 37, 38, 254, 256
Hungarian Revolution, and, 297
Italo-Ethiopian conflict, 124-137, 430
Laos, and, 307
Lester period, and, 177
links with League, 67
Middle East 1956-57, and, 291-293
Princeton transfer, and, 152, 153, 157
Secretariat crisis 1938-39, 142, 143,
143n, 145
Secretariat debate 1928-32, 38-43,
101, 107, 317
Sino-Japanese conflict, and, 123
structural position of SG, and, 426
Yemen, and, 377

J

Jacklin, Seymour, 158, 179-182, 186,
188, 192-194, 197
Jackson, R. G. A., 221
Jadotville, Congo, 358-360
Janacek, George, 380
Japan
Avenol analysis, and, 170
Avenol appointment, and, 109, 111n
Bruce Report, and, 148
construction of League Secretariat,
and, 35
Corfu case, and, 70
decline of League, and, 137
expulsion of Soviet Union, and, 149,
152
Korean War, 239, 242
Laos, and, 307
Lebanon, and, 301-302
Lie peace mission, 233
Secretariat crisis 1938-39, and, 143n,
145
Sino-Japanese conflict, 77-96, 116-124,
136-137, 170, 417, 419, 424, 429,
430, 446, 452, 453
universality of League, and, 18

withdrawal from League, 88, 89, 91,
93-95, 111n, 116-124
Jarring, Gunnar, 397, 454
Jebb, Sir Gladwyn, 100, 196, 210n
Jenks, Wilfred, 186
Jerusalem, 217, 222, 223, 225n, 283n,
376, 396
Jessup, Philip, 227-229
Jèze, Gastion, 126
Johnson, Lyndon B., 385, 396, 402-403,
405-407
Jönköping, 272
Jordan, 222, 222n, 284, 298, 301-304,
332, 394, 396-397
judicial settlement, 126

K

Kaminaville, Congo, 358
Kasavubu, Joseph, 311, 312, 315-316,
320, 352
Kashmir, 198, 230, 261, 386-389, 390,
459
Katanga Province, *see* Congo crisis
financial interests, 354
grants of power to SG, and, 435
Hammarskjold, and, 309-310, 312-315,
320-325
record of SG, and, 429
Thant, and, 344, 348, 350-359
Katzin, Alfred, 239, 241
Kelen, Emery, 273n
Kellogg-Briand Pact 1928, 79, 81, 87, 138
Kelly, Sir David, 155, 156n
Kennedy, John F., 309, 320
Congo crisis, 351-353, 356-357, 361
Cuba missile crisis, 368-373, 375
West New Guinea, 364
Kerno, Ivan, 231
Khan, Ayub, 387
Khiary, Mahmoud, 322-324
Khrushchev, Nikita S., 295, 299, 302,
316-317
Cuba missile crisis, 349, 370, 372, 375,
454
Kimba, Evariste, 353
Kitona, Congo, 352, 353, 358, 361
Kitona Declaration, 352
Kivu Province, Congo, 320
Kolwezi, Congo, 359
Koo, Wellington, 91
Korean War
American Communists in Secretariat,
and, 256

Armistice Agreement, 247, 279, 280
China, 241, 243-246, 250, 446
Chinese representation, and, 231
compared with UNEF and command,
    289, 312
effect on UN and SG Office, 247-251,
    262-263, 266-267
General Assembly, 238, 242-243, 245-
    246, 250, 289
legitimization function, 446
Lie Peace Mission, and, 234-235
Lie term extension and resignation,
    and, 264, 266-267, 269, 272
Lie views on UN and Office, and,
    259-260, 262-263
MacArthur, Douglas, 239-243
neutrality of SG, and, 236-240, 417,
    419
prestige of SG, and, 424
record of SG, and, 429-430
Security Council, 237-242, 244,
    246-247, 250, 289
Soviet Union, 236-237, 241, 243, 247,
    249, 259, 262-263, 266, 429
Unified Command, 239-241, 243-245,
    247
UN and Lie response to the attack,
    236-240
UN prospects, and, 271, 279, 327
UN Commission on Korea, 237-239,
    242
UNCURK, 243, 247
UN invasion of North Korea, 241-244
UN peace terms, 244-247
United States, 236-251, 289, 429-430,
    446
Kosygin, Aleksei N., 389
Kreisler, Fritz, 276
Kremlin, 203
Kuomintang Government, *see* China,
    Nationalist Government
Kuznetsov, A. A., 313

L

La Paz, Bolivia, 74
La Pelouse, 114, 152n, 165, 182
Lake Tsana, Ethiopia, 128
Lansing, Robert, 63
Laos, 305-309, 332, 337
Larus, Joel, 174n
Lash, Joseph, 273n
Latin America
    Avenol appointment, and, 109, 110

Avenol views, and, 139
constituency for SG, and, 433
Cuba missile crisis, and, 374
Drummond functions and role, and,
    30, 51n, 60, 61
Drummond views, and, 46-47
Gran Chaco conflict, 72-75
League universality, and, 18, 46
Leticia Trapeze conflict, 75-77
Lie election, and, 209
Monroe Doctrine issue, 64-67
neutrality of SG, and, 420
record of SG, and, 430
Thant election and re-election, and,
    346-348, 391
Thant support, 343
U.S. League membership, and, 61
Lausanne Economic Conference, 110
Laval, Pierre, 126-128, 130
League of Nations, 17-27, 42-52, 69, 95,
    100, 115-116, 177, 184-185, 201-203,
    209-213, 217, 248, 317, 342, 430
    Archives, 32-33, 43, 46, 52, 113
    Assembly, 25-31, 33, 34, 37, 39-40,
        47-48, 51-53, 96, 98, 102, 108, 112,
        141n, 169, 175n, 179, 195n
    Aland Islands question, 55
    Assembly Committees, 30, 37
    Assembly President, 31, 165, 179,
        195
    Avenol resignation, and, 161-163
    Bruce Report, and, 146-148, 183
    Credentials Committee, 133-135
    Eleventh Assembly, 39
    expulsion of Soviet Union, and, 150-
        152, 152n
    First Assembly, 36
    Fourth Committee, 31, 38-39,
        41-42, 98, 110-111, 148, 150n,
        162, 169
    grants of power to SG, 433
    Italo-Ethiopian conflict, 129,
        132-135
    Last Assembly 1946, 169, 192,
        194-197
    Princeton transfer, and, 153n
    Second Committee, 148
    Secretariat crisis 1938-39, and,
        141, 143n, 145, 180
    Sino-Japanese conflict, 78, 88-94,
        119, 121
    voting procedures, 49, 50
Board of Liquidation, 197-198
collective security, 18, 138-139

Commission on League of Nations
1919, 22-23
Committee of Enquiry (Committee of
Thirteen), 39-42, 110
majority report, 41
minority report, 39-42, 107, 107n
Second Committee of Thirteen,
42, 96-97, 110
Committee on Organization of the
League of Nations, 33-35, 39
Council, 22-23, 25, 27-31, 33-37,
40-41, 44-45, 47-48, 50-53, 102,
111n, 112, 138, 148, 169, 171, 173
Aland Islands question, 54-59
Avenol resignation, 161-163
Bruce Report, 146-147
Corfu case, 68-71
Drummond resignation, 96-99, 108
expulsion of Soviet Union, 150,
150n
financial reconstruction, 106, 107
Gran Chaco conflict, 72-74
grants of power to SG, 433
Greco-Bulgarian conflict, 71-72
Italo-Ethiopian conflict, 125-129,
132-134
Latin American relations, and,
64-66
Lester period, 173-176, 179, 190
Leticia Trapeze, 75-77
mediation function, 452
participation of SG, and, 450
President of, 31, 66n, 70, 72, 80,
86, 162-165, 173, 179
Secretariat crisis 1938-39, and, 144
Sino-Japanese conflict, 77-96, 118,
118n, 119, 121
U.S. League membership, and, 62-63
Covenant, 18, 22, 24, 27-29n, 32-33,
36, 44, 48, 105, 108, 115-116,
122-124, 139, 140, 152, 168, 170,
172, 187, 202, 207
Article 1, 122
Article 1 (3), 89, 121, 122, 187
Article 3, 94
Article 6, 27
Article 6 (2), 112, 195
Article 8, 138
Article 10, 70
Article 11, 28-29, 56, 82, 88-89, 150
Article 12, 70, 138
Article 13, 70, 138
Article 15, 28, 29, 56, 70, 84, 88,
89, 89n, 126, 138, 150

Article 15 (4), 76, 93, 94n
Article 15 (8), 56-57, 70
Article 16, 28, 29n, 90, 93n, 94,
138-140
Article 19, 138
Article 21, 64-66
Aland Islands question, 56-57
Corfu, 69-71
Gran Chaco conflict, 72-74
Greco-Bulgarian conflict, 71
Italo-Ethiopian conflict, 124, 125,
128, 129, 136, 137
Latin American relations, 64-66
neutrality of SG, 417, 419
"reform" of Covenant, 116, 133,
137-139
Sino-Japanese conflict, 79, 82, 83,
88-91, 93, 93n, 95, 121, 122
High Commissioner for Refugees, 181,
188n
Mandates System, 18, 32-33, 60, 122,
187-188
Permanent Mandates Commission,
122
Minorities System, 32-33
Opium Supervisory Body, 180, 184
Permanent Central Opium Board,
181, 184
permanent missions, 47, 48
sanctions, 18, 28, 29, 76, 138-141
Italo-Ethiopian conflict, 124,
129-132, 135-138
Sino-Japanese conflict, 77, 80, 84,
89, 90, 93n, 94
Secretariat, 17, 19, 22, 25-27, 30-40,
42, 47, 49, 51-53, 59-60, 71-72, 100,
108, 112, 115, 118, 118n, 113, 148
Administrative Commissions
Section, 34, 54, 175n
Americans on staff, 60-64
Central Section, 115
Chef de Cabinet, 141, 142
Committee on Budgetary
Economies, 143, 143n
crisis of 1938-39, 141-146
Deputies SG, 35, 39, 106, 109-111,
111n, 113, 146, 175, 175n
Directors, 32, 36, 40, 41, 45, 48-49,
57-58, 61-62, 111n, 130, 143,
152n
Disarmament Section, 144
distribution of nationalities, 36-37,
96
Economic Section, 33-34, 71, 106,

484

110, 143-145, 154, 157-159, 181,
  184, 186
English system, 32, 114, 436
Financial Section, 33-34, 71, 106,
  110, 144-145, 154, 157-159, 181,
  184, 186
French system, 32, 114-115, 437
Haute Direction, 31-32, 35-42,
  48-49, 96, 98, 107, 110-111, 111n,
  112n, 114, 145-146, 161, 171,
  175n, 436, 442
Health Section, 120, 144, 185
Intellectual Cooperation Section,
  111n
Internal Administrative Services,
  175n
International Bureaux, 111n
Latin American Bureau, 66
Latin American correspondents, 66
Latin American relations, 64-67
Latin American staff members, 66,
  67
Legal Section, 34, 60, 110
Mandates Section, 60, 143, 144
Minorities Questions Section, 54,
  11n, 143-144, 175n
national islands, 37n, 110, 112n
Opium Section, 144, 158
Political Section, 33, 111n, 118,
  130, 144
Princeton transfer, 152-158
Public Information Section, 60-61,
  111n, 113, 146n
Sections, 32-33, 36, 40, 45, 52, 111,
  112
Social Section, 144
Transit Section, 144, 157, 181,
  184, 186
Under-Secretaries, 32-33, 35-37,
  39-42, 60, 64, 107n, 110-111,
  11n, 126, 130, 133, 146
Weekly meetings, 32, 40-41, 45, 48,
  57, 61-62, 152n
Supervisory Commission, 31, 39, 140
  Avenol resignation, 161-165
  Lester period, 178-183, 188, 190,
    192-194, 196-197
  Princeton, 155, 177
  Secretariat crisis 1938-39, 141, 141n,
    145, 147n
Treasury, 158, 177, 180
League of Nations Union (London), 108,
  108n, 112
Lebanon, 222, 265, 284, 298-305, 308,

332, 454, 456
Lefever, Ernest W., 323
legitimization function, 220, 226, 236,
  408, 442, 445-447, 448-449, 451
Leith-Ross, Sir Frederick, t186
lend-lease, 214
Leopoldville, 310, 312-313, 315, 320-325,
  352, 353, 357-359, 362, 364
Lester, Sean, 112, 146, 147
  attempted French withdrawal, 187, 188
  Avenol, and, 174-179
  Avenol resignation, and, 159, 161,
    163-165, 165n, 178
  background, 173-175
  becomes Acting SG, 164-165, 175, 178
  becomes Deputy SG, 174, 175
  constitutional theory, 427
  ILO Conference 1944, 186-187
  last Assembly 1946, 195-196
  made SG, 195, 195n, 196
  Princeton, 153-154, 157, 178
  record, 429
  retirement, 198, 199
  San Francisco Conference, at, 193-194
  skilled personnel, 436
  structural position, 426
  technical work during war, 180-185
  transfer to UN, 196-198
  views on UN, 189-191, 195
  Woodrow Wilson Award, 194-195
Leticia Trapeze conflict, 72, 73, 75-77,
  173
Lever, Vera, 114, 167, 167n, 168
liaison functions, 212
Liberal Party (Great Britain), 46, 99, 100
Lie, Trygve
  accomodation function, 453-454
  American Communists in Secretariaat,
    251-256, 266
  Article 98, and, 205
  Avenol resignation, 171
  background, 207-208
  Berlin blockade, 226-229
  Chinese representation, 230-235, 249,
    446
  compared with Drummond, 53, 102,
    211-213, 215, 257
  compared with Hammarskjold, 216-
    217, 225, 249, 251, 260-261, 263,
    276, 279n, 283, 325, 341, 343-344
  compared with Thant, 341, 343-344
  constituency, 431-432
  constitutional theory, and, 427-428
  diplomatic skills, and, 422, 423

election as SG, 207-213
Hammarskjold election, and, 274
integration function, and, 463
Iranian issue, 213-217
Korean War, 236-251, 259-260,
    262-263, 266, 271-272, 429, 466
    effect of on Office, 248-251
later career, 99, 269
League transfer to UN, 197, 198
neutrality, and, 417, 419, 420
Palestine, 217-224
Peace Mission, 230, 232-236
presentations to Assembly and
    Council, 215-216, 258
prestige, 425
quoted, 201
record, and, 429
resignation, 247, 266-268, 271-272,
    274
skilled personnel resource, 436-437
Soviet boycott, 266-268, 271, 414
tangible resources, 439
term extension, 259, 264-267, 268
Thant election, and, 345
UN founding, and, 203
UN Guard, 224-226, 439
views on UN and Office, 256-264,
    412-413
Lima, Peru, 77
Lindstrom, Jan-Gunnar, 183n
Linner, Sture, 323, 353n
Lisbon, Portugal, 158, 181, 181n
Lithuania, 139
Litvinov, Maxim, 135
Lloyd, Selwyn, 286
Lloyd George, David, 44, 62
Lodge, Henry Cabot, 288, 301, 408
London Conference (on Cyprus) 1964,
    382
Loutfi, Omar, 299, 374
Louvain, Catholic University of, 253n
Louvanium, University of, 322
Loveday, Alexander
    Avenol resignation, 159, 164
    Lester period, 184-188, 193-194, 198
    Princeton, 157, 158, 177, 181
Lumumba, Patrice, 311-316, 319-321
Luxemburg, 152, 240
Lytton, Lord, 85
Lytton Commission, 79, 84-86, 88-92;
    see Sino-Japanese conflict
    Lytton Report, 90-94

M

MacArthur, Douglas, 239-243
MacDonald, B. F., 388
Macapagal, Diasdado, 378
Madariaga, Salvador de, 98, 125, 129,
    131
Madrid, Spain, 181n
Makarios, Archbishop, 381, 382
Malagasy Republic, 321
Malaya, 378, 380, 381
Malaysia, 377-381, 390, 453, 454
Mali, 370
Malik, Charles, 265, 266, 299, 300
Malik, Jacob, 228, 229, 240, 246
Manchester Guardian, 34, 34n
Manchester Square, 35
Manchukuo, 90-92, 94, 119
Manchuria, 77-96, 109, 116, 243, 244,
    247
Manchurian Advisory Committee, 119
mandates entrusted to SG, 206, 284-285,
    288-291, 314, 333, 336, 362, 433-435
Mandates System, *see* League of Nations
Manila Accord 1963, 378
Mansfield, Mike, 387
Mantoux, Paul, 33
Marambio, Tulio, 388-389
Markings, 275
Marshall Plan, 202, 273, 274
Masaryk, Thomas, 24
Massigli, René, 110n
Mathu, Eliud, 358
Matsudaira, Baron, 88
Matsuoka, Yosuke, 91-93
Mayfair (London), 35
McCarran, Pat, 253
McCarthy, Joseph, and McCarthyism,
    251, 253, 254, 256
McCoy, Frank, 85
McGhee, George, C., 355
mediation and negotiation functions
    Arab-Israeli War 1967, 400
    Berlin blockade, 226-227, 229
    Drummond contribution, 101, 102
    Gran Chaco conflict, 73
    Hammarskjold Peking mission, 282
    Iranian issue, 214, 216-217
    Korean War, 236, 244, 247
    Leticia Trapeze, 75
    Lie views, 257, 258, 262, 263
    Malaysia, 379
    neutrality of SG, and, 419
    Palestine 1947-49, 221, 223, 224

Peace Mission, 232, 234
prestige of SG, 425
SG function, 449, 451-453
structural position of SG, 426
troika proposal, and, 319
UN SG and San Francisco Conference, 204, 205
Vietnam War, 409
West New Guinea, 308
Mediterranean area, 139
Mediterranean Sea, 385
Melle, France, 106
membership requirements for UN, 231, 235
Menon, Krishna, 281
Merton, Robert K., 440n
Mexico, 65, 66, 73, 186, 265, 274, 374
Mexico City, 186
Michelmore, Laurence V., 379
Middle East, see Arab-Israeli War 1967
  1947-49 Palestine, 217-224, 226
    Armistice Agreements, 222
    Bernadotte, Count Folke, 221, 222, 225
    Bunche, Ralph, 219, 221-223
    General Assembly, 217-220, 223
    Great Britain, 217-219, 221, 224
    Partition Plan, 217-220, 223
    Security Council, 218, 219, 221, 222
    Soviet Union, 217, 218, 220
    UNSCOP, 217
    UNTSO, 221, 222
    United States, 217-221
  1956-57 crisis, 283-295, 296, 298, 356, 370, 383
    accomodation function, 453-454
    Bunche, Ralph, 289-290
    Cordier, Andrew, 288, 293
    Dulles, John Foster, 285, 287-288, 294
    executive functions, 455
    France, 285-288, 290-293, 296, 446, 454
    grants of power, and, 434
    Great Britain, 285-288, 290-293, 296, 446, 454
    Hammarskjold views, and, 329-331, 337
    interposition, and, 458
    Israel, 283-287, 290-294, 454
    legitimization function, and, 446
    mediation function, and, 452
    Nasser, Gamal, 283, 283n, 285, 292, 293, 456
    participation function, and, 451
    Pearson, Lester, 288
    prestige of SG, and, 424
    Soviet Union, 283-284, 286-288, 290, 293-294
    Suez Canal, 285-293, 296, 356
    UNEF, 288-293
    UNTSO, 283, 289
    United States, 283, 286, 287, 290, 293, 294
  League universality, and, 18
  Lebanon crisis 1958, 298-305, 454, 456
  Lester period, 188
Mikoyan, Anastas I., 349, 375
militarism, 202
Military Adviser, see UN Secretary-General
military alliances, 210, 230, 237n
Miller, David Hunter, 22n, 23, 23n, 24, 48n
Miller, Richard, 273n
mini-states, 235
Minorities System, see League of Nations
Mitchell, William, 253n
Mixed Armistice Commissions for Palestine, 222
Moats, Helen M., 34n, 38n
mobilization of resources, 449, 455, 456
Mobutu, Joseph, 315, 316, 320
Modzelewski, Zygmunt, 265n
Mollet, Guy, 286
Monnet, Jean, 33, 35, 39, 106, 109, 113, 172
Monroe Doctrine, 64-66, 70, 72
Monthly Bulletin of Statistics, 184
Montreal, Canada, 158, 181, 183, 184, 194
Morley, Felix, 28, 28n, 29n, 38n
Morocco, 312, 370
Motta, Gieuseppi, 110n, 145
Mukden, China, 78, 91, 96, 117
Munich Agreement, 139, 141, 142, 143n
Munongo, Godefroid, 353
Murphy, Robert, 187, 188n
Museum of Modern Art (New York), 276
Mussolini, Benito, 37, 38n, 99, 254
  Corfu case, 68, 69
  Italo-Ethiopian conflict, 124-126, 128, 129, 131-133, 135, 138
Myrdal, Gunnar, 228

N

Nanking, 83, 107, 117, 119
Naples, Italy, 291
Narasimhan, Chakravarthi V., 319, 346n, 347n, 366, 368, 436, 437
Nasser, Gamal
  Arab-Israeli War 1967, 394-396, 398-399
  Lebanon crisis 1958, 298-300, 303-304
  Middle East 1956-57, 283, 283n, 285, 292, 293, 456
National Geographic Magazine, 275
national islands, *see* League Secretariat
National Liberation Front (South Vietnam), 405
Nazism, 174, 201, 237
Ndola, Northern Rhodesia, 324, 326, 341
Nehru, Brij Kumar, 345
Nehru, Jawaharlal, 345
Nervo, Luis Padilla, 100, 265-266, 274
Netherlands, the, 77, 109n, 111n, 139, 152, 183, 210n, 217, 240, 293
  West New Guinea, 348, 362-368, 454
Neutral Commission (Gran Chaco conflict), 73, 74
neutral intermediary, 101, 203, 223, 229, 251, 262, 269, 272, 282, 289, 294, 305, 325, 332, 364, 413, 451, 458, 463
neutral states, 18, 138, 145, 151, 193, 216, 224-229, 237, 250, 288, 300, 305-309, 318, 341, 361
  Cuba missile crisis, 375
  neutrality of SG, and, 420
  prestige of SG, and, 425
  record of SG, and, 430
  Thant election, 345-347
neutrality and impartiality, 213-214, 226, 236-238, 241, 248-251, 256, 264, 287, 318, 334, 371, 411
  as resource of SG, 416-420, 442
Neville, Robert, 21n
New Delhi, India, 196n, 406
"new order", 105, 135, 157, 158, 160, 167, 170, 176
New York City
  American Communists in Secretariat, 252, 255n
  Arab-Israeli War 1967, 394, 395, 398
  Avenol resignation, 160, 163, 165n, 166, 178, 178n, 179n
  Chinese UN representation, 230
  communications facilities, 439

  Congo crisis, 313, 358
  Cuba missile crisis, 375
  Hammarskjold election, 274
  Hammarskjold Peking mission, 281
  Hungarian revolution, 297
  information resource, 421
  Korean War, 239, 245
  Lebanon 1958, 304
  Lie resignation, 268
  mediation function, 452
  Middle East 1956-57, 284
  participation function, 451
  Peace Mission, 232
  Princeton mission, 156, 178
  Thant, and, 342, 344-345, 390
New York Times, The, 326
New York World's Fair 1939, 146
New Zealand, 240
Nicosia, Cyprus, 385
Nigeria, 354, 365
Nimmo, Robert H., 387
Nine Power Treaty 1922, 79, 91-93
Nitobe, Inazo, 35, 78
Nobel Prize for Peace, 223
Noblemaire Committee, 37
  Noblemaire Report, 37, 175n
Noel-Baker, Philip, 174, 196
non-governmental organizations, 212n, 241
non-proliferation agreement, 235
non-recognition doctrine, *see* Stimson Doctrine
North Africa, 106, 187
North Atlantic Treaty Organization, 262, 316, 360, 373, 385, 388
North Borneo, 378-380
North Korea, 236-251, 446
North Vietnam, 305-307, 400, 402-404, 406-409, 432, 442, 461
Northern Rhodesia, 323, 324
Norway
  Aland Islands question, 54
  Avenol election, 109n
  Bruce Report, 147n
  Congo crisis, 357
  construction of League Secretariat, 34
  Korean War, 237
  Lester period, 181, 198
  Lie background and election, 207-209, 211
  Lie subsequent career, 269
  Lie term extension and resignation, 259, 268
  political constituency, 431

Princeton transfer, 152, 155
Secretariat crisis 1938-39, 144n
Secretariat debate 1928-32, 38
UNEF, 291, 292, 395
Norwegian Labour Party, 208
Nu, U, 342, 390
nuclear free zones, 235
nuclear test ban treaty, 235
nuclear umbrella, 18
"null and void" affair, 163-165; see
Avenol resignation

O

observation missions (UN), 221, 225,
283, 297, 299-300, 306, 336, 376-377,
387-389
authorization, 409
conflict management, 449
contingency planning, 421
field operation function, and, 457
interposition, and, 458
mobilization function, 455-456
policy planning, 456-457
record of SG, and, 431
Olivan, Julio Lopez, 193-194
open-door policy, 87
Operation Grandslam, 359
Operation Morthor, 323-325
Operation Rumpunch, 322-324
Opium Supervisory Body, see League of
Nations
Organization of American States, 369
Organization for European Economic
Cooperation (OEEC), 273, 274
Oriental Province, Congo, 320
Ortiz-Sanz, Fernando, 367
Oslo, Norway, 207, 269
University of, 208
Owen, David, 196
Oxford University, 138, 147n, 333, 337

P

Pace, Julian, 127n
Pacem In Terris Convocation 1965, 409
Pakistan, 225, 244, 281, 291, 365-366
Kashmir dispute, 386-389
Palais des Nations, 35, 107n, 114, 152n,
153, 158-159
Lester period, 180, 183, 190, 192, 199
Palestine, 198, 217-224, 225, 225n, 230,
237n, 261, 454; see Middle East
Commission, 218, 219, 219n

Mandate, 217-219, 454
Mediator, 220-223
neutrality of SG, and, 417
Partition Plan, 217-220, 223, 285
Temporary Trusteeship Plan, 220
UNSCOP, 217
Pan American Arbitration Conference, 73
Pan American Union, 64
Panama, 65, 67, 218
Panmunjom, Korea, 247
Pantanaw, Burma, 342
Paraguay, 72-75, 174
Pardo, Carlos, 140
Paris talks on Vietnam War, 400, 406-408
Paris, University of, 106, 126, 147n
participation function, 215, 285, 303,
449-451, 452-453
Partition Plan for Palestine, 217-220,
223, 285
Pathet Lao, 305, 307-308
Paul-Boncour, Joseph, 209n
Peace Mission 1950, 230, 232-236
peacekeeping, 17-18, 100, 139
peacekeeping (UN), 50, 53, 100, 206,
283, 289, 317, 393, 443; see United
Nations
Pearson, Lester, 210, 268, 274, 288
Peking, China
Chinese representation, 230-233
Hammarskjold mission, 279-283, 329,
434
Korean War, 239, 244-246
Lebanon, and, 302
Lie term extension, 264, 266
Peking formula, 280-281, 337
Pelt, Adrian, 111n, 146n
Permanent Central Opium Board, see
League of Nations
Permanent Court of International
Justice, 39, 50, 57, 64, 97, 109, 181,
184-185, 193-194, 273
Corfu case, 68, 70
Registry, 39, 97, 181, 193, 273
Sino-Japanese conflict, 82, 84
permanent missions, 47, 48, 421, 426
Permanent Norwegian-Swiss Conciliation
Commission, 198
Perse, Saint-John, 275
Pershing, John J., 85
Perth, Earl of, 19, 20, 99, 100
Peru, 67, 72, 74, 147n, 173, 217
Leticia Trapeze conflict, 75-77
Pescadore Islands, 281
Pétain regime, 106, 158-159, 165, 175

Phelan, Edward, 112n, 181, 185-186, 186n, 193-194, 196
Philadelphia, 186-187
Philippines, the, 218, 240, 265, 274, 357
  Malaysia dispute, 378, 380
Phouma, Souvanna, 305
Pilotti, Massimo, 111n, 126, 130n, 131, 133, 145
Pineau, Christian, 286
Plan of National Reconciliation (Congo), 354-357, 361
Plaza, Galo, 383
plebiscite supervision, 225n, 458
pluralistic security community, 459
Poincaré, Raymond, 106
Poitiers, University of, 106
Poland, 58, 120, 142, 210, 214, 265n, 274
policy planning, 449, 456-457
Political and Civil Rights, Covenant on, 235
Politis, Nicolas, 109n
Port Fuad, 292
Port Said, 458
Portugal, 357n
positivism, 17
Possible Plan for a General International Organization 1944, 191n, 203, 210
prestige of SG, 101-102, 220, 285, 302, 304, 319, 350, 361, 379, 399, 410, 414, 419, 424
Pretoria, South Africa, 337
preventive diplomacy, 225, 248, 269, 271, 293, 328, 331-332, 338, 345, 438, 451, 458, 460
Princeton University
  Avenol resignation, 159-160, 162, 164, 166, 171
  Hambro, Carl, and, 155-157
  Institute for Advanced Study, 154, 155n
  Lester period, 177-178, 181, 183-185, 187, 198
  Loveday, Alexander, 157, 158, 177, 181
  Sweetser, Arthur, and, 153, 153n, 154, 155
  Tittmann, Harold, and, 155, 156, 158
  transfer to, from Geneva, 152-158
  U.S. State Department, and, 155-157
Principal Allied and Associated Powers, 33, 44
  Supreme Council, 44, 45
    Aland Islands question, and, 54, 55, 57

propaganda functions, 202, 230, 234, 297, 330
provisional measures, 225n, 387
Pusan, Korea, 241

Q

Quai d'Orsay, 83, 116, 118n, 132, 167, 351, 419
quiet diplomacy, 214, 216-217, 303, 328-330, 443

R

racial discrimination, 412-413, 417
racism, 263
Rahman, Abdul, 378
Rajchman, Ludwik, 86, 120-121, 142-143
Rangoon, Burma, 342, 402
  University of, 342
Ranshofen-Wertheimer, Egon, 30, 30n, 31, 115n, 175n
Rau, Sir Benegal, 265, 266
Reading, Lord, 81, 82
record as SG resource, 428-431
recruitment, 462
Red Cross, 374
regional military alliances, 202, 248, 262-263
regionalism, 64-67, 72-75, 75-77, 139, 248, 263, 303-304
Republican Party, 62
responsiveness, 462-463
Reveillaud, Jean, 144
Rhodes, 222, 451
Rikhye, Indar Jit, 365, 374, 394-395
Rist, Charles, 147n
Rockefeller Foundation, 154, 157
Rockefeller Institute, 154, 155n
Rolz-Bennett, José, 365, 382-383, 385
Romulo, Carlos P., 265-266, 274
Roosevelt, Franklin, 146n, 192, 210n, 411
Rosenberg, Marcel, 145-146
Royal Canadian Air Force, 376
rule-making function, 447-449
Rumania, 109n
Rusk, Dean, 345, 402, 408
Rzymowski, Wincenty, 210

S

Sabah, *see* North Borneo
Salter, Arthur, 33, 71

490

Salvemini, Gaetano, 127n, 130, 130n
San Antonio formula, 406
San Francisco Conference, *see* United
　Nations Conference on International
　Organization
Sananikone, Phoui, 305, 308
sanctions, *see* League of Nations *and*
　United Nations
Sarawak, 378-380
Sato, Naotuke, 78, 88, 89n
Saudi Arabia, 376-377
Scandinavia, 139, 151, 432
Schwebel, Stephen M., 24n, 25, 25n,
　26n, 28n, 29n, 40n, 149n, 159, 167,
　167n, 238, 250, 260
Scotland, 99
Scott, Sir Russell, 144n
secondment, 149, 438
Security Council, *see* United Nations
Selassie, Haile, 128
self-defense, 71, 79, 284, 312-313, 325,
　384
self-determination, 363, 368, 378-380,
　461
Seymour, Charles, 20n, 23n
Shanghai, China, 80, 88-90
Sharm El-Sheikh, 294, 396
Shastri, Lal Bahadur, 387
Simitch, Stanoje, 210
Simon, Sir John, 85
Sinai Peninsula, 286-287, 293, 394-396
Singapore, 378
Sinn Fein movement, 173
Sino-Japanese conflict 1931-33
　Assembly, 78, 88-94, 119, 121
　Avenol election, and, 108, 109, 11n
　Briand, Aristide, 80-82, 84-85
　Committee of Nineteen, 90-94
　Council, 77-96, 118, 118n, 119, 121
　Covenant, Article 1, 89, 121-122;
　　Article 11, 82, 88-89; Article 15, 84,
　　88-89, 89n
　Drummond resignation, and, 97
　face-saving function, and, 453
　France, 80, 83, 85, 88, 93n, 94, 118,
　　118n, 120, 123
　Gilbert, Prentiss, 80-81, 92, 92n, 97,
　　119-121, 123
　Great Britain, 80, 84-88, 90, 93n, 94,
　　103, 120-121, 123
　Japanese withdrawal from League,
　　88-89, 91, 93-95, 111n, 116-124
　Kellogg-Briand Pact, 79, 81, 87
　League prospects, and, 46, 52, 105

League technical aid to China, 117,
　119-121
legitimization function, and, 446
Lester views, and, 174
Lytton Commission, 79, 84-86, 88-92
　Lytton Report, 90-94
mediation function, and, 452
neutrality of SG, and, 417, 419
prestige of SG, and, 424
record of SG, and, 429
Special Committee on Technical
　Collaboration, 119
Stimson, Henry, 79-81, 87-88, 90,
　92-93
　Stimson Doctrine, 87-90, 119
United States, 64, 79-81, 83, 85-88,
　94-95, 118-119
Walters, Frank, 85, 118, 118n, 119, 123
Siotis, Jean, 24n, 160, 160n
skilled personnel as SG resource,
　436-438, 442
Skrzeszewski, Stanislaw, 274
Slim, Mongi, 345, 346
Smuts, Jan, 24, 209n
Sobolev, Arkady, 211, 227
socialization, 462
Sokoline, Vladimir, 146
South Africa, 24, 179, 239-240, 316, 337,
　354, 357, 357n, 417
South Asia, 18
South Korea, 236-251; *see* Korean War
South Vietnam, 400-401, 403-405, 407,
　409
Southeast Asia, 18, 332, 390, 406,
　408-409
southern Africa, 263, 412
Southern Rhodesia, 222, 316, 354, 357,
　357n
　Rhodesian Federation, 358n
Soviet-American cooperation, 193
Soviet Union, 18, 46, 90, 113
　accomodation function, and, 455
　Aland Islands question, and, 54, 58
　Arab-Israeli War 1967, and, 396-397
　articulation function, and, 443
　Avenol resignation, and, 160
　Berlin blockade, 226-229
　boycott of Lie, 266-268
　boycott of UN, 230, 238
　Chinese representation, and, 230-238
　Congo crisis, 310-321, 321n, 325,
　　350-353, 356-357, 359-360
　constituency of SG, and, 431-433
　constitutional theory, and, 428

Cuba missile crisis, 368-375
Cyprus case, and, 382, 384-385
diplomatic skills of SG, and, 423
expulsion from League, 113, 146,
    149-152, 162, 171
financial crisis of UN, and, 348, 356,
    390, 409
grants of power to SG, and, 435
Greek frontier case, and, 258
Hammarskjold election, and, 274
Hammarskjold Peking mission, 279
Hammarskjold views, and, 328, 333,
    336
Hungarian revolution, and, 289-290,
    295-298, 446
Iranian issue, 214-216
Italo-Ethiopian conflict, 135
Kashmir dispute, 387n, 388-389
Korean War, 236-237, 240-241, 243,
    245, 247, 249, 259, 262-264, 266,
    429
Laos, 305-308
Lebanon 1958, 298, 301-304
legitimization function, 446
Lester period, 185-186, 193
Lie election, and, 208-210
Lie Peace Mission, 230, 232, 234
Lie term extension and resignation,
    264-268, 272
Malaysia dispute, 379
Middle East 1956-57, 283-284, 286-
    288, 290, 293-294
neutrality of SG, and, 417, 419-420
Palestine, 217-218, 220
pressures for limited SG Office, 216,
    249, 256, 261, 271-272, 308, 316-
    317, 334, 338, 343-344, 361, 377,
    409, 413-414, 423, 428-429, 431,
    435
prestige of SG, and, 425
record of SG, and, 430-431
Secretariat crisis 1938-39, and, 145
skilled personnel as SG resource, 436
structural position of SG, and, 426
Thant elections, and, 343-350
Thant re-election, and, 391
troika proposal, 256, 316-319, 341,
    344-347, 349, 391-392
UN, and, 201-203, 213, 224n, 225,
    226n, 233, 235, 262-263, 271
UN Secretariat, and, 211, 211n
Vietnam War, and, 401, 403, 406
Yemen, and, 376-377
Spaak, Paul-Henri, 209, 210, 274, 356

Spain, 33, 57, 66, 77, 111n, 112n, 128,
    158, 175n, 181n, 193
    Civil War, 66, 114, 135
Special Committee on Technical
    Collaboration, 119; *see* Sino-Japanese
    conflict
Special War Mission 1917, 20-22
Spinelli, Pier, 304, 377
Stalin, Josef, 228, 232, 234, 269, 279,
    295, 327, 430
Stanleyville, 322
state responsibility, 70
Statistical Year-Book, 184
Stern Group, 222
Stettinius, Edward R., 210
Stevenson, Adlai, 271, 348, 349, 369,
    371-372, 402
Stimson, Henry, 73n, 74, 76
    Sino-Japanese conflict, 79-81, 81n,
        87-88, 90, 92-93
    Stimson Doctrine, 87, 88, 90, 119
Stockholm Sweden, 54, 55, 275
    University of, 273
Stolpe, Sven, 274n
structural-functionalism, 440n
structural position as SG resource,
    426-427, 441-442
sub-troika, 346
Suez Canal, 217, 285-288, 290-293,
    296, 356, 396-397
Sugimura, Yotaro, 78, 85, 93n, 109,
    111n, 118, 118n, 145
Suharto, President, 365
Sukarno, President, 363, 365, 378-380
Sunderland House (London), 35-36, 56,
    60
supervision, 458
Supervisory Commission, *see* League of
    Nations
Supreme Economic Council, 106
Sweden
    Aland Islands question, 54-60
    Avenol election, and, 109n
    Beck-Friss mission, 331, 332
    Congo crisis, 314, 357
    Cuba missile crisis, 374
    Hammarskjold background and
        election, 268, 271-275
    Korean War, 244
    League Secretariat debate 1928-32, 41
    Lebanon, 299
    Middle East 1956-57, 293
    Swedish Academy, 273
    Swedish Royal Museum, 276

Swedish Tourist Association, 275,
    275n
UNEF, 395
UNFICYP, 383
UNYOM, 376
Sweetser, Arthur, 44, 111n, 113-114, 178,
    178n
    Avenol resignation, and, 160, 160n,
        163n, 165n, 166-167, 176, 179n
    Lester period, 182n, 183-185, 185n,
        187n, 189n, 190n, 192n, 193n, 195n,
        197-198
    Princeton transfer, 153-155, 177
    U.S. League membership, 60, 61, 64
Switzerland, 52, 110n, 139, 167, 173,
    177-178, 308, 354, 374
    Aland Islands question, 57-59
    Bruce Report, 148
    Gran Chaco conflict, 73
    Hammarskjold Peking mission, 281
    Lester period, 179-180, 180n, 183
    Princeton transfer, 153
    Secretariat crisis 1938-39, 144-145
    Soviet expulsion, 151
Syria, 222, 284, 298-301, 304, 393-394,
    394n, 396
Sze, Alfred, 78, 81, 82, 85

T

Taft, William H., 62
Taiwan, 244, 279
Taiwan Straits, 279, 281
taksim, 385
Tananarive, 321
Tanner, Valnö A., 151
Tashkent, Soviet Union, 389
Tashkent Declaration, 389
Tavares de Sá, Hernane, 374
technical assistance program, 233, 235
Teclé-Hawariate, Bajirond, 125, 126
Ten Point Memorandum 1950, 230-236,
    263
TenBroeck, Carl, 155n
Tentative Proposals for a General
    International Organization 1944, 191n
Thailand, 240, 332, 342
Thant, U, 216, 249-251, 260-261, 263,
    324, 338
    accomodation function, 454
    Arab-Israeli War 1967, 393-400, 452,
        456
    arbitration function, 453
    articulation function, 443-444
    background, 341-343
    communication function, 442
    Congo crisis, 326, 350-362
    constituency, 431-433
    constitutional theory, 428
    contingency planning, 421-422
    contribution, 343-344
    Cuba missile crisis, 369-375, 442, 454,
        459
    Cyprus, 381-386
    diplomatic skills, 422-423
    election as Acting SG, 344-347
    election as SG, 347-350
    grants of power, 435
    Hammarskjold, compared with, 343-
        344, 361-362, 383-384, 410
    integration, 461, 463
    interposition, 459
    Kashmir dispute, 386-389
    legitimization function, 446-447
    Lie, compared with, 341-344
    Malaysia dispute, 377-381, 453
    mediation, 452
    neutrality, 417, 419-420
    policy planning, 456
    prestige, 424-426
    record, 429-430
    re-election 1966, 390-393
    rule-making, 448
    skilled personnel, 436-437
    tangible resources, 439
    Vietnam war, 400-409, 432-433, 435,
        442, 447, 461
    views on UN and SG, 409-414
    West New Guinea, 362-368, 454
    Yemen, 375-377
Thomas, Albert, 26-27, 31, 108, 114, 170
Thysville, Congo, 310, 320
Tiran, Straits of, 293, 396
Tittmann, Harold, 148-151, 155-156,
    158-159, 161, 180n, 181n
Titulescu, Nicolas, 109n
Tokyo, 79-82, 84-85, 92, 117-118,
    120-122
    Korean War, 240
Toscano, Mario, 128, 130n
transaction flows, 462, 463
transactions volume, 202
Treaty of Guarantee 1959, 381, 382
Treaty of Mutual Assistance, 138
Treaty of Paris of 1856, 55, 58
treaty revision, 138-139
Trendelenberg, Ernst, 111n, 145
tribalism, 310, 325

Trieste, 225n
Tripartite Pact of 1906, 127, 127n, 128
Tripartite Treaty of 1942, 214
troika proposal, 256, 316-319
truce supervision, 221-222, 225n, 247,
    458
Truman, Harry S,. 228, 232, 237n, 239,
    245, 254
    Truman Doctrine, 202
Truman, Louis W., 357, 361
Trusteeship Council, *see* United Nations
Tshombe, Moise, 310, 312-314, 316, 320,
    322-325, 345, 348, 350-360; *see* Congo
    crisis
Tudela, Francisco, 147n
Tunesia, 307, 312-313, 316, 345
Tuomioja, Sakaari, 307, 308, 383
Turkey, 240, 301, 373
    Cyprus case, 381-382, 385-386

U

U-2 reconnaissance planes, 368, 372
Unified Command, *see* Korean War
Union Minière du Haut-Katanga, 309,
    350-355, 357, 358; *see* Congo crisis
United Arab Republic, 298-300, 304,
    370, 374, 376-377, 393-400
United Nations
    Advisory Committee on Administrative
        and Budgetary Questions, 141n, 197
    Avenol, and, 169
    Charter
        Article 2 (4), 70, 70n
        Article 4, 231
        Article 7, 204, 207, 336-338, 428,
            435
        Article 39, 222, 387
        Article 40, 387
        Article 43, 224-225, 233, 235, 238,
            247, 262, 288
        Article 51, 284
        Article 97, 204, 336
        Article 98, 205, 261, 336, 338, 426,
            428
        Article 99, 28-29, 102, 169, 204-205,
            215-216, 221, 237n, 238, 258,
            261, 284, 287, 306-307, 311,
            329-330, 336-338, 392, 043,
            426-428, 435, 450
        Article 100, 207, 268, 335, 335n,
            336, 338
        Article 100 (1), 256
        Article 101, 204

        Article 101 (3), 36, 36n
        Chapter VI, 262
        Chapter VII, 222, 224n, 226, 262,
            289, 312-313, 337, 387-388, 398
        Chapter XV, 204
        American Communists in
            Secretariat, 255, 255n, 256
        Berlin blockade, and, 226, 228
        Chinese representation, 231
        collective security, 213, 224, 298
        compared with League Covenant on
            SG powers, 28, 123
        Congo crisis, 325, 351
        Corfu conflict, 71
        Cuba missile crisis, 369, 371
        Drummond contribution, 101
        Drummond name in Covenant, and,
            24
        geographical distribution, and, 439
        Hammarskjold Peking mission, and,
            281
        Hammarskjold views, and, 278, 287,
            302, 327-339
        Kashmir dispute, and, 388
        Korean War, and, 236-238, 240-241,
            243, 249-250, 262, 264, 429
        Lester views on, 195
        Lie term extension and resignation,
            and, 264, 267-268
        Lie views on, 212, 219, 223, 256-
            264, 269
        Middle East 1956-57, and, 284,
            284n, 287, 294
        neutrality of SG, and, 416-419
        Palestine 1947-49, and, 219, 222-224
        participation function, and, 450
        Peace Mission, and, 233
        skilled personnel, and, 437
        Thant, and, 409, 412
        Thant election, and, 345, 346n
        Thant views on, 409-414
        UN founding and SG articles, 202-
            208
        Vietnam war, and, 403
    Corfu case, and, 70
    Drummond, and, 47-48, 50, 99-100,
        102
    Economic and Social Council, 140,
        148-149, 183, 205, 241
    European Headquarters, 33, 35, 304,
        377
    founding of, and Charters SG articles,
        202-208
    General Assembly, 100, 205-207,

210-211, 212n, 215, 227-229,
235-236, 258, 272, 348
1st Assembly, 208
7th Assembly, 210
15th Assembly, 316, 345
16th Assembly, 344, 363
17th Assembly, 347, 349, 364
21st Assembly, 392
accomodation function, and, 455
aggregation function, and, 445
American Communists in
Secretariat, and, 254, 255
Arab-Israeli War 1967, 395, 396,
398-399
Berlin blockade, 227-229
Congo crisis, 314, 316-321, 321n,
326, 362
constituency, and, 432, 433
constitutional theory, and, 427
financial crisis, and, 356
First Committee, 242
grants of power, and, 433-435
Hammarskjold election, and, 274
Hammarskjold Peking mission,
280-281
Hammarskjold views, and, 328,
330, 336, 338
Hungarian revolution, and, 296-297
Kashmir dispute, and, 388
Korean War, and, 238, 242-243,
245-246, 250, 289
Laos, 309
Lebanon, 302-304
legitimization, and, 446-447
Lie term extension and resignation,
259, 265-267, 269
Malaysia, 378-379
Middle East 1956-57, and, 285,
287-292, 294, 398
Palestine 1947-49, 217-220, 223
policy planning, 456-457
President of, 100, 208-210, 228,
258, 326, 345
prestige of SG, and, 425
rule-making function, and, 447-448
structural position, and, 426
Thant and elections, 343, 345-347,
349
Thant re-election, 391-393
Thant views, and, 409-411
UN Guard, and, 225
Vietnam War, and, 401
West New Guinea, and, 363-365
International Court of Justice, 207,

227, 233, 348, 363, 381
League of Nations, and, 18-19, 36-37,
43
Lester period, 173, 189, 195, 198-199
transfer from League to UN, 189-
198
L'Organisation des Nations Unies au
Congo, Force de (ONUC)
command, 312
financial crisis, and, 409
Hammarskjold, and, 312-315, 320,
325, 350, 383
mobilization, and, 456
participation, and, 450-451
principles of, 312
rule-making, 448
Thant, and, 348, 350-352, 354-360,
439
peacekeeping forces, 217, 219, 219n,
220-221, 223-226, 233, 288, 294,
301, 336, 393
accomodation, 455
articulation, 443
authorization, 409
conflict management, 449
constitutional theory, 428
contingency planning, 421-422
interposition, 458
mediation, 452
mobilization, 455-456
policy planning, 456-457
record of SG, and, 431
rule-making, 448
Preparatory Commission, 196-197,
204-206, 210n, 212
presence, 305-307, 309, 328, 331, 457
sanctions, 71, 221, 222, 325
Congo crisis, 353-357, 361
Kashmir, 387, 387n
Secretariat, 37, 48, 142, 203-304, 206,
211, 213, 225, 257, 335
Administrative and Financial
Services, Department of, 211,
211n
American Communists in, 251-256
Assistant SG's, 196, 211, 211n, 212,
279n
departments, 211, 211n, 212, 212n,
279n
Deputy Under Secretaries, 279n
Economic Affairs, Department of,
198, 211n
geographical distribution, 36, 335,
437, 439, 462

Heads of Office, 279n
Korean War, and, 239
Legal Counsel, 214
Personnel, Department of, 380
Political and Security Council
    Affairs, Department of, 198, 211,
    211n, 437
Social Affairs, Department of, 211n
Staff regulations, 252-256
top-level staff, 207, 211, 228, 279,
    279n, 319, 341, 344, 421, 436, 439
Trusteeship, Department of, 211n,
    312
Under Secretaries, 279n, 319, 343,
    347n, 377
Under Secretaries without portfolio
    (Special Political Affairs), 279n,
    374, 437
Under Secretary for General
    Assembly Affairs, 319
Under Secretary for Public
    Information, 281, 374, 380
Secretary-General, 28, 31, 46, 53, 67,
    100, 123, 171, 203-307, 211, 215-
    216, 220, 223-224, 229, 233, 266,
    272, 283
administrative and executive
    functions, 204
Annual Report, 26-27, 30-31, 102,
    183, 189, 436, 447
    Hammarskjold, 257, 276-277,
        329, 333-334, 337, 447
    Lie, 205-206, 212n, 225n, 231,
        247-248, 257-258, 261-262
    Thant, 413, 421
Congo crisis, effect of, 324-327,
    360-362
Executive Assistant, 196, 211, 212,
    288, 311, 319
Executive Office, 206, 212, 212n,
    290, 364, 421, 439
    aggregation function, 445
    articulation function, 443
    field operation, 458
    policy planning, 457
    skilled personnel, 436-437, 437n
financial functions of, 204
Korean War, effect of, 248-251,
    259-260, 262, 263-267
legal memoranda, use of, 214-216,
    219n, 230, 246, 258
Middle East 1956-57, effect of,
    294-295

Military Adviser, 365, 374, 421-422,
    442
minimalist approach, 211-212
presentations to Council and
    Assembly, 215-216
political role, 204-205, 212, 217,
    233-234, 249, 257, 258-260, 268
procedures for election of, 206
Soviet boycott 1951-52, 266-268
Soviet pressures for limited Office,
    216, 249, 256, 261, 271-272, 308,
    316-317, 334, 338, 343-344, 361,
    377, 409, 413-414, 423, 428-429,
    431, 435
spokesman, as, 258-260, 338
symbol, as, 212, 426
term of office, 206
Security Council, 28, 102, 169, 201,
    204-206, 208-210, 216, 225n, 226n,
    258, 261, 277
Arab-Israeli War 1967, 396-397
Berlin blockade, 227-229
Chinese representation, 230-231,
    232n
Congo crisis, 311-317, 320-322,
    350-353, 359-360, 362
constituency, and, 433
constitutional theory, and, 427
Cuba missile crisis, 369-370, 372,
    375
Cyprus, 382-385
grants of power, and, 433-435
Hammarskjold election, 274
Hammarskjold views, and, 328, 332,
    336-338
Hungarian revolution, 289, 296
Iranian issue, 213-215
Kashmir dispute, 387-389
Korean War, 237-242, 244, 246-247,
    250, 289
Laos, 306-309
Lebanon, 299-302
legitimization function, and, 446,
    447
Lie term extension and resignation,
    265, 267-268
limited SG Office, and, 361, 409,
    410, 423
Malaysia, 378
Middle East 1956-57, 283-288, 290
mobilization, and, 456
Palestine, 1947-49, 218-219, 221-222
Peace Mission, 232-235
policy planning, 456-457

President of, 214-215, 258
prestige, and, 425
record, and, 430
rule-making function, and, 447
structural position, and, 426
Thant elections and re-election,
   345-346, 349, 391-393
Thant views, and, 410-411
Vietnam war, and, 401
Yemen, and, 376-377
specialized agencies, 212n, 233, 235
Trusteeship Council, 205, 225n
UN Commission on Korea, 237-239,
   242; see Korean War
UN Commission for Palestine, 218,
   219, 219n
UN Commission for the Unification
   and Rehabilitation of Korea
   (UNCURK), 243, 247; see Korean
   War
UN Conference on International
   Organization (UNCIO), 26, 53, 71,
   99, 101, 192-194, 202-208, 211, 238,
   247, 288
UN Conference on Trade and
   Development (UNCTAD), 463
UN Correspondents Association, 238
UN Emergency Force (UNEF), 226,
   288-293, 300, 303, 312, 325, 330,
   376, 383
   accomodation function, 454
   Advisory Committee, 291, 315, 395,
      397-398
   Commander, 289, 293
   financial crisis, and, 348, 409
   mobilization, 456
   participation, 450-451
   policy planning, 456
   rule-making, 448
   withdrawal, 292, 393-400, 439, 456
UN Force in Cyprus (UNFICYP),
   381-386, 409, 448, 451
UN Guard (Field Service), 224-226,
   233, 439
UN India-Pakistan Observation
   Mission (UNIPOM), 388-389
UN Military Observation Group in
   India and Pakistan (UNMOGIP),
   386-389
UN Observation Group in Lebanon
   (UNOGIL), 299-302, 304
UN Relief and Rehabilitation
   Administration (UNRRA), 186
UN Security Force (UNSF), 364-365,

366; see West New Guinea
UN Special Committee on Palestine
   (UNSCOP), 217
UN Temporary Executive Authority
   (UNTEA), 364-368, 458
UN Truce Supervision Organization
   (UNTSO), 198, 221, 222, 283, 289,
   376, 458
   Arab-Israeli War 1967, 394, 194n,
      396
UN Yemen Observation Mission
   (UNYOM), 376-377
United States
   accomodation function, and, 454
   Aland Islands question, 58-59
   American Communists in Secretariat,
      251-256
   Arab-Israeli War 1967, 396-397
   articulation function, and, 433
   Avenol, and, 109, 111n, 113, 115, 139,
      160-161, 164, 166
   Berlin blockade, 226-229
   Bruce Report, 146-148
   Chinese representation, 231, 234
   communication, and, 441
   Communist Party of, 251-256
   Congo crisis, 310-311, 315, 318, 325,
      351-361, 447, 454
   Congress and Senate of, 20, 60-62, 74,
      115, 156, 192, 252-254, 280-281,
      351, 387, 391
      Senate Juliciary Committee 252
      Internal Security Subcommittee,
         252-254
   constituency of SG, and, 432
   Constitution of, 252-254
   constitutional theory as SG resource,
      and, 428
   Consul in Geneva, 48, 63, 67, 80, 92,
      97, 109, 121, 130, 142, 148-150, 155,
      180n, 181n
   Cuba missile crisis, 368-375, 454
   Cyprus, 383, 385-386
   Drummond, and, 20, 21, 46, 51n, 97
   financial crisis, and, 348, 409
   Gran Chaco conflict, 72-75
   grants of power, and, 435
   Greek frontier case, and, 258
   Hammarskjold background and
      election, 273-274
   Hammarskjold Peking mission, 279,
      434, 454
   Hammarskjold views, and, 328
   Hungarian revolution, 289, 295-298

Iranian issue, 214-216
Italo-Ethiopian conflict, 130, 134
Joint Chiefs of Staff, 243
Kashmir, 386-388
Korean War, 236-251, 264, 289,
    429-430, 446
Laos, 305-308
League Committee on Budgetary
    Economies, 144n
League membership, 60-64
League prospects, and, 18
League Secretariat, 33, 35, 145
Lebanon, 298-304
Lester period, 181, 183-187, 189,
    191-193, 195-198
Leticia Trapeze, 75-77
Lie election, 208-210
Lie Peace Mission, 230, 232, 232n, 234
Lie term extension, 264-266
Malaysia dispute, 379
Middle East 1956-57, 283, 286-287,
    290, 293-294
National Archives of, 441
National Security Council, 245, 368
neutrality of SG, and, 417, 419-420
Palestine 1947-49, 217-221
prestige of SG, and, 425
Princeton University, 154-158, 177
record of SG, and, 430-431
Seventh Fleet, 239
Sino-Japanese conflict, 79-81, 83,
    85-88, 94-95, 118-119
skilled personnel, and, 436, 438
Soviet expulsion from League, and,
    151-152
State Department, 60-63, 81, 97, 119,
    132, 142, 151, 155-157, 159, 180,
    181n, 187-188, 191-193, 203, 203n,
    211, 251, 254, 352, 357, 361, 364,
    401-402, 441, 454
Thant background and elections, 341,
    343, 345-347, 391
UN, and, 201-203, 224-225, 230,
    262-264, 269, 271
Vietnam war, 401-409, 442, 447, 461
West New Guinea, 364-365
White House, 60, 62, 402
Uniting for Peace Resolution, 287
Universal Declaration of Human
    Rights, 235, 401
universality, 18, 46, 50, 68, 138, 201,
    230, 233-235, 390, 400, 409, 413, 417,
    431, 446
Uppsala, Sweden, 272, 273

University of, 273
Uruguay, 67, 73, 110, 217, 374

V

van Dusen, Henry P., 274n
van Eysinga, Willem, 109, 109n
van Hamel, Joost, 34
van Kleffens, Eelco, 210n
Vance, Cyrus R., 385-386
Varvaressos, K., 147n
Vathana, Savang, King, 306, 308
Vaud, 167
Veldekens, Paul, 253n
Venizelos, Eleutherios, 24, 98
verification, 458
Versailles Conference, 19, 22-24, 27, 33,
    35, 54-55, 202
Versailles Peace Treaty, 36, 62, 69, 116,
    139
Vichy, France, 106, 145, 153, 157, 159,
    161, 164-167, 175, 177, 187
Victoria, Queen, 20, 276
Vienna, Austria, 297
Vietcong, 404, 407-408
Vietnam, 235, 305, 410-411
    War in, 400-409
        accomodation, and, 455
        articulation, and, 443
        communications, and, 442
        constituency, and, 432-433
        grants of power, and, 435
        Geneva Conferences, and, 400
        legitimization, and, 447
        neutrality of SG, and, 420
        Paris talks on, 400, 406-408
        participation, and, 451
        Thant's re-election, and, 390-392
        Thant's three basic points, 404-406
Vigier, Henri, 142, 197-198
Villari, Luigi, 127n
von Horn, Carl, 315-316, 376
Vyshinsky, Andrei, 245, 265, 268, 274

W

Wal-Wal incident 1934, 125, 125n, 128;
    see Italo-Ethiopian conflict
Waldock, Humphrey, 281
Walters, Frank, 32, 66, 66n, 111n, 113,
    113n, 436
    Bruce Report, 147
    Italo-Ethiopian conflict, 129, 130,
        130n, 132

resignation, 153, 154, 154n
Secretariat crisis 1938-39, 142, 143, 146
Sino-Japanese conflict, 85, 118, 118n, 119, 123
Warsaw Pact, 373
weekly meetings, *see* League Secretariat
Weimar Republic, 83
West Bank area (Jordan), 396-397
West Berlin, *see* Berlin blockade
West Germany, 350, 354-356
West Irian, *see* West New Guinea
West New Guinea, 348-349, 362-368, 390, 454, 458
    UN Security Force, 364-366
    UNTEA, 364-368, 458
Western European group, 391
Wheeler, Raymond A., 293
Wiart, Count Carton de, 144n
Wieschhoff, Heinrich, 311-313
Willoughby, Westel W., 87n
Wilson, Hugh, 73-74, 76, 79n, 90, 119
Wilson, Woodrow, 20-24, 60, 63, 91, 194-195, 328
    Woodrow Wilson Foundation and Award, 194-195
Winant, John G., 181
World Economic Survey, 184
World War I, 17, 20, 34, 45, 106, 194
World War II
    Aland Islands question, and, 59

    Avenol, and, 160-161, 167, 170
    Bruce Report, 147-148
    Iranian issue, 213-214
    Katzin, Alfred, 239
    Laos, and, 305
    League, and, 18, 107, 137, 145
    Lester period, 173, 176, 179-181, 183, 193, 194
    Princeton transfer, 152, 154, 157
    Sino-Japanese conflict, and, 90, 99
    Soviet expulsion from League, 151n
    UN early years, 201-202
Wu Hsiu-Chuan, 244-245

Y

Yalta Conference, 192
Yalu River, 243-244
Yemen, 375-377, 390, 459
Yorkshire, England, 19
Yoshizawa, Kenkichi, 78-82, 85
Young, Oran, 415n, 416n, 421
Yugoslavia, 210, 217-218, 238, 243, 258, 265n, 287, 293, 376, 395, 399

Z

Zellweger, Edouard, 308
Zinchenko, Constantin, 239
Zorin, Valerian A., 347, 349, 369, 372
Zurich, 381